Praise for the First Edition

There are already several books about AspectJ—one of its major advantages.... My favorite is AspectJ in Action.

—Rod Johnson, Creator of the Spring Framework
in *J2EE Development without EJB*

One of the clearest expositions of AOP and its benefits that I have seen.... It is obvious that a lot of care and attention has gone into the preparation of the material.

—Adrian Colyer, AspectJ Project Lead, in *The Computer Journal*

I would highly recommend AspectJ in Action *to anyone who is interested in AOP.... I liked the practical angle, and you could tell that Ramnivas has really used AOP/AspectJ on his projects.*

—Dion Almaer at TheServerSide.com

...real solutions to tough problems.

—Chris Bartling, Identix, Inc.

Laddad brings to the professional community a valuable book, to support AOP tutoring and adoption...a well-constructed, well-balanced book that delivers what it promises.

—Computing Reviews at www.reviews.com

I started reading at 11 PM and couldn't stop.... It's a must-read for anyone interested in the future of programming.

—Arno Schmidmeier, AspectSoft

This book is to aspect-oriented programming what the Gang of Four book is to design patterns.

—Computing Reviews at www.reviews.com

...a wonderful job of introducing the new AOP trend...no other book succeeded to present the challenges of AOP so well.

—JavaRanch.com

More Praise for the First Edition

The author succeeds brilliantly in gradually building your understanding of AOP, then AspectJ's own semantics, and then the coding possibilities these offer.... The writing is clear and accessible, the content expertly graduated.

—a reader at Amazon.co.uk

...one of the few technical books that has blown my hair back.... [I] walked away feeling as though I had actually grown as a developer.

—Alex Winston at AlexWinston.com

By far the best programming-related book I have read in a long time.

—a reader at Amazon.co.uk

...a very clear and complete treatment of aspects. Like the other books in the "In Action" series from Manning, it is filled with very good diagrams.... This book will definitely help.

—on The Daily Channel

...I would recommend going with AspectJ in Action*...you will get the most bang for your buck from Ramnivas's work.... The subject-oriented approach in this book lends itself well to future reuse.*

—on jroller.com

...exactly what I needed...fantastic use of diagrams, figures, and annotated code. They solidly add to understanding the content.... I found the book to really be excellent from all viewpoints for getting into the subject matter from many angles and diving down very deep into it.

—Max Spille at TheServerSide.com

This book provides a very good resource both for people starting to learn AOP and AspectJ and for experienced AOP programmers who wish to deepen their knowledge in this new area.

—Valentin Crettaz, JavaRanch

The only resource that presents AOP concepts and real-world examples in an approachable, readable way.

—Jean Baltus, Metafron-Infosys

AspectJ in Action

Second Edition

ENTERPRISE AOP WITH SPRING APPLICATIONS

RAMNIVAS LADDAD

Greenwich
(74° w. long.)

For online information and ordering of this and other Manning books, please visit www.manning.com. The publisher offers discounts on this book when ordered in quantity. For more information, please contact

Special Sales Department
Manning Publications Co.
Sound View Court 3B fax: (609) 877-8256
Greenwich, CT 06830 email: orders@manning.com

Manning Publications Co.
Sound View Court 3B
Greenwich, CT 06830

Development Editor: Cynthia Kane
Copyeditor: Tiffany Taylor
Typesetter: Gordan Salinovic
Cover designer: Marija Tudor

ISBN 978-1-933988-05-4
Printed in the United States of America
1 2 3 4 5 6 7 8 9 10 – MAL – 14 13 12 11 10 09

To Ashish
In our hearts you will always remain

brief contents

contents

PART 2 APPLICATIONS OF ASPECTJ WITH SPRING..............249

foreword

This is a timely book, about a powerful and widely used technology that continues to grow in importance.

Since the first edition of *AspectJ in Action*, much has changed in AspectJ and the broader environment. This comprehensive update squarely addresses these changes.

Among the changes, three issues stand out: important new capabilities of AspectJ, increasing interest in dynamic languages in general and on the JVM, and the emergence of AspectJ as a key practical technology in mainstream enterprise Java.

AspectJ has matured greatly since the first edition. It now has comprehensive support for Java annotations, along with support for other language improvements such as generics, variable-length argument lists, and covariant return types. Annotations fit hand in glove with AOP, providing an ideal way of adding information about program structure and semantics for use by aspects. For example, one concise aspect might add consistent additional behavior to all executions of a method with a given annotation; another might cause a set of classes to be annotated with a particular annotation to direct an enterprise framework to add behavior at runtime. These language enhancements not only simplify the authoring of many aspects—they also make AspectJ an ideal match for modern enterprise Java programming models, and truly a new language.

The last few years has seen a significant rise in interest in dynamic languages—many of which (such as Groovy) provide capabilities for metaprogramming. Although this is a welcome change, it has caused some confusion regarding the role of AOP. Metaprogramming can solve some of the problems solved by AOP, but it doesn't directly offer the ability to exploit program structure in a complementary way to OOP that is core to

AOP. This book will help you understand which approach is appropriate to your everyday problems and how you can use them together. Ramnivas Laddad neatly expresses the relationship between AOP and dynamic languages in Chapter 1: "...statically typed languages use AOP to gain metaprogramming support. In contrast, dynamic languages benefit from AOP as a disciplined application of metaprogramming."

Another important change since the first edition of this book is the rise of modern frameworks, which constitutes a huge validation of AOP. Today, the Spring Framework has become the most popular component model for enterprise Java. Its core benefit—sophisticated provision of declarative services to simple POJOs containing business logic and unpolluted by infrastructure concerns—is built on AOP, and its popularity and proven usefulness demonstrate the benefits of the modularization AOP is designed to achieve. (Indeed, *all* modern enterprise Java technologies follow Spring's approach of providing enterprise services with minimal infrastructure API calls in user code.) Furthermore, Spring 2.0 made the important architectural decision to adopt the AspectJ pointcut expression language—the heart of AspectJ—and a subset of the AspectJ annotation programming model as its preferred AOP programming model—another validation, which exposes more developers to the benefits of AspectJ.

As a result, AspectJ works hand in hand with Spring and is particularly relevant to solving enterprise Java problems. Ramnivas has embraced this synergy in this book: he explains clearly how you can benefit from AspectJ concepts if you're already using Spring, and how AspectJ the language is a natural extension of the AOP concepts supported by Spring. Readers who aren't using Spring will still benefit from the valuable case studies and examples the Spring AOP experience provides.

This practical bent is important and to be commended. Programming languages are only as valuable as their practical usage potential, as history repeatedly shows. Another key to practical usage potential is tool support. In the case of AspectJ, there has recently been a huge step forward in this regard. Improvements to the Eclipse AspectJ plugin (AJDT) have resulted in dramatic performance and stability improvements, making AspectJ easier for less experienced developers to use. Meanwhile, the new Spring Roo project (http://www.springsource.org/roo) makes innovative use of AspectJ in greatly simplifying the authoring of enterprise Java applications. Not only is this a further validation of AspectJ, but it also promises to make the full power of AspectJ available in a large number of applications without developers needing to make an explicit choice to adopt AspectJ.

Together, these advances remove a key *practical* barrier to adopting AspectJ. The remaining barrier to adoption is the effort in learning AOP and AspectJ *concepts*—an effort well worth making. Learning AspectJ is like learning to type: it requires the investment of some time up front to be able to reap ongoing rewards in productivity.

This book will make that effort as easy and as pleasurable as possible. As you learn about AOP and AspectJ, I highly recommend Ramnivas Laddad as your guide.

A long-term advocate of AOP, Ramnivas is outstandingly knowledgeable about his subject. Even more important, he deeply understands how it fits into a broader context.

Through many years of experience as an enterprise architect and consultant, he has gained a deep *practical* knowledge about real-world problems, seeing aspects as just one (albeit an important) weapon in the armory of the modern architect. This experience stands out in the relevance and value of the examples and in the fact that the book is well balanced. Ramnivas isn't a mere cheerleader, and he provides excellent discussion of alternatives to AOP that will help you make the right architectural choices.

Finally, this book, like the previous edition, is a pleasure to read. Clear, concisely worded, and well organized, it will make your navigation of AspectJ and AOP concepts easy.

I wish you great success with AspectJ and the Java platform, and I hope you enjoy reading this book as much as I have.

ROD JOHNSON
CREATOR OF THE SPRING FRAMEWORK

preface

My association with AOP and AspectJ has now lasted more than a decade. I still remember my initial experience with AspectJ around 1998 and more serious exploration in 2002. It felt like a breath of fresh air that finally addressed some of the shortcomings of object-oriented programming. My initial experimentation led me to write an article series in *JavaWorld* in 2002 and the first edition of this book in 2003. After writing the book, I gave talks at many conferences about facets of AOP and AspectJ, and how to use them with the Spring Framework commonly referred to as *Spring*. Over the last few years, as a Spring committer, I have been trying to improve Spring-AspectJ integration. While doing this, I have been actively using these technologies on many projects. This book is a reflection of my experience with the technologies, understanding the best ways to explain them, and finding pragmatic ways to adopt them.

A lot has changed since the publication of the first edition of this book. Back then, AspectJ was a new language, Spring had just come out, and alternative languages on the Java platform were far fewer. Now, AspectJ is a 10-year-old language, Spring is the de facto lightweight framework for developing enterprise software, and new languages on the Java platforms are numerous.

Yet some things haven't changed. Software complexity is still increasing at breakneck speed. Our ability to cope with complexity remains essentially unaltered. As a result, our search for better ways to reduce implementation complexity also remains unchanged. These factors make AOP implemented using AspectJ an important tool in an enterprise Java developer's toolbox.

The changes to AspectJ have been dramatic. It now includes two syntax possibilities: the traditional syntax and the annotation-based @AspectJ syntax, which lowers the barrier to begin using AspectJ. It supports many weaving possibilities, including load-time weaving, making the use of AspectJ for applications such as monitoring and tracing a simple experience. To top it off, Spring has adopted AspectJ's programming model as its AOP solution. This caused the Spring community to be drawn to the power of AOP with AspectJ as the preferred programming model.

Below the surface, significant changes have also taken place. SpringSource (now part of VMWare) is sponsoring AspectJ development. Due to the complexity involved on the compiler and tools front, projects such as AspectJ require serious attention. Full-time development afforded by SpringSource support has been crucial in recent years.

And so, it was time to write a new edition of *AspectJ in Action.* My initial thought was that I would update most chapters with new AspectJ features and update a few examples. I estimated the overall effort would take six months. Boy, was my estimate off the mark! It took more than three years to update and re-update the book. There were many reasons (besides being busy at my day job). AspectJ kept improving over the last three years. The ecosystem surrounding Spring changed dramatically. Through my consulting experience, my understanding of the problems that AOP is trying to solve and its adoption in the real world changed, as well. Therefore, many examples from the first edition wouldn't work any more, even if I gave them a facelift. Like the first edition, I wanted this book to be of immediate practical value. Therefore, I decided to rewrite many of the chapters and most of the examples. I'm glad that I took that path.

I humbly hope that you'll appreciate my effort, like this book, and use it in your applications.

preface to the first edition

I've always felt that implementing a software system is much harder than it needs to be. It is difficult to map requirements to the implementation and then trace the implementation back to the requirements. Although many approaches—such as object-oriented programming, component-oriented programming, and design patterns—help to some extent, none of them satisfactorily addresses the system-level requirements, often referred to as crosscutting concerns, that must be included in multiple modules.

I came across AspectJ version 0.3 in 1998 while looking for better ways to architect a Java-based system. AspectJ was an implementation of aspect-oriented programming (AOP), a new methodology that specifically targeted the management of crosscutting concerns. Even though AspectJ was in its infancy, I became fascinated by its potential. The struggle to keep up with all the new advances in the Java and XML world, along with other priorities in my life, prevented me from pursuing it further. Still, exploring AspectJ was always on my to-do list, and I started looking at it again when it was in version 0.8. By then, AspectJ had evolved into a much more powerful language. I started using AspectJ and found that the more I used it, the more I fell in love with it. Today, the current version of AspectJ (1.1)—which this book is based on—has morphed into a mature, robust language.

In early 2002, I wrote a series of articles for *JavaWorld* describing AOP and AspectJ; the book you are holding grew out of that series. From reader responses, I realized that most developers understand that AspectJ can be used to modularize the crosscutting concern of logging, but they struggle to imagine how it may be applied beyond that. Logging, while an important concern, is not something developers lose sleep over. Logging using AspectJ, therefore, is best characterized as a vitamin and not a painkiller; while vitamins are important, often the need for them is not pressing enough to require immediate action. To further complicate the situation, the examples of AOP that are widely available today either repeat the same logging problem or are too abstract to be of immediate practical value.

My mission statement for this book is "to be a key element in bringing AOP and AspectJ into everyday practice." To accomplish this goal, the book not only presents the AspectJ language but also provides practical AspectJ-based solutions to a wide variety of real-world problems. You will find that you can utilize these solutions to quickly reap the benefits of the language. I have tried to use current technologies as the basis for these solutions so that you can readily apply them to your system. This also demonstrates that these latest technologies by themselves are not enough to manage crosscutting concerns, since combined with AspectJ, they provide a better solution. The book also presents a few original design patterns that increase the power of AspectJ significantly.

It is not often that one gets to write about such an exciting new programming methodology and language. I enjoyed writing this book. I hope you will enjoy reading it.

acknowledgments

Although only one name appears on the cover, many people helped behind the scenes. I'm humbled by all the support I've received in making this book a reality.

Many thanks to Andy Clement, Adrian Colyer, and Andrew Eisenberg for providing a solid implementation of AspectJ and AJDT. Special thanks to Andy and Andrew for meticulously reviewing the manuscript, making many helpful suggestions, and catching subtle issues. Also thanks to past AspectJ teams—without you there would be no AspectJ.

My thanks go to Jackie Carter, Nermina Miller, and Cynthia Kane for helping as development editors. Many thanks to Manning's publisher, Marjan Bace, for his commitment to making this a quality book. I'd like to thank Mary Piergies for managing the production and Tiffany Taylor for doing such an outstanding job at copyediting, making my writing look much better. Also thanks to Maureen Spencer for weeding out errors during proofreading, Gordon Salinovic for putting together the final copy, Karen Tegtmeyer for arranging reviews, and Steven Hong for taking care of the publicity.

My sincerest thanks to Dean Wampler and Colin Yates for reviewing the manuscript with a keen and critical eye; without your reviews, the book wouldn't be as accessible. Thanks to Luke Taylor for reviewing the book, especially security related material. Also thanks to Simone Gianni, Wayne Lund, and Marius Marin for graciously reviewing the manuscript. I am honored to be able to call you my friends.

Thanks to the official reviewers, who provided extremely useful feedback that also led to many improvements: Doug Warren (who served as the technical proofreader as well), Ara Abrahamian, Madhav Ayyagari, Paul Benedict, Thomas Darimont, Dab

Dobrin, Peter Johnson, Amin Mohammed-Coleman, Andrew Oliver, Thomas Palmer, Srini Penchikala, Andrew Rhine, Chris Richardson, Rick Wagner, Craig Walls, and Robert Wenner.

Also thanks to many Author Forum readers who took time to review the Early Access chapters and notified me about bugs as well as offering suggestions for improvement. I'd especially like to thank Swaroop Belur, Adrian Citu, Bhaskar Maddala, and David Wright. Any remaining errors are mine.

I'd like to send a big thank-you to all my colleagues at SpringSource for their support and encouragement. Special thanks to Rod Johnson for writing the foreword and rooting for AOP and AspectJ.

Finally, I'd like to thank my family for their help and support. A special thanks goes to my wife, Kavita, who reviewed the manuscript, tried out multiple versions of code, and helped with the illustrations for the book—never complaining about my many broken promises to spend more time with her. Thanks also to my son Shadaj, a budding computer scientist, for accepting the sacrifice that comes with having a busy dad. Now that the book is complete, I promise to work with you on all the projects we've thought of.

about this book

AspectJ in Action, Second Edition is a comprehensive and practical guide to applying AOP and AspectJ in real-world enterprise applications. Although the book focuses on practical applications, it doesn't skimp on concepts in AOP and constructs in AspectJ. I cover a broad spectrum of solutions—from simple examples that address tracing, monitoring, and policy enforcement to complex ones dealing with caching, concurrency control, transactions, and security. The book also covers how AOP helps improve domain-logic implementation. To make this book immediately useful and provide a practical context of enterprise applications, I use:

- Java (1.6)
- AspectJ (1.6)
- Spring (3.0)
- Spring MVC (3.0)
- Spring Security (3.0)
- Spring Batch (2.0)
- Log4J (1.2)
- JPA (1.0)
- Hibernate (3.3)
- OSCache (2.4)
- EJB (3.0)
- Mockito (1.8)
- JUnit (4.6)
- Ant (1.7)
- Maven (2.2)
- Eclipse (3.5)
- AJDT (2.0)
- SpringSource Tools Suite (2.1)

Regardless of your area of expertise, you'll find examples that you can use in your work immediately.

Roadmap

This book is divided into two parts plus three appendices. Part 1 (chapter 1 through 9) focuses on the technology, although we introduce many practical aspects that you may use in your application. Part 2 (chapter 10 through 17) focuses on applications of AOP. If you're new to AOP and AspectJ, you should read part 1 before reading part 2. If you're familiar with an older version of AspectJ, you may want to read part 1, focusing only on new features such as support for annotations, the @AspectJ syntax, new weaving models, and Spring integration.

Chapter 1 makes a case for AOP. It introduces the problems that aspect-oriented programming aims to address, discusses how current techniques fall short, and explains how AOP handles them. It presents the core concepts of AOP such as the join point model, pointcuts, and advice. It also presents a generic model of AOP to help distinguish it from similar technologies.

Chapter 2 introduces AspectJ at a high level. We'll discuss various language concepts and constructs, weaving choices, and Spring integration. We'll finish the chapter by showing the IDE support for AspectJ.

Chapter 3 gets into the details of the AspectJ language by closely examining its join point model. It introduces the pointcut expression language along with many examples. This chapter should serve as a handy reference for you.

Chapter 4 focuses on dynamic crosscutting that lets you modify the behavior of the system. It introduces various kinds of advice supported by AspectJ. In this chapter, you'll begin to implement aspects to deal with fault tolerance and caching functionality. This chapter provides you with enough information to start writing simple AspectJ programs.

Chapter 5 focuses on static crosscutting that you can use to modify the structure of the system. It examines mechanisms such as inter-type declarations, weave-time errors and warning declarations, and exception softening. It also shows a few examples of AspectJ that you can begin using immediately.

Chapter 6 discusses the unit of modularization in AspectJ: the aspect. We'll put together all the concepts presented so far. Equipped with this new knowledge, we'll update the caching example introduced in chapter 4. Specifically, we'll add automated tests to verify its functionality and expose the aspect over JMX.

Chapter 7 presents the brand-new feature in AspectJ 5: the @AspectJ syntax. In this chapter, we'll map the traditional syntax to the @AspectJ syntax, which is useful with both byte-code-based weaving and Spring's proxy-based implementation. We'll complete this chapter by discussing how you choose between the traditional and the @Aspect syntax.

Chapter 8 discusses weaving models offered by AspectJ, some of which are new features of AspectJ 5. We'll go into detail about build-time and load-time weaving. We'll also show an example that adds monitoring to a web application using load-time weaving.

Chapter 9 focuses on Spring AspectJ integration. We'll discuss using the @AspectJ syntax while avoiding the use of the byte-code-based weaver. We'll dive into how Spring's dependency injection mechanism works in synergy with proxy-based AOP. We'll also discuss a Spring-based variation of load-time weaving along with a complete example.

Next, we'll dive into part 2 to apply the knowledge you gain in part 1 to practical applications of AOP.

Chapter 10 discusses many variations of tracing and monitoring. These aspects represent how most developers begin with AOP. Make no mistake: these aren't toy aspects, and by the end of this chapter you should be able use aspects in your own project and reap immediate benefits.

Chapter 11 continues the journey of exploring another set of aspects that developers use during their initial exploration of AOP: policy enforcement. In this chapter, we'll discuss how policy-enforcement aspects can help keep your design intact. We'll include a wide range of examples: layered architecture, mixing of JDBC with JPA, Swing, and EJB.

Chapter 12 presents a set of design patterns that have been found to be useful in practice and that we'll use in the chapters that follow. We'll present the worker object pattern, the wormhole pattern, the participant pattern, and its variation—the annotation-driven participant pattern.

Chapter 13 applies some of the patterns presented in the previous chapter to a complex crosscutting concern of concurrency control. We'll implement aspects that modularize concurrency control for Swing-based applications. We'll also implement a read-write lock aspect.

Chapter 14 discusses one of the most commonly required crosscutting concern in enterprise applications: transaction management. We'll implement several aspects based on the abstraction offered by Spring. We'll also develop a fault-tolerance scheme that works particularly well with transaction managed operations.

Chapter 15 explains the modularization of another crosscutting concern: security. We'll implement aspects based on abstraction offered by Spring Security.

Chapter 16 introduces how AOP can help you better implement domain logic. We'll discuss how AspectJ can extend dependency injection concepts to domain objects and how to use this possibility of implementing rich behavior in domain objects. We'll also examine improving business logic through aspects, refactoring using aspects, and implementing certain domain-driven design policies using aspects.

Chapter 17 rounds out the book by showing a pragmatic approach to adopting AOP.

The first of the three appendixes presents an e-commerce example that is used in the book. The remaining appendixes explain how to use AspectJ with Ant and Maven.

Who should read this book

AspectJ in Action, Second Edition is aimed at intermediate to advanced Java developers. Whether you develop enterprise applications or architect complex software systems, you'll find this book enjoyable and helpful. If you're developing applications using the Spring Framework, you'll find most of the code developed in this book of immediate value. But even if you aren't using Spring, you'll be able to modify the code to any other framework you may be using. The book focuses heavily on Spring-based applications, but it also includes examples of other technologies such as Swing and EJB.

Although knowledge of object-oriented programming and Java is required, I don't assume that you're familiar with aspect-oriented programming or AspectJ. Basic knowledge of the Spring Framework will help you get the most out of this book. If you aren't familiar with the Spring Framework, you may want to read a few of the many online resources to gain some familiarity. For some of the specific technologies, such as transaction management in Spring and Spring Security, the book presents a short introduction so that you can understand the aspects without needing another source. I also cite resources (both text and online) for those who want to gain in-depth understanding.

Code and typographical conventions

To keep the code short, we don't show most import statements in Java and AspectJ source code, except in chapter 2 and where import statements improve clarity of the code. Similarly, we don't show the namespace and schema declarations in most XML source code. The downloadable code, of course, has unabbreviated code.

The book follows the following typographical conventions:

- *Italic* typeface is used to introduce new terms.
- `Courier` typeface is used to denote code samples as well as program elements.
- **`Courier bold`** typeface is used to denote code of special interest.
- Code-line continuations are indicated by ➥.

Getting the source code

The source code for the example applications in this book is freely available from Manning's web site, www.manning.com/AspectJinActionSecondEdition or www.manning.com/laddad2. Much of the source code is reusable either in its original state or after some customization. The downloadable package contains the source code, instructions on how to set up the environment, and build scripts that automate compiling and running the programs. The source code is organized to promote experimentation, where you can modify code for any of the projects without affecting others.

All of the technologies used in this book are being steadily updated. I expect the code to work without any changes with Java 5 and Java 6, Spring 3.0, and AspectJ 1.6.5. But I'll update source code with significant releases of the technologies used—especially if those break the code.

Author online

The purchase of *AspectJ in Action, Second Edition* includes free access to a private web forum run by Manning Publications, where you can make comments about the book, ask technical questions, and receive help from the author and from other users. To access the forum and subscribe to it, point your web browser to www.manning.com/laddad2 or www.manning.com/AspectJinActionSecondEdition. This page provides information on how to get on the forum once you are registered, what kind of help is available, and the rules of conduct on the forum.

Manning's commitment to our readers is to provide a venue where a meaningful dialogue between individual readers and between readers and the author can take place. It is not a commitment to any specific amount of participation on the part of the author, whose contribution to the AO remains voluntary (and unpaid). We suggest you try asking the author some challenging questions lest his interest stray!

The Author Online forum and the archives of previous discussions will be accessible from the publisher's web site as long as the book is in print.

About the author

RAMNIVAS LADDAD is a well-known expert in enterprise Java, especially in the area of AOP and Spring. He is the author of the first edition of *AspectJ in Action,* the best-selling book on AOP and AspectJ that has been lauded by industry experts for its presentation of practical and innovative AOP applications to solve real-world problems. Ramnivas, a Spring Framework committer, is also a very active presenter at leading industry events and has been an active member of both the AspectJ and Spring communities from their beginnings. He has worked with a wide range of systems, especially dealing with complex and mission-critical applications, in various roles.

Ramnivas shares his thoughts on http://ramnivas.com/blog, and you can follow him on Twitter at http://twitter.com/ramnivas.

about the title

By combining introductions, overviews, and how-to examples, the *In Action* books are designed to help learning and remembering. According to research in cognitive science the things people remember are things they discover during self-motivated exploration.

Although no one at Manning is a cognitive scientist, we are convinced that for learning to become permanent it must pass through stages of exploration, play, and, interestingly, retelling of what is being learned. People understand and remember new things, which is to say they master them, only after actively exploring them. Humans learn *in action.* An essential part of an *In Action* guide is that it is example-driven. It encourages the reader to try things out, to play with new code, and explore new ideas.

There is another, more mundane, reason for the title of this book: our readers are busy. They use books to do a job or solve a problem. They need books that allow them to jump in and jump out easily and learn just what they want just when they want it. They need books that aid them in action. The books in this series are designed for such readers.

about the cover illustration

The figure on the cover of *AspectJ in Action, Second Edition* is an "Ysleno Moluco," an inhabitant of the Molucan Islands, also known as the Spice Islands, a southwestern province of Indonesia. The illustration is taken from a Spanish compendium of regional dress customs first published in Madrid in 1799.

The title page of the Spanish compendium states:

> *Coleccion general de los Trages que usan actualmente todas las Nacionas del Mundo desubierto, dibujados y grabados con la mayor exactitud por R.M.V.A.R. Obra muy util y en special para los que tienen la del viajero universal*

which we translate, as literally as possible, thus:

> *General collection of costumes currently used in the nations of the known world, designed and printed with great exactitude by R.M.V.A.R. This work is very useful especially for those who hold themselves to be universal travelers*

Although nothing is known of the designers, engravers, and workers who colored this illustration by hand, the "exactitude" of their execution is evident in this drawing. The "Ysleno Moluco" is just one of many figures in this colorful collection. Their diversity speaks vividly of the uniqueness and individuality of the world's towns and regions just 200 years ago. This was a time when the dress codes of two regions separated by a few dozen miles identified people uniquely as belonging to one or the other. The collection brings to life a sense of isolation and distance of that period—and of every other historic period except our own hyperkinetic present.

Dress codes have changed since then and the diversity by region, so rich at the time, has faded away. It is now often hard to tell the inhabitant of one continent from another. Perhaps, trying to view it optimistically, we have traded a cultural and visual diversity for a more varied personal life. Or a more varied and interesting intellectual and technical life.

We at Manning celebrate the inventiveness, the initiative, and the fun of the computer business with book covers based on the rich diversity of regional life of two centuries ago? brought back to life by the pictures from this collection.

a real-world perspective of AOP

What is the real deal with AOP? Is it something that you should embrace or ignore? What do you gain with AOP, and what do you risk by adopting it? Let's address these important questions from a practitioner's point of view. We'll start with AOP in the context of the typical hype cycle. This will give us a historical perspective on AOP evolution and indicate what lies ahead. We also look at the landscape, focusing on the current situation and changes since the first edition of this book. While AOP is a more general concept, because our focus is the real world use of it, we'll focus on AspectJ—its most prominent implementation.

Mapping AOP onto the hype cycle

Every technology goes through a cycle that's well illustrated by the Gartner Hype Cycle (http://en.wikipedia.org/wiki/Hype_cycle). AOP is no exception. Understanding the hype cycle and the position of the technology you're considering adopting is important. It allows you to offer a more accurate gauge of the benefits the technology is likely to offer and the risk you expose yourself to. In this section, I'll give my assessment of the hype cycle of AOP in five major phases: technology trigger, peak of inflated expectations, trough of disillusionment, slope of enlightenment, and plateau of productivity. The following figure depicts the hype cycle and how AOP maps to it.

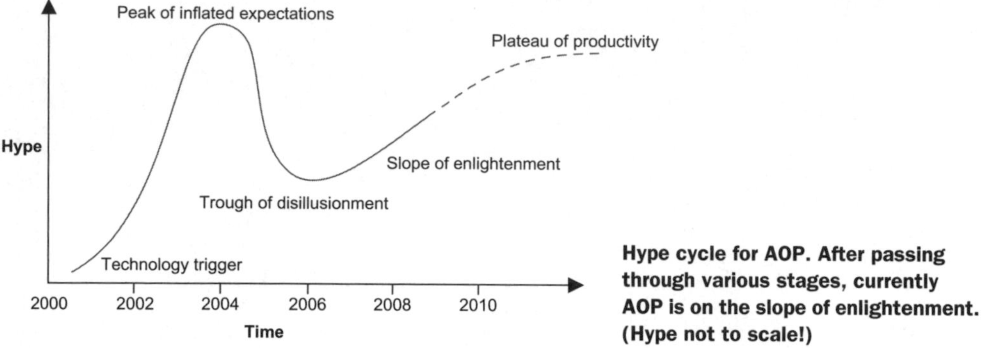

Hype cycle for AOP. After passing through various stages, currently AOP is on the slope of enlightenment. (Hype not to scale!)

Let's look at each of the major phases in the figure.

Technology trigger

In this phase, a new technology appears on the horizon with a promise to solve a set of problems. It may be an announcement of a new product or an actual release of a product. Either way, it may generate some buzz and attract developers towards it.

For AOP, the technology trigger occurred with AspectJ 1.0 release in 2002 followed by a more serious 1.1 release in 2003 (earlier releases, although interesting, didn't receive much attention). Gregor Kiczales and his team, while working at Xerox Palo Alto Research Center (PARC), developed the AOP concepts backed by the AspectJ language. Many technologists could immediately understand the potential for AspectJ, especially for enterprise applications. Aspect-oriented programming using AspectJ was seen as a way to modularize some of the common crosscutting concerns—transaction management, security, caching, concurrency control, and lest we forget, tracing.

For many technologies, especially with substantially new ideas and potential to solve complex problems, the next phase follows.

Peak of inflated expectations

In this phase, the technology gains much hype (warranted or otherwise). Everyone wants to know about it, everyone has an opinion of it, but few people use it in real applications. A few adventurous (or reckless) developers (or *early adopters*) try it. If the technology fits the problem well, and you have good understanding of it, adopting technology during this phase can give you a competitive advantage. It's fascinating to be associated with a technology in this phase. People perceive you as "cool."

For AOP, the peak occurred around 2004. I enjoyed the attention I received as well as the response to the first edition of *AspectJ in Action* (thank you!). Many smaller companies and a few larger ones used AspectJ in a few projects. During this time, most developers working on AspectJ and AspectJ Development Tools (AJDT) were from IBM. This significant investment from IBM helped AspectJ gain solid footing.

But the lack of mass adoption made using the technology an adventure. Fortunately for AspectJ the peak wasn't high due to expectation management by AspectJ evangelists. For example, Gregor Kiczales, the father of AOP, portrayed AspectJ as the

"15% solution" (http://www.ddj.com/architect/184414845): he argues that in a typical project, you'll use AspectJ for about 15% of your coding. Think about it. When was the last time the creator of a language quoted such a small number for his own language? Even the first edition of this book ended with, "However, AOP isn't a silver bullet that will solve all your programming problems. Nevertheless, we have to make progress—one step at a time." This expectation management led to a smaller peak in the hype cycle and, fortunately, a shorter fall in the next phase.

Trough of disillusionment

In this phase, the technology starts to lose the attention it once received. It becomes one of many things vying for attention. In this phase, many early adopters continue to use the technology creatively to gain a competitive advantage. Others begin to look at it with a skeptical eye. The technology sees serious and innovative competition from newer solutions that address part of the same problem space. Interestingly, many of these competing technologies are going through the "peak of inflated expectation" phase. On one extreme, these new technologies can drive the existing one into oblivion (which isn't necessarily a bad thing—if the technology couldn't take on a competition, oblivion is a respectful resting place). On the other side, competition can shake the technology and force it to innovate further.

For AOP, the trough occurred around 2006. In addition to the naturally expected trough that follows a peak, Java 5 also proved to be disruptive to implementing other features needed in making AspectJ an easily acceptable technology—compiler and weaver speed, tools integration, and so on. Although the core AJDT committers kept developing the technology, much more dedicated effort was needed. Furthermore, many users perceived the adoption of AspectJ as a big step due to the requirement of using a brand-new syntax and the need to use a special compiler at the beginning of a project. Eclipse, the main supported IDE for AspectJ, was advancing at a rapid pace, leaving a large gap between its Java support and AspectJ support.

Enterprise Java Beans (EJB) provided serious competition. Through a framework-centric approach, you could implement crosscutting functionality such as transaction management and security in a modular fashion. More serious competition came from dynamic languages such as Ruby and Groovy and associated frameworks such as Rails and Grails. The metaprogramming model available in these technologies provided an alternative solution to modularize crosscutting concerns.

On the tooling side, all new languages suffer from the lack of maturity (although most new language proponents would argue otherwise). In reality, tools always lag behind language creation. I still remember using Emacs with Java for several years after disappointing experiences with many IDEs. But this didn't cause us early Java adopters to discard the language for the lack of tools. A judicious decision requires that you weigh the benefits of the language against the handicaps introduced by immature or nonexisting tools. For AspectJ, the tools side—especially IDEs—has been a weakness, especially if you expected its support to match that of Java.

AspectJ took on all these challenges to enter the next—and most useful—phase.

Slope of enlightenment

This phase results from multiple factors such as changes in the technology to meet real-world requirements, maturing of the technology due to sustained field testing, finding the right context for the technology to make an impact, and disillusionment about other technologies once considered as alternatives. The technology also starts to be used to solve problems in the context of focused application areas.

The slope of enlightenment started for AOP right after its trough. Adrian Colyer, the AspectJ lead, left IBM to join SpringSource. Soon, I joined SpringSource, and I've been contributing to Spring AspectJ integration as a committer. Later, Andy Clement, a lead AspectJ developer, also left IBM to join SpringSource. Recently, Andrew Eisenberg joined SpringSource and is working on improving AspectJ-related tools. Currently, AspectJ is a SpringSource portfolio project and enjoys its sponsorship. All these factors helped bring together Spring and AspectJ and afford sustained development.

During my consulting engagements, I see signs of AspectJ being in this phase. Developers no longer fear it for its perceived complexity but rather show curiosity about exploring the benefits it offers and eagerly want to use AspectJ.

Let's look at the underlying factors that caused AspectJ to enter this phase.

RESPONSE TO USER NEEDS

AspectJ followed a path to enlightenment (pardon the pun) by simplifying its adoption. New syntax and weaving models (in part due to merger with AspectWerkz—a project led by Jonas Bonér and Alexandre Vasseur) removed some of the bumpiest patches on the path. The new syntax choices delayed the use of the weaver as far as executing the application (and, used with Spring, eliminated the weaver altogether). Load-time weaving allowed the introduction of AspectJ without much fuss. Java 5 also made a huge difference with the introduction of annotations. Annotations allow a simple collaboration point between developers of the main-line business logic and developers of aspects. Annotations alleviate the difficulty of writing good pointcuts to a large degree by enabling course-grained pointcuts that identify fine-grained join points in the main-line code.

The promise of good tooling—especially the possibility of visualizing the interaction between aspects and classes—has been an important differentiator from similar technologies (such as metaprogramming). Although AspectJ's support for Eclipse has always been reasonable, it was never as good as that for Java. Part of the problem was fast innovation in the underlying Eclipse JDT, which kept raising user expectations. Furthermore, compilation speed and memory requirement have been less than optimal. Overall, there was a gap between potential and reality when it came to tooling. Lately, the AspectJ and AJDT teams have performed some amazing feats in optimizing the compilation process and IDE integration. The changes in the latest AJDT, where the JDT is woven with AspectJ functionality (using AspectJ itself) make development within Eclipse a pleasant and productive experience. With all these changes, any issues with tooling are a thing of past.

Spring AOP also needed to respond to user needs. Although proxy-based AOP lowered the adoption barrier compared to AspectJ's byte-code based AOP, Spring's programming model wasn't inviting. Aspects written using it were type-unsafe and verbose. As a result, most developers limited themselves to the aspects shipped as part of Spring and other frameworks. Spring responded by adopting the AspectJ programming model with a proxy-based implementation. This new possibility lets you use a subset of the AspectJ syntax without the need for a special compiler or weaver. This significantly reduced the barrier to writing custom aspects to meet the specific needs of an application. Here, too, annotation-based pointcuts helped remove whatever was left of the barrier to its adoption. Currently, Spring considers AspectJ to be its preferred programming model and has relegated the old model to a transitionary technology status.

Spring's adoption of AspectJ also provided AspectJ a much needed context to grow.

FOCUSED CONTEXT: THE SPRING FACTOR

Languages grow within a certain context. C grew in the context of operating system programming, C++ grew in context of UI programming, Java grew in the context of servlets (leading it to be the favored server-side language), and Ruby grew in the context of Rails. AspectJ lacked such a context. It has been used in real-time programming, UI programming, and server-side programming. As a result, there has been a dissipated effort to make AOP a mainstream technology. The Spring Framework has changed it all. It provided the right context—enterprise applications—for AOP to gain prominence.

AOP was already an integral part of Spring, helping with concerns such as transaction management, security, and monitoring. By using an elegant programming model offered by AspectJ, it paved the way for mass adoption.

AVAILABILITY OF A GRADUAL ADOPTION PATH

The adoption of a new technology, especially with significantly new concepts such as AOP, is never easy. You need a path that allows a gradual introduction of the technology. Before AspectJ 5 and Spring AOP, the adoption path for AOP was steep.

Spring's proxy-based AOP with AspectJ syntax is a great way to start with AOP. It yields immediate benefits and provides experience with AOP. Spring even provides a few pre-built aspects to get you started. During this phase, you can start writing simple aspects based on the @AspectJ syntax applied using proxy-based AOP. Later, you can use byte-code-based weaving along with or as a replacement for the proxy-based AOP. Here, you can have several smaller steps available to manage risk. Initially, you can use aspects such as tracing and monitoring for development. Because you don't need to commit to using these aspects in production, there is little risk in trying them. With these aspects, load-time weaving is a great help; you don't need to modify your build system or use a special IDE, making the addition of aspects a much simpler task.

Next, you can begin using policy enforcement aspects. You can get feedback provided by the aspects about any policy violations while remaining uncommitted to their production use. In this phase, you can start using AJDT for immediate feedback right inside the IDE. During this process, you can vastly simplify the writing of the aspects using custom annotations—something you couldn't do before AspectJ 5. By this stage, you should be comfortable with the patterns and practices of AOP. This is the point at which you can make a judicious decision based on real experience.

NEW JVM LANGUAGES

In the last few years, practitioners have distinguished between Java the platform and Java the language. There is a growing recognition that Java the language isn't sufficient for productivity even considering the vast number of tools available for it. You need to choose some other language to gain a competitive advantage. At the same time, there is growing faith in the other part of Java the platform. With all the innovations in the VM as well as the overall platform (OSGi, mature libraries, IDEs), it's compelling to use the Java platform for many projects. Combining these factors has led to innovative new languages such as Groovy, JRuby, Scala, and Clojure on the Java platform. Today, it's not a shock to hear of a project using one of these new languages. As a result, the fear of new languages has gone down substantially. The use of multiple languages within the same project is also common. One of the negatives of AspectJ—that it's a new language—is no longer the case.

Even on the methodology front, there is a growing sense that OOP may have run its course. For today's complex problems, we need more power. We need to use OOP with *something* else: metaprogramming, functional programming, or, as I'll explain in this book, aspect-oriented programming. Furthermore, you may use several additional methodologies along with OOP. For example, you may use Java with Scala to take the functional approach along with AspectJ to deal with crosscutting concerns. This *Polyglot Programming* (http://www.polyglotprogramming.com) approach uses multiple languages in the same application and is steadily gaining traction. AspectJ may have to adopt its join point model, which exclusively targets the Java language, to fit into the polyglot programming scenario. Fun times may lie ahead!

ACCEPTANCE OF ANNOTATIONS

Selecting the required crosscutting points is one of the most critical and difficult tasks in writing aspects. Relying only on naming convention, type hierarchy, and package structure takes you quite a way. But in many case, defining a robust pointcut poses some difficulty. With the introduction of annotations in Java 5, AspectJ provides an easy and transparent way to select the join points you want. With annotations in play, aspect developers can expect class developers to mark program elements with annotations. It makes both camps happy—aspect developers can write simple pointcuts that can select program elements based on annotations they carry. On the other hand, class developers control the application of crosscutting functionality, because they choose what to annotate. The result is simplified and robust adoption of AOP.

DISILLUSIONMENT FROM THE ALTERNATIVE TECHNOLOGIES

The EJB framework appeared to provide a solution to modularizing crosscutting concerns. But most developers realize that the approach it offers is too heavyweight.

Various interceptor-based technologies promised to be alternatives to AOP. For example, EJB3 introduces interceptors as a new mechanism, a concept similar to AOP's advice—a definite step in the right direction, but lacking the join point model, which lies at the core of AOP.

Dynamic languages provide an alternative to AOP. But even with Groovy and Ruby, AOP has a place. Dynamic languages, despite the buzz surrounding them, are still new. As these languages mature and are used more seriously in enterprise applications, I expect AOP to gain prominence. After all, not many people thought anything was lacking in the Java programming language 10 years back! Interestingly, due to the availability of metaprogramming in dynamic languages, implementing AOP is easy.

For AspectJ, this phase is ongoing. It will be interesting to see how it unfolds.

Plateau of productivity

This is a boring phase, where there is little hype. The technology is no longer cool and on the leading or bleeding edge. It starts to appear on resumes and job applications in a substantial way. The technology fulfills its promise of improved productivity, and developers use it for the problems where it's known to really work. Although it's boring to those who are looking for a shot of excitement, this phase is the most appropriate for mass adoption. This phase often includes interesting innovations, but they aren't a hallmark of the phase. Instead, the focus is on best (and worst) practices based on real experience in the technology's adoption and problem-specific premade solutions (libraries).

This is where the Java language is today. AOP and AspectJ should reach this level in a few years.

Where is AOP being used?

We can address the question of how real AOP is by looking at where it's being used. Let's see what kind of applications use AOP.

Enterprise applications

Enterprise applications need to address many crosscutting functionalities: transaction management, security, auditing, service-level agreement, monitoring, concurrency control, improving application availability, error handling, and so on. Many enterprise applications use AOP to implement these functionalities. All the examples in this book are based on real-world problems and their AOP solutions.

Virtually every project that uses Spring uses AOP. Many applications start with prewritten aspects supplied with Spring (primarily transaction management and security). But due to the @AspectJ syntax, writing custom aspects is becoming a common task. After reaching the limits of Spring AOP, many applications move toward AspectJ weaving. The typical trigger point for this change is crosscutting of domain objects or other forms of deeper crosscutting functionalities. At that time, it's common to start with the @AspectJ syntax (which is used with Spring's proxy-based AOP) along with the load-time weaver. Of course, applications that don't use Spring often use AspectJ weaving from the beginning.

The industry sectors in which AspectJ is used in production (with proxy-based and bytecode-based AOP) range from financial companies (banking, trading, hedge funds) and health care to various web sites (e-commerce, customer care, content providers, and so on). If you're implementing enterprise applications and using AOP, you're in good company.

Web and application servers

The open source SpringSource dm Server (http://www.springsource.com/products/dmserver) supports developing enterprise application based on OSGi. It uses AspectJ to implement various crosscutting functionalities, such as First Failure Data Capture (FFDC), context collection, tracing, and policy enforcement. The SpringSource tc Server (http://www.springsource.com/products/tcserver) uses AspectJ to implement monitoring of deployed applications. You can expect a lot more functionality to be implemented using AspectJ in both these products.

Application frameworks

Application frameworks can use AOP effectively to target specific crosscutting functionalities while keeping their structure modularized. As discussed earlier, Spring provides crosscutting solutions such as transaction management and security through aspects. Furthermore, Spring includes aspects for injecting dependencies into domain objects. Frameworks that use AspectJ as their foundation have started to appear as well.

A recently released Spring Roo (http://www.springsource.org/roo) is an open-source, lightweight, and customizable framework that includes interactive and IDE-based tooling to enable rapid delivery of high performance enterprise Java applications. It uses a round-tripping code generator along with AspectJ byte-code weaving to keep generated code separate from user-written code. By judiciously combining annotations with AspectJ's static and dynamic crosscutting, it offers a significant boost in developer productivity without tying the application to Spring Roo. Another AspectJ-based project—Magma (http://cwiki.apache.org/labs/magma.html)—is an Apache lab project that simplifies development of Java web applications. It internally uses AspectJ and exposes it to power users to improve developer productivity and produce maintainable software.

Monitoring tools

AspectJ makes implementing a flexible monitoring scheme a breeze. Therefore, many tools use AspectJ as the underlying technology. Glassbox (http://www.glassbox.com), an open source product, offers ready-to-use aspects and tools to help you get started with application-level monitoring and pinpoint potential bottlenecks. Another open source product, Perf4J (http://perf4j.codehaus.org), uses annotations along with AspectJ weaving to monitor applications. Yet another open source tool, Contract4J (http://contract4j.org), uses AspectJ to monitor contract violations.

Several commercial products also use AspectJ to implement monitoring solutions. SpringSource Application Management Suite (http://www.springsource.com/products/suite/ams) focuses on application-level monitoring such as the time taken by methods in the system specifically targeting Spring-based applications. It also includes functionality such as alerting and trend analysis to let you take corrective actions. JXInsight (http://www.jinspired.com/products/jxinsight) monitors applications to provide insight into potential performance bottlenecks. It uses AspectJ-based probes to weave into various technologies. MaintainJ (http://maintainj.com) uses aspects to monitor system execution and generates sequence diagrams.

Compiler and IDE integration

AspectJ itself uses AspectJ to extend the JDT complier to support AspectJ constructs. AJDT uses AspectJ weaving through OSGi-based weaving service implemented by the Equinox Aspect project (http://www.eclipse.org/equinox/incubator/aspects) to better integrate with the JDT in Eclipse. This recent change enabled AJDT to provide a much better user experience. Scala IDE for Eclipse also followed the same route to provide a better experience for Scala developers.

I hope this discussion has helped put AOP and AspectJ in perspective. Rather than being a niche product, AspectJ has long been considered a standard tool in the developer toolbox. The rest of the book should give you a deeper understanding of what these technologies offer you.

Part 1

Understanding AOP and AspectJ

Part 1 of this book introduces aspect-oriented programming (AOP), the AspectJ language, and how it integrates with Spring. We'll discuss the need for a new programming methodology and the way this methodology is realized in AspectJ. Because AOP is a new methodology, we'll devote the first chapter to introducing it: why it is needed, and what its core concepts are. Chapter 2 shows the overall flavor of the AspectJ language through examples. The next four chapters will delve deeper into the AspectJ syntax. Together, these chapters should give you enough information to start writing simple code and see the benefits that AspectJ offers. Chapters 7 and 8 will explore the alternative syntax and weaving models. Given the mutual importance of Spring and AspectJ, this part of the book ends by devoting chapter 9 to Spring-AspectJ integration. Along the way, we'll examine many examples to reinforce the concepts learned.

You'll find the material in part 1 useful as a reference while reading the rest of the book. If you're new to AOP and AspectJ, we strongly recommend that you read this part first.

1 Discovering AOP

This chapter covers

- Understanding crosscutting concerns
- Modularizing crosscutting concerns using AOP
- Understanding AOP languages

Reflect back on your last project, and compare it with a project you worked on a few years back. What's the difference? One word: *complexity*. Today's software systems are complex, and all indications point to even faster growth in software complexity in the coming years. What can a software developer do to manage complexity?

If complexity is the problem, modularization is the solution. By breaking the problem into more manageable pieces, you have a better shot at implementing each piece. When you're faced with complex software requirements, you're likely to break those into multiple parts such as business functionality, data access, and presentation logic. We call each of these functionalities *concerns* of the system. In a banking system, you may be concerned with customer management, account management, and loan management. You may also have an implementation of data access and the web layer. We call these *core concerns* because they form the core functionality of the system. Other concerns, such as security, logging, resource pooling, caching, performance monitoring, concurrency control, and transaction management, cut across—or *crosscut*—many other modules. We call these functionalities *crosscutting concerns.*

For core concerns, object-oriented programming (OOP), the dominant methodology employed today, does a good job. You can immediately see a class such as `LoanManagementService` implementing business logic and `AccountRepository` implementing data access. But what about crosscutting concerns? Wouldn't it be nice if you could implement a module that you identify as `Security`, `Auditing`, or `PerformanceMonitor`? You can't do that with OOP alone. Instead, OOP forces you to fuse the implementation of these functionalities in many modules. This is where aspect-oriented programming (AOP) helps.

AOP is a methodology that provides separation of crosscutting concerns by introducing a new unit of modularization—an *aspect*. Each aspect focuses on a specific crosscutting functionality. The core classes are no longer burdened with crosscutting concerns. An *aspect weaver* composes the final system by combining the core classes and crosscutting aspects through a process called *weaving*. Thus, AOP helps to create applications that are easier to design, implement, and maintain.

In this chapter, we'll examine the fundamentals of AOP, the problems it addresses, and why *you* need to know about it. In the rest of the book, we'll examine AspectJ, which is a specific implementation of AOP. Let's start by discussing how you manage various concerns without AOP, which will help you understand why you need AOP.

1.1 Life without AOP

How do you implement crosscutting concerns using OOP alone? Typically, you add the code needed for each crosscutting concern in each module, as shown in figure 1.1.

This figure shows how different modules in a system implement both core concerns and crosscutting concerns. Let's illustrate the same idea through a code snippet. Consider the skeleton implementation of a representative class that encapsulates some business logic in a conventional way, shown in listing 1.1. A system consists of many such classes.

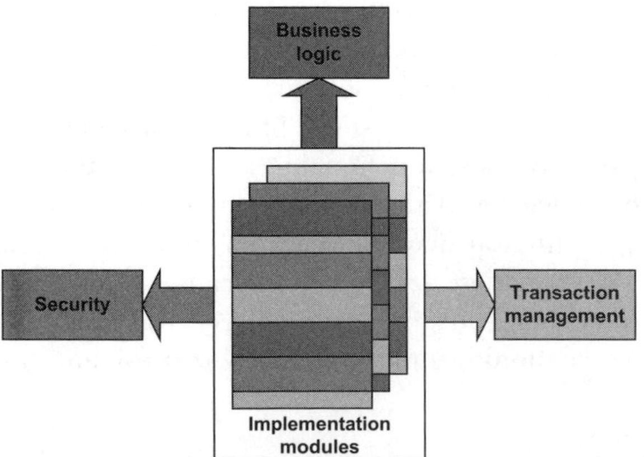

Figure 1.1 Viewing a system as a composition of multiple concerns. Each implementation module deals with some element from each of the concerns the system needs to address.

Listing 1.1 Business logic implementation along with crosscutting concerns

```
public class SomeBusinessClass extends OtherBusinessClass {
    ... Core data members
    ... Log stream
    ... Concurrency control lock

    ... Override methods in the base class

    public void someOperation1(<operation parameters>) {
        ... Ensure authorization

        ... Lock the object to ensure thread-safety

        ... Start transaction

        ... Log the start of operation

        ... Perform the core operation

        ... Log the completion of operation

        ... Commit or rollback transaction

        ... Unlock the object
    }

    ... More operations similar to above addressing multiple concerns
}
```


Although the details will vary, the listing shows a common problem many developers face: a conceptual separation exists between multiple concerns at design time, but implementation tangles them together. Such an implementation also breaks the Single Responsibility Principle (SRP)[1] by making the class responsible for implementing core and crosscutting concerns. If you need to change the invocation of the code related to crosscutting concerns, you must change each class that includes such an invocation. Doing so breaks the Open/Close principle[2]—open for extension, but closed for modifications. The overall consequence is a higher cost of implementing features and fixing bugs.

With conventional implementations, core and crosscutting concerns are *tangled* in each module. Furthermore, each crosscutting concern is *scattered* in many modules. The presence of code tangling and code scattering is a tell-tale sign of the conventional implementation of crosscutting concerns.[3] Let's examine them in detail.

1.1.1 Code tangling

Code tangling is caused when a module is implemented to handle multiple concerns simultaneously. Developers often consider concerns such as business logic, performance, synchronization, logging, security, and so forth when implementing a module.

---

1 See http://www.objectmentor.com/resources/articles/srp.pdf for more details.

2 See http://www.objectmentor.com/resources/articles/ocp.pdf for more details.

3 Note that code tangling and scattering may also stem from poor design and implementation (such as copied/pasted code). Obviously, you can fix such problems within the bounds of OOP. But in OOP the problem of crosscutting concerns is present even in well-designed systems.

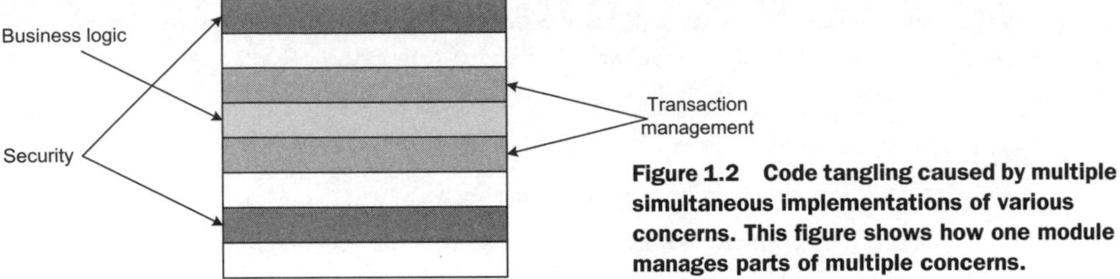

Figure 1.2 Code tangling caused by multiple simultaneous implementations of various concerns. This figure shows how one module manages parts of multiple concerns.

This leads to the simultaneous presence of elements from each concern's implementation and results in code tangling. Figure 1.2 illustrates code tangling in a module.

Another way to look at code tangling is to use the notion of a multidimensional concern space. Imagine that you're projecting the application requirements onto a multidimensional concern space, with each concern forming a dimension. Here, all the concerns are mutually independent and therefore can evolve without affecting the rest. For example, changing the security requirement from one kind of authorization scheme to another shouldn't affect the business logic. But as you see in figure 1.3, a multidimensional concern space collapses into a one-dimensional implementation space.

Because the implementation space is one-dimensional, its focus is usually the implementation of the core concern that takes the role of the dominant dimension; other concerns then tangle the core concern. Although you may naturally separate the individual requirements into mutually independent concerns during the design phase, OOP alone doesn't let you retain the separation in the implementation phase.

We've looked at the first symptom of crosscutting concerns when implemented using traditional techniques; now, let's move on to the next.

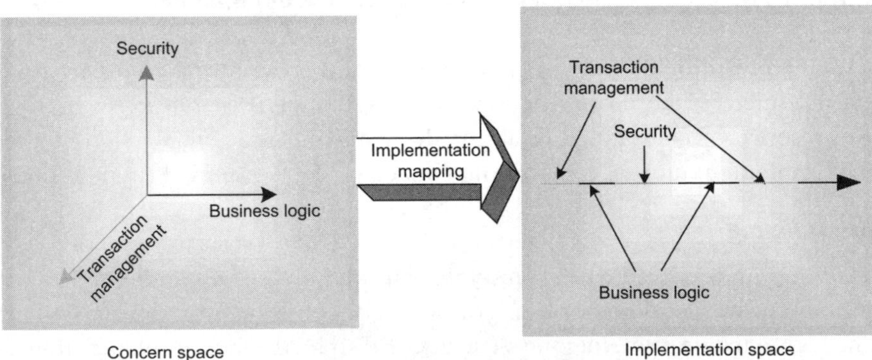

Figure 1.3 Mapping the *n*-dimensional concern space using a one-dimensional language. The orthogonality of concerns in the concern space is lost when it's mapped to the one-dimensional implementation space.

1.1.2 Code scattering

Code scattering is caused when a single functionality is implemented in multiple modules. Because crosscutting concerns, by definition, are spread over many modules, related implementations are also scattered over all those modules. For example, in a system using a database, performance concerns may affect all the modules accessing the database.

Figure 1.4 shows how a banking system implements security using conventional techniques. Even when using a well-designed security module that offers an abstract API and hides the details, each client—the accounting module, the ATM module, and the database module—still needs the code to invoke the security API to check permission. The code for checking permission is scattered across multiple modules, and there is no single place to identify the concern. The overall effect is an undesired tangling between the modules to be secured and the security module.

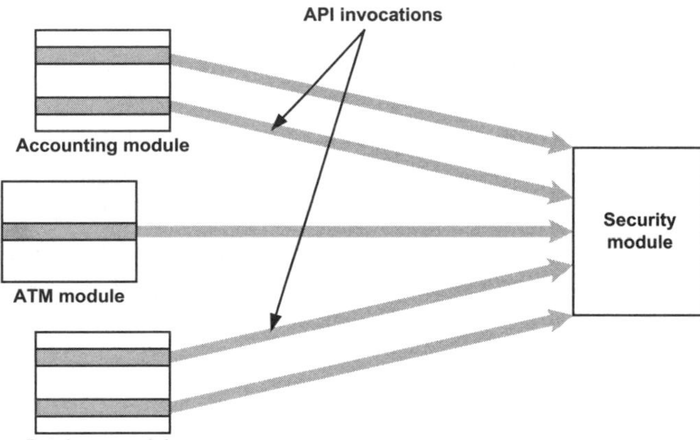

Figure 1.4 Implementation of a security concern using conventional techniques. The security module provides the API for authentication and authorization. But the client modules—accounting, ATM, and database—must embed the code to invoke the API to, say, check permission.

Code tangling and code scattering together impact software design and development in many ways: poor traceability, lower productivity, lower code reuse, poor quality, and difficult evolution. All of these problems lead us to search for better approaches to architecture, design, and implementation. Aspect-oriented programming is one viable solution. In the next section, we'll introduce you to AOP. Later in this chapter, we'll examine alternatives to AOP as well.

1.2 Modularizing with AOP

In OOP, the core concerns can be loosely coupled through interfaces, but there is no easy way to do the same for crosscutting concerns. This is because a concern is implemented in two parts: the server-side piece and the client-side piece. OOP modularizes the server part quite well in classes and interfaces. But when the concern is of a crosscutting nature, the client part (consisting of the requests to the server) is spread over all the clients.

NOTE We use the terms *server* and *client* here in the classic OOP sense to mean the objects that are providing a certain set of services and the objects using those services. Don't confuse them with networking servers and clients.

As an example, let's take another look at the typical implementation of a crosscutting concern in OOP, shown in figure 1.4. The security module provides its services through an interface. The use of an interface loosens the coupling between the clients and the implementations of the interface. Clients that use the security services through the interface are oblivious to the exact implementation they're using; any changes to the implementation don't require changes to the clients themselves. Likewise, replacing one security implementation with another is just a matter of instantiating the right kind of implementation. The result is that you can replace one security implementation with another with little or no change to the individual client modules. But this arrangement still requires that each client have the embedded code to call the API. Such calls must be included in all the modules requiring security and are tangled with their core logic.

Using AOP, none of the core modules contain calls to the security API. Figure 1.5 shows the AOP implementation of the same security functionality shown in figure 1.4. The security concern—implementation and invocations—now resides entirely inside the security module and the security aspect. For now, don't worry about the way in which AOP achieves this; we'll explain in the next section.

The fundamental change that AOP brings is the preservation of the mutual independence of the individual concerns. Implementations can be easily mapped back to the corresponding concerns, resulting in a system that is simpler to understand, easier to implement, and more adaptable to changes.

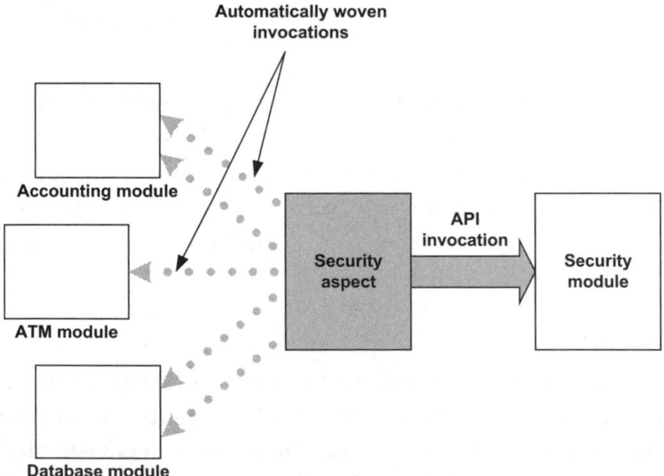

Figure 1.5 Implementing a security concern using AOP techniques: The security aspect defines the interception points needing security and invokes the security API upon the execution of those points. The client modules no longer contain any security-related code.

1.3 Anatomy of an AOP language

The AOP methodology is just that—a methodology. In order to be of any use in the real world, it must be implemented, or realized. Each realization of AOP involves specifying a language or a framework and associated tools. Like any other programming methodology, an AOP implementation consists of two parts:

- The *language specification* describes the language constructs and syntax to express implementation of the core and crosscutting concerns.
- The *language implementation* verifies the code's adherence to the language specification and translates the code into an executable form.

1.3.1 The AOP language specification

Any implementation of AOP must specify a language to implement the individual concerns and a language to implement the weaving rules. Note that an AOP system may offer a homogeneous language that doesn't distinguish between the two parts. This is likely to be the case in future AOP languages. Let's take a closer look at these two parts.

IMPLEMENTATION OF CONCERNS

As in other methodologies, the concerns of a system are implemented into modules that contain the data and behavior needed to provide their services. A module that implements the core part of the caching concern maintains a collection of cached objects, manages the validity of the cached objects, and ensures bounded memory consumption. To implement both the core and crosscutting concerns, we normally use standard languages such as C, C++, and Java.

WEAVING RULES SPECIFICATION

Weaving rules specify how to combine the implemented concerns in order to form the final system. After you implement the core part of the caching concern in a module (perhaps through a third-party class library), you must introduce caching into the system. The weaving rule in this case specifies the data that needs to be cached, the information that forms the key into the cache storage, and so forth. The system then uses these rules to obtain and update cache from the specified operations.

The power of AOP comes from the economical way of expressing the weaving rules. For instance, to modularize tracing concerns in listing 1.1, you can add a few lines of code to specify that all the public operations in the system should be logged. Here is a weaving specification for the tracing aspect:

- Rule 1: Create a logger object.
- Rule 2: Log the beginning of each public operation.
- Rule 3: Log the completion of each public operation.

This is much more succinct than modifying each public operation to add logging code. Because the tracing concern is modularized away from the class, it may focus only on the core concern, as follows:

```
public class SomeBusinessClass extends OtherBusinessClass {
    ... Core data members

    ... Override methods in the base class

    public void someOperation1(<operation parameters>) {
        ... Perform the core operation
    }

    ... More operations similar to above
}
```

Compare this class with the one in listing 1.1: all the code to perform tracing—the ancillary concerns from the class's point of view—have been removed. When you apply the same process to other crosscutting concerns, only the core business logic remains in the class. As you'll see in the next section, an AOP implementation combines the classes and aspects to produce a woven executable.

Weaving rules can be general or specific in the ways they interact with the core modules. In the previous logging example, the weaving rules don't need to mention any specific classes or methods in the system. On the other end of the spectrum, a weaving rule may specify that a business rule should be applied only to specific methods, such as the `credit()` and `debit()` operations in the `Account` class or the ones that carry the `@ReadOnly` annotation. The specificity of the weaving rules determines the level of coupling between the aspect and core logic.

The language used to specify weaving rules can be a natural extension of that language or something entirely different. For example, an AOP implementation using Java as the base language might introduce new extensions that blend well with the base language, or it could use a separate XML-based language to express weaving rules.

1.3.2 The AOP language implementation

The AOP language implementation performs two logical steps: It first combines the individual concerns using the weaving rules, and then it converts the resulting information into executable code. AOP implementation thus requires the use of a processor—*weaver*—to perform these steps.

An AOP system can implement the weaver in various ways. A simple approach uses source-to-source translation. Here, the weaver processes source code for individual classes and aspects to produce woven source code. The aspect compiler then feeds this woven code to the base language compiler to produce the final executable code. This was the implementation technique used in early implementations of AspectJ. The approach suffers from several drawbacks because the executable code can't be easily traced back to the original source code. For example, stack traces indicate line numbers in woven source code.

Another approach first compiles the source code using the base language compiler. Then, the resulting files are fed to the aspect compiler, which weaves those files. Figure 1.6 shows a schematic of a compiler-based AOP language implementation.

An AOP system may also be able to push the weaving process close to execution of the system. If the implementation of AOP is Java-based, a special class loader or a virtual

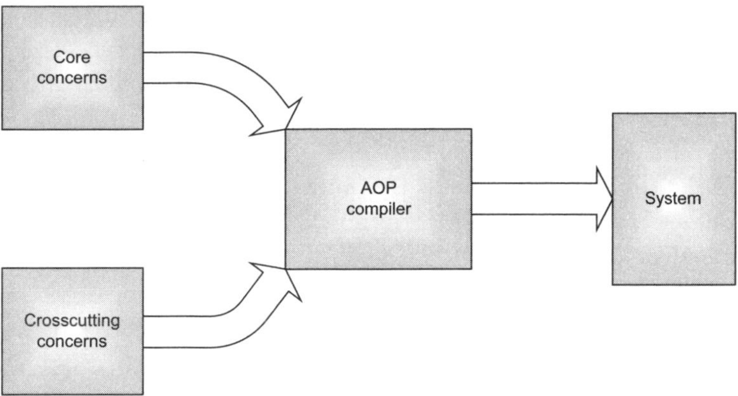

Figure 1.6 An AOP language implementation that provides a weaver in the form of a compiler. The compiler takes the implementation of the core and crosscutting concerns and weaves them together to form the final system.

machine (VM) agent can perform the weaving. Such an implementation first loads the byte code for the aspects, weaves them into the classes as they're being loaded, and supplies those woven versions of the classes to the underlying VM.

Yet another implementation could use automatically created proxies. In this case, each object that needs weaving is wrapped inside a proxy. Such an implementation typically works well in conjunction with another framework that controls the creation of objects. In this way, the framework can wrap each created object in a proxy.

So far, we've looked at the mechanics of an AOP system. Now, let's examine AOP's fundamental concepts.

1.4 Fundamental concepts in AOP

By now, it should be clear that AOP systems help in modularizing crosscutting concerns. But so do many other technologies, such as byte-code manipulation tools, direct use of the proxy design pattern, and meta-programming. How do you differentiate AOP from these options? To find out, we need to distill the core characteristics of AOP systems into a generic model. If a system fits that model, it's an AOP system.

To implement a crosscutting concern, an AOP system may include many of the following concepts:

- *Identifiable points in the execution of the system*—The system exposes points during the execution of the system. These may include execution of methods, creation of objects, or throwing of exceptions. Such identifiable points in the system are called *join points*. Note that join points are present in all systems—even those that don't use AOP—because they're points during execution of a system. AOP merely identifies and categorizes these points.
- *A construct for selecting join points*—Implementing a crosscutting concern requires selecting a specific set of join points. For example, the tracing aspect

discussed earlier needs to select only the public methods in the system. The *pointcut* construct selects any join point that satisfies the criteria. This is similar to an SQL query selecting rows in database (we'll compare AOP with databases in section 1.5.2). A pointcut may use another pointcut to form a complex selection. Pointcuts also collect context at the selected points. For example, a pointcut may collect method arguments as context. The concept of join points and the pointcut construct together form an AOP system's *join point model.* We'll study AspectJ's join point model in chapter 3.

- *A construct to alter program behavior*—After a pointcut selects join points, you must augment those join points with additional or alternative behavior. The *advice* construct in AOP provides a facility to do so. An advice adds behavior before, after, or around the selected join points. Before advice executes before the join point, whereas after advice executes after it. Around advice surrounds the join point execution and may execute it zero or more times. Advice is a form of *dynamic crosscutting* because it affects the execution of the system. We'll study AspectJ's dynamic crosscutting implementation in chapter 4.
- *Constructs to alter static structure of the system*—Sometimes, to implement crosscutting functionality effectively, you must alter the static structure of the system. For example, when implementing tracing, you may need to introduce the logger field into each traced class; *inter-type declaration* constructs make such modifications possible. In some situations, you may need to detect certain conditions, typically the existence of particular join points, before the execution of the system; *weave-time declaration* constructs allow such possibilities. Collectively, all these mechanisms are referred to as *static crosscutting*, given their effect on the static structure, as opposed to dynamic behavior changes to the execution of the system. We'll study AspectJ's static crosscutting support in chapter 5.
- *A module to express all crosscutting constructs*—Because the end goal of AOP is to have a module that embeds crosscutting logic, you need a place to express that logic. The *aspect* construct provides such a place. An aspect contains pointcuts, advice, and static crosscutting constructs. It may be related to other aspects in a similar way to how a class relates to other classes. Aspects become a part of the system and use the system (for example, classes in it) to get their work done. We'll examine AspectJ's implementation of aspect in chapter 6.

Figure 1.7 shows all these players and their relationships to each other in an AOP system.

Each AOP system may implement a subset of the model. For example, Spring AOP (discussed in chapter 9) doesn't implement weave-time declarations due to its emphasis on its runtime nature. On the other hand, the join point model is so central to AOP that every AOP system must support it—everything else revolves around the joinpoint model.

When you encounter a solution that modularizes crosscutting concerns, try to map it onto the generic AOP model. If you can, then that solution is indeed an AOP system. Otherwise, it's an alternative approach for solving the problem of crosscutting concerns.

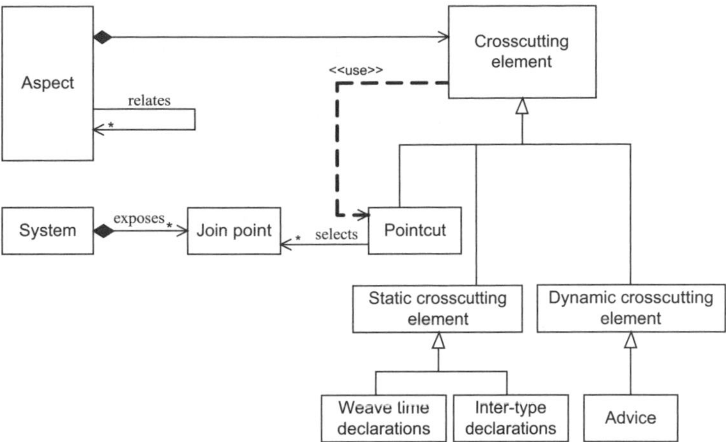

Figure 1.7 Generic model of an AOP system. Note that not every system implements each part of the model.

1.5 AOP by analogy

When you're learning a new technology, it sometimes helps to compare it with existing technologies. In this section, we'll attempt to help you understand AOP by comparing it with Cascading Style Sheets (CSS), database programming, and event-oriented systems. The purpose of this section is to help those familiar with at least one of these technologies to understand AOP by analogy.

1.5.1 Cascading Style Sheets (CSS)

CSS is a widely supported mechanism to separate content from presentation in HTML pages. Without CSS, formatting information is fused with content (causing tangling), and similar content elements have presentational information spread into multiple places (causing scattering). CSS helps the situation by letting the main document focus on content by separating the formatting information into a document called a *stylesheet*.

A core concept in CSS is a *selector* that selects document elements matching a certain specification. For example, the `body p` selector can select paragraphs inside the body element. You can then associate presentational information with a selector and, for example, set the background color of such elements to blue using the `body p {background: blue;}` element.

AOP acts on classes in the same way that CSS acts on documents. AOP lets you separate crosscutting logic from the main-line logic. AOP's pointcuts have the same selection role as CSS selectors. Whereas CSS selectors select structural elements in a document, pointcuts select program elements. Similarly, the blocks describing the formatting information are analogous to AOP advice in functionality.

Often, the selection mechanism requires more information than merely using the inherent characteristics of a structure such as `body p`. It's common practice to supplement content elements with additional metadata through the `class` attribute. For example, you can mark an HTML paragraph element as menu by using the tag `<p class="menu">`. Then, in the stylesheet, you can select such an element by using the `p.menu` selector and apply appropriate presentation characteristics. In AOP, practitioners face the same problem—selection through a pointcut often requires information beyond merely relying on inherent characteristics of the program elements such as class and method names. The use of Java annotations plays a role similar to the class attribute in HTML documents. You can, for example, mark a method as `@Transactional` and utilize it in a pointcut expression.

There are similarities from the adoption perspective as well. Through WYSIWYG HTML editors, it's easy to create a good-looking HTML. That apparent simplicity led to many initial web documents embedded with formatting information. But when we realized that it's difficult to create a consistent look when every element's formatting is specified independently, developers started to look favorably at CSS. AOP has encountered a similar trend. There is a level of comfort in embedding the implementation of crosscutting functionality inside classes; you can see exactly what's going to happen. But you soon realize that creating a consistent implementation is nearly impossible when similar code is scattered in many places. In addition, using CSS requires a level of expertise and understanding of the semantics associated with the elements in a document. Using AOP requires similar understanding of the semantic separation between core and crosscutting elements.

CSS works at the structure level, and database triggers offer similar separation at the programming level. Let's see how that technique compares with AOP.

1.5.2 Database systems

Database systems offer "dynamic crosscutting" targeted toward data access, whereas AOP offers a similar mechanism toward general programming. It offers two good analogies to AOP concepts: SQL with pointcuts and triggers with advice.

SQL AND POINTCUTS

A join point is like a row in a database, whereas a pointcut is like an SQL query. An SQL query selects rows according to a specified criterion such as "rows in accounts table, where the balance is greater than 50". It provides access to the content of the selected rows. Similarly, a pointcut is a query over program execution that selects join points according to a specified criterion such as "method execution in the `Account` class, where the method name starts with 'set'". It also provides access to the join point context (objects available at the join point, such as method arguments).

TRIGGERS AND ADVICE

Database programming often uses triggers to respond to changes made in data. For example, you can use a trigger to audit changes in certain tables. The following snippet calls the `logInventoryIncrease()` procedure when inventory increases:

```
CREATE OR REPLACE TRIGGER inventory_increase_trigger
    AFTER UPDATE OF count ON inventory
    FOR EACH ROW
        WHEN (new.count > old.count)
        CALL logInventoryIncrease(:new.itemID, :old.count, :new.count);
```

The static condition, such as the name of the table and the modified column, as well as the dynamic condition, such as the difference in the column value, are analogous to AOP's pointcut concept. Both describe a selection criterion to "trigger" certain actions. The stored procedure specified in the trigger is analogous to AOP's advice.

Database triggers and AOP's advice both modify the normal program execution to carry additional or alternative actions. But there are some obvious differences. Database triggers are useful only for database operations. AOP has a more general approach that can be used for many other purposes. But note that AOP doesn't necessarily obviate the need for database triggers, for reasons such as performance and bringing uniformity to multiple applications accessing the same tables.

Similar to database triggers, event-oriented programming includes the notion of responding to events.

1.5.3 Event-oriented programming

Event-oriented programming is essentially the observer design pattern (we'll discuss it as an alternative to AOP in section 1.7.3). Each interested code site notifies the observers by firing events, and the observers respond by taking appropriate action, which may be crosscutting in nature.

In AOP, the program is woven with logic to fire virtual events and to respond to the events with an action that corresponds to the crosscutting concern it's implementing. But note this important difference: Unlike in event-based programming, there is no explicit code for the creation and firing of events in the subject classes. Executing part of the program constitutes the virtual-event generation. Also, event systems tend to be more coarse-grained than an AOP solution implements.

Note that you can effectively combine event-oriented programming with AOP. Essentially, you can modularize the crosscutting concern of firing events into an aspect. With such an implementation, you avoid tangling the core code with the event-firing logic.

Now that you have a good understanding of AOP, let's turn our attention to a bit of history and the current status of AOP implementations.

1.6 Implementations of AOP

Much of the early work that led to AOP today was done in research institutions. Cristina Lopes and Gregor Kiczales of the Palo Alto Research Center (PARC), a subsidiary of Xerox Corporation, were among the early contributors to AOP. Gregor coined the term *AOP* in 1996 and started AspectJ, the first implementation of AOP.

But AOP is a methodology with many possible implementations. Each implementation takes a slightly different view on the target use case and programming constructs. Let's see who the dominant players are and how they size up against each other.

1.6.1 AspectJ

AspectJ is the original and still the best implementation of AOP. After a few initial releases, Xerox transferred the AspectJ project to the open source community at eclipse.org. In its early implementations, AspectJ extended Java through additional keywords to support AOP concepts, similar to the way C++ extended C to support OOP concepts. As an implementation, it provided a special compiler.

Until a few years back, AspectJ had a close cousin: AspectWerkz. This AOP system followed the core AspectJ model, except that it used metadata expressed through Javadoc annotations, Java 5 annotations, or XML elements in place of additional keywords. In AspectJ version 5, AspectWerkz merged with AspectJ, offering developers a choice of technologies including a new @AspectJ (pure Java 5 annotation-based) syntax. We'll study that syntax in chapter 7.

AspectJ's primary tool support is an Eclipse plug-in, AspectJ Development Tools (AJDT). One of AJDT's most important features is a tool for visualization of crosscutting, which is helpful for debugging a pointcut specification. Although you write classes and aspects separately, you can visualize the combined effect even before the code is deployed.

> **Scala and AspectJ**
>
> Scala is a new language that compiles source code to the standard Java byte code. Scala maps program elements to byte code in a manner similar to that of Java. This lets you use Scala with AspectJ. You can see a working example at http://blog.objectmentor.com/articles/2008/09/27/traits-vs-aspects-in-scala. Note that, unlike Scala, other JVM languages such as JRuby and Groovy use mapping that heavily relies on reflection. Therefore, AspectJ may not be used as readily with those. Instead, you need specialized languages that work with them, as you'll see in section 1.6.3.

The AspectJ language has an alternative implementation called the AspectBench compiler (abc; http://aspectbench.org). The focus of this project is to provide a flexible implementation to support experimenting with new AspectJ language features and optimization ideas.

1.6.2 Spring AOP

Spring is the most popular lightweight framework for enterprise applications. To satisfy the needs of enterprise applications, it includes an AOP system based on interceptors and the proxy design pattern. Earlier implementations of Spring AOP (prior to Spring 2.0) offered a somewhat complex programming model. The new programming model, based on AspectJ, offers a much better programming experience and enables Spring users to write custom aspects without difficulty.

Like AspectJ, Spring AOP, through the Spring IDE (an Eclipse plug-in), provides support for visualizing crosscutting in the IDE. We'll examine how Spring uses AspectJ in detail in chapter 9 and in examples throughout the book.

Spring.NET is the .NET counterpart of the Spring Framework. It includes AOP support that is similar to Spring AOP.

1.6.3 Other implementations of AOP

Many other implementations of AOP in Java are available. JBoss (http://www.jboss.org/jbossaop), an open source application server, offers an AOP solution that includes a pointcut language similar to that of AspectJ. In addition, the AOP Alliance API is implemented in frameworks such as Guice (http://code.google.com/p/google-guice) and Seasar (http://www.seasar.org). (Spring used to offer a programming model based on the AOP Alliance API, but that model has been designated a transitional technology status due to the availability of the AspectJ-based model.)

AspectJ has been an inspiration for AOP implementations for other languages such as Aquarium for Ruby (http://aquarium.rubyforge.org), Aspect-Oriented C (http://research.msrg.utoronto.ca/ACC), and AspectC++ (http://www.aspectc.org). Groovy, like Ruby, makes it possible to implement an AOP-like functionality through its meta-object protocol (MOP) facility (see http://www.infoq.com/articles/aop-with-groovy for an explanation of this approach). But as with Ruby, efforts are underway to introduce an AspectJ-like syntax to provide a domain-specific language (DSL) to simplify writing aspects (see http://svn.codehaus.org/grails-plugins/grails-aop for the code of the yet-to-be-released grails-aop project).

AOP has generated quite a bit of interest in the .NET world. Due to the use of byte code representations and the possibility of using proxies, .NET offers choices similar to those available in the Java world. In addition to Spring.NET, prominent AOP solutions in .NET include PostSharp (http://www.postsharp.org) and Aspect# (http://www.castleproject.org/aspectsharp). LOOM.NET (http://www.dcl.hpi.uni-potsdam.de/research/loom) is a research project that's exploring static and dynamic weaving in .NET.

1.7 Alternatives to AOP

The problem AOP addresses isn't new. The concerns of auditing, transaction management, security, and so on emerged as soon as we started implementing nontrivial software systems. Consequently, many competitive technologies deal with the same problem: frameworks, code generation, design patterns, and dynamic languages. Let's look at those alternatives.

NOTE Although I'll compare these techniques as alternatives to AOP and (not surprisingly) show how AOP outshines each of them when it comes to dealing with crosscutting concerns, I don't mean that these techniques are useless. Each of these approaches is appropriate for a set of problems. AOP works well alongside these techniques and, in some cases, can enhance their implementation.

1.7.1 Frameworks

Frameworks such as servlets and Enterprise JavaBeans (EJB) offer specific solutions to a focused set of problems. For example, the servlet specification offers filters to deal with requests made using the HTTP protocol. Given that each framework deals with a specific problem, it may also provide some solutions for dealing with the associated crosscutting concerns. For example, with the servlet framework, you may use filters to implement concerns such as security.

Similarly, the EJB framework addresses crosscutting concerns such as transaction management and security. The EJB3 specification even provides limited support for interceptors—which, to an extent, matches the goals of AOP. But as you'll see later, it falls short of being a complete solution.

You can use AOP along with an underlying framework. In such an arrangement, the core framework deals with the target problem and lets aspects deal with crosscutting concerns. For example, the core Spring Framework deals with dependency injection for configuration and enterprise service abstraction to isolate beans from the underlying infrastructure details, while employing AOP to deal with crosscutting concerns such as transaction management and security.

A framework's approach to crosscutting concerns often, but not always, boils down to either employing code generation or implementing appropriate design patterns. Let's examine the two in more details.

1.7.2 Code generation

Code-generation techniques shift some responsibility of writing code from the programmer to the machine. (Of course, programmers do have to write code for the generators.) These techniques represent powerful ways to deal with a wide range of problems and often are helpful in raising the level of abstraction. You can modify the original code to add functionality such as observer notifications or produce additional artifacts such as proxy classes. In the process, code generation takes care of one of the drawbacks of using design patterns directly: manual modifications in many places.

A variation of code generation works at the compiled code level through byte-code manipulation tools. Instead of producing source code that needs to be compiled into machine code, the code generator directly produces machine code. For Java, the difference between source code–level generation and byte-code generation is small, given how directly source code maps to byte code. Many Java technologies, such as Hibernate and JRuby, use byte-code manipulation techniques as the basis for their implementation.

In Java 5, the annotation language feature lets you attach additional information to the program elements. Code-generation techniques can take advantage of those annotations to produce additional artifacts such as Java code or XML configuration files. Java 5 even provides an Annotation Processing Tool (APT), to simplify the process. But APT forces you to understand low-level details such as the syntax tree, and that makes it difficult to use unless you acquire specific skills. It's no surprise that few non-framework programmers use APT. AOP, on the other hand, can provide simpler solutions to process annotations, as you'll see in rest of the book.

Many systems, most notably AspectJ, use byte-code manipulation as the underlying technique in implementing AOP. The difference is how it employs the technique as part of the overall AOP model. First, it provides a much simpler programming model, making it easier for you to create modularized crosscutting implementations without knowing low-level details such as the abstract syntax tree. It essentially provides a DSL targeted at crosscutting concerns. Users are isolated from byte-code manipulation mechanisms, which aren't for the faint of heart. Furthermore, by limiting power, AOP nudges you toward writing better code. In short, although code generation is capable of doing anything AOP can do (and a lot more), AOP brings a level of discipline that is essential for good software engineering when it comes to dealing with crosscutting concerns.

1.7.3 Design patterns

Design patterns also provide solutions to crosscutting concerns. In this section, we'll take a comparative look at some of the design patterns—observer, chain of responsibility, decorator, proxy, and interceptor—that help with crosscutting concerns. You'll see that quite a few similarities exist between design patterns and AOP—you can view a few design patterns as a "poor man's" AOP implementation.

OBSERVER PATTERN

The well-known observer design pattern decouples the subject (an object of interest) from observers (objects that need to respond to changes in the subject). When a subject changes its state, it notifies all observers of the change by calling a method such as `notify<ChangeType>()`, passing it an event object that encapsulates the information about the change. The notification method iterates over all the observers and calls a method on each observer (in message-oriented systems, these details change a bit, but the overall scheme remains the same). The called method in the observer includes the logic appropriate to respond to the event.

AOP's advice may superficially look like an event responder, but there are some important differences. First, you won't see invocations such as `notify<ChangeType>()` in the subject class; thus, advice decouples the observer pattern logic from the subject. As a result, you can produce notifications that weren't planned in advance, making your system extensible over what it was originally designed to be and bringing it new life in some situations. Second, the context collected by pointcuts (equivalent to information carried in an event object) is much more flexible and powerful in AOP. Pointcuts can collect just the right amount of context needed for advice logic. With a typical event model, you end up passing everything that you might possibly need.

CHAIN OF RESPONSIBILITY

The chain of responsibility (COR) pattern, shown in figure 1.8, puts a chain of processing objects in front of a target object. Before or after invoking the target object, the objects in the chain may perform additional work.

Successfully applying the COR pattern has two prerequisites. First, you should have only one or a small number of target methods, whose processing needs to be augmented. Second, the associated framework should already support the pattern. For example, the filter implementation in the servlet framework implements the COR pattern. It works well there because both prerequisites are met: it targets only one method—`doService()`—and the filter-management code is implemented as a part of

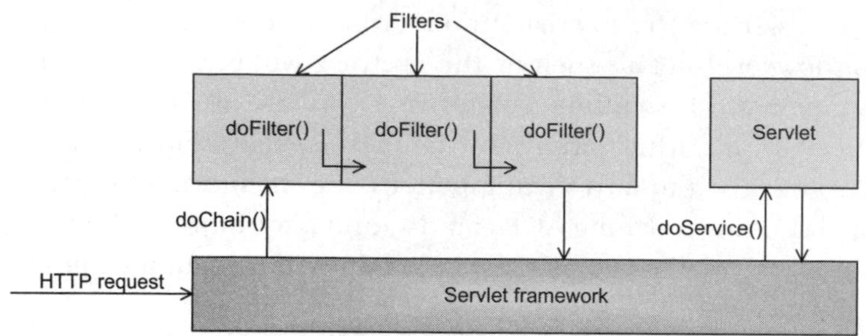

Figure 1.8 Chain of responsibility as implemented by the servlet framework. The filter chain allows applying additional logic such as coarse-grained security around the doService() method.

the framework. In this setup, some coarse-grained crosscutting concerns—ones that deal at the HTTP request level—may be modularized into servlet filters. But for any concern that needs to go beyond the `doService()` method, filters offer no solution.

AOP works in similar ways, except it doesn't have either of the prerequisites. Instead, each aspect deals with the problem head on by advising appropriate code.

DECORATOR AND PROXY

The decorator and proxy[4] design patterns use a wrapper object that can perform some work before, after, or around invocation of the wrapped object or its representation, as shown in figure 1.9. This additional work can be crosscutting in nature. For example, each method may perform a security check before the wrapped object's method is invoked.

Java offers dynamic proxies that reduce the code required for creating wrapper types and routing each method. Using this feature, you dynamically create a proxy for a given set of interfaces, supplying an invocation handler. The proxy implements all the specified interfaces and invokes the invocation handler when any interface method is called. You'll see a full example of dynamic proxies in chapter 9, section 9.2.1.

Implementing crosscutting concerns using dynamic proxies requires control over the creation of each object so that it may be wrapped in a dynamic proxy. Because

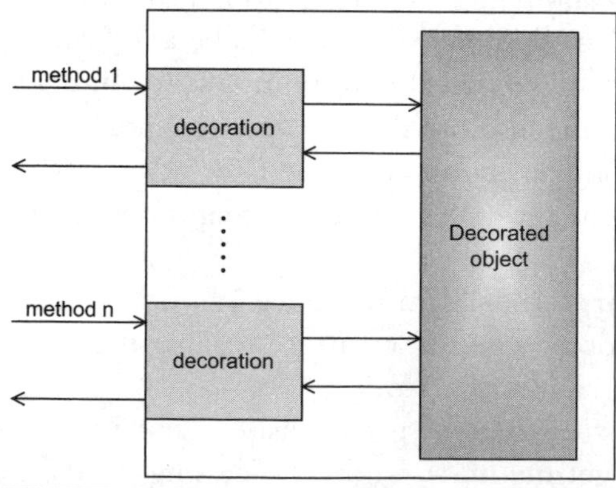

Figure 1.9 The decorator design pattern. The original object is wrapped in the decorator that presents the same interface as the decorated object. Each method passes through the decoration, which can implement functionality such as security and transaction management.

[4] I lump these two patterns together because the distinction between them isn't significant from the AOP perspective. A decorator holds onto a real object that it decorates, whereas a proxy may not necessarily hold any real object but simulates holding one. In a way, the proxy design pattern is a generalization of the decorator design pattern.

proxies invoke the invocation handler for every method, proxies must include logic to apply crosscutting concern selectively. Furthermore, dynamic proxies intercept method invocations only: they can't crosscut object creation, field access, exception handling, and so on.

Direct use of the decorator and proxy design patterns to implement crosscutting concerns requires substantial effort. But you can use these patterns as the underlying implementation technique as a part of an AOP system. The Spring Framework, as you'll see in chapter 9, uses the proxy design pattern internally to avoid exposing it to users. This isn't unlike the byte-code manipulation technique—cumbersome as a programming technique to deal with crosscutting concerns, but a fine underlying technology to implement AOP systems.

Another design pattern, interceptor, is often used along with the proxy design pattern. Let's see how it compares to AOP for crosscutting concerns.

INTERCEPTOR

An interceptor performs additional logic by intercepting method invocations on an object. The interceptor pattern lets you express crosscutting logic in an interceptor object. Used with the proxy or decorator design pattern, this pattern offers a reasonable solution for a wide range of crosscutting problems. For example, Java supports the creation of dynamic proxies, which you can configure with an interceptor. Implementing the interceptor pattern generically and successfully requires a fair amount of machinery; thus it's best to leave such an implementation to a framework.

Let's consider the newest implementation of the interceptor pattern in EJB3. The earlier versions of the EJB framework offered a solution for a specific set of crosscutting concerns: primarily transaction management and role-based security. EJB3 offers a way to modularize user-specific crosscutting concerns through the interceptor approach:

```
public class TracingInterceptor {
    private Logger logger = ...

    @AroundInvoke
    public Object trace(InvocationContext context) throws Exception {
        logger.log("Entering " + context.getMethod().getName()
                   + " in " + context.getBean().getClass().getName());
        return context.proceed();
    }
}
```

Then, you can apply the interceptor to target classes and methods, as shown in the following code snippet:

```
@Stateless
@Interceptors({TracingInterceptor.class})
public class InventoryManagementBean {
      ...
}
```

You can target specific methods by marking each method with the `@Interceptors` annotation. On the other extreme, you can declare an interceptor as a default interceptor that applies to all beans except those that opt out. EJB3's implementation has a few limitations: for example, an interceptor may be applied only to EJBs and not to ordinary types in the system, which may pose restrictions on certain usages. The programming model is also complex and type-unsafe: the intercepted context (intercepted bean, method name, method arguments) is accessed through the `InvocationContext` object, whose method returns `Object` and may require casting before using the context.

But the real problem with the EJB interceptor design (and many similar interceptor implementations) is the missing key abstraction of pointcuts. Classes and methods need to declare that they must be intercepted, reducing the interceptor to a more macro-like facility. As a result, although the logic equivalent to AOP's advice is modularized, the pointcut equivalent logic is spread in all intercepted types. And due to the generic nature of the join point context, the interceptor method may need complex logic to pluck arguments from the context.

Note that the Spring Framework, in versions prior to 2.0, used a mechanism similar to `InvocationContext` and thus suffered from programming complexities similar to EJB3 interceptors. But Spring's AOP always used a pointcut notion to avoid the problem of spreading selection logic in multiple places. The AspectJ integration introduced in Spring 2.0 removes the need for `InvocationContext`-like logic and raises the pointcut implementation to a new level, as you'll see in chapter 9.

1.7.4 Dynamic languages

Dynamic languages have recently gained popularity, and rightly so. A dynamic language, when combined with a framework that takes advantage of the underlying language, can provide powerful solutions for a set of problems. For example, Ruby combined with Rails, or Groovy combined with Grails, provides simpler solutions for certain kinds of web applications. Most dynamic languages offer a meta-programming facility that lets you modify the structure and behavior of a program during its execution. The meta-programming facility may modularize crosscutting concerns. For example, you can modify an existing method's implementation to wrap it with code that performs the crosscutting functionality before or after dispatching the original method.

Although meta-programming is a fine tool for dealing with crosscutting concerns, you must keep in mind a few considerations:

- You need to use a dynamic language that supports meta-programming. The static versus dynamic languages war hasn't concluded, nor will it conclude any time soon, so you'll have to make a considered choice.
- Meta-programming may be too powerful a tool for you; a more disciplined approach may be appropriate.
- Tooling to support crosscutting implementation is difficult to imagine with general-purpose meta-programming facilities offered by dynamic languages.

This is a reason why Dean Wampler, a long-time AOP expert, started the Aquarium project (http://aquarium.rubyforge.org) to bring AOP to Ruby. It shows that although AOP is popular in statically typed languages, it also has a role in dynamically typed languages. Interestingly, as seen from this project, it's relatively easy to build AOP capabilities on top of core meta-programming support provided by the underlying language. By providing an aspect-focused DSL to express pointcuts, Aquarium provides a solution to modularize the pointcut portion of AOP in Ruby.

It's instructive to note that the father of AOP, Gregor Kiczales, who wrote *The Art of the Metaobject Protocol* (MIT Press, 1991), thought that AOP was better suited for crosscutting concerns instead of a direct application of meta-programming.

In a way, statically typed languages use AOP to gain meta-programming support. In contrast, dynamic languages benefit from AOP as a disciplined application of meta-programming.

1.8 Costs and benefits of AOP

Nothing comes free! Software engineering, like any engineering discipline, is all about optimizing costs and benefits. AOP isn't free either. Critics of AOP often talk about how difficult it is to understand. And indeed, AOP takes time, patience, and practice to master. But the main reason behind the difficulty is the newness of the methodology. When was the last time a brand-new programming methodology was accepted without its share of adaptation resistance? AOP demands that you think about system design and implementation in a new way.

When you use AOP, you get a lot of benefits, but you must also understand some costs in order to make informed decisions. In this section, we'll discuss first the costs and then the benefits of AOP.

1.8.1 Costs of AOP

Some of the costs associated with AOP are the usual suspects associated with any new technology:

- Making an investment in learning AOP
- Hiring skilled programmers
- Following an adoption path to ensure that you don't risk the project by overextending yourself
- Modifying the build and other development processes
- Dealing with the availability of tools

Well-understood mitigation techniques are available for some of these issues:

- Making a proper investment in learning the technology (and you already took a step by reading this book)
- Doing due diligence in checking skill availability (which is becoming increasingly easy due to Spring's popularity)
- Following a gradual adoption path, which we'll show in part 2 of the book

Tools for AOP aren't as mature as they are for Java (although they're more mature than for most other languages that run inside the Java VM). Fortunately, a lot of effort is currently under way to improve the tooling around AOP, so this isn't a serious impediment to adopting it.

But one cost, still common to most new technologies, deserves more in-depth treatment: the cost of abstraction. Abstraction lets you hide inessential details and thus reduce the complexity of the underlying system. Good abstraction leads to the creation of well-isolated modules. Because each module represents a much smaller subsystem, abstraction offers a way to contain complexity at a level you can cope with. Modularity is a divide-and-conquer approach to managing complexity. But the abstraction introduced by AOP isn't without costs.

NEED FOR GREATER SKILLS

Creating the right level of abstraction is a highly skilled job (many correct abstractions are possible in a given system). A thorough understanding of the costs and benefits is a hallmark of good software engineering. Merely understanding the implementation mechanisms won't yield useful abstractions.

In the context of AOP, you must understand how to fit the new unit of modularity—aspects—into the system. For that, you must apply decomposition techniques to separate core concerns from crosscutting concerns. All this requires experience that is often best gained by applying AOP in a gradual manner. The second part of the book provides details of this strategy.

On the flip side, crosscutting logic is separated from business logic. This enables you to use developers who understand only the business logic and not the intricacies of the crosscutting functionality.

COMPLEX PROGRAM FLOW

Abstraction, by its nature, hides the details. In software systems, higher levels of abstraction always mean that less information is available at the code level. Looking at a code segment doesn't tell you the whole story that will unfold during system execution. For example, in OOP, due to polymorphic methods, you can't tell the exact method that will be executed at runtime, because the choice of method is based on the type of the object, not the static type of the declared variable. This makes analyzing program flow a complex task. Even in procedural languages such as C, if you use function pointers, the program flow isn't static and requires some effort to be understood.

AOP abstracts away program flow even further. You may not know (except through good tooling support) that a crosscutting action will take place in a certain part of the code. Many programmers new to AOP get stuck until they realize that this separation of concerns is the whole point. If you insist on understanding the exact program flow, it's a sign that you need to reflect a little longer on the core ideas of AOP. But just as OOP requires a few years of practice before you understand the underlying core ideas, most developers get AOP eventually.

1.8.2 Benefits of AOP

Now that you know the costs, let's look at the benefits.

SIMPLIFIED DESIGN

The architect of a system is often faced with underdesign/overdesign issues. If you underdesign, you may have to make massive changes later in the development cycle. If you overdesign, the implementation may be burdened with code of questionable usefulness. With AOP, you can delay making design decisions for future requirements because you can implement those as separate aspects. You can focus on the current requirements of the system.

AOP works in harmony with one of the most popular trends of agile programming by supporting the practice of "You aren't gonna need it" (YAGNI). Implementing a feature just because you may need it in the future often results in wasted effort because you won't actually need it. With AOP, you can practice YAGNI; and if you do need a particular kind of functionality later, you can implement it without having to make system-wide modifications. Even for the feature that you need, agile programming promotes developing them progressively. AOP helps you add features incrementally through the introduction of aspects, often without modifying the rest of the code.

CLEANER IMPLEMENTATION

AOP allows a module to take responsibility only for its core concern, thus following the SRP; a module is no longer liable for other crosscutting concerns. For example, a module implementing business logic is no longer responsible for the security functionality. This results in cleaner assignments of responsibilities, reduced code clutter, and less duplication. It also improves the traceability of requirements to their implementation, and vice versa.

Reduced code tangling makes it simpler to test code, spot potential problems, and perform code reviews. Reviewing the code of a module that implements only one concern requires the participation of an expert in the functionality implemented by that module. Such a simplified process leads to higher-quality code.

Reduced code scattering avoids the cost of modifying many modules to implement a crosscutting concern. Thus, AOP makes it cheaper to implement a crosscutting feature. By letting you focus on the core concern of a module and make the most of your expertise, AOP also reduces the cost of the core concerns.

The end effect is a cheaper overall feature implementation, better time-to-market, and easier system evolution.

BETTER CODE REUSE

The key to greater code reuse is a more loosely coupled implementation. If a module is implementing multiple concerns, other systems requiring similar functionality may not be able to use the module if they implement a different set of crosscutting concerns. With AOP, because you can implement each crosscutting module as an aspect, core modules aren't aware of crosscutting functionality. By modifying the aspects, you can change the system configuration. For example, a service layer may be secured in a project with one security scheme, in another project with another scheme, or in still another project with no security at all by including or excluding appropriate aspects. Without AOP, a service layer tied with a specific security implementation may not be reused in another project.

1.9 Summary

The most fundamental principle in software engineering is that the separation of concerns leads to a system that is simpler to understand and easier to maintain. Various methodologies and frameworks support this principle in some form. For instance, with OOP, by separating interfaces from their implementation, you can modularize the core concerns well. But for crosscutting concerns, OOP forces the core modules to embed the crosscutting concern's logic. Although the crosscutting concerns are independent of each other, using OOP leads to an implementation that no longer preserves independence in the implementation.

Aspect-oriented programming changes this by modularizing crosscutting concerns in a generic and methodical fashion. With AOP, crosscutting concerns are modularized by encapsulating them in a new unit called an aspect. Core concerns no longer embed the crosscutting concern's logic, and all the associated complexity of the crosscutting concerns is isolated into the aspects. AOP marks the beginning of a new way of dealing with a software system by viewing it as a composition of mutually independent concerns. By building on top of existing programming methodologies, AOP preserves the investment in knowledge gained over the last few decades.

In the last few years, AOP has become a practical technology. It has been deployed in many organizations, big and small, to add powerful features that we might have otherwise shied away from or implemented in a laborious manner.

In the next eight chapters, we'll study a specific implementation of AOP for Java, AspectJ, as well as its integration with Spring. Those chapters and the rest of the book will provide examples that use this technology to solve real problems. In chapter 2, you'll see how AspectJ implements AOP for Java.

2 Introducing AspectJ

This chapter covers

- Writing an AspectJ "Hello, world!" application
- Becoming familiar with the AspectJ language
- Weaving mechanisms
- Integrating with Spring

In chapter 1, we focused on general concepts in AOP. With those behind us, we can now look at one specific AOP implementation: AspectJ. AspectJ is an aspect-oriented extension to the Java programming language. Like any AOP implementation, AspectJ consists of two parts: the language specification, which defines the grammar and semantics of the language; and the language implementation, which includes weavers that take various forms such as a compiler and a linker. A weaver produces byte code that conforms to the Java byte-code specification, allowing any compliant Java virtual machine (VM) to execute those class files. The language implementation also offers support for integrated development environments (IDEs), to simplify building and debugging applications.

AspectJ started and initially grew as a special language that extends the Java language with new keywords. It also provided a special compiler that could understand those extensions. But recently, a lot has changed in its form as a language, as well as in the weaver. First, AspectJ offers an alternative syntax based on the Java annotation facility to express crosscutting constructs. This lets you use a plain Java compiler instead of the special compiler. Second, AspectJ offers new options for weaving classes with aspects. Finally, it has gained a strong foothold in the Spring Framework with several integration options. All these changes have made adoption of AspectJ easier than ever before.

In this chapter, we'll examine important facets of AspectJ—starting with language constructs, passing through syntax and weaving choices, peeking into the Spring integration, and ending with tools support—from a high-level perspective. In the chapters that follow, we'll delve deeper into each of these facets.

2.1 Writing your first AspectJ program

You'll begin your journey by writing a simple application. This code introduces a few AspectJ concepts and gives you a feel for the language.

> **Installing AspectJ**
>
> You'll need to install AspectJ to work with the code in this book. Doing so is easy:
>
> 1. Download the AspectJ distribution from http://www.eclipse.org/aspectj/downloads.php.
> 2. Run `java -jar` *`<path-to-downloaded-file>`*. Doing so opens a wizard that will guide you through the installation process. When the wizard finishes, you'll have the AspectJ compiler and other tools, various AspectJ libraries (such as aspectjrt.jar and aspectjweaver.jar), and documentation.
>
> Alternatively, you can use Eclipse along with the AspectJ Development Tools (AJDT) to run these examples in the IDE. See section 2.7.1 for details.

2.1.1 Setting up the example

Let's create a regular Java class, as shown in listing 2.1, which contains two methods that will print messages. Later in this section, you'll create a few aspects to introduce additional behavior without modifying the class.

Listing 2.1 Class encapsulating the message-delivery functionality

```
package ajia.messaging;

public class MessageCommunicator {
    public void deliver(String message) {
        System.out.println(message);
    }

    public void deliver(String person, String message) {
        System.out.println(person + ", " + message);
    }
}
```

The `MessageCommunicator` class has two methods: one to deliver a general message and the other to deliver a message to a specific person. Next, let's write a simple class to exercise the functionality of the `MessageCommunicator` class, as shown in listing 2.2.

Listing 2.2 Class to exercise the message-delivery functionality

```
package ajia.main;

import ajia.messaging. MessageCommunicator;

public class Main {
    public static void main(String[] args) {
        MessageCommunicator messageCommunicator
            = new MessageCommunicator();
        messageCommunicator.deliver("Wanna learn AspectJ?");
        messageCommunicator.deliver("Harry", "having fun?");
    }
}
```

When you compile the `MessageCommunicator` and the `Main` class together using the AspectJ compiler (ajc) and run the `Main` program, the output is as follows (Commands shown in this chapter are for Windows; please change them appropriately for your platform.):

```
> ajc ajia\messaging\MessageCommunicator.java ajia\main\Main.java
> java ajia.main.Main
Wanna learn AspectJ?
Harry, having fun?
```

Running the examples

The main reason behind showing the command-line operations is to remove some of the mystery about how AspectJ works. The downloadable sources include shell scripts that match the commands and also include the necessary setup. But most developers will prefer to run the code through the Ant and Maven scripts also provided with the downloadable sources. See appendixes B and C for detailed instructions on how to use these tools with AspectJ.

Every valid Java program is a valid AspectJ program. Therefore, you could use the AspectJ compiler (ajc) to compile the classes instead of a Java compiler such as javac.

Now that the basic setup is ready, let's add a few aspects to the system to improve the message-delivery functionality.

2.1.2 Adding an aspect

Consider authentication functionality: before delivering a message, you'd like to check whether the user has been authenticated. Without using AOP, you'd have to write code like the following:

```
public class MessageCommunicator {
    private Authenticator authenticator = new Authenticator();

    public void deliver(String message) {
        authenticator.authenticate();
        System.out.println(message);
    }
```

```
    public void deliver(String person, String message) {
        authenticator.authenticate();
        System.out.println(person + ", " + message);
    }
}
```

You have to add a call to authenticate() in each method that needs authentication, which leads to code tangling. Similar code must be present in all classes that require the authentication functionality—leading to code scattering. With AOP, you can do better.

Without changing a single line of code in the MessageCommunicator class from listing 2.1, you can enhance its functionality by adding an aspect to the system. Listing 2.3 shows the traditional syntax. Later, you'll see alternative syntax to implement the same functionality.

Listing 2.3 Aspect to secure access

```
package ajia.security;

import ajia.messaging.MessageCommunicator;

public aspect SecurityAspect {                                    ❶ Aspect declaration
    private Authenticator authenticator = new Authenticator();

    pointcut secureAccess()                                       ❷ Pointcut declaration
        : execution(* MessageCommunicator.deliver(..));

    before() : secureAccess() {                                   ❸ Advice
        System.out.println("Checking and authenticating user");
        authenticator.authenticate();
    }
}
```

The Authenticator class asks for credentials (username and password) when the authenticate() method is called for the first time in a thread. Upon successful authentication, it stores the user in a thread local so it doesn't ask for credentials in the same thread again. Upon failure, it throws a runtime exception. (I don't show the Authenticator here, for brevity's sake. If you like, you can download it from the book's web site: http://manning.com/laddad2/.)

Compile the classes along with the aspect. Now, when you run the program, you see the following output (the use of Java generic feature in the Authenticator class requires specifying the -source 5 option to ajc):

```
> ajc  -source 5 ajia\messaging\MessageCommunicator.java
➥    ajia\main\Main.java
➥    ajia\security\SecurityAspect.aj ajia\security\*.java
> java ajia.main.Main
Checking and authenticating user
Username: ajia
Password: ajia
Wanna learn AspectJ?
Checking and authenticating user
Harry, having fun?
```

The SecurityAspect.aj file declares the `SecurityAspect` aspect. Note that you could have declared the aspect in SecurityAspect.java file, because AspectJ accepts both .aj and .java extensions for input source files. Although the file extension doesn't matter to the compiler, aspects typically use the .aj extension, and Java code uses the .java extension. Let's looks at the listing in more detail:

1. An aspect is a unit of modularization in AOP, much like a class is a unit of modularization in OOP. The declaration of an aspect is similar to a class declaration.
2. A pointcut selects interesting points of execution in a system, called *join points*. The aspect defines a pointcut `secureAccess()` that selects execution of all the methods named `deliver()` in the `MessageCommunicator` class. The `*` indicates that the pointcut matches any return type, and the `..` inside parentheses after `deliver` specifies that it matches regardless of the number of arguments or their types. In this example, the pointcut selects execution of both overloaded versions of `deliver()` in the `MessageCommunicator` class. You'll learn about join points and pointcuts in detail in the next chapter.
3. An advice defines the code to execute upon reaching join points selected by the associated pointcut. Here, you define a piece of advice to execute before reaching the join points selected by the `secureAccess()` pointcut. The `before()` part indicates that the advice should run prior to the execution of the advised join point—in this case, prior to executing any `MessageCommunicator.deliver()` method. In the advice, you authenticate the current user. With the aspect now present in the system, each time `MessageCommunicator.deliver()` is executed, the advice code performs the authentication logic before the method.

Now that you have the flavor of the AspectJ language, it's time for an overview of the language and its core building blocks.

2.2 AspectJ crosscutting construct

Recall the generic AOP model discussed in chapter 1. AspectJ is the most complete implementation of that model, supporting all its elements. In this section, we'll examine how AspectJ maps each model element into program constructs. Note that AspectJ offers two syntax choices: traditional and @AspectJ. This section uses the traditional syntax to study these building blocks. We'll examine the @AspectJ syntax in section 2.3.

We can classify the crosscutting constructs in the AOP model as *common* crosscutting constructs (join point, pointcut, and aspect), *dynamic* crosscutting construct (advice), and *static* crosscutting constructs (inter-type declarations and weave-time declarations). These constructs form the building blocks of AspectJ. Let's study the common crosscutting constructs first.

2.2.1 Common crosscutting constructs

AspectJ supports a few common constructs consisting of the join point, the pointcut, and the aspect. You can use these constructs with both dynamic and static crosscutting.

JOIN POINT

In AOP, and therefore in AspectJ, *join points* are the places where the crosscutting actions take place. Listing 2.1 has join points corresponding to the execution of the `deliver()` methods as well as calls to the `println()` method on the `System.out` object. Listing 2.2 has join points corresponding to the creation of `MessageCommunicator` and calls to the `deliver()` methods.

After you identify join points useful for a crosscutting functionality, you need to select them using the pointcut construct.

POINTCUT

A *pointcut* is a program construct that selects join points and collects context at those points. For example, a pointcut can select a join point that is an execution of a method. It can also collect the join-point context, such as the `this` object and the arguments to the method.

The following pointcut selects the execution of any public method in the system:

```
execution(public * *.*(..))
```

The wildcards `*` and `..` indicate that the pointcut selects regardless of the return type, declaring type, method name, and method parameters. Here, the only condition specified is that the access specification for the method must be `public`.

It's a good idea to name a pointcut so that other programming elements can use it (and so that programmers—including yourself—can understand the intention behind the pointcut). For example, you can name the earlier pointcut `publicOperation`, as follows:

```
pointcut publicOperation() : execution(public * *.*(..));
```

ASPECT

The *aspect* is the central unit in AspectJ, in the same way that a class is the central unit in Java. It contains the code that expresses the weaving rules for both dynamic and static crosscutting. Additionally, aspects can contain data, methods, and nested class members, just like a normal Java class. Let's define an aspect that performs profiling that you'll update as you learn about more elements:

```
package ajia.profile;

public aspect ProfilingAspect {
}
```

Learning about common crosscutting constructs will pay off when you begin using them with dynamic and static crosscutting constructs. Let's see how, starting with the dynamic crosscutting construct.

2.2.2 Dynamic crosscutting construct: advice

AspectJ's dynamic crosscutting support comes in the form of advice. *Advice* is the code executed at a join point selected by a pointcut. Advice can execute before, after, or around the join point. The body of advice is much like a method body—it encapsulates the logic to be executed upon reaching a join point.

Using the `publicOperation()` pointcut from the previous section, you can advise all public methods of `MessageCommunicator` to profile them. Let's update `ProfilingAspect` (shown in listing 2.4) with profiling advice.

Listing 2.4 Profiling all public methods

```
package ajia.profile;

public aspect ProfilingAspect {
    pointcut publicOperation() : execution(public * *.*(..));

    Object around() : publicOperation() {
        long start = System.nanoTime();
        Object ret = proceed();
        long end = System.nanoTime();
        System.out.println(thisJoinPointStaticPart.getSignature()
                           + " took " + (end-start) + " nanoseconds");
        return ret;
    }
}
```

The advice records the start time, calls `proceed()` to continue executing the advised method, records the end time, and prints the time taken by the method execution. The `thisJoinPointStaticPart` variable is one of the three variables available in each advice that carry information about the currently advised join point, such as the method name, the `this` object, and method arguments.

When you compile this aspect along with the other code and execute it, you get the following output:

```
> ajc -source 5 ajia\messaging\MessageCommunicator.java ajia\main\Main.java
➥   ajia\security\SecurityAspect.aj ajia\security\*.java
➥   ajia\profile\ProfilingAspect.aj
> java ajia.main.Main
Checking and authenticating user
boolean ajia.security.Authenticator.isAuthenticated() took 840051
➥   nanoseconds
Username: ajia
Password: ajia
String[] ajia.security.Authenticator.getUserNamePassword() took 5248473759
➥   nanoseconds
void ajia.security.Authenticator.authenticate() took 5250886077 nanoseconds
Wanna learn AspectJ?
void ajia.messaging.MessageCommunicator.deliver(String) took 5252761734
➥   nanoseconds
Checking and authenticating user
boolean ajia.security.Authenticator.isAuthenticated() took 5028 nanoseconds
void ajia.security.Authenticator.authenticate() took 61740 nanoseconds
Harry, having fun?
void ajia.messaging.MessageCommunicator.deliver(String, String) took 307581
➥   nanoseconds
void ajia.main.Main.main(String[]) took 5253861315 nanoseconds
```

While dynamic crosscutting alters the program behavior, static crosscutting alters the programs structure. Let's see AspectJ's support for it.

> **Pseudo keywords in AspectJ**
>
> The `proceed` and other keywords such as `aspect`, `pointcut`, and `before` are really pseudo keywords that gain special meaning only in the right context. For example, it is perfectly legitimate to use a method named 'proceed' in Java classes. But when `proceed` is used in an around advice, it acquires a special meaning. This use of pseudo keywords enables AspectJ to work with any valid Java program that may already include AspectJ keywords.

2.2.3 Static crosscutting constructs

Static crosscutting comes in the form of inter-type and weave-time declarations.

INTER-TYPE DECLARATION

The *inter-type declaration* (ITD) (also referred to as *introduction*) is a static crosscutting construct that alters the static structure of the classes, interfaces, and aspects in the system. For example, you can add a method or field to a class, or declare a type to implement an interface. In an ITD, one type (an aspect) declares the structure for the other types (classes, interfaces, and even aspects)—hence the name.

The following statement makes the weaver assign the `AccessTracked` interface as the parent of the `MessageCommunicator` class:

```
declare parents: MessageCommunicator implements AccessTracked;
```

When this declaration is woven in, it has the same effect as declaring the `MessageCommunicator` class as follows:

```
public class MessageCommunicator implements AccessTracked {
    ...
}
```

Another form of ITD—*member introduction*—offers a way to add new methods and fields to other types. The following declaration adds the `lastAccessedTime` field and the `updateLastAccessedTime()` and `getLastAccessedTime()` methods to the `AccessTracked` type:

```
private long AccessTracked.lastAccessedTime;

public void AccessTracked.updateLastAccessedTime() {
    lastAccessedTime = System.currentTimeMillis();
}

public long AccessTracked.getLastAccessedTime() {
    return lastAccessedTime;
}
```

You can then advise methods in a type that implements `AccessTracked` (directly or through a `declare parents` statement) to update the last-accessed time, as shown in the following snippet:

```
before(AccessTracked accessTracked)
    : execution(* AccessTracked+.*(..))
```

```
        && !execution(* AccessTracked.*(..))
        && this(accessTracked){
      accessTracked.updateLastAccessedTime();
}
```

This code advises all methods of types that implement the `AccessTracked` interface (the + wildcard denotes subtypes) but not the method in `AccessTracked` (such as the introduced `updateLastAccessedTime()` method). The `this()` pointcut collects the tracked object so you can call the `updateLastAccessedTime()` method on it.

Let's put all these snippets in an aspect, as shown in listing 2.5, to see their effect.

Listing 2.5 Tracking the last-accessed time using an aspect

```
package ajia.track;

import ajia.messaging.MessageCommunicator;

public aspect TrackingAspect {
    declare parents: MessageCommunicator implements AccessTracked;

    private long AccessTracked.lastAccessedTime;

    public void AccessTracked.updateLastAccessedTime() {
        lastAccessedTime = System.currentTimeMillis();
    }

    public long AccessTracked.getLastAccessedTime() {
        return lastAccessedTime;
    }

    before(AccessTracked accessTracked)
        : execution(* AccessTracked+.*(..))
          && !execution(* AccessTracked.*(..))
          && this(accessTracked) {
         accessTracked.updateLastAccessedTime();
    }

    private static interface AccessTracked {
    }
}
```

To see the effect, modify the `Main` class to print the last-accessed time for the `messageCommunicator` object, as shown in listing 2.6.

Listing 2.6 Modified `Main` class to print the last-accessed time

```
package ajia.main;

...

public class Main {
    public static void main(String[] args) {
        ...

        System.out.println("Last accessed time for messageCommunicator "
                           + messageCommunicator.getLastAccessedTime());
    }
}
```

When you compile and execute this class, the output is as follows:

```
> ajc -source 5 ajia\messaging\MessageCommunicator.java ajia\main\Main.java
➥    ajia\security\SecurityAspect.aj ajia\security\*.java
➥    ajia\profile\ProfilingAspect.aj ajia\track\TrackingAspect.aj
> java ajia.main.Main
...
Last accessed time for messageCommunicator 1250040714984
...
```

ITDs also offer a way to annotate program elements and deal with checked exceptions in a systematic manner, but we'll defer that discussion until chapter 5.

An important form of static crosscutting allows detecting and flagging the presence of join points, matching a pointcut during compilation. Let's see how.

WEAVE-TIME DECLARATION

The *weave-time declaration* is another static crosscutting construct that allows you to add weave-time warnings and errors when detecting certain usage patterns. Often, weaving is performed during compilation; therefore, these warnings and errors are issued when you compile the classes.

Consider `SecurityAspect` from listing 2.3. With this aspect in place, you might want to warn about direct calls to the `Authenticator.authenticate()` method. The following declaration will cause the compiler to issue a warning if any part of the system calls the prohibited method—except, of course, `SecurityAspect`:

```
declare warning
    : call(void Authenticator.authenticate()) && !within(SecurityAspect)
    : "Authentication should be performed only by SecurityAspect";
```

Note the use of the `call()` pointcut to select a method call (as opposed to selecting the method execution, which is always in the `Authenticator` class) and `!within()` to restrict selection of join points to only those occurring outside `SecurityAspect`. The weaver will report warnings when it detects the specified conditions along with other compile-time warnings such as use of a deprecated method.

Let's see this in action by modifying `SecurityAspect` to add this declaration:

```
package ajia.security;

public aspect SecurityAspect {

    ...

    declare warning
        : call(void Authenticator.authenticate())
          && !within(SecurityAspect)
        : "Authentication should be performed only by SecurityAspect";
}
```

You also modify the `Main` class to add `new Authenticator().authenticate()` (and the associated import statements) to test a violation. When you compile the code, the output is as follows:

```
> ajc -source 5 ajia\messaging\MessageCommunicator.java ajia\main\Main.java
➥    ajia\security\SecurityAspect.aj ajia\security\*.java
...\ajia\main\Main.java:13 [warning]
```

```
➥   Authentication should be performed only by SecurityAspect
new Authenticator().authenticate();
^^^^^^^^^^^^^^^^^^^^^^^^^^^^^^^^^^^

        method-call(void ajia.security.Authenticator.authenticate())
        see also: ...\ajia\security\SecurityAspect.aj:15::0
```

As the output shows, the compiler detects and flags the violation and also points to the aspect with the corresponding `declare warning` statement.

This completes our discussion of various crosscutting constructs in AspectJ. By offering comprehensive support for various elements, AspectJ enables modularization of crosscutting concerns. You'll see examples based on these constructs throughout the book.

Until now, we've restricted ourselves only to the traditional AspectJ syntax and compiler as the weaver. But AspectJ offers an alternative syntax that we'll study next. Later in this chapter, we'll examine alternative weaving models.

2.3 AspectJ alternative syntax

The traditional syntax we've been using so far requires the use of the special ajc compiler early in the development process to compile aspects. This poses a potential barrier to adopting AspectJ. To simplify adoption, starting with AspectJ version 5, alternative syntax and weaving models are available, thanks to the merger of AspectJ with AspectWerkz, another implementation of AOP for Java.

The alternative @AspectJ syntax extends the language using the new annotation facility in Java 5. The main advantage of this syntax style is that you can compile your code using a plain Java compiler (for example, javac). As a result, the code works better with conventional Java IDEs and tools that don't understand the traditional AspectJ syntax. Furthermore, the proxy-based AOP framework in Spring uses this syntax, simplifying adoption of AspectJ if the project is already using Spring. The disadvantage of @AspectJ syntax is its verbosity in expressing the same constructs and its limitations in expressing certain constructs, especially in the static crosscutting category.

Let's create an @AspectJ version of the aspect from listing 2.3, as shown in listing 2.7.

Listing 2.7 Introducing security using the @AspectJ syntax

```
package ajia.security;

import org.aspectj.lang.annotation.Aspect;
import org.aspectj.lang.annotation.Before;
import org.aspectj.lang.annotation.Pointcut;

@Aspect                                                  ❶ Aspect declaration
public class SecurityAspect {
    private Authenticator authenticator = new Authenticator();

    @Pointcut(
        "execution(* ajia.messaging.MessageCommunicator.deliver(..))")
    public void secureAccess() {}
                                                         Pointcut declaration ❷
    @Before("secureAccess()")          ❸ Advice
    public void secure() {
```

```
        System.out.println("Checking and authenticating user");
        authenticator.authenticate();
    }
}
```

❸ **Advice**

Following are the differences between listings 2.3 and 2.7:

❶ Instead of using the `aspect` keyword, you use a class annotated with an `@Aspect` annotation. The ajc compiler, which understands the semantics associated with the `@Aspect` annotation, uses this information to treat the class as if it's an aspect.

❷ Similarly, the `@Pointcut` annotation marks an empty method as a pointcut. You must specify the pointcut expression—the same expression as in the version using the traditional syntax (except for the use of the fully-qualified type name for `ajia.messaging.MessageCommunicator`). The name of the method serves as the pointcut name.

❸ The `@Before` annotation marks a regular method as a before advice. The body of the method consists of the advice logic—this code is executed when a matching join point is executed.

First, let's compile the code using javac and execute the resulting code. Note that annotations such as `@Aspect`, `@Pointcut`, and `@Before` are contained in aspectjrt.jar and must be on your classpath regardless of whether you compile the aspects with ajc or javac:

```
> javac ajia\messaging\MessageCommunicator.java
➥   ajia\security\SecurityAspect.java ajia\security\Authenticator.java
➥   ajia\security\AuthenticationException.java ajia\main\Main.java
> java ajia.main.Main
Wanna learn AspectJ?
Harry, having fun?
```

The code compiled fine, but the aspect had no effect on the output. This may not surprise you; after all, javac has no idea of the meaning of annotations such as `@Aspect` and `@Pointcut`. In general, javac is aware of only a few standard annotations (such as `@Override` and `@SuppressWarnings`). You need to include an aspect weaver somewhere between compiling the source code and executing the byte code in the VM. The simplest way to use the @AspectJ syntax is to use the ajc compiler instead of javac. Alternatives include binary weaving, where code compiled using javac is then woven using ajc; and load-time weaving (LTW), where classes are woven as they're being loaded into the VM. We'll discuss these alternatives in the next section.

Now, let's compile the same sources using ajc:

```
> ajc -source 5 ajia\messaging\MessageCommunicator.java
➥   ajia\security\SecurityAspect.java ajia\security\Authenticator.java
➥   ajia\security\AuthenticationException.java ajia\main\Main.java
> java ajia.main.Main
Checking and authenticating user
Username: ajia
Password: ajia
Wanna learn AspectJ?
Checking and authenticating user
Harry, having fun?
```

The output is the same as that produced by the aspect in listing 2.3. (Note the `-source 5` option to allow Java 5 constructs such as annotations.)

The value proposition of @AspectJ syntax is a simplified adoption curve. The aspect's syntax is expressed using Java constructs, which reduces the mental block commonly associated with using yet another language. You're still using plain Java! In addition, tools such as compilers, IDEs, and code-coverage utilities work more easily with the @AspectJ syntax, because they're working with plain Java code.

So far, we've focused on the AspectJ syntax. Now, let's look at another puzzle piece that completes AspectJ: the weaver.

2.4 Weaving mechanisms

A weaver needs to weave together classes and aspects so that advice gets executed, inter-type declarations affect the static structure, and weave-time declarations produce warnings and errors. AspectJ offers three weaving models:

- Source weaving
- Binary weaving
- Load-time weaving

Regardless of the weaving model used, the resulting execution of the system is identical. The weaving mechanism is also orthogonal to the AspectJ syntax used; any combination of weaving mechanism and AspectJ syntax will produce identical results. In this section, we'll examine the weaving models offered by AspectJ. We'll revisit this topic in chapter 8.

2.4.1 Source weaving

In *source weaving*, the weaver is part of the compiler (all the examples in this chapter so far have used source code weaving). The input to the weaver consists of classes and aspects in source-code form. You can write the aspects in either the traditional syntax or the @AspectJ syntax.

The weaver, which works in a manner similar to a compiler, processes the source and produces woven byte code. The byte code produced by the compiler is compliant with the Java byte-code specification, which any standard compliant VM can execute.

Essentially, when used in this manner, ajc replaces javac. But note that unlike javac, ajc requires that all sources be presented together if you want woven byte code. If you present sources separately, the resulting byte code can be used as input for binary weaving or load-time weaving, discussed next.

2.4.2 Binary weaving

In *binary weaving*, input to the weaver—classes and aspects—is in byte-code form. The input byte code is compiled separately using the Java compiler or the AspectJ compiler. For example, you can use jar files or class files produced using the Java compiler.

Let's see binary weaving in action in a step-by-step manner. The goal is to compile classes and aspects without weaving and then weave the resulting binary (.class) files.

> **Binary weaver and linker**
>
> If you're familiar with languages such as C and C++, think of the weaver as a linker, which is a more accurate comparison. Much the same way a linker takes object files or libraries compiled using a compiler as input to produce an executable or another library, the weaver takes files containing byte code as input and produces woven byte code.

STEP 1: COMPILING THE JAVA SOURCES

Compile the code from listings 2.1 and 2.2 using javac. You could use ajc; but to illustrate the effect of binary weaving clearly, we're staying away from ajc. Use the `-d` option to specify the destination directory for the classes, to help you better understand the effect:

```
> javac -d classes ajia\messaging\MessageCommunicator.java
➥ ajia\security\Authenticator.java ajia\security\AuthenticationException.java
➥ ajia\main\Main.java
```

Unsurprisingly, executing the `Main` class shows that there is no effect of the aspect:

```
> java -classpath classes ajia.main.Main
Wanna learn AspectJ?
Harry, having fun?
```

STEP 2: COMPILING THE ASPECT

Next, compile the @AspectJ-styled aspect from listing 2.7, directing its output to a different directory:

```
> javac -d aspects ajia\security\SecurityAspect.java
```

If you wanted to use the traditional aspect from listing 2.3, you'd have to compile it using ajc:

```
> ajc -d aspects ajia\security\SecurityAspect.aj
```

Executing the `Main` class shows that the output still doesn't have any effect on the aspect:

```
> java -classpath classes;aspects ajia.main.Main
Wanna learn AspectJ?
Harry, having fun?
```

STEP 3: WEAVING THE ASPECT

To weave aspects into classes in binary form, you use binary weaving:

```
> ajc -inpath classes;aspects -aspectpath aspects -d woven
```

The `-inpath` option specifies the path to the classes that are weaving targets. Because you used javac to compile the aspects, you must also pass those to `-inpath` so that ajc can add the necessary support methods. The `-aspectpath` option specifies the path to the aspects to be woven in.

Executing the Main class shows that you've restored security to the system. Because you pass an explicit -classpath option, you must add the CLASSPATH you've set to make the AspectJ runtime available to the VM:

```
> java -classpath woven;%CLASSPATH% ajia.main.Main
Checking and authenticating user
Username: ajia
Password: ajia
Wanna learn AspectJ?
Checking and authenticating user
Harry, having fun?
```

Binary weaving can also take a combination of source and byte-code form as input (classes or aspects). For example, you may have classes compiled into a jar file and aspects available in source form.

An extension of binary weaver is load-time weaving.

2.4.3 Load-time weaving

A load-time weaver takes input in the form of binary classes and aspects, as well as aspects and configuration defined in XML format. A load-time agent can take many forms: a Java VM Tools Interface (JVMTI) agent, a classloader, or a VM- and application server–specific class preprocessor, which weaves the classes as they're loaded into the VM.

Let's use LTW to weave in the SecurityAspect, starting with the output of the first two steps in the previous section. LTW needs an XML file that specifies the weaving configuration. AspectJ supports a few locations for such a file; you'll use one of them by naming the file aop.xml and placing it in a directory named META-INF in a classpath component. Listing 2.8 shows the minimal XML file that serves this purpose.

Listing 2.8 aop.xml file specifying the configuration for LTW

```
<aspectj>
    <aspects>
        <aspect name="ajia.security.SecurityAspect"/>
    </aspects>
</aspectj>
```

This configuration instructs the weaver to weave in the SecurityAspect. As you'll see later in chapter 8, aop.xml can include a lot more configuration information, including pointcut definitions.

You enable LTW by including the -javaagent option when starting the VM:

```
> java -classpath classes;aspects
➥     -javaagent:%ASPECTJ_HOME%\lib\aspectjweaver.jar ajia.main.Main
Checking and authenticating user
Username: ajia
Password: ajia
Wanna learn AspectJ?
Checking and authenticating user
Harry, having fun?
```

The `-javaagent` option specifies that the aspectjweaver.jar file that comes as part of the AspectJ distribution should be used as the JVMTI agent. The weaver uses the information in the aop.xml file in listing 2.8 and weaves the aspects specified in the `<aspects>` section into classes as they're being loaded into the VM.

By now, you must be wondering how AspectJ performs its magic. In the next section, we'll take a quick look at how the source files are compiled into the byte code.

> **Spring-driven LTW**
>
> Spring 2.5 introduces Spring-driven LTW, an alternative way to configure AspectJ LTW for Spring applications. With it, for certain application and web servers, you can avoid modifying the launch script (required to specify the `-javaagent` option); instead, you modify the application context to express the desire to use LTW, and Spring handles the rest. We'll examine this weaving option in chapter 9.

2.5 AspectJ weaving: under the hood

Because the byte code produced by the AspectJ weaver must run on any compliant Java VM, it must adhere to the Java byte-code specification. This means the weaver must map crosscutting elements to Java constructs. In this section, we'll outline how the different elements in an AspectJ program map to pure Java byte code. Note that the discussion that follows presents a simplified view of AspectJ code transformation into pure Java byte code.

Here are the typical ways the AspectJ weaver maps various crosscutting elements to pure Java:

- Aspects map to classes, with each data member and method becoming the members of the class representing the aspect.
- Pointcuts are intermediate elements that map to methods. They may have associated auxiliary methods to help perform matching at runtime.
- Advice usually maps to one or more methods. The weaver inserts calls to these methods at *potential* locations matching the associated pointcut.
- Inter-type declarations of fields and methods are added directly to target classes.
- Weave-time warnings and errors have no real effect on byte code (they're stored in a binary form so that they can be applied through binary weaving). They cause the compiler to print warnings or abort compilation when there's an error.

Each mapped element carries annotations that help the weaver use the crosscutting information, even for aspects presented to it in byte code form. The annotations also help bring symmetry to the @AspectJ syntax discussed in section 2.3.

WARNING Thinking about language semantics in terms of transformed code helps take the mystery out of AspectJ. It also makes you appreciate the hard work the AspectJ weaver performs—and the hard work you no longer need to perform! But such thinking can bog you down in the details of the transformed code. A better approach is to begin thinking in terms of language semantics instead of implementation.

In light of this information, let's see how aspects and classes look after passing through the AspectJ weaver. Note that the weaver produces byte code and not Java code, as shown here. We're showing you this code only to give you an idea of the source code that is roughly equivalent to the byte code produced.

2.5.1 The compiled aspect

First, let's examine the code in a class that is equivalent to `SecurityAspect` from listing 2.3:

```
package ajia.security;

@Aspect
public class SecurityAspect {
    private Authenticator authenticator = new Authenticator();

    public static final SecurityAspect ajc$perSingletonInstance;

    @Pointcut(
        "execution(* ajia.messaging.MessageCommunicator.deliver(..))")
    void ajc$pointcut$$secureAccess$76() {}

    @Before("secureAccess()")
    public final void ajc$before$ajia_SecurityAspect$1$e248afa3() {
        System.out.println("Checking and authenticating user");
        authenticator.authenticate();
    }

    static {
        SecurityAspect.ajc$perSingletonInstance = new SecurityAspect();
    }

    ... method aspectOf() and hasAspect() (discussed in chapter 6) ...
    ... aspect initialization code ...
}
```

`SecurityAspect` is mapped to a class of the same name. By default, an aspect is a singleton, and users don't instantiate it explicitly. The static block in the aspect ensures that the singleton aspect instance is created as soon as the `SecurityAspect` class is loaded into the system—typically, during the execution of code that refers to the aspect. The pointcut is mapped to the `ajc$pointcut$$secureAccess$76()` element. The before advice is mapped to the `ajc$before$ajia_SecurityAspect$1$e248afa3()` method, whose body is identical to the advice body. Notice the annotations on the methods; they make the code identical to that produced by compiling an equivalent @AspectJ aspect. The AspectJ weaver weaves calls to these methods into the advised code, as you'll see next.

2.5.2 The woven class

Now, let's see the equivalent code for the `MessageCommunicator` class (from listing 2.1), after it has been woven with `SecurityAspect`:

```
package ajia.messaging;

import ajia.security.SecurityAspect;

public class MessageCommunicator {
    public void deliver(String message) {
```

```
        SecurityAspect.aspectInstance.
            ajc$before$ajia_SecurityAspect$1$e248afa3();
        System.out.println(message);
    }

    public void deliver(String person, String message) {
        SecurityAspect.aspectInstance.
            ajc$before$ajia_SecurityAspect$1$e248afa3();
        System.out.print(person + ", " + message);
    }
}
```

Recall that the `deliverMessage()` pointcut in `SecurityAspect` is defined to select both of the overloaded `deliver()` methods in `MessageCommunicator`. Accordingly, the `ajc$before$ajia_SecurityAspect$1$e248afa3()` call on the aspect instance `SecurityAspect.aspectInstance` is made from both methods.

Performance implications of AspectJ weaving

"How does it affect the performance of woven code?" is perhaps the most commonly asked question about AspectJ. The inquiring mind wants to know how a hand-woven implementation of crosscutting functionality compares with that implemented with AspectJ.

The code produced by the weaver answers this question well. Because the weaver encapsulates the advice in a method and calls it from appropriate places, there is virtually no overhead from the AspectJ weaver. Furthermore, because advice is well isolated in one place, you can easily add optimizations to that code—something you'd cringe at implementing in hundreds of places.

If you're looking for more details about weaving and its performance implications, read "Advice Weaving in AspectJ" by Erik Hilsdale and Jim Hugunin (http://hugunin.net/papers/aosd-2004-cameraReady.pdf).

We have examined how AspectJ operates under the hood. Now, let's look at a different weaving possibility. The Spring Framework, starting with version 2.0, offers integration with @AspectJ, but without using the AspectJ weaver you've seen so far.

2.6 Spring AspectJ integration

Spring, the most widely used lightweight framework for developing enterprise applications, offers its own form of AOP to modularize crosscutting concerns typically seen in enterprise applications. It uses the proxy design pattern to intercept the execution of methods on the target object. Due to the use of proxies, it exposes method execution join points only for objects created by the Spring container (commonly known as *Spring beans*). But it is a pragmatic solution for its target applications.

Starting with version 2.0, Spring offers several options to leverage AspectJ's power in an incremental manner. For example, it lets you use AspectJ pointcut expressions in addition to its own pointcut expressions. In this section, we'll preview Spring AspectJ integration for aspects written in @AspectJ syntax. This will be helpful to you because you'll see many Spring-based examples in the book.

Let's continue to use the `MessageCommunicator` class from listing 2.1 and the annotation-style aspect from listing 2.7. First, you'll write a minimum application context file to define the needed configuration (see listing 2.9). Please read the Spring Framework documentation for details of the syntax of the application configuration file.

Listing 2.9 Defining the application context (applicationContext.xml)

```
<?xml version="1.0" encoding="UTF-8"?>
<beans xmlns="http://www.springframework.org/schema/beans"
    xmlns:xsi="http://www.w3.org/2001/XMLSchema-instance"
    xmlns:aop="http://www.springframework.org/schema/aop"
    xsi:schemaLocation="http://www.springframework.org/schema/beans
       http://www.springframework.org/schema/beans/spring-beans-2.5.xsd
       http://www.springframework.org/schema/aop
       http://www.springframework.org/schema/aop/spring-aop-2.5.xsd">
    <aop:aspectj-autoproxy/>                      <- (1) Instructing automatic proxy creation

    <bean id="messageCommunicator"
          class="ajia.messaging.MessageCommunicator"/>   (2) Declaring regular bean

    <bean id="securityAspect" class="ajia.security.SecurityAspect"/>   <- (3) Declaring aspect bean
</beans>
```

(1) The `<aop:aspectj-autoproxy>` element tells Spring to automatically create proxies for the beans that can be advised by aspects (which are declared as beans as in (3)).

(2) The `<bean>` element creates a bean for the `MessageCommunicator` class.

(3) The `<bean>` element creates a bean corresponding to the aspect declared using the @AspectJ syntax.

Next, you modify the `Main` class from listing 2.2 to create the application context and obtain the `messageCommunicator` bean from it. Then, you use the bean to deliver a few messages (see listing 2.10).

Listing 2.10 Using the Spring container application context

```
package ajia.main;

import org.springframework.context.ApplicationContext;
import org.springframework.context.support.ClassPathXmlApplicationContext;

import ajia.messaging.MessageCommunicator;

public class Main {
    public static void main(String[] args) {
        ApplicationContext context
            = new ClassPathXmlApplicationContext("applicationContext.xml");
        MessageCommunicator messageCommunicator
            = (MessageCommunicator)context.getBean("messageCommunicator");
```

```
        messageCommunicator.deliver("Wanna learn AspectJ?");
        messageCommunicator.deliver("Harry", "having fun?");
    }
}
```

Now, let's compile all these classes and execute the `Main` class:

```
> javac ajia\messaging\*.java ajia\main\*.java ajia\security\*.java
> java ajia.main.Main
Checking and authenticating user
Username: ajia
Password: ajia
Wanna learn AspectJ?
Checking and authenticating user
Harry, having fun?
```

You see the same output as when you use an AspectJ weaver. Behind the scenes, the Spring container creates a proxy around the `messageCommunicator` bean and intercepts methods called on it according to the `SecurityAspect` defined using the @AspectJ syntax. As a result, you can use the aspects written using @AspectJ in a Spring application without needing the AspectJ weaver. We'll examine the details in chapter 9.

So far in this chapter, you've used only command-line tools to work with aspects. But in real life, virtually no one works without a good IDE. You also need support for documentation so the crosscutting information is available outside the IDE. In the next section, we'll look at the logistical support provided by AspectJ.

2.7 AspectJ logistics overview

AspectJ offers a complete set of tools ranging from a compiler to IDE support. We've already examined the compiler and load-time weaver. Let's look at a few important tools in more detail. This will help you when you download the book's source code and try out the examples.

2.7.1 IDE integration

IDE support offers an integrated approach to editing, compiling, executing, and debugging tasks. AspectJ eases the development process by providing integration with Eclipse. The integration with the IDE is achieved through the AspectJ Development Tools (AJDT) plug-in. Using this integration, you can edit, compile, and debug your project the same way you would a project written in Java.

TIP AJDT offers plug-ins for various versions of Eclipse. You can download an appropriate version from http://www.eclipse.org/ajdt/downloads. Better still, you can use the free SpringSource Tools Suite (STS), which is an Eclipse distribution that includes many useful plugins, including AJDT, targeted for developing Spring-based applications.

Figure 2.1 shows how the example in this chapter looks in the Eclipse IDE. Note that the Spring IDE, an Eclipse plug-in for developing Spring-based applications, offers similar functionality for Spring AspectJ integration, as discussed in section 2.6.

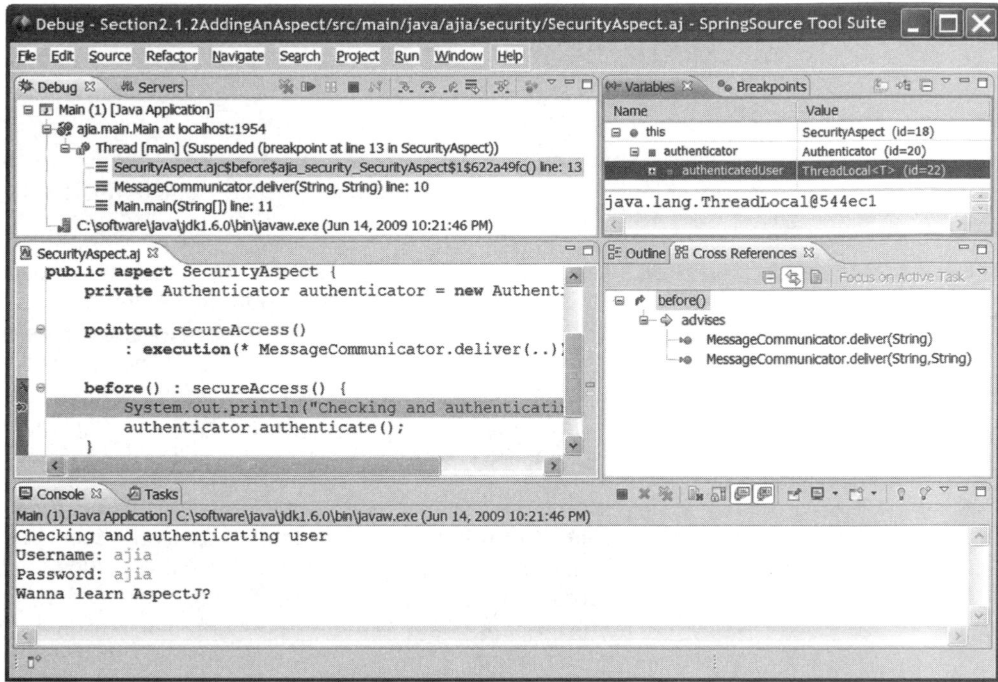

Figure 2.1 Developing applications using Eclipse-AspectJ integration (using STS distribution). The overall feel for editing, building, and debugging is like a plain Java project. The IDE also shows how crosscutting elements affect the various parts of the system.

NOTE AspectJ itself uses AspectJ for its implementation. And AJDT uses AspectJ to weave into Eclipse's Java Development Tools (JDT), to offer AspectJ integration.

In figure 2.1, Eclipse shows the standard views, along with a *Cross References* view that shows how an advice applies to different parts of the code. This view helps in diagnosing problems where advice doesn't apply to the expected set of methods. If you see any mismatch, you can modify the corresponding pointcuts and reexamine the list of the advised methods.

The AJDT plug-in also offers a way to visualize the big picture effects of crosscutting concerns using the *Visualiser.*

> **What about other IDEs?**
>
> Earlier versions of AspectJ supported other IDEs besides Eclipse—NetBeans, JBuilder, and Java Development Environment for Emacs (JDEE)—by offering open source plug-ins for each of them. But those plug-ins haven't been kept up to date. (An effort is currently under way to revive the NetBeans plug-in. See http://www.jroller.com/ramlog/entry/using_the_aspectj_plug_in1 for details.)

What about other IDEs? *(continued)*

This is perhaps a reflection of the market reality—no other IDE is as popular as Eclipse.

One IDE that has a good market and mind share is IntelliJ IDEA. Although an AspectJ plug-in is available for it (http://intellij.expertsystems.se/aspectj.html), it works only with the @AspectJ syntax.

Note that for any IDE without direct support for AspectJ, the possibility of using the @AspectJ syntax makes the lack of direct AspectJ support a less pronounced issue. Because the code is still plain Java, as far as the IDE is concerned, you can edit code, take advantage of code completion, and so on. If the IDE allows you to replace the default compiler, you can replace it with ajc. If not, you can introduce a post-compilation step (often supported in IDEs) to run ajc to perform binary weaving. Debugging works fine too, because the method representing advice is still executed as if there was a real call.

When you use the @AspectJ syntax in an IDE that doesn't support AspectJ directly, you lose the source-code markers that indicate advice applicability, along with the crosscutting references view. You can alleviate this problem to an extent by using ajbrowser (which comes as a part of the AspectJ distribution)—a standalone tool that shows how weaving rules affect different parts of a program.

Although Eclipse IDE integration shows crosscutting information in a crosscutting references view, you'll often need the same information in a static document.

2.7.2 AspectJ documentation tool

The AspectJ documentation tool—ajdoc—extends Javadoc to provide crosscutting information in static form. You invoke ajdoc in a way similar to Javadoc:

```
> ajdoc -source 5 ajia\messaging\*.java ajia\main\*.java ajia\security\*.aj
➥   ajia\security\*.java ajia\profile\*.aj ajia\track\*.aj
```

It produces HTML files similar to the ones produced by Javadoc, except the elements carry additional information showing how aspects and classes interact (see figure 2.2).

The output produced by ajdoc offers a simple way to examine the crosscutting structure without needing an IDE. Because ajdoc isn't tied to a specific IDE, you can use it alongside the IDE of your choice even if it doesn't support AspectJ directly.

The tools offered by AspectJ are indispensable during the development process. If you haven't already done so, download and install AspectJ and AJDT as well as this book's source code.

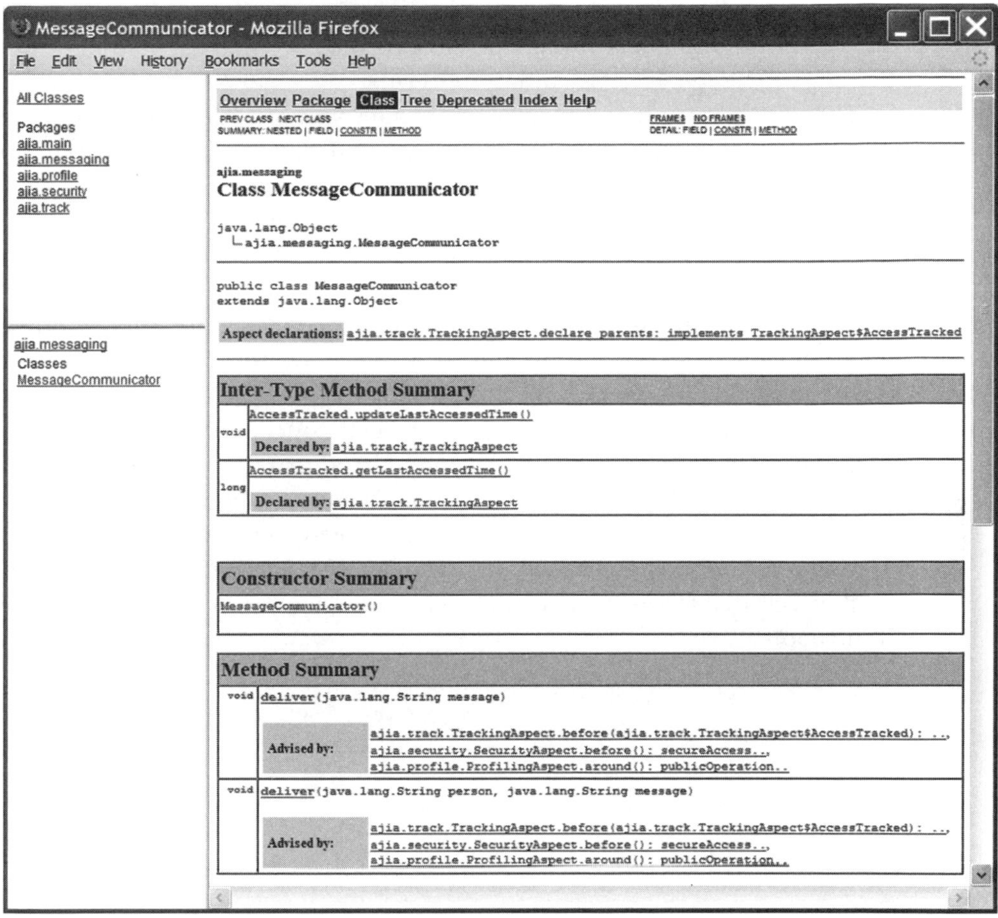

Figure 2.2 Output produced by ajdoc, which works similarly to Javadoc. In addition to the regular documentation, it provides markers to show crosscutting information.

2.8 Summary

AspectJ adds AOP constructs—pointcuts, advice, aspects, inter-type declarations, and weave-time declarations—to Java, creating a powerful language that facilitates modularizing crosscutting concerns while retaining the benefits of Java, such as platform independency. You can add new functionality without changing code in the core modules and without those modules being aware of what you've done.

Aspect-oriented programming in AspectJ is simple: choose where you want to crosscut, choose the kind of action you need to perform, and programmatically specify both of them. The AspectJ language exposes the necessary join points in a Java program. Pointcuts let you choose the join points you want to affect, and advice allows you to specify the action at those join points. The static crosscutting mechanism enables you to modify the static structure of the system. AspectJ complements—and doesn't compete with—Java. By utilizing its power to modularize the crosscutting concerns, Java programmers no longer need to recode multiple modules when implementing or changing a crosscutting concern.

The new additions to AspectJ—the various syntax options, weaving models, and integration with Spring—make adopting AspectJ much easier. It's typical for Spring developers to start with the Spring AspectJ integration, using proxy-based weaving, and to learn the power of AOP and AspectJ through experience. Then, they often move to advanced AOP techniques using AspectJ weaving, often along with the @AspectJ syntax. At this point, load-time weaving is often a common choice due to its simplicity in getting started. Later, when they're looking for even more advanced usages, they may go for the traditional syntax along with a combination of source, binary, and load-time weaving.

In this chapter, we studied the core AspectJ concepts from 20,000 feet. It's now time to get a closer view. The next chapter introduces the join-point model that is at the heart of AOP. The three chapters that follow will discuss dynamic crosscutting, static crosscutting, and aspects. We'll then proceed to examine the @AspectJ syntax, weaving mechanisms, and Spring integration. All this information will enable you to write aspects that are useful in complex Java applications, which we'll explore in part 2 of the book.

3 Understanding the join point model

This chapter covers

- The join point model
- Pointcut details

The join point model is the central concept in AOP, as you've seen in previous chapters. It consists of two parts: join points, the points in the execution of an application; and pointcuts, a mechanism for selecting join points.

AspectJ's pointcut language is sophisticated, expressive, and elegant. It lets you select join points based on structural information such as types, names, arguments, and annotations as well as runtime conditions such as control flow. This allows you to select exactly the join points you need to implement a crosscutting functionality.

In this chapter, you'll learn about the concept of a join point in AOP and discuss the join point model in AspectJ. We'll discuss the join points supported by AspectJ, categorize them, and examine code associated with each kind of join point. Then, you'll build a simple example to reinforce the concepts learned. We'll spend the rest of the chapter discussing pointcuts supported by AspectJ along with many code snippets. We'll also examine various signature patterns that form the basic building blocks of a pointcut.

The Spring Framework supports a subset of AspectJ pointcuts in its proxy-based AOP framework. I'll provide brief notes about this where appropriate.

The focus of this chapter is on concepts and syntax. We'll visit the art of writing pointcuts in part 2 of the book. By then, you'll have seen many simple examples of AspectJ and will be ready to appreciate complex and more interesting applications.

> **How to read this chapter**
>
> This chapter serves a dual purpose: it teaches concepts and provides a reference when you practice AOP. You should at least read section 3.1. Then, if you're reasonably familiar with AspectJ, I suggest that you read this chapter completely before proceeding with the next chapter. If this book is your first introduction to AOP, read the remainder of the chapter focusing on the concepts, but without worrying about nuances of the syntax. Come back and read this chapter fully to excel at AOP.
>
> Think of it this way. You can't become a master database programmer unless you master SQL. The same applies to AOP—you can't claim mastery of AOP unless you master the join point model.

What exactly is the join point model?

3.1 Understanding the join point model

Consider a situation where you need to implement transaction management. If you decide that, due to the crosscutting nature of the functionality, AOP is the preferred approach, how do you go about implementing such functionality? Here is the typical process.

1. You *identify places* where you need to start a transaction before the main-line logic and where you commit or roll back the transaction after the logic finishes, based on the outcome.

   In other words, you identify the join points that require the transaction management functionality.

2. You *write a pointcut* that selects the required join points. For transaction management, the desired join points are likely to correspond to method execution. You try to identify any commonality between those methods. Perhaps they belong to all types in a package or to subclasses of a type, or they share part of the method name. More likely, in the case of transaction management, you may have an `@Transactional` annotation associated with the desired methods. You use this commonality to construct a pointcut. The pointcut may also need to collect join point context (objects such as `this`, arguments, and annotations) to provide to advice.

3 You *write an aspect* that encapsulates the transaction-management functionality. The advice in the aspect uses the pointcut you wrote to start and commit or roll back transactions at the selected join points. The advice uses the collected join point context in its implementation. For example, if the annotation specifies a read-only property, it may start a read-only transaction.

As you can see, the steps to identify join points and implement a pointcut dominate the process. Let's go a level deeper in these all-important concepts.

3.1.1 Join points

A *join point* is an identifiable execution point in a system. A call to a method is a join point, and so is a field access. A `for` loop or an `if` statement is a join point, too.

AspectJ deliberately exposes only a subset of all possible join points. For example, AspectJ exposes join points for a method call and a field access, but not for a loop or an `if` statement. Exposed join points are the only places where you can interject crosscutting actions. The AspectJ join point model encourages you to write robust and maintainable systems by limiting access to more stable program constructs.

In figure 3.1, the UML sequence diagram shows join points in an account transaction, which illustrates some of the places where you can introduce augmentative or alternative crosscutting behavior.

In the sequence diagram, you see several join points that are encountered when an object invokes a `debit()` method on an `AccountService` object. The first join point is

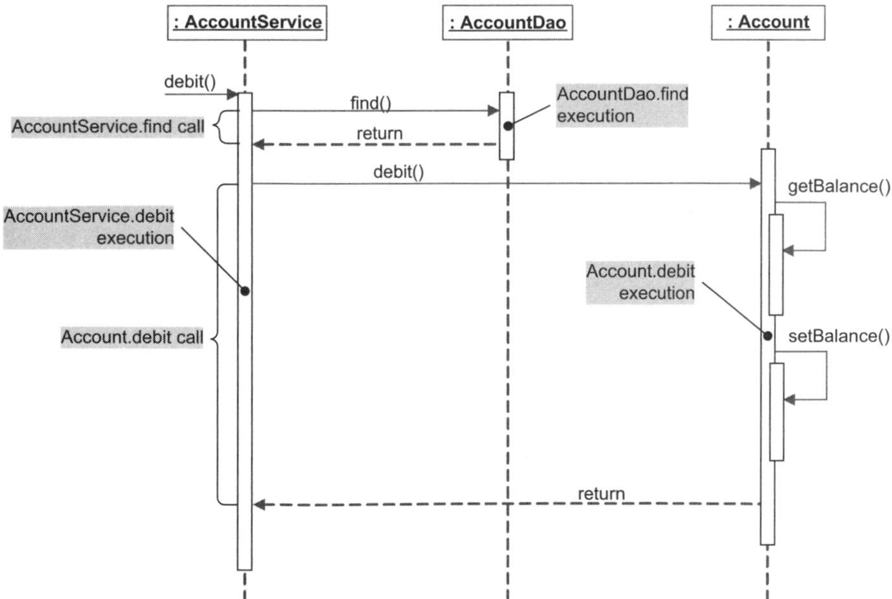

Figure 3.1 Join points in program execution. Method calls and execution are some of the most commonly used join points. (Not all the join points in the sequence diagram are shown in the figure.)

the call to the `debit()` method itself, followed by its execution. Its execution encounters join points for the call and execution of the `find()` method on `AccountDao` and the `debit()` method on `Account`.

Method calls and execution aren't the only join points; an assignment to a field, such as to the `balance` of the `Account` class, is also a join point (not shown in the sequence diagram). You can write advice to perform an action at these join points. For example, you can advise the execution of `setBalance()` to detect and flag a minimum-balance rule violation.

3.1.2 Pointcuts

A *pointcut* is a program construct that selects join points and collects join point context. Let's see the core characteristics of this construct.

SELECTING JOIN POINTS

Pointcuts specify a selection criterion. As you'll see shortly, you use types, methods, fields, and annotations as the primary mechanism to define pointcuts. You can also specify runtime conditions that must be satisfied at a selected join point.

COLLECTING JOIN POINT CONTEXT

A join point has associated runtime information—called *join point context*—in the form of objects such as the executing object and the method arguments. For example, a method call has the caller object, the object on which method is invoked, the arguments, and attached annotations of the method as the join point context. Similarly, for the exception-handler join point, the current object and the thrown exception form its context. As you'll see in chapter 4, certain pointcuts can collect this context and pass it to advice.

USING SIGNATURES

In Java, all program elements have signatures. Pointcuts use patterns for these signatures to specify the selected join points. Figure 3.2 shows the relationship between program elements, signature, join points, and pointcuts.

Signature patterns can specify a few wildcards to match a wide range of program elements. We'll examine signature patterns in section 3.5.

USING RUNTIME SELECTION CRITERION

Often, a signature doesn't offer enough information to specify the selection criterion. AspectJ offers several pointcuts that use runtime information such as the runtime types of the object involved, their values, and the control flow that led to a join point. (For now, think of control flow as the call stack leading up to the join point.)

DETERMINING POINTCUTS STATICALLY

When you specify a pointcut, the weaver needs to use that information to determine whether a program element matches the specified conditions. For a pointcut that specifies only a structural matching criteria, the weaver can determine the match during the weaving process without any runtime checks. Such pointcuts are called *statically determinable pointcuts.* Static crosscutting may use only these kinds of pointcuts, as we'll discuss in chapter 5.

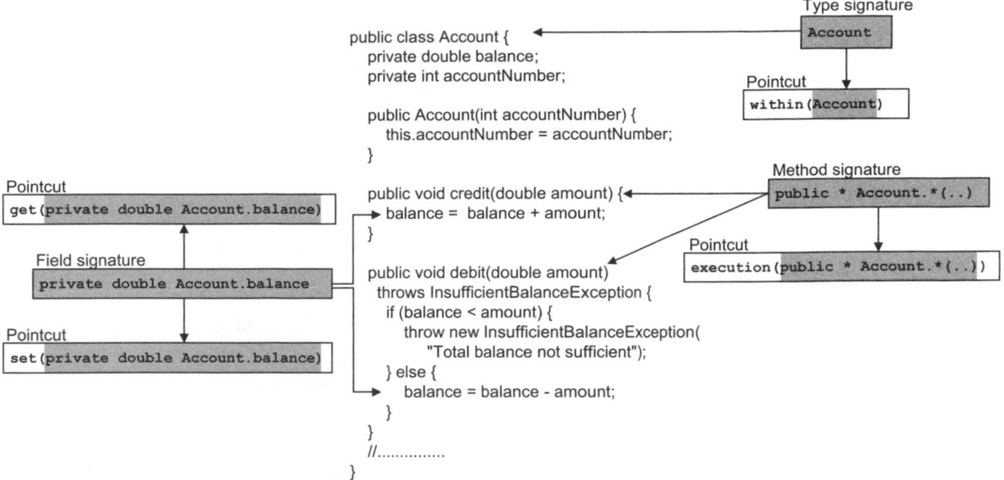

Figure 3.2 Relationship between join points, signature patterns, and pointcuts. Types, methods, and fields all have a signature pattern associated with them (shown with a gray background); it's a way to identify a program element. Pointcuts use signature patterns to select the associated join points.

Learning about pointcuts becomes easier when you understand various join point categories, as we'll discuss next.

3.2 Categorizing exposed join points

AspectJ exposes several categories of join points. It's important to know the join points exposed for a piece of code so that your advice applies properly. Often, you'll encounter a situation where selecting the required join point may not seem possible; but a good understanding of the exposed join points may reveal alternative possibilities. For example, although no exposed join point corresponds to a middle of a method, perhaps a join point corresponding to a call or an exception handler in that method will do the job. This understanding may also guide your refactoring process so that you can expose the needed join points. For example, you can use the Extract Method refactoring to pull out the code so you can select join points corresponding to the extracted method.

NOTE Although I cover a fair amount of detail in this section, I'm limiting my coverage to practical uses. For more in-depth semantics, refer to the AspectJ Programming Guide available from AspectJ's web site (http://www.eclipse.org/aspectj/docs.php).

Let's take a quick look at the categories of the join points exposed by AspectJ and their semantics. Table 3.1 shows each available category and the code it represents. Later, we'll drill down into each of them.

Table 3.1 Overview of join point categories exposed by AspectJ

Category	Exposed join point	Code it represents
Method	Execution	Method body
Method	Call	Method invocation
Constructor	Execution	Execution of an object's creation logic
Constructor	Call	Invocation of an object's creation logic
Field access	Read access	Access to read an object's or a class's field
Field access	Write access	Access to write an object's or a class's field
Exception processing	Handler	Catch block to handle an exception
Initialization	Class initialization	Class loading
Initialization	Object initialization	Object initialization in a constructor
Initialization	Object pre-initialization	Object pre-initialization in a constructor
Advice	Execution	Advice execution

3.2.1 Method join points

In well-written software, each method performs a well-defined behavior. Method-related join points represent useful points to add crosscutting behavior. Consequently, these join points are the most commonly used.

AspectJ exposes two kinds of join points for methods: *execution* and *call* join points. The method-execution join point encompasses the execution of all the code within the body of the method. The following code shows an example of the method execution join point for the `debit()` method:

```
public class Account {

    ...

    public void debit(double amount)
        throws InsufficientBalanceException {
        if (balance < amount) {
            throw new InsufficientBalanceException(
                 "Total balance not sufficient");
        } else {
            balance = balance - amount;
        }
    }
}
```

debit() method execution join point

In this code snippet, the join point for the execution of the `debit()` method encompasses the whole method body. This means you can write advice for this join point to be applied before, after, and around the body.

NOTE Method-execution join points gain extra prominence when using Spring's proxy-based AOP—because they're the only join points available with it!

The method-call join point occurs at the places where a method is being invoked. The following code shows an example of the method-call join point for the `debit()` method:

```
Account account = new Account(200);
account.debit(100);
```

debit() method call join point

In this code, the call join point is the call to the `debit()` method. Note that the code that forms the arguments isn't part of the join point. For example, if the `debit()` method is called in the statement `account.debit(Currency.round(100.2345))`, the call `Currency.round(100.2345)` is *not* part of the `debit()` method call join point.

Execution vs. call: your place or mine?

For most purposes, the difference between the execution and call join points doesn't matter. The most important effect of choosing one over the other relates to weaving. If you advise an execution of a method, the weaver weaves advice into the method body. But if you advise calls to a method, the weaver weaves all method invocation locations. Consider a situation in which you need to advise the `debit()` method in the `Account` class. If you want to weave the `Account` class, you use an execution join point. If you want to affect only the caller classes, you use a call join point.

If your goal is to issue compile-time errors and warnings, where you may want to detect calls made from some parts of the code, using a call join point is the only choice. See chapter 11 for examples of such usage. The call join point also lets you collect the caller object's context—something you can't do easily with the execution join points. We'll discuss context collection in chapter 4.

If you use reflection to invoke a method or constructor, the weaver matches the execution join point the same way as a normal invocation. But the call join point for the invocation corresponds to the reflection API that you use and not the method or constructor.

If your goal is to advise a method's behavior, then in the absence of any requirements posed by weaving or other design considerations, you should prefer execution join points. A typical program has multiple calls to the same method but only one method implementation. Advice to the call join point, then, leads to weaving in all those places, instead of in just one location, as would be the case for an execution join point.

Often, you need to apply crosscutting behavior at object-construction time. AspectJ exposes constructor-related join points to enable such possibility.

3.2.2 Constructor join points

Constructor join points are similar to method join points, except they represent the execution and invocation of object construction. This join point encompasses the execution of the code within the body of a constructor for an object. The following code shows an example of the constructor-execution join point for the `Account` class:

```
public class Account {
    ...

    public Account(int accountNumber) {
        this.accountNumber = accountNumber;     <-- Account constructor
    }                                               execution

    ...
}
```

Similar to the method-execution join point, the execution join point for the `Account(int)` constructor encompasses the entire constructor body.

If you don't have an explicit constructor, the constructor join point exposes the automatically supplied default constructor.

Constructor-call join points represent the points that invoke the creation of an object. The following code shows an example of this join point for the `Account` object:

```
Account account = new Account(200);
```

In this code, the constructor-call join point is the call to the constructor. The discussion of choosing an execution or a call join point for a method applies to constructor join points equally well.

3.2.3 Field access join points

Imagine that you need to perform some crosscutting action whenever a field is accessed. Perhaps the field is cached, and you need to ensure that it contains the latest value before any code reads it. Or, perhaps you want to mark an object dirty whenever a field in it is modified. To enable such possibilities, AspectJ offers field-access join points. These join points correspond to the read and write access to an instance or class member of a class. The following code snippet shows field-access join points in the `Account` class:

```
public class Account {
    private int accountNumber;
    private double balance;
    ...

    public Account(int accountNumber) {             Write-access
        this.accountNumber = accountNumber;     <-- join point
    }

    public String toString() {
        return "Account: "                  Read-access
            + accountNumber;            <-- join point

    }

    ...
}
```

In this code snippet, a join point for a field's read access encompasses reading the field as part of creating the string representation of an object in the `toString()` method. The join point for a field's write access encompasses an assignment to `accountNumber` in the constructor.

A field access join point is similar to the execution join point for the getter and setter methods for the field, except that the former is present at the field level and doesn't need those methods. Therefore, advising field access join points is often a superior approach that doesn't require implementing getters or setters to achieve functionality such as enforcing validation, implementing object-association constraints, and triggering business rules.

Note that AspectJ exposes access to instance variables as well as class variables (static fields) but not to local variables. Furthermore, field access join point doesn't match access through the reflection API.

3.2.4 Exception-handler join points

Imagine that you want to respond to any handled exceptions of certain types. Perhaps you want to log the exception before rethrowing. AspectJ offers exception-handler join points, which represent the handler block (the `catch` block) of an exception type to make such a crosscutting implementation possible. The following code shows an exception-handler join point:

```
try {
    account.debit(amount);
} catch (InsufficientBalanceException ex) {
    postMessage(ex);
    overdraftManager.applyOverdraftProtection(account, amount);
}
```

Exception handler join point

Here, the exception-handler join point encompasses the entire `catch` block—in this case, posting message and overdraft-protection logic.

Let's move on to the next join point category from table 3.1.

3.2.5 Class-initialization join points

Let's say you want to perform class-level crosscutting, such as the initialization of class (static) variables. Class-initialization join points represent the loading of a class, including the initialization of the static portion. Here's an example:

```
public class Account {
    static {
        try {
            System.loadLibrary("accounting");
        } catch (UnsatisfiedLinkError error) {
            ... deal with the error
        }
    }

    ...
}
```

Account class initialization

The class-initialization join point in this code snippet encompasses a call to the `System.loadLibary()` method and the `try/catch` block surrounding it. If there were multiple static blocks, the join point would encompass all of them. This join point is present even when you don't have an explicit static block; in those cases, it represents the loading of the class, and you can use it to weave class load-time actions.

3.2.6 Object initialization join points

Object-initialization join points select the initialization of an object, from the return of a parent class's constructor until the end of the first called constructor. Such a join point, unlike a constructor-execution join point, occurs only in the first called constructor for each type in the hierarchy. Unlike class-initialization that occurs when a class loader loads a class, object initialization occurs when an object is created.

Typically, these join points are used with advice that needs to perform certain additional object initialization, such as injecting its dependencies. For example, Spring's domain-object dependency-injection support (often used through the `@Configurable` annotation) advises the object-initialization join point to inject dependencies. This code shows two object initialization join points:

```
public class SavingsAccount extends Account {
    ...

    public SavingsAccount(int accountNumber, boolean isOverdraft) {
        super(accountNumber);
        this.isOverdraft = isOverdraft;              <-
    }                                                   Object initialization
                                                        join point
    public SavingsAccount(int accountNumber) {
        this(accountNumber, false);
        this.minimumBalance = 25;                    <-
    }

    ...
}
```

In this code snippet, for the first constructor, the object-initialization join point encompasses the assignment to the `isOverdraft` instance member and not `super()`. For the second constructor, the join point encompasses the assignments in the first and second constructor.

3.2.7 Object pre-initialization join points

The object pre-initialization join point is rarely used. It encompasses the passage from the first called constructor to the beginning of its parent constructor. Practically, it encompasses calls made while forming arguments to the `super()` call in the constructor. Here's an example:

```
public class SavingsAccount extends Account {
    ...                                                     Object
    public SavingsAccount(int accountNumber) {              pre-initialization
        super(accountNumber,                                join point
              AccountManager.internalId(accountNumber)   <-
              );
    }

    ...
}
```

In this code snippet, the object pre-initialization encompasses a call to the `AccountManager.internalId(accountNumber)` method only—and *not* the entire `super()` call.

So far, we've examined join points present in Java programs. Let's complete the join point discussion with an additional type that is specific to AspectJ.

3.2.8 Advice execution join points

Not to be outdone by the standard Java constructs, AspectJ offers one of its own join points, which encompasses the execution of any advice in the system. You can advise such join points for purposes such as profiling the advice itself or monitoring executions of advice for unit-testing of aspects. It's often desirable to avoid advising join points while a join point is being advised, to avoid a sort of recursive condition. The advice execution along with a control-flow pointcut (see section 3.6.2) helps implement such requirements. The following code shows an advice-execution join point:

```
public aspect AccountActivityMonitorAspect {
    ...
    before() : accountActivity() {
        logAccountActivity(thisJoinPoint);      <-- Advice-execution join point
    }
}
```

In this code snippet, the advice-execution join point encompasses the before advice in `AccountActivityMonitorAspect`. If you used @AspectJ syntax (discussed in chapter 7) to represent the aspect, it would select the methods representing advice.

Now that you know all the join points AspectJ offers, let's create an example to help you understand them.

3.3 Join point demonstration example

We'll use classes from appendix A to demonstrate join points in a program. First, create a simple driver (listing 3.1) program, which will exercise some of those classes. Later, you'll add a simple aspect to trace join points in the system.

Listing 3.1 Main driver

```
package ajia.main;

import ajia.domain.Order;

public class Main {
    public static void main(String[] args) {
        Order order = new Order();
        order.getTotalPrice();
    }
}
```

Next, let's write a simple tracing aspect.

3.3.1 The aspect

Listing 3.2 shows an aspect that prints the information for all join points as the code executes. Because we haven't discussed the details of various pointcuts, you'll use only a `within()` pointcut along with a negation operator to select all the join points occurring outside the aspect. (You'll learn more about the `within()` pointcut later in this chapter.) The before and after advice print the information about the join points selected by the traced() pointcut. You also use a special variable—thisJoinPoint—that is available in each advice body; thisJoinPoint is a special object that contains information about the join point, as we'll discuss in chapter 4.

Listing 3.2 Tracing all join points in classes

```
package ajia.tracing;

public aspect JoinPointTraceAspect {
    private int callDepth;

    pointcut traced() : !within(JoinPointTraceAspect);      <-- 1 Selects trace points

    before() : traced() {
        print("Before", thisJoinPoint);                     2 Before advice
        callDepth++;
    }

    after() : traced() {
        callDepth--;                                         3 After advice
        print("After", thisJoinPoint);
    }

    private void print(String prefix, Object message) {
        for(int i = 0; i < callDepth; i++) {
            System.out.print("  ");
        }
        System.out.println(prefix + ": " + message);
    }
}
```

1. The pointcut !within(JoinPointTraceAspect) excludes all join points within the aspect, thus selecting all the calls, execution, field access, and so forth outside the JoinPointTraceAspect. This also avoids advising the print() method in the aspect, which would lead to infinite recursion because the advice calls that method.

2. The before advice executes just before each advised join point. The *call depth* is the level in the execution stack of method calls. You use the call depth to get the indentation effect by printing additional spaces corresponding to the call depth before each print statement; this helps you to better understand the output. In the before advice, you increment the call depth to indicate that you're going one level deeper into the call stack. Then, you print the thisJoinPoint object, which contains the text representation of the advised join point.

3. The after advice executes after each advised join point. For the call depth, you perform the action opposite the one in the before advice, because you're now going one level up in the call stack. Just as in the before advice, you print the thisJoinPoint object.

What does this demo aspect show you? Let's look at the output.

3.3.2 The result

When you compile all the classes and the tracing aspect and run the Main class, you get the following output:

```
Before: staticinitialization(ajia.main.Main.<clinit>)
After: staticinitialization(ajia.main.Main.<clinit>)
Before: execution(void ajia.main.Main.main(String[]))
  Before: call(ajia.domain.Order())
    Before: staticinitialization(ajia.util.DomainEntity.<clinit>)
    After: staticinitialization(ajia.util.DomainEntity.<clinit>)
    Before: staticinitialization(ajia.domain.Order.<clinit>)
    After: staticinitialization(ajia.domain.Order.<clinit>)
    Before: preinitialization(ajia.domain.Order())
    After: preinitialization(ajia.domain.Order())
    Before: preinitialization(ajia.util.DomainEntity())
    After: preinitialization(ajia.util.DomainEntity())
    Before: initialization(ajia.util.DomainEntity())
      Before: execution(ajia.util.DomainEntity())
      After: execution(ajia.util.DomainEntity())
    After: initialization(ajia.util.DomainEntity())
    Before: initialization(ajia.domain.Order())
      Before: execution(ajia.domain.Order())
        Before: call(java.util.ArrayList())
        After: call(java.util.ArrayList())
        Before: set(Collection ajia.domain.Order.lineItems)
        After: set(Collection ajia.domain.Order.lineItems)
      After: execution(ajia.domain.Order())
    After: initialization(ajia.domain.Order())
  After: call(ajia.domain.Order())
  Before: call(double ajia.domain.Order.getTotalPrice())
    Before: execution(double ajia.domain.Order.getTotalPrice())
      Before: call(Collection ajia.domain.Order.getLineItems())
        Before: execution(Collection ajia.domain.Order.getLineItems())
          Before: get(Collection ajia.domain.Order.lineItems)
          After: get(Collection ajia.domain.Order.lineItems)
          Before: call(java.util.ArrayList(Collection))
          After: call(java.util.ArrayList(Collection))
        After: execution(Collection ajia.domain.Order.getLineItems())
      After: call(Collection ajia.domain.Order.getLineItems())
      Before: call(Iterator java.util.Collection.iterator())
      After: call(Iterator java.util.Collection.iterator())
      Before: call(boolean java.util.Iterator.hasNext())
      After: call(boolean java.util.Iterator.hasNext())
    After: execution(double ajia.domain.Order.getTotalPrice())
  After: call(double ajia.domain.Order.getTotalPrice())
After: execution(void ajia.main.Main.main(String[]))
```

Here are some keys to interpreting this output:

- The output lines that contain `staticinitialization()` show class-level initialization that occurs when a class is loaded. The `<clinit>` part of the output indicates the class initialization.
- Similarly, lines with `preinitialization()` and `initialization()` show object initialization.
- The output lines that contain `execution()` and `call()` show the execution and call join points of a method or a constructor.
- The output lines that contain `get()` and `set()` show the read and write field access join points.

You can use this code as a starting point for further exploration. Experiment with it to gain a deeper understanding of the join point model.

Now, let's move our attention to writing pointcuts to select join points.

3.4 Understanding pointcut basics

AspectJ's pointcut language is the same in the traditional and @AspectJ syntax. A subset of the language is also available in the Spring Framework. Knowing about possible pointcuts and join points selected will help you decide whether to use AspectJ's weaver-based or Spring's proxy-based AOP.

You can declare a pointcut inside an aspect, a class, or an interface. As with data and methods, you can use an access specifier to restrict access to it.

3.4.1 Named and anonymous pointcuts

In AspectJ, pointcuts can be either *anonymous* or *named*. Named pointcuts are elements that can be referenced from multiple places, making them reusable. Anonymous pointcuts, like anonymous classes, are defined at the place of their usage, such as a part of advice, a part of static crosscutting constructs (discussed in chapter 5), or when another pointcut is defined.

REUSABILITY: NAMED POINTCUTS

Named pointcuts are recommended and therefore the most commonly used pointcuts. Figure 3.3 shows the `accountOperation()` named pointcut that selects calls to any methods in an `Account` class.

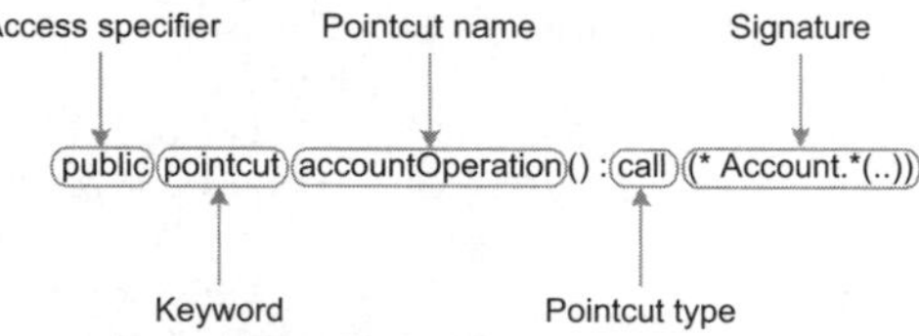

Figure 3.3 Defining a named pointcut. You define a named pointcut using the `pointcut` keyword and a name. The part after the colon defines the selected join points using the pointcut type and signature.

You can use the named pointcut in advice as follows:

```
before() : accountOperation() {
    ... advice body
}
```

> **A special form of pointcut**
>
> A special form of named pointcut omits the colon and the pointcut definition following it. Such a pointcut selects no join points. For example, the following pointcut selects no join points (indicating that there are no thread-safe operations):
>
> ```
> pointcut threadSafeOperation();
> ```
>
> Such pointcuts are useful to supply an implementation for an abstract pointcut from a base aspect (a topic we'll cover in chapter 6) that selects no join points. Think of this form as being analogous to implementing a method with an empty body. Note that the special form of the pointcut differs from an abstract pointcut only in omitting the `abstract` keyword.

In a few circumstances, a pointcut definition is simple and reusability isn't a concern. In those cases, it often suffices to use anonymous pointcuts.

USE ONCE: ANONYMOUS POINTCUTS

You define an anonymous pointcut at the point of its usage. Because you can't reuse such pointcuts, you should avoid using them when the pointcut code is complicated.

You can specify anonymous pointcuts as a part of advice. For example, advice may use an anonymous pointcut as follows:

```
before() : call(* Account.*(..)) {
    ... advice body
}
```

You can also use an anonymous pointcut as part of another pointcut. For example, the following pointcut uses an anonymous `within()` pointcut to limit the call join points selected by `accountOperation()` made from classes with `banking` as the root package:

```
pointcut internalAccountOperation()
    : accountOperation() && within(banking..*);
```

You can combine both named and anonymous pointcuts using pointcut operators, which lets you create complex selection criteria using simpler pointcut definitions.

3.4.2 Pointcut operators

Java provides unary and binary operators to form complex conditional expressions by combining simpler conditional expressions. In a similar spirit, AspectJ provides a unary negation operator (`!`) and two binary operators (`||` and `&&`) to form complex matching rules by combining simple pointcuts:

- *Unary operator*—AspectJ supports only one unary operation—! (negation)—that lets you match all join points *except* those specified by the pointcut. For example, the tracing example in listing 3.2 uses `!within(JoinPointTraceAspect)` to exclude all the join points occurring inside the body of `JoinPointTraceAspect`.
- *Binary operators*—AspectJ offers `||` and `&&` to combine pointcuts. Combining two pointcuts with the `||` operator selects join points that match *either* of the pointcuts, whereas combining them with the `&&` operator selects join points matching *both* pointcuts.

The precedence between these operators is the same as in plain Java. You can use parentheses to override the default operator precedence and make your code more legible.

3.5 Signature syntax

The program-element signature forms the central construct in a pointcut definition. After you learn the signature syntax, learning a set of pointcuts (called *kinded* pointcuts) becomes trivial. Signature patterns, by themselves, are also helpful in static crosscutting.

Given that crosscutting concerns, by definition, span multiple modules and multiple program elements, the language must provide an economical way to express selection criteria. The signature syntax in AspectJ uses wildcards to select program elements that share common characteristics.

AspectJ supports the following three wildcards:

- `*` denotes any number of characters except the period. In a type signature pattern, it denotes a part of the type or package name. In other patterns, it denotes a part of the name such as the method or field name.
- `..` denotes any number of characters including any number of periods. In a type signature pattern, it denotes all direct and indirect subpackages. In method signature patterns, it denotes an arbitrary number of method arguments.
- `+` denotes any subtype of a given type. It may be used only as a suffix to a type signature pattern.

Let's examine the various signature patterns in AspectJ.

3.5.1 Type signature patterns

The term *type* collectively refers to classes, interfaces, annotations, and primitive types. In AspectJ, *type* also refers to aspects. A type signature pattern specifies a set of types and may use wildcards, unary, and binary operators. To simplify understanding this topic, we'll categorize type signature patterns based on how they use Java constructs. Let's look at a few examples.

BASIC TYPE SIGNATURE PATTERN

The basic type signature pattern doesn't use new Java 5 features.

NOTE In traditional syntax, when you don't explicitly specify packages, the weaver matches types against the imported packages and the package of the defining type. In @AspectJ syntax, you must always use fully qualified names except when specifying types in the same package as the aspect itself.

Table 3.2 shows simple examples of matching type signatures.

Table 3.2 Examples of type signatures

Signature pattern	Description	Example types
`Account`	The `Account` type	Only the `Account` type (not its base types or subtypes)
`*Account`	Any type with a name ending with `Account`	`SavingsAccount` and `CheckingAccount`
`java.*.Date`	Type `Date` in any of the direct subpackages of the `java` package	`java.util.Date` and `java.sql.Date`

Table 3.2 Examples of type signatures *(continued)*

Signature pattern	Description	Example types
`java..*`	Any type inside the `java` package or any of its direct and indirect subpackages	Any type in `java.awt` or `java.util`, as well as indirect subpackages such as `java.awt.event` and `java.util.logging`
`javax..*Model+`	All the types in the `javax` package and its direct and indirect subpackages that have a name ending in `Model`, and their subtypes	`TableModel`, `TreeModel`, and so forth, and all their subtypes, such as `AbstractTableModel`, `DefaultTableModel`, and `DefaultTreeModel`

A new language feature in Java 5 offers a way to attach annotations to program elements. Let's see how you can use those annotations in type signature patterns.

ANNOTATION-BASED TYPE SIGNATURE PATTERN

Annotations specify metadata (additional data or information) about the element they're annotating. For example, a type may carry an annotation such as `@Entity` that indicates that the type is persistent. AspectJ allows the use of annotations in type signature patterns. Because the annotations are types too, the type signature patterns in table 3.2 apply to them as well.

Using annotations in pointcuts is proving to be popular among AOP practitioners. When used with custom annotations, writing pointcuts becomes an easy task. For example, you can define the `Sensitive` annotation as follows:

```
@Retention(RetentionPolicy.RUNTIME)
public @interface Sensitive {
    int level();
}
```

The annotation defines one integer attribute to indicate the level of sensitivity. You can then mark all types that represent sensitive information, as shown here:

```
@Sensitive(level=5)
public class MedicalRecord {
    ...
}
```

You can use the annotation in type selection criteria to select all sensitive types.

> **Retention policy of annotations**
>
> Annotations used as a part of a statically determinable pointcut must have at least class-retention policy so the compiler retains them in the class file. Others need runtime retention so the compiler retains them in the class files and the VM makes them available at runtime.

Let's look at some examples of type signatures using annotations, shown in table 3.3.

Table 3.3 Examples of type signatures using annotations

Signature pattern	Description	Example types
@Secured Account	The Account type with the Secured annotation	@Secured class Account {

@Sensitive *	Any type marked with the Sensitive annotation	@Sensitive(level=5)
		class MedicalRecord {
		@Sensitive(level=10)
		class NuclearDesign {

@Business* Customer+	The Customer type or its subtypes that carry an annotation of a type whose name starts with Business	@BusinessEntity
		class Customer {
		@BusinessCritical
		class PlatinumCustomer
		extends Customer {

Note that Java doesn't support annotation inheritance. For example, you can't declare an annotation type, say BusinessEntity, to extend another annotation type Entity. Therefore, AspectJ need not (and doesn't) support the + wildcard with annotation types.

GENERIC-BASED TYPE SIGNATURE PATTERNS

Another major feature in Java 5 is support for generics. Table 3.4 shows a few examples of type signatures using generics.

Note that the type-pattern complexity seen in the last two rows stems from Java; AspectJ uses the same syntax with the type signature patterns in Java.

Table 3.4 Examples of type signatures using generics

Signature pattern	Description	Example types
Map<Long,Account>	The Map type, with the first generic parameter bound to the Long type and second bound to the Account type	Map<Long, Account> (but no other base or subtype)
*<Account>	Any type with Account as the parameter	Collection<Account>, Portfolio<Account>, and so on
Collection <@Sensitive *>	The Collection type, with a type parameter that carries the Sensitive annotation	Collection<MedicalRecord>, if MedicalRecord carries the @Sensitive annotation
Collection <? extends Account>	The Collection type, with a type parameter that is Account or extends Account	Collection<Account>, Collection<SavingsAccount>, Collection<CheckingAccount>, and so on
Collection <? super Account>	The Collection type, with a type parameter that is one of the base type of the Account	Collection<BankEntity> and Collection<Nameable>, assuming Account extends or implements (directly or indirectly) BankEntity and Nameable

COMBINING TYPE SIGNATURE PATTERNS

You can combine type signature patterns using unary and binary operators. Table 3.5 shows some examples.

Table 3.5 Examples of combined type signatures using unary and binary operators

Signature pattern	Description	Example types
`!Collection`	Any type other than `Collection`.	`Account`, `Customer`, `ArrayList` (although it extends `Collection`), and so on
`Collection || Map`	The `Collection` or `Map` type.	`Collection` and `Map` only
`java.util.RandomAccess+ && java.util.List+`	Any type that implements both the specified interfaces.	`java.util.ArrayList`, because it implements both interfaces
`!@Secured *`	Any type that doesn't carry the `Secured` annotation.	`java.util.ArrayList`, `StringUtils` (assuming it isn't marked with `@Secured`), and so on
`@Secured @Sensitive *`	Any type that carries both `@Secured` and `@Sensitive` annotations. Although `@(Secured && Sensitive)` is a valid pattern, it's meaningless because it selects annotations that are simultaneously `Secured` and `Sensitive`—an impossible combination per the Java specification.	`@Secured` `@Sensitive(level=5)` `class MedicalRecord {`
`@(Secured || Sensitive) *`	Any type that carries either an `@Secured` or `@Sensitive` annotation.	`MedicalRecord` (as defined in the previous row), and `@Secured` `class InventoryService {`

Although certain pointcut definitions use a type signature pattern by itself, its more common usage is as a part of method, constructor, and field signature patterns. Let's look at how that works.

3.5.2 Method and constructor signature patterns

These signature patterns identify call and execution join points in methods and constructors. Method and constructor signatures specify the name, the return type (for methods only), the declaring type, the argument types, and modifiers, as shown in figure 3.4.

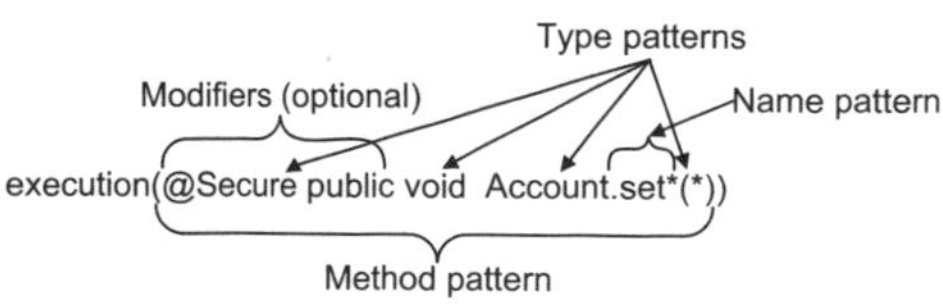

Figure 3.4 Method signature patterns used in pointcuts. A method pointcut specifies a method signature pattern that uses type and name patterns.

As you can see in figure 3.4, a method pattern uses the type signature patterns extensively. The portion before the return value contains modifiers, such as `public`, `private`, `protected`, `static`, and `final` as well as annotations for the method. These modifiers are optional, and the matching process ignores the *unspecified* modifiers. For instance, unless you specify the `final` modifier, the matching process selects both final and nonfinal methods that match the rest of the signature. You can also use the modifiers with the negation operator to specify matching with all but the specified modifier. For example, `!final` matches all nonfinal methods.

When a type is used in the method signature for declaring classes, interfaces, return types, arguments, and declared exceptions, you can specify the type signatures discussed in tables 3.2–3.5 in place of specifying exact types. Note that if a pattern matches a base type method, it also matches the overridden implementations of the same method in subclasses.

BASIC METHOD SIGNATURE PATTERN

In method signatures, the wildcard `..` is used to denote any type and number of arguments taken by a method. Table 3.6 shows examples of matching method signatures.

Table 3.6 Examples of method signatures

Signature pattern	Matched methods	Example methods
`public void Account.set*(*)`	Any public method in the `Account` class with the name starting with `set` that returns `void` and takes a *single argument of any type*. This match is performed regardless of other modifiers, such as `static` and `final`, as well as any annotations associated with the method.	`class Account { public void setBalance(double balance) { public void setCustomer(Customer customer) {`
`public void Account.*()`	Any public method in the `Account` class that returns `void` and takes no arguments.	`class Account { public void update() {`
`public * Account.*()`	Any public method in the `Account` class that takes no arguments and returns any type.	All methods in the previous row as well as methods in `Account` such as `public Date lastUpdate() {`
`public * Account.*(..)`	Any public method in the `Account` class that takes any number (including zero) and type of arguments and returns any type.	All methods in the previous two rows as well as methods in `Account` such as `public void transfer(Account account, double amount) {`
`* Account.*(..)`	Any method in the `Account` class. This matches methods with `public`, `private`, `protected`, and the default access.	All methods in the previous three rows as well as methods in `Account` such as `protected void debit(double amount)`
`* *.*(..)` or `* *(..)`	Any method regardless of return type, defining type, method name, and arguments.	Any method in the system

Table 3.6 Examples of method signatures *(continued)*

Signature pattern	Matched methods	Example methods
`!public * Account.*(..)`	Any method with nonpublic access in the `Account` class. This matches any method with `private`, `protected`, or default access.	`class Account { protected void debit (double amount) {`
`* *(..) throws SQLException`	Any method that declares that it can throw `SQLException`.	`class JDBCUtil { Connection getConnection() throws SQLException {`
`* Account+.*(..)`	Any method in the `Account` class or its subclasses. This matches any additional method in `Account`'s subclasses.	All methods in `Account` as well as all methods in `class SavingsAccount extends Account { ...`
`* java.io.Reader.read (char[],..)`	Any `read()` method in the `Reader` class, regardless of the type and number of arguments to the method, as long as the first argument type is `char[]`.	`read(char[])` and `read(char[], int, int)`, but not `read()` in `java.io.Reader`
`* javax..*.add*Listener (EventListener+)`	Any method whose name starts with add and ends in `Listener` in the `javax` package, or any of the direct and indirect subpackages, that takes one argument of type `EventListener` or its subtype.	`addTableModelListener (TableModelListener)` in `TableModel` `addTreeModelListener(TreeModelListener)` in `TreeModel`
`* java.io.PrintStream. printf(String, Object...)`	The `printf()` method in `java.io.PrintStream` that takes a `String` as the first argument followed by *a variable number of* `Object` arguments. Note the use of `...` (triple dots), which matches how Java specifies variable arguments.	`class PrintStream { PrintStream printf (String format, Object... args) {`
`Account AccountService.*(..)`	Any method in `AccountService` that returns the `Account` type. If a subclass overrides the method that declares to return a subtype of `Account` (using the *covariant return type* feature in Java 5), that is also selected. Note that you don't need a + wildcard to select the overridden method in `SpecialAccountService`, because due to the covariant return type feature, that method matches the base type method's signature (in addition to its own signature).	`class AccountService { public Account getAccount(long id) {` `class SpecialAccountService extends AccountService { public SpecialAccount getAccount(long id) {`

If you're using Java 5, you can use the annotations associated with methods by specifying annotation-based matching criteria in signatures.

ANNOTATION-BASED METHOD SIGNATURE PATTERN

AspectJ supports selecting methods based on the annotations they carry. For example, the following method carries the `@Transactional` annotation:

```
public class Account {
    ...

    @Transactional
    public void credit(double amount) {
        ...
    }

    ...
}
```

Table 3.7 shows examples of method selection based on annotations.

Table 3.7 Examples of method signature patterns based on annotations

Signature pattern	Description	Example methods
`@Secured * *(..)`	Any method marked with the `@Secured` annotation.	`@Secured void credit(double amount)` `@Secured MedicalRecord getRecord()`
`@Secured @Transactional * *(..)`	Any method marked with both `@Secured` and `@Transactional` annotations.	`@Secured @Transactional void credit(double amount)` `@Secured @Transactional(readOnly=true) MedicalRecord getRecord()`
`@(Secured || Transactional) * *(..)`	Any method marked with either an `@Secured` or `@Transactional` annotation.	`@Transactional void credit(double amount)` `@Secured MedicalRecord getRecord()`
`(@Sensitive *) *(..)`	Any method that returns a type marked with an `@Sensitive` annotation.	`MedicalRecord getRecord()` Assuming `MedicalRecord` is annotated with `@Sensitive`
`* (@BusinessEntity *).*(..)`	Any method defined in a type annotated with the `@BusinessEntity` annotation.	All methods in `Account` and `Customer`, if these types are annotated with the `@BusinessEntity` annotation
`* *(@RequestParam (*))`	Any method with one parameter marked with the `@RequestParam` annotation. Note the use of parentheses around that last * to group the parameter type.	`void show(@RequestParam Long id)`

Table 3.7 Examples of method signature patterns based on annotations *(continued)*

Signature pattern	Description	Example methods
`* *(@Sensitive *)` or `* *((@Sensitive *))`	Any method with one parameter whose type carries the `@Sensitive` annotation.	`void create(MedicalRecord mr)`, assuming `MedicalRecord` carries the `@Sensitive` annotation
`* *(@RequestParam (@Sensitive *))`	Any method with one parameter marked with the `@RequestParam` annotation, where the parameter's type is marked with the `@Sensitive` annotation.	`void create(@RequestParam MedicalRecord mr)`, assuming `MedicalRecord` carries the `@Sensitive` annotation

Note that you can use types with generics (as shown in table 3.4) for the type portions in method signatures.

Constructors, owing to their similarities to methods, follow the method signature patterns closely.

CONSTRUCTOR SIGNATURE PATTERN

A constructor signature differs from a method signature in three ways:

- Because constructors don't have a return value, *it doesn't allow the return-value specification.*
- Because constructors don't have names as regular methods do, you need to *substitute* `new` *for the method name* in a signature.
- Because constructors can't be declared static, you may not use the `static` keyword.

For example, the public constructor of the `Account` class, taking no arguments, has the signature `public Account.new()`. Due to the strong resemblance between method and constructor signatures, for brevity's sake, we don't show examples in a table.

We'll complete the discussion of signature patterns with patterns for the fields defined in types.

3.5.3 Field signature patterns

Much like a method signature, a field signature allows you to designate a member field. You can then use field signatures to select join points corresponding to read or write access to the specified fields. A field signature must specify the field's type, the declaring type, and the modifiers. You can use type-signature patterns to specify the types involved. Figure 3.5 shows how a field pointcut uses a field-signature pattern.

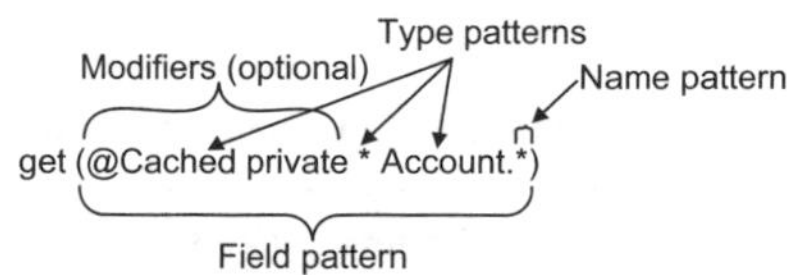

Figure 3.5 Field signature patterns used in pointcuts. A field-access pointcut selects read (get) or write (set) access to fields matching the specified a field signature pattern that, in turn, uses type and name patterns.

As with a method signature, modifiers (access specification, static, and final) are optional. Omitting a modifier selects fields without consideration for the omitted modifier.

BASIC FIELD SIGNATURE PATTERN

The basic field signature, like a method signature, sticks to pre–Java 5 features. Let's dive straight into a few examples in table 3.8.

Table 3.8 Examples of field signature patterns

Signature pattern	Description	Example fields
`private double Account.balance`	Private (instance or static) field `balance` of the `Account` class	`class Account {` `  private double balance;`

`* Account.*`	Any field of the `Account` class, regardless of access modifier, type, or name	`class Account {`
		`  private double balance;`
		`  protected long id;`
		`  ...`

`* Account+.*`	Any field of the `Account` class or its subclasses, regardless of access modifier, type, or name	Fields in the previous rows as well as in `Account`'s subclass such as:
		`class SavingsAccount extends Account {`
		`  private double minimumBalance;`

You can enhance a field signature by specifying annotations associated with the field in addition to other selection criteria.

ANNOTATION-BASED FIELD SIGNATURE PATTERN

In addition to types and methods, Java 5 also supports annotating fields. For example, in the following code, the field `id` is marked with the `@Id` annotation:

```
public class Account {
    @Id private Long id;
    ...
}
```

Not surprisingly, AspectJ can use field-level annotations. Table 3.9 shows some examples.

Table 3.9 Examples of field signature patterns with annotations

Signature pattern	Description	Example fields
`@Sensitive * *.*`	Any field that is marked with the `@Sensitive` annotation, regardless of the field's type, declaring type, or name	`private @Sensitive SSN socialSecurityNumber;`

Table 3.9 Examples of field signature patterns with annotations *(continued)*

Signature pattern	Description	Example fields
`(@Sensitive *) *.*`	Any field whose type is marked with the `Sensitive` annotation	If the type `MedicalRecord` is marked with the `Sensitive` annotation, this pattern selects any field of the `MedicalRecord` type.
`* (@Sensitive *).*`	Any field defined in a type annotated with the `Sensitive` annotation	Fields such as `diagnosis` and `treatment` in the `MedicalRecord` type (assuming `MedicalRecord` is annotated with `@Sensitive`).

As with method signatures, you can use types with generics in field signatures.

Now that you understand the syntax of the signatures, you're ready to use them in pointcuts. That will prepare you to write useful aspects in your application.

3.6 Implementing pointcuts

AspectJ offers several pointcut designators, which when combined with the signatures discussed in the preceding section, form pointcuts. Pointcuts match join points in AspectJ two ways:

- *Kinded pointcuts*—Pointcuts that directly map to join point categories or *kinds*, discussed in section 3.2, to which they belong. For example, AspectJ offers a pointcut designator to match method executions.
- *Non-kinded pointcuts*—Pointcuts that select join points based on information at the join point, such as runtime types of the join point context, control flow, and lexical scope. These pointcuts select join points of any kind as long as they match the prescribed condition. Some of the pointcuts of this type also allow the collection of context at the selected join points.

By learning about various signature patterns, you've already traveled half way toward the goal of understanding kinded pointcuts. Let's complete that journey.

3.6.1 Kinded pointcuts

Kinded pointcuts follow a specific syntax to select each kind of exposed join point in AspectJ. When you understand the categories of exposed join points and signature syntax, you'll find that understanding kinded pointcuts is simple—all you need is their syntax. Table 3.10 shows the syntax for each of the kinded pointcuts.

Kinded pointcuts at a glance

Selects—Join points of the specified kind and signature

Spring—Supports only `execution()`

Statically determinable—Yes

Table 3.10 Mapping of exposed join points to pointcut designators

Join point category	Pointcut syntax
Method execution	`execution(MethodSignature)`
Method call	`call(MethodSignature)`
Constructor execution	`execution(ConstructorSignature)`
Constructor call	`call(ConstructorSignature)`
Class initialization	`staticinitialization(TypeSignature)`
Field read access	`get(FieldSignature)`
Field write access	`set(FieldSignature)`
Exception handler execution	`handler(TypeSignature)`
Object initialization	`initialization(ConstructorSignature)`
Object pre-initialization	`preinitialization(ConstructorSignature)`
Advice execution	`adviceexecution()`

When you understand the pointcut syntax in table 3.10 and the signature syntax as described in section 3.5, you'll be able to write kinded pointcuts. For example, to select any public method in the `Account` class, you write a `call()` pointcut as follows:

```
call(public * Account.*(..))
```

Similarly, to select any write access to the `balance` field of type `double` and with private access in the `Account` class, you write a `set()` pointcut as follows:

```
set(private double Account.balance)
```

A join point can have only one kind

What will `execution(* Account.*(..)) && call(* Account.*(..))` select? Nothing! The pointcut intends to select join points that must be an execution of an `Account` method *and simultaneously* a call to an `Account` method. You can't have a join point that is simultaneously both execution and call. Remember, a call is on the caller side, whereas execution happens on the receiver side—they're two completely different places.

You can't have a join point of multiple kinds; and creating a pointcut to match different kinds always leads to no match. You can avoid this common mistake by remembering a simple rule: don't combine two pointcuts of different kinds with the `&&` operator.

Another common newbie mistake is to be misled by `&&`. In our example, it's a mistake to read the pointcut as "Select executions of `Account` methods *and* calls to `Account` methods." The correct way to read this pointcut is, "Select join points that match *both* conditions: it's an execution of an `Account` method *and* it's a call to an `Account` method."

> **A join point can have only one kind *(continued)***
>
> If you read it this way, the error is easily apparent. Remember another simple rule: pointcuts specify a selection criterion that every matching join point must satisfy. This reading also leads to a solution: use || instead of &&: `execution(* Account.*(..)) || call(* Account.*(..))`. This pointcut correctly reads, "Select join points that match *either* condition: it's an execution of an `Account` method *or* it's a call to an `Account` method."

Now that we've examined the kinded pointcuts, let's look at the other type of pointcut: the kind that selects join points based on specified conditions regardless of the kind of join point. This type of pointcut offers a powerful way to express certain complex weaving rules.

3.6.2 Non-kinded pointcuts

Non-kinded pointcuts select join points based on criteria other than the signature of the join point. For example, with non-kinded pointcuts, you can select all join points occurring inside a class or all join points where the `this` object is of a certain type. In each case, the selected join points may include method executions, calls, exception handlers, field accesses, and so on, as long as they match the specified criteria. In other words, these pointcuts don't consider the kind of join point during selection—hence the name. AspectJ offers non-kinded pointcuts based on a program's control flow and its lexical structure, execution object, arguments, annotations, and conditional expressions.

> **Spring and non-kinded pointcuts**
>
> As we mentioned earlier, Spring supports only one kind of join point: method execution. But it supports many ways to select those join points. Obviously, it supports the `execution()` pointcut, which specifies method signatures. It also supports a few pointcuts based on lexical structure, execution object, arguments, and annotation. Chapter 9 provides a detailed look at what Spring supports; but where appropriate, this chapter also indicates the pointcuts supported by Spring.

Let's discuss each of the non-kinded pointcuts.

CONTROL-FLOW BASED POINTCUTS

These pointcuts select join points occurring in the control flow of join points selected by another pointcut. The control flow of a join point defines the flow of the program instructions that occur as a result of the invocation of the join point. Think of control flow as similar to a call stack. For example, the `Account.debit()` method calls `Account.getBalance()` as part of its execution; the call and the execution of `Account.getBalance()` are said to have occurred in the control flow of the `Account.debit()`

method. In a similar manner, other methods, field access, and exception handler join points also occur in the control flow of the method's join point.

> **Control-flow based pointcuts at a glance**
>
> *Selects*—Join point in control flow or below of join points selected by the specified pointcut
>
> *Spring*—Not supported
>
> *Statically determinable*—No

A control-flow pointcut specifies another pointcut as its argument. There are two control-flow based pointcuts:

- `cflow (<Pointcut>)`—Selects the join points in the control flow of the specified pointcut, including the join points matching the pointcut
- `cflowbelow (<Pointcut>)`—Selects the same join points as `cflow()`, except for the join point that initiated the control flow

The sequence diagram in figure 3.6 shows the graphical representation of the `cflow()` and `cflowbelow()` pointcuts.

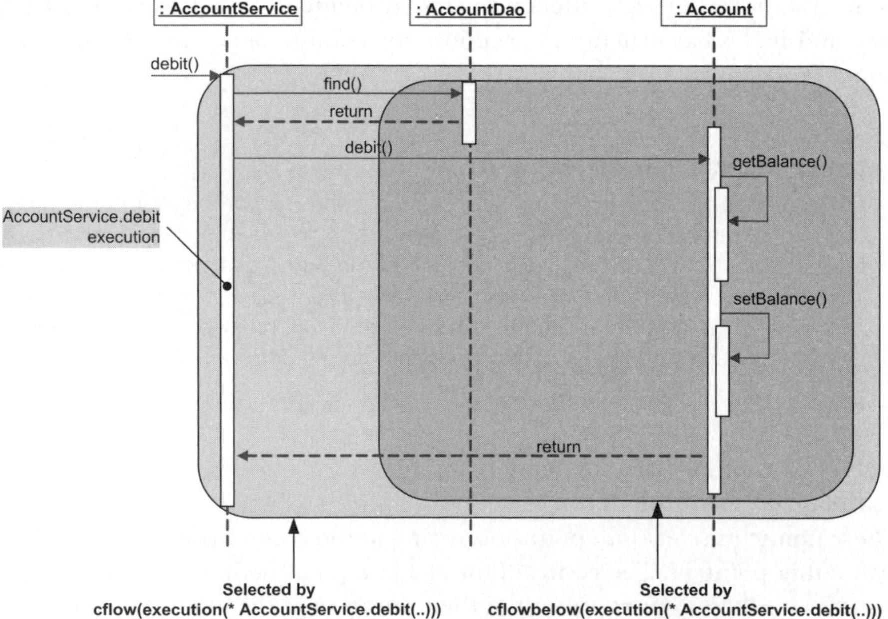

Figure 3.6 Control-flow based pointcuts select every join point occurring in the control flow of join points matching the specified pointcut. The `cflow()` pointcut includes the matched join point, whereas `cflowbelow()` excludes that join point.

Table 3.11 shows some examples of using control-flow based pointcuts.

Table 3.11 Examples of control-flow based pointcuts

Pointcut	Description
`cflow(execution(* Account.debit(..)))`	All join points in the control flow of execution of any `debit()` method in `Account`, including the execution of the `debit()` method
`cflowbelow(execution(* Account.debit(..)))`	All join points in the control flow of execution of any `debit()` method in `Account`, but excluding the execution of the `debit()` method
`cflow(execution(@Transactional * *(..)))`	All join points in the control flow of execution of any method marked with the `@Transactional` annotation
`cflow(transacted())`	Any join point in the control flow of the join points selected by the `transacted()` pointcut

Idiom: top-level join point

One common usage of `cflowbelow()` is to select top-level, nonrecursive join points. For example, `transacted() && !cflowbelow(transacted())` selects the methods that aren't already in the control flow of another method selected by the `transacted()` pointcut. In other words, it selects the outermost transacted method, where typically you'll start and stop transactions.

The control flow leading up to a join point is a runtime concept determined by the path taken during program execution. Consequently, `cflow()` and `cflowbelow()` pointcuts can't be determined at compile time.

LEXICAL-STRUCTURE BASED POINTCUTS

A *lexical scope* is a segment of source code. Lexical-structure-based pointcuts select join points occurring inside the lexical scope of specified classes, aspects, and methods. Because only the lexical structure is considered during evaluation of the selection criteria, unlike with `cflow()` and `cflowbelow()`, these pointcuts are statically determinable.

Lexical-structure-based pointcuts at a glance

Selects—Join points in specified type or method/constructors

Spring—Supports `within()` but not `withincode()`

Statically determinable—Yes

Two pointcuts fall into this category:

- `within(<TypePattern>)`—Selects any join point within the body of the specified *classes* and *aspects*, as well as any nested classes
- `withincode(<ConstructorSignature>)` or `withincode(<MethodSignature>)` —Selects any join point inside a lexical structure of a *constructor* or a *method*, including any local classes in them

Table 3.12 shows some examples of lexical-structure-based pointcuts.

Table 3.12 Examples of lexical-structure based pointcuts

Pointcut	Description
`within(Account)`	Any join point inside the `Account` class's lexical scope including inside any nested classes
`within(Account+)`	Any join point inside the lexical scope of the `Account` class and its subclasses including inside any nested classes
`within(@javax.persistence.Entity *)`	Any join point inside the lexical scope of any type marked with the `javax.persistence.Entity` annotation including inside any nested classes
`withincode(* Account.debit(..))`	Any join point inside the lexical scope of any `debit()` method of the `Account` class including inside any local classes

Idiom: avoiding the advising of aspect elements

One common usage of the `within()` pointcut is to exclude the join points in the aspect. For example, the following pointcut excludes the join points inside `TraceAspect`:

```
traced() && !within(TraceAspect)
```

If you advise this pointcut, the `!within()` part ensures that even if the `traced()` pointcut (such as `execution(* *(..))`) selects join points in the aspect, they won't be advised.

EXECUTION-OBJECT POINTCUTS

These pointcuts select join points based on the types of the objects at execution time. The pointcuts select join points that match either the type of `this`, which is the current execution object, or the `target` object, which is the object on which the method is being called.

Execution object pointcuts at a glance

Selects—Join points matching `this` or the target type. Optionally, collects the matched objects.

Spring—Supports `this()`. Supports `target()` with somewhat different semantics to accommodate the proxy-based implementation.

Statically determinable—No.[1]

Accordingly, there are two execution object pointcut designators:

- `this()`—Takes the form `this(<Type or ObjectIdentifier>)`. It selects join points that have a `this` object associated with them that is of the specified type or the specified `ObjectIdentifier`'s type. In other words, if you specify `Type`, it matches the join points where the expression `this instanceof <Type>` is true, leading to matching subtypes as well. The form of this pointcut that specifies `ObjectIdentifier` collects the `this` object so you can use that object in advice.
- `target()`—Similar to the `this()` pointcut but uses the target of the join point instead of `this`. It takes the `target(<Type or ObjectIdentifier>)` form. The `target()` pointcut is normally used with a method-call join point, and the target object is the one on which the method is invoked.

In addition to matching the join points, these pointcuts can collect the context at the specified join point.

Type vs. object identifier forms for the curious

The two variations of `this()` and `target()` as well as `args()` and various annotation-based pointcuts discussed later in this chapter serve a specific purpose. The forms that specify types restrict the join point selection based on the types of the appropriate objects at a join point. On the other hand, the forms that specify object identifiers restrict the join point selection based on the types of the object identifiers in addition to making the appropriate objects at the join point available to the advice. We'll discuss context collection in chapter 4.

Table 3.13 shows some examples of using execution-object pointcuts.

Note that unlike most other pointcuts that take the `TypePattern` argument, `this()` and `target()` pointcuts take `Type` as their argument. So, you can't use the any wildcards while specifying the type.

---

1 AspectJ can optimize pointcuts such as `this()` in certain scenarios to avoid runtime checks (effectively determining them statically). But such pointcuts still can't be used in static crosscutting, and thus we classify them as statically non-determinable.

Table 3.13 Examples of execution object pointcuts

Pointcut	Description
`this(Account)`	Any join point where `this instanceof Account` evaluates to `true`. This selects all join points, such as methods calls and field assignments, where the current execution object is `Account` or one of its subclasses: for example, `SavingsAccount`.
`target(Account)`	Any join point where the object on which the method is being called is `instanceof Account`. This selects all join points where the target object is `Account` or one of its subclasses: for example, `SavingsAccount`.

Further, due to Java's use of erasure for generics implementation, AspectJ doesn't allow the type pattern for these pointcuts to be a generic type along with its parameters. For example, it is an error to specify `target(List<Account>)`. However, you may specify a generic type without the parameters such `target(List)`.

Because static methods don't have the `this` object associated with them, the `this()` pointcut won't select the execution of such a method. Similarly, because static methods aren't invoked on an object, the `target()` pointcut also won't match calls to such a method.

There are a few important differences in the way `within()` and `this()` perform matching. The former matches when the object in the lexical scope matches the type specified in the pointcut, whereas the latter matches when the current execution object is of a type that is specified in the pointcut or its subclass. The code snippet that follows shows the difference between the two pointcuts. The `SavingsAccount` class extends the `Account` class, and the `Account` class contains a nested `Helper` class:

```
public class Account {
    ...

    public void debit(double amount)
        throws InsufficientBalanceException {
        ...
    }

    private static class Helper {
        ...
    }
}

public class SavingsAccount extends Account {
    ...
}
```


In this example, `within(Account)` selects any join point in the `Account` class, including any nested classes, but no join points inside its subclasses, such as `SavingsAccount`. On the other hand, `this(Account)` selects any join point in the `Account` class as well as `SavingsAccount`, but excludes any join points inside either class's nested classes.

Also note that the two pointcuts `execution(* Account.*(..))` and `execution(* *.*(..)) && this(Account)` don't select the same set of join points. The first selects

> **Idiom: selecting join points only in subclasses**
> You can match all the join points only in subclasses of a type by using the `this(Type) && !within(Type)` idiom. You can also use the `within(Type+) && !within(Type)` pointcut, but it also selects join points in the nested classes in the subclasses.

all the instance and static methods defined in the `Account` class, whereas the latter picks up the instance methods in the class hierarchy of the `Account` class but none of the static methods.

ARGUMENT POINTCUTS

These pointcuts select join points based on the argument object's *runtime* type of a join point. Objects considered as argument objects differ depending on the join point kind:

- For method and constructor join points, the argument objects are the method and constructor arguments.
- For exception-handler join points, the argument object is the handled exception.
- For field write access join points, the argument object is the new value to be set.

Argument-based pointcuts take the form `args(Type or ObjectIdentifier, ..)`. Note that the selection is based on runtime type (similar to the `this()` or `target()` pointcuts) and not the declared type in program element.

> **Argument pointcuts at a glance**
> *Selects*—Join points matching argument types. Optionally, collects the matched arguments.
>
> *Spring*—Supported.
>
> *Statically determinable*—No.

Similar to execution object pointcuts, these pointcuts can be used to collect the context, but we'll say more about this in chapter 4. Table 3.14 shows some examples of using argument pointcuts.

Table 3.14 Examples of argument pointcuts

Pointcut	Description
`args(Account, .., int)`	Any method or constructor join point where the first argument is of type `Account` and the last argument is of type `int`. This matches methods such as `print(Object, float, int)` as long as the first argument passes the `instanceof Account` test.
`args(RemoteException)`	Any join points with a single argument of type `RemoteException`. It matches a method or constructor taking a single `RemoteException` argument, a field-write access setting a value of type `RemoteException`, or an exception handler of type `RemoteException`.

With Java 5, the use of annotations is proving to be a popular choice. Let's see what AspectJ offers in this regard.

ANNOTATION-BASED POINTCUTS

AspectJ allows selection based on annotations carried by types, methods, and fields. Like the execution object and argument pointcuts, annotation-based pointcuts come in two forms: selection based on matching annotation types and collection of the matching annotation. For example, if `MedicalRecord` is annotated with `@Sensitive`, `@this(Sensitive)` selects all join points where `this` is of `MedicalRecord` type. If the `@Sensitive` annotation is marked as `@Inherited` (see the Java Language Specification for the semantics associated with the `@Inherited` meta annotation), it also matches join points where `this instanceof MedicalRecord` is true.

> **Annotation based pointcuts at a glance**
>
> *Selects*—Join points based on annotations. Optionally, collects the matched annotations.
>
> *Spring*—Supports all except `@this()`.
>
> *Statically determinable*—Yes, except for `@this()`, `@target()`, and `@args()`.

Table 3.15 summarizes these pointcuts and explains the version that performs only selection without collecting the matching annotation. We'll discuss the version that collects the matching annotation in the next chapter.

Table 3.15 Annotation-based pointcuts in AspectJ

Pointcut	Selection
`@this(TypePattern or ObjectIdentifier)`	Any join point where the `this` object's type carries the annotation of the `TypePattern` type.
`@target(TypePattern or ObjectIdentifier)`	Any join point where the target object's type carries the annotation of the `TypePattern` type.
`@args(TypePattern or ObjectIdentifier, ..)`	Any join point where the arguments' type carries annotations of the `TypePattern`.
`@within(TypePattern or ObjectIdentifier)`	Any join point in the lexical scope of a type that carries an annotation matching the specified `TypePattern`.
`@withincode(TypePattern or ObjectIdentifier)`	Any join point where the matching program element (method or constructor) carries an annotation matching the `TypePattern`.
`@annotation(TypePattern or ObjectIdentifier)`	Any join point where the subject carries the specified annotation. For method, constructor, and advice-execution join points, the subject is the same as the program element. For field-access and exception-handler join points, the subject is the field or exception being accessed. For initialization and pre-initialization join points, the subject is the first called constructor matching the specified signature. For static initialization join points, the subject is the type being initialized.

Note that the annotations used in a statically determinable pointcut in table 3.15 must have either class or runtime retention, whereas annotations used in the remaining pointcuts must have runtime retention.

So far, we've explored pointcuts that use join point signatures. AspectJ also offers a way to select based on arbitrary conditions.

CONDITIONAL CHECK POINTCUTS

This pointcut selects join points based on some conditional check at the join point. It takes the form of `if(BooleanExpression)`. Table 3.16 shows some examples of using conditional check pointcuts.

Table 3.16 Examples of conditional check pointcuts

Pointcut	Description
`if(debug)`	Any join point where the `debug` static field (in the defining aspect) is set to `true`.
`if(System.currentTimeMillis() > triggerTime)`	All the join points occurring after the current time has crossed the `triggerTime` value.
`if(circle.getRadius() < 5)`	All the join points where the `circle`'s radius is less than 5. The `circle` object must be a context collected by the other parts of the pointcut or a static field in the defining aspect. See section 4.4.1 for details of the context-collection mechanism.

Conditional check pointcuts at a glance

Selects—Join points matching a condition

Spring—Doesn't support

Statically determinable—No

The `if()` pointcut is often combined with other pointcuts to selectively apply dynamic crosscutting. For example, you can use `execution(* *(..)) && if(debug)` to apply a trace advice only if debug flag has been set to `true`. We'll examine such usage in chapter 10.

3.7 Summary

The real innovation in AspectJ is the pointcut expression language; it's powerful, expressive, and well thought out. Although we focused solely on AspectJ's pointcut language, you'll find that applying it to other AOP systems such as Spring and JBoss AOP is easy—the concepts remain the same, even though different mechanisms are used. Furthermore, in Spring 2.0, you can use the AspectJ pointcut expressions directly without using the AspectJ weaver.

AspectJ's pointcut support offers many possibilities to facilitate writing good pointcuts:

- You can write pointcuts exploiting program elements' core components such as name, defining types, and access modifier. If you use generics, you can specify those to further restrict in your selection criteria.
- You can also use dynamic conditions such as runtime types involved at the join point as well as the control flow that led to the execution of the join point.
- You can also use annotations associated with the join points. During your initial exploration of AOP, annotation-based crosscutting will be particularly attractive. If the program elements of your interest carry annotations, it's trivial to define a pointcut based on those annotations.

For some developers, AspectJ's pointcut language may seem daunting at first. But in my experience, explaining pointcuts systematically—starting with simple pointcuts and then progressing to various signature patterns—invokes an "I see" expression without fail. When I give talks introducing AOP, I often show a few examples of simple pointcuts, explain the wildcards for a couple of minutes, and then ask attendees to tell me pointcuts for more complex selection. I am happy to report nearly 100% correct answers. The reason for such a good response is the consistent nature of the AspectJ language; when you understand the basics, complex patterns become obvious and intuitive.

Now that you know how to write type, method, and field signature patterns and how to utilize them in pointcuts to select the relevant join points, you're ready to put them to good use. In the next chapter, we'll discuss dynamic crosscutting, where additional or augmentative behavior is associated with the selected join point.

4 Modifying behavior with dynamic crosscutting

This chapter covers

- Learning advice basics
- Using three advice types
- Writing a caching example

In the previous chapter, we presented the join point model and examined the pointcut construct as the way to select join points of interest. In this chapter, you'll put that knowledge to practical use as we discuss dynamic crosscutting. Dynamic crosscutting constructs provide a way to affect the behavior of a system, whereby you can alter behavior at join points selected by pointcuts. After reading this chapter, you should be able to start writing meaningful programs in AspectJ.

As we discussed in chapter 2, AspectJ supports multiple syntaxes: traditional and @AspectJ. Although the details vary a bit, all of these syntaxes share a common base. After you learn the traditional syntax, you can easily learn the @AspectJ syntax. Spring-AspectJ integration also uses many of the same base constructs, so when you know an AspectJ syntax form, you can easily apply it in Spring. In this chapter, we'll continue to focus on the traditional syntax.

4.1 Advice overview

Dynamic crosscutting weaving rules consist of two parts: *advice* (what to do) and *pointcuts* (when to apply the advice). AspectJ supports dynamic crosscutting through advice—a method-like construct that defines crosscutting action at the join points selected by a pointcut. We'll begin with discussing three kinds of advice followed by the general anatomy of advice.

4.1.1 Advice classification

If you're implementing a security check, you want that check to take place before executing the join point. On the other hand, if you're implementing exception logging, you want to log after executing the join point and only if it threw an exception. If you're implementing caching, you want to surround the original code with the caching logic: obtain a value from the cache, execute the original code if the cache doesn't contain a value, and add the value to the cache after executing the original code. To take care of all these scenarios, AspectJ offers three kinds of advice:

- *Before advice* executes prior to the join point's execution.
- *After advice* executes following the join point's execution. After advice has three variations based on the outcome of the join point execution:
  - *After (finally)* executes after execution of the join point, regardless of the outcome.
  - *After returning* executes after successful execution of the join point—that is, without throwing an exception.
  - *After throwing* executes after failed execution of the join point—that is, throwing an exception.
- *Around advice* surrounds the join point's execution. This advice is special in that it has the ability to continue the original execution with the same or altered context, zero or more times.

Join points exposed by AspectJ are the only points where you can apply advice. Figure 4.1 shows various join points in an execution sequence at which you can introduce a new behavior via advice.

Let's see how you can implement each kind of advice.

4.1.2 Advice syntax

Although details vary, all instances of advice share a good portion of syntax. Let's look at the general syntactical structure of an advice. The advice construct can be broken into three parts:

- *Advice declaration*—Specifies if the advice will run before, after, or around the join points
- *Pointcut specification*—Specifies which join points will be advised
- *Advice body*—Contains the code to execute upon reaching a selected join point

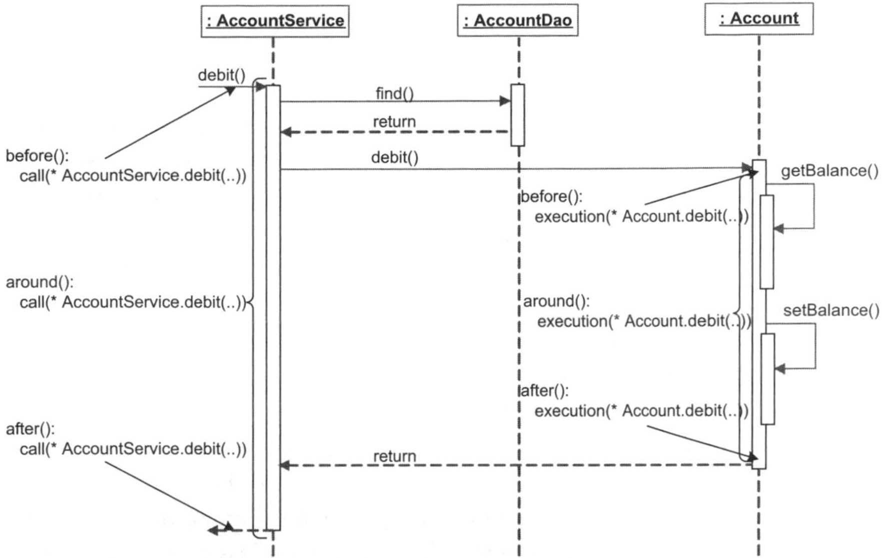

Figure 4.1 Various points in a program flow where you can advise the join point (not all possible points are shown)

Before we show an example, let's review the pointcut that you'll use in an advice:

```
pointcut connectionOperation(Connection connection)
    : call(* Connection.*(..) throws SQLException)
      && target(connection);
```

This named pointcut consists of two anonymous pointcuts:

- `call()`—Selects calls to any method of the `Connection` class.
- `target()`—Collects the target object of the method calls. We'll discuss context collection in section 4.4.

Now, let's look at an example of an around advice using the named pointcut shown earlier:

```
Object around(Connection connection)                    <-❶ Advice declaration
    : connectionOperation(connection) {                 <-❷ Pointcut specification
    long startTime = System.nanoTime();
    Object ret = proceed(connection);
    System.out.println("Operation " + thisJoinPoint           ❸ Advice body
                    + " on " + connection + " took "
                    + (System.nanoTime() - startTime));
    return ret;
}
```

❶ The part before the colon is the advice declaration, which specifies when the advice executes relative to the selected join point—before, after, or around it. The advice declaration also specifies the context information available to the advice body, such as the execution object and arguments, which the advice body can use to perform its logic in the same way a method would use its parameters. It also specifies any checked exceptions thrown by the advice. A `before()` or `after()` advice doesn't declare a return type, but an `around()` advice declares the return type.

❷ The part after the colon is the pointcut; the advice executes whenever a join point matching the pointcut is encountered. You can use an advice not just with methods but also with any other kind of join point. For example, you can advise a constructor invocation, field write-access, exception handler, and so forth.

❸ Just like a method body, the advice body contains the actions to execute. In the example, the around advice prints the time elapsed during advised connection operations. `thisJoinPoint` is a special variable available in each join point; we'll discuss it in section 4.5. In around advice, the `proceed()` statement is a special syntax to carry out the advised operation, as we'll examine in section 4.3.3.

Normally, the advice doesn't have a name. This makes sense because you never call advice directly; it's the system's responsibility to execute the advice body upon reaching the selected join points. But you can assign advice a name using a special annotation. For example, you can use the following snippet to assign `profileConnection` as the advice name:

```
@AdviceName("profileConnection")
Object around(Connection connection) throws SQLException
    : connectionOperation(connection) {
    ...
}
```

The main purpose of naming advice is to add the same capability offered by annotation-style advice that we'll discuss in chapter 7. Tools such as aspect-aware unit-testing frameworks may also use the name of the advice.

Looking at the advice construct, you're probably thinking that it looks an awful lot like a method. Let's compare the two.

4.2 Comparing advice to methods

Because advice and methods both express behavior, AspectJ keeps advice syntax close to that of methods. But because advice logic applies automatically in a crosscutting manner instead of through explicit calls to a method, there are some differences.

4.2.1 Similarities between advice and methods

Let's compare the three categories of similarities: declaration, body, and behavior. The advice declaration part looks much like a method signature:

- It optionally has a name (through the `@AdviceName` annotation).
- It takes arguments in the form of join point context that the advice body can use to perform its logic, just like in a method.
- It may declare that it can throw exceptions.

The advice body looks much like a method body:

- The code inside the advice body follows the same access-control rules as a method to access members from other types and aspects.
- Advice can refer to the aspect instance using `this`.
- An around advice can return a value and therefore declares the return type.
- Advice must declare checked exceptions that may be thrown by its implementation.

Advice behaves in a similar way to a method overriding the advised join point—it can augment or alter the overriding methods behavior. In fact, the exception-declaration rules for advice follow the Java specification for overridden methods. Like overridden methods, advice

- Can't declare that it may throw a checked exception that isn't already declared by *all* advised join points. The weaver will issue an error if this condition isn't met. For example, you aren't allowed to declare that the advice may throw `SQLException` unless all the advised methods declare that they throw it.
- May omit a few checked exceptions declared by the advised join points. For example, if all advised join points throw `IOException` and `SQLException`, an advice may declare that it can throw only one of them.
- May declare that it can throw more specific checked exceptions than those declared by the advised join points. For example, if all advised join points throw `IOException`, an advice may declare that it can throw a subtype—say, `FileNotFoundException`.
- May throw any runtime exceptions.

Despite these similarities, advice aren't methods.

4.2.2 Differences between advice and methods

Advice differs from methods in several ways. Compared to methods, advice

- Only optionally has a name.
- Can't be called directly. (It's the system's job to execute it.)
- Doesn't have an access specifier. (This makes sense because you can't directly call advice anyway.)
- Doesn't include a return type in the signature of before and after advice.
- Has access to a few special variables besides `this` that carry information about the advised join point: `thisJoinPoint`, `thisJoinPointStaticPart`, and `thisEnclosingJoinPointStaticPart` (we'll examine these variables in section 4.5).
- May use the keyword `proceed` in around advice to proceed with the advised join point.

Let's look at each kind of advice in more details.

4.3 Advice in depth

Armed with information about the advice classification and general syntax, it's a good time to dive deeper into each type of advice. In this section, we'll start with the simplest kind of advice: before. Then, we'll look into all variations of the after advice followed by the around advice. We'll finish this section with a complete example.

4.3.1 Before advice

Before advice executes before the execution of the advised join point. In the following code snippet, the advice performs authorization prior to the execution of any method annotated with the `@Secured` annotation:

```
before() : execution(@Secured * *(..)) {
    ... authorize the user
}
```

If you throw an exception in the before advice, the advised operation won't execute. For example, if the authorization logic in the previous advice throws an exception, the advised method won't execute. Before advice is typically used for performing pre-operation tasks, such as policy enforcement, tracing, and security.

4.3.2 After advice

After advice executes after the execution of a join point. Because it's often important to distinguish between normal returns from a join point and those that throw an exception, AspectJ offers three variations of after advice:

- After, regardless of the outcome
- After returning normally
- After throwing an exception

Let's see how each kind of after advice works.

AFTER (FINALLY)

The following code snippet shows the basic form of after advice that executes regardless of the join point's outcome: returning normally or throwing an exception. This plain form of the after advice is often referred to as *after (finally)* advice due to its behavioral resemblance to a `finally` block, which executes regardless of the outcome of the corresponding `try` block:

```
after() : call(* Account.*(..)) {
    ... log the return from operation
}
```

This advice executes after any call to any method in the `Account` class, regardless of how it returns—normally or by throwing an exception.

AFTER RETURNING

You often need to apply advice only after a successful completion of advised join points. AspectJ offers *after returning* advice that is executed after the successful execution of join points. The following code shows the form for after returning advice:

```
after() returning : call(* Account.*(..)) {
    ... log the successful completion
}
```

This advice executes after the successful completion of a call to any method in the `Account` class. If the advised method throws an exception, the advice doesn't execute. AspectJ offers a variation of the after returning advice that collects the return value. It has the following syntax:

```
after() returning(<ReturnType returnObject>)
```

You can use the collected return object in the advice as shown in figure 4.2. Although you can modify the collected return object (for example, remove elements from a collection), there is no way to return a new object. If you need such possibility, you'll have to use the around advice.

```
after() returning(Connection conn) :
    call(Connection DriverManager.getConnection(..)) {
    System.out.println("Obtained database connection: "
                       +conn);
}
```

Figure 4.2 Passing a return object context to an advice body. The return object is collected in `returning()` by specifying the type and object identifier.

In figure 4.2, you collect the return value of `DriverManager.getConnection()` by specifying the type and the name of the return object in the `returning()` part of the advice specification. You then use the return object in the advice body to print its value.

After advice implicitly limits join point selection to only those that are compatible with the specified return type inside `returning()`. For example, in figure 4.2, if you used the `call(* DriverManager.*(..))`, it still would select only methods that return a type that is `Connection` or its subtype.

Another variation of the after advice advises join points upon throwing an exception.

AFTER THROWING

Similar to after returning advice, AspectJ offers *after throwing* advice. Such advice executes only when the advised join point throws an exception. The following code shows the form for after throwing advice:

```
after() throwing : execution(* Controller+.*(..)) {
    ... log the failure
}
```

This advice executes after execution of any method in the `Controller` class or its subtype (note the +) if it throws an exception. If a method returns normally, the advice doesn't execute. Similar to the variation of the after returning advice, AspectJ offers a variation of the after throwing advice that captures the thrown exception object. The advice has the following syntax:

```
after() throwing (<ExceptionType exceptionObject>)
```

You can use this form of the after throwing advice when you want to collect the exception thrown by the advised method so that you can use it in the advice body. In figure 4.3, you collect the exception thrown by any method by specifying the exception type and a name in the `throwing()` part. Much like the return value and any other context, you can use this exception object in the advice body.

Note that `thisJoinPoint` is a special type of variable that carries join point context information. We'll look at these types of variables in section 4.5. Similar to the after returning type, the selected join points are implicitly limited to the join points that throw exceptions compatible with the type specified inside `throwing()`.

```
after() throwing(Throwable ex)
        : execution(* *(..)) {
        System.out.println("Exception" + ex
        + "while executing"
        + thisJoinPoint);
}
```

Figure 4.3 Passing a thrown exception to an advice body. The exception object is captured in `throwing()` by specifying the type and object identifier. Advice may access the special variables such as `thisJoinPoint` in a similar manner to the `this` variable inside an instance method.

Unless the after throwing advice itself throws an exception, the original exception processing continues up the call stack. Specifically, after throwing advice can't swallow an exception, and the caller of the join point receives the exception thrown by the join point.

Now, let's move on to the omnipotent around advice that is capable of implementing all other types of advice.

4.3.3 Around advice

Around advice surrounds join points. It has the ability to execute the join point with the same or different context any number (including zero) of times. This implies that an around advice may bypass the advised join point or execute the advised join point multiple times, each with different context. Some typical usages of around advice are as follows:

- Perform additional logic before and after the advised join point (for example, profiling)
- Bypass the original operation and perform some alternative logic (for example, caching)
- Surround the operation with a `try/catch` block to perform an exception-handling policy (for example, transaction management)

Around advice is the most potent form in that it can be always used instead of before or after advice; but in order to precisely express programming intent, it's best to use the simplest form of advice appropriate for the task.

Around advice has explicit control over the advised join point's execution. Let's see how.

PROCEEDING WITH ADVISED JOIN POINT

If within the around advice you want to execute the advised join point, you must use a special keyword—`proceed()`—in the body of the advice. Unless you call `proceed()`, the advised join point is bypassed. When using `proceed()`, you can pass the context collected by the advice, if any, as the arguments; or you can pass a different set of arguments. The important thing to remember is that you must pass the same number and types of arguments as collected by the advice. Because `proceed()` causes the execution of the advised join point, it returns the same value returned by the advised join point. For example, advising a method that returns a `float` value, invoking `proceed()` returns the same `float` value as the advised method. We'll discuss the details of returning a value from an around advice later in this section.

> **Around advice and the @AspectJ syntax**
> The rules of engagement are different when you implement around advice in the @AspectJ syntax, as you'll see in chapter 7. But the overall theme is consistent with the concepts presented here.

In the following snippet, the around advice invokes `proceed()` with a `try/catch` block to handle exceptions. This snippet also collects the context of the operation's target object and argument. We'll discuss that part in section 4.4:

```
void around(Account account, float amount)
    throws InsufficientBalanceException
    : call(void Account.debit(float) throws InsufficientBalanceException)    ❶
    && target(account)                                                        ❷
    && args(amount) {
    try {
        proceed(account, amount);
    } catch (InsufficientBalanceException ex) {
        if (!processOverdraft(account, amount)) {                             ❸
            throw ex;
        }
    }
}
```

Let's zoom into the parts of this snippet:

❶ The pointcut selects any call to the `Account.debit()` method that throws `InsufficientBalanceException`.

❷ The `target()` and `args()` pointcuts collect join point context: the account and the amount.

❸ In the advice body, you surround the call to `proceed()` with a `try/catch` block, with the `catch` block performing overdraft-protection logic. The result is that when the advice is executed, it in turn executes the advised method using `proceed()`. If the method throws `InsufficientBalanceException`, the `catch` block executes the overdraft-protection logic using the collected join point context. If the overdraft-protection logic fails, it rethrows the caught exception.

The join point's execution may return a value. Let's see how around advice deals with it.

RETURNING A VALUE FROM AROUND ADVICE

Each around advice must declare a return value (which can be `void`). It's typical to declare the return type to match the return type of the advised join points. For example, if you advise a set of methods that are returning an integer, you declare the advice to return an `int`. For a field-read join point, you match the advice's return type to the accessed field's type.

In some cases, an around advice applies to join points with different return types. For example, if you advise all the methods needing transaction support, the return values of all those methods are likely to be different. To resolve such situations, the around advice may declare its return value as—catch all—`Object`. In those cases, AspectJ accommodates return types in the following manner:

- If a join point returns a primitive type, AspectJ boxes it in its corresponding wrapper type and performs the opposite, unboxing after returning from the advice. For instance, if a join point returns an integer and the advice declares that it will return `Object`, AspectJ boxes the integer value in an `Integer` object and returns it from the advice. Upon assignment of such a value, the object is first unboxed to an integer. This feature is similar to the auto-boxing feature introduced in Java 5, but AspectJ doesn't need Java 5 for this feature to work.
- If a join point returns a non-primitive type, AspectJ performs appropriate typecasts before assigning the return value. The scheme of returning the `Object` type works even when a captured join point returns a `void` type.

Note that the AspectJ weaver issues an error if you specify a return type that isn't compatible with any of the advised join points.

Invoking `proceed()` returns the value returned by the join point. Unless you need to manipulate the returned value, you can return the value that was returned by the `proceed()` statement. If you don't invoke `proceed()`, you must still return an appropriate value.

THROWING AN EXCEPTION FROM AROUND ADVICE

An around advice, like other advice, must declare any checked exceptions it throws during advice execution. But any exception thrown by calling `proceed()` need not be declared. For example, although `proceed()` in the following code may throw the checked `InsufficientBalanceException`, because the advice code itself doesn't explicitly throw that exception, the advice need not declare it:

```
void around()
  : call(void Account.debit(float) throws InsufficientBalanceException) {
    long start = System.nanoTime();
    proceed();
    long end = System.nanoTime();
    System.out.println("The debit method took "
                       + (end-start) + " nanoseconds");
}
```

Compare this to the advice at the beginning of section 4.3.3, which throws `InsufficientBalanceException`; in that case, the advice must declare that it may throw that exception. When you're advising join points that all throw the same exceptions, this works fine. But in situations such as transaction management, selected join points throw a variety of exceptions, and an `around()` advice may need to catch the thrown exception and rethrow the caught exception after taking some action. This need, combined with the rules governing which exceptions an advice may declare, make the situation complicated. In these cases, you need to use other techniques, including throwing a runtime exception or wrapping the original exception.

Let's look at an example that uses around advice to handle failures.

EXAMPLE: IMPLEMENTING FAULT TOLERANCE

In a distributed environment, dealing with a network failure is often an important task. If the network is down, clients often reattempt operations. The following example examines how an aspect with around advice can implement the functionality to handle a network failure.

Listing 4.1 simulates the network and other failures by making the method throw an exception randomly.

Listing 4.1 Simulated remote service with high failure rate

```
package ajia.remoting;

import org.springframework.remoting.RemoteAccessException;
import ajia.faulttolerance.Idempotent;

public class RemoteService {
    @Idempotent
    public int getReply(){
        if(Math.random() > 0.25) {
            throw new RemoteAccessException("Simulated failure occurred");
        }
        System.out.println("Replying");
        return 5;
    }
}
```

By checking against a randomly generated number, the `getReply()` method simulates a failure that results in an exception (statistically, the method fails approximately 75 percent of the time—a high failure rate!). When it doesn't fail, it prints a message and returns 5. Note the use of `org.springframework.remoting.RemoteAccessException`: an unchecked exception that is thrown by Spring proxy when you implement RMI using Spring's remoting solution. This example doesn't use Spring to create proxies, because the local invocation suffices for illustration.

Let's also create an annotation type (as shown in listing 4.2) that you can use to denote *idempotent* methods—operations that may be retried safely.

Listing 4.2 Marker annotation to denote methods that may be retried

```
package ajia.faulttolerance;

import java.lang.annotation.Retention;
import java.lang.annotation.RetentionPolicy;

@Retention(RetentionPolicy.RUNTIME)
public @interface Idempotent {
}
```

Next, let's write a simple client (listing 4.3) that invokes the idempotent method in RemoteService.

Listing 4.3 Client of the remote service

```
package ajia.remoting;

public class RemoteClient {
    public static void main(String[] args) {
        RemoteService service = new RemoteService();
        int retVal = service.getReply();
        System.out.println("Reply is " + retVal);
    }
}
```

Now, let's write an aspect to handle failures by reattempting the operation three times before giving up and propagating the failure to the caller (listing 4.4).

Listing 4.4 Aspect that handles failure by retrying

```
package ajia.faulttolerance;

import org.springframework.remoting.RemoteAccessException;

public aspect FailureHandlingAspect {
    private final int MAX_RETRIES = 3;

    Object around() : call(@Idempotent * *(..)) {      ❶ Advice declaration
        int retry = 0;
        while(true){
            try{
                return proceed();                       ❷ Execution of advised join point
            } catch(RemoteAccessException ex){
                System.out.println("Encountered " + ex);
                if (++retry > MAX_RETRIES) {
                    throw ex;
                }
                System.out.println("\tRetrying...");
            }
        }
    }
}
```

❶ You declare that the around advice returns `Object` to accommodate potential different return value types in the selected join points. The pointcut part of the advice uses an anonymous pointcut to select calls to all methods with the `@Idempotent` annotation.

❷ You return the value returned by the invocation of `proceed()`. Although the join point is returning an `int`, AspectJ takes care of the boxing and unboxing logic.

When you compile and run the program, you get output similar to the following:

```
Encountered org.springframework.remoting.RemoteAccessException:
➥    Simulated failure occurred
        Retrying...
Encountered org.springframework.remoting.RemoteAccessException:
```

```
➥   Simulated failure occurred
       Retrying...
Replying
Reply is 5
```

The output shows a few failures, some retries, and eventual success. (Your output may be different due to the randomness introduced.) It also shows the correct assignment to the `retVal` member in the `RemoteClient` class, even though the advice returned the `Object` type.

In chapter 3, we alluded to an important function of a pointcut: collecting join point context. Now is a good time to understand how pointcuts collect context so that you can use it in dynamic crosscutting.

4.4 Collecting join point context

Consider data-driven security. The permission-check logic needs access to the method and objects involved—referred to as *join point context*—to make a decision if the caller possesses the authority to access the objects. Pointcuts, therefore, need to expose the context at the point of execution to pass it to the advice implementation. Join point context comes in two forms:

- Objects (including primitives) involved at the join point
- Annotations associated with the join point

AspectJ provides the `this()`, `target()`, and `args()` pointcuts to collect the objects at the advised join points. It provides `@this()`, `@target()`, `@args()`, `@annotation()`, `@within()`, and `@withincode()` pointcuts to collect annotations associated with the advised join points.

4.4.1 Collecting objects at the join point

You'll recall from chapter 3 that you can specify each of the context-collecting pointcuts two ways:

- Using the type of the objects
- Using `ObjectIdentifier`, which is the name of the object

When advice needs the join point context, you use a pointcut that uses the `ObjectIdentifier`. With this form, you need to remember two things:

- The advice declares the collected objects in much the same way as a method would—each argument specifies a type and name. Then, you use pointcuts to bind each argument to a join point context.

  For example, in figure 4.4, the anonymous pointcut in the before advice declares all the arguments to be collected by the pointcut. The declaration for collected context specifies the type of each collected object. The `target()` pointcut specifies `account` as the object identifier for the collected object, whose type is specified in the pointcut declaration as `Account`.

- The matched pointcuts are implicitly restricted to an equivalent pointcut that uses the type of the object identifier specified.

  For example, in figure 4.4, the matched join points are limited to `target (Account)`, because the type of the account identifier is `Account`. This restricts any matching to join points, where the target object is of the `Account` type (even if you omitted the `call()` portion of the pointcut expression). See section 3.6.2 for details of how matching works.

Figure 4.4 shows an example of collecting join point context and using it in an advice. The `target()` pointcut collects the objects on which the `credit()` method is being invoked, whereas the `args()` pointcut collects the argument to the method. The part of the advice before the colon specifies the type and name for each of the collected arguments. The body of the advice uses the collected context in the same way that the body of a method would use the parameters passed to it. The object identifiers in the code in the figure are `account` and `amount`.

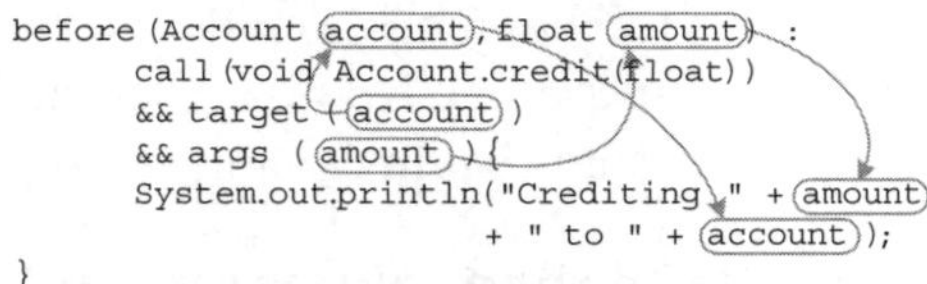
before (Account account, float amount) :
call (void Account.credit(float))
&& target (account)
&& args (amount) {
System.out.println("Crediting " + amount
+ " to " + account);
}

Figure 4.4 Passing an executing object and an argument context from the join point to the advice body. The target object in this case is collected using the `target()` pointcut, whereas the argument value is collected using the `args()` pointcut.

When you use named pointcuts, those pointcuts must collect the context and pass it to the advice. Figure 4.5 shows the collection of the same information as in figure 4.4 but uses named pointcut to capture the context and make it available to the advice.

```
pointcut creditOperation(Account account, float amount) :
    call (void Account.credit(float))
    && target (account)
    && args (amount);

before (Account account, float amount) :
    creditOperation(account, amount) {
    System.out.println("Crediting" + amount
                       + " to " + account);
}
```

Figure 4.5 Passing an executing object and an argument captured by a named pointcut. This code snippet is functionally equivalent to figure 4.4 but uses a named pointcut. For the advice to access the join point's context, the pointcut must collect the context, as opposed to the advice collecting the context when using anonymous pointcuts.

The pointcut `creditOperation()`, besides selecting join points, collects the context so that the advice can use it. You collect the target object and the argument to the `credit()` operation. Note that the pointcut declares the type and name of each collected element, much like a method call. The names of the arguments in the first part of the advice match those in the pointcut definition.

Let's look at some more examples of passing context. In figure 4.6, you collect the security annotation associated with the method and use its property to perform authorization.

As we discussed earlier in this section, when you're collecting context, an implicit restriction on matched join points limits you to only those that can satisfy the collected context. In this example, only join points that carry an `@Secured` annotation

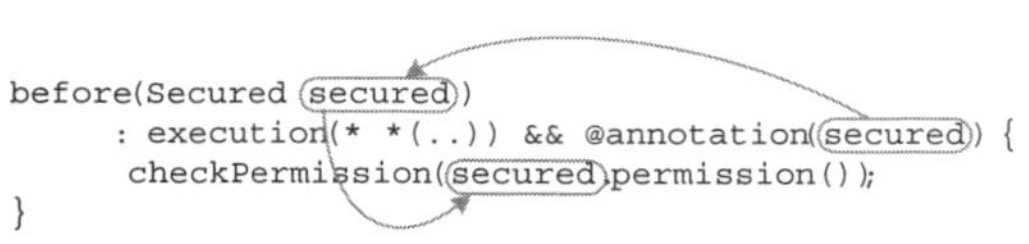

```
before(Secured secured)
    : execution(* *(..)) && @annotation(secured) {
    checkPermission(secured.permission());
}
```

Figure 4.6 Collecting the annotation associated with the join point. Here, you collect the annotation associated with the advised method. After it's collected, the annotation can be used like any other object.

are matched. After you collect the annotation, you can use it like any other object; specifically, you can access annotation properties. In figure 4.6, you access the `permission` property to perform an authorization check.

> **Retention policy for annotations**
>
> Note that annotations accessed during runtime must be marked with a runtime retention policy using the `@Retention(RetentionPolicy.RUNTIME)` meta-annotation. This requirement is common to any runtime usages of annotations (such as through reflection) and not specific to AspectJ.

Let's look at all available pointcuts that let you collect the required context. Table 4.1 summarizes all the context-collecting pointcuts in AspectJ.

Table 4.1 AspectJ pointcuts for collecting join point context

Pointcut	Collected context
`this(obj)`	`this` object at the matching join point.
`target(obj)`	Target object at the matching join point. For a method call join point, the target object is the object on which the method is being invoked. For a method-execution join point, the target object is the `this` object (the same as that collected using `this()`). For field-access join points, the target object is the object whose field is being accessed. For other join points, no target object is available.
`args(obj1, obj2, ...)`	Objects that represent arguments at the matching join points. For method-call or -execution and constructor-call or -execution join points, it collects the arguments to the method or constructor. For exception-handler join points, it collects the handled exception. For field-modification join points, it collects the new value being set.
`@this(annot)`	Annotation associated with the type of the `this` object at the matching join point.
`@target(annot)`	Annotation associated with the target object.
`@args(annot1, annot2, ...)`	Annotations associated with the arguments.
`@within(annot)`	Annotation associated with the type enclosing the matching join point.
`@withincode(annot)`	Annotation associated with the method enclosing the matching join point.
`@annotation(annot)`	Annotation associated with the current join point subject. See the `@annotation` entry in table 3.15 for information about the subject for each kind of join point.

Let's utilize the context-collecting functionality in an example that implements a simple caching strategy.

4.4.2 *Implementing simple caching*

Consider a stock-market service that provides charts for a given stock for a given number of preceding days. The service computes the contents for the chart (such as a GIF or PNG file's content), given the ticker symbol for the stock. Assume that creating a chart is an expensive operation, and you'd like to cache the chart. Listing 4.5 shows the example service.

Listing 4.5 Service that provides stock charts

```
package ajia.stock;

import ajia.caching.Cachable;

public class StockService {
    @Cachable(cacheStore="Chart")
    public byte[] getQuoteGraph(String ticker) {
        // Simulate creation of graph
        return ticker.getBytes();
    }
}
```

Notice the use of an annotation to indicate the methods whose return values may be cached. The annotation type `@Cachable` shown in listing 4.5 specifies a `cacheStore` attribute that specifies a part of the key. As discussed in section 4.4.1, given that you'll need to access the annotation during runtime, you mark it with runtime retention, as shown in listing 4.6.

Listing 4.6 Annotation to mark methods returning cachable content

```
package ajia.caching;

import java.lang.annotation.Retention;
import java.lang.annotation.RetentionPolicy;

@Retention(RetentionPolicy.RUNTIME)
public @interface Cachable {
    String cacheStore();
}
```

In order to develop an aspect based only on the constructs you've learned so far, let's make a series of assumptions (some of them not realistic—we'll revisit the solution later in this chapter and again in chapter 6). First, we assume that the cached methods take only one argument. Second, we assume that a concatenation of the `cacheStorage` attribute (in annotation) and the method argument form the cache key. Third, some external service will manage cache expiration.

Now, let's develop an aspect that implements caching in such scenarios. You'll use OSCache as the underlying caching solution. You could modify the solution to use any other product, such as EHCache, Oracle Coherence, or even a good-old in-memory map. Regardless, the aspect must advise any cached operation, compute the cache key, and query the cache with that key. If it finds a cached value, it needs to return it and bypass the original operation. Otherwise, it must proceed with the advised method and put its return value in the cache. An around advice fits the bill, given the need to potentially bypass the original operation.

Listing 4.7 implements a caching scheme through an aspect.

Listing 4.7 Aspect that implements the caching logic

```
package ajia.caching;

import com.opensymphony.oscache.base.Cache;
import com.opensymphony.oscache.base.NeedsRefreshException;

public aspect CacheAspect {
    private Cache cache = new Cache(true, true, false);

    public pointcut cachedAccess(Object arg, Cachable cachable)
        : execution(@Cachable * *(*))
          && args(arg) && @annotation(cachable);          ❶ Collects context

    Object around(Object arg, Cachable cachable)
        : cachedAccess(arg, cachable) {
        if(arg == null) {
            return proceed(arg, cachable);
        }                                                  ❸ Passes context to proceed()

        String key = cachable.cacheStore() + ":" + arg;

        Object cachedValue = null;
        try {
            cachedValue = cache.getFromCache(key);
        } catch (NeedsRefreshException ex) {               ❷ Uses pointcut's context
            // either the value isn't in the cache,
            // or the value is stale
            cachedValue = proceed(arg, cachable);
            cache.putInCache(key, cachedValue);
        }
        return cachedValue;
    }
}
```

❶ The `cachedAccess()` pointcut selects the execution of methods that take a single argument and are marked `@Cachable`. It collects the argument to the method using the `args()` pointcut. To accommodate arguments of various types, including primitives, you declare the collected argument's type as `Object`. It also collects the annotation to the method using the `@annotation()` pointcut.

❷ The around advice implements the caching logic. It declares that it uses the context collected by the pointcut by declaring the advice parameters. In the advice body, if the argument to the advised method is `null`, it calls `proceed()` to continue with the original method. This ensures that the advice doesn't alter the behavior of a call when it can't effectively deal with it.

The caching logic is simple. First, it computes the cache key by appending the argument to the `cacheStore` attribute of the annotation; this forms keys such as `Chart:GOOG`. Next, it tries to retrieve the cached value for the key. If it gets a value, it returns it. If not (detected by caching exception), it calls `proceed()` to continue with the advised method and puts the return value in the cache before returning it.

3 The around advice passes the collected context to `proceed()`. Recall that the number and type of arguments to `proceed()` must match the advice declaration.

Let's write a simple tracing aspect so that you can see the effect of the aspect in action. Listing 4.8 shows an aspect that produces a trace on cache hits and misses.

Listing 4.8 Monitoring cache usage

```
package ajia.caching;

import com.opensymphony.oscache.base.Cache;
import com.opensymphony.oscache.base.NeedsRefreshException;

public aspect CacheMonitoring {
    pointcut cacheRetrieval(String key)
        : call(* Cache.getFromCache(String)) && args(key);

    after(Object key) returning(Object value)
        : cacheRetrieval(key) {
        System.out.println("Cache hit.  Key: " +  key
                          + " Value: " + value);
    }

    after(Object key) throwing(NeedsRefreshException ex)
        : cacheRetrieval(key) {
        System.out.println("Cache miss. Key: " +  key);
    }
}
```

Finally, let's write a simple class that exercises the service, as shown in listing 4.9.

Listing 4.9 Class to exercise caching functionality

```
package ajia.main;

import ajia.stock.StockService;

public class Main {
    public static void main(String[] args) {
        StockService service = new StockService();
        service.getQuoteGraph("GOOG");
        service.getQuoteGraph("GOOG");
        service.getQuoteGraph("YHOO");
        service.getQuoteGraph("YHOO");
        service.getQuoteGraph("GOOG");
    }
}
```

When you compile and run the code using the build script supplied with the downloadable sources, you get the following output:

```
Cache miss. Key: Chart:GOOG
Cache hit.  Key: Chart:GOOG Value: [B@18558d2
Cache miss. Key: Chart:YHOO
Cache hit.  Key: Chart:YHOO Value: [B@18a47e0
Cache hit.  Key: Chart:GOOG Value: [B@18558d2
```

As soon as the aspect finds a cached value, it uses that value instead of recomputing.

> **Testing an aspect**
> Ideally, you should write a test for your aspect so you can run it automatically. Developing such tests, however, require injecting a mock or stub object in the `CacheAspect` instance to set its `cache` property. Then we can control and observe interaction with the `cache` property to verify correctness. We haven't yet examined the mechanism to access an aspect instance that you need to in order to inject dependencies. You'll learn that mechanism in chapter 6, where you'll improve this aspect and write tests for it.

AspectJ offers an alternative way to collect context through the special variables available in each advice. Let's see why we need this alternative mechanism.

4.5 Accessing join point context via reflection

AspectJ offers an alternative way to access the static and dynamic context associated with the join points through a reflection API. For example, through this API, you can access the name of the currently advised method as well as the argument objects to that method. The most common use of this reflective information is to implement tracing and similar aspects. You've already used simple reflection support to write the `JoinPointTraceAspect` in chapter 3. In this section, we'll examine the details of reflection support.

AspectJ provides reflective access to join point context by making three special objects available in each advice body: `thisJoinPoint`, `thisJoinPointStaticPart`, and `thisEnclosingJoinPointStaticPart`. These objects are much like the special variable `this` that is available in each instance method in Java to provide access to the execution object. The information contained in these three objects is of two types:

- *Static information*—Doesn't change between multiple executions. For example, the name and source location of a method remain the same during different invocations of the method.
- *Dynamic information*—Changes with each invocation of the same join point. For example, two different calls to the method `Account.debit()` will probably have different account objects and debit amounts.

Each join point provides one object that contains dynamic information and two objects that contain static information about the join point and its enclosing join point. Let's examine the information in each of these special objects:

- `thisJoinPoint`—This object of type `JoinPoint` contains the dynamic information of the advised join point. It gives access to the target object, the execution object, and the method arguments. Through these objects, you can access annotations associated with their types as well. It also provides access to the static information for the join point, using the `getStaticPart()` method. You use `thisJoinPoint` when you need dynamic information related to the join point. For example, if you want to log the execution object and method arguments, you use the `thisJoinPoint` object.
- `thisJoinPointStaticPart`—This object of type `JoinPoint.StaticPart` contains the static information about the advised join point. It gives access to the source location, the kind (method-call, method-execution, field-set, field-get, and so forth), and the signature of the join point. You use `thisJoinPointStaticPart` when you need the structural context of the join point, such as its name, kind, source location, associated annotations, and so forth. For example, if you need to log the name of the advised method, you use the `thisJoinPointStaticPart` object.
- `thisEnclosingJoinPointStaticPart`—This object of type `JoinPoint.StaticPart` contains the static information about the enclosing join point, which is also referred to as the *enclosing context*. The enclosing context of a join point depends on the kind of join point. For example, for a method-call join point, the enclosing join point is the execution of the caller method, whereas for an exception-handler join point, the enclosing join point is the method that surrounds the catch block. You use the `thisEnclosingJoinPointStaticPart` object when you need the context information of the join point's enclosing context. For example, while logging an exception, you can log the enclosing context information as well.

To use the special variables available in advice, you need to know the API for the associated types. We'll now examine the reflection API offered by AspectJ.

4.5.1 The reflection API

The reflection API in AspectJ is a set of interfaces that together form the programmatic access to the join point information. These interfaces provide access to dynamic information, static information, and various join point signatures. In this section, we'll examine these interfaces and their relationship with each other. Figure 4.7 shows the structural relationship between the interfaces of the reflection API in a UML class diagram.

The `org.aspectj.lang` package and its subpackage `org.aspectj.lang.reflect` provide support for accessing the join point information:

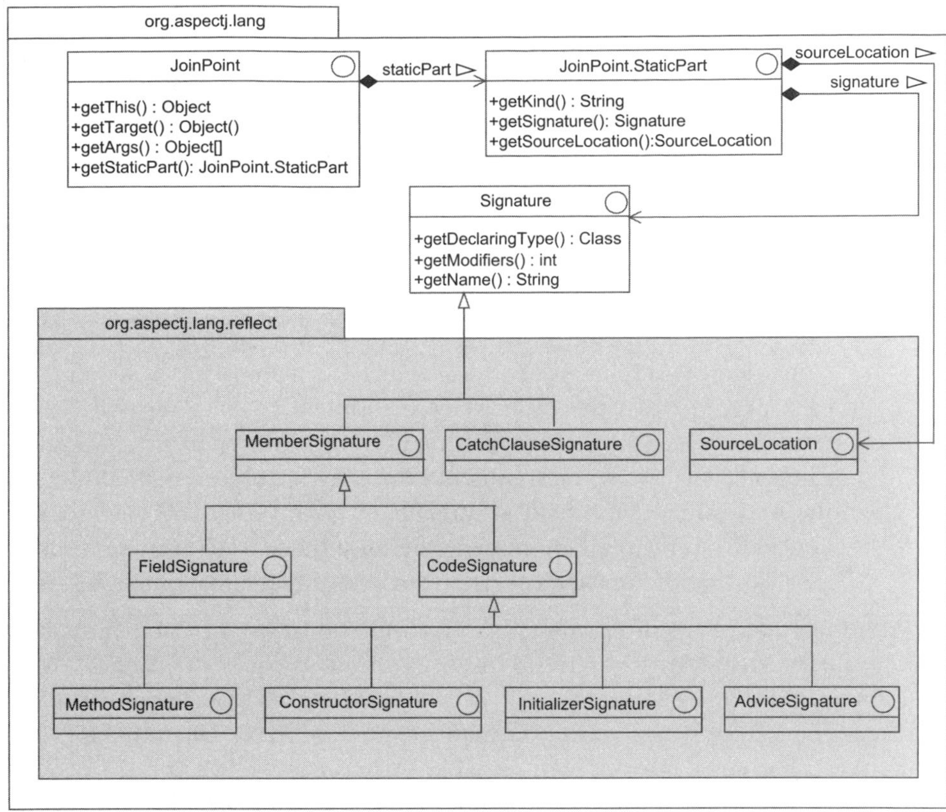

Figure 4.7 The structural relationship among various interfaces supporting reflection

- The `JoinPoint` interface models dynamic information associated with an advised join point.
- A `JoinPoint` object also contains an object of type `JoinPoint.StaticPart` that can be accessed through the method `getStaticPart()`. This object provides access to the join point's static information. This static information consists of the join point's kind, signature, and source code location.
- A `JoinPoint.StaticPart` object is composed of a `String` object (that represents the kind), a `Signature` object, and a `SourceLocation` object.
- The `Signature` object provides access to the join point's signature, and the `SourceLocation` object provides access to the join point's source-code location.
- The `org.aspectj.lang.reflect` subpackage contains interfaces for various join point signatures connected through an inheritance relationship, as well as the `SourceLocation` interface.

NOTE The purpose of the API discussion in this section is to give you an overview. For more details, refer to the AspectJ API documentation.

Now, let's examine the API for accessing dynamic join point information.

THE ORG.ASPECTJ.LANG.JOINPOINT INTERFACE

This interface provides access to the dynamic information associated with the currently advised join point. It specifies two methods for obtaining the currently executing object, target object, and arguments, as well as the static information:

- The `getThis()` method returns the currently executing object, whereas the `getTarget()` method is used to obtain the target object for a called join point. The `getThis()` method returns null for join points occurring in a static method, whereas `getTarget()` returns `null` for the calls to static methods.
- The `getArgs()` method returns the arguments for the join point. For method and constructor join points, `getArgs()` returns an array of each element referring to each argument in the order they're supplied to the join point. The AspectJ weaver wraps each primitive argument in the corresponding wrapper type. For example, it wraps an `int` argument in an `Integer` object. For field-set join points, the new value of the field is available in `getArgs()`. For field-get join points, `getArgs()` returns an empty array, because there is no argument for the operation. For handler execution, `getArgs()` returns the exception.

Although there is no direct API to obtain annotations, you can obtain the corresponding objects through the reflection API and then use Java's reflection API to access annotations. For example, you can get the annotations associated with the currently executing object (`this`) using `thisJoinPoint.getThis().getClass().getAnnotations()`. For more information, see table 4.2 in section 4.5.3.

In addition to providing access to the dynamic information, the `JoinPoint` interface offers direct access to the static information of the advised join point. There are two ways to obtain the static information through the `thisJoinPoint` variable of type `JoinPoint`:

- By using the direct methods (`getKind()`, `getSignature()`, and `getSourceLocation()`) with the `thisJoinPoint` object. The next section discusses these methods because they're also defined in the `JoinPoint.StaticPart` interface, where they perform identical tasks.
- Through the object obtained with `getStaticPart()`, which contains the same information as `thisJoinPointStaticPart`.

Let's move our attention to accessing join point's static information.

THE ORG.ASPECTJ.LANG.JOINPOINT.STATICPART INTERFACE

This interface allows the API to access the static information associated with the currently advised join point. It specifies three methods to obtain the kind of join point, the join point signature, and the source location information corresponding to code for the join point:

- The `getKind()` method returns the kind of join point. The method returns a string such as "method-call", "method-execution", or "field-set" that indicates the kind of the advised join point. The `JoinPoint` interface defines one constant for each of the available kinds of join points.

- The `getSignature()` method returns a `Signature` object for the executing join point. Depending on the nature of the join point, it can be an instance of one of the subinterfaces shown in figure 4.7. Although the base `Signature` interface allows access to common information such as the name, the declaring type, and so forth, you have to cast the object obtained through `getSignature()` to a subinterface if you need finer information (the type of method argument, its return type, its exception, and so on).
- The `getSourceLocation()` method, which returns a `SourceLocation` object, allows access to the source-location information corresponding to the join point. The `SourceLocation` interface contains a method for accessing the source filename, line number, and so forth.

Each of the `JoinPoint`, `JoinPoint.StaticPart`, and `Signature` interfaces specifies three methods for obtaining string representation of the object with varied descriptiveness: `toString()`, `toLongString()`, and `toShortString()`.

NOTE The `thisJoinPoint` object, *if used in an advice*, is allocated every time an advice is executed to capture the current dynamic context. In contrast, `thisJoinPointStaticPart` is allocated only once per join point during the execution of a program. Therefore, using dynamic information is expensive compared to static information. You should be aware of this fact while designing aspects such as tracing.

To demonstrate the use of reflection APIs, let's modify the caching example from section 4.4.2.

4.5.2 Improving caching using reflection APIs

Recall from the caching example in section 4.4.2 that we made a series of assumptions. Particularly onerous ones were that cached methods take only one argument and that the argument would be sufficient to form the key. Alas, the real world doesn't confirm to such assumptions: methods routinely take more than one argument, and a key may need to be a complex composition of arguments. For example, if the arguments to a method that retrieves a statement are of type `Account` and duration, forming the cache key may require composing the account id (but not its balance) and duration. Now that you know more about join point context, you can improve the solution.

The important mechanism we'll introduce in the new solution is using annotations to support specifying a script that computes the key and letting the script use the join point context. For example, the modified `StockService` specifies the caching information, as shown in listing 4.10. For the purpose of illustration, the example uses Spring's expression language as the scripting language.

Listing 4.10 Caching specification using scripts

```
package ajia.stock;

import ajia.caching.Cachable;

public class StockService {
```

```
    @Cachable(cacheStore="Chart", keyScript="#ticker + ':' + #days")
    public byte[] getQuoteGraph(String ticker, int days) {
        // Simulate creation of graph
        return ticker.getBytes();
    }
}
```

This class specifies the key to be computed by augmenting the `ticker` argument with the days argument, separated by a colon. Note how the script uses variables that match the method parameter names. Obviously, you need to modify the annotation type to include the `keyScript` attribute, as shown in listing 4.11.

Listing 4.11 Cachable annotation that includes the `keyScript` attribute

```
package ajia.caching;

import java.lang.annotation.Retention;
import java.lang.annotation.RetentionPolicy;

@Retention(RetentionPolicy.RUNTIME)
public @interface Cachable {
    String cacheStore();
    String keyScript();
}
```

Let's modify the aspect to use the key script, as shown in listing 4.12.

Listing 4.12 Caching scheme that uses script for key computation

```
package ajia.caching;

import ...

public aspect CacheAspect {
    private Cache cache = new Cache(true, true, true);
    private ExpressionEvaluator expressionEvaluator
        = new SpelExpressionEvaluator();

    public pointcut cachedAccess(Cachable cachable)
        : execution(@Cachable * *(..))  && @annotation(cachable);

    Object around(Cachable cachable) : cachedAccess(cachable) {
        Map<String, Object> jpContextMap
            = JoinPointContextUtil
                  .getJoinPointContextMap(thisJoinPoint);
        String key = null;

        try {
            key = cachable.cacheStore() + ":"
                  + expressionEvaluator.evaluate(cachable.keyScript(),
                                                 jpContextMap);
        } catch (Exception ex) {
            System.out.println("Exception evaluating expression " + ex);
            return proceed(cachable);
        }

        Object cachedValue = null;
        try {
```

```
            cachedValue = cache.getFromCache(key);
        } catch (NeedsRefreshException ex) {
            cachedValue = proceed(cachable);
            cache.putInCache(key, cachedValue);
        }
        return cachedValue;
    }
}
```

Evaluating a script expression requires you to specify a context—a map with keys set to the variable names and values set to the variable objects. In order to use scripts for caching, you must create a map with keys set to parameter names and values set to arguments. Using reflection API, this is a simple task, as shown in listing 4.13.

Listing 4.13 Utility class that creates a map from the join point object

```
package ajia.util;

import ...

public class JoinPointContextUtil {
    public static Map<String, Object>
            getJoinPointContextMap(JoinPoint jp) {
        Map<String, Object> context = new HashMap<String, Object>();

        context.put("_jp", jp);

        // convenience binding
        context.put("_this", jp.getThis());
        context.put("_target", jp.getTarget());
        context.put("_args", jp.getArgs());

        Signature sig = jp.getSignature();
        if (sig instanceof CodeSignature) {
            CodeSignature codeSig = (CodeSignature) sig;
            String[] paramNames = codeSig.getParameterNames();
            Object[] args = jp.getArgs();
            for(int i = 0; i < paramNames.length; i++) {
                context.put(paramNames[i], args[i]);
            }
        }
        return context;
    }
}
```

The `getJoinPointContextMap()` method uses the signature of the join point to retrieve parameter names and the `getArgs()` method to access method arguments. The code also binds a few other variables such as `this`, target, and arguments, as well as the join point, so that a script can use them. For example, a script can use the `#_jp.signature.name` expression to obtain the method name. Note that merely binding the join point object will suffice, because you can navigate to all the objects from it; but scripts written using it alone aren't as elegant.

The `SpelExpressionEvaluator` class shown in listing 4.14 is executes a script written in Spring Expression Language. Its main purpose is to isolate code related to evaluating expression from the aspect. Note that the ExpressionEvaluator interface (not shown) contains the evaluate() method.

Listing 4.14 Class to evaluate Spring Expression language scripts

```
package ajia.expression;

import ...

public class SpelExpressionEvaluator implements ExpressionEvaluator {
    private ExpressionParser parser = new SpelExpressionParser();

    public Object evaluate(String script, Map<String, Object> context)
        throws ParseException, EvaluationException {
        Expression expression = parser.parseExpression(script);
        EvaluationContext evalContext = new StandardEvaluationContext();
        for(String key : context.keySet()) {
            evalContext.setVariable(key, context.get(key));
        }
        return expression.getValue(evalContext);
    }
}
```

Finally, let's modify the Main class, as shown in listing 4.15, to exercise new additions, mainly using the second argument to the getQuoteGraph() method that specifies the duration of the chart.

Listing 4.15 Class to exercise caching functionality

```
package ajia.main;

import ajia.stock.StockService;

public class Main {
    public static void main(String[] args) {
        StockService service = new StockService();
        service.getQuoteGraph("GOOG", 1);
        service.getQuoteGraph("GOOG", 1);
        service.getQuoteGraph("YHOO", 5);
        service.getQuoteGraph("YHOO", 365);
        service.getQuoteGraph("GOOG", 365);
        service.getQuoteGraph("GOOG", 365);
    }
}
```

Now, when you execute the new code, you get the following output:

```
Cache miss. Key: Chart:GOOG:1
Cache hit.  Key: Chart:GOOG:1 Value: [B@17172ea
Cache miss. Key: Chart:YHOO:5
Cache miss. Key: Chart:YHOO:365
Cache miss. Key: Chart:GOOG:365
Cache hit.  Key: Chart:GOOG:365 Value: [B@12f6684
```

The output shows the effect of caching that considers both the ticker and the specified duration. We'll revisit this example in chapter 6 to improve it further.

In addition to showing the use of reflection API, the example demonstrates how AspectJ works nicely with other solutions: a caching product and a scripting engine, in this case. For most nontrivial problems (such as the ones you'll see in part 2 of this book), such combinations often lead to elegant and reusable solutions.

> **Aspect as a controller**
> It can be tempting to start putting too many concerns into the advice, making the advice difficult to test and causing maintenance headaches. Best practice would indicate that the aspect should be treated as a controller, delegating to other services (like the cache and expression-evaluator utility classes). With such an arrangement, you can test classes separately from aspects. The tests for aspects only need to verify correct invocations of the collaborating classes. You'll use this arrangement in chapter 6, when you write a test for an improved version of the caching aspect.

As you can see, using the reflection API is easy. But it isn't always the preferred solution.

4.5.3 *Comparing the reflection API to pointcuts*

An alternative to using the reflection API to collect dynamic context is to use pointcuts provided for that specific purpose, such as `this()`, `target()`, `@this()`, and `@target()`. Although you can always use reflection to obtain the dynamic context, this approach has some downsides:

- It has poorer performance.
- It lacks static type checking.
- It's cumbersome to use.

But sometimes you need to use reflection because little information is available or required about the advised join points. For instance, you can't easily use an `args()` pointcut to collect all arguments for all traced methods, because each method may take a different number and type of arguments. Further, the tracing aspect's advice doesn't need to care about the type of the argument objects because the only interaction of the tracing aspect with those objects is to print them. In such cases, the reflection API is the appropriate mechanism to access the join point context.

Table 4.2 compares the two ways to access the join point context. This table doesn't show all possibilities, because the purpose is to give you a quick idea about ways to access join point information.

The preceding table makes it clear that using the pointcut approach is simpler and type-safe. Therefore, when possible, it's best to avoid the reflection API.

Table 4.2 Comparing styles for accessing join point context

Pointcut-style context collection	Reflection-style context collection
pointcut pc(Account acc) : this(acc);	Account acc = (Account)thisJoinPoint.getThis();
pointcut pc(Account acc) : target(acc);	Account acc = (Account)thisJoinPoint.getTarget()

pointcut pc(Account acc,
            Customer cust)
    : args(acc, cust);
	Object[] arguments = thisJoinPoint.getArgs();
	Account acc = (Account)arguments[0];
	Customer cust = (Customer)arguments[1];

poincut pc(Secure sec) : @this(annot);	Secure sec = thisJoinPoint.getThis().getClass(). getAnnotation(Secure.class)
poincut pc(Secure sec) : @target(sec);	Secure sec = thisJoinPoint.getTarget().getClass(). getAnnotation(Secure.class);

pointcut pc(Secure sec,
            Transactional tx)
    : @args(sec, tx);
	Object[] arguments = thisJoinPoint.getArgs();
	Secure sec = arguments[0].getClass().
	getAnnotations(Secure.class);
	Transactional tx = arguments[1].getClass().
	getAnnotations(Transactional.class);

poincut pc(Sensitive sens) : @annotation(sec);	Assuming the join point is a field join point: FieldSignature sig = (FieldSignature)thisJoinPointStaticPart. getSignature(); Sensitive sens = sig.getField().getAnnotation (Sensitive.class);
pointcut pc(Secure sec) : @within(sec);	thisJoinPointStaticPart.getSignature(). getDeclaringType().getAnnotation(Secure.class);
pointcut pc(Secure sec) : @withincode(sec);	Assuming the join point is a method join point: MethodSignature sig = (MethodSignature)thisJoinPointStaticPart. getSignature(); Secure sec = sig.getMethod().getAnnotation (Secure.class);

4.6 Summary

Dynamic crosscutting in AspectJ modifies the behavior of the modules and consists of both pointcut and advice constructs. The advice constructs provide a way to express actions at before, after, or around the desired join points. With context-collecting pointcuts, advice can support static typing that is natural to a Java programmer.

The reflection support in AspectJ provides access to the join point's static and dynamic information through a small number of interfaces. You can use this context to tailor the advice based on the actual values (method parameters or return value) being used at runtime. Alternatively, you can use this information in tracing aspects to gain more insight into the system's inner workings. The dynamic and static information together can produce an enriched log output with a simple tracing aspect.

Although dynamic crosscutting forms a major part of support for crosscutting functionality, elegant solutions need to modify the static structure of the system. Such support comes in the form of static crosscutting, which we'll explore in the next chapter.

5 Modifying structure with static crosscutting

This chapter covers

- Using member introduction
- Supplementing annotations
- Modifying type hierarchies
- Responding to compile-time errors and warnings
- Softening exceptions

Altering the dynamic behavior of the system in a crosscutting manner dominates the use of AOP. But often you'll also need to alter the static structure of the system in a crosscutting manner. Whereas dynamic crosscutting modifies the behavior of the program, static crosscutting modifies the static structure of the types—the classes, interfaces, and other aspects—and their weave-time behavior. There are three broad classifications of static crosscutting:

- *Inter-type declaration (ITD)*—One type (an aspect) makes declarations for another type (an interface, a class, or even an aspect). It consists of support for member introduction, type-hierarchy modification, and annotation supplementation.

- *Weave-time error and warning declarations*—This form of static crosscutting detects the presence of a join point and issues errors and warnings during the weaving process.
- *Exception softening*—This approach lets you deal with checked exceptions in a crosscutting manner.

In this chapter, we'll examine all these constructs and present several examples. As in the previous chapters, we'll discuss the traditional syntax here and visit the @AspectJ syntax in chapter 7 (part of which is supported in Spring as well). Let's start with AspectJ's support for introducing members.

5.1 Introducing members

Consider a situation where you want to implement the observer design pattern, where *observers* are notified about any modifications to the observed object—the *subject*. In enterprise applications, such an arrangement is common with systems that react to changes in certain objects. For example, rule engines like Jess and Drools are capable of observing objects that participate in evaluating a rule. Whenever any observed object's state changes, the rule engine reevaluates the applicability of rules. Supporting such a scenario requires each subject class to include code to add and remove listeners as well as notification code in each property. This can be a lot of boilerplate code. Through the member-introduction facility, a form of ITD, you can avoid the code duplication and create an elegant implementation.

Let's start with an example that needs change-notification support.

5.1.1 Scattering and tangling

Consider the `Customer` class shown in listing 5.1. For brevity, we show only one property: `address`.

Listing 5.1 `Customer` class without property change–notification support

```
package ajia.domain;

public class Customer {
    private String address;

    public String getAddress() {
        return address;
    }

    public void setAddress(String address) {
        this.address = address;
    }
}
```

To support property change notifications, you must add methods to add and remove a listener and fire a property change event in each setter. A conventional implementation looks similar to listing 5.2.

Listing 5.2 `Customer` class with property change–notification functionality

```
package ajia.domain;

import ...

public class Customer {
    private String address;

    private PropertyChangeSupport propertyChangeSupport;

    public Customer() {
        propertyChangeSupport = new PropertyChangeSupport(this);
    }

    public String getAddress() {
        return address;
    }

    public void setAddress(String address) {
        propertyChangeSupport.firePropertyChange("address",
                                                 this.address, address);
        this.address = address;
    }

    public void addPropertyChangeListener(
            PropertyChangeListener listener) {
        propertyChangeSupport.addPropertyChangeListener(listener);
    }

    public void
        removePropertyChangeListener(PropertyChangeListener listener) {
        propertyChangeSupport.removePropertyChangeListener(listener);
    }
}
```

The property change–notification code is scattered in each subject class and tangled with the core functionality implemented in the class. These are classic symptoms of a crosscutting concern. Although dynamic crosscutting can take care of notification by advising setters, you need another mechanism to eliminate methods such as `addPropertyChangeListener()` and `removePropertyChangeListener()`.

You can push the common methods to a base class, but such a technique doesn't work in cases where the subject class already extends another class. AspectJ's static crosscutting offers an elegant solution that, when combined with dynamic crosscutting, yields untangled code as in listing 5.1 and avoids any duplication across multiple classes. In the next section, we'll focus on removing tangling using aspects. In section 5.2, we'll extend the aspect to remove scattering as well.

5.1.2 Untangling with aspects

Before we proceed, let's write a quick test case to allow you to monitor your progress. Listing 5.3 shows a test case that verifies that listeners get notifications when the `address` property is modified.

Listing 5.3 Verifying change-notification functionality

```
package ajia.domain;

import ...

public class CustomerBeanTest {
    @Test
    public void addressChangeNotifications() {
        Customer testCustomer = new Customer();
        testCustomer.setAddress("oldAddress");
        final AtomicInteger counter = new AtomicInteger();
        testCustomer.addPropertyChangeListener(
          new PropertyChangeListener() {
             public void propertyChange(PropertyChangeEvent evt) {
                 assertEquals("address", evt.getPropertyName());
                 assertEquals("oldAddress", evt.getOldValue());
                 assertEquals("newAddress", evt.getNewValue());
                 counter.incrementAndGet();
             }});
        testCustomer.setAddress("newAddress");
        assertEquals(1, counter.get());
    }
}
```

This test case passes with listing 5.2. Your goal is to make it pass with listing 5.1. At this point, the test case doesn't even compile, due to the lack of the `addPropertyChangeListener()` method in the `Customer` class from listing 5.1. Let's fix it by writing an aspect shown in listing 5.4 that uses *member introduction* to introduce such members into the specified classes and interfaces in a crosscutting manner.

Listing 5.4 Aspect to add change-notification functionality in the `Customer` class

```
package ajia.bean;

import org.apache.commons.beanutils.BeanUtils;
import ...

public aspect BeanMakerAspect {
    private PropertyChangeSupport Customer.propertyChangeSupport;

    public void Customer.addPropertyChangeListener(
            PropertyChangeListener listener) {
        propertyChangeSupport.addPropertyChangeListener(listener);
    }

    public void Customer.removePropertyChangeListener(
            PropertyChangeListener listener) {
      propertyChangeSupport.removePropertyChangeListener(listener);
    }

    pointcut beanCreation(Customer bean)
        : initialization(Customer+.new(..)) && this(bean);

    pointcut beanPropertyChange(Customer bean, Object newValue)
        : execution(void Customer+.set*(*))
```

Introduces data member ❶

Introduces method ❷

```
        && args(newValue) && this(bean);

    after(Customer bean) returning : beanCreation(bean) {
        bean.propertyChangeSupport = new PropertyChangeSupport(bean);   <-- Uses introduced data member ❸
    }

    void around(Customer bean, Object newValue)
        : beanPropertyChange(bean, newValue) {
        String methodName
            = thisJoinPointStaticPart.getSignature().getName();
        String propertyName
            = Introspector.decapitalize(methodName.substring(3));
        Object oldValue = getPropertyValue(bean, propertyName);
        proceed(bean, newValue);
        bean.propertyChangeSupport.firePropertyChange(          ❹ Uses introduced method
                    propertyName, oldValue, newValue);
    }

    private static Object getPropertyValue(Object bean,
                                           String propertyName) {
        try {
            return BeanUtils.getProperty(bean, propertyName);
        } catch (Exception ex) {
            return null;
        }
    }
}
```

❶ The aspect introduces a member `propertyChangeSupport` of type `PropertyChange-Support` into the `Customer` class. Note that introduced members can be marked with an access specifier, because you've marked `propertyChangeSupport` with `private` access. AspectJ interprets the access specifiers for the introduced members with respect to the introducing aspect. For example, the members marked `private` are accessible *only* from the introducing aspect, as in ❸.

❷ Similarly, you introduce two new methods `addPropertyChangeListener()` and `removePropertyChangeListener()` with `public` access. The use of `public` access makes these methods part of the API for the `Customer` class. Other classes and aspects may freely use these methods much the same way as the public `getAddress()` method. With these two changes, you should be able to compile the test case successfully. But there will be no notifications, and the test will fail.

❸ It's typical for the introducing aspect to use the introduced members to support dynamic crosscutting. Here, the after advice to the bean-creation join point sets `propertyChangeSupport` to a newly created object, effectively augmenting the construction logic. Note the use of `initialization()` pointcut to select only the first called constructor of the object being created.

❹ The around advice uses the introduced field to notify the listeners. I haven't taken care of mapped and indexed properties and assume that a getter exists for each setter. You can improve this part of the functionality before you use this aspect in real systems.

Note that the around advice uses reflection to obtain old values. In many cases, observers don't need the old values, because they're interested in knowing that a property has changed. If that is the case, you can remove the attendant code and make the aspect more efficient.

The test case should pass once again.

A holistic approach toward member introduction

In object-oriented programming, the fundamental paradigm—which is often lost in implementation mechanics—is that of sending messages to an object and the object processing those messages. A typical implementation of this concept maps message-sending to a method call and message-processing to a method implementation. The location of the code that processes the message isn't a core concept.

In languages like Java, the message-processing logic, implemented as a method, resides in the class or in a base class in the inheritance hierarchy. You can apply this conceptual framework to member introduction in AOP: think of a method introduced by an aspect as an alternative location to process the message—the aspect body instead of the class or its base type. In other words, an aspect introducing a method responds to the messages on behalf of the class.

In a real-world system, you won't have just one class that needs change-notification support. Let's extend the solution to encompass many classes.

5.1.3 Mixing with mixins

A *mixin* is a program construct that lets you mix certain functionality into other classes. Depending on the programming language, it may be implemented in a variety of ways: a class in C++, a trait in Scala, and a module in Ruby. In Java, there is no way to implement a mixin in a useful manner. In AspectJ, interfaces with inter-type declarations offer the mixin functionality.

Instead of introducing the listener-management methods in each class using a separate aspect, you create an interface and introduce methods to it through an aspect. Such an interface provides the mixin functionality. The classes implementing the interface automatically have those methods' implementation available. Listing 5.5 shows the `BeanSupport` marker interface (marker interface is an interface without methods).

Listing 5.5 Marker interface for classes supporting bean functionality

```
package ajia.bean;

public interface BeanSupport {
}
```

The classes that need to support change notification must implement the `BeanSupport` interface, as shown for the `Customer` class in listing 5.6 (in the section that follows, you'll remove this requirement).

Listing 5.6 Example bean class: `Customer`

```
package ajia.domain;

public class Customer implements BeanSupport {
    private String address;

    public String getAddress() {
        return address;
    }

    public void setAddress(String address) {
        this.address = address;
    }
}
```

Next, the modified version of the `BeanMakerAspect` in listing 5.7 shows how the aspect uses the `BeanSupport` interface instead of a hard-coded `Customer` class.

Listing 5.7 Aspect implementing bean functionality in a crosscutting manner

```
package ajia.bean;

import ...

public aspect BeanMakerAspect {
    private PropertyChangeSupport BeanSupport.propertyChangeSupport;

    public void BeanSupport.addPropertyChangeListener(
            PropertyChangeListener listener) {
        propertyChangeSupport.addPropertyChangeListener(listener);
    }

    public void BeanSupport.removePropertyChangeListener(
            PropertyChangeListener listener) {
        propertyChangeSupport.removePropertyChangeListener(listener);
    }

    pointcut beanCreation(BeanSupport bean)
        : initialization(BeanSupport+.new(..)) && this(bean);

    pointcut beanPropertyChange(BeanSupport bean, Object newValue)
        : execution(void BeanSupport+.set*(*))
          && args(newValue) && this(bean);

    after(BeanSupport bean) returning : beanCreation(bean) {
        bean.propertyChangeSupport = new PropertyChangeSupport(bean);
    }

    void around(BeanSupport bean, Object newValue)
        : beanPropertyChange(bean, newValue) {
        String methodName
            = thisJoinPointStaticPart.getSignature().getName();
        String propertyName
            = Introspector.decapitalize(methodName.substring(3));
        Object oldValue = getPropertyValue(bean, propertyName);
        proceed(bean, newValue);
        bean.propertyChangeSupport.firePropertyChange(
                propertyName, oldValue, newValue);
```

```
    }

    private static Object getPropertyValue(Object bean,
                                           String propertyName) {
        try {
            return BeanUtils.getProperty(bean, propertyName);
        } catch (Exception ex) {
            return null;
        }
    }
}
```

The code segments in bold are the only changes we've made compared to listing 5.4. Rerunning the tests should lead to a green bar.

Now, if you want to add the change-notification functionality to another class, you need to make that class implement the `BeanSupport` interface. For example, to add the functionality to the `Account` class, all you need to do is modify the declaration of the class as shown in the following snippet:

```
public class Account implements BeanSupport {
    ...
}
```

Spring Roo and ITDs

Spring Roo (http://www.springsource.org/roo) is a new framework based on Spring and AspectJ that promotes domain-driven design. It uses ITDs to separate automatically maintained generated code from user code.

In section 5.2, you'll see another kind of ITD to get the same effect of implementing an interface without modifying the class.

5.1.4 Member introduction rules

Now that you've seen one complete example, let's go over the rules of engagement when an aspect introduces a member:

- *An aspect may only introduce members with* `public` *or* `private` *access specification.* When it uses `public` access, as `BeanMakerAspect` does for `addPropertyChangeListener()` and `removePropertyChangeListener()`, the introduced member is visible to other parts of the system (plain Java classes or aspects). If it uses `private` access, as `BeanMakerAspect` does for `propertyChangeSupport`, the introduced member is visible only to the introducing aspect. When using a `private` introduction, the name of the member woven into the types is a mangled version. The name change caused by mangling may be significant in a few cases where tools and frameworks rely on specific names or name patterns. If you're curious, see the implementation of the `AnnotationBeanConfigurerAspect` from the Spring Framework for one such case.

- *Multiple aspects may introduce the same named members as long as they have* `private` *access.* It's an error to introduce the same `public` member through multiple aspects.
- *An aspect may introduce fields (final as well as non-final), methods, and constructors to classes as well as interfaces.* Notice that the aspect may introduce methods *along with their implementations* to an *interface.* This is contrary to standard Java rules, where interfaces may contain only method declarations (but not their implementations) and may contain only final fields.
- *If a class contains a method, and an aspect introduces the same method to its base interface, the implementation in the class takes precedence.* Intuitively, you may think of this rule as matching the override semantics. But note this caveat: unlike a regular override, there is no way to call the logical `super()` method (which would be the introduced implementation). This prevents you from implementing an augmentative override, where you call `super()` before or after additional code. If you encounter such a situation, consider advising the introduced method to augment behavior.
- *A member-introduction declaration can use only one type.* Specifically, the use of wildcards such as `private PropertyChangeSupport *.propertyChangeSupport` is prohibited. But as you'll see in the next section, you can combine a member declaration with a type modification to get the effect of introducing a member into multiple types.

Let's complete our discussion of member introduction with a popular idiom used in AspectJ projects.

5.1.5 *Idiom: Providing a default interface implementation*

Plain Java doesn't allow interfaces to contain implementation code; only classes can implement methods. Sometimes, it would be useful to have a default implementation for interfaces as well. Without AspectJ, the usual strategy is to create a default implementation class for the interface and let the classes extend this class. This works fine as long as the implementing classes need to extend this class alone, but the solution starts to break down if you need to implement two or more such interfaces. Similarly, it breaks down if you need to extend another class and implement an interface using its default implementation. You can make the task somewhat easier with the delegation pattern by delegating each method to an instance of the default implementation class. Nevertheless, you end up with several one-line methods, which causes code scattering—one of the symptoms of a crosscutting concern.

Consider the simple interface in listing 5.8. We'll use this interface to show how AspectJ can simplify the job of providing the default implementation for an interface.

Listing 5.8 An interface for entities with a name

```
package ajia;

public interface Nameable {
    public void setName(String name);
    public String getName();
}
```

With pure Java, you have to implement the two methods in each class that implements this interface, as in listing 5.9.

Listing 5.9 Entity class implementing the `Nameable` interface in a conventional way

```
package ajia;

public class Entity implements Nameable {
    private String name;

    public void setName(String name) {
        this.name = name;
    }

    public String getName() {
        return this.name;
    }
}
```

With this idiom, you create an aspect that introduces the default implementation of the methods to the interface. Listing 5.10 shows the implementation of the methods in the `Nameable` interface.

Listing 5.10 `Nameable` interface with the default implementation

```
package ajia;

public interface Nameable {
    public void setName(String name);
    public String getName();

    static aspect Impl {
        private String Nameable.name;

        public void Nameable.setName(String name) {
            this.name = name;
        }

        public String Nameable.getName() {
            return this.name;
        }
    }
}
```

The classes implementing the `Nameable` interface no longer have to contain these methods. Listing 5.11 shows the new version of `Entity` that works with the `Nameable` interface in listing 5.10.

Listing 5.11 `Entity` class implementing the `Nameable` interface the AspectJ way

```
package ajia;

public class Entity implements Nameable {
}
```

Using pure Java, you could achieve a similar effect by creating a class—say, `DefaultNameable`—that provides the default implementation and making `Entity` extend that class. But this approach would work only when you implemented a single interface.

Consider another interface, `Identifiable`, in listing 5.12.

Listing 5.12 `Identifiable` interface without any default implementation

```
package ajia;

public interface Identifiable {
    public void setId(String id);
    public String getId();
}
```

If `Entity` were to implement both `Nameable` and `Identifiable` without using AspectJ, you'd have to implement one of the interfaces and extend the other's default implementation. When you use the default-interface idiom, you declare that the `Entity` class implements both the interfaces, and you're done. As you can see in listing 5.13, the nested aspect inside `Identifiable` is similar to the one in `Nameable`.

Listing 5.13 `Identifiable` with a default implementation

```
package ajia;

public interface Identifiable {
    public void setId(String id);
    public String getId();

    static aspect Impl {
        private String Identifiable.id;

        public void Identifiable.setId(String id) {
            this.id = id;
        }

        public String Identifiable.getId() {
            return this.id;
        }
    }
}
```

The `Entity` class implements both interfaces, as shown in listing 5.14. The effect is the same as extending the default implementation for both (if multiple inheritance was allowed in Java).

Listing 5.14 `Entity` class implementing `Nameable` and `Identifiable`

```
package ajia;

public class Entity implements Nameable, Identifiable {
}
```

This idiom not only saves you from writing code, but it also facilitates making changes. If you need to modify the default implementation, all you need to do is change the nested aspect.

Although the classes that implement these interfaces no longer have to implement their methods, in some cases you may need to customize a few methods. When such methods are directly implemented in classes, they override the default implementation introduced by the aspect, just as you'd expect.

Another variation you can use provides only a partial default implementation for an interface. For example, consider a situation where the default implementation needs information from the concrete classes or where you want to force the implementing class's developers to think about the correct semantics for a certain method. In such cases, this idiom lets you implement as many methods as appropriate in the interface, and lets the concrete classes implement the rest.

Yet another variation provides a choice to the class implementers if they want to use the introduced implementation or provide their own. With such an idiom, instead of introducing the fields directly to the interface, the aspect introduces them to a subinterface. Listing 5.15 shows an implementation of this variation for the `Nameable` interface.

Listing 5.15 `Nameable` with the default implementation

```
package ajia;

public interface NameableMixin extends Nameable {
    static aspect Impl {
        private String NameableMixin.name;

        public void NameableMixin.setName(String name) {
            this.name = name;
        }

        public String NameableMixin.getName() {
            return this.name;
        }
    }
}
```

The mixin implementation for `Identifiable` is similar. Note that with this idiom, the `Nameable` and `Identifiable` interfaces are left in their original state, as shown in listings 5.8 and 5.12.

Now, the classes that want to utilize the mixin implementation introduced through an aspect extend the mixin interfaces instead of the original interface, as shown in listing 5.16.

Listing 5.16 Explicit use of mixins implemented through aspects

```
package ajia;

public class Entity implements NameableMixin, IdentifiableMixin {
}
```

The next time you encounter an interface whose implementation is boilerplate, consider using this idiom to save code.

So far, we've focused on one form of static crosscutting: member introduction. The next form lets you modify the type hierarchy in a crosscutting manner.

5.2 Modifying the type hierarchy

The implementation in listing 5.7 requires that any class that wants to participate must declare that it implements the `BeanSupport` interface. Sometimes, such modifications aren't possible—for example, when you're working with a third-party library. In a few cases, the modifications may be undesirable, as when too many classes need such behavior.

With AspectJ, you can modify the inheritance hierarchy of existing classes and interfaces through use of the `declare parents` construct. AspectJ offers two forms:

```
declare parents : [TypePattern] implements [InterfaceList];
```

and

```
declare parents : [TypePattern] extends [Class or InterfaceList];
```

The declaration of parents must follow the regular Java object-hierarchy rules. For example, you can't declare a class to be the parent of an interface. Similarly, you can't declare parents in such a way that it results in multiple inheritance.

> **Evaluation order: static and dynamic crosscutting**
>
> AspectJ applies all static crosscutting *prior* to dynamic crosscutting. For example, it applies all `declare parents` statements before evaluating matches for a pointcut. This way, matching isn't affected by how a static structure came to be: it could be due to the way classes were written or due to a static crosscutting construct.

Let's use this new information to remove one of the issues with the example implementation and make ordinary classes acquire the change-notification functionality. The `declare parents` feature can help by using some characteristics of the types to select them and supply a base class or interface. For example, if you want all the classes in `banking.entities` to have the notification functionality, you add the following aspects:

```
package ajia;

public aspect BankingBeanParticipationAspect {
    declare parents: banking.entities.* implements BeanSupport;
}
```

Now, classes like `Customer` don't have to include `implements BeanSupport` as part of their declaration.

Although the preceding declaration relies on the package structure, you can use any other characteristics. For example, if you want to add the change-notification functionality to any class with the `@Entity` annotation, you can easily do so by using the following declaration in an aspect:

```
package ajia;

public aspect EntityBeanParticipationAspect {
    declare parents: @Entity * implements BeanSupport;
}
```

Similarly, you can create and use your own annotation to mark classes that need change-notification support.

> **Experimental features: hasmethod() and hasfield()**
>
> The current version of AspectJ includes an experimental feature that defines a type pattern based on the methods and fields a target type contains (enabled through the `-XhasMember` compiler flag). Such a type pattern works only in a `declare parents` construct. For example, you can use the following statement to declare `BeanSupport` as the parent of types that contain a method with the `@Observed` annotation:
>
> ```
> declare parents: hasmethod(@Observed * *(*)) implements BeanSupport;
> ```
>
> With this statement, including a method with `@Observed` annotation leads to supporting bean-notification functionality (the pointcut as written also expects a one-argument method to match the setter semantics and let it collect the old value). In a complete implementation, you must refactor the `BeanMakerAspect` aspect to modify the `beanPropertyChange()` pointcut to account for the `@Observed` annotation.

Let's pause to look at an example using the constructs you've learned so far.

5.3 *Introducing members to multiple types*

A combination of member introduction and type-hierarchy modification provides a useful idiom to introduce members to multiple types. In such cases, you create an interface, introduce members to it, and declare it the parent of the target types. The overall scheme is similar to creating default implementations of interfaces, as discussed in section 5.1.5, except that here you use an interface as an intermediary to introduce members.

Let's say you want to trace the last-accessed time for each service class. Further, assume that a service class is marked with the `@Service` interface. You need to introduce a field for the last-accessed time in all service classes. As discussed in section 5.1.4, you can't use wildcards in a member-introduction statement. Therefore, you'll need to use another type as an intermediary, as shown in listing 5.17.

Listing 5.17 Combining member introduction and type-hierarchy modifications

```
package ajia.tracking;

import ...

public aspect TimeTracker {
```

```
    private static interface LastAccessedTimeHolder {
        static aspect Impl {
            private long LastAccessedTimeHolder.lastAccessedTime;

            public long LastAccessedTimeHolder.getLastAccessedTime() {
                return lastAccessedTime;
            }

            public void
                LastAccessedTimeHolder.setLastAccessedTime(long time) {
                lastAccessedTime = time;
            }
        }
    }

    declare parents : @Service * implements LastAccessedTimeHolder;

    before(LastAccessedTimeHolder service)
        : execution(* LastAccessedTimeHolder+.*(..)) && this(service)
          && !within(TimeTracker) {
        service.setLastAccessedTime(System.currentTimeMillis());
    }
}
```

With this arrangement, you can call the `getLastAccessedTime()` and `setLastAccessedTime()` methods on any service object as you do in the before advice. But other parts of the system may also call those methods. For example, you can expose the methods through a JMX console using an exporter as if the method was present in each service class.

Now, let's move our attention to another form of inter-type declaration that helps you associate annotations with program elements.

5.4 Supplying annotations

Annotations have gained support in many frameworks such as Enterprise JavaBeans (EJB), Java Persistence API (JPA), Spring, and JUnit. These frameworks support program elements to carry annotations that are meaningful to the framework. For example, a method may carry an `@TransactionAttribute` annotation, which an EJB 3 application server can use to execute the method inside a transaction context.

AspectJ provides support for selecting join points based on annotations carried by the program elements. In many cases, several program elements repeat the same annotation, leading to annotation clutter. To avoid this kind of clutter and provide support for many interesting design patterns (such as the annotation-driven participant pattern discussed in chapter 12), AspectJ offers static crosscutting constructs to supply annotations in a crosscutting manner.

Let's say you need to annotate all public methods in the `Account` class with the `@Secured` annotation, with its `role` property set to `"ROLE_TELLER"`. You can use AspectJ's `declare @method` construct as follows to get the job done:

```
declare @method: public * Account.*(..): @Secured(role="ROLE_TELLER");
```

This statement has the same effect as individually annotating each method with the @Secured(role="ROLE_TELLER") annotation.

AspectJ lets you associate annotations with methods, constructors, fields, and types. The constructs for supplying annotations share the following general form:

```
declare @<target-kind>:
    <Target-element-pattern>:
    @<Annotation-type>[Annotation-properties];
```

This declaration has three parts.

- declare @<*target-kind*>—Declares the kind of elements annotated by the statement
- <*Target-element-pattern*>—Uses a signature pattern (see chapter 3) to select the program elements to be annotated
- @<*Annotation-type*>[*Annotation-properties*]—Declares the annotation, which may contain any properties available for the annotation

Table 5.1 shows all the constructs in AspectJ for annotating program elements:

Table 5.1 AspectJ constructs for annotating program elements

Construct	Example
declare @method: <*Method signature pattern*>: <*Annotation*>;	declare @method: * AccountService.*(..): @Transactional(Propagation.Required);
declare @constructor: <*Constructor signature pattern*>: <Annotation>	declare @constructor: AccountService+.new(): @ConfigurationOnly;
declare @field: <*Field signature pattern*>: <*Annotation*>;	declare @field: * MissileInformation.*: @Classified;
declare @type: <*Type signature pattern*>: <*Annotation*>;	declare @type: banking..* : @PrivacyControlled;

Like normal annotations, declare statements must use annotations that are compatible with the elements being annotated. For example, in table 5.1, the @Transactional annotation must be defined with an @Target meta-annotation with a value that includes ElementType.METHOD (or it can skip the @Target annotation to make it compatible with any target element). See the Java 5 documentation for details.

One interesting use of the declaring annotations is creating annotation *bridging* by supplying an annotation when another annotation is detected. For example, the following statement marks all types carrying the @PrivacyControlled annotation with the @Tracked annotation:

```
declare @type: @PrivacyControlled * : @Tracked;
```

> **Domain-object dependency injection and static crosscutting**
>
> Spring's support for domain-object dependency injection (often known through the `@Configurable` annotation associated with it) lets you inject dependencies into any object (not just Spring beans). It also serves as a good real-world use of static crosscutting. Its implementation uses a member introduction, parent hierarchy modification, supplying annotations, and the `hasmethod()` type pattern (in a commented block of code due to its experimental nature). Check it out by downloading Spring's source code.

Now, any aspect using a pointcut based on the `@Tracked` annotation, such as `execution(* (@Tracked *).*(..))`, will also select methods in types with the `@PrivacyControlled` annotation, because the `declare` statement attaches the `@Tracked` annotation to those types.

Program elements annotated using the `declare` statement can be used the same way as normally annotated program elements. For example, if a pointcut specifies an annotation as part of the matching specification, program elements annotated using a `declare` statement will match the same way as methods directly marked with an annotation. Furthermore, annotations introduced using a `declare` statement will be available to tools such as persistence frameworks (like Hibernate and JPA) and EJB application servers just like annotations directly supplied to a program element.

5.5 Declaring weave-time errors and warnings

AspectJ provides a static crosscutting mechanism to declare weave-time errors and warnings based on certain usage patterns. This mechanism is often used with the AspectJ compiler as the weaver and therefore is also referred to as a compile-time error and warning construct. With this mechanism, you can implement behavior similar to the `#error` and `#warning` preprocessor directives supported by some C/C++ preprocessors; you can also implement more complex and powerful directives.

The `declare error` construct provides a way to declare a weave-time error when the compiler detects the presence of a join point matching a given pointcut. The compiler issues an error, prints the given message for each detected use, and aborts the compilation process:

```
declare error : <pointcut> : <message>;
```

Similarly, the `declare warning` construct provides a way to declare a compile-time warning, but it doesn't abort the compilation process:

```
declare warning : <pointcut> : <message>;
```

Note that because these declarations affect compile-time behavior, you must use only *statically* determinable pointcuts in the declarations. In other words, you cannot use the pointcuts that use runtime checks to select the matching join points—`this()`, `target()`, `args()`, `@this()`, `@target()`, `@args()`, `if()`, `cflow()`, and `cflowbelow()`—in such a declaration.

A typical use of these constructs is enforcing rules, such as prohibiting calls to certain unsupported methods, or issuing a warning about such calls. The following code example causes the AspectJ compiler to produce a compile-time error if a join point matching the `callToUnsafeCode()` pointcut is found anywhere in the code that is being compiled:

```
declare error : callToUnsafeCode()
    : "This third-party code is known to result in a crash";
```

The following code is similar, except it produces a compile-time warning instead of an error:

```
declare warning : callToBlockingOperation()
    : "Please ensure you are not calling this from an AWT thread";
```

You'll see more examples of how to use compile-time errors and warnings for policy enforcement in chapter 11.

Let's complete our discussion of static crosscutting support in AspectJ by examining a construct that lets you demote checked exceptions to unchecked at selected join points.

5.6 Softening checked exceptions

Java specifies two categories of exceptions that a method may throw: checked and unchecked. When an exception is checked, callers must deal with it either by catching the exception or by declaring that they can throw it. When an exception is unchecked (which directly or indirectly extends `RuntimeException` or `Error`), callers need not deal with it explicitly and the exception is automatically propagated up the call stack. Exception softening lets you treat checked exceptions thrown by specified pointcuts as unchecked ones and thus eliminates the need to explicitly deal with them in the caller code.

The exception-softening feature helps modularize the crosscutting concerns of exception handling. For example, you can soften a `RemoteException` thrown in a Remote Method Invocation (RMI)-based system to avoid handling the exception at each level. This may be a useful strategy in some situations. For instance, if you know you're using local objects of RMI-capable classes that won't throw any `RemoteException`, you can soften those exceptions.

To soften exceptions, you use the `declare soft` construct, which takes the following form:

```
declare soft : <ExceptionTypePattern> : <pointcut>;
```

If a method is throwing more than one checked exceptions, you must soften each one individually. In listing 5.19, the aspect declares the softening of an exception thrown by the `TestSoftening.perform()` method in listing 5.18. The method behaves as if it's throwing an `org.aspectj.lang.SoftException`, which extends `RuntimeException`.

Listing 5.18 TestSoftening.java: code for testing the effect of softening an exception

```
package ajia;

import java.rmi.RemoteException;
```

```
public class TestSoftening {
    public static void main(String[] args) {
        TestSoftening test = new TestSoftening();
        test.perform();
    }

    public void perform() throws RemoteException {
        throw new RemoteException();
    }
}
```

Compiling the `TestSoftening` class by itself results in a compiler error, because `main()` neither catches the exception nor declares that it's throwing that exception:

```
> ajc ajia\TestSoftening.java
  ...\src\ajia\TestSoftening.java:10
   [error] Unhandled exception type RemoteException
   test.perform();
   ^^^^^
```

Listing 5.19 shows `SofteningTestAspect`, which softens the `RemoteException` thrown by the join point that corresponds to the call to the `TestSoftening.perform()` method.

Listing 5.19 Aspect to soften `RemoteExceptions`

```
package ajia;

import ...

public aspect SofteningTestAspect {
    declare soft : RemoteException : call(void TestSoftening.perform());
}
```

By softening the exception, you can compile the code without errors. When you run the program, you see a call stack due to a thrown `SoftException`:

```
> ajc ajia\TestSoftening.java ajia\SofteningTestAspect.aj
> java ajia.TestSoftening
  Exception in thread "main" org.aspectj.lang.SoftException
        at ajia.TestSoftening.main(TestSoftening.java:10)
  Caused by: java.rmi.RemoteException
        at ajia.TestSoftening.perform(TestSoftening.java:13)
        ... 1 more
```

Exception softening is a quick way to avoid tangling the concern of exception handling with the core logic. But be careful about overusing this technique: one of the reasons to use checked exceptions is that it forces you to handle them by making a conscious decision about processing the exceptions or propagating them to the caller. The use of exception softening short-circuits this.

5.7 Summary

Static crosscutting offers ways to affect the static structure of the system. Static crosscutting, which you can use by itself or in support of dynamic crosscutting, includes the following constructs: member introduction, annotation supplementation, type hierarchy modification, weave-time declarations, and exception softening.

The member-introduction facility helps with code scattering and tangling resulting from duplicated common structure needed across multiple types. The ability to modify the type hierarchy offers a way to deal with multiple types uniformly even though the types don't share a common type. The annotation-declaration feature allows aspects to reduce annotation clutter by encapsulating annotations from multiple elements into one concise statement. Annotations declared in this manner can be consumed using dynamic crosscutting through annotation-based pointcuts. Weave-time errors and warnings provide a way to detect the presence of join points that may be in violation of some programming wisdom. Last, exception softening simplifies dealing with checked exceptions. The overall result is a simple, programmer-friendly language that supports AOP in Java. You'll see many of these facilities used to implement complex crosscutting concerns in part 2 of this book.

In the next chapter, we'll discuss the construct of an aspect that provides a unit to express both dynamic and static crosscutting elements.

6 Aspects: putting it all together

This chapter covers

- Formally introducing aspects
- Creating reusable aspects with aspect association
- Using aspect precedence to coordinate multiple aspects
- Bypassing access-specification rules using privileged aspects

Aspects represent the unit of modularization in AOP and AspectJ. They provide a way to include crosscutting constructs such as pointcuts and advice. You've already seen quite a few aspects in the preceding chapters' examples.

In this chapter, we'll take a closer look at the core *aspect* construct. We'll begin by examining the aspect construct in a formal way and compare it to the *class*—the most similar concept in object-oriented programming. Next, we'll examine the aspect association that provides a mechanism needed to write reusable aspects. We'll follow that by considering the effects of multiple aspects in a system advising the same join point, and ways to control ordering. We'll complete this chapter by examining a way aspects can override the standard access-specification rules.

Like the preceding three chapters, we'll focus on aspects expressed using the traditional syntax. As you'll see in the next chapter, the concepts you learn here can be easily mapped into aspects expressed using the @AspectJ syntax as well as Spring AOP.

6.1 Working with aspects

An *aspect* encapsulates the implementation of a crosscutting functionality. The AspectJ weaver takes the rules specified in each aspect and uses them to modify the behavior of the core modules in a crosscutting manner. Syntactically, an aspect declaration looks much like a class declaration:

```
[access specification] [abstract] aspect <AspectName>
    [extends class-or-aspect-name] [implements interface-list]
    [[<association-specifier>(Pointcut)]|[pertypewithin(TypePattern)]]  {
    ... aspect body
}
```

The keyword `aspect` declares an aspect. Each aspect declaration has the following characteristics:

- It has a name to enable the other parts of the program to refer to it and its elements.
- It may have an access specification.
- It may be marked as abstract.
- It may extend another aspect or a class, and implement interfaces.
- It may specify an instantiation model using either of the optional specifiers `[<association-specifier>(Pointcut)]` or `[pertypewithin(TypePattern)]`.
- Its body contains pointcuts, dynamic and static crosscutting constructs, data members and methods, as well as nested types.

Because the simplest way to look at aspects is to see them as analogous to classes in Java, let's look at the similarities and differences between aspects and classes.

6.1.1 Similarities between aspects and classes

Aspects are similar to classes in many ways. Both may

- Have data and members
- Have access specifications
- Be marked abstract
- Implement or extend other types
- Be nested inside other types

Let's see each of the similarities in detail.

ASPECTS CAN INCLUDE DATA MEMBERS AND METHODS

The data members and methods in aspects have the same role as in classes. For instance, an aspect can manage its state using data members, whereas methods can implement behavior that supports the crosscutting concern's implementation or can be utility methods. Aspects may also include constructors. But if a concrete aspect includes a constructor, it must also include a no-argument constructor to allow the system to instantiate the aspect. You shouldn't instantiate an aspect directly using any constructor. Therefore, only the no-argument constructor can call constructors that take arguments.

ASPECTS CAN HAVE ACCESS SPECIFICATIONS

An aspect's access specifier governs its visibility following the same rules as classes and interfaces. Top-level aspects can have only `public` or package (specified by omitting the access specifier) access. Nested aspects, like nested classes, can have a `public`, `private`, `protected`, or package access specifier.

ASPECTS CAN BE ABSTRACT

With abstract aspects, you can create reusable units of crosscutting by deferring some of the implementation details to subaspects. An abstract aspect can mark any pointcut or method as abstract and refer to it from other constructs.

Like a class, an aspect that contains abstract pointcuts or methods must declare itself as an abstract aspect. Any subaspect of an abstract aspect that doesn't define every abstract pointcut and method in the base aspect, or that adds additional abstract pointcuts or methods, must also declare itself abstract. The mechanism of creating abstract aspects is useful for library aspects, such as for transaction management.

The following example shows an abstract aspect that contains an abstract pointcut and an abstract method:

```
public abstract aspect AbstractTracing {
    public abstract pointcut traced();          <— Abstract pointcut

    public abstract Logger getLogger();          <— Abstract method

    before() : traced() {                                  <— Advice to abstract pointcut
       getLogger().log(Level.INFO, "Before: " + thisJoinPoint);   <—
    }                                                      Uses abstract method
}
```

In this aspect, the `traced()` pointcut is declared abstract to let subaspects provide its definition. Similarly, the abstract method `getLogger()` defers providing the logger object to subaspects. The advice that logs the message uses both these abstract entities to perform its task. The net effect is the encapsulation of the tracing logic in the base aspect. Each subaspect fills in the details of the trace points and the logger object.

Let's see how a concrete aspect provides a definition for abstract pointcuts and methods.

ASPECTS CAN EXTEND CLASSES AND ABSTRACT ASPECTS, AS WELL AS IMPLEMENT INTERFACES

The following concrete aspect extends the `AbstractTracing` aspect you've just seen. It provides definitions for its abstract pointcut and method, matching the requirements of tracing the banking system:

```
public aspect BankingTracing extends AbstractTracing {
    public pointcut traced()                              | Pointcut
        : execution(* banking..*.*(..));                  | definition
```

```
    public Logger getLogger() {                          Method
        return Logger.getLogger("banking");              definition
    }
}
```

This aspect defines the `traced()` pointcut to select the execution of any method in classes that are part of the `banking` root package. The `getLogger()` method implementation returns the logger that is specific to the banking system. You can have many such subaspects, each providing the required definitions. The result is that the code in the base aspect is shared, whereas the subaspects provide the application-specific details.

Note that an aspect may extend a class and implement interfaces. Such an aspect can access the base-class functionality in the same way as a subclass.

ASPECTS CAN BE EMBEDDED IN CLASSES AND INTERFACES AS NESTED ASPECTS

You can embed aspects into classes and interfaces when the aspect's implementation is intimately tied to its enclosing class or interface (such as refactoring aspects, as you'll see in chapter 16). Because the aspect resides in the same source file, this simplifies the modifications required for the aspect's implementation when the enclosing entity changes. Note that an embedded aspect must be marked as `static`.

6.1.2 *Differences between aspects and classes*

Despite their similarities, aspects aren't classes. Here are some of the ways that aspects are different from classes:

- Their instantiation model is different.
- They have additional restrictions on inheritance.
- They may have relaxed access rules.

Let's examine each difference in detail.

ASPECTS CAN'T BE DIRECTLY INSTANTIATED

The system instantiates aspects appropriately. In other words, you *never* use `new` to create an aspect instance.

> **Explicit aspect creation**
>
> A typical dependency injection (DI) framework by default uses a constructor to instantiate objects. When using an aspect with such a framework, you often need to inject dependencies into the aspect instance as well. But the fact that an aspect shouldn't be constructed directly using a constructor poses a problem. Fortunately, most DI frameworks support an alternative mechanism that uses a factory method; and aspects provide a factory method—`aspectOf()`—that we'll discuss in section 6.2.6.

ASPECTS CAN'T INHERIT FROM CONCRETE ASPECTS

Although aspects can inherit from abstract aspects, they can't inherit from concrete aspects. This limitation exists to reduce complexity. For example, with this rule in place, the AspectJ compiler considers only concrete aspects for weaving. If subaspects of a concrete aspect were allowed, the language would have to specify how such subaspects interact with the weaving specified by their base aspect. In practice, this restriction usually doesn't pose any significant problem.

CONCRETE ASPECTS MAY NOT DECLARE GENERIC PARAMETERS

Because the system instantiates an aspect, there would be no way to bind a generic-type parameter during such instantiation. Consequently, only abstract aspects may declare the generic-type parameters. Any concrete aspect extending such an aspect must bind the generic parameters in its declaration.

ASPECTS CAN BE MARKED AS PRIVILEGED

Aspects can have a special `privileged` access specifier. This gives them access to the private members of the classes they're crosscutting. You'll learn more about this in section 6.4.

Let's turn our focus to an advanced feature of AspectJ—aspect association—which comes in handy when you're developing reusable aspects for certain crosscutting functionality.

6.2 Aspect association

By default, only one instance of an aspect type exists—much like a singleton class. The state of such an aspect is effectively global. Usually, this arrangement is fine and even desirable for stateless aspects as well as aspects with an inherently global state, such as a resource pool. But in some situations, especially when you're creating reusable aspects, you want to associate the aspect's state with an individual object, a specific class, or a control flow. The aspect-association mechanism offers various ways to associate aspect instances. This mechanism offers many interesting and powerful design choices.

AspectJ offers four different kinds of aspect association:

- Singleton (default)
- Per object
- Per control-flow
- Per type

Although an aspect is a singleton aspect by default, you can explicitly specify so by using the following form:

```
aspect <AspectName> [issingleton()] {
    ... aspect body
}
```

For per-object and per–control-flow association, you can specify association by modifying the aspect declaration that takes the following form:

```
aspect <AspectName> [<perthis|pertarget|percflow|percflowbelow>(<Pointcut>)] {
    ... aspect body
}
```

The part in bold specifies how the aspect is associated with the join points selected by the specified pointcut.

For per-type association, you use a modification to the previous syntax:

```
aspect <AspectName> [pertypewithin(TypePattern)] {
    ... aspect body
}
```

WARNING Aspect association is perhaps the most advanced topic in AspectJ, and some effort is required to understand it fully. This is especially true if you haven't had much experience with AspectJ. But it's an important topic for developers engaged in writing reusable library aspects. If you're relatively new to AspectJ, you may want to skim until section 6.2.8 (where I show how to use Spring to configure an aspect and implement automated testing for the caching example we have been developing in previous chapters). After you've gained more experience, you can revisit this section.

Let's explore all these aspect association choices in detail; then, we'll examine how each affects the join point selection. We'll also compare the per-object aspect association with the member-introduction mechanism shown in the previous chapter.

6.2.1 Default singleton association

Default association is in effect when you don't include an association specification. Alternatively, you can use `issingleton()` in the aspect declaration; but such explicit declaration isn't a common practice. All the aspects you've seen so far in this book are of this type. This type of association creates one instance of the aspect for an aspect type.

For our discussion of aspect association in this section, let's create an aspect, `AssociationDemoAspect`. (Later, you'll modify this aspect to see the effect of other aspect associations.) Listing 6.1 shows the default (singleton) association aspect that illustrates aspect instance creation. You'll use the `Account` class along with `SavingsAccount`, which extends `Account` (not shown here, but provided as a part of this book's downloadable sources). The aspect logs a message in its constructor to designate its creation. Then, it prints the aspect's instance and the `this` object at the advised join point.

Listing 6.1 `AssociationDemoAspect` with the default association

```
package ajia;

public aspect AssociationDemoAspect {
    public AssociationDemoAspect() {
        System.out.println("Creating aspect instance");     ❶ Aspect constructor
    }

    pointcut accountOperationExecution(Account account)
        : (execution(* Account.credit(..))
           || execution(* Account.debit(..)))              ❷ Account operation pointcut
          && this(account);
```

```
    before(Account account)
        : accountOperationExecution(account) {
        System.out.println("JoinPoint: " + thisJoinPointStaticPart
                           + "\n\taspect: " + this
                           + "\n\tobject: " + account);
    }
}
```

Advice that prints the aspect and account instance ❸

❶ You print a simple message in the aspect constructor to keep track of when the aspect instance is created.

❷ The `accountOperationExecution()` pointcut selects the execution of the `credit()` and `debit()` methods in the `Account` class. It also collects the `Account` object using the `this()` pointcut so that you can print it in the advice.

❸ The advice to `accountOperationExecution()` prints the static context of the captured join point, the aspect instance, and the `Account` object collected by the pointcut. Note that when used from advice, the object `this` refers to the instance of an aspect and not the execution object at a join point.

Next, let's write a simple driver program (listing 6.2) that creates two `Account` objects and calls methods on them.

Listing 6.2 Driver to examine aspect associations

```
package ajia.main;

public class Main {
    public static void main(String[] args) throws Exception {
        SavingsAccount account1 = new SavingsAccount(12245);
        SavingsAccount account2 = new SavingsAccount(67890);
        account1.credit(100);
        account1.debit(50);

        account2.credit(100);
        account2.debit(50);
    }
}
```

When you compile the classes and run the driver program, you see output similar to the following:

```
Creating aspect instance
JoinPoint: execution(void ajia.Account.credit(float))
        aspect: ajia.AssociationDemoAspect@e09713
        object: ajia.SavingsAccount@de6f34
JoinPoint: execution(void ajia.Account.debit(float))
        aspect: ajia.AssociationDemoAspect@e09713
        object: ajia.SavingsAccount@de6f34
JoinPoint: execution(void ajia.Account.credit(float))
        aspect: ajia.AssociationDemoAspect@e09713
        object: ajia.SavingsAccount@156ee8e
JoinPoint: execution(void ajia.Account.debit(float))
        aspect: ajia.AssociationDemoAspect@e09713
        object: ajia.SavingsAccount@156ee8e
```

Creates aspect instance

The output shows that only one instance of the aspect is created, and that instance is available to the advice in the aspect and shared among all the Account objects.

Now, let's move our attention to other aspect associations that allow more than one instance of an aspect to exist in an application.

6.2.2 Per-object association

Consider a situation where you need to apply the read-write lock pattern, which needs a lock per object. Ideally, you'd like to create a reusable aspect given that the pattern itself is reusable. The per-object association feature provides a mechanism to associate a new aspect instance with each execution or target object. In the following snippet, a new aspect instance is associated with each new execution object using perthis(), which matches the abstract access() pointcut (see chapter 13 for a complete example of this pattern implemented using AspectJ):

```
public abstract aspect ReadWriteLockAspect perthis(access()) {
    // ... aspect's state - the read-write lock

    public pointcut access() : readOperation() || writeOperation();

    public abstract pointcut readOperation();
    public abstract pointcut writeOperation();

    // ... advice to readOperation() and writeOperation() pointcut
    // ... to take/release lock
}
```

As an example, you can enable read-write concurrency control for the banking-related classes by creating a subaspect that provides a definition for the abstract pointcuts:

```
public aspect BankingReadWriteLockAspect extends ReadWriteLockAspect {
    public pointcut readOperation() : ... ;
    public pointcut writeOperation() : ...;
}
```

Now, whenever a join point that is selected by the access() pointcut executes, and the this object at the join point isn't previously associated with a BankingReadWrite-LockAspect instance, a new instance of the aspect is created and associated with the this object. Effectively, the aspect's state forms a part of each execution object's state. The advice in the base and derived aspects may then use the state of the aspect as if it were the advised object's state.

With per-object associations, an aspect instance is associated with each object matching the association specification. You can specify two kinds of per-object associations:

- perthis()—Associates a separate aspect instance with the execution object (this) for the join point matching the pointcut specified in perthis()
- pertarget()—Associates a separate aspect instance with the target object for the join point matching the pointcut specified in pertarget()

With object associations, the aspect instance is created when executing a join point of a matching object for the first time. After an association is created between an object

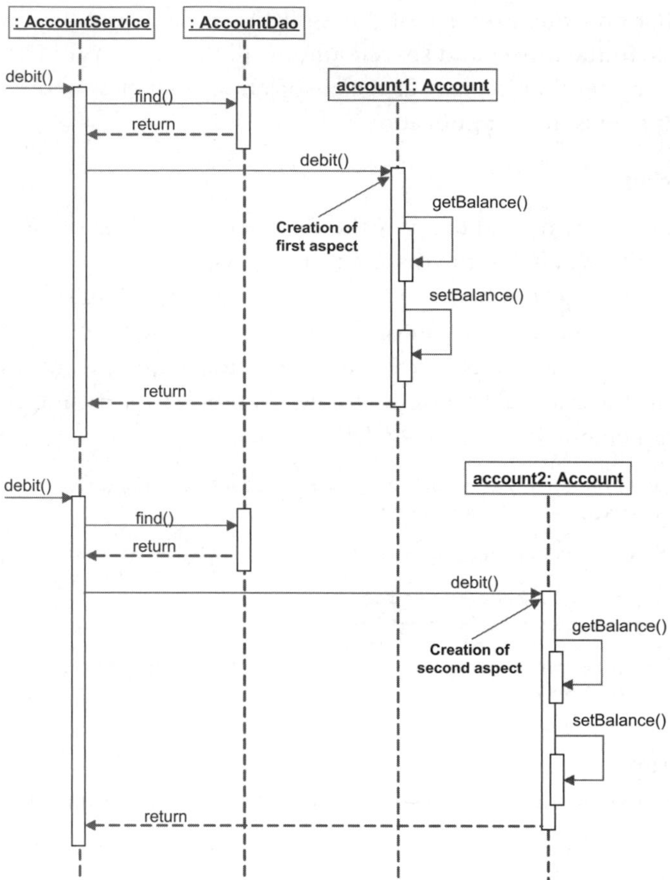

Figure 6.1 This sequence diagram shows aspect-creation and -association points for object-based association. For this illustration, we specify the `perthis(execution (* Account.*(..)))` association.

and an instance of the declaring aspect, the association is good for the lifetime of that object. Specifically, executing another matching join point on the same object doesn't create a new aspect with the object. Figure 6.1 illustrates object association using a UML sequence diagram.

As the figure shows, an aspect is created for each object when the join point matching the pointcut is executed the first time for that object. The aspect association remains valid during the lifetime of the object. Notice that no new aspect instance is created when the `getBalance()` or `setBalance()` method is invoked on the `account1` or `account2` object because an aspect is already associated with their execution objects.

Let's modify the aspect `AssociationDemoAspect` (listing 6.1). Listing 6.3 shows the use of the `perthis()` association with the `accountOperationExecution` pointcut.

Listing 6.3 `AssociationDemoAspect` with `perthis()` association

```
package ajia;

public aspect AssociationDemoAspect
```

```
    perthis(accountOperationExecution(Account)) {

    // ... unchanged from listing 6.1
}
```

When you compile this using the modified aspect and run the driver program (listing 6.2), you get the following output:

```
Creating aspect instance                                    <-- Creates aspect for first object
JoinPoint: execution(void ajia.Account.credit(float))
        aspect: ajia.AssociationDemoAspect@de6f34
        object: ajia.SavingsAccount@156ee8e                     Aspect instance
JoinPoint: execution(void ajia.Account.debit(float))            for advice to
        aspect: ajia.AssociationDemoAspect@de6f34               first object
        object: ajia.SavingsAccount@156ee8e
Creating aspect instance                                    <-- Creates aspect for second object
JoinPoint: execution(void ajia.Account.credit(float))
        aspect: ajia.AssociationDemoAspect@47b480
        object: ajia.SavingsAccount@19b49e6                     Aspect instance
JoinPoint: execution(void ajia.Account.debit(float))            for advice to
        aspect: ajia.AssociationDemoAspect@47b480               second object
        object: ajia.SavingsAccount@19b49e6
```

Two instances of `AssociationDemoAspect` are created, one for each `SavingsAccount` object. Each aspect is created just before the execution of the first join point with each `Account` object. In each advice body, the same aspect instance is available for each join point on an object.

To associate an aspect instance with the target object for a matching join point instead of the execution object, you use `pertarget()` instead of `perthis()`.

6.2.3 Per-control-flow association

Consider a transaction-management aspect. You need to maintain the transactional resource (JDBC connection, Hibernate session) from the point at which the transaction starts until it ends. The per-control-flow aspects offer a possibility of associating an aspect instance with each control flow associated with a join point. The following snippet of a base aspect shows a transaction-management aspect that needs to maintain some state during the control flow of a transaction:

```
public abstract aspect TransactionManagementAspect percflow(transacted()) {

    // ... aspect state:
    // ...    instance members such as the connection object used

    abstract pointcut transacted();

    // ... advice using the aspect state
}
```

You can introduce a transaction-management capability in a banking application by extending this aspect and providing a definition for the abstract `transacted()` pointcut:

```
public aspect BankingTransactionManagementAspect
    extends TransactionManagementAspect {
```

```
    pointcut transacted() : execution(* AccountService.*(..))
                            || execution(* ReportingService.*(..));
}
```

As an alternative to using `percflow()` aspects, you can use thread-specific storage such as `ThreadLocal` to manage the control flow's state. But in many cases, using an aspect association creates a simpler implementation.

As figure 6.2 shows, an aspect is created as soon as each matching control flow is entered for the first time. The aspect association then remains valid during the lifetime of the control flow. Each gray area in the figure indicates the scope of the aspect instance that was created upon entering the area.

You can specify two kinds of per-control-flow object associations:

- `percflow()`—Associates a separate aspect instance with the control flow at the join point matching the pointcut specified in `percflow()`
- `percflowbelow()`—Associates a separate aspect instance with the control flow below the join point matching the pointcut specified inside `percflowbelow()`

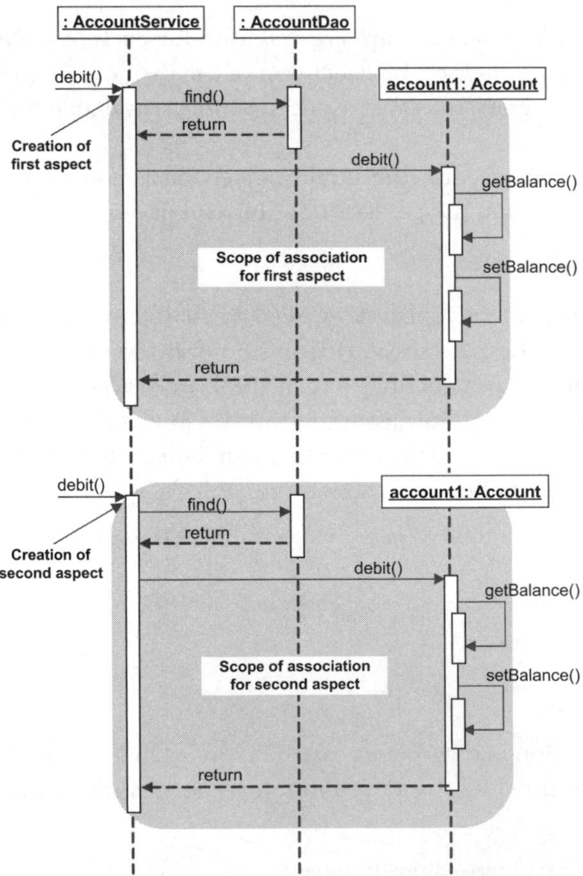

Figure 6.2 This sequence diagram shows aspect-creation and -association points for control-flow-based associations. This illustration shows the `percflow(execution(* AccountService.*(..)))` association.

Much like the `perthis()` and `pertarget()` cases, after an association is made between a control flow and an aspect instance, it continues to exist for the lifetime of that control flow. Figure 6.2 also illustrates the effect of control-flow-based association.

In the figure, an aspect associates the aspect instance with the control flow of join points that match the execution of the `debit()` method in the `AccountService` class. Two aspect instances are created—one each for the invocation of `debit()` execution. Each aspect instance continues to exist until its join point's execution completes.

To help you better understand control-flow-based association, let's modify `AssociationDemoAspect` again. You'll also modify the pointcut in the before advice to include the `setBalance()` execution, as shown in listing 6.4.

Listing 6.4 `AssociationDemoAspect` with `percflow()` association

```
package ajia;

public aspect AssociationDemoAspect
    percflow(accountOperationExecution(Account)) {

    // ... unchanged from listing 6.1

    before(Account account)
        : accountOperationExecution(account)
        || (execution(* Account.setBalance(..)) && this(account)) {
        System.out.println("JoinPoint: " + thisJoinPointStaticPart
                           + "\n\taspect: " + this
                           + "\n\tobject: " + account);
    }
}
```

When you compile and run the program, you see output similar to the following:

```
Creating aspect instance
JoinPoint: execution(void ajia.Account.credit(float))
        aspect: ajia.AssociationDemoAspect@6ca1c
        object: ajia.SavingsAccount@1bf216a
JoinPoint: execution(void ajia.Account.setBalance(float))
        aspect: ajia.AssociationDemoAspect@6ca1c
        object: ajia.SavingsAccount@1bf216a
Creating aspect instance
JoinPoint: execution(void ajia.Account.debit(float))
        aspect: ajia.AssociationDemoAspect@12ac982
        object: ajia.SavingsAccount@1bf216a
JoinPoint: execution(void ajia.Account.setBalance(float))
        aspect: ajia.AssociationDemoAspect@12ac982
        object: ajia.SavingsAccount@1bf216a
Creating aspect instance
JoinPoint: execution(void ajia.Account.credit(float))
        aspect: ajia.AssociationDemoAspect@1389e4
        object: ajia.SavingsAccount@c20e24
JoinPoint: execution(void ajia.Account.setBalance(float))
        aspect: ajia.AssociationDemoAspect@1389e4
        object: ajia.SavingsAccount@c20e24
Creating aspect instance
```

```
JoinPoint: execution(void ajia.Account.debit(float))
        aspect: ajia.AssociationDemoAspect@2e7263
        object: ajia.SavingsAccount@c20e24
JoinPoint: execution(void ajia.Account.setBalance(float))
        aspect: ajia.AssociationDemoAspect@2e7263
        object: ajia.SavingsAccount@c20e24
```

Four instances of the aspect are created: two corresponding to the `credit()` method and two corresponding to the `debit()` method executions initiated by the `Main` class. Each execution of the `credit()` and `debit()` methods called from the `Main` class resulted in a new control flow matching the join point specified in the aspect association pointcut, resulting in a new aspect instance being created.

Each instance is created just before the execution of the `credit()` and `debit()` methods, because a new control flow matching the pointcut specified starts with their execution.

The `setBalance()` method that is called from the control flow of `debit()` and `credit()` methods is associated with the same aspect as its caller. Because the `setBalance()` method falls in the control flow of `debit()` and `credit()` methods, the instance created for the caller continues to be associated with any method called by this caller. Note that if you include the `setBalance()` method in the `accountOperationExecution()` pointcut, it will result in the creation of a new aspect instance upon each execution of the `setBalance()` method, similar to the aspect instances (for execution of the `debit()` method) shown in figure 6.2.

AspectJ offers one more type of association: per-type. Let's see how it compares with the other association types.

6.2.4 Per-type association

Associating an aspect instance with the type (class, interface, or aspect) is similar to object association, except the aspect instance is associated with the class instead of its objects. You can think of per-type association as being similar to a static member defined in a class, whereas per-object association is like an instance member.

Let's look at the general structure of per-type association (see chapter 10 for a more complete example):

```
public abstract aspect TracingAspect pertypewithin(ajia.services.*) {

    // ... aspect state:
    // ...    instance members such as the logger object used

    abstract pointcut traced();

    // advice to initialize the aspect state
    after() : staticinitialization(*) {
        logger = Logger.getLogger(getWithinTypeName());
    }

    // ... advice to use the aspect state such as
    before() : traced() {
        logger.log(...);
    }
}
```

With such a declaration, the state in the aspect effectively becomes the static (class-bound) state of any class matching any type in the `ajia.services` package. It's typical to advise the static initializer to initialize the aspect state and use that state in other advice. Because the static-initialization join point is invoked only once per class (when the class is loaded), the advice to a static initializer ensures that the state is initialized only once, and the `pertypewithin()` association ensures the association of that state with each matching type.

Also notice the use of the `getWithinTypeName()` method when obtaining a logger. For each `pertypewithin()` aspect, the weaver adds this method, which returns the type name associated with the aspect instance. Any other advice then effectively uses the class-specific state (logger, in this case).

Let's continue to modify `AssociationDemoAspect` to better understand the `pertypewithin()` association. Listing 6.5 modifies the aspect in listing 6.1 to associate the aspect with types matching `Account+` type pattern—in this case, the `Account` and `SavingsAccount` types.

Listing 6.5 `AssociationDemoAspect` with per-type association

```
package ajia;

public aspect AssociationDemoAspect pertypewithin(Account+) {
    // ... unchanged from listing 6.1
}
```

To illustrate the effect of the aspect association, make a small modification to `SavingsAccount` to override the implementation of the `debit()` method, as shown in Listing 6.6.

Listing 6.6 Modification to illustrate `pertypewithin()` association

```
package ajia;

public class SavingsAccount extends Account {
    private static final float MINIMUM_BALANCE = 25.0f;

    public SavingsAccount(int accountNumber) {
        super(accountNumber);
    }

    public void debit(float amount)
        throws InsufficientBalanceException {
        if (getBalance() < (amount + MINIMUM_BALANCE)) {
            throw new InsufficientBalanceException(
                      "Minimum balance not maintained");
        }
        super.debit(amount);
    }
}
```

When you compile and execute the code, you see output similar to the following:

```
Creating aspect instance
Creating aspect instance
```

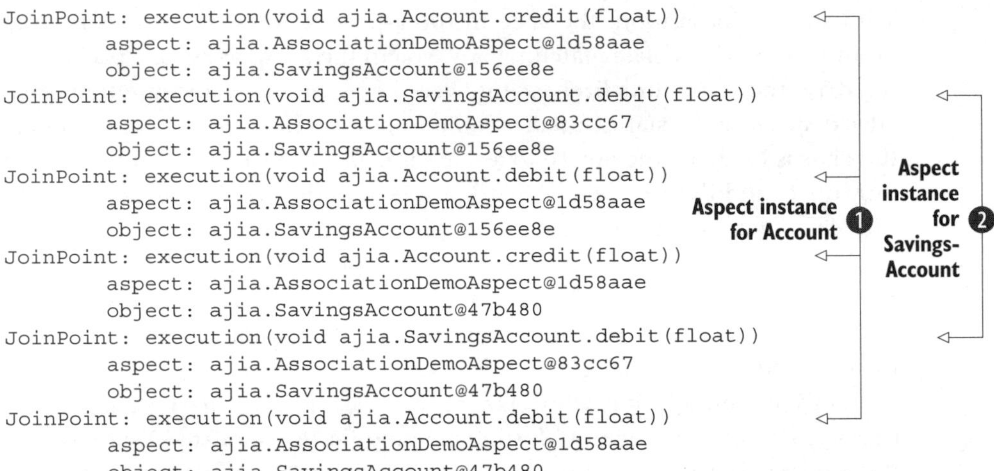

JoinPoint: execution(void ajia.Account.credit(float))
aspect: ajia.AssociationDemoAspect@1d58aae
object: ajia.SavingsAccount@156ee8e
JoinPoint: execution(void ajia.SavingsAccount.debit(float))
aspect: ajia.AssociationDemoAspect@83cc67
object: ajia.SavingsAccount@156ee8e
JoinPoint: execution(void ajia.Account.debit(float))
aspect: ajia.AssociationDemoAspect@1d58aae
object: ajia.SavingsAccount@156ee8e
JoinPoint: execution(void ajia.Account.credit(float))
aspect: ajia.AssociationDemoAspect@1d58aae
object: ajia.SavingsAccount@47b480
JoinPoint: execution(void ajia.SavingsAccount.debit(float))
aspect: ajia.AssociationDemoAspect@83cc67
object: ajia.SavingsAccount@47b480
JoinPoint: execution(void ajia.Account.debit(float))
aspect: ajia.AssociationDemoAspect@1d58aae
object: ajia.SavingsAccount@47b480
Aspect instance for Account 1
Aspect instance for Savings-Account 2

The most important observation is that there are two aspect instances, and the aspect instance available at a join point corresponds to the type in which the join point is defined. Let's examine the output in more detail:

1. An aspect instance is created for the `Account` class. In the current AspectJ implementation, the aspect instance is created when the class is loaded, which also corresponds to the static initialization join point for the class. When a join point with corresponding code defined in the `Account` type is advised, the aspect instance available at that point is the one created for the `Account` type.
2. An aspect instance is similarly created for the `SavingsAccount` class. When a join point with the corresponding code defined in `SavingsAccount` is advised, the aspect instance accessed is the one created for `SavingsAccount`. For example, for the `debit()` method, when the code defined in `SavingsAccount` executes, the aspect instance accessed is the one for `SavingsAccount`. But when the superclass's code is executed for the same method, the aspect instance accessed is the one created for the `Account` type.

The lexical scope in which the join point's program element is defined governs the aspect instance available at a join point. In particular, the dynamic type of the object doesn't play any role here. Although the type of the advised object is always `SavingsAccount`, the aspect instance corresponding to `Account` or `SavingsAccount` is made available depending on where the code resides. This behavior lets you implement the common logging idiom by using the logger instance associated with the class from which the logging code is executed. You'll use this facility when we examine tracing using AspectJ in chapter 10.

6.2.5 *Implicit limiting of join points with aspect associations*

Using the per-object, per-control-flow, or per-type association has the side effect of implicitly limiting the advice in the aspect to only join points that match the scope of an aspect instance. The scope of an aspect instance is the set of join points that have an aspect instance associated with them. For example, for the `percflow()` association, the scope of an aspect instance is all the join points occurring inside the control flow of the specified pointcut. This means that even if a pointcut specified for an advice matches a join point, the advice to that join point won't apply unless the join point also matches the scope of the aspect. This side effect often surprises developers when they refactor an aspect to create reusable parts and need to use `per-` associations.

The aspect association implies that advice in an aspect will apply to join points only if:

- For `perthis()` associations, the join point's execution object matches the aspect instance's associated object.
- For `pertarget()` associations, the join point's target object matches the aspect's associated object.
- For `percflow()` associations, the join point is in the control flow of the aspect's associated control flow.
- For `percflowbelow()` associations, the join point is below the control flow of the aspect's associated control flow.
- For `pertypewithin()` associations, the type matching the join point's definition matches the type pattern declared in the aspect association.

Aspect instances are created automatically by the system according to the association specification. To access their state from outside the aspect, you need to get its instance.

6.2.6 *Accessing aspect instances*

Consider a profiling aspect that collects durations for the execution of profiled methods. You'd typically keep the profile data inside the profile aspect. When you need to retrieve this data—say, from another thread that prints the latest profile information—you have to get the aspect instance first. For all types of aspect associations, you can get the aspect instance using the static method `aspectOf()` that is available for each aspect. The method returns an instance of the aspect. For a profiler case, you can retrieve the data as follows:

```
profileData = ProfilerAspect.aspectOf().getProfileData();
```

The `aspectOf()` method returns the aspect instance associated with the aspect on which the method is invoked.

Each aspect contains two static methods: `aspectOf()`, to obtain the associated aspect instance; and `hasAspect()`, to check if an instance is associated. These methods take different arguments depending on the aspect association. Table 6.1 shows the arguments taken by different aspect associations.

In all cases, the `aspectOf()` method returns the instance of an aspect if one is associated. In the case of the default association, it creates an instance if none is associated, and returns it. You can use this fact to inject dependencies into aspects (you'll use it in an example later in this section). In all other cases, if an instance isn't associated, `aspectOf()` throws a `NoAspectBoundException`.

Table 6.1 Using the `aspectOf()` and `hasAspect()` methods

Aspect association	Argument to methods	Example
Default (`issingleton()`)	None	`LoggingAspect.aspectOf()`
Per-object(`perthis()` and `pertarget()`)	Object instance	`BankingReadWriteLockAspect.aspectOf(myObject)`
Per-control flow (`percflow()` or `percflowbelow()`)	None	`TransactionManagementAspect.aspectOf()`
Per-type (`pertypewithin()`)	Class	`LoggingAspect.aspectOf(MyClass.class)`

The method `hasAspect()` returns `true` if an aspect instance is associated; otherwise, it returns `false`. Note that because an aspect instance with a control-flow-based association lives only during the control flow (or below, for `percflowbelow()`), you can get the aspect instance only in the control flow associated with the aspect.

6.2.7 Comparing per-object association and member introduction

The member-introduction mechanism introduced earlier in this section is often considered an alternative to per-object association. They share some commonality, but there are a few important differences. Let's examine the differences between these two mechanisms.

You can avoid using per-object association by judiciously using static crosscutting with introduced fields. In that case, instead of keeping the state in an aspect, you introduce that state to the object being advised. This kind of modification often leads to simpler design. For example, consider the following aspect, which associates an aspect instance with each `Account` object. The aspect's state—`minimumBalance`—effectively becomes part of the `Account` object's state:

```
public aspect MinimumBalanceAspect perthis(this(Account)) {
    private float minimumBalance;
    ... methods and advice using minimumBalance
}
```

To use a member introduction instead of an association, you can change the aspect in the following way:

```
public aspect MinimumBalanceAspect {
    private float Account.minimumBalance;

    ... methods and advice using minimumBalance
}
```

In this snippet, you use the member-introduction mechanism to associate a new member—`minimumBalance`—with each `Account` object. The result is identical in both snippets—a new state is associated with each `Account` object.

Certain reusable aspects (such as a read-write lock management aspect) that need to work with diverse types of objects may not have a common shared type. For example, `Customer` and `Account` probably have no class or interface common to their inheritance hierarchy. Therefore, to introduce a state, you must first specify a common type using `declare parent`. For instance, you can declare the interface `ReadWriteLockManaged` to be a parent type of `Account` and `Customer`. Then, you can introduce the required state to `ReadWriteLockManaged`. This way, you get the same effect as per-object association using a simple introduction mechanism.

Developing reusable aspects using introduction instead of per-object association can get tricky. The main reason is that a reusable base aspect, unaware of the application-specific classes, can't use the `declare parent` construct to specify a common type. Although you can get around this issue by using a complex design, per-object association can offer an elegant alternative solution. When you use per-object association, the base aspect includes an abstract pointcut that associates the aspect with the object at the matching join points. All that a derived aspect needs to do is provide a definition for that pointcut so that it selects join points whose associated objects need an additional per-object state. Section 13.3.2 will provide a concrete example of simplifying a reusable aspect using per-object association.

The choice between using per-object association and member introduction is a balance between elegance and simplicity. Experience is usually the best guide.

Let's put the knowledge you've gained regarding the aspect-instantiation model to good use through an example.

6.2.8 Improving the caching aspect

In chapter 4, the caching solution used a hard-coded instance of the cache object. A better design choice is to use a DI mechanism to inject a cache instance in the aspect. Let's modify the example to use Spring's DI with the aspect. You'll then externalize the cache configuration and expose a few objects through the Java Management Extension (JMX) so you can change the cache configuration in a running application. You'll also use this arrangement to write automated tests.

USING DEPENDENCY INJECTION WITH ASPECTS

Let's modify the aspect to remove the hard-coded creation of the cache field and add a setter so that you can use the Spring container to configure that property. This also enables you to inject the aspect with mock objects for testing purposes. You also add a flag to enable the aspect. If that flag is set to `false`, the advice bypasses the caching logic. Listing 6.7 shows the modified aspect.

Listing 6.7 Preparing the aspect for DI

```
package ajia.caching;

import ...

public aspect CacheAspect {
    private Cache cache;
```

```
    private boolean enabled = true;

     ... pointcut and other fields unchanged from listing 4.12

    Object around(Cachable cachable) : cachedAccess(cachable) {
        if(!enabled) {
            return proceed(cachable);
        }

      ... remaining advice unchanged

    }

    public Cache getCache() {
        return this.cache;
    }

    public void setCache(Cache cache) {
        this.cache = cache;
    }

    public boolean getEnabled() {
        return this.enabled;
    }

    public void setEnabled(boolean enabled) {
        this.enabled = enabled;
    }
}
```

The `setCache()` method lets the cache property be injected through an external configuration such as the one in listing 6.8, which defines an application context to be used by the Spring container.

Listing 6.8 Configuring the aspect to inject dependencies

```
<?xml version="1.0" encoding="UTF-8"?>
<beans xmlns="http://www.springframework.org/schema/beans"
    xmlns:xsi="http://www.w3.org/2001/XMLSchema-instance"
    xsi:schemaLocation=
     "http://www.springframework.org/schema/beans
      http://www.springframework.org/schema/beans/spring-beans-2.5.xsd">

    <bean id="cacheAspect" class="ajia.caching.CacheAspect"
          factory-method="aspectOf">
        <property name="cache" ref="cache"/>
    </bean>

    <bean id="cache" class="com.opensymphony.oscache.base.Cache">
        <constructor-arg value="true"/>
        <constructor-arg value="true"/>
        <constructor-arg value="true"/>
    </bean>

    <bean class="org.springframework.jmx.export.MBeanExporter">
        <property name="beans">
            <map>
                <entry key="ajia:service=cacheAspect"
                       value-ref="cacheAspect"/>
                <entry key="ajia:service=cache"
```

(1) Bean corresponding to aspect

(2) Injects cache property

(3) Declares cache bean

(4) Exposes aspects and caches bean through JMX

```
                        value-ref="cache"/>
            </map>
        </property>
    </bean>
</beans>
```

❹ **Exposes aspects and caches bean through JMX**

The example has beans corresponding to the aspect and the cache object that you expose through JMX. Whereas in a typical Spring application, even `StockService` is configured as a bean, here we've left it unchanged to maintain our focus on the main theme of this section. Let's examine the entities in the application context:

❶ You use `aspectOf()` as the factory method when defining the bean corresponding to the aspect. The Spring container uses that method to instantiate the aspect instead of using `new`.

❷ The bean corresponding to the aspect is like any other bean. Here, you inject the `cache` bean into it.

❸ The `cache` bean is an instance of the `Cache` class with all constructor arguments set to `true`.

❹ The use of DI allows aspects to leverage the Spring Framework's power. You expose the cache aspect and the cache bean to JMX by adding this snippet to an application context file. Similarly, you could utilize other functionality offered by Spring, such as transaction management and security.

UPDATING THE PROGRAM TO CHECK CACHE BEHAVIOR

Let's modify the `Main` class to load the Spring application context that will lead to configuring the aspect instance. You'll also add a loop around the code, which exercises caching functionality to let you play with it while you modify properties through a JMX console. Listing 6.9 shows the modified class. Note that the aspect has the needed support in place to write an automated test. We will do that in the section that follows.

Listing 6.9 Modified main class to load Spring's application context

```
package ajia.main;

import ...

public class Main {
    public static void main(String[] args) throws IOException {
        new ClassPathXmlApplicationContext("applicationContext.xml");
        StockService service = new StockService();

        while(true) {
            service.getQuoteGraph("GOOG", 1);
            service.getQuoteGraph("GOOG", 1);
            service.getQuoteGraph("YHOO", 5);
            service.getQuoteGraph("YHOO", 365);
            service.getQuoteGraph("GOOG", 365);
            service.getQuoteGraph("GOOG", 365);

            System.in.read();
        }
    }
}
```

When you run this program, you can connect to it using a JMX console. Figure 6.3 shows the JConsole tool that is shipped with JDK 5 and newer version.

Executing this program leads to a few warnings due to our taking the simplest possible approach and exposing all properties of the beans. In practice, you'll use one of the `MBeanInfoAssemblers` provided by Spring to limit the exposure. (See the Spring

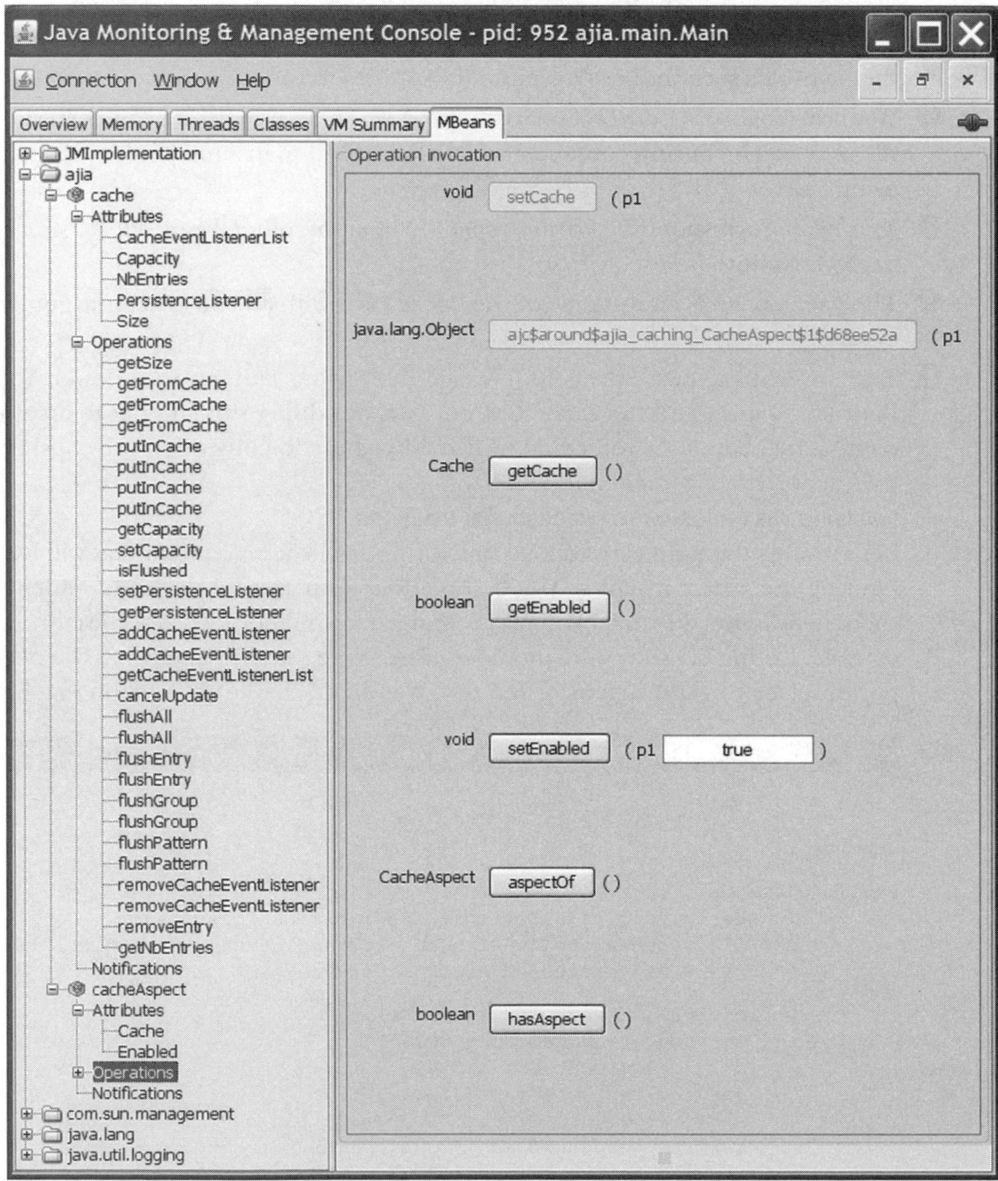

Figure 6.3 JMX console for the caching example. Notice how the `cache` and `cacheAspect` beans are available as MBeans. Also notice how the aspect's `enabled` property is exposed, which lets you enable or disable the caching logic.

reference manual or a book such as *Spring in Action*, 2nd edition, by Craig Walls [Manning, 2007] for more information.)

Let's see how you can use this new functionality. The following output shows an interaction, with commentary regarding the input and JMX console interaction in italics:

```
Cache miss. Key: Chart:GOOG:1
Cache hit.  Key: Chart:GOOG:1 Value: [B@96cf11
Cache miss. Key: Chart:YHOO:5
Cache miss. Key: Chart:YHOO:365
Cache miss. Key: Chart:GOOG:365
Cache hit.  Key: Chart:GOOG:365 Value: [B@f47bf5

[Disable aspect by setting the enabled attribute
of the cacheAspect MBean to false through JConsole]
[Enter]
       No output since caching is disabled
[Enter]
[Re-enabled aspect by setting the enabled attribute
of the cacheAspect MBean to true through JConsole]
[Enter]
Cache hit.  Key: Chart:GOOG:1 Value: [B@96cf11
Cache hit.  Key: Chart:GOOG:1 Value: [B@96cf11
Cache hit.  Key: Chart:YHOO:5 Value: [B@1823918
Cache hit.  Key: Chart:YHOO:365 Value: [B@7262b6
Cache hit.  Key: Chart:GOOG:365 Value: [B@f47bf5
Cache hit.  Key: Chart:GOOG:365 Value: [B@f47bf5
Cache hit.  Key: Chart:GOOG:1 Value: [B@96cf11
Cache hit.  Key: Chart:GOOG:1 Value: [B@96cf11
Cache hit.  Key: Chart:YHOO:5 Value: [B@1823918
Cache hit.  Key: Chart:YHOO:365 Value: [B@7262b6
Cache hit.  Key: Chart:GOOG:365 Value: [B@f47bf5
Cache hit.  Key: Chart:GOOG:365 Value: [B@f47bf5

[Clear cache for GOOG 1-day chart by invoking
the removeEntry() operation on cache MBean
with Chart:GOOG:1 as the argument]
[Enter]
Cache miss. Key: Chart:GOOG:1
Cache hit.  Key: Chart:GOOG:1 Value: [B@15e236a
Cache hit.  Key: Chart:YHOO:5 Value: [B@1823918
Cache hit.  Key: Chart:YHOO:365 Value: [B@7262b6
Cache hit.  Key: Chart:GOOG:365 Value: [B@f47bf5
Cache hit.  Key: Chart:GOOG:365 Value: [B@f47bf5
Cache hit.  Key: Chart:GOOG:1 Value: [B@15e236a
Cache hit.  Key: Chart:GOOG:1 Value: [B@15e236a
Cache hit.  Key: Chart:YHOO:5 Value: [B@1823918
Cache hit.  Key: Chart:YHOO:365 Value: [B@7262b6
Cache hit.  Key: Chart:GOOG:365 Value: [B@f47bf5
Cache hit.  Key: Chart:GOOG:365 Value: [B@f47bf5
```

Play around with it to get a better understanding of interacting with the cache object.

WRITING AN AUTOMATED TEST FOR CACHING

To ensure that the aspect continues to behave correctly in the future, let's write tests that can be run automatically. Because you've modified the aspect to allow injecting dependencies, you can inject it with mock objects and verify correct interactions.

Listing 6.10 shows a test class to verify the caching behavior. Note that it uses the Mockito framework (http://mockito.googlecode.com); you can use any other mock framework, such as JMock or EasyMock, if you prefer.

Listing 6.10 JUnit test for checking cache behavior

```
package ajia.caching;

import static org.mockito.Mockito.*;

import ...

public class CacheAspectTest {
    private CacheAspect cacheAspect = CacheAspect.aspectOf();
    private TestService testService = new TestService();

    @Mock private Cache mockCache;
    @Mock private TestServiceHelper mockHelper;

    @Before
    public void setUp() {
        MockitoAnnotations.initMocks(this);
        cacheAspect.setCache(mockCache);
        testService.helper = mockHelper;
    }

    @Test
    public void cacheHit() throws Exception {
        testService.get("testArg");
        verify(mockCache).getFromCache("test:testArg");
        verifyZeroInteractions(mockHelper);
    }

    @Test
    public void cacheMiss() throws Exception {
        when(mockCache.getFromCache("test:testArg"))
            .thenThrow(new NeedsRefreshException("miss"));
        testService.get("testArg");
        verify(mockHelper).get();
    }

    private static class TestService {
        private TestServiceHelper helper;

        @Cachable(cacheStore="test", keyScript="#arg1")
        public Object get(String arg1) {
            return helper.get();
        }
    }

    private static interface TestServiceHelper {
        Object get();
    }
}
```

(1) Sets up test

(2) Tests cache hit

(3) Tests cache miss

(1) Sets up test

(1) You obtain the instance of the `CacheAspect` using the `aspectOf()` method. You also use a `TestService` object whose method is marked with the `@Cachable` annotation. The

TestService class uses a helper object, whose interaction you monitor to verify correct caching behavior. You annotate the Cache and TestServiceHelper fields with the @Mock annotation, so that you can create them by calling MockitoAnnotations.initMocks(). (See the Mockito documentation for details.) You inject the mock object for TestServiceHelper into the TestService object. Similarly, you inject the mock object for Cache into the aspect.

2 The test for a cache hit invokes the method that should be cached. It verifies that the cache is queried with the right key. It also verifies that no interaction took place with the helper object, because a cache hit should lead to bypassing that object.

3 The test for a cache miss specifies the behavior for the cache to throw an exception. After calling the cached method, this test verifies that the helper method has been called, because a cache miss should lead to its invocation.

Run this test, and you should see a green bar. You should test classes such as JoinPointContextUtil and SpelExpressionEvaluator separately, using regular testing techniques.

6.3 Aspect precedence

Because a system may consist of multiple advice in the same or different aspects that interact with the same join point, an obvious question arises: how does AspectJ determine the order in which advice are applied, and how can you control this order? To understand the need for controlling the advice execution order, let's look at the example in listing 6.11. Consider a class representing a home, with methods for entering and exiting the home.

Listing 6.11 Simple class representing a home

```
package ajia;

public class Home {
    public void enter() {
        System.out.println("Entering");
    }

    public void exit() {
        System.out.println("Exiting");
    }
}
```

Now, let's create a security aspect (listing 6.12) consisting of advice for engaging the security system in the home when you exit and disengaging it when you enter.

Listing 6.12 Aspect securing a home

```
package ajia;

public aspect HomeSecurityAspect {
    before() : execution(void Home.exit()) {
        System.out.println("Engaging");
```

```
    }

    after() : execution(void Home.enter()) {
        System.out.println("Disengaging");
    }
}
```

Another aspect (listing 6.13) conserves energy by switching off the lights before you leave the home and switching them on after you enter.

Listing 6.13 Aspect implementing an energy-saving functionality

```
package ajia;

public aspect SaveEnergyAspect {
    before() : execution(void Home.exit()) {
        System.out.println("Switching off lights");
    }

    after() : execution(void Home.enter()) {
        System.out.println("Switching on lights");
    }
}
```

The simple driver in listing 6.14 shows the effects of multiple advice on a join point.

Listing 6.14 Simple class to show the effect of multiple advice on a join point

```
package ajia.main;

public class Main {
    public static void main(String[] args) {
        Home home = new Home();
        home.exit();
        System.out.println();

        home.enter();
    }
}
```

When you compile these files together passing the compiler the `-Xlint:warning` flag, you get the following warnings:

```
[WARNING] at this shadow method-execution(void ajia.Home.enter())
➥   no precedence is specified between advice applying from aspect
➥   ajia.HomeSecurityAspect and aspect ajia.SaveEnergyAspect
    [Xlint:unorderedAdviceAtShadow]
[WARNING] at this shadow method-execution(void ajia.Home.exit())
➥   no precedence is specified between advice applying from aspect
➥   ajia.HomeSecurityAspect and aspect ajia.SaveEnergyAspect
    [Xlint:unorderedAdviceAtShadow]
```

When execute the `Main` program, you see the following output:[1]

[1] It's possible to get output that differs from what is shown here, depending on several factors, including the version of the AspectJ compiler you're using. Your output may match the desired output, but such a match is accidental: precedence is arbitrarily determined, unless you specify the advice precedence.

```
Switching off lights
Engaging
Exiting

Entering
Disengaging
Switching on lights
```

The exhibited behavior may not be desirable, considering that switching off lights prior to securing the home may make you fumble in the dark. Also, trying to disarm the security system without the lights on when you enter may cause similar trouble, and any delay in disarming the system may result in security being called. The preferred sequence when entering the home is Enter > Switch on lights > Disarm; and while exiting, Arm > Switch off lights > Exit. From an implementation perspective, you would like the following:

- The before advice in `SaveEnergyAspect` should run before the `HomeSecurityAspect`'s before advice.
- The after advice in `SaveEnergyAspect` should run after the `HomeSecurityAspect`'s after advice.

In the next few sections, we'll discuss the rules of precedence and ways you can control precedence. Later, you'll apply this information to the previous problem to learn how you can achieve the correct advice ordering.

6.3.1 Ordering of advice

As you've just seen, with multiple aspects present in a system, pieces of advice in the different aspects can often apply to a single join point. When this happens, AspectJ uses the following precedence rules to determine the order in which the advice is applied. Later, you'll see how to control precedence:

1. The aspect with higher precedence executes its before advice on a join point *before* the aspect with lower precedence.
2. The aspect with higher precedence executes its after advice on a join point *after* the aspect with lower precedence.
3. The around advice in the higher-precedence aspect encloses the around advice in the lower-precedence aspect. This kind of arrangement allows the higher-precedence aspect to control whether the lower-precedence advice will run by controlling the call to `proceed()`. If the higher-precedence aspect doesn't call `proceed()` in its advice body, not only will the lower-precedence aspects not execute, but the advised join point also won't execute.

Figure 6.4 illustrates the precedence rules.

It's often necessary to change the precedence of advice applied to a join point. Let's see what mechanisms AspectJ provides to meet such needs.

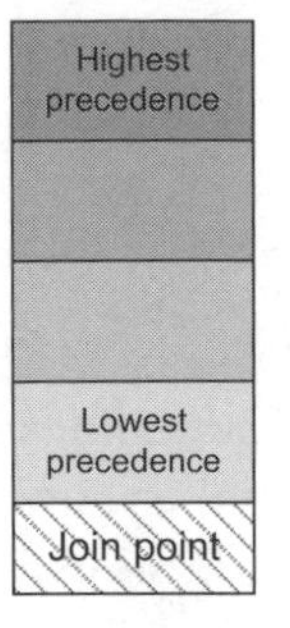

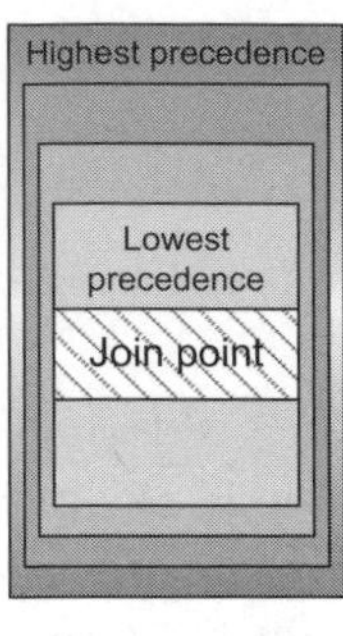

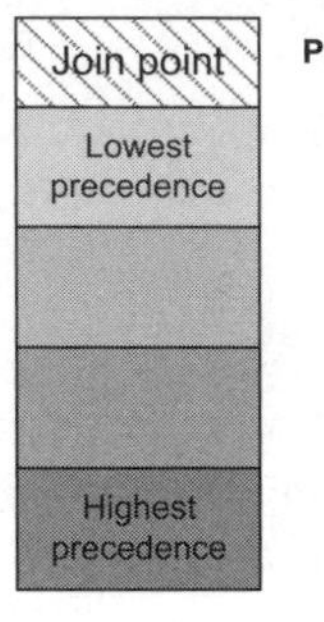

Figure 6.4 Ordering the execution of advice and join points. The darker areas represent the higher-precedence advice. You can think of the around advice as the higher-precedence advice running the lower-precedence advice in a nested manner.

6.3.2 *Explicit aspect precedence*

AspectJ provides a construct—`declare precedence`—for controlling aspect precedence. The `declare precedence` construct must be specified inside an aspect. The construct takes the following form:

```
declare precedence : TypePattern1, TypePattern2, ...;
```

The result of this kind of declaration is that aspects matching the type pattern on the left dominate the ones on the right, thus taking a higher precedence. In this example, the precedence of `TypePattern1` is higher than the precedence of `TypePattern2`.

Precedence ordering considers only concrete aspects when matching the type pattern and ignores all abstract aspects. By controlling aspect precedence, you can control the order in which advice is applied to a pointcut. For example, the following declaration causes `AuthenticationAspect` to have a higher precedence than `AuthorizationAspect`:

```
declare precedence : AuthenticationAspect, AuthorizationAspect;
```

Let's use this declaration to correct the precedence between `HomeSecurityAspect` and `SaveEnergyAspect` in the `Home` class example.

USING PRECEDENCE TO CONTROL ORDERING

You want to run the before advice to arm the security system prior to the before advice to switch off the lights, and the after advice to disarm the system following the after advice to switch on the lights. This means you need `HomeSecurityAspect` to have a higher precedence than `SaveEnergyAspect`. You achieve this goal by writing another aspect (listing 6.15) that declares the correct and explicit precedence between the two.

Listing 6.15 Aspect coordinating security and energy-saving aspects

```
package ajia;

public aspect HomeSystemCoordinationAspect {
    declare precedence: HomeSecurityAspect, SaveEnergyAspect;
}
```

When you compile your code and run the driver program, you see the following output:

```
Engaging
Switching off lights
Exiting

Entering
Switching on lights
Disengaging
```

This is exactly what you wanted. You could have added the `declare precedence` clause in either `HomeSecurityAspect` or `SaveEnergyAspect` and gotten the same result. But this kind of modification would cause the declaring aspect to know about the other aspect and thus cause an undesirable coupling between the two.

WARNING In the absence of any special precedence control, the order in which the advice is applied is unpredictable. The AspectJ compiler can help you spot situations where the advice order is unpredictable—all you need to do is pass it the `-Xlint:warning` flag.

Let's examine some more examples of the `declare precedence` clause, to help you better understand it.

TYPICAL PRECEDENCE CONTROL PATTERNS

Because the clause expects a list of `TypePatterns`, you can use wildcards in aspect names. The following declaration causes all aspects whose names start with `Auth`, such as `AuthenticationAspect` and `AuthorizationAspect`, to have higher precedence than `PoolingAspect`:

```
declare precedence : Auth*, PoolingAspect;
```

But in this declaration, the precedence between two aspects starting with `Auth` is unspecified. If controlling the precedence between two such aspects is important, you must specify both aspects in the desired order.

Because declare precedence takes a type list, you can specify a sequence of precedence. For example, the following declaration causes aspects whose names start with `Auth` to have precedence over both `PoolingAspect` and `LoggingAspect`, while also causing `PoolingAspect` to take precedence over `LoggingAspect`:

```
declare precedence : Auth*, PoolingAspect, LoggingAspect;
```

It's common for certain aspects to have higher precedence among all aspects. You can use the `*`, `+`, and `..` wildcards to indicate such an intention. The following declaration causes `AuthenticationAspect` to dominate all the remaining aspects in the system:

```
declare precedence : AuthenticationAspect, *;
```

It's also common for certain aspects to have lower precedence among all aspects. You can use a wildcard to achieve this as well. The following declaration causes `CachingAspect` to have the lowest precedence:

```
declare precedence : *, CachingAspect;
```

It's an error if a single `declare precedence` clause causes circular dependency in the ordering of aspect precedence. The following declaration produces a compile-time error because `Auth*` matches `AuthenticationAspect`, causing a circular dependency:

```
declare precedence : Auth*, PoolingAspect, AuthenticationAspect;
```

But it's legal to specify a circular dependency that causes precedence in multiple clauses. You can use this to enforce that two different, potentially conflicting or redundant aspects, such as two pooling aspects, share no join points. You get a compile-time error if the two aspects in question share a join point. The following declarations won't produce an error unless `PoolingAspect` and `AuthenticationAspect` share a join point:

```
declare precedence : AuthenticationAspect, PoolingAspect;
declare precedence : PoolingAspect, AuthenticationAspect;
```

You can include a `declare precedence` clause inside any aspect. A common usage idiom is to add such clauses to a separate coordination aspect (such as the one you used in the previous `HomeSystemCoordinationAspect` example) so that aspects are unaware of each other. Such a separation is particularly important for third-party, off-the-shelf aspects where you may not have the control over source files that you would need to add such clauses. Separating precedence control also avoids the tangling of the core functionality in the precedence relationship with other aspects.

Aspect inheritance and precedence

AspectJ implicitly determines the precedence between two aspects related by a base-derived aspect relationship. The rule is simple: the derived aspect implicitly has higher precedence than the base aspect. Because only concrete aspects in the `declare precedence` clause are designated for precedence ordering, declaring a base aspect (which is always abstract) to have higher precedence over subaspects has no effect. In other words, there is no way to declare higher precedence for base aspects.

The precedence control offered by AspectJ is simple yet powerful and is immensely helpful for a complex system. You can now create multiple aspects independently as well as use aspects developed by others without requiring modifications to any aspects.

Let's now examine the rules that govern the precedence of advice within an aspect.

6.3.3 *Ordering advice in a single aspect*

It's also possible to have multiple advice in one aspect that you want to apply to a pointcut. Because the advice reside in the same aspect, aspect-precedence rules can no longer apply. In such cases, the advice that appears first lexically inside the aspect executes first. Note that the only way to control precedence between multiple advice in an aspect is to arrange them lexically. Let's illustrate this rule through a simple example (listing 6.16) that shows both the effect of the precedence rule and its interaction between different types of advice.

Listing 6.16 Illustrating advice ordering in an aspect

```
package ajia.main;

public aspect InterAdvicePrecedenceAspect {
    public pointcut performCall() : call(* Main.perform());

    after() returning : performCall() {
        System.out.println("<after1/>");
    }

    before() : performCall() {
        System.out.println("<before1/>");
    }

    void around() : performCall() {
        System.out.println("<around>");
        proceed();
        System.out.println("</around>");
    }

    before() : performCall() {
        System.out.println("<before2/>");
    }
}
```

In listing 6.17, the `Main` class sets up the scenario to check the precedence by calling the `perform()` method from the `main()` method.

Listing 6.17 Main driver to check precedence within an aspect

```
package ajia.main;

public class Main {
    public static void main(String[] args) {
        Main main = new Main();
        main.perform();
    }

    public void perform() {
        System.out.println("<performing/>");
    }
}
```

After compiling the aspect with the `Main` class, when you run the code, you get this output:

```
<before1/>
<around>
<before2/>
<performing/>
<after1/>
</around>
```

The output shows the following:

- The first before advice is followed by around advice, due to their lexical ordering.
- The second before advice runs after the around advice starts executing but before executing the captured join point. Note that, regardless of precedence, all before advice for a join point must execute before the advised join point.
- The after advice executes before completing the around advice, because it has higher precedence than the around advice. Note that the earliest an after advice can run is after the join point's execution.

Now that you know all about precedence control between multiple aspects and advice within an aspect, you should be able to control how aspects and advice apply at any given join point. Let's complete this chapter by discussing a way to bypass the normal Java access-specification rules.

6.4 Privileged aspects

For the most part, aspects have the same standard Java access-control rules as classes. For example, an aspect normally can't access any private members of other classes. This is usually sufficient and is desirable on most occasions. But in a few situations, an aspect may need to access certain data members or operations that aren't exposed to outsiders. You can gain such access by marking the aspect `privileged`.

Let's see how this works in the following example. The `Main` class (listing 6.18) contains a private data member.

Listing 6.18 Driver to illustrate privileged aspects

```
package ajia.main;

public class Main {
    private int id;

    public static void main(String[] args) {
        Main main = new Main();
        main.method1();
    }

    public void method1() {
        System.out.println("Main.method1");
    }
}
```

Consider a situation where `PrivilegeTestAspect` (listing 6.19) needs to access the class's private data member to perform its logic.

Listing 6.19 Aspect that accesses private member of a class

```
package ajia.main;

public aspect PrivilegeTestAspect {
    before(Main callee) : call(void Main.method1())
                          && target(callee) {
```

```
            System.out.println("PrivilegeTestAspect:before objectId="
                               + callee.id);
        }
    }
```

If you try to compile this code, you get a compiler error for accessing the `Main` class's private member `id`:

```
...PrivilegeTestAspect.aj:9
➥   [error] The field Main.id is not visible
+ callee.id);
  ^^^^^^^^^^

1 error
```

But if you mark the aspect as `privileged` (as follows), the code compiles without error and behaves as expected:

```
privileged public aspect PrivilegeTestAspect {
    ...
}
```

With the privileged aspect, you can access the internal state of a class without changing the class.

Privileged aspects have access to implementation details, so you should exercise restraint when using this feature. If the classes change their implementation—which they're legitimately entitled to do—the aspect accessing such implementation details will need to be changed as well.

6.5 Summary

Aspect-association constructs offer elegant ways to manage the state of an aspect with respect to the associated object, control flow, or type. This mechanism—although a little difficult to understand at first—provides the necessary machinery to write complex aspects. Using this feature, you can create reusable aspects more effectively while knowing only minimal information about the target systems.

As you begin to realize the benefits of aspect-oriented programming, you may find that multiple aspects, such as authorization and transaction management, affect the same parts of the system. Aspect precedence will help you coordinate these aspects so that they function correctly.

The privileged-aspect feature will help you handle situations where you need to access the private members of classes. But in this case, it's perhaps more important to understand the negative implications of using the technique.

So far, we've mainly focused on the traditional AspectJ syntax and compile-time weaving. But AspectJ provides alternative syntax and weaving models that can be valuable for certain kinds of applications. We'll devote the next three chapters to exploring these new features.

7 Diving into the @AspectJ syntax

This chapter covers

- Mapping pointcuts
- Mapping dynamic and static crosscutting
- Understanding the limitations of the syntax

One-size-fits-all usually fits nothing! Over the last few years, the AspectJ community realized that a single syntax style and one weaving model didn't meet all the needs of real-world AOP usage. AspectJ responded to the real world's needs by offering pragmatic choices for syntax and weaving models. With the new choices, using AspectJ is easier than ever before. In this chapter, we'll examine a major alternative to the traditional syntax. The next chapter will deal with weaving models.

Until now in this book, we've focused on the traditional syntax, which excels in its power, expressiveness, and compactness. But using it requires a leap of faith, due to the need to use a different compiler and other tools (mainly an IDE) that can understand such syntax. For a pragmatic adoption, we need a smoother path and reduced dependency on specialized tools. The @AspectJ (often pronounced as "at

AspectJ") syntax offers the option of compiling source code with a plain Java compiler and makes it easier to work with any Java IDE. If you're in a situation where you can't afford to make an outright switch to the AspectJ compiler, the @AspectJ syntax offers you a compelling alternative.

The @AspectJ syntax was added due to the merging of AspectWerkz with AspectJ. The users of AspectWerkz made it clear that the syntax aided in simplifying AOP adoption. The @AspectJ syntax uses plain Java along with annotations to express crosscutting elements. Although the syntax tends to be somewhat verbose and slightly less powerful, aspects written in @AspectJ syntax can be compiled using a plain Java compiler. Later, you can use the binary or load-time weaver to weave classes and aspects together. The @AspectJ syntax thus provides a pragmatic balance between compactness and toolability.

The Spring Framework heavily utilizes the @AspectJ syntax within its proxy-based AOP framework without needing an AspectJ weaver—not even binary or load-time. Another new syntax in Spring—schema-style AOP—was inspired by @AspectJ, making it possible to use @AspectJ-style aspects without the need for annotations so that they can be used in projects using a version prior to Java 5. We'll explore how Spring utilizes the @AspectJ syntax and schema-style AOP in chapter 9, which uses the information in this chapter as its basis.

In chapter 2, we looked at a simple example illustrating the @AspectJ syntax. In this chapter, we'll delve deeper into this syntax. We'll examine the purpose of the @AspectJ syntax, mapping of the various crosscutting constructs, and limitations of the syntax. We'll then put all this information together to help you choose the right syntax given your situation. Let's start with an overview of @AspectJ syntax.

7.1 Syntax overview

The most important driving force and raison d'être of the @AspectJ syntax is keeping the code plain Java. It does so by keeping crosscutting information in annotations on Java elements. This allows Java compilers and tools expecting plain Java code to work with aspects. Figure 7.1 shows the general mapping between the traditional and the @AspectJ syntax.

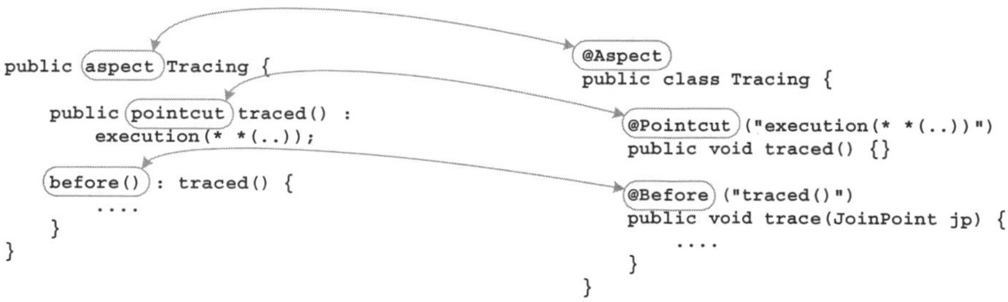

```
public aspect Tracing {

    public pointcut traced() :
        execution(* *(..));

    before() : traced() {
        ....
    }
}
```

```
@Aspect
public class Tracing {

    @Pointcut("execution(* *(..))")
    public void traced() {}

    @Before("traced()")
    public void trace(JoinPoint jp) {
        ....
    }
}
```

Figure 7.1 The mapping between the traditional and @AspectJ syntax. Each crosscutting element is mapped to a Java element carrying a specific annotation. Any information that can't be expressed in Java alone is expressed as parameters to the annotations.

As figure 7.1 shows, the general idea behind the design of the @AspectJ syntax is to find a suitable Java element and annotate it to express the crosscutting characteristic. The driving principles behind the @AspectJ syntax are the natural mapping of crosscutting elements, compatibility with Java, and early error detection. Let's see the reasons for each of these.

7.1.1 Natural mapping

The @AspectJ syntax uses similarities between AOP and OOP constructs to find a natural mapping for crosscutting constructs. For example, given the similarity between aspects and classes, (as discussed in section 6.1.1) a class with an annotation can serve as an aspect. Also, because a pointcut can be abstract and may declare parameters, a method makes a good candidate that can represent these characteristics. Most elements find a direct mapping from the traditional syntax into the @AspectJ syntax. But elements such as inter-type declarations need some adjustment. A few features, such as the privileged aspect, can't be mapped at all within the constraint of compiling using javac. Table 7.1 summarizes the mapping used by the @AspectJ syntax.

NOTE The annotations used by the @AspectJ syntax are a part of the aspectjrt.jar file. You'll need to put this jar in the classpath when you compile aspects written in this syntax.

The @AspectJ syntax utilizes many concepts from the traditional syntax. For example, although it doesn't use the `pointcut` keyword to define a pointcut, it uses the same pointcut expression language (with minor differences) inside an annotation. This makes learning the @AspectJ syntax easy after you understand the traditional syntax; all you need to know is the mapping between the traditional and the @AspectJ syntax.

Table 7.1 Crosscutting elements supported by the @AspectJ syntax and their mapped elements

Feature	Mapped element
Aspects	Class with `@Aspect` annotation
Pointcuts	Method with `@Pointcut` annotation
Advice	Method with `@Before`, `@After`, `@AfterReturning`, `@AfterThrowing`, or `@Around` annotation
Declaring parents	Field with `@DeclareMixin` and `@DeclareParents` annotation
Declaring errors and warnings	Field with `@DeclareError` and `@DeclareWarning` annotation
Introducing data and methods	Not supported
Exception handling	Not supported
Privileged aspects	Not supported

7.1.2 Java compatibility

Aspects expressed using the @AspectJ syntax can be compiled using regular javac. This lets existing IDEs work better with such code, because they can always treat aspects as regular Java code. The IDE can compile the code using a Java compiler and weave in the classes and aspects in a post-processing step (you can also use the load-time weaver). Other tools, such as code-coverage tools (such as Clover) and code analyzers (for example, PMD and FindBugs) work well, again due to the fact that they treat the code as plain Java code. Obviously, these tools won't understand the semantics of the annotations; but the tools won't balk at @Aspect-expressed aspects, and that is sufficient in most cases.

Although you can compile the code for @AspectJ aspects using javac, the Java compiler can't understand the semantics associated with the @AspectJ annotations. As a result, you still need the AspectJ weaver to perform binary weaving during build-time or load-time. Note that if you use ajc to compile the aspects written using @AspectJ syntax, it performs weaving at build-time, obviating the need for a special weaving step.

7.1.3 Early error detection

The @AspectJ syntax is designed to give as many errors and warnings as soon as possible even when you compile using the javac compiler. This design dictates using the Java constructs as much as possible instead of using expressions buried in strings. Consider a *hypothetical* plain-Java AspectJ syntax that uses a string whose value is the text for the corresponding aspect defined using the traditional syntax (note that there are many other possibilities for this kind of syntax). For example, the following class could represent an aspect *in plain Java*:

```
@Aspect("public aspect SQLPeformanceMonitoring {"
      + "    public pointcut monitored() : call(* java.sql.*.*(..)); "
      + "    Object around() : monitored() {"
      + "        ... "
      + "    }"
      + "}")
public class SomeClass {
}
```

This hypothetical syntax could work, and it's trivial to learn once you understand the traditional syntax. But a big drawback would be the lack of compile-time checks for the code expressed using the string, if you use javac to compile such code. Any syntactical (or even spelling) errors in code expressed in the string will be reported only at the weave time, which may be as late as deployment time if you use load-time weaving (discussed in the next chapter). For example, any errors in the body of the `around()` advice will go undetected during compilation using javac. This consideration has led to a few deviations from a straightforward mapping from the traditional syntax (a good example is the `if()` pointcut, discussed in section 7.3.2).

Let's examine the various crosscutting elements expressed in the @AspectJ syntax.

7.2 Mapping aspects

In AspectJ, an aspect is the unit of modularization for crosscutting concerns and consists of elements such as pointcuts and advice. In @AspectJ, a class marked with the `@Aspect` annotation represents an aspect. Such a class can contain other crosscutting elements such as pointcuts and advice, also expressed using the @AspectJ syntax. Here is the general form of aspect declaration using @AspectJ syntax:

```
@Aspect(["<perthis|pertarget|percflow|percflowbelow>(Pointcut) |
          [pertypewithin(TypePattern)]"])
[access specification] [abstract] [static] class <AspectName>
    [extends class-or-aspect-name]
    [implements interface-list] {
    ... aspect body
}
```

One difference from a regular class is the annotation attached to the class that indicates to an AspectJ weaver that the class is to be treated as an aspect. Let's look at a few examples. The following snippet declares a singleton abstract aspect:

```
@Aspect
public abstract class Monitoring {
    ...
}
```

This declaration is equivalent to the following aspect expressed using the traditional syntax:

```
public abstract aspect Monitoring {
    ...
}
```

The next snippet declares a subaspect of the previous abstract aspect:

```
@Aspect
public class BankingMonitoring extends Monitoring {
    ...
}
```

The equivalent aspect expressed using the traditional syntax is as follows:

```
public aspect BankingMonitoring extends Monitoring {
    ...
}
```

NOTE Only classes, not other types such as interfaces and enums, can be marked with the `@Aspect` annotation.

Due to the special semantics associated with aspects, there are a few restrictions on the class declaration to match the aspect semantics. (See section 6.1.2 for a discussion of differences between aspects and classes.) In particular, the class must do the following:

- Include a non-arg public constructor if the class defines a constructor.
- Not extend a concrete class carrying the `@Aspect` annotation. This matches the restriction that an aspect can't extend another concrete aspect.

- Not declare a generic parameter unless it's an abstract aspect. This matches the restriction that only abstract aspects are allowed to declare generic type parameters.
- Be marked `static` if it's a nested class. This matches the restriction that an inner aspect must be `static` (that is, not bound to an instance of the enclosing type).

The `@Aspect` annotation has an optional property that you can use to specify aspect association, as we'll discuss next.

7.2.1 Specifying aspect association

The aspect association construct lets you express association with objects, control flow, and types. The aspect-association information is specified using the optional `value` attribute. For example, in the following aspect, the aspect specifies a `perthis()` association:

```
@Aspect("perthis(execution(* ajia.Account.*(..)))")
public class ConcurrencyControl {
    ...
}
```

You can similarly specify associations such as `pertarget()`, `percflow()`, and `percflowbelow()` as well as `pertypewithin()`.

You may need to access associated aspect instances. Let's see how you do that with the @AspectJ syntax.

7.2.2 Accessing the aspect instance

When you're using traditional-style aspects, you can access an aspect instance using the automatically added `aspectOf()` method (see section 6.2.6 for details). But the same scheme doesn't work when you're using the @AspectJ syntax, because a Java compiler can't understand the automatically added `aspectOf()` method and therefore will produce a compile-time error for code such as `ProfileAspect.aspectOf()`. The same issue exists with the `hasAspect()` method. @AspectJ syntax provides an alternative using the `org.aspectj.lang.Aspects` class, which contains `aspectOf()` and `hasAspect()` methods. Compared to the traditional syntax, there are two differences. You do the following:

- Invoke the method on the `Aspects` class instead of on the aspect.
- Pass the aspect's class as the first argument to each method.

For example, if you need an instance of the `ProfileAspect` aspect, you use `Aspects.aspectOf(ProfileAspect.class)`. For per-object or per-type aspects, you pass the object or the class for the type as the second argument. (See table 6.1 for details.) All other semantics match the traditional syntax.

7.2.3 Declaring aspect precedence

The traditional syntax offers the `declare precedence` construct to control precedence between aspects, as discussed in section 6.3.2. @AspectJ syntax offers the `@DeclarePrecedence` annotation for the same purpose, which you use as follows:

```
@Aspect
@DeclarePrecedence("ajia.HomeSecurityAspect, ajia.SaveEnergyAspect")
public class HomeSystemCoordinationAspect {
}
```

The `@DeclarePrecedence` annotation must be attached only to an aspect (a class with the `@Aspect` annotation). You set the annotation's `value` attribute to aspect type patterns separated by a comma—following the same rules as the traditional syntax. Note that you must use fully qualified aspect types unless the aspect resides in the same package as the aspect declaring precedence.

> **Not quite a direct mapping**
>
> Because the `value` attribute is of the `String` type, you can declare only one precedence per aspect. This is unlike the traditional syntax, where an aspect may include any number of `declare precedence` statements. Equivalent functionality in the @AspectJ syntax requires using multiple aspects, with each declaring a single precedence. In a future version of AspectJ, the attribute type may change to `String[]`, thus resolving this difference.

Crosscutting elements in an @AspectJ aspect must be expressed using annotated elements. Let's examine how the various crosscutting elements map to the @AspectJ syntax.

7.3 Mapping pointcuts

After you've defined your aspects, you'll want to add pointcuts to select join points and collect context at the selected join points. The @AspectJ syntax uses a method with a `@Pointcut` annotation to represent a pointcut. The `value` parameter of the annotation represents the pointcut expression. All other pointcut characteristics such as the name, access specification, abstractness, and parameters match with the corresponding characteristics of the method representing it. The pointcut expression used is the same as in the traditional syntax (see tables 3.11 to 3.16 for pointcut expression examples) except for two differences: the use of fully qualified type names and a special treatment of the `if()` pointcut.

Let's examine the syntax for abstract and concrete pointcuts.

7.3.1 Mapping abstract pointcuts

Abstract pointcuts allow you to write reusable aspects by letting subaspects provide a definition for those pointcuts. The @AspectJ syntax maps abstract pointcuts to an abstract method with the `@Pointcut` annotation without any annotation parameters (using the default value, instead). Here is the general form of abstract pointcut expressed in the @AspectJ syntax:

```
@Pointcut
[access specifier] abstract void pointcut-name([args]);
```

Because an abstract pointcut doesn't need a pointcut expression, the default value for the pointcut annotation suffices. The method representing the abstract pointcut must be declared to return `void`. Method parameters define the pointcut parameters that a concrete pointcut must collect as the join point context.

Let's look at a few examples. The following pointcut defines an abstract pointcut that doesn't declare any parameters:

```
@Pointcut
public abstract void readOperation();
```

This pointcut is equivalent to the following pointcut expressed in the traditional syntax:

```
public abstract pointcut readOperation();
```

The following pointcut declares two pointcut parameters:

```
@Pointcut
public abstract void accountOperation(Account account,
                                      float amount);
```

This pointcut is equivalent to the following pointcut expressed in the traditional syntax:

```
public abstract pointcut accountOperation(Account account,
                                          float amount);
```

The method-access specification can be `public`, `package` (default), or `protected`, but not `private`, following the rules for an abstract method.

7.3.2 Mapping concrete pointcuts

A concrete pointcut uses a pointcut expression to specify a join point selection criterion and collect join point context. The @AspectJ syntax maps concrete pointcuts to a concrete method with the `@Pointcut` annotation, which specifies the pointcut expression. The method body for a concrete pointcut is empty, because the method is a placeholder without any significance for the code inside it (except the `if()` pointcut, which we'll discuss shortly). Here is the general form for the pointcut:

```
@Pointcut("<pointcut-definition>")
[access specifier] void <pointcut-name>([args]) {}
```

Here is an example of a simple concrete pointcut:

```
@Pointcut("execution(public void set*(*))")
public void setter() {}
```

This pointcut is equivalent to the following pointcut expressed using the traditional syntax:

```
public pointcut setter() : execution(public void set*(*));
```

We'll now examine the specific requirements for pointcuts written using the @AspectJ syntax.

REQUIREMENTS FOR POINTCUT EXPRESSIONS

The pointcut expression for a concrete pointcut is the same as in the traditional syntax (as described in section 3.4), except for two differences:

- Type names, if any, must be fully qualified, unless the type resides in the same package as the aspect or belongs to the `java.lang` package. You can't use imported type names.
- If you use an `if()` pointcut, it must be of the `if(true)`, `if(false)`, or `if()` form. If you use the last form, the method body must specify the selection criteria for the pointcut, as we'll discuss later in this chapter.

You're required to use fully qualified type names because `import` statements aren't retained in compiled byte code. That makes it impossible for the Aspect weaver to deduce the type from the pointcut expression string. For example, the following pointcut must specify the fully qualified type names even if the corresponding types are part of `import` statements:

```
@Pointcut("call(* java.sql.Connection.*(..))")
public void connectionOperation() {}
```

This pointcut is equivalent to the following pointcut:

```
public pointcut connectionOperation()
    : call(* java.sql.Connection.*(..))
```

It's also equivalent to the following pointcut defined in a file that imports the used type:

```
import java.sql.*;
...

public pointcut connectionOperation ()
    : call(* Connection.*(..))
```

> **Weaving and error detection**
>
> Although the @AspectJ syntax promotes early error detection, due to the fact that pointcut expressions are strings, errors in them aren't reported until those strings are parsed. If you use ajc to compile the aspects, it parses pointcuts immediately and issues any errors. If you use AJDT, it also reports any errors immediately. But if you use the binary or load-time weaver, parsing and (consequently) error detection occur at that time.

REQUIREMENTS FOR COMPILATION

Pointcut parameters expressed as part of the method parameters must be bound using the same pointcut expression. For example, the following pointcut binds the pointcut context using the `this()` and `args()` pointcuts:

```
@Pointcut("execution(public * ajia.banking.domain.Account.*(float))"
        + " && this(account) && args(amount)")
public void accountOperation(Account account, float amount) {}
```

If you use javac to compile code that uses method parameters (such as in the previous snippet), you must use either the `-g:vars` (or `-g`, which is a superset of `-g:vars`) flag or the `argNames` parameter to the `@Pointcut` annotation. This is required because the Java compiler doesn't preserve argument names in the compiled code. As a result, the AspectJ weaver can't determine the correspondence between the method parameter names (which are lost in the byte code) and identifiers used in the pointcut expression (which, being part of the annotation value, are preserved). Using `-g:vars` instructs the compiler to preserve argument names in the compiled byte code. The use of this flag leads to slightly larger class files; but no degradation occurs in the runtime performance of such a class, making the use of this flag a non-issue in real-world applications.

If you can't (or prefer not to) use the `-g:vars` flag, you need to use the `argNames` parameter to preserve the same information. For example, the following pointcut redefines the `accountOperation()` pointcut to use the `argNames` pointcut parameter:

```
@Pointcut(value="execution(public * ajia.banking.domain.Account.*(float)) "
              + "&& this(account) && args(amount)",
          argNames="account, amount")
public void accountOperation(Account account, float amount) {}
```

The value of the `argNames` parameter is a comma-separated list of the method parameter names in the same order as defined by the method. Because `argNames` duplicates parameter names, there is a chance that it may become inconsistent when, for example, method parameters are rearranged without rearranging the `argNames` parameters value. Therefore, I recommend that you use the `-g:vars` (or `-g`) flag to compile @AspectJ-styled aspects.

Let's complete our discussion of pointcuts by examining the special treatment provided to the `if()` pointcut.

SPECIAL TREATMENT OF THE IF() POINTCUT

In the traditional syntax, you include the conditional statement in the `if()` pointcut definition. With @AspectJ, you must provide the same statement in a method. This difference in style allows more checks to be performed at compile-time even when you use a Java compiler. For example, consider the pointcut defined using the traditional syntax:

```
pointcut debugEnabled() : if(logLevel >= DEBUG);
```

The same pointcut in @AspectJ is expressed as follows:

```
@Pointcut("if()")
public static boolean debugEnabled() {
    return logLevel >= DEBUG;
}
```

The pointcut expression in the @AspectJ syntax is `"if()"` as part of the annotation value. The method declares that it returns a `boolean` and the body is the expression used in the traditional syntax. The method used for the `if()` pointcut must be `public` and static. You can then use this named pointcut as a part of other pointcuts, such as the following:

```
@Pointcut("traced() && debugEnabled()")
public void debugTraced() { }
```

You can also rewrite the same pointcut to avoid the explicit debugEnabled() pointcut, as follows:

```
@Pointcut("traced() && if()")
public static boolean debugTraced() {
    return logLevel >= DEBUG;
}
```

Here, the if() pointcut is part of the expression and supplies the condition that goes with it as part of the method body.

Note that the if() pointcut can use pointcut context as well as the reflective join point objects same way as in the traditional syntax. For example, the following pointcut uses the collected context in evaluating the condition:

```
@Pointcut("if() "
        + "&& execution(public void "
        + "             ajia.banking.domain.Account.debit(float)) "
        + "&& args(amount)")
public static boolean largeWithdrawl(float amount) {
    return amount > LARGE_AMOUNT_THRESHOLD;
}
```

Similarly, if the pointcut logic needs to utilize a join point object equivalent to thisJoinPoint, thisJoinPointStaticPart, or thisEnclosingJoinPointStaticPart, it must declare a parameter of the corresponding types (JoinPoint, JoinPoint.StaticPart, or JoinPoint.EnclosingStaticPart) and use it inside the method body. For example, the following pointcut selects the execution of join points whose return type is a primitive:

```
@Pointcut("if() && execution(* *(..))")
public static boolean returnsPrimitive(JoinPoint.StaticPart jp) {
    return ((MethodSignature)jp.getSignature())
            .getReturnType().isPrimitive();
}
```

Because the method corresponding to a pointcut that uses if() must be static, and because an advice may not be declared as a static method (as we'll discuss in section 7.4), an if() pointcut may not be part of pointcut expression specified with an advice. For example, the following code leads to weave-time errors:

```
@Before("traced() && if()")
public void trace(JoinPoint jp) { // error
    ...
}
```

You can use two special forms of the if() pointcut without the accompanying method body: if(true) and if(false). This simplifies turning an advice on or off. For example, the inclusion of `&& if(false)` in the following snippet provides a quick way to turn off the advice:

```
@Before("traced() && if(false)")
public trace(JoinPoint jp) {
    ...
}
```

Why the special treatment for if()?

Consider the following code segment, using a hypothetical alternative that follows the same style of expressing the pointcut expression as an annotation value:

```
// not a real syntax; spelling and code errors are deliberate
@Pointcut("if(logLeval >== DEBUGG)")
public void debugEnabled() { }
```

The two spelling mistakes and the use of a non-existent operator will go unnoticed by a plain Java compiler, for whom the annotation value carries no meaning other than being a string value. The errors will be revealed only at weave-time. AspectJ chooses syntax that lets such errors be caught at compile-time.

Now that we've completed our discussion of pointcuts, we'll move on to advice expressed using @AspectJ syntax, which builds on the pointcut syntax.

7.4 Mapping dynamic crosscutting constructs

Like a pointcut, an advice is represented with a method. This shouldn't be surprising considering the commonality between advice and methods, as discussed in section 4.2.1. The method representing an advice carries a `@Before`, `@After`, `@AfterReturning`, `@AfterThrowing`, or `@Around` annotation to denote the kind of advice the method is implementing. The `value` attribute of the annotation denotes the associated pointcut (which can be named or anonymous), whereas the method body denotes the advice to be executed.

As in the traditional syntax, methods that stand in for advice

- Should not return a value (they must return `void`), except for the around advice. This matches the traditional syntax, where advice may not return a value unless it's an around advice.
- May declare that it throws an exception similar to the traditional syntax.
- Should not be declared `static`. This matches the traditional syntax, where advice behaves like an instance method, because it has access to the `this` variable that points to the aspect instance.

Because a method has a name, that name is also the advice's name. Note that in the traditional syntax, advice doesn't have an inherent name. But advice in the traditional syntax may be annotated with `@AdviceName` to assign it a name, thus matching the @AspectJ syntax.

Although all advice constructs follow common ideas, each has a few peculiarities. We'll consider them separately.

7.4.1 The before advice

The before advice is created using a method with the `@Before` annotation. It takes the following general form:

```
@Before("<pointcut>")
public void <advice-name>([arguments]) {
    ... advice body
}
```

The value of the `@Before` annotation specifies the pointcut associated with the advice. The pointcut may be named (referring to a pointcut defined in the same or a different aspect) or may be a pointcut expression. The method used as advice must be `public` and must return `void`. The advice name doesn't matter from AspectJ's point of view; but you should provide a meaningful name that represents the logic carried by the advice. The optional arguments to the method represent the join point context.

NOTE The downloadable sources contain JUnit tests that may come in handy when you experiment with source code.

Let's look at a few examples of the before advice with anonymous and named pointcuts as well as with reflective access to join point information.

ADVISING WITH ANONYMOUS POINTCUTS

The first example specifies an anonymous pointcut and uses no join point context. The aspect in listing 7.1 advises the execution of any method in the system to produce a heartbeat so that monitoring tools can check if the system is alive.

Listing 7.1 System monitoring: using an anonymous pointcut

```
package ajia.monitoring;

import org.aspectj.lang.annotation.Aspect;
import org.aspectj.lang.annotation.Before;

@Aspect
public class SystemHealthMonitor {
    HeartBeatListener heartBeatListener
        = new HeartBeatListener();

    @Before("execution(* *(..)) && !within(ajia.monitoring.*)")
    public void beatHeart() {
        heartBeatListener.beat();
    }
}
```

The anonymous pointcut selects all the methods except those in the `ajia.monitoring` package to avoid infinite recursion that would result from advising the `beat()` method. Anonymous pointcuts are useful if they're short and simple. But in most cases, you'll want to use a named pointcut.

> **An advice join point isn't a method join point**
>
> The snippet `execution(* *(..)) && !within(ajia.monitoring.*)` in listing 7.1 won't select the `beatHeart()` method that stands in for an advice. Although `beatHeart()` is a method, from AspectJ's perspective, it really is an advice. Hence, the join point corresponds to its advice-execution join point and not a method execution. You could select such a "method" using the `adviceexecution()` pointcut discussed in chapter 3.

ADVISING WITH NAMED POINTCUTS

By separating the definition of the pointcut from the advice that uses it, you create a reusable pointcut and make your code more readable. The @AspectJ syntax provides a natural way to express this recommended approach. Let's modify the previous aspect to use a named pointcut, as shown in listing 7.2.

Listing 7.2 System monitoring: using a named pointcut

```
package ajia.monitoring;

import org.aspectj.lang.annotation.Aspect;
import org.aspectj.lang.annotation.Pointcut;
import org.aspectj.lang.annotation.Before;

@Aspect
public class SystemHealthMonitor {
    HeartBeatListener heartBeatListener
        = new HeartBeatListener();

    @Pointcut("execution(* *.*(..)) && !within(ajia.monitoring.*)")
    public void aliveOperation() {}

    @Before("aliveOperation()")
    public void beatHeart() {
        heartBeatListener.beat();
    }
}
```

Because you use a named pointcut, you may use it for more than one advice and use it as part of other pointcut definitions. Note that, as discussed in section 7.3.2, because @AspectJ requires that an `if()` pointcut must be named—except for special cases of `if(true)` and `if(false)`—using a named pointcut is the only choice.

USING A REFLECTIVE JOIN POINT CONTEXT

So far, you've avoided using the join point context, which worked fine for the simple heartbeat-monitoring example. But most advice need the join point context. Let's first consider reflective access to join point information, which, in traditional style, you obtain using the `thisJoinPoint`, `thisJoinPointStaticPart`, and `thisEnclosingJoinPointStaticPart` special variables that are available in every advice. In @AspectJ styled aspects, you can't use these variables due to the fundamental design constraint on @AspectJ syntax: the code must be compilable using a plain Java compiler. Such a compiler won't understand special variables. Therefore, AspectJ requires the advice to declare method parameters of the corresponding type and use those parameters inside advice. The weaver ensures that those parameters are appropriately passed when advice is executed.

The simple aspect shown in listing 7.3 prints entry into each method. This requires the method name to be available in the join point's static context.

Listing 7.3 Tracing aspect utilizing the join point context

```
package ajia.tracing;

import ...

@Aspect
public class Tracing {
    @Pointcut("execution(* *.*(..))")
    public void traced() {}

    @Before("traced()")
    public void trace(JoinPoint jp) {
        System.out.println("Entering " + jp);
    }
}
```

In the advice, you get reflective access to the dynamic context of the current join point by declaring a method parameter of type `JoinPoint`. When the advice is executed, the information in this variable is exactly the same as you get in `thisJoinPoint` in the traditional syntax. The equivalent advice in the traditional style would use the special `thisJoinPoint` variable available in every advice as follows:

```
before() : traced() {
    System.out.println("Entering " + thisJoinPoint);
}
```

You can similarly declare a parameter of type `JoinPoint.StaticPart` to obtain static information associated with the current join point, logically the same as the `thisJoinPointStaticPart` (which would make more sense in the previous example, because the advice isn't using the dynamic information anyway). Obtaining the enclosing context (equivalent to `thisEnclosingJoinPointStaticPart` in the traditional syntax) is interesting. Because the type of both `thisJoinPointStaticPart` and `thisEnclosingJoinPointStaticPart` is `JoinPoint.StaticPart`, the weaver can't determine the objects you intend if it sees two variables of the same type. If the advice needs to obtain the enclosing join point context, it must declare a variable of type `JoinPoint.EnclosingStaticPart` (which is a subtype of `JoinPoint.StaticPart`).

USING A TYPED JOIN POINT CONTEXT

You can always obtain the join point context using reflective access, but this approach suffers from issues such as lack of compile-time safety, reduced performance, and difficult programming (see section 4.5). A better approach is to use pointcuts such as `this()` and `args()`, which expose the join point context with more specific types. The @AspectJ syntax requires that the needed join point context be declared as method

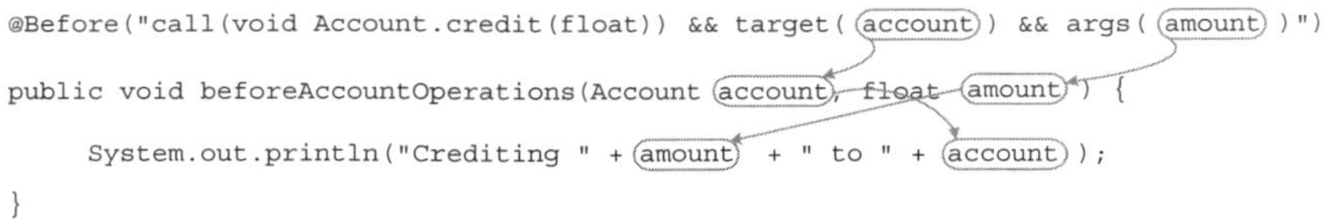

```
@Before("call(void Account.credit(float)) && target( account ) && args( amount ) ")

public void beforeAccountOperations(Account account, float amount ) {

    System.out.println("Crediting " + amount + " to " + account );

}
```

Figure 7.2 Collecting context using anonymous pointcuts. The method parameter declares the needed context, and the context-collecting pointcut binds those parameters to the join point context.

parameters the same way a traditional advice declares advice parameters. The pointcut must then use the same parameter names to collect context in pointcut. Figure 7.2 shows the scheme for collecting context using anonymous pointcuts.

Let's consider an example where the goal is to log all operations on a JDBC connection (see listing 7.4). The log statement should contain information about the connection object.

Listing 7.4 Collecting the join point context using an anonymous pointcut

```
package ajia.monitoring;

import ...

@Aspect
public class ConnectionMonitor {
    @Before("call(* java.sql.Connection.*(..)) && target(connection)")
    public void monitorUse(Connection connection) {
        System.out.println("About to use " + connection);
    }
}
```

In this aspect, the advice needs access to the target of any call to `Connection`. Therefore, the advice declares a method parameter of the `Connection` type with `connection` as the variable name. The pointcut then uses a `target()` pointcut to bind that variable. You can, of course, use a named pointcut, where the pointcut binds the context and makes it available to the advice. Figure 7.3 shows the scheme for collecting context using named pointcuts.

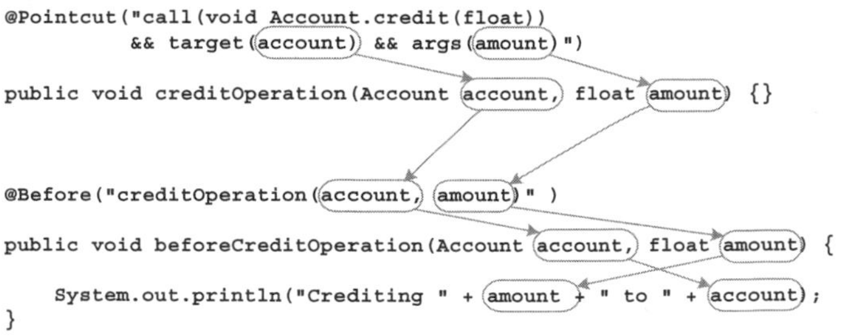

```
@Pointcut("call(void Account.credit(float))
        && target(account) && args(amount)")

public void creditOperation(Account account, float amount) {}


@Before("creditOperation(account, amount)" )

public void beforeCreditOperation(Account account, float amount) {

    System.out.println("Crediting " + amount + " to " + account);
}
```

Figure 7.3 Context collection using named pointcuts. The pointcut method parameter declares the needed context, and the context-collecting pointcut binds those parameters to the join point context. The advice then maps that context.

Listing 7.5 shows the modified aspect that uses a named pointcut.

Listing 7.5 Collecting the join point context using a named pointcut

```
package ajia.monitoring;

import ...

@Aspect
public class ConnectionMonitor {
    @Pointcut("call(* java.sql.Connection.*(..)) "
            + "&& target(connection)")
    public void connectionOperation(Connection connection) {}

    @Before("connectionOperation(connection)")
    public void monitorUse(Connection connection) {
        System.out.println("About to use " + connection);
    }
}
```

In the preceding aspect, the `connectionOperation()` pointcut binds the connection variable using a `target()` pointcut. Note that you can mix reflective access to join point information with that obtained using context-binding pointcuts by including one or more variables of appropriate reflective access types. For example, Listing 7.6 shows enhanced connection monitoring through use of static context available with the join point as well as the information about the surrounding join point.

Listing 7.6 Mixing reflective access with collected context

```
package ajia.monitoring;

import ...

@Aspect
public class ConnectionMonitor {
    @Pointcut("call(* java.sql.Connection.*(..))"
            + " && target(connection)")
    public void connectionOperation(Connection connection) {}

    @Before("connectionOperation(connection)")
    public void monitorUse(JoinPoint.StaticPart jpsp,
                           JoinPoint.EnclosingStaticPart jpesp,
                           Connection connection) {
        System.out.println("About to use " + connection
                           + " to perform " + jpsp.toShortString()
                           + " called from " + jpesp.toShortString());
    }
}
```

That completes our exploration of the before advice along with many common concepts applicable to all kinds of advice in @AspectJ. Let's now move our attention to other kinds of advice, starting with the after advice.

7.4.2 The after advice

In AspectJ, the after advice has three variations: after (finally), after returning, and after throwing. The after (finally) advice, which executes regardless of how the join point execution completes (normally or by throwing an exception), is similar to before advice from the code point of view because the information available to the advice is exactly the same. The only difference is the annotation used: `@After`. In all the examples in the previous section, replacing `@Before` with `@After` will modify the application of the advice; everything else can remain the same. For example, listing 7.7 shows listing 7.5 modified to use the advice (modifications are in bold).

Listing 7.7 Using after advice with @AspectJ syntax

```
package ajia.monitoring;

import ....

@Aspect
public class ConnectionMonitor {
    @Pointcut("call(* java.sql.Connection.*(..)) && target(connection)")
    public void connectionOperation(Connection connection) {}

    @After("connectionOperation(connection)")
    public void monitorUse(Connection connection) {
          System.out.println("Just used " + connection);
    }
}
```

The other two variations of after advice (after returning and after throwing) come in two sub-variations. The first variation uses the fact that the join point executes normally or by throwing an exception. The second variation collects either the returned object (for the after-returning advice) or the thrown exception (for the after-throwing advice).

EXPRESSING AFTER RETURNING AND AFTER THROWING

The first variation requires a trivial change: instead of using `@After`, you use `@AfterReturning` or `@AfterThrowing`, as shown in listing 7.8 (differences from listing 7.7 are in bold).

Listing 7.8 Using after returning and after throwing advice

```
package ajia.monitoring;

import ....

@Aspect
public class ConnectionMonitor {
    @Pointcut("call(* java.sql.Connection.*(..))"
          + " && target(connection)")
    public void connectionOperation(Connection connection) {}

    @AfterReturning("connectionOperation(connection)")
    public void monitorSuccessfulUse(Connection connection) {
        System.out.println("Just used " + connection
                          + " successfully");
    }

    @AfterThrowing("connectionOperation(connection)")
    public void monitorFailedUse(Connection connection) {
```

```
        System.out.println("Just used " + connection
                           + " but met with a failure");
    }
}
```

Often, you need to collect the result of the join point execution. The variation discussed next explains how to accomplish this.

COLLECTING THE RETURN VALUE AND THROWN EXCEPTION

The second variation of the after advice—the one that needs access to the returned object or the thrown exception—must be expressed differently. For the after-returning advice, you can specify an additional parameter to the method and use the parameter name as the value of the `returning` attribute of the annotation to that parameter name. The after-throwing advice is similar: you specify an exception type as the method parameter and use the name of the parameter as the value of the `throwing` attribute.

Let's modify the example in the listing 7.8 to collect the return value and thrown exception. Listing 7.9 shows the resulting aspect.

Listing 7.9 Collecting the return value and thrown exception

```
package ajia.monitoring;

import ....

@Aspect
public class ConnectionMonitor {
    @Pointcut("call(* java.sql.Connection.*(..))"
            + " && target(connection)")
    public void connectionOperation(Connection connection) {}

    @AfterReturning(value="connectionOperation(connection)",
                    returning="ret")
    public void monitorSuccessfulUse(Connection connection,
                                     Object ret) {
        System.out.println("Just used " + connection
                           + " successfully which returned " + ret);
    }

    @AfterThrowing(value="connectionOperation(connection)",
                   throwing="ex")
    public void monitorFailedUse(Connection connection,
                                 Exception ex) {
        System.out.println("Just used " + connection
                           + " but met with a failure of kind " + ex);
    }
}
```

In the code, you explicitly use the `value` attribute. This is required because the annotation specification in Java lets you omit the attribute name only if a single value is specified and the attribute name is `value`. Also, note that the `pointcut` attribute is available, which you can use in place of `value`. If both `pointcut` and `value` attributes are specified, the `pointcut` attribute takes precedence.

The type of the return value or the exception specified limits the advice applicability to where the return object or the thrown exception is assignable to the specified type. For example, instead of specifying `Object` as the return value type, if you specify `Statement`, only methods that return `Statement` or its subtype will be selected. This behavior is identical to that seen with the traditional syntax.

The last kind of advice—around advice—comes with interesting peculiarities owing to its power. Let's look at it to complete our discussion of dynamic crosscutting support in @AspectJ.

7.4.3 The around advice

An around advice in @AspectJ is represented by a method with an `@Around` annotation. The method must be `public` and may return a value. The rules governing the return value are the same as the rules in the traditional syntax. Specifically, the return value must be compatible with all matching join points. For example, the method may return `void` only if all matching join points return `void`. Similarly, the method may return `Collection` only if all matching join points return `Collection` or its subtype. The method may also return `Object`, where the matching join points may return any type and the weaver takes care of necessary unboxing and casting.

PROCEEDING WITH THE ORIGINAL JOIN POINT EXECUTION

What happens when you want to implement the advice logic and want to proceed with the original join point? In the traditional syntax, you do so by using the special keyword `proceed()` in around advice. No such special keyword exists in @AspectJ-styled around advice. Instead, you must take the same approach as with `thisJoinPoint` and related variables. If you need to proceed with the original join point, you must declare the method to take a parameter of the `ProceedingJoinPoint` type (which extends `JoinPoint`).

The `ProceedingJoinPoint` interface provides two methods: `proceed()` and `proceed(Object[])`. The no-argument `proceed()` proceeds with the original join point with unaltered join point context (the execution object, method arguments, and so on). This approach is useful in the majority of cases, where there is no need to alter the context. Listing 7.10 shows a use of no-argument `proceed()` (you'll use this aspect in a running example in the next chapter, where you'll define a concrete subaspect for it).

Listing 7.10 Performance monitoring aspect using an `around()` advice

```
package ajia.monitoring;

import ...

@Aspect
public abstract class Monitoring {
    @Pointcut
    public abstract void monitored();

    @Around("monitored()")
    public Object measureTime(ProceedingJoinPoint pjp)
```

```
            throws Throwable {
        long startTime = System.nanoTime();
        Object ret = pjp.proceed();
        long endTime = System.nanoTime();
        System.out.println("Method "
                       + pjp.getSignature().toShortString()
                       + " took " + (endTime-startTime));
        return ret;
    }
}
```

Notice that the `measureTime()` method declares that it throws a `Throwable`. This is required because `proceed()` declares that it throws `Throwable` to accommodate for exceptions a join point may throw. For example, a join point invoked by calling `proceed()` may throw `SQLException` or `IOException`. The generic `ProceedingJoinPoint.proceed()` can't know about the join points' exception characteristics and, to accommodate every join point, declares that it may throw a `Throwable`.

The rules of engagement are different if you need to proceed with the join point with altered context. Let's discuss those.

ALTERING THE JOIN POINT CONTEXT

In a few use cases of the around advice, the original join point must be invoked with an altered context. In those cases, you need to use the other form—`proceed(Object[])`—to pass the new context. The array passed to the call must contain elements in the following order:

- The `this` object or its replacement (only if you collected context using `this()`).
- The target object or its replacement (only if you collected context using `target()`).
- The join point's arguments or its replacements, in the same order as needed by the join point (even if you did *not* use the `args()` pointcut to collect them). A simple way to pass all arguments is to use the `getArgs()` method on the `ProceedingJoinPoint` object.

This logic is best illustrated by the following utility method, which takes care of these rules to form the array that can be passed to `proceed(Object[])`. The method expects that the caller passes in the objects to be used as `this`, target, and arguments. If you don't collect either of the first two, the caller passes a `null` for them:

```
public static Object[] formProceedArguments(Object thiz, Object target,
                                            Object[] arguments) {
    int argumentsOffset = 0;
    if(thiz != null) { argumentsOffset++; }
    if(target != null) { argumentsOffset++; }
    Object[] jpContext = new Object[arguments.length + argumentsOffset];

    int currentIndex = 0;
    if(thiz != null) { jpContext[currentIndex++] = thiz; }
    if(target != null) { jpContext[currentIndex++] = target; }
```

```
    System.arraycopy(arguments, 0,
                     jpContext, argumentsOffset, arguments.length);
    return jpContext;
}
```

This scheme of proceeding with altered context is different from that used in the traditional style, where you pass objects matching the collected context. The @AspectJ style is especially weak when you need to alter the context collected by arguments, because you're forced to know the exact position of the argument you want to alter, in turn forcing the advice to know too much about the join point. For example, imagine an advice to two methods, with the first method taking a `PaymentService` object as the first argument and the other method taking it as the second argument. If you want the methods to proceed with an alternative payment service, you must set the first parameter for the first method and the second parameter for the second method, forcing the advice to examine details of the join point. In the traditional syntax, you invoke `proceed()` with the parameter corresponding to the service collected. In that case, the decision of collecting the `PaymentService` argument from the two methods resides with the pointcut, which is the right place to know more about the selected join point.

That completes our discussion of dynamic crosscutting. To summarize, dynamic crosscutting is well supported in the @AspectJ syntax. All the things that you can do in the traditional syntax can be done with the @AspectJ syntax. Yes, the approach has a few differences, such as the `if()` pointcut and the invocation of `proceed()` in an around advice; but overall, @AspectJ is a fairly easy syntax to learn once you understand the traditional syntax.

Static crosscutting, on the other hand, has some significant differences imposed by the core design constraint of compilation with javac. Although some features are implemented in a straightforward way, others are complex. In addition, a few features aren't implemented in @AspectJ. Let's investigate.

7.5 Mapping static crosscutting

Recall that static crosscutting modifies the structure of a program. It comes in many forms: introducing members, declaring new types as parent type, attaching annotations, compile-time errors and warnings, and exception softening. Static crosscutting significantly relies on compile-time behavior. As a result, not all features can be implemented in @AspectJ.

We'll first look at mapping of weave-time declarations. Then, we'll examine how @AspectJ maps the `declare parents` feature. In the section that follows, we'll examine the features that aren't available with the @AspectJ syntax.

7.5.1 Mapping weave-time declarations

You declare weave-time errors and warnings in @AspectJ by declaring a `static final` member of the `String` type annotated with a `@DeclareError` or `@DeclareWarning` annotation. The value of the string is the message emitted by the weaver upon detecting the occurrence of a matching join point; the annotation attribute specifies the pointcut for which errors and warning are to be emitted. For example, the following snippet results in the issue of an error for every join point matching the `callToUnsafeCode()` pointcut:

```
@DeclareError("callToUnsafeCode()")
static final String unsafeCodeUsageError
          = "This third-party code is known to result in a crash";
```

Similarly, the following snippet leads to a warning for each join point matching the `callToBlockingOperations()` pointcut:

```
@DeclareWarning("callToBlockingOperations()")
static final String blockingCallFromAWTWarning
          = "Please ensure you are not calling this from the AWT thread";
```

Note that AspectJ requires you to mark the field associated with the `@DeclareError` or `@DeclareWarning` as `static` and `final`. This ensures that the variable remains unmodified during program execution. Otherwise, confusion may exist between the message in the source file and its runtime value. Further, the string specified must be a literal and not a result of a call to a `static` method. For example, the following code is in error:

```
@DeclareWarning("callToBlockingOperations()") // error
static final String blockingCallFromAWTWarning
                   = Warnings.blockCallWarning();
```

This constraint ensures that the weaver can access the message string without executing any methods.

7.5.2 Mapping declare parents

The @AspectJ syntax offers limited but useful support for static-crosscutting constructs aimed at type modification. With the traditional syntax, it's possible to use `declare parents` statements to add new parent types (class or interface) to a set of existing types (see section 5.2 for details). An AspectJ weaver can then take into account the effect of such statements during code compilation.

For example, if the `Account` type is declared to have `Entity` as a parent, the AspectJ compiler lets an `Account` object be assigned to a variable of `Entity` type. The Java compiler, on the other hand, can't understand the meaning behind a declaration expressed in an annotation and won't allow such assignments without an explicit typecast. Therefore, you'll see some significant differences in how `declare parents` is supported in the two syntaxes.

The support for declaring parents comes though the `@DeclareMixin` annotation. This annotation mixes an interface into a matching set of types and delegates the implementation to a specified object. To mix in a set of types, you annotate a factory method with this annotation and specify a type-pattern to select types being mixed-in as its `value` attribute. The return type of the method (which must be an interface) is mixed in with the matched types. The AspectJ weaver uses the object returned by the method to delegate the implementation for the mixed-in interface.

Note that @AspectJ syntax also supports the `@DeclareParents` annotation. But because `@DeclareParents` can't implement the exact equivalent of the `declare parents` construct and may mislead developers into believing they're equivalent, `@DeclareMixin` is the preferred approach. In the future, `@DeclareParents` may be deprecated.

DECLARING PARENTS FOR MARKER INTERFACES

Declaring parents for marker interfaces (interfaces without any methods) requires that the factory method return a `null` (you may return any other object, but since there is nothing to delegate to, the object will remain unused). For example, the following snippet declares all the types in the `ajia.banking.domain` package to implement `java.io.Serializable`:

```
@DeclareMixin("ajia.banking.domain.*")
public Serializable serializableMixin() {
    return null;
}
```

The declaration is equivalent to

```
declare parents: ajia.banking.domain.* implements Serializable;
```

If the interface isn't a marker interface, you need to consider additional constraints, as we'll discuss next.

DECLARING PARENTS FOR NON-MARKER INTERFACES

If the interface used in `@DeclareMixin` isn't a marker interface, either the classes selected by the type pattern must already implement the methods for the interface or the factory method must return an object to delegate the implementations for the interface methods. For example, consider the interface in listing 7.11.

Listing 7.11 The interface for any types that need the `id` property

```
package ajia.tracking;

public interface Identifiable {
    public Long getId();
    public void setId(Long id);
}
```

Now, consider the aspect in listing 7.12, which declares the `Identifiable` interface as the parent for each type in the `ajia.banking.domain` package.

Listing 7.12 Account-tracking aspect declaring parents to the tracked types

```
package ajia.tracking;

import ...

@Aspect
public class AccountTracking {
    @DeclareMixin("ajia.banking.domain.*")
    public Identifiable identifiableMixin() {
         return null;
```

```
    }

    ... advice

}
```

This snippet produces a `NullPointerException` unless all classes in the `ajia.banking.domain` package implement the `getId()` and `setId()` methods to satisfy the interface. Of course, requiring classes to already include an implementation isn't useful in most situations. Therefore, the method annotated with `@DeclareMixin` annotation must return an object that is used as the delegate. Listing 7.13 shows a modified aspect that doesn't require the selected types to implement the methods in the parent interface.

Listing 7.13 Declaring parents to use a default implementation

```
package ajia.tracking;

import org.aspectj.lang.annotation.Aspect;
import org.aspectj.lang.annotation.DeclareMixin;

@Aspect
public class AccountTracking {
    @DeclareMixin("ajia.banking.domain.*")
    public Identifiable identifiableMixin() {
        return new IdentifiableDefaultImpl();
    }
}
```

The AspectJ weaver uses the return object to delegate implementation of the interface to the types specified.

The annotated factory method is public and may be declared static. If it's an instance method, it can use aspect instance members while creating the delegate object. For example, if an aspect is injected with a dependency, that dependency may be passed on to the delegate object.

The method annotated with the `@DeclareMixin` annotation can declare a single parameter. In that case, AspectJ passes the object being mixed in as that parameter. You can pass this parameter to the delegate object being created if it needs access to the object being mixed in. In the following snippet, the `mixedIn` parameter is the object into which the `Auditor` interface is being mixed in:

```
@DeclareMixin("ajia.banking.domain.*")
public Auditor auditorMixin(Object mixedIn) {
    return new AuditorImpl(mixedIn);
}
```

By default, the return type of the factory method is the type to be mixed in. Only methods that belong to that interface are delegated to the returned object. You can control the interfaces to be mixed in by specifying the `interfaces` attribute of the annotation. In the following snippet, even if the `AuditorMonitoringAgent` interface implements the `Auditor` and `MonitoringAgent` interfaces and a few others, the matched types are mixed in only with the `Auditor` and `MonitoringAgent` interfaces:

```
@DeclareMixin(value="ajia.banking.domain.*",
              interfaces="{Auditor.class, MonitoringAgent.class}")
public AuditorMonitoringAgent mixin() {
    return new AuditorMonitoringAgentImpl();
}
```

So far, you've seen ways to introduce a parent type. But how do you use the introduced type? Specifically, how can you invoke methods specified in the declared parent interface on regular objects?

UTILIZING THE INTRODUCED TYPE

With a `@DeclareMixin` statement, the weaver modifies the byte code for the child types to make them implement the parent type. For example, the statement in the previous section modifies the `Account` class to implement the `Identifiable` interface. But the Java compiler doesn't know this. As a result, you'll get compilation errors if you assign an `Account` object to a variable of the `Identifiable` type. You can fix these errors by specifying a typecast, as shown in listing 7.14.

Listing 7.14 Using a typecast to use the new declared parent interface

```
package ajia.main;

import ...

public class Main {
    public static void main(String[] args) {
        Account account = new Account(1);
        Identifiable identifiableAccount = (Identifiable)account;
        identifiableAccount.setId(6L);
        System.out.println("Id is " + identifiableAccount.getId());
    }
}
```

Most likely, an advice will use the new parent type. In that case, you can avoid typecasts by using an appropriate context-collecting pointcut. For example, the code in listing 7.15 assigns the desired type to the collected context without the need for a typecast.

Listing 7.15 Using the declared parent in advice

```
package ajia.tracking;

import ...

@Aspect
public class AccountTracking {
    @DeclareMixin("ajia.banking.domain.*")
    public Identifiable identifiableMixin() {
        return new IdentifiableDefaultImpl();
    }

    @AfterReturning("execution(* ajia.banking.domain.*.*(..))"
                  + " && this(identifiable)")
    public void track(Identifiable identifiable) {
        System.out.println("Object with id " + identifiable.getId());
    }
}
```

Because the types in the `ajia.banking.domain` package are declared to have `Identifiable` as the parent interface, you know that the `this` instance associated with execution of the methods in those types will also match `Identifiable`. You therefore use an `Identifiable` variable in the advice declaration and bind it using the `this()` pointcut.

In summary, the `declare parents` feature comes with a few interesting twists. For most usages, the @AspectJ-based syntax offers sufficient power. But when you need full power, you must use the traditional syntax. There are other reasons to use the traditional syntax—primarily the lack of equivalent constructs in the @AspectJ syntax. Let's discuss the AspectJ features that aren't available with the @AspectJ syntax.

7.6 Features not implemented in @AspectJ

AspectJ strives hard to offer a reasonable and intuitive mapping to @AspectJ syntax for most features. But one feature—associating annotations—isn't implemented in the current version. A few other features—introducing data and methods, softening exceptions, and privileged aspects—will never be implemented due to the fundamental design constraints of playing by the rules laid out by the plain Java compiler. Let's start with the feature that is currently not implemented.

7.6.1 Associating annotations

As discussed in section 5.4, the various ways to declare annotations offer means to attach annotations to program elements in a crosscutting manner. The current version of AspectJ doesn't offer the same facility with the @AspectJ feature. This feature isn't implemented because there isn't an elegant mapping that allows compilation using javac and performs as much compile-time checking as reasonably possible. In a future version, this feature may be implemented.[1]

Let's discuss the features that *can't* be implemented in @AspectJ due to the fundamental constraints of compiling code using a plain Java compiler.

7.6.2 Introducing data and methods

With the traditional syntax, you can introduce additional members (data and methods) directly to other types. The introduced member can then be used like any other member (without consideration for whether the member existed because the type declared it or because an aspect introduced it). When an introduced member is encountered, the AspectJ compiler treats it correctly because it understands the semantics behind the member. A plain Java compiler, oblivious to such semantics, can't compile such code.

For example, consider the following code, which uses a hypothetical syntax to introduce a data member:

```
// Not real syntax
@Aspect
public class DirtyTracker {
```

[1] If you're wondering about the possible syntax considered for this feature, or if you have interesting alternative proposals, see the associated enhancement request: https://bugs.eclipse.org/bugs/show_bug.cgi?id=103646.

```
    ... hypothetical syntax equivalent of:
    ... private boolean DirtyTracked.dirty = false;

    @AfterReturning("set(* DirtyTracked+.* *) && this(tracked)")
    public void markDirty(DirtyTracked tracked) {
        tracked.dirty = true;
    }
}
```

A plain Java compiler won't realize that the dirty field has been introduced by an aspect, making such an introduction useless, even if it were possible. Thus the @AspectJ syntax doesn't offer this feature. But note that as discussed in section 7.5.2, the @AspectJ syntax lets you introduce parent interfaces, which supports implementing the same functionality in a different (and recommended) way.

The next feature is also useless due to the Java compatibility constraint, even if implemented.

7.6.3 Softening exceptions

Exception softening lets you treat specified checked exceptions as unchecked at certain join points. This feature relies on the AspectJ compiler's ability to use directives to treat exceptions thrown by join points as runtime exceptions during compilation and hence not force handling of the exceptions. A plain Java compiler can't understand the expected compile-time behavior. Consider the following hypothetical implementation:

```
// Not real syntax
@DeclareSoft("call(void TestSoftening.perform())")
RemoteException remoteException;
```

Although you can declare an intent that the AspectJ compiler should be able to understand, a Java compiler won't modify its compile-time behavior. Hence, the Java compiler will consider the call to the TestSoftening.perform() method to be in error.

The exception-softening feature has two parts: modifying compile-time behavior to avoid explicit handling of a checked exception and throwing a SoftException instead of the softened checked exception. The latter part can be implemented with @AspectJ. But the same part can also be implemented easily using an AfterThrowing advice:

```
@AfterThrowing(value="call(void TestSoftening.perform())",
               throwing="ex")
public void soften(RemoteException ex) {
    throw new SoftException(ex);
}
```

Note that an advice alters *only* the runtime behavior and will still force the caller to handle the exception even if RemoteException will never be thrown. The real value of declare soft is its compile-time behavior. If that can't be provided, there is little left in the feature to be a useful addition.

The next unimplemented feature isn't supported for identical reasons.

7.6.4 Privileged aspects

As discussed in section 6.4, privileged aspects are allowed to bypass the regular Java access rules. Because a pure Java compiler won't understand the modified access-control rules, a privileged aspect doesn't make sense with the @AspectJ syntax and can't be implemented in @AspectJ. In most systems, this isn't a burden, because you shouldn't use this feature too often anyway. But if you need equivalent functionality, consider using Java's reflection (along with `AccessibleObject.setAccessible()` method).

That completes our discussion of the @AspectJ syntax. We'll now compare this syntax with the traditional syntax.

7.7 Comparing syntax styles

Let's compare the syntax choices with regard to ease of learning, code verbosity, crosscutting expression power, tool friendliness, and ease of adoption. This will help you choose the right syntax based on your specific needs:

- *Ease of learning*—It's a myth that the @AspectJ syntax is easier because it's "plain Java." The reality is that @AspectJ isn't significantly easier or more difficult than the traditional syntax. The syntax is "plain" in that a Java compiler doesn't choke on it. From a programmer's perspective, you still have to learn the pointcut syntax and advice semantics. When choosing one syntax over the other, ease of learning isn't a factor.
- *Verbosity*—The traditional syntax is the most compact because it's specifically designed to express AOP constructs. Further, the traditional syntax can use types referring to `import` statements, shortening the pointcut expressions. But the @AspectJ syntax must always use fully qualified types, which can lead to difficult-to-read pointcut expressions. When you're choosing a syntax style, verbosity is never a deciding factor, but it deserves some consideration—especially if you plan to use aspects heavily.
- *Crosscutting expression power*—Because the traditional syntax requires the use of a special compiler, it liberates the program elements from a few Java rules (such as allowing ITDs and exception softening) and facilitates advanced applications of AOP. Depending on the application, the difference in power may be a deciding factor. If all you need is dynamic crosscutting, you won't feel that the @AspectJ syntax is much less powerful than the traditional syntax. But if you must use advanced static crosscutting, you may have to use the traditional syntax.
- *Tool friendliness*—The traditional syntax is foreign to most Java tools and will cause difficulties for those tools. The @AspectJ syntax, owing to the fact that aspects may be treated as regular Java classes, offers tool friendliness. The @AspectJ syntax works reasonably well in an environment without specific support for AspectJ (IntelliJ IDEA, for example), because such environments can treat the AspectJ code as the Java code. It also works great in environments that support AspectJ. For example, in Eclipse, you get all the goodies, such as the

crosscutting reference view. Certain tools, such as Emma (http://emma.sourceforge.net), work at the byte-code level; in those cases, because aspects compile to standard-compliant byte code, there is no difference in tool friendliness for either syntax.

Note that even with @AspectJ, you still need an AspectJ-aware IDE to see the crosscutting reference view and visualize the relationship between program elements and aspects. For example, IntelliJ IDEA users don't get this functionality easily (AspectJ includes a standalone ajbrowser tool and ajdoc, but the user experience isn't the same).

- *Adoption ease*—The simplified adoption of a new technology requires a pay-as-you-go approach that offers a way to introduce the technology with minimal impact on your development tools and processes. The @AspectJ syntax offers a gradual path to AOP adoption that may follow these lines:
  - If your application is based on the Spring Framework, you can use Spring's proxy-based AOP, which supports the @AspectJ syntax. As you'll see in chapter 9, you can express aspects using the @AspectJ syntax and apply them to Spring beans without build-time or load-time weaving. Instead, Spring uses the information in an aspect to create proxies around beans to implement the crosscutting functionality. Further, the Spring IDE (an Eclipse plug-in) offers the cross-reference view that lets you visualize the interaction between beans and aspects. Using the @AspectJ syntax along with proxy-based weaving is popular in Spring applications and experiences virtually no resistance during adoption.
  - When you need more power than that offered by Spring's proxy-based AOP, you can continue to use the @AspectJ syntax along with a build-time or load-time AspectJ weaver. The @AspectJ syntax used this way requires minimal changes to your tool chain or build and deployment processes, thus simplifying its inclusion.
  - When you need even more power, you can write a few aspects using the traditional syntax.

I'll make a few more recommendations about choosing syntax in the next chapter, after you've learned about weaving choices.

7.8 Summary

AspectJ's approach to providing an AOP solution for Java is a pragmatic one. The real world is full of varied needs and preferences. To respond to these needs, AspectJ provides choices for the syntax.

On the language side, a one-size-fits-all approach, which seems attractive because it reduces the size of the language, may not work well. The annotation-based @AspectJ syntax offers most features of the traditional syntax approach while staying within the limits of plain Java. Combined with an AspectJ weaver, the @AspectJ syntax offers a great way to use AspectJ without making any significant modifications to tools.

AspectJ's approach to creating an annotation-based syntax fully leverages the Java language, making it possible to flag programming errors as soon as possible. When it comes to dynamic crosscutting, where runtime behavior is affected, @AspectJ offers the full power of AOP. With static crosscutting, given the use of a Java compiler, a subset of features is offered, which should be sufficient to implement most applications of AOP.

We aren't finished with choices yet! The next chapter discusses another set of decisions regarding weaving models and a related additional syntax based on XML.

8 AspectJ weaving models

This chapter covers

- Classifying weaving models
- Using build-time weaving
- Using load-time weaving

Until now, we've focused on *writing* aspects. But for aspects to have effect, you need to *weave* them. Weaving, a fundamentally critical mechanism in implementing AOP, composes classes and aspects into an executable system.

The most basic form of weaving is build-time source-code weaving, where the AspectJ compiler compiles source files to produce a woven system. Although this form offers the best experience by providing immediate feedback for source-code errors and by eliminating deployment modifications, using a new compiler can impede AOP adoption. One alternative is build-time byte-code weaving, which lets you delay the introduction of the special compiler until after you compile the code. It also offers a way to weave even when you don't have access to the source code for classes or aspects. Load-time weaving goes further by eliminating the weaving step from the build process. Instead, it weaves classes as they're loaded into the VM. Load-time weaving is often the first choice for AspectJ-based tools that want to add new functionality in a minimally invasive fashion. All these choices make adoption of AspectJ easier than ever before.

In this chapter, we'll examine various weaving models. We'll also discuss the XML syntax, which offers a simpler way to modify aspects without requiring recompilation. We'll end the chapter by comparing all the choices and creating guidelines for choosing the appropriate weaving model in a given situation. Let's start with the weaving models offered by AspectJ.

8.1 Classifying weaving models

You can classify an AspectJ weaving model based on when it performs weaving and which kind of input it processes. Based on when it performs weaving, AspectJ offers two weaving models:

- *Build-time weaving* weaves classes and aspects together during the build process *before deploying the application.*
- *Load-time weaving (LTW)* weaves just in time *as the classes are loaded by the VM,* obviating any pre-deployment weaving.

Based on the kind of input a weaver processes, you can classify weaving models two ways:

- *Source code weaving* accepts input in the source-code form.
- *Byte-code (binary) weaving* that accepts input in byte code form produced by a compiler.

Table 8.1 shows the weaving possibilities supported by the AspectJ weaver.

Table 8.1 Weaving models supported by AspectJ

Weave time	Weaver input	
	Source code	Byte code (binary)
Build-time	Yes	Yes
Load-time	Source using XML syntax only	Yes

AspectJ supports build-time weaving that can take either source code or byte code. For LTW, the primary supported input is the byte code. LTW supports source code in a limited manner for aspects expressed in XML syntax (discussed in section 8.3.2). AspectJ lets you combine these weaving models. For example, you may have a few aspects woven in using source-code build-time weaving and a few more (say, third-party aspects) using byte-code build-time weaving. Then, you can use XML-based aspects using source-code load-time weaving. You may also weave in aspects (again, perhaps, third-party aspects) using the byte-code load-time weaver.

Let's examine the details of each supported weaving model, starting with build-time weaving.

8.2 Build-time weaving

The AspectJ compiler—ajc—enables build-time weaving.[1] It can take input in the form of source files, class files, and jar files, each of which may contain classes and aspects. The compiler produces woven byte code (as class files or as a jar depending on the compiler options). You can then deploy the resulting byte code in any standard compliant VM. Except for adding aspectjrt.jar to the classpath, you don't need to make any changes in deployment. The aspectjrt.jar file contains definitions for the various user accessible AspectJ types such as `JoinPoint` and `Signature`, various @AspectJ annotations, as well as internal AspectJ types utilized during runtime.

Build-time weaving is most suitable if you're learning AOP. The quick feedback you get from the compiler is invaluable. Build-time weaving is the only choice when it comes to certain static crosscutting usages. For example, consider an aspect that introduces a method to a class using an ITD. Such a method must be woven in to successfully compile the classes that use the introduced method. Waiting until LTW will lead to compilation errors in the accessing classes aborting any further steps. Build-time weaving is also attractive for refactoring aspects, where the classes often embed aspects. We'll examine refactoring aspects in chapter 16.

Build-time weaving can work with either source or binary code. Let's see how.

8.2.1 Build-time source code weaving

In this most common weaving mechanism, the weaver accepts classes and aspects in the source format (written using the traditional syntax or the @AspectJ syntax). The compiler produces byte code, which you can execute in any standard VM. This option is similar to using javac to compile Java sources. In this book, we've so far used this model to compile all the examples. Figure 8.1 shows the schematic for build-time source-code weaving.

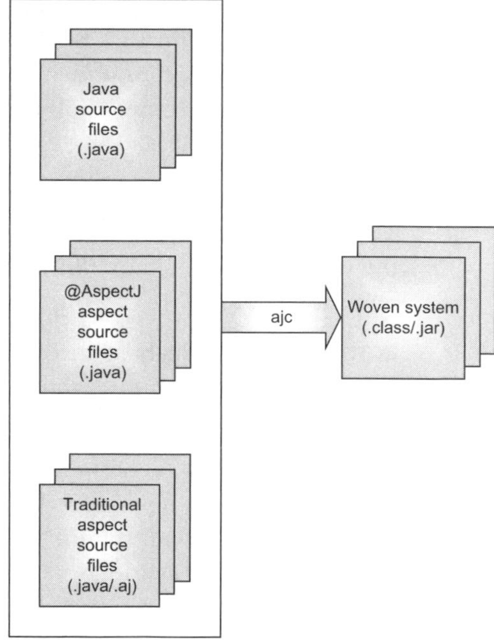

Figure 8.1 Build-time source-code weaving. Java sources and aspect sources are provided as the input to ajc, which produces the woven system.

Using build-time source-code weaving essentially involves replacing javac with ajc. Most options available to javac

[1] The AspectJ compiler is based on the Eclipse Java compiler.

are available to ajc. For example, to weave the tracing logic in all banking classes, you supply sources as follows:

```
> ajc ajia\banking\*.java ajia\tracing\TraceAspect.aj
```

Javac vs. ajc: Similar but not the same

Note one important difference between javac and ajc: with javac, you can compile all source files together or each source file individually without any difference in the output. This isn't the case with ajc; instead, you must pass all the input files together in one invocation. For example, the following two commands will *not* produce the same result as the earlier command:

```
> ajc ajia\banking\*.java
> ajc ajia\tracing\TraceAspect.aj
```

The apparent intention is to weave the tracing aspect into the banking-related classes. But TraceAspect.aj isn't included while compiling the banking classes, so no such weaving occurs.

You can also specify the root directories of the source files you want to compile by passing the list of directories to the `-sourceroots` option. The AspectJ compiler then compiles all source files under each specified directory and its subdirectories. The following command compiles all the source files under the c:\ajia-book\banking\src and c:\ajia\tracing\src directories:

```
> ajc -sourceroots C:\ajia-book\banking\src;c:\ajia-book\tracing\src
```

The separator character between the multiple source directories specified must match the native path separator. On Windows systems, it's a semicolon (`;`); and on UNIX systems, it's a colon (`:`).

NOTE You're unlikely to invoke ajc directly as shown in this chapter. Instead, you'll use Ant or Maven as discussed in appendixes B and C, which shows all the options in this chapter using build scripts.

The AspectJ compiler supports additional options such as `-showWeaveInfo`, to show information about how AspectJ is weaving classes with aspects, and `-Xlint`, to produce useful warnings about potential programming mistakes. See the AspectJ documentation (http://www.eclipse.org/aspectj/doc/released/devguide/ajc-ref.html) for the full list of options.

Internally, source weaving utilizes binary weaving. Even when you present source files as input to the compiler, the AspectJ compiler first compiles the code into byte-code form and then weaves the resulting byte code together. Let's examine binary weaving to understand this process.

8.2.2 Build-time binary weaving

Often, you don't have access to the source code for the classes or aspects or both. For example, you may be using a third-party library for classes or aspects. Build-time source-code weaving won't be useful for such a scenario. AspectJ's build-time binary weaving offers a solution in such cases. With this option, you perform the following steps:

- *Use already-compiled classes.* These classes may have been compiled using either a Java compiler or the AspectJ compiler; it doesn't matter.
- *Use already-compiled aspects.* Aspects written using the @AspectJ syntax may have been compiled using either the Java compiler or the AspectJ compiler. Much the same as for classes, using the Java or AspectJ compiler makes no logical difference. You must use the `-g:vars` or `-g` option, as described in section 7.3.2, when compiling aspects using javac. Aspects written using the traditional syntax, of course, must have been compiled using the AspectJ compiler, because javac won't understand the syntax.
- *Weave classes with aspects by presenting their byte code to another invocation of ajc, which produces a set of classes or a jar file depending on the options provided.* Any standard VM may then execute the resulting byte code.

Figure 8.2 shows the schematic for build-time binary weaving.

From a usage perspective, the difference between source code weaving and binary weaving is minor. With either approach, you still use the ajc compiler. The only difference is the flags that specify sources or byte-code input. The following command uses the classes in services.jar as input to be woven in with aspects in monitoring.jar:

```
> ajc -inpath services.jar -aspectpath monitoring.jar
```

You can combine source-code and binary weaving in a single command. For example, the following command uses source-code weaving for files with a .java extension in the

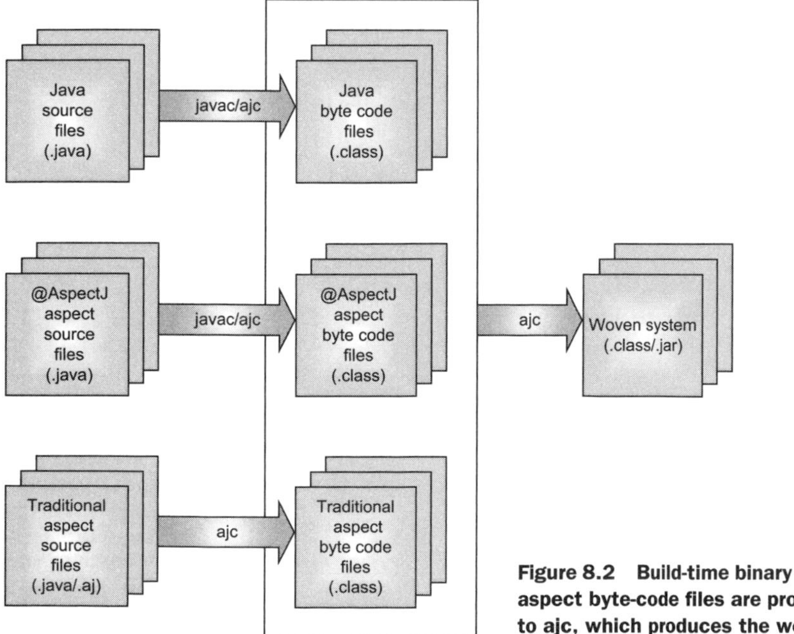

Figure 8.2 Build-time binary weaving. Java and aspect byte-code files are provided as the input to ajc, which produces the woven system.

banking directory and a .aj extension in the tracing directory along with the jar files used in the earlier command:

```
> ajc ajia\banking\*.java tracing\*.aj -inpath services.jar
➥    -aspectpath monitoring.jar
```

You can use the `-outjar` option of ajc to produce a jar file. This jar file can be used as a part of the final system. It may also be used as input to another invocation of ajc, as byte code input to be woven in (using `-inpath`) or aspects to weave in (using `-aspectpath`).

> **Jar by –outjar: nothing special**
>
> Note that the jar file produced by using `-outjar` is a packaged version of the class files that would be produced if you didn't specify the flag. In other words, no additional information is added to the packaged jar file when you use this flag.

Figure 8.3 shows how you can create an aspect library using javac or ajc and how you can use such a library with binary weaving.

Binary weaving is especially attractive with the @AspectJ syntax. You can compile the source code (including aspects expressed using the @AspectJ syntax) using javac. Then, you can use binary weaving to produce the final system. You can utilize this style in IDEs that don't directly support AspectJ, where you let the IDE compile all sources using javac and then use a post-compilation step (often implemented as an Ant or

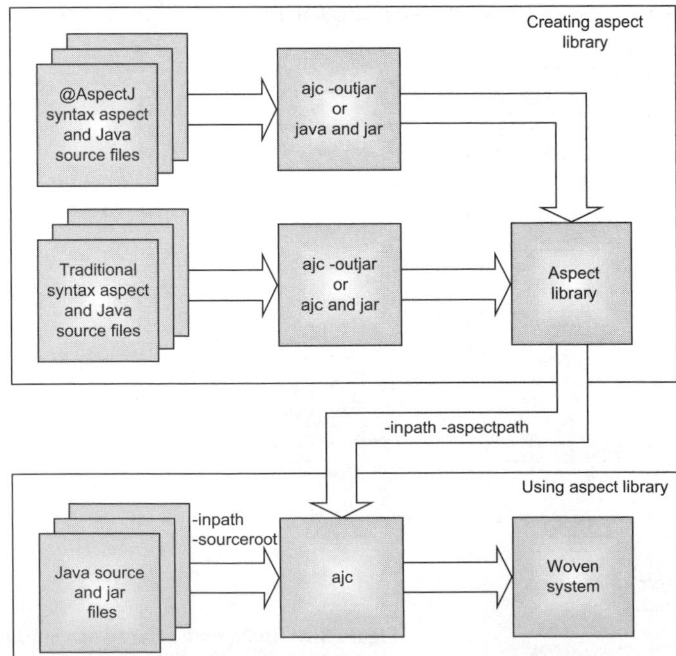

Figure 8.3 Creating an aspect library involves using `-outjar` or explicitly using the jar tool. When you use the library, you need the `-aspectspath` and `-inpath` options. The output of the system can be multiple class files or a jar file, depending on how you use the `-outjar` option.

Maven target) to weave classes and aspects. This style also helps keep your build process unchanged up to the point of creating jar files for plain Java source files. You can then augment the build process with an additional build step that weaves in the needed aspects. Figure 8.4 depicts this process.

As shown in the figure, the existing build system produces a jar file. The AspectJ compiler weaves aspects into that jar file to produce a woven jar.

> **Support for XML syntax in build-time weaving**
>
> The current version of AspectJ doesn't support XML syntax (described in section 8.3.2) with build-time weaving. There is no fundamental reason for this, so expect a future version of AspectJ to support aspects defined using XML-based syntax.

Build-time weaving can be easy or difficult to start, depending on your perspective. You may perceive it as easier for these reasons:

- You're just replacing javac with ajc. If you use build-time binary weaving, you can even leave your build system or IDE setup intact except for an additional post-compilation step.
- When it comes to deployment, except for including aspectjrt.jar in the classpath, you can ignore the fact that the system was built using the AspectJ compiler.

But you may also perceive it as difficult because it affects how you build your system; and, for a certain class of crosscutting concerns, it may be a bit burdensome. LTW, discussed in the next section, offers a solution in those cases.

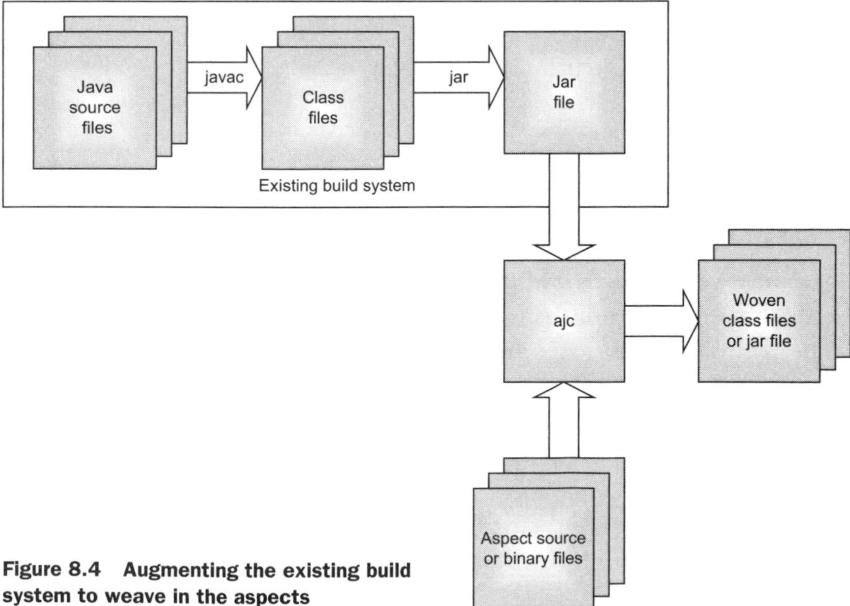

Figure 8.4 Augmenting the existing build system to weave in the aspects

8.3 Load-time weaving

Let's say you want to monitor the behavior of your application to see if there are any performance bottlenecks. Or, perhaps you want to include a concurrency monitoring aspect to debug a deadlock situation. In either case, you don't expect to keep the aspects in the system after they have served their purpose (finding the code responsible for performance bottlenecks and deadlocks). Modifying the build system only to weave aspects that you don't intend to keep in the system for a long time can be a hindrance. For such cases, load-time weaving provides a way to leave your build system intact and still weave aspects as needed.

The mechanism used for LTW is an extension of binary weaving. LTW, much like binary weaving, takes byte code as input. The difference is that unlike with binary weaving, there is no explicit weaving step. Instead, the VM is set up to perform weaving as the VM *loads* the classes—hence the name *load-time* weaving.

The load-time weaver uses the Java Virtual Machine Tools Interface (JVMTI) facility—a new feature introduced in Java 5. JVMTI allows a *JVMTI agent* to, in addition to many other things, intercept the loading of a class. The load-time weaver is a JVMTI agent that uses this functionality to weave in classes as the VM loads them. This agent, of course, works only with Java 5 and newer VMs. For pre-Java 5, you can use a classloader-based version, because a classloader, too, offers a way to intercept the loading of a class and modify its byte code before the VM loads it. But unlike the JVMTI solution, a classloader-based solution is often application-server specific.

Spring-native load-time weaving

Spring version 2.5 supports LTW that obviates the use of a JVMTI agent on certain application and web servers. It also supports the use of an alternative JVMTI agent that serves other purposes (specifically, to aid Java Persistence API (JPA) based implementations). We'll examine this possibility in the next chapter.

Let's look in more depth at LTW.

8.3.1 Load-time weaving overview

The load-time weaver needs additional information to decide which aspects to weave. Although the weaver could examine the classpath to detect aspects present, that would be a prohibitively expensive approach because every class on the classpath would have to be checked to see if it was an aspect. Weaving all aspects found on the classpath may not be desirable, anyway. Therefore, the weaver requires that you explicitly specify each aspect in an aop.xml file in the META-INF directory on the classpath. Because many classpath entries (jar files and directories) may contain an aop.xml file, the weaver uses them all by combining the information in them.

Figure 8.5 shows the overview of arrangement used by LTW.

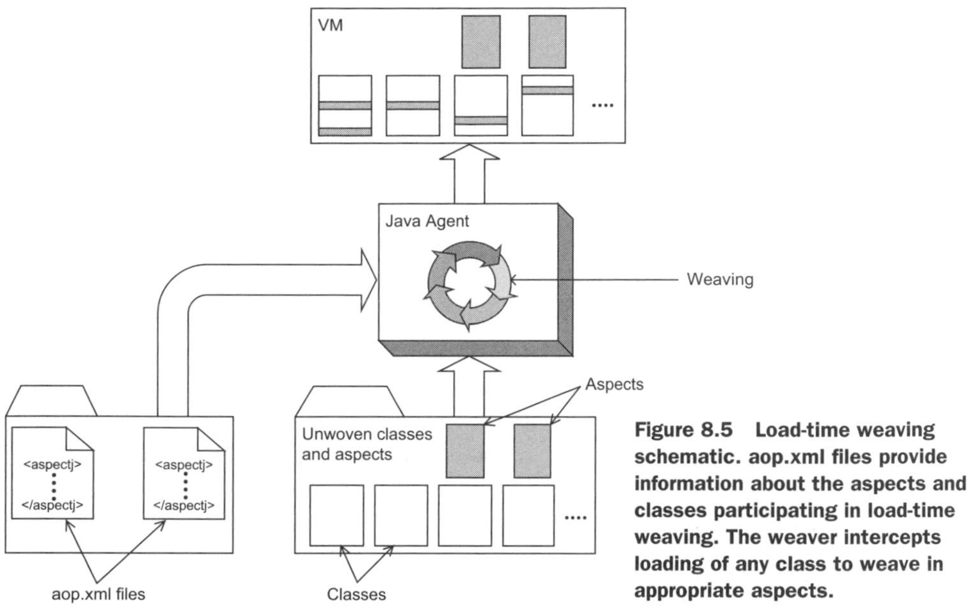

Figure 8.5 Load-time weaving schematic. aop.xml files provide information about the aspects and classes participating in load-time weaving. The weaver intercepts loading of any class to weave in appropriate aspects.

> **Alternative to aop.xml**
>
> You can use META-INF/aop-ajc.xml or org/aspectj/aop.xml as alternatives to META-INF/aop.xml. You can also use the `-Dorg.aspectj.weaver.loadtime.configuration` VM option to specify an explicit list of files instead of using the default ones on the classpath. This option is useful when you want to try multiple load-time weaver configurations quickly. In this book, when I refer to aop.xml, the discussion applies to the alternative files as well.

Here are the steps performed when you use LTW:

1. You deploy an application to use the load-time weaver by using the `-javaagent` option to `java` to specify aspectjweaver.jar as an agent, as shown in the following command:

```
> java -javaagent:<path-to>/aspectjweaver.jar [other options] <Main-Class>
```

2. The VM initializes the agent. During initialization, the agent loads all the files matching META-INF/aop.xml in the classpath. It examines each aop.xml file for the list of aspects. It also examines any inclusion or exclusion filter specified (see the next section for more details). If the agent finds multiple aop.xml files in META-INF directory on the classpath, it logically combines them.
3. The agent loads the listed aspects that also match the inclusion and exclusion conditions.
4. The agent registers its interest in the class-loading event so that the VM gives it an opportunity to examine and possibly modify a class being loaded.

5. The system starts its normal execution. The VM then loads classes as needed during execution.
6. The VM notifies the agent whenever it loads a class. The agent, in turn, inspects the class to determine if any of the loaded aspects need to be woven in. If so, it weaves the class and hands over the modified byte code to the VM.
7. The VM uses the woven byte code to realize the class.

As you may guess from these steps, LTW has a definite impact on load-time performance. Specifically, the time to load the application and the memory consumed by it are higher. But after a class is loaded into the VM, there is no additional performance penalty. The woven byte code produced by LTW is identical to the byte code you would obtain using build-time weaving. In a way, you need to pay for weaving at some point between writing code and executing the system. For build-time weaving, you pay at build time; and for load-time weaving, you pay at class-loading time. Although significant optimizations are being added to LTW, depending on your usage, you may get performance improvements by offloading the weaving step away from deployment.

> **OSGi and LTW**
>
> OSGi defines an architecture for dynamic and modular Java applications. Eclipse, of course, is a well-known application based on the OSGi platform. On the server side, too, OSGi is gaining popularity through application servers such as the SpringSource dmServer (http://www.springsource.org/dmserver).
>
> An OSGi application consists of a set of bundles. Typically, a bundle includes Java types as well as metadata to export and import types and services. The Equinox Aspects project (http://www.eclipse.org/equinox/incubator/aspects) lets you add aspects to a bundle. It can then weave those aspects into other bundles as they're deployed into the OSGi container. Equinox Aspects uses LTW as the underlying implementation.
>
> Recently, the AJDT project has started using Equinox Aspects to weave AspectJ tooling functionality into JDT. The Scala plug-in has taken a similar approach based on Equinox Aspects.

An important component of LTW is the aop.xml files that configure the weaver. Let's examine how you write such a file.

8.3.2 Configuring the load-time weaver

The LTW configuration specifies the aspects and classes participating in the weaving process, the definitions of pointcuts for abstract aspects, and various debugging options. Logically, the XML files are a kind of source code useful only for LTW. Except for the XML files, all other input must be first compiled using the Java or AspectJ compiler. This is similar to how Java Server Pages (JSP) work; although the web container will compile JSP files to byte code (typically, after first compiling to source code), all other Java code must have been already compiled. Let's examine how you specify various configuration elements.

SPECIFYING ASPECTS TO BE WOVEN

Often, you need to supply a reusable concrete aspect to the load-time weaver. XML syntax offers a simple element for this purpose, as shown in listing 8.1.

Listing 8.1 Basic aop.xml enlisting aspects to be woven

```
<aspectj>
    <aspects>
        <aspect name="ajia.tracing.Tracing"/>
        <aspect name="ajia.transaction.TransactionManagementAspect"/>
        ...
    </aspects>
</aspectj>
```

The <aspects> section specifies the aspects to be woven. This section is analogous to the -aspectpath compiler option. Each <aspect> section specifies an aspect to be woven. The name attribute of the element is a fully qualified type name. Note that a type pattern isn't allowed as an attribute value. Here, the agent weaves in ajia.tracing.Tracing and ajia.transaction.TransactionManagementAspect aspects (unless other parts in the system indicate their exclusion, as discussed later in this section).

XML syntax also lets you express concrete aspects written using the traditional or @AspectJ syntax.

DEFINING CONCRETE ASPECTS

Aspect libraries often contain abstract aspects. You must define concrete subaspects for those aspects to be woven in. Although you can always use code to define subaspects and use the <aspect> elements as discussed in the earlier section, an easier solution is to define concrete aspects using the <concrete-aspect> element. Listing 8.2 shows an example of a concrete aspect defined using AspectJ's XML syntax by providing a definition for the abstract pointcut in the base aspect.

Listing 8.2 Specifying concrete aspects using XML syntax

```
<aspectj>
  <aspects>
     <!-- Assume ajia.monitoring.Monitoring is an abstract aspect with
          an abstract monitored() pointcut -->
     <concrete-aspect name="ajia.monitoring.JDBCMonitoring"
                      extends="ajia.monitoring.Monitoring">
        <pointcut name="monitored"
                  expression="call(* java.sql.*.*(..))"/>
     </concrete-aspect>
     ...
  </aspects>
  ...
</aspectj>
```

The ajia.monitoring.Monitoring aspect includes an abstract monitored() pointcut that it advises to implement the monitoring functionality. The <concrete-aspect>

element defines the ajia.monitoring.JDBCMonitoring aspect, which includes a nested element to provide a definition for the abstract pointcut.

The use of XML to define pointcuts offers an easy way to modify the definition and affect system behavior without recompilation. For example, if you need to monitor the execution of methods in banking classes along with JDBC, you change the pointcut to the following definition:

```
<pointcut name="monitored"
          expression="call(* java.sql.*.*(..))
                      || execution(* ajia.banking..*.*(..))"/>
```

Note that you can replace the binary operators || and && with OR and AND for pointcuts written using XML. This substitution is especially helpful for writing the && operator, which in XML is written &&.

XML syntax is purposefully limited to define subaspects and pointcuts in those aspects. Unlike with traditional or @AspectJ syntax, you can't define or override methods in the base aspect. Pointcuts specified in aop.xml also have a few limitations:

- *The pointcuts can't collect a join point's context.*

  You can't, for example, use an args() pointcut to collect arguments to a method. This limitation makes aspects expressed using XML suitable only for scoping purposes. For instance, you may have a base class that defines a pointcut to do the primary selection along with an abstract-scope pointcut. You can then provide the definition for the scope pointcut in XML.
- *The pointcut must use fully qualified type names similar to @AspectJ syntax and for the same reason: XML syntax doesn't support a feature comparable to Java import statements.*

  For example, if you want to select only the Account class in the ajia.banking.domain package, you must specify ajia.banking.domain.Account as the type name. But note that you can always use wildcards to select a set of types as usual. For example, if you use *..Account as the type pattern, it matches ajia.banking.domain.Account and Account types defined in other packages, if any.

Given these restrictions, you may have situations where you need to use the traditional or @Aspect syntax to define concrete aspects.

DEFINING ASPECT PRECEDENCE

As you may recall from chapter 6, without explicit declarations, the order in which advice from multiple aspects apply is arbitrary. AspectJ provides a mechanism to control precedence among multiple aspects. Typically, aspect precedence is a system-level consideration specified in a precedence-coordination aspect. LTW provides a way to specify aspect precedence in the load-time configuration that already acts at the system level.

To specify aspect precedence, you define a <concrete-aspect> element and specify the precedence sequence in its precedence attribute. For example, the following snippet specifies that ajia.security.AuthorizationAspect has a higher precedence over ajia.transaction.TransactionManagementAspect:

```
<concrete-aspect name="ajia.SystemLevelPrecedenceCoordinator"
                 precedence="ajia.security.AuthorizationAspect,
➥                ajia.transaction.TransactionManagementAspect"/>
```

The concrete aspect specified in this manner is merely a placeholder that should not extend any abstract aspect or define any pointcuts.

SPECIFYING WEAVING OPTIONS IN AOP.XML

For more advanced use of LTW, you need more control. Specifically, you need to specify aspects and classes participating in the weaving process. The `<include>` and `<exclude>` elements nested inside `<aspects>` and `<weaver>` elements help with this. Listing 8.3 shows an aop.xml file with these elements.

Listing 8.3 aop.xml with weaving options

```
<aspectj>
    <aspects>
        <aspect ....
        <concrete-aspect ....

        <include within="ajia..*"/>                          ❶ Included aspects
        <include within="org.springframework..*"/>

        <exclude within="@ajia.util.Untested *"/>            ❷ Excluded aspects
        <exclude within="ajia.concurrency.DeadLockDetection+"/>
    </aspects>
                                                             ❸ Weaver options
    <weaver options="-verbose -showWeaveInfo">
        <include within="ajia.banking..*"/>                  ❹ Included classes
        <exclude within="org.springframework..*"/>           ❺ Excluded classes

        <dump within="banking..*" beforeandafter="true"/>    ❻ Woven classes to be dumped
    </weaver>
</aspectj>
```

The `<aspects>` element specifies the aspects to weave in. In contrast, the `<weaver>` section specifies the classes to weave into, in addition to controlling other weaver parameters. In a sense, the `<aspects>` section plays a role similar to the `-aspectpath` option to the compiler, whereas the `<weaver>` section plays a role similar to the `-inpath`, `-verbose`, and `-showWeaveInfo` options. Let's see these elements in detail:

❶ The optional `<include>` elements in the `<aspects>` section specify the aspects to be considered for weaving. Each `<include>` element specifies a type pattern for the `within` attribute. A common use of the `<include>` element is to weave only a subset of aspects declared in other aop.xml files. For example, the aop.xml in an aspect library may list all its aspects. Without an `<include>` (or `<exclude>`) element, this leads to weaving of all those aspects. But another aop.xml may limit weaving to only a subset of those aspects by using an `<include>` element. In this case, you include all aspects in the `ajia` and `org.springframework` packages as well as their direct and indirect subpackages. When you don't specify an `<include>` element, all aspects declared using `<aspect>` and `<concrete-aspect>` are candidates to be woven in.

Why <include> and <exclude>?

The main practical reason to use `<include>` and `<exclude>` elements is to control the weaving of aspects specified in other aop.xml files. If you have only one aop.xml file, you can control inclusion and exclusion by listing only the aspects to be woven in using the `<aspect>` and `<concrete-aspect>` elements. Many developers also use `<include>` and `<exclude>` to perform quick experimentation around aspects to weave in.

2 Similarly, optional `<exclude>` sections specify type patterns for the aspects to be excluded. A common use of `<exclude>` is to exclude aspects defined in other aop.xml files. It serves a purpose similar to that of the `<include>` element, except that it allows exclusion instead of inclusion. Only aspects that are listed are woven if they match the types specified in the `<include>` but not those in the `<exclude>` elements. In this case, you're excluding deadlock-detection aspects by specifying a type pattern that selects all subaspects of `DeadLockDetection`. You also exclude all aspects that carry the `@Untested` annotation. When you don't specify an `<exclude>` element, all aspects declared using `<aspect>` and `<concrete-aspect>` that match `<include>` elements, if any, are woven in.

3 The `<weaver>` element controls the classes to be woven in along with a few other characteristics of the weaving process. The `<weaver>` element can specify the options passed to the weaver using the `options` attribute. Most of these options are the same as those for the compiler, such as `-verbose`, `-showWeaveInfo`, `-nowarn`, `-XmessageHandlerClass`, and `-Xlint`. See the AspectJ documentation (available at http://www.eclipse.org/aspectj/doc/released/devguide/ltw-configuration.html#weaver-options) for details.

4 The `<include>` element specifies a type pattern for the types exposed to the weaver, which is thus available to be woven in. By default, the weaver weaves in all types exposed to it. Here, you expose all banking-related types to the weaver.

5 The `<exclude>` element specifies a type pattern for the types that shouldn't be exposed to the weaver. By default, nothing is excluded. The combination of `<include>` and `<exclude>` control the types exposed to the weaver. Here, you exclude any types from the Spring Framework using the `org.springframework..*` type pattern. Note that the weaver excludes all types in direct or indirect subpackages of `java`, `javax`, and `org.aspectj` by default.

6 Finally, the `<dump>` section can specify woven types that should be written to the disk for diagnostic purposes. The optional `beforeandafter` parameter specifies whether the unwoven classes should be dumped as well. This may be useful to examine generated classes such as those for JSP pages.

You may run into a situation where you have multiple aop.xml files. Let's see how AspectJ handles such a case.

> **Automatically generating aop.xml**
>
> AspectJ offers `-outxml` and `-outxmlfile` compiler options to create weaver configuration files. `-outxml` results in the creation of a META-INF/aop-ajc.xml file that lists all the concrete aspects in the input sources. With `-outxmlfile`, you specify the name for the file.
>
> These options are especially important for aspect libraries. You can include the generated file in the aspect library jar. When you include the resulting jar in the classpath for the system, the load-time weaver automatically considers all the aspects in the library for weaving. Of course, if you don't want a particular aspect, you can add an `<exclude>` element in another aop.xml file. Because `<include>` and `<exclude>` allow type patterns, selecting a precise set of aspects is easy.

USING MULTIPLE AOP.XML FILES

When you have multiple aop.xml files in various components in the classpath, AspectJ's load-time weaver logically combines all those files. Because the net effect is the logical combination, it may have surprising results. For example, if an aop.xml file specifies an `<exclude>` element inside an `<aspects>` element, it excludes any aspect matching the pattern (and not just from the classpath component associated with the aop.xml file that specifies it).

The recommended practice is that the aop.xml file associated with each library should only list aspects using the `<aspect>` elements and not exclude any aspects using wildcards. Although excluding specific aspects in the library isn't a problem, using a wildcard can end up choosing aspects in other libraries and may lead to surprises. Instead, you should use an additional aop.xml file to choose aspects to be woven in. Think of such an aop.xml file as application-level configuration.

Let's put all the information in this chapter to good use by seeing an example in action.

8.4 Load-time weaver in action

Let's use LTW to monitor a web application. (In the next chapter, we'll use the same example to illustrate Spring-driven LTW.) You'll use the jpetstore sample web application based on the Spring Framework and Tomcat as the web server. But as you'll see, you can easily modify the example to use with any application and server. Follow these steps:

1. *Deploy the normal application.* Start with the copy of jpetstore provided in the downloadable sources. Alternatively, you can use Subversion to check it out from https://src.springsource.org/svn/spring-samples/jpetstore. (In the following text, I assume a Windows system. The downloaded sources contain scripts for Windows and UNIX platforms.).

   From the org.springframework.samples.jpetstore directory, execute the following commands:

```
> mvn package
> copy target\org.springframework.samples.jpetstore-1.0.0-SNAPSHOT.war
➥    %TOMCAT_HOME%\webapps\jpetstore.war
```

Many times, especially when you're learning to use LTW, you'll encounter issues that have little to do with LTW but are rather due to errors in the application. Therefore, it's prudent to run the application without LTW as the first step. Start the HSQL server by executing db\hsqldb\server.bat from the jpetstore directory, and then run Tomcat by executing %TOMCAT_HOME%\bin\startup.bat. Assuming the default Tomcat settings, this will also explode the war file that you'll need for the next step. Visit the web page for the application (with default settings, at http://localhost:8080/jpetstore), and buy a few pets. If everything goes fine, follow the next steps to add LTW.

2 *Prepare the aspects.* To enable monitoring, use the aspect from listing 7.10 and the concrete subaspect defined using the XML syntax from listing 8.2. Compile the aspect, and copy the resulting class and aop.xml file to the deployed web application using the following commands:

```
> mvn package
> copy target\Section8.4LoadTimeWeaver-1.0-SNAPSHOT.jar
➥    %TOMCAT_HOME%\webapps\jpetstore\WEB-INF\lib
```

In this step, you copy the compiled aspect and aop.xml file (packaged in Section8.4LoadTimeWeaver-1.0-SNAPSHOT.jar) to the deployed application. Alternatively, you could copy the resulting class file and META-INF/aop.xml into the classes directory in the application's WEB-INF directory. You could also bundle the same files as part of the war file. The only things that matter are that the class files corresponding to the aspect be available on the classpath and that aop.xml be included in a META-INF directory in a classpath component.

3 *Configure the startup script.* To enable LTW in Tomcat, first copy %TOMCAT_HOME%\bin\startup.bat to %TOMCAT_HOME%\bin\startup-aspectj-ltw.bat so you can easily switch between different ways to start the server. Next, modify the new file by adding the following snippet at the top, to add the AspectJ LTW agent to the Java VM used by Tomcat:

```
set ASPECTJ_HOME=<Directory where you installed AspectJ>
set JAVA_OPTS=-javaagent:%ASPECTJ_HOME%\lib\aspectjweaver.jar
```

4 *Start the server.* Using the new launch script, start the server. To see the effect of the aspects, revisit the application's web page, and buy a few pets:

```
> startup-aspectj-ltw.bat
...
Method DriverManager.registerDriver(..) took 2110603
Method DriverManager.getDriver(..) took 114539
Method DriverManager.getLogWriter() took 12571
```

```
Method DriverManager.getDriver(..) took 45815
Method Driver.connect(..) took 6869588
Method Connection.getAutoCommit() took 100669778
Method Connection.getAutoCommit() took 100941042
Method Connection.isClosed() took 22070
Method Connection.isClosed() took 646451
Method Connection.getAutoCommit() took 464026
Method Connection.getAutoCommit() took 15171481
Method Connection.clearWarnings() took 13130
...
```

As you can see, you get monitoring of every call on any JDBC object. Play around—in particular, modify the `monitored()` pointcut in aop.xml to monitor different parts of the system. Also, if you have a web application running with Java 5 or above, try adding LTW-based monitoring to it. We'll revisit the monitoring solution using AOP in chapter 10.

8.5 Choosing syntax and weaving

Which weaving model is best suited: build-time or load-time? Which syntax is the best: traditional or @AspectJ? All these choices have pros and cons, with no clear winner in all situations. This realization is behind AspectJ's support for multiple syntaxes and weaving models. In this section, we'll look at some guidelines you can follow to help choose the right syntax and weaving model in a given situation. Although these guidelines are somewhat prescriptive in nature, their main purpose is to help you simplify the decision-making process. Considering your unique circumstances, you may want to deviate from these guidelines:

- *The team is using Eclipse, and AspectJ is a core part of the design.* Use the traditional syntax, because it will lead to the most compact code and provide the full power of AspectJ. You can use build-time weaving, because the plug-in makes its usage easy. Although plug-ins are available for other IDEs (NetBeans, for example), in the short term, they won't be as good as the Eclipse plug-in.
- *The team isn't using Eclipse, and AspectJ is a core part of the design.* Use the @AspectJ syntax if you must work in non-Eclipse environments. Let the IDE compile classes and aspects through its normal build process. Use a post-build step to weave classes and aspects together. Even though the IDE isn't AspectJ aware, debugging won't be a problem. You can set breakpoints in normal classes as well as those carrying the `@Aspect` annotation.
- *The team is exploring AspectJ for non-production use.* This is a situation where you've just started with AspectJ, and one of the development aspects (such as those discussed in chapters 10 and 11) catches your attention. You're also likely to use pre-built third-party (open source or otherwise) aspects instead of developing your own. In this situation, because you aren't yet sure about the scope of AspectJ usage in your project, it's best to not alter your build environment.

If you're using Java 5, due to the simple configuration to set up the weaving agent, LTW should receive your first consideration. All you'll need to do is make a few modifications to your startup script (add the `-javaagent` option) and create an aop.xml file (to define aspects to weave in and define concrete subaspects). If you're using pre-Java 5, although you may use a classloader-based LTW, it can be difficult to set up correctly at first. Binary weaving is your choice in this case. As in figure 8.4, let the main build system produce jar files. Create another build script to take that input and weave aspects into it. Binary weaving is also a good choice when you can't modify the application-startup script.

Whenever you face choices for AspectJ usage, start with these basic recommendations. After you gain sufficient experience, you'll figure out needed improvisations.

8.6 Summary

AspectJ's approach to providing an AOP solution for Java is pragmatic. The real world is full of varied needs and preferences. The weaving models offered by AspectJ simplify its use in a wide variety of applications. Build-time weaving is the easiest approach for many applications due to the experience provided by AspectJ-aware tools such as the Eclipse AJDT plug-in. But it requires an upfront cost that can sometimes be prohibitive, especially while you're still deciding if you want to go the AOP route. Binary weaving offers a choice of keeping the build environment largely unchanged by requiring a post-build weaving task. The other weaving model, load-time weaving, offers a simpler alternative. LTW leaves the build system unchanged and offers a possibility of quick deployment-time modifications.

You aren't yet finished with choices! The next chapter discusses another possibility that is both an alternative syntax and an alternative weaving model: Spring-AspectJ integration.

9 Integration with Spring

This chapter covers

- Understanding Spring AOP basics
- Using @AspectJ integration
- Working with schema-style AOP
- Weaving aspects using Spring

The Spring Framework, a widely used enterprise application framework, is based on three core ideas: dependency injection, enterprise services abstraction, and aspect-oriented programming. Dependency injection (DI) is at the heart of Spring. It allows components to be wired in a declarative manner. The enterprise services abstraction encourages isolating stable application logic from volatile infrastructure code. Of course, our main interest here is the use of AOP in Spring. AOP lets you separate the implementation of crosscutting concerns from business concerns. All of these features work together to offer a compelling solution.

The central theme in Spring is the use of *plain old Java objects* (POJOs) as the primary backbone of an application. Each POJO is just that—a plain old Java object that isn't tied to any framework artifacts. POJOs let you focus on the core concerns of a class and isolate the stable business logic from the volatile infrastructure. The result is the creation of a loosely coupled system that is faster to develop, easier to test, and simpler to evolve. But for a typical enterprise application, POJOs alone can't provide all the needed functionality. Specifically, POJOs can't deal with crosscutting concerns without duplicating code and tying into infrastructural code. Spring offers AOP as the way to deal with the crosscutting concerns.

In this chapter, we'll look at the Spring integration options for AspectJ and provide guidelines for choosing the right form for a given scenario. We assume that you have some knowledge of Spring. If not, please read a good book such as *Spring in Action*, 2nd edition by Craig Walls and Ryan Breidenbach (Manning, 2007). Of course, you should also read the comprehensive documentation that comes with the Spring Framework (http://www.springsource.org/documentation).

9.1 Spring AOP fundamentals

As we discussed in chapter 1, various AOP systems can implement the general AOP concepts in a variety of ways. Although their styles and capabilities differ, all the systems aim at the same problem of modularizing crosscutting concerns and share the core concepts. Spring provides its own way of implementing AOP: the main highlight is the use of proxies that avoid the need for explicit weaving (build-time or load-time). This kind of solution offers the lowest barrier to adoption, because you're still programming in plain Java. Spring's AOP, although not as powerful as AspectJ, offers a pragmatic solution to modularize commonly encountered crosscutting concerns in a typical enterprise application. If you need more power, you can always use AspectJ byte-code weaving, because AspectJ works with any Java application. Spring provides a few options to simplify AspectJ usage, as well.

Spring has always included AOP as a fundamental component of the framework. But the programming model used to be a bit complex due to the exposure of low-level constructs directly to developers. As a result, most aspects using that model were a part of Spring itself or written by advanced Spring developers. Starting with version 2.0, Spring simplifies the programming model through AspectJ integration that still works within the proxy-based framework (and hence doesn't require explicit byte-code weaving). Specifically, under this model, you can write aspects using

- A subset of the @AspectJ syntax you learned in chapter 7.
- Plain Java (without annotations), with AOP constructs expressed in XML (the schema-style AOP). This is an especially useful alternative if you can't use Java 5 or above and, hence, annotations.

Spring also simplifies the use of full-power AspectJ that relies on byte-code modification techniques. Specifically, it supports

- Configuring aspect instances as Spring beans
- Simplifying load-time weaving (LTW) without requiring modifications to the launch script (to add the weaving agent) for a few web and application servers

Let's dive straight into a simple example that illustrates the use of the @AspectJ syntax with Spring. In later sections, we'll delve deeper into nuances of AspectJ integration.

> **Dependency injection**
>
> Objects need collaborating objects to implement their behavior. For example, an MVC controller needs service objects so that it can invoke business functionality in response to user interaction.
>
> An important consideration is how an object gets access to its collaborating objects. You can create the collaborating objects inside an object that needs them, but this is undesirable due to the strong coupling with a specific implementation of the collaborating classes and difficulty in sharing the collaborating objects. Alternatively, you can use a locator (essentially, a map) to locate a collaborating object by its key. This is called *dependency lookup*. The objects that need dependencies often use an interface to specify the type of a collaborating object to avoid dependency on a particular implementation. Although this improves the situation a bit, objects now have a dependency on the locator object. Consequently, such objects can be used only in environments that support the locator implementation.
>
> DI offers further improvement. Objects declare their dependency on collaborating objects through constructor parameters, setter methods, or annotated methods and fields. An external configuration specifies the wiring information, and a container uses that configuration to construct the objects and inject them with their dependencies. With such an arrangement, objects have no direct dependency on the environment. For example, in a unit test, you can directly construct an object, call its setters (perhaps with mock objects), and test it.
>
> See http://martinfowler.com/articles/injection.html for more information on the principles behind DI. We'll discuss DI in more detail in chapter 16, where we examine how AOP can help implement it for domain objects.

9.1.1 *Setting up the application*

We'll start with a stub implementation of the `InventoryService` interface (developed as a part of the code in appendix A) in listing 9.1. It prints a message as the implementation of each method.

Listing 9.1 Stub implementation of `InventoryService`

```
package ajia.service.impl;

import ajia.service.InventoryService;
import ajia.domain.Product;

public class InventoryServiceStubImpl implements InventoryService {
    public void addProduct(Product product, int quantity) {
        System.out.println("InventoryServiceImpl.addProduct "
                + product.getName() + " " + quantity);
    }

    public void removeProduct(Product product, int quantity) {
        System.out.println("InventoryServiceImpl.removeProduct "
                + product.getName() + " " + quantity);
```

```
    }

    public boolean isProductAvailable(Product product, int quantity) {
        System.out.println("InventoryServiceImpl.isProductAvailable "
                + product.getName() + " " + quantity);
        return true;
    }
}
```

Listing 9.2 shows an application context file that declares a bean of the InventoryServiceStubImpl type with inventoryService as the id.

Listing 9.2 application-context.xml: application context file

```
<beans ...>
    <bean id="inventoryService"
          class="ajia.service.impl.InventoryServiceStubImpl"/>
</beans>
```

If necessary, you can inject other beans as dependencies in the inventoryService bean as well as inject this bean as into other beans. Finally, listing 9.3 shows a simple driver program to exercise the setup created so far.

Listing 9.3 Driver program to exercise Spring AOP functionality

```
package ajia.main;

import org.springframework.context.ApplicationContext;
import org.springframework.context.support.ClassPathXmlApplicationContext;
import ...

public class Main {
    public static void main(String[] args) throws Exception {
        ApplicationContext applicationContext
            = new ClassPathXmlApplicationContext(
                                "application-context.xml");

        InventoryService inventoryService
            = (InventoryService)
                applicationContext.getBean("inventoryService");
        Product ajiaBook = new Product("AJIA", "AspectJ in Action", 44.99);
        inventoryService.addProduct(ajiaBook, 1000000);
        inventoryService.removeProduct(ajiaBook, 1000000);
    }
}
```

The driver program creates an application context and obtains the inventoryService bean from it. The program then invokes a few methods on it. When you compile and run this program, you see the following output:

```
InventoryServiceImpl.addProduct AJIA 1000000
InventoryServiceImpl.removeProduct AJIA 1000000
```

It's time to add aspects written using the @AspectJ syntax into this Spring application.

9.1.2 *Utilizing the @AspectJ syntax*

Let's see @AspectJ integration in action. The aspect in listing 9.4 should come as no surprise if you read the @AspectJ syntax in chapter 7. Functionally, the aspect is auditing the use of the inventory service.

Listing 9.4 Auditing bean using @AspectJ syntax

```
package ajia.auditing;

import ...

@Aspect
public class InventoryAuditing {
    @Pointcut("execution(* *(ajia.domain.Product, int)) "
            + "&& args(product, quantity)")
    public void audited(Product product, int quantity) {}

    @Before("audited(product, quantity)")
    public void audit(JoinPoint jp, Product product, int quantity) {
        System.out.println("Audit: operation = "
                + jp.getSignature().getName()
                + " product = " + product.getName()
                + " quantity = " + quantity);
    }
}
```

`InventoryAuditing` is an @AspectJ aspect consisting of a pointcut and an advice. Next, you need to let Spring's container know about the aspect, as shown in listing 9.5.

Listing 9.5 application-context.xml: configuration for using @AspectJ aspect

```
<beans ....>

    <bean id="inventoryService"
          class=" ajia.service.impl.InventoryServiceStubImpl"/>

    <bean id="auditAspect"
          class="ajia.auditing.InventoryAuditing"/>

    <aop:aspectj-autoproxy/>
</beans>
```

In the configuration, you declare a bean corresponding to the `InventoryAuditing` type. To instruct Spring to use an advice declared in such a bean, you use the `<aop:aspectj-autoproxy/>` element (we'll examine it in detail in section 9.2.4). Now, when you compile the classes using the javac compiler and execute the program, you get the following output:

```
Audit: operation = addProduct product = AJIA quantity = 1000000
InventoryServiceImpl.addProduct AJIA 1000000
Audit: operation = removeProduct product = AJIA quantity = 1000000
InventoryServiceImpl.removeProduct AJIA 1000000
```

Without using a special compiler, you could implement auditing in the system. But for complete development support, you need a tool similar to AspectJ Development Tools (AJDT), discussed in chapter 2. Spring IDE provides just that.

9.1.3 Spring IDE

Spring's AspectJ integration provides IDE support through a set of Eclipse plugins in the form of Spring IDE (see http://springide.org/project/wiki/SpringideInstall for installation instructions). This indispensable plugin for any project using Spring lets you visualize the effects of crosscutting concerns in a way similar to that provided by AJDT. Note that the SpringSource Tools Suite (STS) includes Spring IDE in addition to many other plug-ins. For this example, when you view the code developed so far inside Eclipse, you get the crosscutting information presented in a nice form, as shown in figure 9.1.

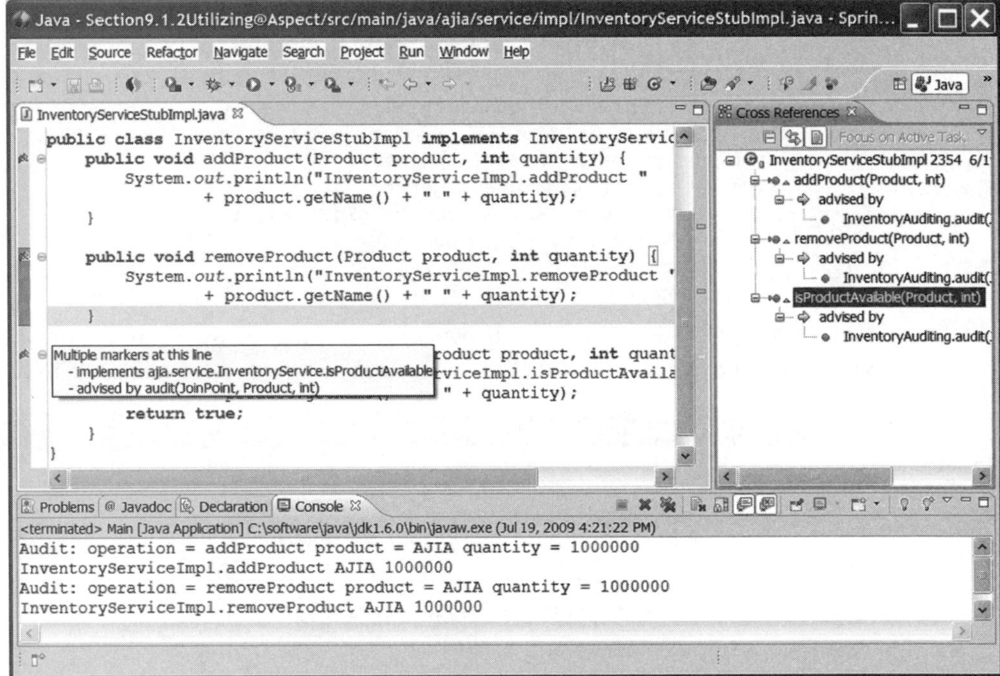

Figure 9.1 Eclipse integration for Spring showing the aspect-bean interaction

As you can see, it isn't difficult to integrate @AspectJ aspects with Spring. You may be curious about how it all works without needing a byte-code weaver. Let's deal with that question.

9.2 Spring AOP under the hood

Spring AOP is a proxy-based AOP system that modularizes crosscutting concerns. Based on the configuration instructions, Spring automatically creates a proxy for each bean that matches the criteria specified in pointcuts. The proxy intercepts calls to the original object. In this section, we'll examine the mechanics of Spring AOP, its under-the-hood implementation, and its limitations. This information will give you a better understanding of Spring AOP and guide you in deciding whether to use Spring AOP or AspectJ AOP.

Because the use of dynamic proxies is central to Spring AOP implementation, let's get a quick introduction to it.

9.2.1 A quick introduction to dynamic proxies

Starting with JDK 1.3, Java offers a mechanism to create proxies for interfaces. Given a set of interfaces, you can use the `Proxy` class to create a proxy. The creation method takes an invocation handler of the `InvocationHandler` type (which defines a single `invoke()` method). The dynamically created proxy dispatches each method to the invocation handler. You can start modularizing crosscutting functionality directly with proxies by writing an `InvocationHandler` whose `invoke()` method implements the crosscutting logic. For example, to trace method invocations, you can write a handler as shown in listing 9.6.

Listing 9.6 Tracing invocation handler to be used in a proxy

```
package ajia.proxy;

import ...

public class TracingInvocationHandler implements InvocationHandler {
    private Object target;

    public TracingInvocationHandler(Object target) {
        this.target = target;
    }

    public Object invoke(Object proxy, Method method, Object[] args)
            throws Throwable {
        System.out.println("Entering " + method);
        return method.invoke(target, args);
    }
}
```

The handler implements the crosscutting logic in the `invoke()` method. This arrangement is similar to around advice, with `method.invoke()` taking the place of the `proceed()` call. Next, you must wrap each object that you want to trace in a proxy, using the code in listing 9.7.

Listing 9.7 Creating a proxy to associate an invocation handler

```
package ajia.main;

import ...

public class Main {
    public static void main(String[] args) {
        InventoryService inventoryService = new InventoryServiceStubImpl();

        InventoryService inventoryServiceProxy
            = (InventoryService) Proxy.newProxyInstance(
                  InventoryService.class.getClassLoader(),
```

```
                        new Class[]{InventoryService.class},
                        new TracingInvocationHandler(inventoryService));

            Product ajiaBook = new Product("AJIA", "AspectJ in Action", 44.95);
            inventoryServiceProxy.addProduct(ajiaBook, 1000000);
            inventoryServiceProxy.removeProduct(ajiaBook, 1000000);
    }
}
```

Sure enough, when you execute this class, you get the following output:

```
Entering public abstract void
➥        ajia.service.InventoryService.addProduct(ajia.domain.Product,int)
InventoryServiceImpl.addProduct AJIA 1000000
Entering public abstract void
➥        ajia.service.InventoryService.removeProduct(ajia.domain.Product,int)
InventoryServiceImpl.removeProduct AJIA 1000000
```

Note that JDK dynamic proxies work only with interfaces; but you can use the Code Generation Library (CGLIB) and other byte-code engineering libraries to create proxies based on classes.

Although the proxy creation provides enough support to implement simple crosscutting functionalities, programming using proxies is too low level for typical needs of enterprise applications. Specifically, you face the following difficulties:

- *Lack of a pointcut language*—There is no pointcut language with plain proxy usage. This forces the invocation handlers to perform two roles: selecting the join point, and implementing crosscutting logic. For example, if you wanted to trace only a few specific methods, the logic to select those methods would have to reside in the `invoke()` method.
- *Explicit creation of proxies*—You must control the creation of each object that needs crosscutting functionality, in order to create a proxy and wrap the original object in it.
- *Weakly typed access to join point context*—Inside the `invoke()` method, join point context (the target object and method arguments) is available only as the raw `Object` type. This forces potentially erroneous typecasts if you need to invoke any methods on them.

All these shortcomings of the raw use of proxies make them unsuitable for implementing complex crosscutting concerns. We need is a higher level programming model—and that is exactly what Spring offers.

9.2.2 Proxy-based AOP with Spring

Spring AOP utilizes proxies as the underlying implementation while simplifying the associated programming model. The result is an AOP solution geared toward enterprise applications. Spring's programming model overcomes issues with the raw use of proxies in the following ways:

- *Pointcut language*—Spring supports multiple possibilities for selecting join points. The regular expression–based mechanism was a popular choice in pre-Spring 2.0 days. If you're using Spring 2.0 or a newer version, AspectJ as the pointcut expression language is the preferred way to express the selection criterion.
- *Automatic proxy creation*—The Spring container already controls the creation of beans for the purpose of dependency injection (DI). Spring can extend the creation logic to wrap those beans in an automatically created proxy. The result is reduced programming burden for developers.
- *Strongly typed access to join point context*—Through @AspectJ and schema-style aspect integration, due to use of context-collecting pointcuts (as discussed in section 4.4), advice can access join point context in a strongly typed manner. For example, you can use the `args()` pointcut to make the `product` argument to `InventoryService` methods available as the `Product` type. This reduces typecasts and associated `ClassCastExceptions`.

Let's look at how Spring offers all these advantages and how it fits into the overall DI mechanism.

9.2.3 Spring AOP internals

Spring uses proxies configured with pointcuts and advice as a mechanism to implement AOP while staying with the overall mechanism dictated by proxies. Figure 9.2 illustrates the overall scheme.

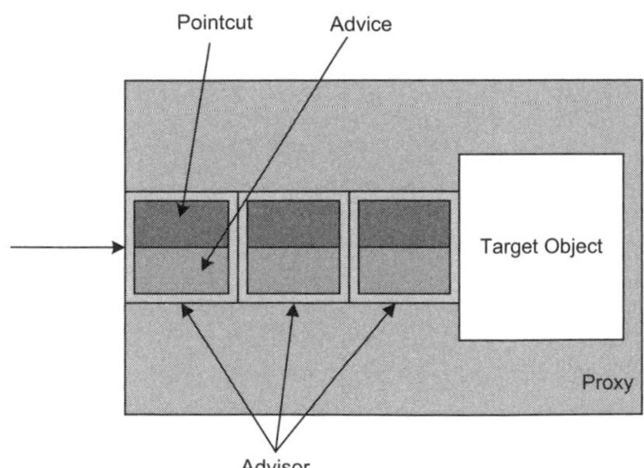

Figure 9.2 A simplified schematic of Spring AOP with pointcuts and advice. The proxy object is a wrapper around the target object and advisors. Each advisor contains a pointcut and an advice. The pointcut decides whether the invoked method is to be advised, and the advice contains the crosscutting functionality.

Let's see the roles played by each component:

- A proxy implements the same interfaces as those implemented by the target object. Alternatively, the proxy may extend the class of the target object. Either way, the external code may use the proxy as a drop-in replacement for the target object.

- Each proxy contains advisors. *Advisor* is an internal Spring concept that developers using AspectJ integration need not be familiar with (with the older Spring AOP, the advisor concept was explicit). Each advisor, in turn, contains two parts: pointcut and advice.
- The pointcut selects the join points, to decide if the advice should execute.
- The advice implements the logic needed for the crosscutting functionality.

By default, Spring uses JDK dynamic proxies. Of course, it works only when the target class implements one or more interfaces. If this isn't the case, or you explicitly want to avoid JDK proxies, Spring offers CGLIB-based proxies, where it dynamically creates a subclass of the target class. Because Java prevents overriding final methods, the dynamically created proxy can't advise final methods in the target class. Spring produces a warning if it detects such a situation. If a final method is invoked, it can lead to inconsistency between the target and proxy object state. If you see such a warning, you should consider avoiding CGLIB proxies.

Let's see how Spring handles the creation of a proxy and blends it with the core DI mechanism.

9.2.4 Proxy-based AOP in DI framework

Spring AOP fits well with the overall DI mechanism that is at the heart of the Spring framework. You declare configuration only for the primary injection. For example, you can use the following snippet to inject an `OrderServiceImpl` into an `OrderController`:

```
<bean id="orderController" class="ajia.web.OrderController">
    <property name="orderService" ref="orderService"/>
</bean>

<bean id="orderService" class="ajia.service.impl.OrderServiceImpl">
    ...
</bean>
```

With this configuration, Spring injects the raw `orderService` bean into the `orderController` bean, as shown in the upper part of figure 9.3.

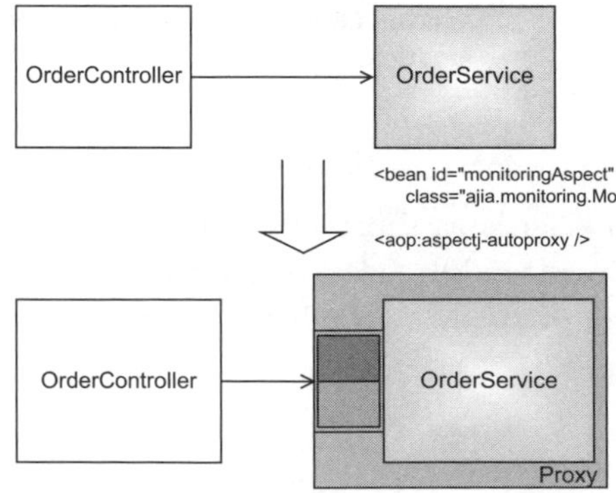

Figure 9.3 Proxy-based AOP working with DI. You declare the configuration, such as the injection of the `OrderService` bean into the `OrderController` bean. Spring's proxy-based AOP creates proxies around any bean that needs to be advised and injects that bean instead of the original.

To implement a crosscutting concern, you declare a bean for an aspect and configure the application context to have Spring's autoproxy mechanism use that aspect:

```
<bean id="monitoringAspect"
      class="ajia.monitoring.MonitoringAspect"/>

<aop:aspectj-autoproxy/>
```

The declaration `<aop:aspectj-autoproxy/>` is an instruction to Spring that it should do the following:

- Examine each bean to check if it's an aspect (by checking for the @Aspect annotation associated with it). If so, check pointcuts and advice in it.
- For each bean in the application context, check if the advice would apply to a method in that bean.
- For each matching bean, automatically create a proxy (hence the name *auto-proxy*) wrapping the original bean—the target object. The proxy implements the same interfaces or extends the same class as the target object.
- Replace the original bean in the application context with its proxy. When Spring's DI performs injection, the proxied bean—and not the target bean—is injected.

The DI mechanism makes proxy-based AOP transparent to the programmer. The result is a clean separation of core injection logic and crosscutting logic.

9.2.5 *Limitations of Spring AOP*

Now that you have a good understanding of the mechanism employed by Spring AOP, let's understand some of its limitations. All of these limitations are due to the use of proxies as the underlying mechanism.

METHOD EXECUTION-ONLY JOIN POINTS

Spring AOP works only for method execution join points, because proxies can intercept only method executions. For many crosscutting concerns seen in enterprise applications, this may not be an immediate problem. For example, transaction management and security often need to intercept at the method execution level. Even in implementations using AspectJ, which supports a whole range of join points, method execution is by far the most commonly used join point.

BEAN-ONLY CROSSCUTTING

The proxy creation requires that the Spring container create the objects that need to be advised. Because Spring controls the instantiation of beans, Spring AOP works naturally with beans. Although you can apply Spring AOP programmatically to any object, as long as you can control its instantiation, this isn't often done in practice. The main reason to avoid programmatic use of Spring AOP is to limit dependency on the Spring Framework.

This limitation dictates the architecture utilized. For example, you can't apply transaction management and security at the domain entities level, because domain entities typically aren't Spring beans. In practice, this means you need to employ a service layer, expose the service objects as Spring beans, and apply crosscutting at that level. In chapter 16, we'll examine the use of AspectJ-based crosscutting to overcome this limitation.

EXTERNAL CALL–ONLY INTERCEPTION

With Spring's proxy-based AOP, the calls to the self (the `this` object) made from the target object aren't advised. Unless the object on which a method is invoked is a proxy, the advisor chain doesn't come into the picture. For example, consider the following implementation of the `removeProduct()` method:

```
public void removeProduct(Product product, int quantity) {
    if (isProductAvailable(product, quantity)) {
        ...
    }
}
```

The execution of `isProductAvailable()` called from the `removeProduct()` method won't be advised even if the pointcut selects it. The call is being made on the `this` object, which is the raw target object and not the proxy. Figure 9.4 shows illustrate the external call-only limitation.

You can get around the self-call limitation by obtaining the proxy to the self object and invoking a method on it. For example, you can modify the code as follows:

```
((InventoryService)AopContext.currentProxy()).isProductAvailable(product,
➥   quantity)
```

The `AopContext.currentProxy()` method returns the current proxy, if any. Essentially, it gives access to the proxy for the current target. Although the method gets the job done, this approach has one serious issue: you just made the business objects aware of the use of the proxy. Therefore, you should use such an approach only in extreme situations. If you find that you need to advise self-calls often, it may be the time to think about using the AspectJ weaver. Note that AspectJ doesn't have this problem because no dichotomy exists between the target and proxy object and self-calls are no different from calls to outside objects.

Now that you have a basic understanding of Spring AOP, let's discuss @AspectJ integration in full.

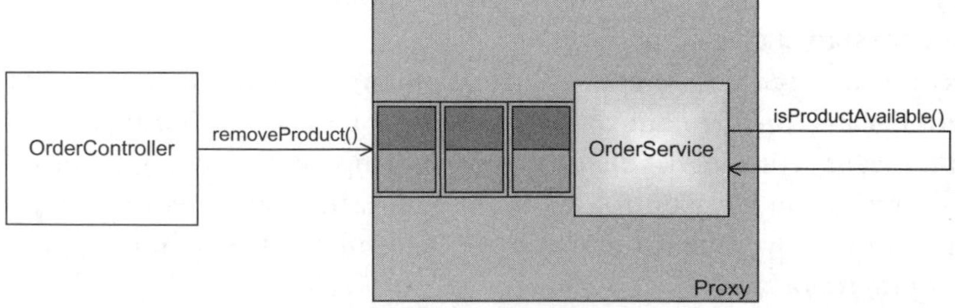

Figure 9.4 Spring AOP advises method execution resulting from an external call. When the object invokes methods on the self object, the proxy chain is bypassed. Thus no advice applies to such calls.

9.3 @AspectJ support in depth

Spring offers integration with aspects expressed in the @AspectJ syntax that we discussed in chapter 7. You get the full expressive power of the syntax while still staying within the proxy-based AOP. Further, such syntax facilitates easy migration to full-power AspectJ, when needed, by switching to AspectJ weaving. Because Spring AOP uses the proxy-based implementation, Spring supports only a subset of the @AspectJ language. For example, because a proxy-based AOP supports only method execution join points, Spring's @AspectJ integration doesn't support pointcuts such as `call()` and `handler()`. In addition, some of the static crosscutting constructs, such as compile-time errors and warnings, aren't supported either. But given the primary importance of the "bean" concept in Spring, there is an additional pointcut to select join points in specific beans. In this section, we'll look at the parts of the @AspectJ language that Spring AOP supports.

To integrate an aspect with Spring, you declare a bean corresponding to the @AspectJ aspect in the same way as any other bean. If needed, you can even inject dependencies into this bean and use them in the advice logic. Then, you instruct Spring through XML to use those beans to advise Spring beans. Figure 9.5 shows the general scheme of @AspectJ integration.

By default, Spring includes all beans with the `@Aspect` annotation for the proxy-creation purpose. If you'd rather control which aspects should be automatically applied, you can specify the `<aop:include>` element with a list of bean names nested in `<aop:aspectj-autoproxy>`:

```
<aop:aspectj-autoproxy>
    <aop:include name="auditAspect"/>
</aop:aspectj-autoproxy>
```

With such a declaration, Spring uses only the listed beans for autoproxying.

By default, Spring uses JDK dynamic proxies as described in section 9.2.1. But if a class being advised doesn't implement any interfaces, you can't use JDK dynamic proxies. In those situations, or if you wish to use CGLIB-based proxies, you can set the optional `proxy-target-class` attribute to `true`:

```
<aop:aspectj-autoproxy proxy-target-class="true"/>
```

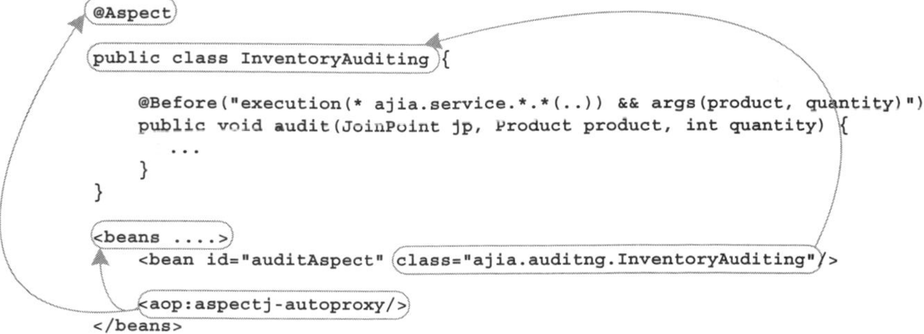

Figure 9.5 The @AspectJ integration. You can use any class written using the @AspectJ syntax. In the application context, you must instantiate a bean of that class. The `<aop:aspectj-autoproxy>` element indicates application of the aspects defined using the @AspectJ syntax.

Doing so lets you advise beans that don't implement any interfaces. It also lets you advise a class that implements interfaces, but that you want to advise methods declared in the class that aren't declared in any of the interfaces.

Equipped with the general structure of @AspectJ integration, let's see how this integration supports two specific forms of crosscutting.

9.3.1 Dynamic crosscutting

Dynamic crosscutting comes in the form of advice that utilizes pointcuts. Spring uses the @AspectJ syntax and semantics to the extent possible given the constraint of a proxy-based implementation. In some cases, it deviates a bit to simplify certain usage patterns found in typical Spring applications.

POINTCUTS

Due to Spring's proxy-based mechanism, which restricts the selected join points to method execution only, you can't use AspectJ's full power. Specifically, you can't use `call()`, `initialization()`, `preinitialization()`, `staticinitialization()`, `get()`, `set()`, `handler()`, `adviceexecution()`, `withincode()`, `cflow()`, `cflowbelow()`, `if()`, `@this()`, and `@withincode()` pointcuts. Table 9.1 shows the AspectJ pointcuts that you can use in Spring. The same pointcuts are also available in schema-style AOP, as you'll see in section 9.4. Note that all context-collecting pointcuts may specify types or identifiers as the parameters. If an expression specifies an identifier in place of type, then in addition to performing selection, the pointcut also collects the matching object that advice may use in the same way as the core @AspectJ syntax. For examples of each of the pointcut, see chapter 7.

Table 9.1 Pointcuts available in AspectJ pointcut expression

Pointcut	Selection
`execution(Method-pattern)`	Select methods that match the specified pattern. This pointcut behaves the same way as in AspectJ, except the pattern specified can't be a constructor pattern, because Spring-AOP can't advise object construction.
`this(TypeOrIdentifier)`	Select methods where the proxy object's type matches the specified type.
`target(TypeOrIdentifier)`	Select methods where the target object's type matches the specified type pattern. Note an important difference between Spring's matching from that of AspectJ. In AspectJ, the `target()` pointcut matches the same objects matched by `this()` for an execution join point. In Spring, `this()` matches the proxy, whereas `target()` matches the target object.
`args(TypeOrIdentifier1, TypeOrIdenifier2, ..)`	Select methods where the method argument's types match the specified type patterns.

Table 9.1 Pointcuts available in AspectJ pointcut expression *(continued)*

Pointcut	Selection
`within(Type-pattern)`	Select methods within the lexical scope of the types mathcing the specified pattern.
`@target(AnnotTypeOrIdentifier)`	Select methods where the annotation with the target object's type matches the specified annotation type patterns. Note that use of `@this()` isn't allowed, because the proxy object is automatically generated and selecting annotations based on it isn't useful.
`@args(AnnotTypeOrIdentifier1, AnnotTypeOrIdentifier2, ..)`	Select methods where the annotations with the method parameters' type match the specified annotation type patterns.
`@within(AnnotTypeOrIdentifier)`	Select methods where the annotation with the defining type matches the specified annotation type pattern.
`@annotation(AnnotTypeOrIdentifier)`	Select methods that carry the specified annotation type pattern.

You can compose pointcuts using unary and binary operations to form a complex join-point selection criterion much the same way with the @AspectJ syntax.

Spring also offers an additional pointcut to select Spring beans.

SELECTING SPRING BEANS

Bean is the most fundamental concept in Spring. An application is a composition of beans created as per the configuration instructions. Beans are also the objects that can be proxied to apply aspects. It's therefore appropriate that there be a way to select specific beans based on their identifiers. Starting with version 2.5, Spring offers a new pointcut designator: `bean(<name-pattern>)`. The name-pattern follows the AspectJ matching rules for a name pattern with * being the only allowed wildcard. This pointcut represents a Spring-specific extension to the AspectJ expression language and as such is useful only with Spring AOP.

This pointcut designator offers two interesting ways to select beans if you follow an appropriate naming convention:

- *Selecting a vertical slice of beans*—If you follow a convention where bean names include a string indicating their role from the business perspective, a `bean()` pointcut can select beans based on business functionality. For example, you can use the `bean(inventory*)` pointcut to select all inventory related beans such as `inventoryRepository`, `inventoryService`, and `inventoryController`.
- *Selecting a horizontal slice of beans*—If you follow a convention where bean names include a string indicating their role from the architectural perspective, a `bean()` pointcut can select beans based on their architectural role. For example, you can use `bean(*Repository)` to select all repository beans. Without the `bean()` pointcut, you have to rely on the package structure or type-based pointcuts, which can sometimes be too restrictive.

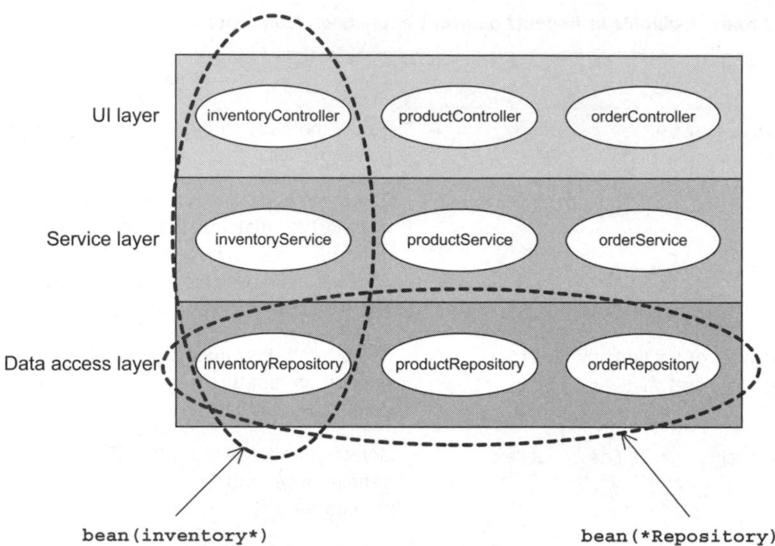

Figure 9.6 Selecting horizontal and vertical slices of beans based on their names using the `bean()` pointcut designator

Figure 9.6 illustrates selecting bean slices using `bean()` pointcuts.

Let's see a few examples of this pointcut. Table 9.2 shows pointcuts and join points selected by them.

You can use unary and binary operators to negate or combine `bean()` pointcuts in the same way as with other pointcuts.

Table 9.2 Examples of `bean()` pointcut and join points selected

Pointcut	Join points selected in
`bean(inventoryRepository)`	The bean named `inventoryRepository`
`bean(*)`	Any bean
`bean(inventory*)`	Any bean whose name starts with `inventory`
`bean(*Repository)`	Any bean whose name ends with `Repository`
`bean(inventory/showInventory)`	The bean named `inventory/showInventory` (designating, say, a controller handling that URL)
`bean(inventory/*)`	Any bean whose name starts with `inventory/` (designating, say, any controller handling inventory-related URLs)
`bean(inventory/*/edit)`	Any bean whose name starts with `inventory/` and ends with `/edit` (designating, say, any controller handling the edit operation functionality related to inventory)
`bean(service:name=monitoring)`	The bean named `service:name=monitoring` (designating, say, a JMX bean)

After you select join points of interest, you can advise them with crosscutting logic as you see next.

ADVICE

Spring's @AspectJ integration supports all advice types: before, after (including after returning and after throwing variations), and around. They all follow the same syntax and semantics as the @AspectJ that we discussed in chapter 7, except for a few differences for the around advice. Therefore, in this section, we'll examine only the around advice.

Following the core @AspectJ semantics, around advice in Spring integration must declare an argument of type `ProceedingJoinPoint` so that it can call the `proceed()` method on it. If the around advice needs to proceed with the same context, it can call the no-arg version of `proceed()`, again matching the core @AspectJ semantics. But the difference comes when it wants to proceed with an altered context. In Spring, you must pass arguments to `proceed()` matching the join-point arguments. Specifically, contrasting with discussion in section 7.4.3, you don't need to and can't pass the `this` and target objects even though you collect them as join point context. For example, in the following contrived example, the advice doubles the quantity to check when `isProductAvailable()` method is executed:

```
@Pointcut("execution(* isProductAvailable(ajia.domain.Product, int)) "
        + "&& this(service)")
public void checkAvailability(InventoryService service) {}

@Around("checkAvailability(service)")
public Object doubleForInventoryCheck(ProceedingJoinPoint pjp,
                                      InventoryService service)
        throws Throwable {
    Object[] args = pjp.getArgs();
    Integer quantity = (Integer)args[1];
    args[1] = quantity * 2; // double the quantity
    return pjp.proceed(args); // check for doubled quantity
}
```

Note that there is no way to modify the service (collected using the `this()` pointcut) with which the advice should proceed. In reality, in a typical Spring application, proceeding with altered context is uncommon (which is why I needed a contrived example)—more so with altered `this` and target objects. You'll use the no-arg version of `proceed()` on most occasions.

ASPECT ORDERING

Unlike core @AspectJ, Spring's integration doesn't support aspect precedence rules using `@DeclarePrecedence` annotation (this may change in a future version of Spring). Instead, it employs a scheme based on the `Ordered` interface (which is a general scheme that applies to other Spring concepts such as `BeanFactoryPostProcessor` and `BeanPostProcessor` as well). If an aspect needs to control ordering, it implements the `Ordered` interface and the configuration sets its `order` property, which specifies the relative order. For example, if you need `SecurityAspect` to have higher precedence than `AuditingAspect`, you have both implement the `Ordered` interface as follows:

```
@Aspect
public class SecurityAspect implements Ordered {
    private int order;

    ... pointcut and advice etc.

    public void setOrder(int order) {
        this.order = order;
    }
}
```

The `AuditingAspect` similarly implements the `Ordered` interface. Then, you set the `order` property of bean for both aspects, as follows:

```
<bean id="securityAspect" class="ajia.security.SecurityAspect">
    <property name="order" value="1"/>
</bean>

<bean id="auditingAspect" class="ajia.auditing.AuditingAspect">
    <property name="order" value="2"/>
</bean>
```

An aspect with a lower value for the `order` property has higher precedence over an aspect with a higher value. In the previous snippet, advice in `SecurityAspect` has higher precedence than advice in `AuditingAspect`.

An alternative to the `Ordered` interface is `@Order`. The aspect is marked with the `@Order` annotation, whose value specifies the aspect's relative order. For example, to get the same ordering as earlier, you mark the `SecurityAspect` as follows:

```
@Aspect
@Order(1)
public class SecurityAspect {
    ...
}
```

Similarly, you mark the `AuditingAspect` with the `@Order` annotation and specify a higher value (lower precedence):

```
@Aspect
@Order(2)
public class AuditingAspect {
    ...
}
```

Essentially, with the `@Order` annotation, the responsibility to specify the order shifts from configuration to code. You choose the `Ordered` interface if you wish to control order through configuration; otherwise, you use the `@Order` annotation.

ASPECT INSTANTIATION MODELS

Spring's AspectJ integration supports the per-object aspect instantiation models through `perthis()` and `pertarget()` aspect associations (specified using the `value` property of the `@Aspect` annotation). An aspect with `perthis()` has a separate aspect instance bound for each Spring bean's `this` object (the proxy around the bean), whereas `pertarget()` has a separate aspect instance bound to each Spring bean's target object (the original bean). Spring doesn't support other instantiation models: `percflow()`, `percflowbelow()`, and `pertypewithin()`.

This completes our discussion of dynamic crosscutting. Spring supports a limited form of static crosscutting as well.

9.3.2 Static crosscutting

The @AspectJ integration supports the static crosscutting construct of declaring parent types by offering the `@DeclareParents` functionality (a future version of Spring may support `@DeclareMixin` as well). For example, as shown in listing 9.8, you can rewrite the aspect in listing 9.4 to use @AspectJ style.

Listing 9.8 Using declare parents with @AspectJ style

```
package ajia.auditing;

import ...

@Aspect
public class InventoryAuditing {
    @DeclareParents(value="ajia.service.*+",
                    defaultImpl=AuditRecorderDefaultImpl.class)
    private AuditRecorder mixin;

    @Pointcut("execution(* *(ajia.domain.Product, int))"
              + "&& this(auditRecorder)"
              + "&& args(product, quantity)")
    public void audited(AuditRecorder auditRecorder,
                        Product product, int quantity) {}

    @Before("audited(auditRecorder, product, quantity)")
    public void audit(JoinPoint jp, AuditRecorder auditRecorder,
                      Product product, int quantity) {
        auditRecorder.record("Operation = "
                + jp.getSignature().getName()
                + " product = " + product.getName()
                + " quantity = " + quantity);
    }
}
```

The `AuditRecorder` interface declares the `record()` method, whereas the `AuditRecorderDefaultImpl` implements the method to print to a logger (these types are available in the book's downloadable sources).

Statelessness (not holding any conversational state) of a typical Spring bean is at odds with the typical use of declaring a parent to add new state. This limits the practical use of declaring a parent for a Spring bean only to introduce a simple state exposed to JMX (usage statistics, performance metrics) or the state that is immediately persisted (metering, audit records).

Although @AspectJ support is powerful and easy to use, it's useful only when you're working with Java 5 or later. To support Java 1.4, Spring provides an XML-based alternative that we discuss next.

9.4 Schema-style AOP support

Schema-style AOP support offers a way to turn a plain Java class into an aspect by specifying the aspect-related metadata using XML. The idea is similar to the @AspectJ syntax you've seen in the previous section, except here the crosscutting information is in XML form. By avoiding the use of Java annotations, the schema-styled AOP makes it possible to express AOP constructs in a form suitable to Java versions prior to Java 5, where there is no language support for annotations.

Figure 9.7 shows the general structure of schema-style AOP support.

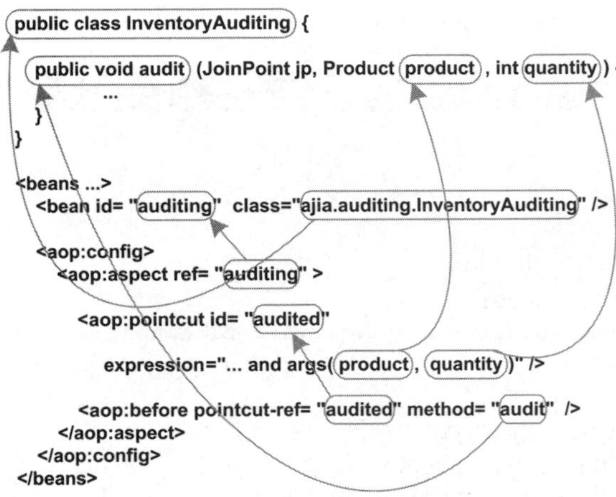

Figure 9.7 Schema-style AOP. Aspects stand in for class, methods stand in for advice, and pointcuts are described in XML. The use of context-collecting pointcuts such as args() lets you collect join point context and makes it available to advice in a strongly type manner.

Light treatment of schema-style AOP

Because @AspectJ offers a better programming model for Java 5 and later, and the mapping from @AspectJ to schema-style AOP is straightforward, I give only an overview of this syntax and show salient differences without going into all the details. Spring 3.0 requires that you use Java 5 or better, further limiting the usefulness of the schema-style AOP. If you must use the schema-style AOP, read the Spring documentation for full details.

The overall idea behind the schema-style AOP is simple: express the state and behavior part in classes, while expressing the crosscutting rules in XML. The various crosscutting elements map as follows.

9.4.1 Mapping aspects

Plain classes along with metadata expressed in XML represent aspects in schema-style AOP. You create a bean of the class representing an aspect and declare an aspect based on that bean. In figure 9.5, the `InventoryAuditing` class is a plain Java class; it extends no special class, implements no special interfaces, and carries no special annotations. This style therefore extends Spring's POJO philosophy to aspects.

An `<aop:aspect>` element inside an `<aop:config>` element declares the intention to use the bean referred by the `ref` attribute as an aspect. The `<aop:advisor>` element offers a way to use advisors written using Spring's traditional AOP API.

Declaring an `<aop:config>` element is an indication to Spring's application context loader that the aspects defined need to be applied to beans. This element may also declare an attribute `proxy-target-class` to instruct Spring to use class-based proxies created using CGLIB. The default value for this attribute is `false`, indicating the choice of JDK dynamic proxies.

Unlike the @AspectJ integration discussed in section 9.3.1, schema-style AOP supports only the singleton instantiation model. In other words, it doesn't support `perthis()` or `pertarget()` instantiation models.

9.4.2 Mapping pointcuts

An `<aop:pointcut>` element inside `<aop:config>` or `<aop:aspect>` elements defines a pointcut. Any aspect may refer to the pointcuts defined at the `<aop:config>` level, thus making them global pointcuts. In contrast, only the enclosing aspect may refer to the pointcuts defined at the `<aop:aspect>` level.

Each `<aop:pointcut>` element has two mandatory attributes: `id` and `expression`. The `id` attribute assigns an identifier that an advice may later use to refer to the pointcut. The `expression` attribute specifies a pointcut expression. No associated Java code is required to define pointcuts. This is a purposeful deviation from the @AspectJ syntax because once the metadata is removed from the method standing in for a pointcut, the only thing left is the pointcut name; this can be easily expressed in XML using the `id` attribute. In other words, the method serves no interesting purpose.

In figure 9.7, we declare the `audited` pointcut. As with @AspectJ syntax, the pointcut may collect context using pointcuts such as `args()`. You can then use this pointcut in advice declarations.

A pointcut expression may use any of the supported pointcut designators shown in table 9.1. Although each pointcut is assigned an id, unlike the @AspectJ integration, it isn't possible to use those ids to compose pointcuts the way you can using the traditional or @AspectJ syntax. For example, consider the `inService()` pointcut defined using the schema-style AOP. It's an error to use this pointcut in the definition of another pointcut:

```
execution(* *(..) throws RemoteException) && inService()
```

The sole use of the id is to refer to the pointcut from advice elements, as we'll discuss in the next section. Note that although you can't use the pointcut defined in the XML itself for composition purposes, you can use pointcuts defined using the @AspectJ style aspects. But because the main usage of the schema-style AOP is for pre-Java 5 versions, using @AspectJ aspects is ruled out, making this possibility of little practical use.

9.4.3 Mapping advice

A method along with an XML element designating the kind of advice defines an advice in the schema-style AOP. The method's arguments serve as the join-point context, and the body serves as the advice implementation. Methods standing in for an advice don't have any special requirements beyond what makes sense for an advice: methods must be public, non-static, and return `void` unless they represent an around advice. Following the @AspectJ syntax, a method may declare variables of `JoinPoint` or `JoinPoint.StaticPart` to obtain the join-point information. An around advice may also declare a variable of `ProceedingJoinPoint` to proceed with the advised join point.

A before advice is mapped using an `<aop:before>` element. An after advice is mapped using an `<aop:after>`, `<aop:after-returning>`, and `<aop:after-throwing>` element following the corresponding advice kind in AspectJ. Similarly, an around advice is mapped using an `<aop:around>` element. Each of these elements may define the following attributes:

- `pointcut`—This attribute specifies a pointcut expression. The expression may use any pointcut from table 9.1. In addition, the context-collecting pointcuts may specify identifiers, instead of just types. Any identifier used must match one of the parameter names in the advice method. Further, the pointcut expression must map all identifiers used in the advice method except those of `JoinPoint`, `JoinPoint.StaticPart`, and `ProceedingJoinPoint` type.
- `pointcut-ref`—This attribute specifies an id attribute to a `<aop:pointcut>` element. The id must match a `<aop:pointcut>` element defined in the same `<aop:aspect>` definition as the advice or a global pointcut defined in an `<aop:config>` element. The expression associated with the referred pointcut must match the same criteria of context-matching as described for the pointcut attribute.
- `method`—This attribute specifies the name of the method in the class of the referred bean (specified by the `ref` attribute of the enclosing `<aop:aspect>` element).
- `arg-names`—This optional attribute specifies the name of the arguments for the method. It lets you map the name of the context collected by pointcut to the method parameters. It serves the same purpose as the `argNames` attribute in @AspectJ syntax (see section 7.3.2). If you don't specify this parameter, you must compile the class standing for the referred aspect using either –g or –g:vars. As a last resort, Spring tries to deduce arguments from the parameter's type. For example, if the method takes one parameter of type `Product` and another of type `int`, Spring can correctly bind the `Product` and `int` context. This scheme, of course, doesn't work if you have multiple parameters of the same type.

Each advice kind may offer additional attributes and have additional peculiarities. The following points should make sense, because they map well from the @AspectJ syntax:

- The `<aop:before>` element doesn't specify any additional attributes.
- The `<aop:after-returning>` element may specify the `returning` attribute to collect and pass the return value to the advice. The value of this attribute must be one of the method arguments. The type of the argument must be compatible with the value returned by the advised join point.

  For example, consider the following `recordShipment()` method to be used as an after returning advice:

  ```
  public void recordShipment(Order order, String trackingNumber) {
      ... email shipment notification
  }
  ```

  The method needs the order as well as the tracking number. The order is available as the parameter to the advised method, so you use an `args()` pointcut to collect it. The tracking number is the return value of the advised method that you'll pass as the `trackingNumber` argument to the advice. Hence, you specify `trackingNumber` as the value of the `returning` attribute:

  ```
  <aop:after-returning pointcut="execution(String ship(ajia.domain.Order))
  ➥                                && args(order)"
                       method="recordShipment"
                       returning="trackingNumber">
  ```

  You can specify `Object` as the type to capture the return value of any type. Spring AOP boxes any primitives, if needed.

  The `<aop:after-throwing>` element is similar to the after returning advice, except you use the `throwing` attribute instead of `returning` attribute. The identifier specified by the `throwing` attribute gives access to the thrown exception.
- An around advice is mapped using an `<aop:around>` element. The method must declare a return value compatible with the selected join points. The return type `Object` is treated in the same way as in the @AspectJ syntax; it's compatible with any return type including primitives and `void`. The method typically declares a parameter of `ProceedingJoinPoint` type. This parameter lets you call `proceed()` when it wants to proceed with the advised join point. The invocation of the `proceed()` method must follow the rules described in section 9.3.1.

Schema-style AOP also supports a limited form of static crosscutting that we'll examine next.

9.4.4 *Mapping static crosscutting*

With this feature, you can declare a new interface as the parent for beans matching a certain type pattern and delegate the implementation to a default implementation. This feature is much like the `declare parents` and `@DeclareParents` feature in AspectJ, with appropriate modifications to work with Spring AOP. An XML element maps to static crosscutting that offers a way to declare new interfaces as parent types.

The declared interface and its default implementation are, of course, implemented in Java.

For example, the following snippet declares `ajia.auditing.AuditRecorder` to be a parent of all types in the `ajia.service` package. It also instructs Spring to use `ajia.auditing.AuditRecorderDefaultImpl` as the implementation for the interface:

```
<aop:declare-parents types-matching="ajia.service.*"
                implement-interface="ajia.auditing.AuditRecorder"
                default-impl="ajia.auditing.AuditRecorderDefaultImpl"/>
```

The aspects can then safely cast any bean of the `ajia.service` type as `ajia.auditing.AuditRecorder`.

Schema-style AOP is a big improvement over old-style Spring AOP that simplifies writing aspects even for newcomers to the AOP field. But as noted at the beginning of the section, you should consider @AspectJ as your first choice if you're using Java 5 or a later version.

9.5 Tapping into the full power of AspectJ

So far in this chapter, we've focused on Spring's proxy-based AOP. But you can use Spring applications with the regular AspectJ weaver to get the full-power of AOP. You can then use the full AspectJ syntax and crosscut join points other than method execution. You also don't have to limit yourself to Spring beans. In this section, we'll look into configuring aspects using Spring DI and leveraging Spring-driven load-time weaving (LTW). Another usage extends Spring's DI to objects that aren't Spring beans; we'll discuss that possibility in chapter 16 because it represents a specific use of AspectJ.

9.5.1 Configuring aspects using Spring DI

When you use the AspectJ weaver, you may need to inject dependencies into aspect instances much the same way as for other Spring beans. For example, you may need to inject a monitoring agent into a monitoring aspect. When you use aspects in a Spring application, the best practice is to use Spring's DI to inject dependencies.

You saw an example of such usage in section 6.2.8 to inject the cache bean into the caching aspect. Aspects can't be instantiated manually using the constructor (which is Spring's default mechanism for creating beans), so you must use the `aspectOf()` method to create the aspect or access one that is already created. Spring provides the `factory-method` attribute to specify a static method that should be used instead of the constructor. Combining this information leads to using `factory-method="aspectOf"` as an additional specification for the bean corresponding to the aspect. This mechanism works for aspects written using the traditional syntax as well as the @AspectJ syntax (in which case the `aspectOf()` method is introduced in such an aspect by the weaver). Note that aspects used with the proxy-based AOP (declared using @AspectJ or XML-based syntax) are Spring beans and shouldn't use the `aspectOf()` approach to instantiation.

The use of `aspectOf()` as the factory method works only for singleton aspects. It doesn't work for other kinds of aspect instantiation: `perthis()`, `pertarget()`, `percflow()`, `percflowbelow()`, and `pertypewithin()`. For these aspect associations, you can use the domain object DI aspects to configure each newly created aspect instance. We'll discuss this technique in chapter 16.

9.5.2 Spring-driven LTW

AspectJ's support for load-time weaving, described in chapter 8, uses a Java VM Tool Interface (JVMTI) agent. But using the agent requires modifying the launch script to add `-javaagent:<path-to>/aspectjweaver.jar`. Often, a different set of developers (Operations) controls the launch script. Starting with version 2.5, Spring makes using LTW simpler and puts more power in the hands of application developers. All you need to do is add the `<context:load-time-weaver/>` element in one of the application configuration files. We'll look at this arrangement in detail later in this section. First, let's see this in action through a simple example.

SPRING-DRIVEN LTW IN ACTION

We'll start with the same jpetstore application (shipped as a part of Spring download) and the same setup as in chapter 8, section 8.4. But instead of making modifications to the deployed application, you'll make the same modifications to the application before deploying it to better show that you don't need changes to the deployment environment (except that if you're using Tomcat or GlassFish, you need to copy a jar to the server's lib directory, as you'll see in a moment). Note that it's valid to make changes in the deployed application as well.

> **No proxies, really!**
>
> Let's make one point clear, which is often a source of confusion: Spring-driven LTW isn't a proxy-based AOP; it's just a way to simplify AspectJ's LTW in Spring applications. It does so by leveraging the server's infrastructure or by augmenting that infrastructure to introduce AspectJ's byte-code weaver such that classes pass through it while being loaded into the VM.

Follow these steps to have the application work with Spring-driven LTW:

1 Prepare the application for Spring-driven LTW. In this step, you create a separate XML file to enable the load-time weaver. By using a separate file, you can easily enable or disable LTW by including or excluding the file from application context. Listing 9.9 shows code that declares the use of LTW.

Listing 9.9 Context file (weaverContext.xml) to enable Spring-driven LTW

```
<beans ...>
    <context:load-time-weaver/>
</beans>
```

To enable LTW, you need to add this file when creating the application context as shown in step 2.

2 Update the application context to include LTW configuration. You need to include weavingContext.xml as a part of the application context. Because you're working with a web application, the Spring way of doing this is to add the file to the `contextConfigLocation` parameter in web.xml. Modify web.xml to add src/main/webapp/WEB-INF/weaverContext.xml, as shown in listing 9.10

Listing 9.10 Modifications to web.xml to add Spring-driven LTW

```
<context-param>
    <param-name>contextConfigLocation</param-name>
    <param-value>/WEB-INF/dataAccessContext-local.xml
                 /WEB-INF/applicationContext.xml
                 /WEB-INF/weaverContext.xml
    </param-value>
</context-param>
```

Although the first two steps are sufficient for a few application servers (we'll discuss those in the section that follows), Tomcat and GlassFish need an extra step. If you're using other supported servers, you can skip to step 4.

3 (Tomcat and GlassFish only.) Prepare the server. Tomcat by default doesn't support the instrumentation capability. But it supports replacing its classloader with one specified by the user. Spring already provides such a classloader. Create a new META-INF directory *parallel to the WEB-INF* directory, and add the context.xml file shown in listing 9.11.

Listing 9.11 Configuration to replacing Tomcat's classloader (META-INF/context.xml)

```
<Context path="/jpetstore" reloadable="false">
  <Loader loaderClass=
            "org.springframework.instrument.
➥                 classloading.tomcat.TomcatInstrumentableClassLoader"
          useSystemClassLoaderAsParent="false"/>
</Context>
```

You also need to make `TomcatInstrumentableClassLoader` available to the server. You do that by copying org.springframework.instrument.classloading-*.jar (or spring-instrument-classloading-*.jar, if you use Maven downloaded dependencies) to %TOMCAT_HOME%/lib. Now you need to prepare the aspects and associated configuration.

4 Prepare the aspects. This is logically the same step as in section 8.4. As you did there, you use the aspect from chapter 7, listing 7.10 and the concrete subaspect defined using the XML syntax from listing 8.2. First, copy ajia/monitoring/Monitoring.java to jpetstore's source directory and aop.xml to the META-INF directory. The directory structure looks like this:

```
org.springframework.samples.jpetstore/
    src/
        main/
            java/
                ajia/
                    monitoring/
                        Monitoring.java
            resources/
                META-INF/
                    aop.xml
            webapp/
                WEB-INF/
                    web.xml
                    weaverContext.xml
                META-INF/
                    context.xml
```

5 Build the war file, and deploy the application. Now that everything is set up, you're ready to deploy the application. From the jpetstore directory, execute the following commands, visit the pet store using a browser, and buy a few pets:

```
> mvn package
> copy target\org.springframework.samples.jpetstore-1.0.0-SNAPSHOT.war
➥    %TOMCAT_HOME%\webapp\jpetstore.war
> %TOMCAT_HOME%\bin\startup.bat
Method DriverManager.registerDriver(..) took 2116750
Method DriverManager.getDriver(..) took 108394
Method Driver.connect(..) took 108744826
Method Driver.connect(..) took 1827048
Method jdbcConnection.close() took 14030834
Method Connection.setReadOnly(..) took 320152
Method Connection.getAutoCommit() took 241372
Method Connection.setAutoCommit(..) took 183543
```

This output is similar to what you saw with AspectJ's LTW using JVMTI in chapter 8.[1] But how does this work?

SPRING-DRIVEN LTW: UNDER THE HOOD

Spring-driven LTW is a variation of AspectJ LTW that we discussed in chapter 8. It interacts with classloaders to set up the LTW. The bean backed by the `<context:load-time-weaver/>` element registers AspectJ's instrumentation agent with the classloader. The classloader passes the byte code for an unwoven class to the instrumentation agent and uses the woven byte code to define the class. Figure 9.8 shows a schematic view of Spring-driven LTW.

Spring-driven LTW requires that the classloader loading the application be capable of accepting an instrumentation agent. A few implementations of Java Persistence API (JPA) also require load-time instrumentation. Therefore, many recent versions of application and web servers already provide such a classloader. A few others provide a

---

1 If you get an `OutOfMemoryException`, you will need to increase the maximum memory Tomcat's JVM may allocate by adding `JAVA_OPTS=-Xmx1024m` to %TOMCAT_HOME%\bin\startup.bat.

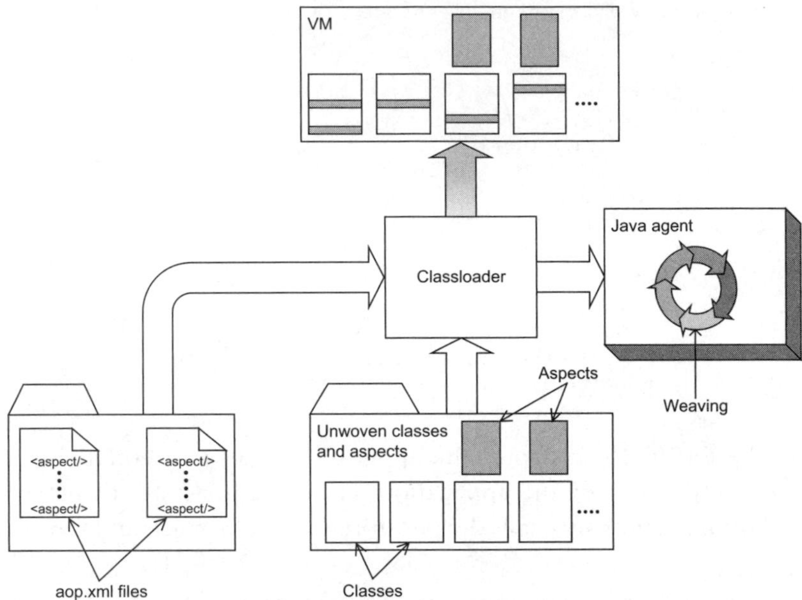

Figure 9.8 Schematic of Spring-driven LTW. The classloader passes unwoven byte code to AspectJ's instrumentation agent. The classloader then loads the woven byte code into the VM.

way to specify the classloader to be used. In such cases, Spring-driven LTW configures that classloader with AspectJ's instrumentation agent. For other servers, you can specify a simple JVMTI agent (that Spring includes) that provides the same capability in any server.

Note that AspectJ's instrumentation agent works only with Java 5 and above. Consequently, Spring-driven LTW works on Java 5 or above. Currently, the following servers support Spring-driven LTW:

- Tomcat 5.5.20+ (with additional application-level changes as outlined in step 3 in the previous section)
- GlassFish 2.0+ web applications (which use Tomcat and therefore match Tomcat in the required application-level changes)
- WebLogic 10.0+
- OC4J 10.0+

With other application servers, if Spring's agent for JPA is used, Spring-driven LTW can utilize it instead of needing the AspectJ LTW. In that case, you must modify the VM options to use the JVMTI agent provided by Spring (replace `<version>` in the following command with the Spring version you're using, such as 3.0.0):

```
> java -javaagent:<path-to>/org.springframework.instrument-<version>.jar ...
```

The org.springframework.instrument-<version>.jar (or spring-instrument-<version>.jar, if you use Maven downloaded dependencies) file is a JVMTI agent that saves the needed instrumentation-related objects so that Spring's load-time weaver can use them later to add AspectJ's instrumentation agent. Note that the Spring agent doesn't, by itself, perform any weaving.

> **Spring-driven LTW without Spring**
>
> It's possible to use the approach taken by Spring-driven LTW even when you don't use Spring. As long as you can access the classloader and add the instrumentation agent to it, you can use LTW. You must add the agent before any of the classes to be woven are loaded, because once a class is loaded into the VM, the classloader and the instrumentation agent are out of picture. If you're using Spring, all the hard work is already done for you.

Now that you understand AspectJ and Spring AOP, let's discuss which AOP system is appropriate in a given situation.

9.6 Choosing an appropriate AOP system

Spring AOP lets you use several styles to express aspects. In this section, we'll compare these choices and establish guidelines for their use. Note that it's legitimate to use multiple styles simultaneously. For this discussion, we assume that Spring is already the architectural basis for your system.

Note that you can always use AspectJ weaving with Spring. After all, a Spring application is just a Java application, and AspectJ works with any Java application. We'll first compare Spring AOP with AspectJ AOP. Then, we'll compare the syntax options within Spring AOP. Armed with this information, we'll create a set of guidelines to help you through the decision process of choosing the right AOP system and syntax.

9.6.1 Comparing AspectJ to Spring AOP

AspectJ represents a powerful system that requires you to use a weaver. Spring AOP, on the other hand, represents a simpler system that works within the machinery offered by Java. The two systems differ in the following ways:

- *The join point model*—Spring AOP exposes only one kind of join point: execution of public non-static methods. AspectJ exposes several in addition to method execution, such as object construction, class loading, method call, exception handler, and field access. Spring AOP also implicitly limits exposed join points to those for the beans. AspectJ, as you've seen in all the chapters so far, has a far-reaching crosscutting capability.
- *Adoption complexity*—Spring AOP has little adoption cost. You don't need to employ any special tools or modify the build or execution environment. Even the AOP concepts you need to learn are far fewer in Spring AOP. Further, Spring AOP's limited power can be seen as a benefit; fewer things can go wrong while you're learning how to use AOP!

- *Configurability*—Spring AOP is an object-based AOP and thus offers an easy way to configure crosscutting functionality for an individual bean. AspectJ is type-based AOP and thus offers simple configuration at the type level. Spring's autoproxy mechanism makes it possible to apply uniform crosscutting across multiple beans on the same type. AspectJ needs to rely on some form of object identity (name, id and so on) to distinguish between multiple instances of the same type.
- *Performance*—Spring's proxy-based AOP, due to the use of reflection necessitated by proxies, has lower performance than byte-code weaving implemented by AspectJ. But most applications of Spring AOP involve advising already expensive operations (database accesses, message queue operations, or network operations). In those cases, the overhead added by Spring's proxy is negligible. In general, Spring AOP's applications are self-selecting regarding performance characteristics—if Spring AOP is suitable for functionality, the performance characteristics are likely to be acceptable.

If you decide to use Spring AOP, you have a few choices about the syntax: traditional interceptor syntax, schema-style AOP, and @AspectJ.

9.6.2 Comparing Spring AOP syntax

The biggest advantage of schema-style AOP is the possibility of using it with Java 1.4 and earlier versions. Unless you're using Java 5 or above, the @AspectJ syntax isn't even a choice. Another advantage of schema-style AOP is that you can look at the configuration file and know about all the aspects in the system. For example, you can understand pointcuts used by security and transaction management aspects just by looking at an XML file. A disadvantage of schema-style AOP is that to understand an aspect, you need to examine both configuration files and Java code. The biggest drawback of schema-style AOP is the lack of a way to compose pointcuts (as discussed in section 9.4.2).

The @AspectJ syntax is the preferred syntax when you're using Java 5 or above. It makes it easy to understand a single aspect; the advice logic and pointcuts are in the same place. It also lets you write pointcuts the way they're supposed to be written—simple pointcuts composed to form complex pointcuts. A disadvantage of @AspectJ compared to schema-style AOP is that examining the XML files forming the application context doesn't reveal the big picture of aspects and their interaction. In practice, this doesn't pose a significant problem. First, Spring's best practice to use multiple XML files to form a Spring application context requires viewing all those files to get the big picture anyway. Second, using the Spring IDE provides the big picture in a much nicer form, as you saw in figure 9.1.

9.6.3 It's decision time

Let's put all this information together to create guidelines for choosing the right AOP system for the right job. Like the guidelines in chapters 6 and 7, although they appear prescriptive in nature, their main purpose is to give you a way to arrive at a first decision quickly.

- *If your aspects need to be applied to Spring beans, use Spring AOP.* In practice, Spring AOP works fine for crosscutting concerns for Spring beans such as service objects, Data Access Objects (DAOs), and UI controllers. Because there is no special weaver, you don't need to change your tool chain. Specifically, you don't need to switch to a particular IDE to build Spring applications. Some of the limitations you're likely to encounter are advising self calls and advising object instantiation join points.
- *If you're using Java 5 or above and Spring AOP suffices, use @AspectJ syntax integration.* This syntax is easy to understand and offers a possibility of moving to full-fledged AspectJ usage should such a need arise in the future.
- *If your AOP needs to extend beyond Spring beans, use AspectJ.* In practice, this means you need fine-grained crosscutting functionalities that extend to domain entities. In those cases, the benefit added by AspectJ outweighs the added logistical complexity (modifications to build or launch scripts).
- *If you need to advise join points beyond method execution, use AspectJ.* If you need to advise join points exposed by AspectJ, but not exposed by Spring AOP, such as method calls, object instantiation, exception handlers, and field access, you need to tap into the power of AspectJ.
- *If you need the best performance possible, use AspectJ.* But make sure the extra performance gained makes a difference in your overall system performance. For example, it's unlikely that a transaction-management aspect will make any noticeable difference if you use Spring AOP or AspectJ.
- *If you need weave-time errors and warnings to enforce architectural policies, use AspectJ.* You'll probably want to use build-time weaving to flag any policy violations as early as possible.

The choices, while overwhelming at first, offer you a solution that matches your needs in any situation. Start with these guidelines, and make changes to match your unique constraints.

9.7 Summary

Spring's integration with AspectJ is drawing a lot of attention. In its simplest form, it lets you use the AspectJ language to express pointcuts. The XML-based aspect configuration further leverages the AspectJ syntax to turn a regular bean into an aspect. The @AspectJ syntax takes an additional step by modularizing the AOP-related configuration right into the beans themselves. Spring accomplishes all these syntax possibilities while staying within the limits of its proxy-based AOP framework. Of course, you can always use an AspectJ weaver with Spring as with any Java application.

These concepts, along with the ones presented in the earlier chapters, complete our introduction to the AspectJ language. Now that you understand the concepts and constructs in AspectJ as well as how it works with Spring, we're ready to dive into practical examples in areas such as tracing, concurrency control, transaction management, and security. The material presented so far will serve as a reference while you read the remainder of the book.

Part 2

Applications of AspectJ with Spring

Part 2 puts the knowledge you gained in the first part to practical use by showing how AspectJ and the Spring Framework simplify enterprise applications. Although Spring provides dependency injection and enterprise service abstraction, AspectJ completes the picture by modularizing crosscutting concerns. We'll explore the two ways Spring integrates with AspectJ: through dynamic proxies and through byte-code weaving. You should be able to use most of the example code in your applications without much modification. Even if you aren't using Spring, you'll find that you can adopt these examples to suit your applications. We include a few examples from outside of Spring—specifically Swing and EJB—to show that AOP concepts are applicable in any kind of applications.

We begin by examining a classic application of AOP: monitoring and tracing. Then, we'll modularize the policy-enforcement concerns to create a safety net that ensures you won't get into trouble by violating programming policies. The examples in chapters 10 and 11 demonstrate how you can use AOP to improve your personal productivity during the development phase. You can take out these aspects when you deploy your system without affecting the correctness of the core system. Of course, as we explain, you can continue using these aspects in the deployed system and gain even more benefits.

We'll then implement complex functionality though AOP. First, chapter 12 introduces a few AOP design patterns that are used in the remaining chapters. Chapters 13 through 16 deal with functionality such as concurrency control, security, transaction management, and domain logic. In each case, you'll put

Spring dependency injection and enterprise abstraction to good use. Chapter 17 concludes this book with a discussion of how you can incorporate AOP into your organization.

10 Monitoring techniques

This chapter covers

- Noninvasive tracing
- Performance monitoring
- Spring AOP for monitoring

Monitoring encompasses a variety of techniques such as tracing important events in an application, profiling performance-critical portions of the app, and observing a system's vital parameters. You need to monitor enterprise applications in all phases of their lifecycle: development, deployment, and production. During the development phase, monitoring helps you understand the interactions between components in the system and spot any deviations from what is expected. During the deployment phase, it lets you profile the application under load to plan the hardware needed for a successful deployment. During production, monitoring helps you verify that the system is working within the expected range of operating parameters; it alerts you about any impending problems and lets you extract useful diagnostic information when things go wrong.

All monitoring techniques share some common problems when implemented using conventional techniques. First, their implementations cut across multiple modules, causing code scattering. Second, the code for monitoring intertwines with business logic, causing code tangling. The sheer amount of code needed is often a reason not to implement monitoring in many applications. Furthermore, even if a determined team is ready to add the needed code, implementing monitoring functionality consistently is a tall order that is seldom achieved with the needed precision.

Recent advances in AspectJ, such as load-time weaving (LTW), make deploying monitoring aspects a much simpler task while providing control over the monitored points without needing recompilation. Spring's AspectJ integration also provides simpler opportunities to implement monitoring functionality for the key components in a typical enterprise application without any changes to build or deployment environments.

In this chapter, we'll examine ways to introduce monitoring in a systematic and noninvasive manner through use of aspects. We'll start with the perennial favorite of AOP: tracing! By introducing simple aspects, you can consistently trace important events in the system, such as execution of and calls to selected methods and throwing of exceptions. For each of these techniques, we'll examine common patterns in implementing tracing the AOP way. We'll also discuss how AOP can enhance conventional logging. Then, we'll extend these techniques to performance monitoring. You should be able to use the information provided in this chapter immediately during development. The experience gained in this process will help you decide about further use of AOP.

10.1 Tracing in action

Tracing is one of the most common monitoring techniques used to understand a system's behavior. In its simplest form, tracing logs messages that describe the occurrence of interesting events during the execution of a system. For example, in a banking system, you would log each account transaction with information such as the nature of the transaction, the account number, and the transaction amount. You could also log exceptions that occurred during execution of the system along with the context under which they occurred.

During the development cycle, tracing plays a role similar to a debugger. It's also usually the only reasonable choice for debugging distributed systems or concurrency-related problems. By examining the log, you can spot unexpected system behavior and correct it. A log also helps you see the interactions between different parts of a system to detect exactly where the problem might be. Likewise, in fully deployed systems, tracing acts as a diagnostic assistant for finding the root cause of the problem.

A poster child of AOP

Tracing has always been a poster child of AOP applications (as well as a popular target of the myth that all AOP can do is tracing—something I'll debunk throughout this book by providing a vast range of applications other than tracing). Tracing and other monitoring techniques are good examples of crosscutting functionality at its extreme. AOP makes implementing monitoring techniques a breeze. It not only saves a ton of code but also establishes centralized control, consistency, and efficiency.

Let's examine an AOP implementation of tracing in action through a simple console application based on code provided in appendix A. In listing 10.1, you add a product to an order.

Listing 10.1 The Main class: a simple test driver

```
package ajia.main;

import ...

public class Main {
    public static void main(String[] args) {
        ApplicationContext context
            = new ClassPathXmlApplicationContext("META-INF/spring/*.xml");

        OrderService orderService
            = (OrderService) context.getBean("orderService");
        ProductService productService
            = (ProductService)context.getBean("productService");
        Order order = new Order();
        Product product = productService.findProduct(1001L);
        orderService.addProduct(order, product, 1);
    }
}
```

Now, let's look at tracing implemented using AspectJ; later, we'll compare it with conventional techniques.

10.1.1 Tracing the aspect-oriented way

Let's use AspectJ to introduce the tracing functionality into each method in all the classes in the example. All you need to do is add the aspect in listing 10.2 to your system and compile it with the classes using the AspectJ compiler (note that you could have written the aspect using @AspectJ syntax without losing any functionality). That's it! You'll have tons of output to impress your colleagues.

Listing 10.2 Tracing method entries

```
package ajia.tracing;

import ...

public aspect TraceAspect {
    private Logger logger = Logger.getLogger(TraceAspect.class);

    pointcut traced()
        : execution(* *.*(..)) && !within(TraceAspect);          ❶ Selects methods to trace

    before() : traced() {
        Signature sig = thisJoinPointStaticPart.getSignature();
        logger.log(Level.INFO,
                   "Entering [" + sig.toShortString() + "]");       ❷ Advises traced methods
    }
}
```

❶ The `traced()` pointcut selects methods to trace—in this case, it selects all the methods in the system. You also follow a common idiom in AspectJ to exclude join points in the aspect itself to avoid a potential problem of infinite recursion. The `!within(TraceAspect)` part helps you avoid recursion caused by tracing method calls in the aspect itself. Although such exclusion won't matter in the current version of the aspect because there are no methods in the aspect itself, it's never too early to start using good practices.

❷ You use `thisJoinPointStaticPart` to get information about the method selected by the pointcut. The method `getSignature()` on `thisJoinPointStaticPart` returns the signature of the selected method. You use the `toShortString()` method to obtain the shorter version description. If needed, you could obtain the longer version using the `toLongString()` method or obtain individual parts of the signature and assemble the output yourself. You could also obtain the line number by using `thisJoinPointStaticPart.getSourceLocation().getLine()`. Note that the weaver creates static information about the join point at weave time, and neither compiler optimization nor the presence of the Just in Time (JIT) and hotspot virtual machine alters this information. See chapter 4 for detailed information about using reflection in an advice body.

When you compile this aspect together with the classes and run the test program, you get output similar to this:

```
Entering [Main.main(..)]
Entering [ProductServiceImpl.findProduct(..)]
Entering [JpaGenericRepository.find(..)]
Entering [OrderServiceImpl.addProduct(..)]
Entering [InventoryServiceImpl.removeProduct(..)]
Entering [InventoryServiceImpl.isProductAvailable(..)]
Entering [JpaInventoryItemRepository.findByProduct(..)]
Entering [InventoryItem.getQuantityOnHand()]
Entering [JpaInventoryItemRepository.findByProduct(..)]
Entering [InventoryItem.deplete(..)]
Entering [JpaGenericRepository.update(..)]
Entering [Order.addProduct(..)]
Entering [Order.isPlaced()]
Entering [Order.getItemFor(..)]
Entering [Product.getPrice()]
Entering [LineItem.setQuantity(..)]
Entering [OrderServiceImpl.updateOrder(..)]
Entering [JpaGenericRepository.update(..)]
```

With the tracing aspect, you get good insight into the system's execution just by writing a simple tracing aspect. Later in this chapter, you'll see improvements that will help you gain an even deeper understanding of the system's inner workings.

To truly appreciate the AOP implementation, let's examine how you could implement the same functionality without it.

Standard logging toolkit vs. log4j vs. commons logging

Throughout this chapter, we use log4j as the primary logging API. Although the use of Jakarta Commons Logging or slf4j would offer a more abstract solution, a few examples use facilities available in log4j without the associated API in Commons Logging and slf4j. Specifically, Commons Logging doesn't support Nested Diagnostic Context (NDC) and Mapped Diagnostic Context (MDC); slf4j supports MDC but not NDC. Because the focus of this chapter is combining AspectJ with a logging toolkit, discussing multiple logging toolkits would distract us from that goal. The good news is that with AspectJ, switching from one logging toolkit to another is a simple task.

10.1.2 Tracing the conventional way

If you were to implement tracing without using AspectJ, you'd end up with code such as in listing 10.3. To illustrate the additional work needed on your part, let's look at the modifications to the `Order` class required using the log4j API.

You instrument each method of the class to log the entry into it. You log each method at the `Level.INFO` level because you're writing informational entries. Listing 10.3 shows the changed `Order` class.

Listing 10.3 The `Order` class with conventional tracing

```
package ajia.domain;

import ...

...
public class Order extends DomainEntity {
    ...
    private Logger logger = Logger.getLogger("trace");

    public void addItem(Product product, int quantity) {
        logger.log(Level.INFO,
                   "Entering [Order.addItem]");
        ...
    }

    public void removeItem(Product product, int quantity) {
        logger.log(Level.INFO,
                   "Entering [Order.removeItem]");
        ...
    }

    public boolean isPlaced() {
        logger.log(Level.INFO,
                   "Entering [Order.isPlaced]");
        ...
    }

    public void place() {
        logger.log(Level.INFO,
                   "Entering [Order.place]");
```

```
            ...
        }
        ...
}
```

Every class in the system would have similar duplication. That would be quite a task, right? Granted, the job would be mostly mechanical—you'd probably copy and paste code. After pasting, you'd have to be sure you changed each argument to the `log()` method correctly; if you didn't, you'd end up with a log message that was inconsistent with the operation being performed. Furthermore, if you wanted entry *and* exit traced rather than just a log message for entry, it would be even worse.

NOTE The code in listings 10.2 and 10.3 isn't exactly equivalent; the former uses an aspect-specific logger, whereas the latter uses a class-specific logger. We'll examine a way to eliminate the difference in section 10.4.5.

Now, consider how long it would take to introduce tracing in a real system with hundreds of classes. How sure could you be that the methods would log the right information? This is a typical scenario with any crosscutting concerns: too much effort to implement them, and too many opportunities for bugs.

Logging toolkit and automatic extraction of caller information

When you're using log4j, avoid using it with `%C`, `%F`, `%L`, `%M`, or a combined `%l` layout pattern. These patterns examine the call stack to extract the caller information (such as the class name, method name, and line number) at the location of the `log()` method invocation. The performance hit from using the call stack to deduce a caller is significant, because it involves obtaining the call stack and parsing its contents—not a trivial job. The log4j documentation explicitly warns against using these patterns ("WARNING Generating caller location information is extremely slow. Its use should be avoided unless execution speed isn't an issue."). Further, in the presence of an optimizing compiler and hotspot/JIT-enabled virtual machine, the deduced caller may be incorrect. When you don't use these formats, you need to supply the caller information yourself the way you did in listing 10.3. But note that this isn't a log4j-specific issue; the same issue exists in any logging kit that offers to deduce the caller from the call stack.

Alas, the need for caller information is too common; without such information, the log output is much less useful. But adding location information to each log invocation adds additional code to something that is already complex. AOP tracing, as you saw in listing 10.2, provides an efficient and accurate means to obtain local information. In section 10.7.1, we'll examine a way to obtain the caller information in the same manner even when you use conventional logging.

Now that you've seen tracing using conventional and AspectJ-based techniques, let's compare the two approaches.

10.2 Conventional vs. AOP tracing

The base implementation technique used in conventional tracing involves a logging toolkit and calls to its APIs. The logging toolkit simplifies the job of categorizing and formatting the log message. It also provides runtime control over the messages logged. For example, with log4j, you can have a logger associated with a category (typically the class name). You can then specify a log4j.xml file to control the level for each log category. Figure 10.1 illustrates this schematic of conventional tracing solutions.

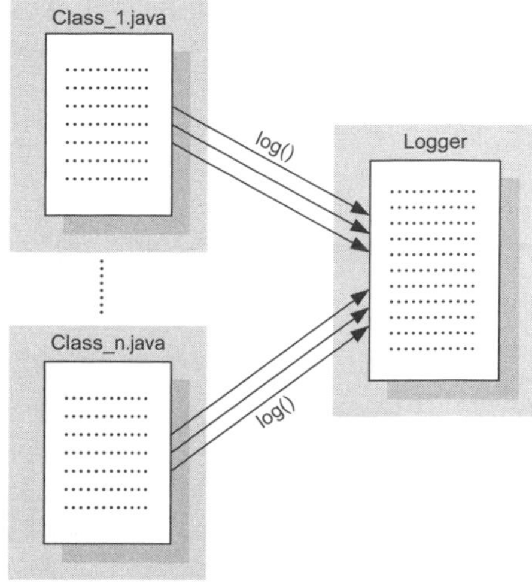

Figure 10.1 Conventional tracing, where all log points issue calls to the logger explicitly

As you can see, the tracing calls are all over the core modules. When a new module is added to the system, all of its methods that need tracing must be instrumented. Such instrumentation is *invasive*, causing tangling of the core concerns with the tracing concern.

> **Logging vs. tracing**
>
> There is some confusion about the use of terms *logging* and *tracing*. Most developers (and this book) refer to logging as an act of producing messages specific to the logic carried by a piece of code. Tracing is commonly considered as the act of producing messages for lower-level events: method entry and exits, object construction, exception handling, state modification, and so on. Both techniques often use a logging toolkit to simplify their implementation.

Consistency is the single most important requirement of tracing. If the tracing specification requires that a certain kind of operations be logged, then the implementation must log *every* invocation of those operations. When things go wrong in a system, doubting the tracing consistency is probably the last thing you want to do. Missed tracing calls can make output hard to understand and sometimes useless. For example, if you were expecting a certain method to have been invoked, and you didn't see a log output for that method, you couldn't be sure if the method wasn't called or wasn't logged due to inconsistent implementation.

Achieving consistency using conventional tracing is a lofty goal; and although systems can attain it initially, it requires continuous vigilance to maintain. For example, if you add new classes to the system or new methods in existing classes, you must ensure that they implement tracing that matches the current tracing strategy.

AOP fixes problems with conventional tracing by combining the logging toolkit with dynamic crosscutting. Essentially, AOP modularizes the invocation of the logging toolkit's APIs. The beauty of this approach is that you don't need to instrument any log points; writing an aspect does a functional equivalent automatically. Further, because there is a central place to control tracing operations, you achieve consistency easily. Figure 10.2 shows an overview of AspectJ-based tracing.

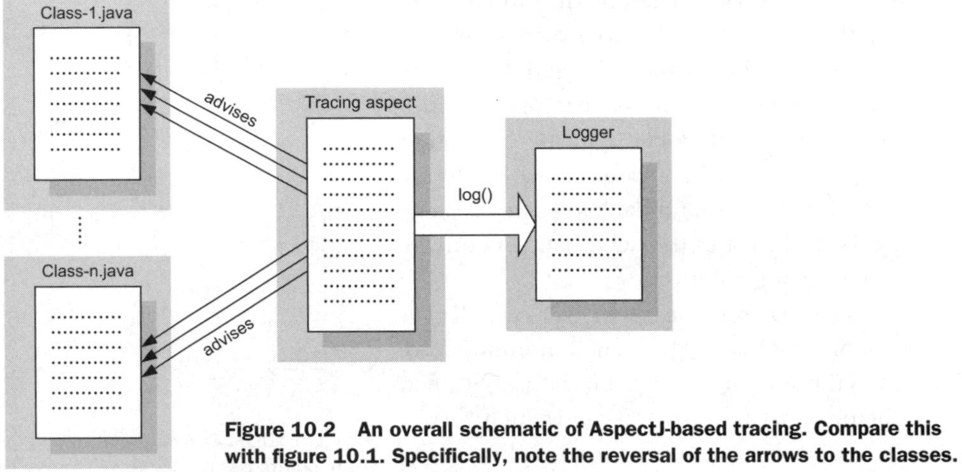

Figure 10.2 An overall schematic of AspectJ-based tracing. Compare this with figure 10.1. Specifically, note the reversal of the arrows to the classes.

With AspectJ-based tracing, the tracing aspect separates the core modules and the logger object. Instead of the core modules' embedding the `log()` method invocations in their source code, the aspect weaves the logging invocations into the core modules when they're needed. AOP-based tracing reverses the dependency between the core modules and the logger; the aspect encodes how the operations in the core modules are logged instead of each core module deciding for itself. This kind of arrangement is known as the *Dependency Inversion Principle* (see http://aosd.net/2007/program/industry/I6-AspectDesignPrinciples.pdf for more details). Furthermore, as we'll show later in this chapter, extending tracing to other events in the system, such as throwing an exception and modifying or accessing important object state, can be implemented easily owing to the powerful pointcut language.

As you can distill from the discussion so far, monitoring through AOP boils down to two parts:

- Selecting join points of interest
- Advising them with monitoring logic

The first part requires some considerations that we'll discuss next. We'll discuss the second part in sections that follow.

10.3 Selecting join points of interest

Typically, you'll want to select a list of monitored methods to make output more understandable and avoid degrading performance. You can achieve this goal by implementing the pointcut to select join points based on their static and dynamic characteristics. Let's look at several design options that will be useful for many pervasive aspects, like tracing.

10.3.1 Selection based on static structure

A simple way to select a set of monitored join points is based on their static structure. You can use characteristics such as the package hierarchy of the types, inheritance structure, method name patterns, and method return type. Leveraging annotations associated with various programming elements is also a powerful way to select the trace points. Typically, you'll use a combination of all these techniques to define your tracing pointcuts. Let's examine each one separately.

LEVERAGING PACKAGE STRUCTURE

A well-defined package structure is central to any good software system. It's common to have the package hierarchy reflect high-level design elements. For example, a software system following the Model-View-Controller (MVC) pattern has a package structure that dedicates a package element to each of the three concepts, leading to packages such as `ajia.domain` and `ajia.web`. Choosing monitoring points using packages therefore makes it easy to select elements based on the function they're playing. With such a selection, you can capture coarse-grained monitoring requirements such as "trace all domain model interactions." Listing 10.4 illustrates a selection based on static structure.

Listing 10.4 Trace aspect utilizing pointcuts based on package structure

```
package ajia.tracing;

import ...

public aspect TraceAspect {
    private Logger logger = Logger.getLogger(TraceAspect.class);

    pointcut domainOp()
        : execution(* ajia.domain..*.*(..))
          || execution(ajia.domain..*.new(..));

    pointcut controllerOp()
        : execution(* ajia.web..*.*(..))
          || execution(ajia.web..*.new(..));

    pointcut repositoryOp()
        : execution(* ajia.repository..*.*(..))
          || execution(ajia.repository..*.new(..));

    pointcut traced()
        : domainOp() || controllerOp() || repositoryOp();

    ... advice to traced() ...
}
```

Note how you construct the final pointcut using simple pointcuts, each selecting a specific set of types. This style—a best practice in AOP—simplifies understanding and maintenance because you can focus on a simple concept at each level. It also makes the pointcut useful.

An alternative style is to use package scopes to define pointcuts, as shown in listing 10.5.

Listing 10.5 Trace aspect utilizing package scopes

```
package ajia.tracing;

import ...

public aspect TraceAspect {
    private Logger logger = Logger.getLogger(TraceAspect.class);

    pointcut inDomainType()
        : within(ajia.domain..*);

    pointcut inControllerType()
        : within(ajia.web..*);

    pointcut inRepositoryType()
        : within(ajia.repository..*);

    pointcut inTracedType()
        : inDomainType() || inControllerType() || inRepositoryType();

    pointcut traced()
        : (execution(* *(..)) || execution(new(..)))
          && inTracedType();

    ... advice to traced() ...
}
```

Here, the first three pointcuts select all the join points within a certain package structure and combine them with pointcuts selecting all methods and constructors. Of course, nothing prevents you from further refining the `traced()` pointcut to, say, separate the selection of method executions from the selection of object creations.

Refactoring in action

Notice how you're progressively modifying the pointcuts to make them simpler and reusable. This is a typical refactoring process applied to aspects. Start by focusing on the problem at hand, and improve it as you go along. With experience, you'll develop your own style whereby you'll start with an implementation following the best practices and thus skip a few initial stages of refactoring.

With either style, typically, you promote pointcuts corresponding to high-level functionality and reusable concepts to a library aspect. For example, you can include the aspect shown in listing 10.6. Such an aspect is usable not only from a monitoring aspect but also from other aspects, as you'll see in the next chapter, where you use it to enforce system-level policies.

Listing 10.6 Reusable aspect to define the system architecture

```
package ajia.architecture;

import ...

public aspect SystemArchitecture {
```

```
    public pointcut inDomainType ()
        : within(ajia.domain..*);

    public pointcut inControllerType()
        : within(ajia.web..*);

    public pointcut inRepositoryType()
        : within(ajia.repository..*);
}
```

Then, the tracing aspect can use these pointcuts to compose its own pointcuts, as shown in listing 10.7.

Listing 10.7 Trace aspect based on reusable aspect defining the system architecture

```
package ajia.tracing;

import ...

public aspect TraceAspect {
    private Logger logger = Logger.getLogger(TraceAspect.class);

    pointcut inTracedType()
        : SystemArchitecture.inDomainType()
          || SystemArchitecture.inControllerType()
          || SystemArchitecture.inRepositoryType();

    pointcut traced()
        : (execution(* *(..)) || execution(new(..)))
          && inTracedType();

    ... advice to traced() ...
}
```

Although the package structure provides a coarse-grained selection of join points, you need to use other information to select join points to match tracing needs more precisely. Let's examine one such approach: using type-related information.

LEVERAGING TYPE STRUCTURE

Type-structure information, such as the naming pattern and inheritance hierarchy, provides useful techniques to select trace join points. If you use a consistent naming pattern for your types, you can leverage type names to define patterns using wildcards. For example, if all your types representing a controller are suffixed with `Controller`, you can use `*Controller` as the pattern to select them.

But because you're relying on a programmer's due diligence in adhering to a naming convention, it's best to find other ways before resorting to using a name pattern. One such way is to use the type hierarchy. For example, if you're using the traditional Spring MVC (that doesn't use the `@Controller` annotation), you can use `org.springframework.web.servlet.mvc.Controller+` as the pattern to select all controllers in your system. You can also use your own type hierarchy. For example, if all your domain entities extend the `DomainEntity` class, you can use `DomainEntity+` as the type pattern.

LEVERAGING ANNOTATIONS

You can leverage annotations to select types. For example, if you choose to use the Java Persistence API (JPA), you can use an annotation such as `@Entity` to select only persistent objects; or if you use JAX-WS Web Services, you can use an annotation such as `@WebService` to choose only web services, as shown in the following pointcut:

```
pointcut entityOp() : execution(* (@Entity *).*(..));
pointcut webServiceOp() : execution(* (@WebService *).*(..));
```

Similarly, if you were to use Spring's annotation-based MVC, you could use the following pointcut:

```
pointcut controllerOp() : execution(* (@Controller *).*(..));
```

It's a best practice to implement pointcuts that utilize technology-specific type hierarchies and annotations in a separate library aspect (similar to listing 10.6). This lets you reuse them in multiple aspects or even in multiple projects using the same set of technologies.

You can even create your own custom annotations and use them for selection. For example, you can use the `@Audit` annotation to implement the tracing functionality required for a regulatory compliance. Such annotations may even specify the compliance code so the audit record can include it:

```
pointcut auditedAuditCode(Audit audit) : execution(@Audit * *(..))
                                         && @annotation(audit);
```

Similar to types, you can use annotations marked not only for the method but also for the return type, parameters, and declared exceptions. For example, the following pointcut selects all methods that return a type that is marked with the `@HIPPAData` annotation:

```
execution((@HIPPAData *) *(..))
```

When using custom annotations, you should avoid the use of tracing-specific annotations such as `@TraceMe`. Although such annotations provide a better degree of separation than a direct use of a logging API, it goes against the core idea of noninvasiveness behind AOP.

LEVERAGING METHOD SIGNATURE

Methods represent even finer granularity. Like type patterns, using name patterns is a possibility, and the same caveat of an unstable naming convention applies. But certain naming patterns—such as all setter methods starting with `set`—prove to be general, especially because other technologies such as dependency injection (DI) and persistence frameworks utilize those conventions.

When you're defining methods using a name pattern, exercise some care to specify the exact criteria needed. For example, although `execution(* set*(..))` certainly selects all setters, it may also end up selecting setters that take multiple arguments. A better pointcut for selecting setters would consider characteristics such as public access, `void` return type, and a single argument: `execution(public void set*(*))`. You still risk selecting a method such as `settle`, should it have public access, a `void` return type, and a single argument. If you want to be even more defensive, you can further tighten the definition to ensure that the character that follows `set` is an uppercase letter. You can then settle the score with the `settle` method! Here is a pointcut that does the job (marginal improvements are possible to minimize typing, but you still need all 26 lines—one per each letter of the alphabet in English):

```
public pointcut setter()
    : execution(public void setA*(*))
      || execution(public void setB*(*))
      ...
```

You can similarly write a pointcut for getter methods that uses `!void` as the return type pattern for methods starting with `get` and `boolean` return type for methods starting with `is`. You must also ensure that the method doesn't take any arguments. You definitely want such pointcuts nicely tucked away in a reusable aspect so you can reap the benefits of the many lines of code you diligently typed!

Other method signature constituents, such as return type, parameter types, and thrown exceptions, can often help you select the right kind of join points. For example, the following pointcut selects all Remote Method Invocation (RMI) operations:

```
execution(public !static * Remote+.*(..) throws RemoteException+)
```

This pointcut leverages the type pattern `Remote+` along with the exception declaration in method to select all public non-static methods defined in the `Remote` type or its subtypes. This also illustrates how to use just the essential characteristics of join points to specify a precise selection criterion. This kind of selection is particularly useful when you're working with standard technologies such as Swing, SWT, Spring, and EJB. You'll see examples of such use throughout this book.

Through a judicious combination of package, type, and method patterns, you can select join points needed for most tracing functionalities mirroring their conventional equivalent. It's important to strike a balance between too general and too specific: the latter runs into the *fragile pointcut problem* because names change and it's easy to forget to change pointcuts.

AspectJ can offer additional possibilities by leveraging dynamic context that would be practically unattractive to implement conventionally.

10.3.2 Selection based on dynamic context

Consider a scenario in which you're utilizing repository classes through various services and you want to trace calls only if a web service originated those calls. The `cflow()` and `cflowbelow()` pointcuts can allow such a criterion. For example, the following pointcut selects all join points in the control-flow of any web service execution:

```
pointcut duringWebServiceOp() : cflow(webServiceOp());
```

You can then combine this pointcut with another that selects repository operations:

```
pointcut repositoryOp()
    : execution(* (@Repository *).*(..));

pointcut repositoryOpDuringWebServicesOp()
    : repositoryOp() && duringWebServiceOp();
```

This pointcut selects any repository method regardless of its lexical location and call depth if it's inside the control-flow of a web service operation.

The control-flow-based pointcuts are also useful in limiting tracing to only the top-level operations in a recursive call stack. For example, the following pointcut selects all top-level transaction-managed operations (assuming that all transactional methods are marked with a `@Transactional` annotation—we'll discuss other possibilities when we deal with transaction management aspect in chapter 14):

```
pointcut transactional()
    : execution(@Transactional * *(..));

pointcut topLevelTransactional()
    : transactional() && !cflowbelow(transactional());
```

By now, you should be convinced that you can select appropriate join points matching a specific monitoring requirement. It does take some experience to master writing good pointcuts, but be assured that it's easier than it may seem at first.

Let's examine the second part involved in each monitoring technique: the monitoring logic. We'll first complete our discussion of tracing. Then, we'll discuss exception monitoring, improving conventional logic, and performance monitoring.

10.4 Tracing

As you saw at the beginning of this chapter, the basic tracing implementation through AOP is easy. But AOP also offers some unique possibilities. In this section, we'll look at indenting trace calls, sharing aspect functionality, tracing intra-method activities, logging method parameters, and using type-specific loggers.

Now, get ready to do something that is practically impossible to do without aspects in any reasonable manner.

10.4.1 Indenting trace calls

You can make trace output tremendously more useful by exposing the caller-callee relationship in some fashion. Not only do you get to see the execution of join points, but you can also visualize the call graph—kind of like a sequence diagram. You may expose this relationship in a variety of forms. A simple way is to include the call-depth value in the log message. Alternatively, a visually more appealing way is to indent the log output to indicate the call-depth value.

Let's develop an aspect to illustrate how easy it is to accomplish this using AspectJ. The core idea here is to keep track of call depth on a per-thread basis and use it when logging a message. The implementation involves advising the traced method with a before advice to increment the depth as you enter the method and with an after advice to decrement it as you exit the method.

A simple way to keep the call depth is to use a thread-local wrapping an integer and update it from before and after advice. Then, when you log, compute the whitespace characters required, and prefix those whitespaces to the message.

Nested Diagnostic Context and Mapped Diagnostic Context

Log statements typically include information available in the local context, such as method names and parameters. To make log output more useful, certain logging toolkits let you set additional context. A log statement then may include that context in its output.

Nested Diagnostic Context (NDC) lets you arrange information in a hierarchical manner. Consider a layered enterprise application. Using NDC, you can push information identifying each layer as you enter it and pop that information when you exit. The log statement then may include the trail of layers that led up to that statement.

Mapped Diagnostic Context (MDC) lets you arrange information in a map. Consider a web application, where you need the log statements in the data access layer to include information such as the accessing user and the remote IP address available in the web layer. Using MDC, the web layer can add the needed information in a map. A log statement in the data layer may then include this information along with its local context.

When using log4j, you can leverage its capability to set up NDC for the same purpose to simplify the implementation. Here, each method pushes whitespaces in the nested context upon entry and pops them upon exit. The log statements then include all the accumulated whitespaces in the nested context. Listing 10.8 shows the aspect that implements the indentation functionality.

Listing 10.8 Indentation using log4j's nested diagnostic context

```
package ajia.tracing;

import ...

public aspect TraceAspect {
    private Logger logger = Logger.getLogger(getClass());

    pointcut traced()
        : execution(* *.*(..)) && !within(TraceAspect);

    before() : traced() {
        Signature sig = thisJoinPointStaticPart.getSignature();
        logger.log(Level.INFO,
                "Entering [" + sig.toShortString() + "]");
        NDC.push("  ");
    }

    after() : traced() {
        NDC.pop();
    }
}
```

You need to make a small change to the output format configuration in the log4j.xml file to include the nested context, as shown in the following snippet. The only difference is the inclusion of the `%x` pattern, which stands for the nested context:

```
<layout class="org.apache.log4j.PatternLayout">
    <param name="ConversionPattern" value="%x%m%n"/>
</layout>
```

When you compile this aspect along with the classes and execute the system, you get output as follows:

```
Entering [Main.main(..)]
  Entering [ProductServiceImpl.findProduct(..)]
     Entering [JpaGenericRepository.find(..)]
  Entering [OrderServiceImpl.addProduct(..)]
     Entering [InventoryServiceImpl.removeProduct(..)]
        Entering [InventoryServiceImpl.isProductAvailable(..)]
           Entering [JpaInventoryItemRepository.findByProduct(..)]
           Entering [InventoryItem.getQuantityOnHand()]
        Entering [JpaInventoryItemRepository.findByProduct(..)]
        Entering [InventoryItem.deplete(..)]
        Entering [JpaGenericRepository.update(..)]
     Entering [Order.addProduct(..)]
        Entering [Order.isPlaced()]
        Entering [Order.getItemFor(..)]
        Entering [Product.getPrice()]
        Entering [LineItem.setQuantity(..)]
     Entering [OrderServiceImpl.updateOrder(..)]
        Entering [JpaGenericRepository.update(..)]
```

Take a moment to pause and consider how you might implement this functionality without using aspects. In every method, you might have to do something like:

```
try {
    NDC.push("   ");
    ... Log statements
    ... Business logic
} finally {
    NDC.pop();
}
```

This kind of code is an invitation to create bugs. First, you might forget to use a `try/finally` arrangement to perform NDC operations, thus missing `NDC.pop()` when an exception is thrown. Second, you might forget to include the NDC logic in every method, making the overall indentation scheme unreliable.

When you add functionality such as indentation logic, the trace aspects are no longer trivial, and it's desirable to share the tracing logic to avoid duplication and simplify maintenance. We'll examine such a possibility in the next section.

10.4.2 Sharing tracing aspect functionality

Tracing requirements come from multiple sources. Ideally, a separate aspect should implement each requirement to ease implementation and maintenance. But you'll still want to share all common tracing functionality. A good way to achieve both these goals is to create a reusable base aspect containing the core tracing functionality and one or more abstract pointcuts. You then create multiple subaspects targeting each related set of requirements. Let's illustrate this idea by refactoring the aspects in listing 10.9 to create a reusable indentation-capable aspect.

Listing 10.9 Abstract aspect for indentation functionality

```
package ajia.tracing;

import ...

public abstract aspect IndentationTraceAspect {
    private Logger logger = Logger.getLogger(IndentationTraceAspect.class);

    public abstract pointcut traced();

    ... before and after advice remain unchanged since listing 10.8
}
```

Compared to listing 10.8, you make only two changes: you mark the aspect as abstract and mark `traced()` as a public abstract pointcut, and you remove the implementation body from the abstract pointcut. The advice remains unchanged. Each subsystem can now extend this aspect. For example, listing 10.10 shows an aspect that logs only the model classes.

Listing 10.10 Concrete aspect to trace domain classes

```
package ajia.tracing;

public aspect TraceAspect extends IndentationTraceAspect {
    public pointcut traced()
        : execution(* ajia.domain..*.*(..));
}
```

With reusable parts in place, you can create simple subaspects and include them as required.

So far, we've limited ourselves to tracing at the entry and exit of a method. But you often need more granularity than that. For example, you may want to trace all remote calls occurring from within specified methods. Let's see how AspectJ can help with such requirements.

10.4.3 Tracing intra-method activities

AspectJ-based tracing helps to modularize logging invocations that are crosscutting in nature. A judicious combination of tracing options presented in this chapter will take care of a majority of the cases. For example, while processing an order, you may want to log specific steps such as securing payment, checking inventory, contacting the shipping division, and so on. If you implemented all these steps in one method, you would be able to use `call()` pointcuts perhaps in combination with `withincode()` to select individual calls. But some steps may encompass multiple calls, further reducing the possibility of selecting the required join points and hence tracing those steps. The first response in such situations should be to break each step into a separate method through Extract Method and similar refactoring (for details, see *Refactoring: Improving the Design of Existing Code* by Martin Fowler [Addison-Wesley, 1999]). You can then select those methods for tracing purposes. This process yields an improved implementation, which is a good thing even without considering the benefits of simplifying tracing.

But real life isn't always considerate enough to offer such a choice. Sometimes you can't refactor a large method like this. Perhaps the requirements may call for logging specific states of the system instead of just the `this` object or the method arguments. In those cases, your only practical choice is to log the intra-method calls the conventional way, with in-line code. As you'll see in section 10.7, AspectJ can help even when you use conventional logging.

10.4.4 Logging the method parameters

Often, you not only want to log the method calls but also the invoked object and the method parameters. You can implement this requirement easily by using the `thisJoinPoint` reference. In each advice body, a special `thisJoinPoint` object is available that includes information about the advised join point and its associated context.

The aspect in listing 10.11 modifies the before advice in `TraceAspect` to log the method parameters.

Listing 10.11 `TraceAspect`: modified to log method parameters

```
package ajia.tracing;

import ...;

public aspect TraceAspect {
    private Logger logger = Logger.getLogger(getClass());

    pointcut traced()
        : execution(* *.*(..)) && !within(TraceAspect);

    before() : traced() && !execution(* Object.*(..)) {
        Signature sig = thisJoinPointStaticPart.getSignature();

        logger.log(Level.INFO,
                   "Entering [" + sig.toShortString() + "]"
                   + createParameterMessage(thisJoinPoint));
    }

    private String createParameterMessage(JoinPoint joinPoint) {
        StringBuffer paramBuffer = new StringBuffer("\n\t[This: ");
        paramBuffer.append(joinPoint.getThis());

        Object[] arguments = joinPoint.getArgs();
        paramBuffer.append("]\n\t[Args: (");
        for (int length = arguments.length, i = 0; i < length; ++i) {
            Object argument = arguments[i];
            paramBuffer.append(argument);
            if (i != length-1) {
                paramBuffer.append(',');
            }
        }
        paramBuffer.append(")]");
        return paramBuffer.toString();
    }
}
```

1 Augments pointcut to avoid infinite recursion

2 Formats log message

1. You augment the pointcut with `!execution(* Object.*(..))` to avoid the recursive invocation that is caused by executing methods defined in `Object` such as `toString()` and `hashCode()`. Without this modification, the logger will prepare the parameter string in `createParameterMessage()` when it calls `toString()` for each object. But when `toString()` executes, it first attempts to log the operation, and the logger will prepare a parameter string for it again when it calls `toString()` on the same object, and so on, causing an infinite recursion. By avoiding the join points for `toString()` execution, you avoid infinite recursion. But you generalize it a bit further, to avoid tracing calls such as `equals()` and `hashCode()` as well by excluding all methods in the `Object` class. Note that the `!within(TraceAspect)` pointcut isn't sufficient here because it only selects the *calls* to `toString()` methods made within the aspect; the execution of the methods is still advised.
2. The `createParameterMessage()` helper method returns a formatted string containing the object and arguments.

Now, when you compile the classes with this aspect and execute the `Main` class, you get output similar to the following that includes the invoked object and the method parameters:

```
Entering [Main.main(..)]
      [This: null]
      [Args: ([Ljava.lang.String;@119298d)]
Entering [ProductServiceImpl.findProduct(..)]
      [This: ajia.service.impl.ProductServiceImpl@e0fcac]
      [Args: (1001)]
Entering [JpaGenericRepository.find(..)]
      [This: ajia.repository.impl.JpaProductRepository@ecb3f1]
      [Args: (1001)]
Entering [OrderServiceImpl.addProduct(..)]
      [This: ajia.service.impl.OrderServiceImpl@c135d6]
      [Args: (ajia.domain.Order@b5ad68,Product: ProductA,1)]
Entering [InventoryServiceImpl.removeProduct(..)]
      [This: ajia.service.impl.InventoryServiceImpl@18baf36]
      [Args: (Product: ProductA,1)]
Entering [InventoryServiceImpl.isProductAvailable(..)]
      [This: ajia.service.impl.InventoryServiceImpl@18baf36]
      [Args: (Product: ProductA,1)]
Entering [JpaInventoryItemRepository.findByProduct(..)]
      [This: ajia.repository.impl.JpaInventoryItemRepository@19c4091]
      [Args: (Product: ProductA)]
Entering [InventoryItem.getQuantityOnHand()]
      [This: ajia.domain.InventoryItem@4b12d9]
      [Args: ()]
Entering [JpaInventoryItemRepository.findByProduct(..)]
      [This: ajia.repository.impl.JpaInventoryItemRepository@19c4091]
      [Args: (Product: ProductA)]
Entering [InventoryItem.deplete(..)]
      [This: ajia.domain.InventoryItem@4b12d9]
      [Args: (1)]
Entering [JpaGenericRepository.update(..)]
      [This: ajia.repository.impl.JpaInventoryItemRepository@19c4091]
```

```
     [Args: (ajia.domain.InventoryItem@4b12d9)]
Entering [Order.addProduct(..)]
     [This: ajia.domain.Order@b5ad68]
     [Args: (Product: ProductA,1)]
Entering [Order.isPlaced()]
     [This: ajia.domain.Order@b5ad68]
     [Args: ()]
Entering [Order.getItemFor(..)]
     [This: ajia.domain.Order@b5ad68]
     [Args: (Product: ProductA)]
Entering [Product.getPrice()]
     [This: Product: ProductA]
     [Args: ()]
Entering [LineItem.setQuantity(..)]
     [This: ajia.domain.LineItem@11ed166]
     [Args: (1)]
Entering [OrderServiceImpl.updateOrder(..)]
     [This: ajia.service.impl.OrderServiceImpl@c135d6]
     [Args: (ajia.domain.Order@b5ad68)]
Entering [JpaGenericRepository.update(..)]
     [This: ajia.repository.impl.JpaOrderRepository@45aa2c]
     [Args: (ajia.domain.Order@b5ad68)]
```

So far, you've used a logger specific to the aspect. Let's see how you can use the logger specific to the types being traced.

10.4.5 Choosing a type-specific logger

A common logging idiom is to use a type-specific logger so that a configuration file can control the information being logged by specifying the log level for each type or a set of types. For example, the following snippet in a log4j.xml file declares that the minimum required log level for a message to appear from types in `ajia.web` package is `warn`:

```
<logger name="ajia.web">
    <level value="warn"/>
</logger>
```

The aspects so far in this chapter haven't had this kind of type-specific control through configuration. Instead, you have one logger per aspect. This arrangement provides aspect-specific control. If you have multiple tracing aspects, you can control them separately using configuration such as the following:

```
<logger name="ajia.tracing.JDBCTraceAspect">
    <level value="warn"/>
</logger>

<logger name="ajia.tracing.ExceptionMonitorAspect">
    <level value="error"/>
</logger>
```

But if you want class-level control, you can do so easily using the `pertypewithin()` aspect association. Recall from section 6.2.4 that `pertypewithin()` associates the aspect state with a type. If you include an aspect member for the logger, a separate aspect instance and therefore a separate logger are associated with each advised type. Listing 10.12 shows a tracing aspect that uses type-specific loggers.

Listing 10.12 `TracingAspect`: tracing using type-specific logger

```
package ajia.tracing;

import ...

public aspect TraceAspect pertypewithin(*) {          <-- 1 Aspect association
    private Logger logger;

    after() returning: staticinitialization(*) {
        logger = Logger.getLogger(getWithinTypeName());   2 Initializes logger
    }

    pointcut traced()
        : execution(* *.*(..)) && !within(TraceAspect);

    before() : traced() {
        Signature sig = thisJoinPointStaticPart.getSignature();
        logger.log(Level.INFO,
                   "Entering [" + sig.toShortString() + "]");
    }
}
```

1. The `pertypewithin()` aspect association selects all types to avoid filtering due to the type pattern specified, if any. This way, the pointcut alone determines the selected join points (otherwise, implicit limiting of join points comes into effect, as discussed in section 6.2.5).

2. After loading any class being logged, you initialize the `logger` member to get the logger object corresponding to that class. Note that `getWithinTypeName()` returns the name of the type with which the aspect instance is being associated. Because a separate aspect instance is associated with each matching type, the logger initialized this way is type-specific.

So far, we've focused on build-time source-code weaving. But a popular approach is to use AspectJ LTW and Spring AOP. Let's discuss these deployment options before we resume discussing additional monitoring techniques.

10.5 A detour: deployment options for monitoring aspects

AspectJ load-time weaving (LTW) introduces a weaver into the runtime system without affecting the build system, thus simplifying its use. Similarly, if your application is based on Spring, you can use Spring's proxy-based AOP that also obviates any build-time changes and goes a step further by avoiding any deployment changes. Let's use tracing as a specific technique to see how AspectJ LTW and Spring AOP can be used with monitoring.

10.5.1 Utilizing load-time weaving

When you're just starting to play with AspectJ, a tracing or performance-monitoring aspect (which we'll discuss in section 10.8) is a good starting point. As we discussed in chapter 8, utilizing LTW at this stage simplifies the deployment task quite a bit. LTW weaving along with XML definitions for the concrete aspects let you change part of the system being monitored without any recompilation. This choice requires that you have a base aspect that declares the monitored pointcut as an abstract pointcut. When you're defining concrete aspects in XML, you provide a definition for the pointcut. Refer to section 8.3.2 for details.

Let's apply the trace aspect you developed in listing 10.9 to your web application through LTW. First, you'll need to write an aop.xml file describing the aspects to weave in and target classes to be woven in. Listing 10.13 shows an example aop.xml that you'll use for the example.

Listing 10.13 aop.xml to weave in trace aspect

```
<aspectj>
    <aspects>
        <concrete-aspect name="ajia.tracing.SystemWideTraceAspect"
                         extends="ajia.tracing.IndentationTraceAspect">
            <pointcut name="traced" expression="execution(* *.*(..))"/>
        </concrete-aspect>
    </aspects>                                               Aspect to weave in ❶

    <weaver>
        <include within="ajia..*"/>
        <exclude within="*..*EnhancerByCGLIB*..*"/>               ❷ Classes to weave in
        <exclude within="*..*.*$$EnhancerByCGLIB$$*"/>
        <exclude within="*..*.*$$FastClassByCGLIB$$*"/>
    </weaver>
</aspectj>
```

❶ In the aspects section, you specify that a subaspect of `IndentationTraceAspect` should be woven in. You use a `<concrete-aspect>` element along with a pointcut definition that selects all join points in the system. Note that as explained in section 8.3.2, the aspects declared using `<concrete-aspect>` elements such as `ajia.tracing.SystemWideTraceAspect` doesn't exist in the Java or AspectJ source code.

❷ You specify types to be woven in. You include all types in direct and indirect subpackages of the `ajia` package. Because you use Hibernate as the JPA implementation, it generates additional classes dynamically (with either `EnhancerByCGLIB`, `$$EnhancerByCGLIB$$`, or `$$FastClassByCGLIB$$` as part of their names). You exclude those classes through a series of `<exclude>` elements.

When you deploy the code using LTW (either through the aspectjweaver.jar discussed in chapter 8 or Spring-driven LTW discussed in chapter 9) and add a few items to the cart using the web interface, you get the output similar to the following:

```
Entering [OrderController.addToCart(..)]
  Entering [OrderController.getCurrentOrder(..)]
     Entering [OrderServiceImpl.updateOrder(..)]
        Entering [JpaGenericRepository.update(..)]
  Entering [ProductServiceImpl.findProduct(..)]
     Entering [JpaGenericRepository.find(..)]
```

```
  Entering [OrderServiceImpl.addProduct(..)]
     Entering [InventoryServiceImpl.removeProduct(..)]
        Entering [InventoryServiceImpl.isProductAvailable(..)]
           Entering [JpaInventoryItemRepository.findByProduct(..)]
           Entering [InventoryItem.getQuantityOnHand()]
        Entering [JpaInventoryItemRepository.findByProduct(..)]
        Entering [InventoryItem.deplete(..)]
        Entering [JpaGenericRepository.update(..)]
     Entering [Order.addProduct(..)]
        Entering [Order.isPlaced()]
        Entering [Order.getItemFor(..)]
        Entering [Product.getPrice()]
        Entering [LineItem.setQuantity(..)]
     Entering [OrderServiceImpl.updateOrder(..)]
        Entering [JpaGenericRepository.update(..)]
Entering [ProductController.productSummary()]
  Entering [ProductServiceImpl.findProducts()]
     Entering [JpaGenericRepository.findAll()]
Entering [DomainEntity.getId()]
Entering [Product.getName()]
Entering [DomainEntity.getId()]
Entering [Product.getName()]
Entering [DomainEntity.getId()]
Entering [Product.getName()]
Entering [DomainEntity.getId()]
Entering [Product.getName()]
```

I strongly recommend that you play with this configuration and see the effects.

If you're still new to AspectJ but already using Spring as an architectural basis, you may want to start simple by utilizing Spring's proxy-based weaving.

10.5.2 Utilizing Spring AOP for tracing

Consider a situation where you need to trace the internal workings or monitor the performance of controllers and repositories in a web application. Although AspectJ-based weaving will work, you can get the functionality without needing an AspectJ weaver (build-time or load-time). This can significantly reduce resistance in getting started with writing your own aspect. If you're using the Spring Framework, you're probably already using aspects shipped with the framework; but many projects could gain a lot from custom aspects to meet their specific needs.

You can use Spring AOP to introduce tracing without any logistical overhead. The downside is that you can only trace public method execution on Spring beans, but this is often sufficient in many enterprise applications.

Let's implement a tracing aspect as shown in listing 10.14. This aspect differs from listing 10.8 only in its use of the @AspectJ syntax to make it work with Spring AOP.

Listing 10.14 Tracing aspect written in @AspectJ

```
package ajia.tracing;

import ...

@Aspect
```

```
public class TraceAspect {
    private Logger logger = Logger.getLogger(TraceAspect.class);

    @Pointcut("execution(* *.*(..))")
    public void traced() {}

    @Before("traced()")
    public void trace(JoinPoint jp) {
        Signature sig = jp.getSignature();
        logger.log(Level.INFO,
                   "Entering [" + sig.toShortString() + "]");
        NDC.push("  ");
    }

    @After("traced()")
    public void exit() {
        NDC.pop();
    }
}
```

You can apply this aspect by adding the configuration file in listing 10.15, which is a part of the application context.

Listing 10.15 Configuration to use the trace aspect: monitoring-context.xml

```
<beans ...>

    <aop:aspectj-autoproxy/>

    <bean id="traceAspect" class="ajia.tracing.TraceAspect"/>
</beans>
```

When you execute the web application and exercise the functionality, you get output such as the following (the shown output is produced when adding a product to the cart):

```
Entering [TransactionAttributeSource.getTransactionAttribute(..)]
Entering [PlatformTransactionManager.getTransaction(..)]
  Entering [EntityManagerFactoryInfo.getNativeEntityManagerFactory()]
  Entering [DataSource.getConnection()]
Entering [ProductService.findProduct(..)]
  Entering [GenericRepository.find(..)]
Entering [PlatformTransactionManager.commit(..)]
Entering [TransactionAttributeSource.getTransactionAttribute(..)]
Entering [PlatformTransactionManager.getTransaction(..)]
  Entering [EntityManagerFactoryInfo.getNativeEntityManagerFactory()]
  Entering [DataSource.getConnection()]
Entering [OrderService.addProduct(..)]
  Entering [TransactionAttributeSource.getTransactionAttribute(..)]
  Entering [PlatformTransactionManager.getTransaction(..)]
  Entering [InventoryService.removeProduct(..)]
    Entering [InventoryItemRepository.findByProduct(..)]
    Entering [InventoryItemRepository.findByProduct(..)]
    Entering [GenericRepository.update(..)]
  Entering [PlatformTransactionManager.commit(..)]
  Entering [GenericRepository.update(..)]
Entering [PlatformTransactionManager.commit(..)]
```

Notice that you see output corresponding to the services, repositories, transaction manager, JPA manager, and datasource objects—all of those are Spring beans. But you don't see any calls for the domain objects such as `Product` and `LineItem`. This is due to the use of Spring AOP, which only applies to Spring beans.

Now you can have monitoring enabled in your application without needing the AspectJ weaver. When your tracing needs to expand beyond what can be handled by Spring's proxy-based weaving—say, to enable intra-method call tracing—you can consider using the full power of AspectJ weaving.

10.6 Exception monitoring

Because exception throwing is an important event in the system, tracing such occurrences is typically desirable. Exception monitoring is an extension of the method-tracing concept, except the focus is on exceptional conditions in a program rather than the execution of methods. The conventional way to trace exceptions involves surrounding the interesting parts of code with a `try/catch` block and instrumenting each `catch` block with a log statement. With AspectJ, it's possible to log exceptions thrown by a method without any modification to the original code.

> **First-failure data capture**
>
> First-failure data capture (FFDC) functionality requires logging all the data (`this`, arguments, method information) at the point of the first failure. By combining the aspect in this section with that in section 10.4.4, you can easily implement FFDC.

In this section, you'll develop an aspect that enables the logging of thrown exceptions in the system. The aspect in listing 10.16 logs any method in the system that throws an exception.

Listing 10.16 `ExceptionTraceAspect`: tracing exceptions using log4j

```
package ajia.tracing;

import ...

public aspect ExceptionTraceAspect {
    private Logger logger = Logger.getLogger("exceptions");

    private ThreadLocal<Throwable> lastLoggedException
        = new ThreadLocal<Throwable>();

    pointcut exceptionTraced()
        : execution(* *.*(..)) && !within(ExceptionTraceAspect);

    after() throwing(Throwable ex) : exceptionTraced() {
        if (lastLoggedException.get() != ex) {
            lastLoggedException.set(ex);
            Signature sig = thisJoinPointStaticPart.getSignature();
            logger.log(Level.ERROR,
```

1 Tracks last handled exception

2 Selects traced method pointcut

3 Advises exceptions thrown

```
                    "Exception trace aspect ["
                    + sig.toShortString() + "]", ex);      ❸ Advises
            }                                                 exceptions
        }                                                     thrown
    }
```

❶ To avoid logging the same exception at each level in the call stack, you keep track of the last logged exception. If another thread throws the same exception object, you want it to be considered a new exception and logged. The use of thread-local ensures such behavior. Note that you could keep all exceptions thrown in a collection, instead of storing just the last exception. But the most common way to handle an exception is catching and rethrowing the same or a wrapped exception. Therefore, you don't need to worry about an old exception being thrown after throwing a new exception. In those situations, the aspect ends up logging the old exception multiple times, which may be a good idea anyway.

❷ The `exceptionTraced()` pointcut selects all the methods that need exception logging. Here, you're defining this as an execution of any method in the system. You can modify this pointcut to include a subset of methods, as described in section 10.3.1.

❸ The after throwing advice collects the thrown object as context. The advice uses `thisJoinPointStaticPart` to log the information about selected join points. You check and set the `lastLoggedException` member to avoid repeated logging of the same exception.

Let's write a simple program (listing 10.17) to exercise your aspect. You use a nested method that throws an exception to show the behavior of avoiding repeated logging of the same exception.

Listing 10.17 A driver that tests exception logging

```
package ajia.main;

public class Main {
    public static void main(String[] args) {
        try {
            perform();
        } catch (Throwable ex) {
            System.out.println("Error occurred during execution");
        }
    }

    public static void perform() {
        nestedPerform();
    }

    public static void nestedPerform() {
        nestedNestedPerform();
    }

    public static void nestedNestedPerform() {
        throw new IllegalStateException("Simulated exception");
    }
}
```

When you compile the Main class along with ExceptionTraceAspect and run the driver program, you get the following output:

```
Exception trace aspect [Main.nestedNestedPerform()]
java.lang.IllegalStateException: Simulated exception
    at ajia.main.Main.nestedNestedPerform(Main.java:24)
    at ajia.main.Main.nestedPerform(Main.java:20)
    at ajia.main.Main.perform(Main.java:14)
    at ajia.main.Main.main(Main.java:7)
Error occurred during execution
```

The output shows that IllegalStateException, which was thrown by the nestedNestedPerform() method, is logged once, but never logged again. All customizations discussed for method tracing in section 10.4 apply here equally well, including using a type-specific logger and creating reusable aspects.

As discussed in section 10.4.3, sometimes you have to resort to conventional logging. Even then, AspectJ won't quit helping you; it's such a good friend, as we'll discuss next.

10.7 Improving conventional logging

Unlike tracing, logging tends to be specific to the application. For example, you can log all the steps in processing an order. In many situations, common parts of logging in a class or a set of classes can be extracted into aspects. Further, because you can log calls and not just execution, you can target calls made from a few specific classes to modularize those calls. Essentially, you can try to reduce logging into somewhat specific tracing. In any case, these aspects tend to be specific to those classes.

With all that said, you're still left with situations where there is no apparent commonality that can be extracted. In those cases, you implement logging in a conventional manner and use AspectJ to enhance the logging functionality and simplify the implementation. Specifically, you can modularize setting up NDC and MDC.

10.7.1 Modularizing NDC with conventional logging

Consider a long method with several log statements. You'll like setting up NDC around that method so that all statements use that context (for example, to provide the indentation effect). If you perform this functionality using conventional coding alone, you must ensure that you call NDC.push() upon entering and NDC.pop() before exiting each method. This usually involves using a finally block such as the following:

```
public void processOrder(Order order) {
    try {
        NDC.push("  ");

        ... business logic and logging

    } finally {
        NDC.pop();
    }
}
```

If you don't need the indentation effect but rather wish to obtain nested caller information associated with each log statement, you use a string identifying the operation as the argument to the `NDC.push()` method. For example, you can use `NDC.push("processOrder")`. If done consistently, you get nested context in output such as "placeOrder processOrder", if the `placeOrder()` method calls the `processOrder()` method.

This kind of arrangement is error prone. In particular, it's common to see a call to `NDC.pop()` without using the `finally` block (thus not clearing the context in case of an exception). AOP can help simplify such an implementation and provide consistency. As shown in listing 10.18, you can set up NDC to perform the indentation in a way similar to the indentation from listing 10.8.

Listing 10.18 Context indentation aspect

```
package ajia.logging;

import org.apache.log4j.NDC;

public abstract aspect ContextIndentationAspect {
    public abstract pointcut logContextOp();

    before(): logContextOp() {
        NDC.push("  ");
    }

    after(): logContextOp() {
        NDC.pop();
    }
}
```

The aspect declares an abstract pointcut and advises it to push and pop a few spaces. The derived aspects provide a definition for the `logContextOp()` pointcut to select the caller of the log method. If you need to establish nested context corresponding to the caller method, you can push `thisJoinPointStaticPart.getSignature().getName()` instead of spaces. You implement a subaspect as shown in listing 10.19 to apply the context indentation to all service types.

Listing 10.19 System context indentation aspect

```
package ajia.logging;

public aspect SystemContextIndentationAspect
    extends ContextIndentationAspect {
    public pointcut logContextOp(): execution(* ajia.service..*.*(..));
}
```

To exercise this class, let's add the `ShippingServiceImpl` class (listing 10.20), which performs manual logging. It uses a few classes that we don't show, because all they do is log a message in each method.

Listing 10.20 Shipping service implementation

```
package ajia.service.impl;

import ...
```

```
public class ShippingServiceImpl implements ShippingService {
    private Logger logger = Logger.getLogger(ShippingServiceImpl.class);
    private CourierService courierService = new CourierServiceImpl();
    private EmailerService emailer = new EmailerServiceImpl();

    public void processOrder(Order order) {
        logger.log(Level.INFO,
            "[ShippingServiceImpl.processOrder] Processing order "
          + order.getId());

        Package packageToSend = createPackage(order);

        logger.log(Level.INFO,
            "[ShippingServiceImpl.processOrder] Notifying courier "
          + "service with " + packageToSend);
        Tracking tracking = courierService.send(packageToSend);

        logger.log(Level.INFO,
            "[ShippingServiceImpl.processOrder] Sending email with "
          + tracking);
        emailer.send(tracking);

        logger.log(Level.INFO,
            "[ShippingServiceImpl.processOrder] Finished processing");
    }

    private Package createPackage(Order order) {
        logger.log(Level.INFO,
            "[ShippingServiceImpl.createPackage] Creating package");
        return new Package("1234");
    }
}
```

When you call the processOrder() method from a driver class, you get the following output:

```
[ShippingServiceImpl.processOrder] Processing order 1000
   [ShippingServiceImpl.createPackage] Creating package
[ShippingServiceImpl.processOrder] Notifying courier service with
➥   Package number: 1234
   [CourierServiceImpl.send] Sending package
[ShippingServiceImpl.processOrder] Sending email with
➥   Tracking number: 12341234
[ShippingServiceImpl.processOrder] Finished processing
```

As you can see, the indentation makes output easier to comprehend by clarifying the caller-callee relationship. Note that following the warning in section 10.1 against using %C, %F, %L, %M, and %l layout patterns, you explicitly pass the class and method name to each log statement. Let's simplify that using AOP and MDC.

10.7.2 Modularizing MDC with conventional logging

You can also use MDC to enhance log messages. In the simplest form, you can register the caller method name and the defining the type as the context. This is a much cheaper way to include the caller information without having to use a pattern that deduces the information by examining the call stack. Listing 10.21 shows an aspect that sets the caller name using thisEnclosingJoinPointStaticPart.

Listing 10.21 MDC establishment aspect

```
package ajia.logging;

import ...

public aspect MDCEstablishmentAspect {
    private static final String MDC_KEY = "caller";

    pointcut logCall() : call(* Logger.log(..));

    before() : logCall() {
         MDC.put(MDC_KEY,
          thisEnclosingJoinPointStaticPart.getSignature().toShortString());
    }

    after() : logCall() {
        MDC.remove(MDC_KEY);
    }
}
```

Next, because the aspect establishes the caller context, you don't need to add that information in each log statement. For example, the following log statement from the ShippingServiceImpl in listing 10.20 changes from

```
logger.log(Level.INFO,
          "[ShippingServiceImpl.processOrder] Processing order "
         + order.getId());
```

to a much simpler:

```
logger.log(Level.INFO,
          "Processing order " + order.getId());
```

Now you can use a pattern such as [%X{caller}] to log this context information. When you invoke the processOrder() method, you see output similar to the following:

```
[ShippingServiceImpl.processOrder(..)] Processing order 1000
[ShippingServiceImpl.createPackage(..)] Creating package
[ShippingServiceImpl.processOrder(..)] Notifying courier service with
➥   Package number: 1234
[CourierServiceImpl.send(..)] Sending package
[ShippingServiceImpl.processOrder(..)] Sending email with
➥   Tracking number: 12341234
[ShippingServiceImpl.processOrder(..)] Finished processing
```

You can combine MDC with NDC (discussed in the previous section). Furthermore, you can use any other diagnostic context to be automatically available for logging. For example, in the following snippet, we use Spring Security API to add context information related to the accessing user:

```
MDC.push("user",
  SecurityContextHolder.getContext().getAuthentication.getPrincipal());
```

The other context that you can establish using MDC includes the ongoing transaction's identifier, the business-specific context such as the shopping card identifier, and so on. Imagine the kind of tangling that would result if you were to provide diagnostic context using conventional means alone. With AspectJ helping with crosscutting functionality, you can concentrate on only the bare minimum work.

That completes our discussion of tracing. Let's now move our focus to another kind of common technique—performance monitoring.

10.8 Performance monitoring

Performance monitoring involves measuring the time taken by interesting parts of the system as well as the number of times a particular method is invoked. Depending on how it's used, you can monitor activities at various levels. For example, in a web application, you can monitor requests by measuring time taken at the servlet and controller layers. You can also monitor the service layer to gain more fine-grained information. For development purposes, you can focus on parts suspected of slowing down the system. For example, you can monitor JDBC or ORM calls to monitor database access. You can also monitor the concurrency characteristics of the system to determine parameters such as thread pool size and throttling.

Performance monitoring of an application involves recording vital parameters of parts of the system: how long it takes to execute certain functionality, how many calls have been made for a particular method, and so on. You can extend the basic idea of tracing to implement performance monitoring. The idea is to compute the difference in timestamps before and after each monitored operation and record that difference against the currently advised join point. You can also count the number of invocations for each advised operation.

Let's develop a simple aspect to show this functionality. You'll also use @AspectJ syntax to show that most monitoring aspects can be implemented easily in either the traditional syntax or the @AspectJ syntax. The use of the @AspectJ syntax will also allow you to use the aspect through Spring's proxy-based weaving.

> **Prebuilt solutions for monitoring**
>
> The purpose of aspects in this section is to illustrate the core performance monitoring technique. For a more complete solution, you may want to consider prebuilt solutions such as Glassbox and the SpringSource Application Monitoring Suite (AMS) that use AspectJ internally as an implementation technology.

Listing 10.22 shows an abstract aspect that uses `System.nanoTime()` as the way to get timing information.

Listing 10.22 `AbstractPerformanceMonitoringAspect`: monitoring operations

```
package ajia.monitoring;

import ...

@Aspect
public abstract class AbstractPerformanceMonitoringAspect {
```

```
    private Logger logger
        = Logger.getLogger(AbstractPerformanceMonitoringAspect.class);

    @Pointcut
    public abstract void monitoredOp();

    @Around("monitoredOp()")
    public Object monitor(ProceedingJoinPoint pjp) throws Throwable{
        long start = System.nanoTime();
        try {
            return pjp.proceed();
        } finally {
            long complete = System.nanoTime();
            logger.log(Level.INFO,
                       "Operation " + pjp.getSignature().toShortString()
                       + " took " + (complete-start) + " nanoseconds");
        }
    }
}
```

You're using the timing API directly. But it's best to encapsulate such functionality into a separate interface to allow a pluggable implementation. For example, you can use Jamon (http://jamonapi.sourceforge.net) or Simon (http://code.google.com/p/javasimon) to simplify gathering data and computing statistics. It's also best to leverage a DI mechanism to make such pluggability a configuration option.

Let's enable monitoring of repository classes by creating a subaspect as shown in listing 10.23.

Listing 10.23 `SystemMonitoringAspect`: monitoring repository operations

```
package ajia.monitoring;

import ...

@Aspect
public class SystemMonitoringAspect extends
      AbstractPerformanceMonitoringAspect {
    @Pointcut("execution(* ajia..*.*(..)) && !within(ajia.tracing..*)")
    public void monitoredOp() {}
}
```

You can now enable this aspect though AspectJ LTW using an `<aspect>` element inside aop.xml. Alternatively, you can define a subaspect of `AbstractPerformanceMonitoringAspect` using an `<concrete-aspect>` element to the same effect. You may also use build-time weaving to weave the aspect prior to deployment. Either way, when a user adds an item to a cart, you get output similar to the following:

```
Operation InventoryItem.getQuantityOnHand() took 14760 nanoseconds
Operation InventoryServiceImpl.isProductAvailable(..) took
➥   54309707 nanoseconds
Operation JpaInventoryItemRepository.findByProduct(..) took
➥   762442 nanoseconds
Operation InventoryItem.deplete(..) took 10447 nanoseconds
Operation JpaGenericRepository.update(..) took 52935 nanoseconds
Operation InventoryServiceImpl.removeProduct(..) took 58732125 nanoseconds
```

```
Operation Order.isPlaced() took 8793 nanoseconds
Operation Order.getItemFor(..) took 26898 nanoseconds
Operation Product.getPrice() took 2481 nanoseconds
Operation LineItem.setQuantity(..) took 13210 nanoseconds
Operation Order.addProduct(..) took 610647 nanoseconds
Operation JpaGenericRepository.update(..) took 7343705 nanoseconds
Operation OrderServiceImpl.updateOrder(..) took 7466786 nanoseconds
Operation OrderServiceImpl.addProduct(..) took 67595893 nanoseconds
Operation OrderController.addToCart(..) took 102952612 nanoseconds
Operation JpaGenericRepository.findAll() took 675822 nanoseconds
Operation ProductServiceImpl.findProducts() took 853805 nanoseconds
Operation ProductController.productSummary() took 1350510 nanoseconds
...
```

You can play with the aspect to make the output more interesting and useful. For example, you may

- Modify the pointcuts to select join points of your interest.
- Modify the base aspect to log more information about the join points.
- Apply NDC context to examine how much time is spent in each constituent method.

The same aspect can be applied using Spring AOP by adding the code in listing 10.24 into a file that forms the application context.

Listing 10.24 Adding performance monitoring through Spring AOP

```
<beans ...>
    <context:component-scan base-package="ajia" >
        <context:exclude-filter expression="ajia.web..*" type="aspectj"/>
    </context:component-scan>

    <aop:aspectj-autoproxy/>

    <bean id="monitoringAspect"
          class="ajia.monitoring.SystemMonitoringAspect"/>
</beans>
```

Now, when you run the web application and add a product to the shopping cart, you get output similar to the following:

```
Operation GenericRepository.find(..) took 36026925 nanoseconds
Operation ProductService.findProduct(..) took 39170621 nanoseconds
Operation InventoryItemRepository.findByProduct(..) took
➥    160806192 nanoseconds
Operation InventoryItemRepository.findByProduct(..) took
➥    4458387 nanoseconds
Operation GenericRepository.update(..) took 86045 nanoseconds
Operation InventoryService.removeProduct(..) took 166793545 nanoseconds
Operation GenericRepository.update(..) took 16229158 nanoseconds
Operation OrderService.addProduct(..) took 184289344 nanoseconds
```

Notice that only Spring beans and not other classes such as domain entities are being monitored. This is due to the proxy-based AOP being applied only to the Spring beans.

You can also extend AspectJ-based profiling functionality to implement modular dynamic service-level monitoring. For example, let's say that you're using some third-party services such as credit-card approval processing over the internet. You may have an agreement that provides you with certain performance guarantees. You can collect the time before and after each invocation of the services. When the service gets near or below the agreed level, you can alert the provider as well as use the information to collect penalties, if the agreement so specifies. If you're on the provider side, you can use the profile information to create alerts when the level of service approaches the agreed level. Such alerts may help you fix the problem before it reaches a critical level.

Let's complete the discussion of AOP-based monitoring by examining how you can control aspects once they're deployed.

10.9 Runtime control of monitoring aspects

Monitoring aspects often need to be turned on or off in production. This reduces the overhead associated with monitoring and the amount of data reported, thus improving comprehension.

A simple way to control an aspect is by using an `if()` check evaluating a `boolean` field and exposing that field through JMX. If you need to control the applicability of the aspect at application startup, you can assign the `boolean` field a system property (or a property read from a property file). You can also combine these two techniques to control the default applicability of the aspect as well as allow runtime control, as shown in listing 10.25.

Listing 10.25 Enabling and disabling monitoring at runtime

```
package ajia.monitoring;

import ...

@Aspect
public abstract class AbstractPerformanceMonitoringAspect {
    private Logger logger
        = Logger.getLogger(AbstractPerformanceMonitoringAspect.class);
    private boolean enabled = Boolean.getBoolean("ajia.monitoring.enable");

    @Pointcut
    public abstract void monitoredOp();

    @Around("monitoredOp()&& !within(AbstractPerformanceMonitoringAspect)")
    public Object monitor(ProceedingJoinPoint pjp) throws Throwable {
         if(!isEnabled()) {
             return pjp.proceed();
         }
         long start = System.nanoTime();
         try {
             return pjp.proceed();
         } finally {
             long complete = System.nanoTime();
             logger.log(Level.INFO,
                        "Operation " + pjp.getSignature().toShortString()
                        + " took " + (complete-start) + " nanoseconds");
         }
    }
```

```
    public void setEnabled(boolean enabled) {
        this.enabled = enabled;
    }

    public boolean isEnabled() {
        return this.enabled;
    }
}
```

The aspect includes a `boolean` field so that it can be exposed to a JMX console. You assign this field the value of the `ajia.monitoring.enable` system property so that unless you start the application with the `-Dajia.monitoring.enable=true` argument, monitoring is disabled. You use this field inside the advice to control its application. Note that you can use an `if()` pointcut, if the aspect is woven using the AspectJ weaver (which can then perform certain optimizations to avoid creation of the `pjp` object if the condition in the pointcut evaluates to `false`). But because Spring AOP doesn't support the `if()` pointcut, you embed the check inside the advice.

For runtime control, you need to expose the field through JMX. If you're using the Spring Framework, exposing the aspect through JMX is a trivial task, as shown in listing 10.26 (assumes AspectJ LTW deployment).

Listing 10.26 Exposing the monitoring aspect using Spring's JMX support

```
<beans ...>
    <bean id="monitorAspect"
          class="ajia.monitoring.SystemMonitoringAspect"
          factory-method="aspectOf"/>                        ❶ Aspect as Spring bean

    <bean class="org.springframework.jmx.export.MBeanExporter">
        <property name="beans">
            <util:map>
                <entry key="ajia:name=monitorAspect"         ❷ Exposes aspect over JMX
                       value-ref="monitorAspect"/>
            </util:map>
        </property>
    </bean>
</beans>
```

❶ You create a Spring bean corresponding to the aspect. Note that if you use Spring's proxy-based AOP, you omit the `factory-method="aspectOf"` part.

❷ You use Spring support for exporting beans to JMX to export the aspect instance under the `ajia:name=monitorAspect` object name.

Now, when you connect to the application using a JMX console such as JConsole, as shown in figure 10.3, you see a bean named `monitorAspect` and can modify its `enabled` property. (You may have to specify `-Dcom.sun.management.jmxremote` to the VM, depending on your web server and the VM).

As you can see, implementing performance monitoring using AspectJ is just as easy as tracing. At this point, if you haven't already done so, I urge you to download the source code for the book and try it yourself before proceeding to the next chapter.

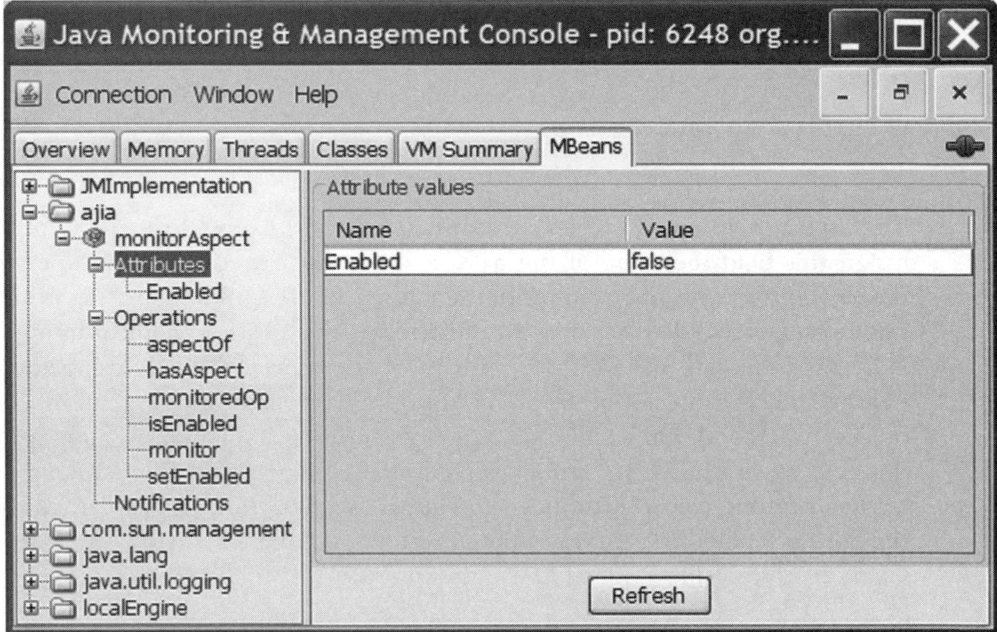

Figure 10.3 JConsole to monitor and control aspect exposed through JMX.

10.10 Summary

Software developers and management often look for a killer application: one that is so well suited that it makes adopting a new technology worthwhile, despite the risks. The reason behind this conservative approach is to balance the considerable investment associated with any new technology against the benefits it offers. A killer application supposedly provides enough benefits to outweigh the risks. But such applications are hard to find. Add to that the difficulty in measuring largely qualitative benefits, such as productivity improvements, cleaner design, ease of evolution, and improved quality. Such qualitative benefits make proving the advantages of a new approach to a skeptic challenging. The more practical approach is to find ways to reduce the investment involved with the new technology. If you can achieve such reduction, you no longer have to wait until you see a bonanza of benefits.

AspectJ-based tracing and monitoring techniques offer low-investment, low-risk ways to begin using AspectJ. The aspects and idioms presented in this chapter may be all that you need to start applying them in real world applications. These aspects also offer a unique plug-and-play nature. LTW offers an attractive way to weave aspects while leaving your build environment intact. The use of LTW further enhances the plug-and-play nature of the solution; a simple modification to the startup script is all you need to add aspects to or remove them from your system.

If this chapter has convinced you of the benefits of using AspectJ for monitoring, you may start out by using it for tracing and performance monitoring to understand system interaction and performance bottlenecks. Later, you can demonstrate to your team the benefits you've experienced, which may lead them to adopt AspectJ as well. At any point, including during the final shipment, you can exclude the AspectJ and monitoring aspects. The overall effect is that you can start using AspectJ with minimal risk.

When you commit to AspectJ-based monitoring, you'll start seeing even more benefits. You can use AspectJ-based solutions for auditing and production performance monitoring. Implementation of all these concerns is now nicely modularized. This solution leads to increased flexibility, improved accuracy, and better consistency. It saves you from the laborious and boring task of writing nearly identical log statements in code all over your system. The use of AspectJ also makes the job of switching logging toolkits an easy task. You can start with any one that you're familiar with and feel comfortable that changing the choice later on will require modifying only a few statements.

Although it isn't a killer application, monitoring may be the perfect way to introduce yourself and your organization to AspectJ.

11 Policy enforcement: keeping your design intact

This chapter covers

- Understanding AOP policy enforcement patterns
- Enforcing EJB programming restrictions using AspectJ
- Enforcing Swing policies using AspectJ

Imagine that you're convinced public access to a data member of a class isn't a good idea. Or, imagine that you've realized layered architecture is the way to go. Or, suppose you've just finished reading the Enterprise JavaBeans (EJB) specification and realize that the specification prohibits working directly with files from an EJB. Clearly, you'd like to ensure that the projects you work on don't violate these principles and restrictions. What are your choices? You could send emails to your team asking them to check for these violations, or you could add this information to a knowledge base. But these solutions are hard to maintain. Even if you somehow manage to detect any violations, perhaps through regular code reviews, what if you start a new project with a new team? Educate them again? OK, you get the point.

Policy enforcement is a mechanism for ensuring that system components follow certain programming practices, comply with specified rules, and meet any assumptions. If there is no enforcement, errors may go undetected during development and show up only in the deployed system. How would you enforce such policies today? Perhaps you'd use a static code-analysis tool such as PMD or FindBugs that looks for specific code patterns to flag potential programming problems. These tools detect violations of commonly accepted practices. You may also be able to write simple custom policies if you learn the tool's specific programming language. Even then, you're limited to policies that static code analysis can detect. Specifically, you can't enforce policies that need information available only at runtime. Although these tools are excellent additions to most development environments, they aren't adequate for catching all scenarios.

AOP provides an elegant way to encapsulate policies in aspects, allowing enforcement with little human diligence. You can also reuse those aspects and apply them to other projects without incurring additional development cost, thus building a company-wide library of accepted policies. Policy enforcement with AOP falls in the developmental aspect category. You can include these aspects during the development phase to help detect policy violations; and for deployment, you can exclude them without affecting the core system behavior. This can be part of an incremental adaptation of AOP; you don't have to commit to using AOP in the deployed system in order to get the benefits from it.

This chapter presents many examples that illustrate how you can detect violations by compiling your code along with a few prewritten aspects. The examples include enforcement of layering in a typical application, enforcing good programming practices and idioms, as well as enforcing framework and concurrency control policies. You'll use AspectJ byte-code weaving as well as Spring AOP to implement various policies. Because the code-analysis tools provide an alternative way to implement some of these policies, we'll compare them with AOP-based solutions and provide guidelines for choosing the right tool for the job. Let's start with an overview of the AOP way of enforcing policies.

11.1 AOP-based policy enforcement overview

Consider a commonly accepted policy in a layered architecture, as shown in figure 11.1. The core idea is that each layer can access functionality only of the layer directly beneath it. This policy, if implemented correctly, can simplify understanding and maintenance of the system. Initially, most applications adhere to these policies. But later, a drift begins from the layering discipline. Over time, many applications reach a point where the layered architecture has no discipline at all.

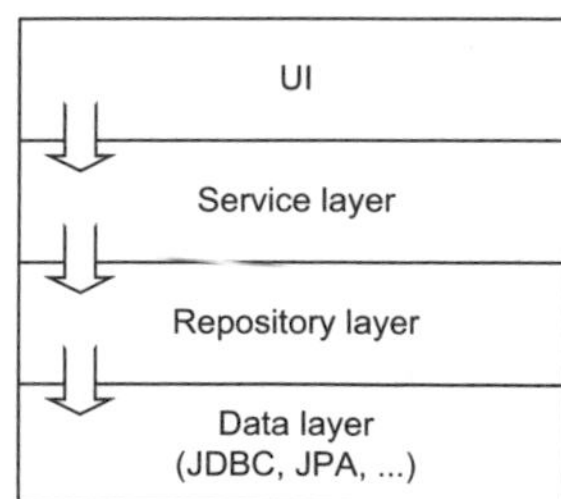

Figure 11.1 A typical layered architecture for enterprise applications. The arrows indicate the allowed interaction. Any other interaction is in violation of the layering policy.

With AspectJ, you can write a simple aspect, as shown in listing 11.1, to enforce the layering policy.

You do it by detecting calls to specific layers and ensuring that they don't occur outside the allowed layer.

Listing 11.1 Enforcement of layered architecture

```
package ajia.architecture;

public aspect LayeringViolation {
    declare error
      : SystemArchitecture.dataLayerCall()
        && !SystemArchitecture.inRepositoryLayer()
      : "Only the repository layer is allowed to access the data layer";

    declare error
      : SystemArchitecture.repositoryLayerCall()
        && !SystemArchitecture.inRepositoryLayer()
        && !SystemArchitecture.inServiceLayer()
      : "Only the service layer is allowed to access the repository layer";

    declare error
      : SystemArchitecture.serviceLayerCall()
        && !SystemArchitecture.inServiceLayer()
        && !SystemArchitecture.inWebLayer()
      : "Only the UI layer is allowed to access the service layer";

    declare error
      : SystemArchitecture.webLayerCall()
        && !SystemArchitecture.inWebLayer()
      : "Only the UI layer is allowed to access itself";
}
```

Each statement declares that a call to a layer occurring outside the same layer or the layer above it is in error. Note that the first statement doesn't check for calls made in the same layer, because you won't weave into the code for the data layer. Similarly, the last statement doesn't check for the layer above the web layer, because no such layer exists.

The aspect itself doesn't define any pointcuts. Instead, it uses the aspect shown in listing 11.2, which describes the system architecture. Other aspects in the same system may reuse this aspect.

Listing 11.2 Aspect defining system architecture pointcuts

```
package ajia.architecture;

import ...

public aspect SystemArchitecture {
    pointcut webLayerCall()
        : call(* ajia.web..*.*(..));

    pointcut inWebLayer()
        : within(ajia.web..*);

    pointcut serviceLayerCall()
        : call(* ajia.service..*.*(..));

    pointcut inServiceLayer()
```

```
        : within(ajia.service..*);

    pointcut repositoryLayerCall()
        : call(* ajia.repository..*.*(..));

    pointcut inRepositoryLayer()
        : within(ajia.repository..*);

    pointcut dataLayerCall()
        : JDBCPointcuts.jdbcCall()
          || JPAPointcuts.jpaCall()
          || SpringPointcuts.jdbcTemplateCall();
}
```

In this aspect, you assume that the application's package structure follows the layering arrangement shown in figure 11.1. For example, you assume that types belonging to the service layer reside in the `ajia.service`'s direct or indirect subpackages. This separation of pointcuts also simplifies modifications to the pointcuts when you perform refactoring such as renaming a package. You can also use an alternative style—for example, to use annotations (such as `@Service` and `@Repository` in Spring) instead of package names. In any case, the pointcuts are well modularized in a single place.

Crosscut Programming Interface

The `SystemArchitecture` aspect represents a kind of interface to a system that exposes its crosscutting structure. This approach is formally called Crosscut Programming Interface (XPI). With this approach, a set of aspects exposes XPI through pointcuts, and other aspects program to that XPI. See http://www.cs.virginia.edu/papers/ieee_software2006.pdf for more details.

The `SystemArchitecture` aspect uses yet another set of reusable aspects. Listing 11.3 shows the aspect that implements JDBC pointcuts.

Listing 11.3 Reusable aspect defining JDBC pointcuts

```
package ajia.jdbc;

public aspect JDBCPointcuts {
    public pointcut jdbcCall()
        : call(* java.sql..*.*(..))
          || call(* javax.sql..*.*(..));

    public pointcut jdbcExecution()
        : execution(* java.sql..*.*(..))
          || execution(* javax.sql..*.*(..));
}
```

You don't need the `jdbcExecution()` pointcut in this section, but it will come in handy as a reusable pointcut. Similarly, listing 11.4 shows an aspect that implements JPA pointcuts.

Listing 11.4 Reusable aspect defining JPA pointcuts

```
package ajia.jpa;

public aspect JPAPointcuts {
    public pointcut jpaCall()
        : call(* javax.persistence..*.*(..));

    public pointcut jpaExecution()
        : execution(* javax.persistence..*.*(..));
}
```

Note that you could easily add all these aspects to a separate library, because they don't include any application-specific code. Next, listing 11.5 defines Spring pointcuts. Specifically, you define a pointcut that selects calls that use Spring JDBC support classes. Of course, if you access JDBC functionality through other means (say, through iBatis), you can add more aspects.

Listing 11.5 Aspect providing Spring-related pointcuts

```
package ajia.spring;

import ...

public aspect SpringPointcuts {
    public pointcut jdbcTemplateCall()
        : call(* JdbcOperations+.*(..))
          || call(* SimpleJdbcOperations+.*(..));

    public pointcut jdbcTemplateExecution()
        : execution(* JdbcOperations+.*(..))
          || execution(* SimpleJdbcOperations+.*(..));
}
```

The aspect could have specified `JdbcTemplate` and `SimpleJdbcTemplate` directly. But it uses the base types `JdbcOperations` and `SimpleJdbcOperations` combined with the + wildcard to select any additional subtypes as well as custom extension to these types.

Notice how elegantly and unambiguously you define each layer. Let's consider the code snippet in listing 11.6, which violates the layering policy by using JDBC from the UI layer.

Listing 11.6 A UI layer class that violates the layering rules

```
package ajia.web;

import...

public class ListInventoryController implements Controller {
    public ModelAndView handleRequest(
        HttpServletRequest request,
        HttpServletResponse response) throws Exception {
        Connection conn =
            DriverManager.getConnection(
                "jdbc:hsqldb:file:ecommerce", "sa", "");
        ... use connection
```

```
            return null;
        }
    }
```

When you compile this class with aspects and the rest of your classes, you get errors like this one:

```
error at DriverManager.getConnection(
^^^^^^^^^^^^^^^^^^^^^^^^^^^^^

...\ajia\web\ListInventoryController.java:20:0::0
➥   Only the repository layer is allowed to access the data layer
        see also: ...\ajia\architecture\LayeringViolation.aj:5::0
```

After you add this aspect to your project's build facility to compile it with the AspectJ compiler, you never have to remind your team members about avoiding layer crossing or accessing the layers in a wrong direction; the aspect does the job for you. Although these types of policy violations *may* be caught by a thorough code review, the immediate feedback of tool-based policy enforcement is incredibly valuable. You're notified about the policy violation as soon as you build code. Indeed, if you're using the AspectJ Development Tools (AJDT) in Eclipse, it will notify you about the violations soon as you enter the code!

Figure 11.2 shows the overall scheme of policy enforcement using AspectJ. Although the figure shows the use of build-time source weaving, other mechanisms such as load-time weaving work as well. See chapter 8 for more information about adding the AspectJ weaver into your system. Aspects implement policy enforcement to identify any violations in a software system. With Spring AOP, you can implement violation detection only during runtime.

The solution presented in this chapter opens a new possibility for application frameworks and library creators. Instead of (or in addition to) shipping the documentation specifying the restrictions, such products can now ship aspects that capture parts of the specification along with their framework. Developers using the framework can detect most violations at compile time by including the aspects in their build system. The

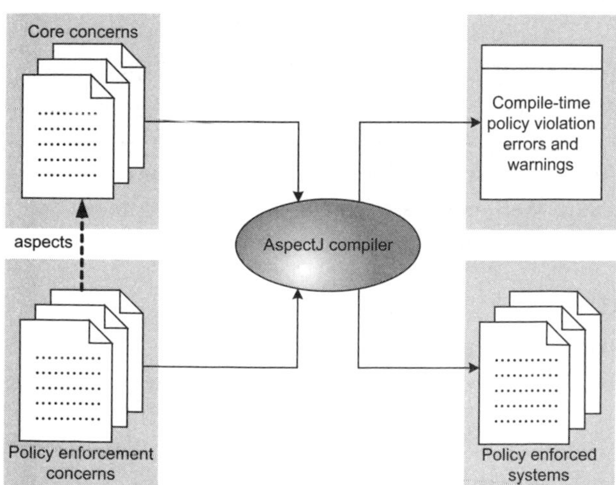

Figure 11.2 The overall scheme of policy enforcement using AspectJ. Aspects implementing policy enforcement are compiled together with the implementation of the core business logic. Compile-time errors/warnings are issued immediately. Runtime enforcement detects violations when the system executes the violating code.

aspects detect other violations at runtime with a clear message indicating where things went wrong. Because aspects are program constructs, they also serve as precise documents. These aspects watch the users over their shoulders to check whether the assumptions made by the library developers are satisfied. Avoiding incorrect usages leads to higher-quality applications, which results in higher user satisfaction.

Now that you have a general understanding of enforcing policies using AOP, let's take a step back and examine how policies originate, why it's important to invest in enforcing those policies, and how you can enforce them.

11.2 Policy origins and destinations

Policies represent accumulated knowledge about how to create higher-quality software. They originate from a variety of sources:

- Consensus among the developer community about generally accepted programming design patterns, idioms, and best practices (yes, it's hard to believe that we developers can agree on anything!)
- Your own ideas about what a good architecture looks like, requirements of the underlying framework, and core architecture of the specific project
- Specific design choices made by the team on a project

What you do with these policies is up to you. If the policies encapsulate design decisions, the software system that follows will stand the test of time. But if you let one violation go through, more violations will soon follow. Code that violates policies can be mistaken for design decisions by new programmers unaware of the real policies, which in the worst case can lead to repetition of those violations as those new programmers ironically try to follow "the company standard". Eventually, such an application loses the implicit architecture that was once its foundation.

The preceding narrative doesn't represent any newfound wisdom. There have been several attempts to create ways to implement these policies. The most common way of documenting these policies relies too much on programmers' due diligence. Regularly conducted code reviews offer a way to share knowledge with others in the team and to look out for policy violations. Although such reviews have a definite place in the software-development process, using them for mundane tasks such as simple policy checks is wasteful. Code reviews should instead focus on the subtler nuances of design and implementation. Automated tools offering static analysis of code to find out potential violations offer excellent solutions in some cases. These tools share a few characteristics with AOP-based policy enforcement. We'll compare the two approaches in section 11.4. For now, let's examine the core ideas in policy-enforcement implementation using AspectJ.

11.3 Enforcement using AOP

Fundamentally, policy enforcement requires flagging conditions that violate certain principles and assumptions, such as accessing the state of a class in a thread-unsafe way or from undesirable classes. Detecting and correcting these conditions is vital for the quality of the overall system. As we alluded to earlier, policy enforcement using AOP involves creating a few aspects that detect all usages that violate the required policies.

You can use many of the aspects developed in this chapter directly, without any modifications. This reusability makes AOP-based policy enforcement highly cost effective. You have two choices for implementing policies: compile-time checking and runtime checking. Each kind of enforcement has its appropriate usages and limitations. In this section, we'll discuss the AOP implementation for both kinds of checking.

11.3.1 Compile-time enforcement

Compile-time checking implies performing policy-violation checks during the compilation phase. Compile-time checks are powerful—they allow you to perform checks even before running the system. In strongly typed languages such as Java and C++, compilers already perform certain compile-time checking, such as type matching, access control, and so forth. With AspectJ, you can take such checking to a new level; you can specify custom checks. Now the compiler is your best friend; it can save you from a potentially time-consuming bug-fix cycle by minimizing the time between creating a bug and finding it.

Note that you may prefer to keep your build system unchanged but still benefit from AOP policy enforcements. All you need to do is use binary weaving, as shown in chapter 8. The regular build system produces artifacts such as jar files. Then, either an additional build step or a separate build system weaves in those artifacts with policy enforcement aspects, producing errors and warnings during the build process as well as woven artifacts with runtime policy checks embedded in them.

Implementing compile-time enforcement using AspectJ involves the use of `declare error` and `declare warning` constructs. These mechanisms provide a way to detect the presence of a matching join point during the compilation phase and to issue an error or a warning. Although its early-detection capability is powerful, compile-time checking has limitations on the kinds of checks it can perform:

- *The only pointcuts you can use are statically determinable pointcuts.* Pointcuts such as `this()`, `if()`, and `cflow()` can't be used for this purpose. You can learn more about these constructs in chapter 5.
- *You can't detect the absence of a join point.* Pointcuts select join points and therefore can't indicate a lack of a join point. For example, you can't detect an empty `catch` block (absence of a join point embedded in a handler join point).
- *You can't use analysis based on multiple join points to declare an error or warning.* A `declare error` or `warning` construct issues an error or warning upon detecting a matching join point. The use of statically determinable pointcuts precludes selecting a join point based on a matching criterion at another join point. Therefore, compile-time enforcement can't implement policies such as checking that a method is correctly releasing a concurrency lock that it acquired earlier in that method. Checking for such a condition requires expressions that encompass two join points: one for acquiring the lock and another for releasing it.
- *You can't detect stylistic violations.* For example, a pointcut can't select methods that are over a certain size, methods that lack documentation, or methods with too many `return` statements.

Runtime policy enforcement can overcome many of these limitations. Further, certain kinds of behavior, such as checking for ranges in values of certain arguments, can be performed only during the execution of a program.

11.3.2 Runtime enforcement

In contrast to compile-time checking, runtime enforcement performs violation detection during system execution. In languages such as Java, the VMs already perform certain runtime checks, such as cast-correctness and null-reference access checks. Runtime policy enforcement is a similar idea, except that you can specify custom checks.

Upon detecting a policy violation at runtime, the usual approach is to log the violation along with the context in which it occurred. If the system malfunctions, the logs can offer insight to potential precursors. Even without malfunctions, periodically examining the logs can provide useful information so you can avoid potential problems in the next release—a sort of built-in QA.

Alternatively, you can implement a *fail-fast* strategy, where you throw an exception upon detecting a violation. Such a strategy ensures that system integrity isn't compromised due to continued execution of the system after a violation has occurred. It also forces the team to fix violations immediately. Of course, you should have a complete, automated test suite to catch violations during the testing phase instead of causing abrupt failures in production.

Contract enforcements

Design-level contracts include pre-conditions, post-conditions, and invariants of form policies that let you express programming intentions. Contract4J (http://www.contract4j.org) is a Java-based library that expresses contracts through Java annotations and enforces them at runtime using AspectJ.

Runtime enforcement involves verifying the policies using dynamic crosscutting constructs. For instance, you can write advice to detect the violation of Swing's thread-safety rule. Because such checking detects violations after the fact, logging for auditing purposes is usually the best option. For major violations, it may be desirable to let the system shut down gracefully to avoid further damage. The choice of action ultimately depends on the nature of the violation. You can use either AspectJ weaving or Spring's proxy-based AOP depending on the policies being enforced (the criterion to use one or the other is the same as discussed in chapter 9).

Runtime policy enforcement comes with a limitation. You need to hit the code path leading to a violation for the enforcement aspect to warn you about the problem. For example, unit or integration tests must exercise code that violates the policy for the Swing single thread policy to be able to flag the violation. In practice, this means having enough testing to exercise many scenarios, so you gain confidence in the code's adherence to policies.

In many situations, it's possible to fix policy violations using an aspect instead of issuing warnings or errors at either runtime or compile time (you'll see examples of such possibilities in sections 11.6 and 11.7). But fixing the problem will force you to include the aspects in the deployed system, and that will remove the choice of using AOP in the deployed system. If you want to preserve that choice, it's important that the policy enforcements don't change the core program behavior in any way. They should be side-effect free and add notifications to inform you about policy violations.

While you have all the information ready to start developing a few examples, let's address a lingering question—how code-analysis tools compare with the AOP way for policy enforcement.

11.4 Comparison with code-analysis tools

Policy enforcement is so important that a few recently developed tools such as FindBugs (http://findbugs.sourceforge.net), Checkstyle (http://checkstyle.sourceforge.net) and PMD (http://pmd.sourceforge.net) address it. These tools use code analysis to find violations of common coding practices. They predefine a few commonly accepted practices. Some even make it easy for you to write your own rules. These tools can be tremendously valuable in improving the quality of your software. Further, IDE integration of these tools makes it easy to use them. How does an AOP solution compare to these tools?

Code-analysis tools can detect code patterns spanning multiple methods and classes. For example, code-analysis tools are capable of detecting duplicated code fragments, concurrency-related issues such as incorrect acquire-release of a lock, inconsistently implemented concurrency policy across multiple methods of a class, and so on. They can also detect code patterns such as empty `catch` blocks. Some of the tools operate at the source-code level (instead of the byte-code level) and therefore can detect a lack of documentation and even violations of coding conventions.

Some policies, such as avoiding public non-final fields in a class, can be enforced by either code-analysis tools or aspects. If the code-analysis tool you use includes a policy of your choice, there isn't much point in duplicating that enforcement using an AOP-based solution. But in other cases, AspectJ's simpler and more expressive programming model is attractive. For the set of problems where AspectJ's join point model is sufficient, writing a couple of pointcuts is all it takes to implement a new policy. This makes it attractive to write policies specific to your code base.

In a few other cases, a code-analysis tool can detect violations of policies at compile-time, whereas with AOP you have to wait until runtime—for example, acquiring and releasing a concurrent lock. In these cases, if the code-analysis tool of your choice implements the needed policy, you should favor its use over AOP.

Code-analysis tools offer no way to detect policies that require a runtime context. For example, the Swing thread-safety violation that requires runtime knowledge (the caller thread, specifically) can't be detected by any code-analysis tool. In those cases, AOP offers a compelling solution.

In summary, you should use code-analysis tools as the first line of defense for enforcing common programming wisdom. For custom, project-specific enforcements, consider using AOP. For runtime enforcement, AOP is often the only reasonable choice. Now that you have a good understanding of AOP policy enforcement as well as its power and limitations, let's examine a series of examples to put this information to good use.

11.5 Implementing flexible access control

Access control is a kind of enforcement that limits access to certain functionality. Preventing access to certain parts of the API enables future modifications. It also simplifies assumptions made on the caller, further simplifying the implementation. But you can reap these benefits only if you can be sure that the whole system follows the access control.

AspectJ lets you define access control in far more precise terms than those offered by the standard Java access specifiers of public, protected, package (default), and private. For package access, for example, Java offers only two categories: the owner package and all other packages. But you may need to define access at a much finer package granularity—such as user interface, networking, and database—so that you can control which packages can access a certain class or method.

In this section, we'll discuss three examples—restricting exposure, limiting collaboration, and implementing the factory pattern—that should give you ideas about how to implement your own access controls.

11.5.1 Restricting exposure

Consider the best practice of not exposing the internal implementation of a class. Minimally, this practice translates to assigning nonpublic access to any (nonfinal) members. Let's see how AspectJ can help implement this rule. In listing 11.7, the aspect warns you about using public access to any nonfinal field.

Listing 11.7 Aspect that detects public access to members

```
package ajia.enforcement;

aspect DetectPublicAccessMembers {
    declare warning :
        get(public !final * *) || set(public !final * *) :
        "Please consider using nonpublic access";
}
```

The aspect, per se, doesn't detect the presence of public fields in a class. But it detects read or write access to any such field. The pointcut `get(public !final * *)` selects read access to any nonfinal public field of any class. The use of `!final` prevents the code from issuing warnings for access to final fields, which usually isn't considered bad practice. Similarly, the pointcut `set(public !final * *)` selects all write access to any nonfinal public field of any class. We don't consider setting a final field to be in error, because that can happen only when the field is being initialized.

The class file in listing 11.8 shows the effect of the enforcement aspect.

Listing 11.8 Class to illustrate the violation of publicly exposed fields

```
package ajia;

public class Accessor {
    public void set() {
        Exposer exposer = new Exposer();
        int exposureCount = exposer.count;
        exposer.count = 10;
    }
}

class Exposer {
    public final int CONST = 56;
    public int count;
}
```

Now, when you compile the DetectPublicAccessMembers aspect along with these classes, you get warnings similar to the following:

```
...\ajia\Accessor.java:7
➥   [warning] Please consider using nonpublic access
int exposureCount = exposer.count;
^^^^^^^^^^^^^^^^^^^^^^^^^^^^^^^^^^
        field-get(int ajia.Exposer.count)
        see also:
➥       ...\ajia\enforcement\DetectPublicAccessMembers.aj:5::0
...\ajia\Accessor.java:8
➥   [warning] Please consider using nonpublic access
exposer.count = 10;
^^^^^^^^^^^^^^^^^^
        field-set(int ajia.Exposer.count)
        see also:
➥       ...\ajia\enforcement\DetectPublicAccessMembers.aj:5::0

2 warnings
```

You can then assign appropriate nonpublic access control to the field and introduce getter and/or setter methods. The next time someone writes code that contains a public field, this aspect will catch the violation immediately.

Try this aspect in your own system; you may get some surprises.

11.5.2 Limiting collaboration

Consider the e-commerce example from appendix A. It appears that the programmer intended to allow the manipulation of the Order class only through implementation of the OrderService interface, which ensures correct inventory updates. But what is there to prevent direct access to an Order object?

Leaving the situation as it is downgrades the programmer's "intention" to a programmer's "wish." Java's access-control mechanism isn't enough in this case. Note that because the Order and OrderService implementation classes are likely to reside in different packages, you need to make the Order methods public. You need a way to implement access control that disallows calls to certain operations on an Order object from anywhere except in OrderService. With AspectJ, writing a simple aspect such as the one in listing 11.9 ensures the intended access control.

Listing 11.9 OrderAccessAspect.java: enforcing access control

```
package ajia.enforcement;

import ...

public aspect OrderAccessAspect {
    declare error
        : (call(* Order.add*(..))|| call(* Order.remove*(..))
           || call(* Order.place(..))|| call(* Order.cancel(..)))
        && !within(OrderService+)
        : "Illegal manipulation to Order; "
        + "Only OrderService or its subtypes may perform such operations";
}
```

You can see the violation detection in action by using the class in listing 11.10, which directly accesses the prohibited methods of the Order class.

Listing 11.10 Class to illustrate the violation

```
package ajia;

import ajia.domain.Order;

public class CustomerService {
   public void manipulateOrder(Order order) {
       order.place();
       order.cancel();
   }
}
```

Compiling OrderAccessAspect along with the CustomerService class detects any illegal access and issues a compile-time error like this:

```
error at order.place();
^^^^^^^^^^^^^^

...\ajia\CustomerService.java:8:0::0 Illegal manipulation to Order;
➥    Only OrderService or its subtypes may perform such operations
        see also: ...\ajia\enforcement\OrderAccessAspect.aj:8::0
error at order.cancel();
^^^^^^^^^^^^^^^

...\ajia\CustomerService.java:9:0::0 Illegal manipulation to Order;
➥    Only OrderService or its subtypes may perform such operations
        see also: ...\ajia\enforcement\OrderAccessAspect.aj:8::0
```

Spring AOP applicability

Due to the need to use the call() pointcut and the declare error statement, you can't use proxy-based Spring AOP to enforce this policy.

With pure Java, this type of complex access control—allowing communication only between collaborating classes—isn't possible.

11.5.3 Enforcing the factory pattern

Consider the factory pattern to create objects of the `Product` class. Let's say you want only the factory to create the `Product` objects. With Java's access-control mechanism, the best you can do is force the `Product` class and the factory class to reside in the same package and assign package access to the `Product` class's constructors. This is over-restrictive and, in some cases, impossible to implement. For example, if the factory is in a package and the `Product` class is in a subpackage, it isn't possible to implement the pattern correctly. Further, other classes in the same package can freely create `Product` objects. The usual solution is to let the `Product` class's constructors have public access and document the restriction. If a developer misses this documentation, you're out of luck.

With AspectJ, you can implement and enforce the needed access-control properly. The usage is similar to `friend` access in C++. With AspectJ, you can implement the friend functionality in Java as well as far more powerful access control. Listing 11.11 shows the `ProductFactory` class that contains a nested aspect that implements the factory pattern policy.

Listing 11.11 `ProductFactory` class, with an aspect that controls its creation

```
package ajia.domain;

import ...

public class ProductFactory {
    // product factory methods

    static aspect FlagNonFactoryCreation {
        declare error
            : call(Product.new(..))
              && !within(ProductFactory+)
            : "Only ProductFactory can create Products";
    }
}
```

The nested aspect declares that invoking any of the `Product` class's constructors from any class other than `ProductFactory` or one of its subclasses will result in a compile-time error.

The class in listing 11.12 creates a `Product` without going through its factory.

Listing 11.12 Class to illustrate a factory pattern violation

```
package ajia;

import ajia.domain.Product;

public class CustomerService {
    public void createProduct(String name, String description,
```

```
                                  double price) {
        Product product = new Product(name, description, price);
    }
}
```

When you compile this class with the ProductFactory class (and therefore its nested aspect), you see an error as follows.

```
error at Product product = new Product(name, description, price);
^^^^^^^^^^^^^^^^^^^^^^^^^^^^^^^^^^^^^^^^^^^^^^^^^^^^^^^^^^^
...\ajia\CustomerService.java:9:0::0
➥   Only ProductFactory can create Products
        see also: ...\ajia\domain\ProductFactory.java:10::0
```

You could further restrict the access to various createProduct() methods in ProductFactory by replacing the within() pointcut with withincode(). See table 3.12 for more details about the withincode() pointcut:

```
declare error
    : call(Product.new(..))
      && !withincode(Product ProductFactory.createProduct(..))
    : "Only ProductFactory.createProduct() can create Products";
```

Now, if you call a constructor of the Product class from anywhere other than a createProduct() method in ProductFactory or its subclass, you get a compile-time error.

Spring AOP applicability

Due to the need to advise constructors, you can't enforce this policy using Spring's proxy-based AOP.

Note that you're using a nested aspect, FlagNonFactoryCreation, to implement the access control in the example. If you've adopted AspectJ as your project's programming language, this is often a better approach because it tightly connects the enforced class and enforcing aspect. Such tight coupling allows you to update the enforcement aspect when the implementation of the access-controlled class changes. But when you use this approach, you lose the choice of compiling the project with a pure Java compiler for deployment builds. If such a choice is important to you, you should move the aspect to a separate file that can be excluded from the final build. Alternatively, you can express the same aspect using the @AspectJ syntax. If you compile the class with ajc, you'll get enforcement. But you're still free to compile the same class using javac. Of course, in that case, you won't see any enforcement.

The examples have shown how to implement precise access control using AspectJ. You can use this pattern to implement the access control that is suitable for your purposes.

The examples so far have been simple and used only static crosscutting. Now you'll work with more complex and technology-specific examples that use a combination of static and dynamic crosscutting.

11.6 Enforcement idiom: return-value restriction

In a software system, you often decide to use a certain set of practices and follow certain guidelines. When every part of the system follows them, the code's clarity and maintenance improve significantly.

Let's consider an idiom to never return a null collection and instead return an empty collection. This simple idea has an interesting effect on code in that callers don't have to check for null before iterating over a collection. But if this pattern is implemented inconsistently, it quickly loses its value. A developer using a class can never be sure if they should test against null before iterating over a collection. As a result, some part of the code will perform the check and others won't, without any necessary correlation with the code that requires checking. This leaves messy code that the pattern tried to prevent in the first place. AspectJ's runtime policy enforcement can help with this situation.

Let's apply this policy to the repository or Data Access Object (DAO). You'd like to enforce that methods don't return a null collection or map. For illustration purposes, assume that all repository classes end in `Repository` (you should be able to modify the example easily to use any other mechanism, such as the `@Repository` annotation in Spring). Listing 11.13 shows an aspect that enforces this idiom.

Listing 11.13 `NullReturnDetector` aspect that enforces the idiom

```
package ajia.enforcement;

import ...

public aspect RepositoryNullReturnDetector {
    private Logger logger =
        Logger.getLogger(RepositoryNullReturnDetector.class);

    after() returning(Object mapOrCollection)
        : execution((Map+ || Collection+) *..*Repository.*(..)) {
        if(mapOrCollection == null) {
            logger.error("Null detected: "
                 + thisJoinPointStaticPart.getSignature(),
                 new Throwable());
        }
    }
}
```

This aspect advises all join points in repository classes corresponding to methods that return `Collection`, `Map`, or their subtypes with an after returning advice. The advice collects the return value, examines it for `null`, and logs a message upon detecting a `null` value. The class shown in listing 11.14 illustrates the violation.

Listing 11.14 Repository that violates the policy of not returning a null collection

```
package ajia.repository;

import java.util.Collection;

public class StubInventoryRepository {
```

```
    public Collection findAll() {
        return null;
    }
}
```

Now, when you compile this class with the `RepositoryNullReturnDetector` aspect and invoke the `findAll()` method from a class (not shown), you get the following output:

```
Null detected: Collection ajia.repository.StubInventoryRepository.findAll()
java.lang.Throwable
at ajia.enforcement.RepositoryNullReturnDetector.ajc$afterReturning
➥       $ajia_enforcement_RepositoryNullReturnDetector$1$c25d8165
➥       (RepositoryNullReturnDetector.aj:18)
at ajia.repository.StubInventoryRepository.
➥       findAll(StubInventoryRepository.java:8)
at ajia.main.Main.main(Main.java:10)
```

> **Spring AOP applicability**
> You can translate this aspect to use @AspectJ syntax and use it with Spring AOP.

Note that AspectJ can also help implement the pattern by advising the target method, check against `null`, and return an empty collection. But as we discussed at the beginning of this chapter, using aspects for such a purpose forces you to use aspects in production.

11.7 Enforcing JPA-JDBC integration policies

Consider listing 11.15, which tests the `JpaProductRepository` class from appendix A. The listing shows a test that uses JPA to update an entity and JDBC to check whether the update was made to the database. (The test uses the `@Autowired` annotation from Spring to cut down the code required. See the Spring documentation for this annotation and Spring's support for JUnit 4 tests.)

Listing 11.15 Testing a JPA-based repository implementation

```
package ajia.repository.impl;

import ...

@RunWith(SpringJUnit4ClassRunner.class)
@ContextConfiguration
@Transactional
public class ProductRepositoryTest {
    private @Autowired ProductRepository productRepository;
    private @Autowired SimpleJdbcOperations jdbcTemplate;

    @Test
    public void update() {
        Product product = productRepository.find(1001L);
```

```
        product.setName("foo");
        productRepository.update(product);

        String updatedName
            = jdbcTemplate.queryForObject(
                "select name from products p where p.id = ?",
                String.class, 1001L);
        assertEquals("foo", updatedName);
    }
}
```

When you run the test, it fails. I assure you that there is nothing wrong with the repository implementation, at least from the test's perspective. Even the core idea behind the test is fine. What gives? Well, I forgot to flush the entity manager before making the JDBC call. Adding `em.flush()` before the `queryForObject()` method fixes the problem. But would you always be lucky enough to notice the problem so quickly? I, for sure, would have first suspected the mapping (isn't it always a mapping problem?) and then perhaps my SQL. Only after some digging would I have realized the real problem. Anyway, that time would be better spent elsewhere. As you'll see shortly, with AOP, you can develop a reusable aspect that ensures that you catch such a mistake right away.

For performance and other reasons, it's common to mix ORM with JDBC. For example, you can update a few objects using JPA followed by JDBC calls to perform bulk object updating. JPA implementations such as Hibernate use a write-behind strategy and therefore may not issue SQL commands needed to reflect the updates until they need to do so (which may be as far out as the transaction commit time). Therefore, you must explicitly flush the entity manager before performing any JDBC operation. This policy is easy to understand and equally easy to forget, causing a lot of headache down the line. You can use an aspect to detect the violation of such a policy.[1] You can implement this policy using AspectJ AOP and Spring AOP. I'll show you both, to highlight the differences.

JPA and bulk update and delete

When you use JPA bulk update or delete (using `Query.executeUpdate()`), because these operations are performed directly against the database, they bypass the first-level cache. This means any queries made through JPA may result in stale or incorrect data. In general, barring a few carefully considered situations, you should perform bulk operations by themselves in a separate transaction. Based on the material presented in this chapter, you should be able to write an aspect that detects such situations and produces a warning.

---

[1] I first saw my colleague Alef Arendsen implement such a policy, which he has used in his consulting engagements. Seeing this common violation leading to mysterious results, he needed a way to detect any violations. The AOP solution, similar to the one in this section, was a good fit.

The example aspect assumes Hibernate as the JPA implementation.[2] You need to make such an assumption because JPA lacks the API to detect a dirty entity manager. Listing 11.16 shows an aspect that checks whether an entity manager is dirty (indicating the need to flush) and issues an error.

Listing 11.16 Aspect to detect dirty session state (AspectJ weaving)

```
package ajia.jpa.enforcement;

import ...

@Aspect
public class JpaJdbcPolicyEnforcement {
    private static Logger logger = Logger.getLogger(
            JpaJdbcPolicyEnforcement.class);

    @PersistenceContext private EntityManager em;        <-- 1 Declares dependency

    @Pointcut("ajia.jdbc.JDBCPointcuts.jdbcCall() " +
            "|| ajia.spring.SpringPointcuts.jdbcTemplateCall()")
    public void jdbcCall() {}                             2 Selects JDBC calls

    @Before("jdbcCall()")
    public void checkFlushedSession() {
        Session currentSession = (Session)em.getDelegate();
        if(currentSession != null
            && currentSession.isOpen()
            && currentSession.isDirty()) {                3 Enforces rule
            logger.error("Dirty session detected before "
                      + "a JDBC call, use EntityManager.flush()",
                        new Throwable());
        }
    }
}
```

1. The aspect needs the entity manager. Therefore, it declares a dependency by including a field of the `EntityManager` type and marking it with the `@PersistenceContext` annotation (see the Spring documentation for more details about this annotation). Using the Spring Framework, you can create a bean for this aspect and have it automatically injected with an `EntityManager` (see listing 11.17 for the configuration).
2. The `jdbcCall()` pointcut uses JDBC and Spring library aspects to select calls made using raw JDBC API or Spring's JDBC template class. Due to the use of the `call()` pointcut, you must use the AspectJ weaver. Note that you could use the `execution()` pointcut, but that would force weaving into JDBC, JPA, and Spring. LTW is better suited for weaving into such libraries. With the use of the `call()` pointcut, you can use build-time weaving (see section 3.2 for details of `call()` vs. `execution()` pointcuts).

[2] For other implementations, you can use specific APIs available for those implementations. For example, with EclipseLink, you can detect a dirty session by calling `getCurrentChanges().hasChanges()` on the `UnitOfWork` object.

3 The before advice in the aspect obtains the current entity manager and casts it to Hibernate `Session`. If the session isn't null (indicating there is a current session), it's open, and it's dirty (indicating there is a need to flush the session), you issue an error log.

Listing 11.17 shows the Spring configuration needed to instantiate a bean for the aspect and have Spring inject its dependencies. Note that due to the use of `@PersistenceContext`, you don't need to define any `<property>` elements.

Listing 11.17 Spring configuration to initialize an aspect (AspectJ weaving)

```
<beans ...>
    <bean class="ajia.jpa.enforcement.JpaJdbcPolicyEnforcement"
          factory-method="aspectOf"/>
</beans>
```

When you run the test, you get the following helpful error:

```
Dirty session detected before a JDBC call, use EntityManager.flush()
java.lang.Throwable
    at ajia.jpa.enforcement.JPAJDBCIntegrationPolicyEnforcement.
➥       checkFlushedSession(JPAJDBCIntegrationPolicyEnforcement.java:28)
    at ajia.repository.impl.ProductRepositoryTest.
➥       update(ProductRepositoryTest.java:74)
```

Note that is it easy to fix the problem by calling `em.flush()` in place of issuing an error. But doing so forces inclusion of that aspect in production.

You can modify the aspect to use the `execution()` pointcut to make it suitable for Spring AOP. Listing 11.18 shows the modified aspect.

Listing 11.18 Aspect to detect dirty session state (Spring weaving)

```
package ajia.jpa.enforcement;

import ...

@Aspect
public class JpaJdbcPolicyEnforcement {
    ... unchanged since listing 11.16

    @Pointcut("ajia.spring.SpringPointcuts.jdbcTemplateExecution()")
    public void jdbcExecution() {}

    @Before("jdbcExecution()")
    public void checkFlushedSession() {
       ... unchanged since listing 11.16
    }
}
```

In a typical Spring application, you won't have beans of raw JDBC types such as `Statement`. Therefore, the pointcut doesn't select methods of those types. Note that this aspect detects violations due to invocation on beans of `JdbcOperations` and `SimpleJdbcOperations` types only. For a more comprehensive enforcement, you should use the solution based on the AspectJ weaver.

Using traditional-style aspect from Spring AOP

You may have noticed that you use `SpringPointcuts` written using the traditional syntax in the `JpaJdbcPolicyEnforcement` aspect that is integrated using Spring proxy-based AOP. This kind of combination is allowed and even makes sense. The reusable aspects containing pointcuts can be in a separate project and compiled using ajc. The plain Java project that uses Spring only deals with the .class files produced by ajc, so it can remain a plain Java project.

You also need to change the Spring configuration to remove the `factory-method` attribute, as shown in listing 11.19.

Listing 11.19 Spring configuration to initialize an aspect (Spring weaving)

```
<beans ...>
    <aop:aspectj-autoproxy/>

    <bean class="ajia.jpa.enforcement.JpaJdbcPolicyEnforcement"/>
</beans>
```

Because the aspect is instantiated as a Spring bean without the AspectJ weaver, it won't have the `aspectOf()` method. Therefore, you use the default constructor to instantiate the bean. When you run the test case, you get the same warning as with AspectJ weaving.

We'll now move to another framework—EJB—to see how AspectJ can help with enforcing its policies.

11.8 Implementing EJB policies

Frameworks often pose a few restrictions on user code. This allows the framework to make a few assumptions and simplify its implementation. In this section, we'll examine programming restrictions imposed by the EJB specification on a bean.

To allow application servers to utilize nodes in a server cluster without any behavioral change in the system, the EJB programming model expects beans to follow certain guidelines. For example, it doesn't let you make AWT operations, work directly with networking resources, or use thread-synchronization primitives from a bean. Because most of these situations occur during heavy loads, you may not run into them during the development phase, and failure may occur only in real deployment situations and stress testing. Refer to section 20.1.2 of the EJB 3.0 core (or 24.1.2 of the EJB 2.0) specification for more details.

No EJB bashing

This section isn't about bashing EJBs. Instead, it's an illustration of how AspectJ can help enforce its policies. If you're using EJBs, these policies will help you use them correctly. Even if you aren't using EJBs, you'll see interesting AspectJ idioms, especially related to the use of custom annotations, that will help you enforce policies of other frameworks.

A first step in implementing a policy-enforcement aspect is to identify the target classes. For EJB 3, that also presents a first challenge. EJB 3 has two options to implement EJBs: using annotations or using XML. In either approach, EJBs no longer need to implement any specific interfaces or extend specific classes. With annotation-based EJBs, identifying the classes implementing EJBs is easy. But the AspectJ compiler can't check deployment descriptors to identify the EJB classes.

In this section, we'll emphasize policy enforcement for annotation-based EJBs, because they represent the promoted approach in the EJB 3 world and they're easy to enforce with AspectJ. Later, we'll present a few ideas about how to extend the solution to XML-based EJBs. For good information on EJB 3, see *EJB 3 in Action* by Debu Panda, Reza Raqhman, and Derek Lane (Manning 2007).

11.8.1 Developing a core EJB enforcement aspect

Our way to detect violations of the EJB specification, like most of the solutions presented in this book, works in a plug-and-play style and is reusable. Compiling your code with the aspect in listing 11.20 gets you the benefit. You can use AspectJ to catch violations at compile time and runtime in a nonintrusive manner, as we discussed in section 11.3.

Let's dive straight into an aspect. Listing 11.20 shows an EJB policy-enforcement aspect that enforces two rules: no AWT code from EJBs and no nonfinal static field access (note that you could write separate aspects for each violation).

Listing 11.20 DetectEJBViolations.java: ensuring EJB policy enforcement

```
package ajia.ejb;

import ...

public aspect DetectEJBViolations {
    Logger logger = Logger.getLogger(getClass());

    pointcut uiCall() : call(* java.awt..*+.*(..));

    declare error : uiCall() && EJBPointcuts.inEJB()
        : "UI calls are not allowed from EJB beans."
        + "See EJB 3.0 specification section 20.1.2";

    before() : uiCall() && cflow(EJBPointcuts.inEJB()) {
        logger.log(Level.ERROR,
             "Detected call to AWT from EJB."
           + "See EJB 3.0 core specification section20.1.2",
                   new Throwable());
    }

    pointcut staticMemberAccess() :
        set(static !final * *) && EJBPointcuts.inEJB();

    declare error : staticMemberAccess()
        : "EJBs are not allowed to have nonfinal static variables."
        + "See EJB 3.0 core specification section 20.1.2";
}
```

1 Selects UI call

2 Detects compile-time UI call violation

3 Detects runtime UI call violation

4 Selects static member modification

5 Detects nonfinal static variable

❶ The `uiCall()` pointcut selects calls to any method in any class that extends a class in `java.awt` or its subpackage. This is probably over-restrictive because it's okay to access classes such as `java.awt.Rectangle`. Nevertheless, you err on the side of safety. You can easily exclude a few classes by modifying the pointcut.

❷ You make it an error to have UI calls made from within EJB. You use a library pointcut `inEJB()` from the `EJBPointcuts` aspect (see listing 11.21). This pointcut selects all join points in an EJB.

❸ To detect violations through indirect calls, you advise the UI calls in the aspect to check a call occurring in the control flow of a join point in an EJB. It detects violations, for example, if a bean calls a method in a utility class, which in turn calls one of the prohibited methods. Bear in mind that this advice may not always catch the violations, because the code path leading to the violating calls may not be executed in a particular sequence. Therefore, you should first try to enumerate all the classes and packages that make UI calls and include those classes in the `uiCall()` pointcut. This way, you'll catch any violations at compile time and won't have to wait until you run the system for problems to occur.

❹ Another EJB programming restriction disallows the use of nonfinal static fields by a bean. With AspectJ, you can indirectly implement this restriction by selecting write access to such fields. This solution doesn't implement the policy in exact terms, but it implements the spirit of it. The `staticMemberAccess()` selects field-write join points for static fields in an EJB.

❺ You issue a compile-time error for a join point matched by `staticMemberAccess()`.

This aspect in listing 11.20 uses another library aspect, `EJBPointcuts`, which defines EJB-related pointcuts. Let's develop that aspect next.

11.8.2 Defining EJB pointcuts

The EJB 3 specification lets you define EJBs by annotating classes. There are three kinds of annotations for stateless, stateful, and message-driven bean. Because you aren't interested in the specific type of bean, you need a way to select classes that are marked with any of the annotations. Listing 11.21 shows an aspect that uses a bridge annotation to simplify selection of an EJB.

Listing 11.21 Library aspect for EJB pointcuts

```
package ajia.ejb;

import ...

public aspect EJBPointcuts {
    declare @type: @Stateless *: @PolicyEnforcedEJB;
    declare @type: @Stateful *: @PolicyEnforcedEJB;
    declare @type: @MessageDriven *: @PolicyEnforcedEJB;

    declare @type: EntityBean+: @PolicyEnforcedEJB;

    pointcut inEJB() : within(@PolicyEnforcedEJB *);
```

```
    @Retention(RetentionPolicy.RUNTIME)
    public static @interface PolicyEnforcedEJB {
    }
}
```

This aspect uses AspectJ constructs to supply annotations in a crosscutting manner (see section 5.4 for details about the `declare @type` construct). You use a simple `PolicyEnforcedEJB` annotation without any properties as an intermediary bridge annotation to select all EJB types. Without such an annotation, you'll get a long-winded pointcut to select types carrying any of the EJB annotations.

Let's see how this aspect helps you detect violations. Consider listing 11.22, which violates some of the EJB programming restrictions.

Listing 11.22 ViolationBean.java: a bean that violates the EJB rules

```
package ajia.ejb;

import ...

@Stateless
public class ViolationBean {
    private static int subscriptionCount;

    // ...

    public void addSubscription(String subscriptionKey) {
        try {
            Subscription subscription =
                find(subscriptionKey);
            // ... business logic
        } catch (Exception ex) {
            JOptionPane.showMessageDialog(null,
                "Exception while adding subscription");
            ex.printStackTrace();
        }
        subscriptionCount++;
    }

    // ...find method etc.
}
```

When you compile the `ViolationBean` class along with the `DetectEJBViolations` aspect, you get the following output:

```
error at JOptionPane.showMessageDialog(null,
^^^^^^^^^^^^^^^^^^^^^^^^^^^^^^^^^^^^^
...\ajia\ejb\ViolationBean.java:21:0::0 UI calls are not allowed
➥         from EJB beans.
➥         See EJB 3.0 specification section 20.1.2
        see also: ...\ajia\ejb\DetectEJBViolations.aj:14::0
error at subscriptionCount++;
^^^^^^^^^^^^^^^^^^^^
...\ajia\ejb\ViolationBean.java:25:0::0 EJBs are not allowed
➥         to have nonfinal static variables.
➥         See EJB 3.0 core specification section 20.1.2
        see also: ...\ajia\ejb\DetectEJBViolations.aj:28::0
```

You're now forced to address the problem (which may involve a simple fix or may require design modifications) before the system can be compiled without errors again. This is a huge improvement in productivity, because fixing errors found at compile-time takes much less effort than if the same bugs are found during code review, testing, or production.

You can extend this aspect to implement other restrictions, such as no calls to `Thread`'s methods, socket creation, `System.in` access, native library loading, or reflection use. For each such restriction, you must provide a pointcut definition to select the join points corresponding to the restricted operations. You also need to include a declare error clause for those pointcuts. To select indirect calls, you have to advise the join point occurring in the control flow of the bean method and log the violation.

11.8.3 Dealing with XML-based EJBs

To select EJBs developed using XML-based metadata, you need additional aspects to mark the EJBs with the `@PolicyEnforcedEJB` annotation. For example, if `Inventory` is an EJB that uses the XML-based metadata, you can include an aspect such as the one in listing 11.23 to make it participate in EJB policy enforcement.

Listing 11.23 XMLBasedEJBs aspect

```
package ajia.ejb;

public aspect XMLBasedEJBs {
      declare @type: Inventory: @EJBPointcuts.PolicyEnforcedEJB;
      ... more statements like this
}
```

The aspect uses the bridge annotation as a way to inform the `EJBPointcuts` that the marked class is an EJB. Note that although you could use an appropriate EJB annotation in the `declare @type` expression, using a bridge annotation lets you avoid interfering with the EJB tools and frameworks. You can include any number of such aspects to treat classes as EJBs for enforcement purposes. You can even select non-EJB classes that are known to be exclusively used by EJBs to maximize compile-time errors (as discussed in ❸ accompanying listing 11.20).

Sometimes, a policy must enforce that a project may not use certain types or methods. Let's use EJBs as an example to illustrate implementing such a policy.

11.8.4 Implementing a "no EJBs" policy

Let's complete this section by implementing a fun policy that specifies that you shall not use EJBs in a project. I call it a "fun" policy that is of little practical importance, because accidentally *slipping in* an EJB is practically impossible. Therefore, the value of this example lies in showing how to implement policies that prohibit accidental use of a certain set of classes. Listing 11.24 shows how you can implement the policy to avoid using EJBs.

Listing 11.24 No-EJB policy enforcement aspect

```
package ajia.ejb;

public aspect NoEJBPolicyEnforcement {
   declare error
       : staticinitialization(*) && EJBPointcuts.inEJB()
       : "EJBs are not allowed in this project.";
}
```

The `staticinitialization(*)` pointcut restricts the warning to only the static initializer of a class. Combining it with `EJBPointcuts.inEJB()` selects static initializers in EJBs and thus issues only one error per EJB. Without the static initialization restriction, you'd get one error per join point in such a class.

11.9 Detecting Swing concurrency control policy violations

Concurrency is a complex topic that is seldom well understood (For an excellent source of information on concurrency control, see *Java Concurrency in Practice* by Brian Goetz et al. [Addison-Wesley, 2006]). You can put concurrent computing resources to good use as long as you understand the rules of engagement. But failing to use them correctly can cause headaches to no end. Any enforcement in this area can be of tremendous importance. This section uses Swing's concurrency rules as an example to illustrate how AspectJ can detect violations.

Swing, currently the most popular Java GUI library, uses a simple thread-safety pattern: use a single thread to access the component! This pattern requires accessing all the Swing components only through the event-dispatching thread (also called the AWT thread). By limiting access to the preassigned thread, the pattern moves the issue of thread-safe access away from the components. When another thread needs to access a Swing component, it must request the event-dispatching thread to carry out the operation on its behalf instead of doing so itself.

In simple applications that don't use any user-created threads, single-thread access usually isn't a major concern. Because the components are updated in response to user actions, which are called in the event-dispatching thread, the single-thread rule is automatically observed. For example, you don't have to worry about this rule when you're deleting a row in `JTable` in direct response to a user clicking a button.

But in complex applications that need access to UI components from a nonevent-dispatching thread, the single-threaded restriction becomes a problem. A typical example is a thread performing network- or I/O-intensive operations or database-related activities. In such cases, these nonevent-dispatching threads may need to update the UI. For example, consider a situation where you need to update the UI based on information from a server (a table's contents in a database, for instance). You make a request to the server, wait for a response, and update the UI based on that response. You don't want the event-dispatching thread to be blocked for the response, because doing so locks your whole GUI until the server responds. A simple solution is to let some other thread wait for the server to respond and update the UI once the response is obtained. Bingo! You just encountered Swing's single-thread rule problem.

You aren't supposed to update any UI component in a nonevent-dispatching thread. If the thread waiting for the server to respond updates the component while the AWT thread is repainting the UI component, it may result in UI anomalies or even worse—a crash. Even more dangerous is the fact that these issues aren't immediately visible—it may be that you never see this problem on your machine. As with most multithreading-related problems, these problems are hard to reproduce and therefore hard to fix. Murphy's Law seems to work well with the single-thread rule: if you violate the single-thread rule, the problems always seem to occur during the customer demo of your product!

> **Not just Swing**
>
> The Standard Widget Toolkit (SWT) used in Eclipse has essentially the same concurrency policy as Swing. But unlike Swing, SWT enforces this policy, thus obviating the need for an external enforcement mechanism.

In this section, we'll examine a way to detect these violations.

11.9.1 Understanding the problem

Swing's single-thread rule states: "Once a Swing component has been realized, all code that might affect or depend on the state of that component should be executed in the event-dispatching thread" (see http://java.sun.com/docs/books/tutorial/uiswing/overview/threads.html). The term *realized* in this context refers to making a component visible. When a component is visible, the event-dispatching thread is the only thread that can safely access or update the state of the realized component. The rule exempts certain methods, allowing them to be safely called from any thread. The important ones are `repaint()`, `revalidate()`, and listener-management methods.

The simple program in listing 11.25 illustrates a violation of this policy.

Listing 11.25 Test code violating the policy

```
package ajia.main;

import ...

public class Main{
    public static void main(String[] args) {
        JFrame appFrame = new JFrame();
        appFrame.setDefaultCloseOperation(JFrame.EXIT_ON_CLOSE);

        DefaultTableModel tableModel = new DefaultTableModel(4,2);
        JTable table = new JTable(tableModel);

        appFrame.getContentPane().add(table);

        appFrame.pack();
        appFrame.setVisible(true);

        System.out.println("Frame is now visible");
```

```
        tableModel.setValueAt("[0,0]", 0, 0);
        tableModel.removeRow(2);
    }
}
```

The two lines in bold violate the rule requiring that after the components are put onto the screen (using `pack()` and `setVisible()`), any access or modification must take place only from the event-dispatching thread by calling either `invokeLater()` or `invokeAndWait()` in the main thread. In this case, you call the `setValueAt()` and `removeRow()` methods on the table model. In practice, this type of violation occurs because of calls made from another user thread, such as a thread reading data from a network or database.

We'll discuss the solution to the problem in more detail in chapter 13, where we'll also examine the AOP way of modularizing it. For now, let's focus on detecting the violation.

11.9.2 Detecting the violation

You'll now develop a dynamic checking aspect to catch any violation of Swing's single-thread rule. The fundamental idea is simple: check whether a thread other than the event-dispatching thread accesses a Swing component's state. In listing 11.26, `DetectSwingSingleThreadRuleViolationAspect` flags the call to the Swing component's methods from a nonevent-dispatching thread. The aspect itself uses a library aspect—Swing—that defines a few pointcuts.

Listing 11.26 Aspect that detects the Swing single-thread rule

```
package ajia.swing;

import ...

public aspect DetectSwingSingleThreadRuleViolationAspect {
    before() : Swing.uiCall()
               && !Swing.threadSafeCall()
               && if(!EventQueue.isDispatchThread()) {
        System.err.println(
            "Violation: Swing method called from nonAWT thread"
            + "\nCalled method: "
            + thisJoinPointStaticPart.getSignature()
            + "\nCaller: "
            + thisEnclosingJoinPointStaticPart.getSignature()
            + "\nSource location: "
            + thisJoinPointStaticPart.getSourceLocation()
            + "\nThread: " + Thread.currentThread()
            + "\nChange code to use EventQueue.invokeLater() "
            + "or EventQueue.invokeAndWait()\n");
    }
}
```

The aspect `DetectSwingSingleThreadRuleViolationAspect` advises the join points selected by the `Swing.uiCall()` pointcut to check whether the caller thread of the selected join points is the event-dispatching thread. The advice logs a message with the information about the call, the caller method, and the caller thread, if any join points aren't called from the event-dispatching thread. This helps you analyze the root cause of the problem. In practice, instead of printing a message onto a console, you'll want to log it into a file; there is little point in telling the user that your program did something wrong.

The bulk of the heavy lifting lies in defining the Swing-related pointcuts. Listing 11.27 shows the library aspect that defines the relevant pointcuts. You'll reuse this aspect when you develop a way to take care of the thread-safety problem in chapter 13.

Listing 11.27 Swing library aspect

```
package ajia.swing;

import ...

public aspect Swing {
    public pointcut threadSafeCall()
        : call(void JComponent.revalidate())
          || call(void JComponent.repaint(..))
          || call(void Component.invalidate())
          || call(void add*Listener(EventListener+))
          || call(void remove*Listener(EventListener+));

    public pointcut viewCall()
        : call(* javax..JComponent+.*(..))
          || call(* javax..JFrame+.*(..));

    public pointcut modelCall()
        : call(* javax..*Model+.*(..))
          || call(* javax.swing.text.Document+.*(..));

    public pointcut uiCall()
        : viewCall() || modelCall();
}
```

(1) Calls to thread-safe methods

(2) Calls to UI component methods

(3) Calls to UI model methods

(4) Calls to UI methods

(1) The pointcut threadSafeCall() selects method calls that are considered safe as per the JComponent documentation. Specifically, it selects calls to repaint(), revalidate(), and invalidate(). It also uses naming patterns to select all listener management methods.

(2) The pointcut viewCall(), which selects the method calls on a view object, is defined as a call to any method of JComponent or its subclasses.

(3) The pointcut modelCall(), which selects operations on a model, is defined as a call to any method of any class with a name ending in Model within the javax package or its subpackages; it also selects subclasses of such a class. In addition, it selects calls to javax.swing.text.Document or its subclasses, because the pointcut that requires the type name to end in Model wouldn't select such methods. By the way, notice the importance of following a consistent naming convention; if you name all your models ending in Model, then selecting join points based on name becomes easy.

4 The pointcut `uiCall()` combines the `viewCall()` and `modelCall()` pointcuts to select all the method calls that are involved in Swing's thread-safety rule. You could have defined the `uiCall()` to directly select all the required methods calls, but the use of separate pointcuts helps improve overall understanding.

When you compile the classes and aspect together and run the driver program, you get the following output:

```
Violation: Swing method called from nonAWT thread
Called method: void javax.swing.JFrame.setDefaultCloseOperation(int)
Caller: void ajia.main.Main.main(String[])
Source location: Main.java:11
Thread: Thread[main,5,main]
Change code to use EventQueue.invokeLater() or EventQueue.invokeAndWait()

Violation: Swing method called from nonAWT thread
Called method: Container javax.swing.JFrame.getContentPane()
Caller: void ajia.main.Main.main(String[])
Source location: Main.java:14
Thread: Thread[main,5,main]
Change code to use EventQueue.invokeLater() or EventQueue.invokeAndWait()
Frame is now visible

Violation: Swing method called from nonAWT thread
Called method: void javax.swing.JFrame.pack()
Caller: void ajia.main.Main.main(String[])
Source location: Main.java:15
Thread: Thread[main,5,main]
Change code to use EventQueue.invokeLater() or EventQueue.invokeAndWait()

Violation: Swing method called from nonAWT thread
Called method: void javax.swing.JFrame.setVisible(boolean)
Caller: void ajia.main.Main.main(String[])
Source location: Main.java:16
Thread: Thread[main,5,main]
Change code to use EventQueue.invokeLater() or EventQueue.invokeAndWait()

Violation: Swing method called from nonAWT thread
Called method: void javax.swing.table.DefaultTableModel.setValueAt(Object,
➥    int, int)
Caller: void ajia.main.Main.main(String[])
Source location: Main.java:18
Thread: Thread[main,5,main]
Change code to use EventQueue.invokeLater() or EventQueue.invokeAndWait()

Violation: Swing method called from nonAWT thread
Called method: void javax.swing.table.DefaultTableModel.removeRow(int)
Caller: void ajia.main.Main.main(String[])
Source location: Main.java:19
Thread: Thread[main,5,main]
Change code to use EventQueue.invokeLater() or EventQueue.invokeAndWait()
```

You can see from the output that `DetectSwingSingleThreadRuleViolationAspect` flags both the violations in accessing the Swing component from the main thread. Note that you're getting false positives before the frame is visible. You can suppress them by modifying the advice to ignore the class or method that is constructing the UI or by advising `Frame.setVisible()` to turn on logging.

11.10 Summary

As you introduce AOP to your project, one of the problems you can face is resistance to committing to it. People will demand proof that AOP is worth the *perceived* effort and complexity. This can become a Catch 22 situation—you can't show its usefulness to your project because you can't use it, and you won't be able to use it unless you show its usefulness. Well, policy enforcement offers you a way to overcome this issue. Even if your organization or team isn't yet committed to AOP, you can still use AOP-based enforcement to improve your personal productivity. Then, you can show others what you've gained. If that convinces your colleagues about the benefits that AOP offers, good. Otherwise, continue using the aspects in your own development world, and exclude them in the final builds. The plug-and-play nature of policy-enforcement aspects provides you an opportunity to play with AOP without requiring a full commitment.

Start with the aspects presented in this chapter. The next time you encounter a novel programming wisdom or best practice, consider writing an enforcement aspect encapsulating the knowledge. Over time, you'll have a repository of policy-enforcement aspects that will help you in all your projects. When you start using a new framework, you can create policy-enforcement aspects specifically targeted to the framework. If you're in a mentoring role, you can provide your aspects to your team. You'll then no longer have to sit down and repeat the policies with each team member.

AOP offers a simple and yet powerful way of implementing system-wide policy-enforcement concerns. The policy-enforcement aspects you develop are reusable, lowering your per-project development cost. These aspects use the AspectJ compiler to enforce as many policies as possible at compile time and use dynamic crosscutting to understand the runtime violations in more detail. You can even use Spring AOP to implement certain runtime policy enforcements. With such aspects in place, you're assured of better-quality code, and you can spend your time on more exciting issues. Note, though, that the mechanisms presented here don't substitute for code reviews. But with policy enforcement in place, the code reviews can focus on the subtler nuances of design and implementations.

When you start enforcing policies in a significant way by using AOP, you'll find AOP to be your best friend; it always watches you, reminds you of common pitfalls, and lets you spend time on the more creative aspects of life.

12 Learning design patterns

This chapter covers

- Using worker object pattern
- Using the wormhole pattern
- Using the participant pattern
- Using the annotation-driven participant pattern

Design patterns define solutions to recurring problems. Familiarity with these patterns often leads to a quick and proven solution; no wonder several books and articles are devoted to design patterns in every major technology. Patterns also carry names like *factory*, *visitor*, and *decorator* to simplify the communication of design concepts. Pattern names also convey the designer's intent and decisions succinctly and accurately without providing all the details.

This chapter presents AOP design patterns that can help you define solutions when you start applying AOP. They can also help you start thinking about problems in more abstract terms. Although this book covers problems from many domains, you'll no doubt encounter new problems as you begin using AOP in your projects. When that happens, you'll find that a combination of these design patterns will lead you to a solution more quickly.

In this chapter, we'll examine four design patterns: the worker object pattern, the wormhole pattern, the participant pattern, and the annotation-driven participant pattern. We'll use AspectJ to illustrate each pattern. Except for the wormhole pattern, you can implement them using Spring AOP as well. In the chapters that follow, we'll use these patterns for more advanced crosscutting implementations.

12.1 The worker object pattern

A *worker object* is an instance of a class that encapsulates a method (called a *worker method*). A worker object can be passed around, stored, and invoked.

In Java, a common implementation of a worker class implements `Runnable`, where the `run()` method invokes the worker method. When you execute such an object, it in turn executes the worker method. The worker object pattern offers a way to generate worker objects automatically for join points selected by a pointcut. You can then pass around these objects to implement various functionalities. When you use this pattern, you ensure a consistent behavior in your system—and you save a ton of code.

I first discovered this pattern while adding thread safety to a Swing-based project, where a network reader thread was performing some UI updates. To comply with Swing's single-thread rule (discussed in chapter 11), the network reader thread couldn't directly call the UI update methods. Early on, I decided to use an aspect that would advise the join points performing the UI updates to route the calls through `EventQueue.invokeLater()`. But in the first solution, I used one hand-coded worker class to route each update method individually. The thread-safety aspect advised each method to pass an instance of the corresponding worker class to the event queue instead of directly invoking the method. Although AspectJ clearly helped to avoid polluting the core code with the logic to comply with the Swing rules, writing the boilerplate classes for each kind of update was boring, to say the least. Feeling that something was amiss, I experimented and created a single aspect that advised all the update methods with an around advice that invoked `proceed()` in an unconventional manner (as I'll describe shortly). The result was that a single aspect consisting of only a few lines replaced all the hand-coded classes.

Soon, I was encountering problems of authorization and transaction management where the same solution could help. Then, I realized that I could use the same approach to execute certain time-consuming operations in a separate thread and thus improve the responsiveness of the UI application. What I had on my hands was a scheme that solved a recurring set of problems—in other words, a pattern. Discovering this pattern was one of my "Aha!" moments.

12.1.1 The current solution

If you were to solve the problem of creating worker objects without using the pattern, you'd have to address two chief tasks for each method involved:

- Implement a class that invokes the work method and creates an object of that class.
- Use that object in place of the original method.

The following snippet shows the scheme:

```
Runnable worker = new Runnable() {
    public void run() {
        ... invoke the work method
    }
}
... use the worker object:
    - send the worker object to a queue for execution,
    - or pass it to another subsystem for execution,
    - or simply call run() directly
```

NOTE Although our discussion uses the `Runnable` interface for illustration purposes, any interface with a method that executes the operation will work equally well.

Depending on the situation, you may use either named or anonymous classes. In either case, you implement an interface such as `Runnable` that contains a `run()` method for invoking the work method. If you use named classes, you must add a constructor to accept arguments matching those of the work method. If you use anonymous classes, you don't (and can't) write a constructor. Instead, you create the class locally and pass the variables from the outer context (where the class is implemented) as the arguments to the work method. You need to mark each local variable passed as `final` because local classes can't access non-final local variables.

With either style, you need to replace the normal method call with the creation of a worker object and invoke that object. The sheer amount of code makes implementation a daunting task; it also increases the risk of missing certain changes, which may result in undesirable system behavior. For example, if you don't reroute certain calls to Swing components that originate in a non-event-dispatching thread, you may observe hard-to-explain UI anomalies or even outright crashes.

As you'll see in the next section, the worker object pattern encapsulates these steps into an aspect, eliminating the need to create multiple worker classes.

12.1.2 An overview of the worker object pattern

In this pattern, you use an aspect to create objects of anonymous classes (which are the worker objects) automatically. You write a pointcut selecting all the join points that need routing through a worker object, and advice that executes the selected join point inside the `run()` method of the anonymous worker class. Normally, when `proceed()` is called directly from within around advice, it executes the selected join point. But with the worker object pattern, you create a worker object, have its `run()` method call `proceed()`, and invoke the `run()` method later, perhaps in another thread, to execute the selected join point.

12.1.3 The worker object pattern template

Let's write a pattern template that you can use to create your own implementation easily. First, you write a pointcut selecting the needed join points. You don't need to collect any context in this pointcut (but you may collect context—it doesn't matter from the pattern's perspective). Next, you advise this pointcut with an around advice to create and use the worker object, as shown in the following snippet:

```
void around() : <pointcut> {
    Runnable worker = new Runnable () {
        public void run() {
            proceed();
        }
    }
    ... use the worker object
}
```

Let's use a simple example to illustrate the worker object pattern. Assume that you've decided that cache pre-fetching and saving a backup copy of a project are expensive operations that can be better executed in a separate thread. (Later, in chapter 13, we'll expand this example to demonstrate how you can avoid locking the UI when calling a time-consuming task.)

Let's set up the example with three classes; then, you'll apply the pattern to them. The class `CachePreFetcher` in listing 12.1 contains one method that simulates the cache fetching operation by printing a message.

Listing 12.1 CachePreFetcher.java

```
package ajia.example;

public class CachePreFetcher {
    public static void fetch() {
        System.out.println("Fetching in thread "
                           + Thread.currentThread());
    }
}
```

Similarly, the `ProjectSaver` class in listing 12.2 contains a single method that simulates backing up a project by printing a message.

Listing 12.2 ProjectSaver.java

```
package ajia.example;

public class ProjectSaver {
    public static void backupSave() {
        System.out.println("Saving backup copy in thread "
                           + Thread.currentThread());
    }
}
```

Now, you write a simple driver (listing 12.3) to exercise these classes.

Listing 12.3 Main.java: exercising the simulated expensive operations

```
package ajia.main;

import ...

public class Main {
```

```
    public static void main(String[] args) {
        CachePreFetcher.fetch();
        ProjectSaver.backupSave();
    }
}
```

When you compile these classes and run the main program, you get following output:

```
Fetching in thread Thread[main,5,main]
Saving backup copy in thread Thread[main,5,main]
```

The output shows that the main thread executes both methods. Consequently, the main thread is blocked for the period that the method is running.

Now, let's write a simple reusable aspect that executes selected join points in a separate thread. The aspect AsynchronousExecutionAspect in listing 12.4 defines a pointcut that selects operations to be routed asynchronously. It also contains an advice to the pointcut.

Listing 12.4 Aspect to route join points asynchronously

```
package ajia.example;

import ...

public aspect AsynchronousExecutionAspect {
    private Executor executor = Executors.newCachedThreadPool();

    public pointcut asyncOperation()
        : execution(* CachePreFetcher.fetch())
          || execution(* ProjectSaver.backupSave())
          /* || ... */;

    void around() : asyncOperation() {
        Runnable worker = new Runnable() {
            public void run() {
                proceed();
            }
        };
        executor.execute(worker);
    }
}
```

In the aspect, the asyncOperation() pointcut selects join points to be routed asynchronously. The around advice creates an object—worker—of an anonymous class that implements the Runnable interface. In the run() method, it calls proceed() to execute the advised join point. Because worker performs the operation selected by the advised join point, it's the worker object here. The advice executes the work by passing the worker object to the execute() method of the executor object. Although you use a thread pool–based executor, you can use any other implementation (such as the one obtained through your application server). The effect of this advice is that instead of directly invoking the join point, the aspect routes the join point execution in a new thread. Note that you can extract a reusable base aspect to route operations asynchronously.

> **Continuations and worker objects**
>
> A *continuation* represents an object form of some code to be executed. Because a continuation is an object, it may be passed around or stored. Then, it may be executed in a different context. A worker object also represents the same concept that can be implemented in Java with the help of AspectJ.

When you compile all these classes and aspects and run the driver program, you get this output:

```
Fetching in thread Thread[pool-1-thread-1,5,main]
Saving backup copy in thread Thread[pool-1-thread-2,5,main]
```

As you can see, by introducing a simple aspect to the system, you ensure that each operation runs in a new thread instead of the main thread.

12.1.4 Getting the return value

Some of the routed calls could be returning a value to the caller. In that case, `proceed()` returns the value of the method when the operation has completed. You can keep this value in the worker object and later return it from the around advice. Of course, for the value to make sense, the caller must wait until the execution of the worker object finishes.

To facilitate managing the return value in a generic fashion, let's write a simple abstract class, `RunnableWithReturn`, that implements `Runnable`. The `run()` method in the implementing classes must set the `returnValue` property to the return value of the `proceed()` statement, which is the return value of the executed join point. Listing 12.5 shows the `RunnableWithReturn` class.

Listing 12.5 RunnableWithReturn.java

```
package ajia.pattern.worker;

public abstract class RunnableWithReturn implements Runnable {
    private Object returnValue;

    public Object getReturnValue() {
        return this.returnValue;
    }

    public void setReturnValue(Object returnValue) {
        this.returnValue = returnValue;
    }
}
```

Instead of using `Runnable`, you use the class shown in listing 12.5 as the base class for an anonymous class inside the advice, as in the code snippet that follows. You also set the return value to the value returned by `proceed()`. After the worker object is executed, you return `worker.getReturnValue()`:

```
Object around() : <pointcut> {
    RunnableWithReturn worker = new RunnableWithReturn() {
        public void run() {
            setReturnValue(proceed());
        }
    }
    ... use the worker object
    return worker.getReturnValue();
}
```

Note that for the return value to make sense, you must wait for the work to complete before invoking `getReturnValue()`. If you call the worker object's `run()` method object in the same thread, you don't need to do anything special. You'll see examples of such situations in chapter 14, when you apply this pattern to transaction management–related concerns. If you call the `run()` method in a separate thread, you have to wait until that thread has a chance to execute the work. You'll see examples of such situations in chapter 13, when you apply this pattern to implement Swing's thread-safety policy.

As discussed in chapter 4, specifying `Object` as the return value causes the around advice to wrap the primitive return values before they're returned from the advice and unwrapping and casting the objects correctly after they're returned from the advice. For example, if the selected method returns a `float`, the AspectJ weaver takes care of it by creating a wrapper object to be returned by `proceed()` and unwrapping it when you assign the advice's return value to a `float` variable.

Let's look at a simple example using this mechanism. You'll implement an aspect as shown in listing 12.6 that uses a worker class to route the advised methods synchronously.

Listing 12.6 SynchronousExecutionAspect.java

```
package ajia.example;

import ...

public aspect SynchronousExecutionAspect {
    public pointcut syncOperation()
        : call(* Math.max(..))
          || call(* List.*(..))
          /* || ... */;

    Object around() : syncOperation() {
        RunnableWithReturn worker = new RunnableWithReturn() {
            public void run() {
                setReturnValue(proceed());
            }};
        System.out.println("About to run " + worker);
        worker.run();
        return worker.getReturnValue();
    }
}
```

The aspect implements the template shown earlier in the section. `syncOperation()` selects calls to `Math.max()` and to all methods of the `List` type to create worker objects. I chose these methods to illustrate that the aspect handles returning a primitive type, returning `void`, and returning an object.

The advice creates a worker object and calls the `run()` method on it. Then, it logs a message when it's about to execute the worker object. Typically, you'd pass the worker object to another thread and wait for the execution of the worker. For example, you'd pass it to `EventQueue.invokeAndWait()` when using Swing, as you'll see in chapter 13.

Finally, let's write a simple driver program (listing 12.7), which prints the result of each operation as it executes.

Listing 12.7 Main.java

```
package ajia.main;

import ...

public class Main {
    public static void main(String[] args) {
        int intMax = Math.max(1, 2);
        System.out.println("intMax = " + intMax);
        double doubleMax = Math.max(3.0, 4.0);
        System.out.println("doubleMax = " + doubleMax);

        List<String> list = new ArrayList<String>();
        list.add(0, "AspectJ");
        String str = list.get(0);
        System.out.println("str = " + str);
    }
}
```

First, you compile the program without aspects and see the output:

```
intMax = 2
doubleMax = 4.0
str = AspectJ
```

Now, when you compile and run the program with the aspects, you see output similar to the following:

```
About to run SynchronousExecutionAspect$1@affc70
intMax = 2
About to run SynchronousExecutionAspect$1@1e63e3d
doubleMax = 4.0
About to run SynchronousExecutionAspect$1@1b90b39
About to run SynchronousExecutionAspect$1@18fe7c3
str = AspectJ
```

As illustrated by the output, the resulting program's behavior is unchanged from the original program that didn't include any aspects. You now have a mechanism for routing direct calls through worker objects that requires writing only a few lines of code.

12.1.5 A summary of the worker object pattern

The worker object pattern offers a new opportunity to deal with otherwise complex problems. You can use this pattern in a variety of situations: from implementing thread safety in Swing applications and improving the responsiveness of UI applications to performing authorization and transaction management. Initially, I was fascinated by the time I saved by not having to write as much code. Later, I felt that the pattern's real value lies in the sheer elegance and consistency it brings to the solution. I am sure your experience will be similar.

12.2 The wormhole pattern

The wormhole pattern makes context information from a caller available to a callee—without having to pass the information as a set of parameters to each method in the control flow. For example, consider an authorization system, where many methods need to know who invoked them to determine if the caller should be allowed to execute the operation. The wormhole allows the methods to access the caller object and its context to obtain such information.

By creating a direct route between two levels in the call stack, you create a wormhole and avoid linearly traveling through each layer. This saves you from having to modify the call chain when you want to pass additional context information, and it prevents API pollution.

12.2.1 The current solution

If you don't use AspectJ, there are two ways to pass the caller's context in a multi-threaded environment:

- Pass the context as additional parameters to methods, which subsequently pass it on. This continues until the context reaches the place of its use. This causes API pollution—every method in the execution stack must have extra parameters to pass on the context collected.
- Use thread-local storage to set and access the context information. This requires the caller to create a `ThreadLocal` variable to store the context information. Although this approach avoids API pollution, it entails changes in both caller and callee implementation and requires an understanding of how the context is stored. You must also clear the context correctly. This is especially important in an environment that uses thread pools (practically, that includes every application and web server). If you forget to clear a thread local, you run the risk of exposing old information to the next user of that thread. Therefore, even if you don't use the wormhole pattern, consider using an aspect to set and clear thread locals. (Hint: use a before advice to set the context and an after advice to clear it—much the same as the indentation aspects in chapter 10.)

In either case, multiple modules are involved in the logic to manage the context.

12.2.2 An overview of the wormhole pattern

The basic idea behind the wormhole pattern, shown in figure 12.1, is to specify two pointcuts: one for the caller and the other for the callee, with the former collecting

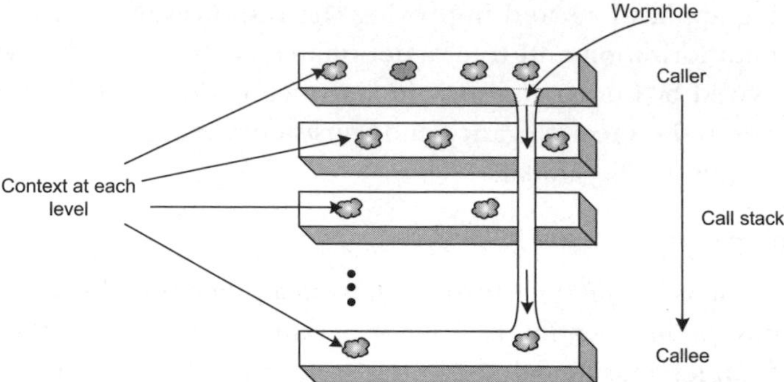

Figure 12.1 The wormhole pattern. Each horizontal bar shows a level in the call stack. The wormhole makes the object in the caller plane available to the methods in the called plane without passing the object through the call stack.

the context to be transported through the wormhole. Then, you specify the wormhole as the execution of the callee's join points in the control flow of a caller's join points.

Figure 12.1 depicts each level in the call stack as a plane in the space. To transport context from one plane to another, you'd normally have to pass it to the next plane until it reached the desired location. The wormhole pattern provides a path that cuts directly through the planes, which avoids having the context trickle through the levels from caller to callee.

12.2.3 The wormhole pattern template

Let's create a template for the pattern that will allow you to plug the pattern into your system by replacing the entities in the template with the specific ones in your system:

```
public aspect WormholeAspect {
    pointcut callerSpace(<caller context>)
        : <caller pointcut>;

    pointcut calleeSpace(<callee context>)
        : <callee pointcut>;

    pointcut wormhole(<caller context>, <callee context>)
        : cflow(callerSpace(<caller context>))
          && calleeSpace(<callee context>);

    // advice to wormhole
    before(<caller context>, <callee context>)
        : wormhole(<caller context>, <callee context>) {
        ... advice body
    }
}
```

In this template, you define a pointcut in the caller's space that collects the associated context. Similarly, you define a pointcut in the callee's space. The collected context in both cases could be an execution, a target, arguments to the callee join point, or any associated annotations. You then create a wormhole through these two spaces using a pointcut that selects the join points selected by the `calleeSpace()` pointcut in the control flow of the join points selected by the `callerSpace()` pointcut. Because you have the context available for both of these join points, you can write advice to the `wormhole()` pointcut using this information.

> **Only with AspectJ**
>
> Due to the use of the `cflow()` pointcut, the wormhole presented here works only with AspectJ weaving. With Spring AOP, you may get a similar effect using `ThreadLocals`.

Let's look at a simple example using this pattern; for more complex and complete examples, see chapter 16. The aspect in listing 12.8 creates a wormhole between a transaction system such as an ATM, a teller, or an Internet bank and the actual account operations. Due to the use of a wormhole, it doesn't matter how many layers exist between a transaction system and the account objects.

Listing 12.8 AccountTransactionAspect.java

```
package ajia.banking.auditing;

public aspect AccountTransactionAspect {
    pointcut transactionSystemUsage(TransactionSystem ts)
        : execution(* TransactionSystem+.*(..))
          && this(ts);

    pointcut accountTransaction(Account account, float amount)
        : this(account) && args(amount)
          && (execution(public * Account.credit(float))
              || execution(public * Account.debit(float)));

    pointcut wormhole(TransactionSystem ts,
                      Account account, float amount)
        : cflow(transactionSystemUsage(ts))
          && accountTransaction(account, amount);

    before(TransactionSystem ts,
           Account account, float amount)
        : wormhole(ts, account, amount) {

        ... log the operation along with information about
        ... transaction system, perform authorization, etc.

    }
}
```

❶ Selects transaction system operations

❷ Selects account operations

❸ Creates wormhole through #1 and #2

❹ Uses wormholed context

❶ The `transactionSystemUsage()` pointcut selects execution join points in a `TransactionSystem` class or its subtypes. It collects the `this` object as the context that you want to pass through the wormhole. Note that only context that can be collected using a pointcut can be passed through the wormhole. In other words, objects such as local variables can't be passed.

❷ The `accountTransaction()` pointcut selects the execution of the `credit()` and `debit()` methods in the `Account` class. It collects the account and the amount as the context.

❸ The `wormhole()` pointcut creates a wormhole between the transaction system and the account operation by selecting join points that match `accountTransaction()` that occur in the control flow of `transactionSystemUsage()`. The pointcut also collects the context selected by the constituent pointcuts, so that advice to it may use it.

4 The advice to the `wormhole()` pointcut can now use the context. The advice knows not only the account and the amount but also the transaction system responsible for causing the account activity. For example, the advice may log this information, perhaps to a database, so that it can be used to generate monthly statements showing transaction systems accessed by customer for each transaction.

The wormhole pattern offers you the flexibility to introduce new join points in the caller space. For example, in a banking system, activities performed in crediting an account may depend on which kind of system invoked them. If a debit action is initiated through a check-clearance system, you can fire overdraft protection logic. But if the same actions were invoked through an ATM machine, you limit the withdrawal amount—it doesn't matter which specific ATM machine initiated the transaction; it's enough that an ATM machine did it. Using a wormhole pattern in these cases helps to avoid passing an extra parameter to the account operations to indicate the type of the transaction system. This not only avoids API pollution but also offers a nonintrusive change if the system adds a new kind of caller. In this banking example, you can implement additional rules when a new kind of the account-access system is added, such as internet banking, without making any system-wide changes.

12.2.4 A summary of the wormhole pattern

The wormhole pattern removes the need to modify multiple modules for passing the caller's context. With the caller context available at the callee's join point execution, you can easily implement functionalities that require both contexts.

12.3 The participant pattern

Selecting join points with common characteristics across a system is essential in ensuring consistent system behavior. For example, you may want to surround all slow operations in the system with a wait cursor. The common AOP approach for accomplishing this is to define pointcuts based on the type and name patterns. For example, a method throwing an `IOException` is potentially performing some IO operation. This information, in conjunction with a hypothesis that IO operations are slow, lets you identify and select a few slow methods. Similarly, you can consider all methods whose name starts with `set` as potentially state-altering operations. But you often can't select all the join points sharing a similar characteristic just by using the type and name patterns. For example, although you characterized all IO operations as potentially slow, how do you select other operations that are slow because they perform complex computations?

Many crosscutting concerns, such as transaction management and authentication, tend to span operations that can't be selected by pointcuts relying solely on type and name patterns. Developers usually assign the name of a method based on its core operation. Therefore, the method's name doesn't reflect the method's peripheral characteristics.

Consider a transaction-management problem: the methods that need to be in a transaction are likely to be named after the business logic they perform, such as `processOrder()`. The name in this case gives no indication that the method needs transaction-management support. Therefore, selecting transactional join points that rely on method names isn't possible.

The participant pattern helps select the methods based on their characteristics and requires the participating classes to collaborate with the aspects explicitly. Keep in mind, though, that the participant pattern and its variations require modifications to the core classes, and there is a possibility that you may not identify all the operations. For this reason, you should use the regular pointcuts to the fullest extent possible.

12.3.1 Current solutions

In this section, we'll look at characteristics-based crosscutting using AOP. First, we'll look at a simple technique that allows you to advise join points that share certain characteristics. Then, we'll improve the solution to make it easier to maintain. We'll use the example where a wait cursor needs to be set around any slow operation.

TAKE ONE

Let's write an aspect, `WaitCursorManagementAspect` (listing 12.9), that advises all the join points that take a long time to execute.

Listing 12.9 WaitCursorManagementAspect.java: the first version

```
package ajia.example;

public aspect WaitCursorManagementAspect {
    public pointcut slowOperation() :
           execution(* Analytics.monteCarloSimulation())
        || execution(* Analytics.updateDatabase())
        || execution(* Document.save())
        || execution(* Document.backupSave())
        /* || ... */;

    before() : slowOperation() {
        WaitCursor.set();
    }

    after() : slowOperation() {
        WaitCursor.unset();
    }
}
```

The aspect defines a pointcut that lists all the methods that have the characteristics of being slow. The problem with this approach is that tight coupling exists between the aspect, all the classes, and the methods in the list. If a new class is added to the system containing a method with the same characteristics, it won't be advised until it's added to the list. Similarly, if a method that is originally part of the list changes its implementation so that it's no longer slow, it will continue to be advised until the aspect is changed to remove the method from the pointcut definition. Both the classes and aspects need to be aware of the existence of each other to remain coordinated. Essentially, you have a fragile pointcut definition.

TAKE TWO

Another fundamental problem is that characteristics such as the expected execution time are implementation-dependent and may change as the system evolves. Let's see if you can tie the pointcut definitions to the classes themselves.

Recall that a class can include pointcuts (but not advice). Because a class knows about the characteristics of its methods, it can specify pointcuts identifying those characteristics. Listing 12.10 shows how `Analytics` includes a pointcut that selects its slow methods.

Listing 12.10 Analytics.java

```
package ajia.example;

public class Analytics {
    // Analytics' implementation

    public pointcut slowOperation() :
        execution(* Analytics.monteCarloSimulation())
        || execution(* Analytics.updateDatabase());
}
```

Similarly, `Document` in listing 12.11 includes a pointcut that selects its slow methods.

Listing 12.11 Document.java

```
package ajia.example;

public class Document {

    // Document's implementation

    public pointcut slowOperation() :
        execution(* Document.save())
        || execution(* Document.backupSave());
}
```

Now you can write an aspect to advise both `slowOperation()` pointcuts defined in `Analytics` and `Document`. Listing 12.12 shows the second version of `WaitCursorManagementAspect`, which advises pointcuts specified in `Analytics` and `Document`.

Listing 12.12 WaitCursorManagementAspect.java: the second version

```
package ajia.example;

import ...

public aspect WaitCursorManagementAspect {
    public pointcut slowOperation() :
           Analytics.slowOperation()
        || Document.slowOperation();

    // advice code
}
```

This version is better than the earlier solution. Instead of being aware of classes and methods, the aspect is now aware of only the classes because it uses the pointcuts defined in them to select the methods. Nevertheless, the need to be explicitly aware of all the classes doesn't make it an optimal solution. If a new class is added to the system, the aspect won't advise the new class until you add it to the aspect.

NOTE It's illegal to specify a pointcut such as `*.slowOperation()`. You must explicitly enumerate all the pointcuts you want to advise from each class.

12.3.2 An overview of the participant pattern

The participant pattern builds on the idea of classes that contain a pointcut denoting certain characteristics. Instead of including a pointcut definition directly inside each class and using those pointcuts in an aspect, the classes define a subaspect that extends the advising aspect and provides the pointcut definition. In a way, this pattern reverses the roles—instead of making aspects aware of classes, it makes the classes aware of the aspects.

Let's examine the structural overview of the pattern:

1. You write an abstract aspect that contains abstract pointcut(s) denoting join points with the desired characteristics. These pointcuts form a kind of *aspectual interface.* The aspect also advises each pointcut (or a combination of them) with the required behavior. You can think of this aspect as an *inviting* aspect—it invites others to participate in the functionality it offers. Such an offer is strictly an invitation or opt-in only.
2. Each class that wants to participate in such a behavior includes a concrete subaspect extending the abstract inviting aspect. Each of these subaspects provides the implementation of the abstract pointcut for the enclosing class. Note that the concrete subaspects don't have to be nested aspects of the class—they can be peer aspects. This way, each class that wants to participate in the collaboration needs to do so explicitly—hence the name of the pattern.

Let's put this information in a template form.

12.3.3 The participant pattern template

In this section, you'll develop a template for the pattern. Listing 12.13 shows the abstract aspect that contains the core logic for implementing the concern; but it defers the definition of the `slowOperation()` pointcut to subaspects.

Listing 12.13 AbstractWaitCursorManagementAspect.java: the base

```
package ajia.example;

import ...

public abstract aspect AbstractWaitCursorManagementAspect {
    public abstract pointcut slowOperation();

    before() : slowOperation() {
        WaitCursor.set();
```

```
    }

    after() : slowOperation() {
        WaitCursor.unset();
    }
}
```

The required crosscutting behavior is in the advice to the abstract pointcut. Listing 12.14 contains a version of Analytics that includes a nested subaspect of AbstractWaitCursorManagementAspect; the subaspect defines the base aspect's abstract pointcut.

Listing 12.14 Analytics.java: participating in the collaboration

```
package ajia.example;

import ...

public class Analytics {

    // Analytics' implementation

    private static aspect WaitCursorManagementParticipant
        extends AbstractWaitCursorManagementAspect {
        public pointcut slowOperation() :
            execution(* Analytics.monteCarloSimulation())
            || execution(* Analytics.updateDatabase());
    }
}
```

In listing 12.15, the nested subaspect declares that the Analytics.monteCarloSimulation() and Analytics.updateDatabase() methods have the desired characteristics to participate in the functionality offered by the base aspect. The effect of this aspect is that the advice to slowOperation() in the base aspect is applied to the specified methods. Document in listing 12.15 participates in the collaboration in the same way.

Listing 12.15 Document.java: participating in the collaboration

```
package ajia.example;

import ...

public class Document {

    // Document's implementation

    private static aspect WaitCursorManagementParticipant
        extends AbstractWaitCursorManagementAspect {
        public pointcut slowOperation() :
            execution(* Document.save())
            || execution(* Document.backupSave());
    }
}
```

There can be many more participants in addition to Analytics and Document. Each of the participating nested subaspects provide a definition to select the join points in their enclosing class, thus applying the functionality of the base aspect to those join points. Note that it's perfectly legitimate for a subaspect to use a naming pattern or other signature components to define the pointcut instead of enumerating the methods. Figure 12.2 depicts the structure.

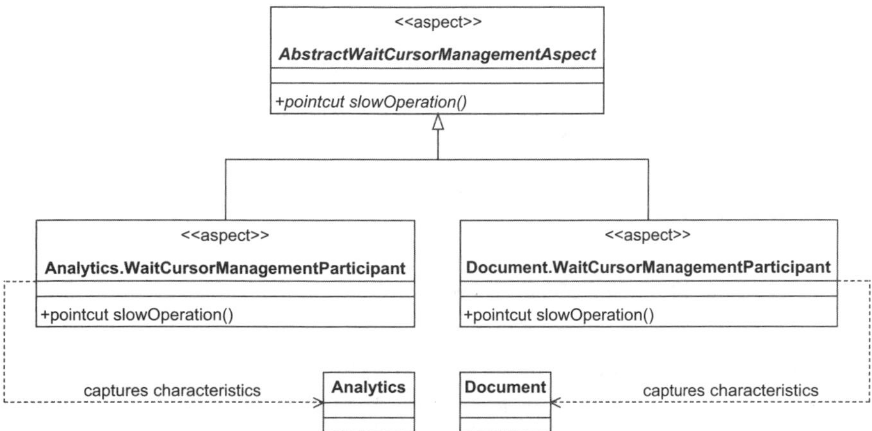

Figure 12.2 A typical structure using the participant pattern. For each class, a nested subaspect exists to make the class participate in the collaboration offered by the base aspect.

With the participant pattern, the collaborating classes explicitly participate in the implementation of the crosscutting concerns by extending an inviting abstract aspect and providing the definition for its abstract pointcut.

SCOPING PARTICIPATION

Although we've shown a one-class/one-participant kind of collaboration, the participant pattern doesn't require it. It's possible, for example, to have one participant per class hierarchy or package. But in such cases, because the aspect isn't nested in the class, you must remember to modify the pointcut in the participant aspect whenever the list of methods matching the desired characteristic changes.

AUGMENTING BEHAVIORAL PARTICIPATION

Crosscutting concern implementations often require some behavior specific to the advised type to be invoked from advice. For example, an authorization aspect may need the roles that are authorized to access specific functionality. In many cases, the base aspect can leverage join point context to deduce the needed behavior. For example, the authorization aspect might use a method name as a key into a map to obtain the security role (you'll use such a scheme in chapter 15). But in other cases, complex logic may be needed to obtain the role. Perhaps the amount involved in a banking transaction determines the role needed to perform the operation. In such cases, you need collaboration from classes not only in supplying the pointcuts but also in augmenting the behavior.

The setup for the participant pattern easily accommodates such scenarios. You include one or more abstract methods in the base aspect. Each participating aspect can then implement these methods. In a sense, this pattern applies the template method design pattern in an aspect setting: the abstract methods form the template method, and the base aspect invokes them as a part of some template logic.

12.3.4 Consequences of the participant pattern

The participant pattern provides a good solution, but it suffers from a couple of shortcomings:

- It requires participants to be directly aware of the base aspect.
- It makes it difficult to remove the aspect. Because the classes refer to the base aspect, you always need it to successfully compile the classes.

You can overcome some of these limitations with a variation of the pattern that uses annotations, as you'll see shortly.

12.3.5 A summary of the participant pattern

The participant pattern lets you implement characteristic-based crosscutting by embedding the knowledge of such characteristics where it belongs—in the classes. Only classes have the potential to know such information, so the pattern makes tracking changes in the class a local affair. Although the pattern requires explicit participation by classes in the aspect collaboration, their knowledge of the aspect is limited to defining the implementation of the abstract aspect.

The biggest consequence of using this pattern is a reversal of the collaboration flow. In the participant pattern, the aspect makes the class participate in the aspect collaboration, whereas in other cases, aspects affect classes without their knowledge.

12.4 Annotation-driven participant pattern

The core concept in the participant pattern is explicit participation by the participants (classes, typically). With the growing popularity of language support for metadata, there is a variation of the classical participant pattern: the annotation-driven participant pattern (ADPP). The key to annotation-driven participation is changing how the participants show interest in the functionality offered by an aspect. Whereas the classical version of the pattern uses a pointcut, the ADPP uses one or more annotation types and expects the participants to attach the annotations to appropriate elements. Figure 12.3 shows the general arrangement implemented in ADPP.

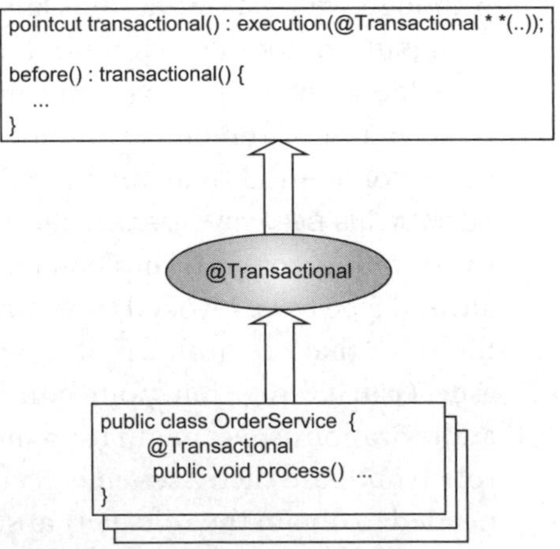

Figure 12.3 The annotation-driven participant pattern uses an aspect that expects program elements to carry certain annotations. The classes participate in the functionality offered by marking program elements with the expected annotation.

As shown in the figure, the aspect advises join points for the methods annotated with the `@Transactional` annotation. Classes such as `OrderService` participate in this functionality by marking appropriate program elements with that annotation.

12.4.1 Current solution

The classical participant pattern discussed in the earlier section is the most common current solution that addresses the problem of selecting join points of the desired characteristics. Obviously, it represents one of the best options when there isn't a way to use annotations. But note that the classical participant pattern offers a few customization possibilities that are harder to achieve with ADPP. For example, in the classical pattern, you can create multiple subaspects, each to suit a specific need. Each subaspect can also provide a variation of a certain behavior by overriding methods in the base aspect. You should preserve the use of an abstract base aspect even in ADPP to allow for such customization.

12.4.2 The annotation-driven participant pattern template

Let's develop a template for the ADPP. We'll use the same example of managing wait cursor around slow methods. Listing 12.16 shows an aspect that uses an annotation to select slow operations and advises them to manage the wait cursor around them.

Listing 12.16 Annotation-driven aspect to manage the wait cursor

```
package ajia.example;

import ...

public aspect SlowAnnotationDrivenWaitCursorManagementAspect
    extends AbstractWaitCursorManagementAspect {
    public pointcut slowOperation()
        : execution(@Slow * *(..)) || execution(* (@Slow *).*(..));
}
```

The aspect extends the base aspect you developed in listing 12.14. The `slowOperation()` pointcut selects methods with the `@Slow` annotation or methods in the classes with the `@Slow` annotation.

Note how you still use the base aspect that doesn't use any annotations and a subaspect that defines the pointcuts using annotations. This arrangement provides freedom regarding the type of annotation used and lets you fall back to the classical participant pattern, if necessary.

The subaspect uses the `@Slow` annotation as shown in listing 12.17. The annotation specifies that it may be used to annotate types and methods.

Listing 12.17 @Slow annotation

```
package ajia.characteristics;

import...

@Target({ElementType.TYPE,ElementType.METHOD})
public @interface Slow {
}
```

Now, you need to mark methods or classes with the `@Slow` annotation. Listing 12.18 shows an `Analytics` class that chooses to mark individual methods with the `@Slow` annotation.

Listing 12.18 Analytics class annotated to participate in the collaboration

```
package ajia.example;

public class Analytics {
    @Slow
    public void monteCarloSimulation() {
        ...
    }

    @Slow
    public void updateDatabase() {
        ...
    }

    ...

}
```

In contrast, you mark the `Document` class (listing 12.19) itself as `@Slow`, thus designating all methods as slow.

Listing 12.19 Document.java: annotated to participate in the collaboration

```
package ajia.example;

@Slow
public class Document {
    public void save() {
        ...
    }

    public void backupSave() {
        ...
    }

    ...

}
```

The annotation type used needs careful consideration to produce the right level of abstraction. Let's discuss it in more detail.

12.4.3 Annotation type abstraction

Writing software is mostly about working at the correct level of abstraction. In the context of ADPP, you have a few possible abstraction choices for the annotation type: from a narrowly defined functionality-specific annotation (such as `@WaitCursor`) to a more general characteristic-specific annotation (such as `@Slow`). Let's discuss the levels of abstraction in detail. Keep in mind that the right abstraction is always in the eye of the beholder.

Although I'll specify three levels of abstraction and discuss criteria, it may not always be clear which level a particular annotation belongs to. The good news is that the levels matter less than the thought process that leads to *a* correct level. Further, the use of an abstract base aspect lets you use multiple levels of abstraction that are suitable for a given task. You can then write subaspects to do either direct participation as with the classical pattern or annotation-driven participation using any annotation of your choice.

FUNCTIONALITY-SPECIFIC ANNOTATION

At this level of abstraction, the goal is to avoid a direct coupling of aspects with classes by using an annotation as an intermediary. The classes and aspects agree on a narrowly defined annotation type whose sole goal is to facilitate the join point selection for a specific functionality. For example, in the case of wait-cursor management, using the `@WaitCursor` annotation defines a collaboration point: classes must use the `@WaitCursor` annotation to apply this functionality.

When classes use functionality-specific annotations, the collaboration they seek is in the form of a specific demand. For example, in the case of the wait-cursor management functionality, aspects are required to set and unset the wait cursor. In environments where a wait cursor makes no sense (say, a server-side application), the aspect is in a fix: should it ignore the demand or fulfill it anyway?

Essentially, with this level of abstraction, you get a macro-like facility. It offers a better alternative than directly embedding crosscutting code inside the classes. It also provides a level of consistency by isolating the functionality in an aspect. For example, you won't run into issues such as a few methods forgetting to unset the wait cursor in a `finally` block (because methods contain no code related to setting and unsetting the wait cursor). But you can often use a better level of abstraction, as you'll see next.

SUBJECTIVE CHARACTERISTIC-BASED ANNOTATION

At this level of abstraction, the focus is on using annotations to describe characteristics of the program element, keeping in mind its specific usages by aspects. This level of abstraction allows program elements to express characteristics within the context of a specific crosscutting functionality. For example, you can use the `@Slow` annotation because slowness is a characteristic of a method that may be used to manage the wait cursor. The use of a characteristic-based annotation type lets you use the same annotation for other concerns that deal with slow methods. Yet this kind of annotation is insufficient for describing characteristics in a functionality-independent way. Specifically, these kinds of annotations make certain assumptions about how they will be used. In the case of wait-cursor management with the `@Slow` annotation, the slowness represents a subjective criterion with an eye on a target usage. It's unlikely that a UI application and a robotics application can agree on the same criterion to define slowness!

For all its limitations, in some cases a subjective characteristic is the best you can do. Consider, for example, a security aspect. There may not be a better abstraction than using a `@Secured`-like annotation—especially when you consider additional information needed, such as roles to implement the security functionality. Note that a method doesn't have an inherent characteristic of being secure; it's only in the context of a system that a method needs to be secured. But subjectively, in the context of a secured application, methods have security attributes that annotations may describe.

In some cases, you may do better and avoid subjective characteristics when using annotations, as you'll see next.

OBJECTIVE CHARACTERISTIC-BASED ANNOTATION

At this level of abstraction, annotations purely describe program elements' characteristics, which aspects may use in any possible way. In other words, annotations describe the objective characteristics of a program element that hold true in any context. For example, for the wait-cursor management functionality, you can use purely timing-related annotations that specify the expected execution time; see listing 12.20.

Listing 12.20 Characteristic-specific annotation

```
package ajia.characteristics;

import ...

@Retention(RetentionPolicy.RUNTIME)
@Target(ElementType.METHOD)
public @interface Timing {
    long value();
}
```

Then, the aspect can select join points based on timing information; see listing 12.21.

Listing 12.21 Timing annotation-driven wait-cursor management aspect

```
package ajia.example;

import ...

public aspect TimingAnnotationDrivenWaitCursorManagementAspect
      extends AbstractWaitCursorManagementAspect {
    private static final int SLOW_THRESHOLD = 1000;

    pointcut timedSlowOperation(Timing timing)
        : execution(@Timing * *(..))
          && @annotation(timing) && if(timing.value() > SLOW_THRESHOLD);

    public pointcut slowOperation() : timedSlowOperation(*);
}
```

You can use the same annotation for a variety of purposes. For example, you can write an aspect that performs monitoring to ensure that a slow operation (with an appropriate threshold) doesn't occur in a critical path.

> **Language keywords in disguise**
>
> One of the tell-tale signs of objective characteristic-specific annotations is that it feels like it could have been a language keyword. For example, consider the `@ReadOnly` annotation to describe read-only methods and objects. This annotation essentially nudges toward replicating the `const` keyword feature in C++.

Defining characteristic-specific annotations often poses some difficulty. For example, what should be the unit of the value property of the `Timing` annotation? Any wall-clock based unit will be wrong on a machine with a different speed. Perhaps you can use milliseconds on a particular setup that serves as a benchmark, or the number of CPU cycles on a benchmark CPU. Can you easily compute such a measurement? If this kind of decision becomes a problem, moving to a subjective characteristic-based annotation is often a pragmatic choice.

No abstraction makes sense in all situations, and providing freedom in choosing a specific implementation is always desirable. Using an abstract base aspect that doesn't use any annotations addresses this issue by letting subaspects make the right choice of abstraction.

Let's examine a variation of ADPP that bridges these abstraction levels and works with elements that aren't annotated.

12.4.4 Variation: bridged participation pattern

A few annotations make some developers uncomfortable. They have the sense that using annotations (especially framework-specific annotations) strips Plain Old Java Objects of their plainness. For example, consider the `@Configurable` annotation in the Spring Framework. Although most developers venturing into domain-object dependency injection (DI) are fine with marking their classes with the `@Configurable` annotation, others feel a bit of uneasiness due to coupling between their domain classes and the Spring Framework. On the one hand, Spring's aspects expect classes to be marked with that annotation. On the other hand, marking your domain classes with the annotation makes them less plain.

The bridged participation pattern helps to overcome this dilemma. In this case, you can use an aspect that supplies the annotation expected by a framework aspect. The core idea of this pattern is to use some characteristic of existing program elements to supply the expected annotations to those elements using `declare @type`, `declare @method`, `declare @constructor`, or `declare @field` statements in AspectJ. With this arrangement, the classes don't directly depend on the framework, yet they benefit from its functionality. This pattern also helps when you can't modify existing source code to add annotations.

Consider a situation where domain classes that need DI are already extending a class—say, `DomainEntity`. You can use the following declaration to supply the `@Configurable` annotations:

```
declare @type: DomainEntity+ : @Configurable;
```

The Spring Framework will now behave as if the domain classes carry the `@Configurable` annotation.

Alternatively, if the classes don't share a common characteristic, you can use your own interface (say, `IConfigurable`) to modify the classes and use it in supplying annotation as follows:

```
declare @type: IConfigurable+: @Configurable;
```

Note that the classes will now be coupled with `IConfigurable`. But if it's your own interface, the coupling isn't as onerous.

You can also use an existing annotation to the same effect. For example, if the domain classes are marked with the `@Entity` annotation, you can piggyback on it to supply the `@Configurable` annotation as follows:

```
declare @type: @Entity * : @Configurable;
```

Figure 12.4 shows the overall scheme used in the bridged participation pattern.

As shown in the figure, the aspect advises methods whose return type is marked with the `@Sensitive` annotation. The bridging aspects use `declare` statements to attach the `@Sensitive` annotation to the existing types, thus making them participate in the collaboration offered by the aspect.

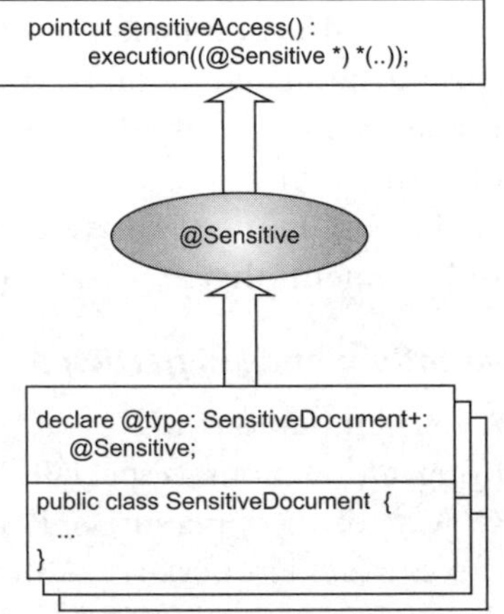

Figure 12.4 Bridged participation pattern, where the aspect advises join points based on the associated annotations just as in ADPP. But instead of marking program elements with annotations, additional aspects attach annotations to those elements through `declare` statements.

Annotation bridging has a few limitations when implemented in AspectJ. In particular, there is no way for a bridge to transfer annotation property values. Furthermore, there is no way to use annotation values in making decisions to supply annotations. For example, you can't supply the `@Slow` annotation if the `@Timing` annotation's value attribute exceeds 1000. A future version of AspectJ may remove these limitations.

12.4.5 Role of ADPP in library aspects

ADPP provides tremendous benefits in writing library aspects by simplifying the collaboration needed by the library users. The aspects in the library often use the bridged participation pattern discussed in the previous section. Instead of writing subaspects and pointcuts (which can be a daunting task for programmers not yet experienced with AOP), library users mark program elements with annotations to participate in the collaboration. Our use of the `@Cachable` annotation in chapter 4 fits this purpose of creating a reusable solution.

The Spring Framework, for example, uses a few annotations to simplify how library users participate in the provided functionality. As you'll see in chapter 14, the `@Transactional` annotation lets you designate classes and methods that need to be executed in a transactional context. As we'll discuss in chapter 15, the `@Secured` annotation lets you designate a secured method and specify the authorization requirements. The `@Configurable` annotation offers a way for objects that aren't Spring beans to have their dependencies injected, which we'll examine in chapter 16.

12.5 Summary

The existence of design patterns—knowledge in a condensed form—reflects the maturity of programming methodologies and languages. The patterns we introduced in this chapter are merely the beginning; and a lot more patterns are waiting to be discovered.

The worker object pattern helps simplify the creation and usage of worker objects. You can use this pattern in implementing functionalities such as concurrency control schemes (discussed in the next chapter) and retrying a failed operation (discussed in chapter 14). The wormhole lets you cut through a call-stack layer to make objects at a layer available to another layer without any help from the intermediate layers. You can use this pattern to make decisions based on context from multiple layers (discussed in chapter 16). The participant pattern and annotation-driven participant patterns help select the desired join points with a minimal coupling between aspects and classes (discussed in chapters 13 through 16).

When you encounter problems, knowing how to apply these patterns will help you solve them efficiently. Instead of thinking about each problem afresh, you can determine whether one of the patterns will fit your situation.

Experiment with these patterns, gain an understanding of them, and think about places you may be able to apply them. When you know these patterns, instead of being surprised by a problem, you'll probably respond by saying, "Yes, I can use the *<name-the-pattern>* pattern."

13 Implementing concurrency control

This chapter covers

- Ensuring Swing's thread-safety rule
- Improving responsiveness of UI applications
- Implementing a reusable read-write lock pattern

If the commonplace usage of multicore processors, the advent of specialized languages such as Erlang and Haskell, the heated discussions in developer communities, and the popularity of books on the subject are any indication, software systems are rapidly embracing ever-higher levels of concurrency. Yet concurrency control remains a mysterious topic to many developers. Even when you gain sufficient knowledge, implementing a concurrency-control scheme correctly and consistently is extremely complex because the implementation spans multiple modules. This can lead to poorly implemented systems with visual anomalies, mysterious crashes, compromised data integrity, and deadlocks—all embarrassingly common problems.

Concurrency control is best implemented using appropriate design patterns. Instead of analyzing ad hoc implementations, you start with proven ways to address thread safety and liveliness problems. A pattern, for example, can specify when and how to obtain locks on an object to avoid deadlocks, provide maximum concurrency, and minimize overhead. Of course, each pattern suits a particular kind of problem, and you must analyze your problem to choose the right pattern.

Many concurrency-control patterns exhibit symptoms of crosscutting concerns, and AOP can help simplify their implementation. In this chapter, we'll examine how AOP can provide a level of consistency that is seldom achieved in conventional implementations. Specifically, we'll discuss modularizing the implementation of two patterns: a Swing thread-safety pattern and the read-write lock pattern.

13.1 Modularizing Swing's single-thread rule

In chapter 11, we developed an AspectJ-based solution for catching violations of Swing's single-thread rule and logging the context under which they occurred. When you understand the violations, you can use conventional solutions to fix them. But fixing the violations in a conventional way can be a daunting task that requires significant modifications in multiple modules. Let's develop a way to fix the problem by adding a couple of aspects to your system; no modifications to the core classes are required. This solution also provides a useful example of the worker object pattern presented in chapter 12. (I discovered that pattern while trying to solve this problem in an application.) Later in this chapter, we'll explore other ways you can use this pattern, such as executing time-consuming tasks in separate threads to improve the responsiveness of the user interface.

In chapter 11, we discussed this problem. Now, let's investigate the solution in more detail so you can modularize its implementation using aspects. If you're already familiar with the problem and solution, you can go directly to section 13.1.3.

Swing requires that only the preassigned event-dispatching thread can access a UI component. To allow other threads to access the component, Swing provides a mechanism to pass a request to the preassigned thread. Threads can pass the requests to perform operations to the event-dispatching thread through `EventQueue.invokeLater()` or `EventQueue.invokeAndWait()`. (You'll see the difference between the two shortly.) With either method, you pass a `Runnable` object whose `run()` method performs the intended operation.

Such a solution requires you to write a class extending `Runnable` for each method that needs to be called from a non-event-dispatching thread and use those classes instead of direct calls. This poses two issues:

- Writing a class for each method is cumbersome.
- You must ensure that the class, in combination with `EventQueue`, replaces any call from a non-event-dispatching thread.

The first limitation is easier to deal with—you can create a library of such classes and use it in your projects. The second issue isn't trivial. It isn't always easy to statically determine if the method call is being made from a non-event-dispatching thread. Missing a few such calls can lead to unexplainable UI problems. Dynamically determining the callers' thread ensures correct behavior if employed consistently, but those checks and the routing logic result in hard-to-read code. Let's set up an example to understand the problem and see how AspectJ can help with it.

13.1.1 A test problem

The class in listing 13.1 exhibits the multithreading problem. This class modifies the class shown in chapter 11 (listing 11.25) to include additional code that illustrates a few specific issues. Later, you'll use the same program to show how the conventional and AspectJ solutions work.

Listing 13.1 Test program showing incorrect usage of the UI update call

```
package ajia.main;

import ...

public class Main {
    public static void main(String[] args) {
        JFrame appFrame = new JFrame();
        appFrame.setDefaultCloseOperation(JFrame.EXIT_ON_CLOSE);

        DefaultTableModel tableModel = new DefaultTableModel(4,2);
        JTable table = new JTable(tableModel);

        appFrame.getContentPane().add(table);

        appFrame.pack();
        appFrame.setVisible(true);

        String value = "[0,0]";
        tableModel.setValueAt(value, 0, 0);          <- 1 Updates UI

        JOptionPane.showMessageDialog(appFrame,
                                  "Press OK to continue");   2 Requests user input

        int rowCount = tableModel.getRowCount();
        System.out.println("Row count = " + rowCount);

        Color gridColor = table.getGridColor();
        System.out.println("Grid color = " + gridColor);     3 Accesses return value
    }
}
```

The last four UI accesses in this program are made from the main thread (which isn't an event-dispatching thread). To correct this situation, you need to route such calls through the event-dispatching thread. Although you're making these calls in the main thread, in real situations such calls typically occur from some other thread, such as a networking thread.

1 The call to set the value of a cell ultimately results in updating the table component. This call can typically be invoked asynchronously—the caller doesn't have to wait until the execution is carried out, because showing the new values doesn't occur until the AWT thread repaints the table.

2 The call to display a message must be made synchronously—the caller must wait until the call has completed the execution, which means after the user has seen and responded to the message.

❸ These calls must also wait before returning to the caller. Only after the method execution can you obtain and assign the return value.

The simple aspect in listing 13.2 monitors UI access calls and the thread executing them.

Listing 13.2 Aspect to log UI activities

```
package ajia.swing;

public aspect LogUIActivitiesAspect {
    before() : Swing.uiCall() {
        System.out.println("Executing:\n\t"
                           + thisJoinPointStaticPart.getSignature()
                           + "\n\t"
                           + Thread.currentThread() + "\n");
    }
}
```

The logging aspect uses the reusable `Swing` aspect you implemented in chapter 11 (listing 11.27). This aspect advises join points selected by the `Swing.uiCall()` pointcut to print the method signature and the caller thread.

When you compile and run the `Main` class with the logging aspect, you get output similar to the following:

```
Executing:
        void javax.swing.JFrame.setDefaultCloseOperation(int)
        Thread[main,5,main]

Executing:
        Container javax.swing.JFrame.getContentPane()
        Thread[main,5,main]

Executing:
        void javax.swing.JFrame.pack()
        Thread[main,5,main]

Executing:
        void javax.swing.JFrame.setVisible(boolean)
        Thread[main,5,main]

Executing:
        void javax.swing.table.DefaultTableModel.setValueAt(Object,
➥      int, int)
        Thread[main,5,main]

Executing:
        void javax.swing.JOptionPane.showMessageDialog(Component,
➥      Object)
        Thread[main,5,main]

Executing:
        int javax.swing.table.DefaultTableModel.getRowCount()
        Thread[main,5,main]

Row count = 4
Executing:
        Color javax.swing.JTable.getGridColor()
        Thread[main,5,main]

Grid color = javax.swing.plaf.ColorUIResource[r=153,g=153,b=153]
```

The output shows that all the calls are made by the main thread. The calls made after the call to `setVisible()` are in violation of the single-thread rule. The correct usage requires them to be executed only in the event-dispatching thread.

> **Automated testing**
>
> How would you automatically test that a conventional or AspectJ-based solution works as expected? With an aspect similar to `LogUIActivitiesAspect`, such a test is easy to write. All you need to do is replace the log statement with `assertTrue(EventQueue.isDispatchThread())`. This is essentially the same approach you used in chapter 11, where you reported any calls not made in the event-dispatching thread. The test code exercises components to be tested, whereas the aspect checks for adherence to the thread-safety rule. For example, the test code calls methods such as `updateStockQuote()`. Any misrouted calls lead to a test failure due to the advice. Although you could have used such a test in this chapter, the logging approach is easier to understand.

Now that you have a simple program illustrating the problem, let's see how to solve it using the conventional solution.

13.1.2 Solution: the conventional way

Before we discuss the AspectJ solution, let's look at a conventional solution; this will help you see the complexity and crosscutting nature of such a solution. You'll also understand the behavior expected from an AspectJ-based solution; ultimately, you want both solutions to behave identically. Listing 13.3 shows the modified `Main` class that implements the thread-safety rule using conventional techniques.

Listing 13.3 Conventional implementation of the Swing thread-safety rule

```
package ajia.main;

import ...

public class Main {
    public static void main(String[] args) {
        final JFrame appFrame = new JFrame();
        appFrame.setDefaultCloseOperation(JFrame.EXIT_ON_CLOSE);

        final DefaultTableModel tableModel
            = new DefaultTableModel(4,2);
        final JTable table = new JTable(tableModel);

        appFrame.getContentPane().add(table);

        appFrame.pack();
        appFrame.setVisible(true);              <-- Trigger point for single-thread rule
        final String value = "[0,0]";
        EventQueue.invokeLater(new Runnable() {
            public void run() {
                tableModel.setValueAt(value, 0, 0);     Asynchronous routing
            }
        });
```

```
        try {
            EventQueue.invokeAndWait(new Runnable() {
                public void run() {
                    JOptionPane.
                     showMessageDialog(appFrame,
                                "Press OK to continue");
                }
            });
        } catch (Exception ex) {
            // ignore...
        }

        final int[] rowCountValueArray = new int[1];
        try {
            EventQueue.invokeAndWait(new Runnable() {
                public void run() {
                    rowCountValueArray[0] = tableModel.getRowCount();
                }
            });
        } catch (Exception ex) {
            // ignore...
        }
        int rowCount = rowCountValueArray[0];

        System.out.println("Row count = " + rowCount);

        final Color[] gridColorValueArray = new Color[1];
        try {
            EventQueue.invokeAndWait(new Runnable() {
                public void run() {
                    gridColorValueArray[0] = table.getGridColor();
                }
            });
        } catch (Exception ex) {
            // ignore...
        }
        Color gridColor = gridColorValueArray[0];

        System.out.println("Grid color = " + gridColor);
    }
}
```

Synchronous routing to get user input

Synchronous routing to get primitive return value

Synchronous routing to get object's return value

In listing 13.3, you route all the calls that access or update the UI components' state by posting a request in `EventQueue`. You wrap each method call made after making the frame visible in an anonymous `Runnable` class, also known as a *routing class*. The `run()` method calls the intended operation. Although you use anonymous classes here, you could use named classes. You then call either `EventQueue.invokeLater()` or `EventQueue.invokeAndWait()` and pass an instance of the routing class. For calls that can be performed in a nonblocking manner, you use `invokeLater()`, whereas for calls that must block the caller, you use `invokeAndWait()`. Note the use of the `final` variables to comply with the Java rules that anonymous classes may access only the `final` variables from the outer method.

You could call all the methods after the frame is realized through a single worker object. It certainly would work here. Nevertheless, to mimic the real programming setup, where different parts of the program may make different calls, you deal with each operation independently.

I haven't handled exceptions, to limit the code's complexity. In most implementations, you'll need to deal with exceptions. In section 13.1.4, I'll show you how to deal with exceptions with the AspectJ-based solution (where the base solution and the exception-handling task are vastly simpler).

> **SwingWorker**
>
> Java 6 includes the `SwingWorker` class to simplify the conventional implementation of Swing concurrency control. It still requires manual coding for every Swing component operation called from a non-event-dispatching thread. The solution in this section doesn't use this class, to better mirror how you'll use AspectJ, which doesn't use or need the `SwingWorker` class.

When you compile the previous class along with the logging aspect and run it, you get the following output:

```
Executing:
        void javax.swing.JFrame.setDefaultCloseOperation(int)
        Thread[main,5,main]
Executing:
        Container javax.swing.JFrame.getContentPane()
        Thread[main,5,main]
Executing:
        void javax.swing.JFrame.pack()
        Thread[main,5,main]
Executing:
        void javax.swing.JFrame.setVisible(boolean)
        Thread[main,5,main]
Executing:
        void javax.swing.table.DefaultTableModel.setValueAt(Object,
➥       int, int)
        Thread[AWT-EventQueue-0,6,main]
Executing:
        void javax.swing.JOptionPane.showMessageDialog(Component,
➥       Object)
        Thread[AWT-EventQueue-0,6,main]
Executing:
        int javax.swing.table.DefaultTableModel.getRowCount()
        Thread[AWT-EventQueue-0,6,main]
Row count = 4
Executing:
        Color javax.swing.JTable.getGridColor()
        Thread[AWT-EventQueue-0,6,main]
Grid color = javax.swing.plaf.ColorUIResource[r=153,g=153,b=153]
```

As you can see, your hard work has paid off. All the calls made after making the frame visible are called in the event-dispatching thread (note the thread ID printed in the log). You no longer violate Swing's single-thread rule. But the complexity of the program is overwhelming. Let's see if you can use AspectJ to get rid of this complexity.

13.1.3 Solution: the AspectJ way

The key element of the solution is to use the worker object pattern explained in chapter 12. You select calls to all the required methods, use the pattern to create a new `Runnable` object, and hand over the object to the event queue for execution. Before releasing the object to the queue, you also check whether the caller thread is already the event-dispatching thread; in that case, you let the original method execute directly.

With the AspectJ-based solution, you'll implement Swing's single-thread rule without making any change to the `Main` class in listing 13.1. This aspect automatically routes any method call that accesses or modifies a Swing component through a non-event-dispatching thread.

You'll implement multiple versions of the solution, with each new solution building on the prior version. Note that each version of the solution uses the original `Main` class from listing 13.1 and `LogUIActivitiesAspect` from listing 13.2. In addition to making the final solution easy to understand, this step-by-step approach suggests a typical way you may want to develop an AspectJ-based solution that tackles new problems: start simple, and handle more issues as you progress.

Each version consists of an abstract aspect. Although you could implement one concrete aspect in each case, using an abstract aspect offers flexibility that can be important when you use the solutions in your system. For instance, you can include the unaltered abstract aspect in your system and write a simple subaspect, similar to the ones shown here, to handle your system-specific requirements. In section 13.1.4, we'll examine the kinds of customization you may need.

THE FIRST VERSION

In the first version of the solution, you route all the calls through `EventQueue.invokeAndWait()`. With this arrangement, the caller is blocked until the event-dispatching thread executes the operation. In practice, blocking the caller is often undesirable and should be limited to situations that warrant its usage. But the implementation does provide a simple solution to ensure compliance with Swing's single-thread rule. Later, you'll improve on this solution. Listing 13.4 shows the base abstract aspect that routes all join points selected by the `uiCall()` pointcut synchronously.

Listing 13.4 Base swing thread-safety aspect: first version

```
package ajia.swing;

import ...

import ajia.pattern.worker.*;

public abstract aspect SwingThreadSafetyAspect {
    public abstract pointcut uiCall();

    pointcut nonRoutedCall()
        : Swing.threadSafeCall()
          || within(SwingThreadSafetyAspect)
          || if(EventQueue.isDispatchThread());
```

❶ Pointcut selects UI method calls

❷ Pointcut selects all excluded join points

```
    pointcut routedCall()
        : uiCall() && ! nonRoutedCall();            ❸ Methods that need routing

    Object around() : routedCall() {
        RunnableWithReturn worker = new RunnableWithReturn() {
            public void run() {
                setReturnValue(proceed());
            }};

        try {
            EventQueue.invokeAndWait(worker);               ❹ Advice routes calls
        } catch (Exception ex) {
            // ... log exception
            return null;
        }
        return worker.getReturnValue();
    }
}
```

This abstract aspect provides the basic functionality of routing all the required calls through `EventQueue.invokeAndWait()` using the worker object pattern. Let's discuss the implementation in detail:

❶ The aspect declares `uiCall()` as an abstract pointcut. The concrete subaspects must provide a definition for this pointcut that selects all the calls to the Swing components.

❷ The `nonRoutedCall()` pointcut selects join points selected by either the `Swing.threadSafeCall()` pointcut or the join points in the aspect or those executed in the event-dispatching thread.

❸ The `routedCall()` pointcut combines the `uiCall()` pointcut with the negation of `nonRoutedCall()` to select the join points that needs to be routed through the event-dispatching thread.

❹ The advice calls `EventQueue.invokeAndWait()` with an anonymous class extending the `RunnableWithReturn` class. The `run()` method calls `proceed()` to carry out the original operation. The `invokeAndWait()` method makes the request and is blocked until the event-dispatching thread executes the `run()` method. The event-dispatching thread eventually calls the `run()` method, resulting in the invocation of the original call, and then unblocks the caller thread. The advice assigns the return value of the `proceed()` statement to the return value property of the worker object. It later obtains this return value by calling the `getReturnValue()` method on the worker object. This return-value management is a result of directly applying the worker object pattern discussed in chapter 12.

The `invokeAndWait()` method can throw `InterruptedException` and `InvocationTargetException`. For now, you'll ignore the exceptions and revisit this issue in section 13.1.4.

Now that you have the base aspect taking care of all the details, let's create a subaspect. The `DefaultSwingThreadSafetyAspect` subaspect defines the `uiCall()` pointcut, which select all methods in Swing components. Because you already have the reusable Swing aspect, defining the pointcut is an easy task. Listing 13.5 shows the `DefaultSwingThreadSafetyAspect` implementation.

Listing 13.5 The subaspect

```
package ajia.swing;

public aspect DefaultSwingThreadSafetyAspect
        extends SwingThreadSafetyAspect {
    public pointcut uiCall() : Swing.uiCall();
}
```

This subaspect ensures adherence to Swing's single-thread rule as long as all your UI components are based on Swing's components and models. If you have additional custom components that don't use any of the standard Swing models as a base class, you need to write a subaspect similar to the one in listing 13.5 and define the pointcut corresponding to all the appropriate methods in your classes. You may want to use the participant pattern (discussed in chapter 12) and write the subaspect as a nested aspect in the classes, which makes it easy to modify the pointcut when the implementation of the enclosing class changes.

Seeing is believing. To see that the calls are indeed routed as intended, you need an additional logging aspect that prints a log message before executing any UI operation in the control flow of `RunnableWithReturn.run()`. Listing 13.6 shows `LogRoutingDetailsAspect`, which implements such logging.

Listing 13.6 LogRoutingDetailsAspect.java

```
package ajia.swing;

import ...

public aspect LogRoutingDetailsAspect {
    pointcut duringSyncRouting ()
        : cflow(execution(* RunnableWithReturn.run()));

    before() : Swing.uiCall()
               && duringSyncRouting() {
        System.out.println("Executing operation synchronously");
    }
}
```

Because advice in all three aspects—`DefaultSwingThreadSafetyAspect`, `LogRoutingDetailsAspect`, and `LogUIActivitiesAspect`—share common join points, you need to control their precedence. You'd like the advice in `DefaultSwingThreadSafetyAspect` to apply first so that the routing takes place prior to any logging. You'd also like `LogRoutingDetailsAspect`'s advice to apply before that of `LogUIActivitiesAspect` so that you can see the routing information prior to execution. `PrecedenceControlAspect` (listing 13.7) implements this precedence control.

Listing 13.7 PrecedenceControlAspect.java

```
package ajia.swing;

public aspect PrecedenceControlAspect {
    declare precedence:
        DefaultSwingThreadSafetyAspect,
        LogRoutingDetailsAspect,
        LogUIActivitiesAspect;
}
```

The aspect in listing 13.7 declares that `DefaultSwingThreadSafetyAspect` has the highest precedence and that `LogUIActivitiesAspect` has the lowest precedence. Refer to chapter 6 for more details of aspect-precedence control.

Let's continue to use the driver program from listing 13.1. When you compile all the classes and aspects and run the test program, you get output similar to this:

```
Executing operation synchronously
Executing:
    void javax.swing.JFrame.setDefaultCloseOperation(int)
    Thread[AWT-EventQueue-0,6,main]

Executing operation synchronously
Executing:
    Container javax.swing.JFrame.getContentPane()
    Thread[AWT-EventQueue-0,6,main]

Executing operation synchronously
Executing:
    void javax.swing.JFrame.pack()
    Thread[AWT-EventQueue-0,6,main]

Executing operation synchronously
Executing:
    void javax.swing.JFrame.setVisible(boolean)
    Thread[AWT-EventQueue-0,6,main]

Executing operation synchronously
Executing:
    void javax.swing.table.DefaultTableModel.setValueAt(Object, int, int)
    Thread[AWT-EventQueue-0,6,main]

Executing operation synchronously
Executing:
    void javax.swing.JOptionPane.showMessageDialog(Component, Object)
    Thread[AWT-EventQueue-0,6,main]

Executing operation synchronously
Executing:
    int javax.swing.table.DefaultTableModel.getRowCount()
    Thread[AWT-EventQueue-0,6,main]

Row count = 4
Executing operation synchronously
Executing:
    Color javax.swing.JTable.getGridColor()
    Thread[AWT-EventQueue-0,6,main]

Grid color = javax.swing.plaf.ColorUIResource[r=122,g=138,b=153]
```

You can see from the output that all UI operations are executed in the event-dispatching thread. Further, all calls are executed in the control flow of `RunnableWithReturn.run()` synchronously with the caller. The return values printed are correct, too—for both primitive and object return types.

This first version of the solution lets you adhere to the Swing's single-thread rule, and you didn't have to touch any of the core classes. But this solution has the shortcoming of routing all the calls through `EventQueue.invokeAndWait()`, causing the caller to be blocked until the event-dispatching thread picks up the request and executes it. In the next section, you'll address this shortcoming.

THE SECOND VERSION

The central idea behind the second version is to detect the need to route a method synchronously or asynchronously based on its return type. If the method is returning a non-`void` type, you must execute the method synchronously. For these calls, you use `EventQueue.invokeAndWait()` along with `RunnableWithReturn`, just as you did in the first version. For all other operations, you assume that it's fine to invoke those operations asynchronously. For those calls, you use `EventQueue.invokeLater()` along with `Runnable`.

Listing 13.8 shows the second version of the `SwingThreadSafetyAspect` base aspect, which routes methods synchronously or asynchronously based on the return type of the method.

Listing 13.8 Base Swing thread-safety aspect: second version

```
package ajia.swing;

import ...

public abstract aspect SwingThreadSafetyAspect {
    ... uiCall(), nonRoutedCall(), and routedCall()
    ... unchanged from listing 13.4.

    pointcut voidReturnValueCall()                    ❶ Selects methods
        : call(void *.*(..));                            returning void

    pointcut syncRoutedCall()                                  ❷ Selects synchronous
        : routedCall() && !voidReturnValueCall();                 routing methods

    pointcut asyncRoutedCall()                                 ❸ Selects asynchronous
        : routedCall() && voidReturnValueCall();                  routing methods

    Object around()
        : syncRoutedCall() {
      RunnableWithReturn worker = new RunnableWithReturn() {
            public void run() {
                setReturnValue(proceed());
            }};                                                      ❹ Synchronous
                                                                       routing
        try {                                                          advice
            EventQueue.invokeAndWait(worker);
        } catch (Exception ex) {
            // ... log exception
```

```
                return null;
            }
            return worker.getReturnValue();
        }

        void around()
            : asyncRoutedCall() {
            Runnable worker = new Runnable() {
                public void run() {
                    proceed();
                }};

            EventQueue.invokeLater(worker);
        }
    }
```

4 Synchronous routing advice

5 Asynchronously routing advice

❶ You define the `voidReturnValueCall()` pointcut to select all the methods that don't return a value.

❷ You need to synchronously route the join points that return a value. For this purpose, you define `syncRoutedCall()`, which combines `routedCall()` with the negation of the `voidReturnValueCall()` pointcut.

❸ You need to asynchronously route join points that don't return a value. You define the `asyncRoutingCall()` pointcut by combining the `routedCall()` pointcut with the `voidReturnValueCall()` pointcut.

❹ You advise the `syncRoutedCalls()` pointcut to route the join point synchronously. Except for the pointcut used, the advice remains unchanged from the first version.

❺ You add a new advice to route calls asynchronously for the join points that don't return a value. The advice body is similar to the synchronous routing advice. You use `Runnable` instead of `RunnableWithReturn` to implement the worker object, because you don't need to consider the return value. To route asynchronously, you use `EventQueue.invokeLater()` instead of `EventQueue.invokeAndWait()`. Because `EventQueue.invokeLater()` doesn't throw a checked exception, you don't need the exception-handling logic in this advice.

The subaspect in listing 13.5 (which provides the definition for a pointcut corresponding to all UI operations) continues to work fine with this aspect.

Before you check how the solution works, let's include additional advice in the `LogRoutingDetailsAspect` aspect (listing 13.9) to differentiate between synchronously and asynchronously routed calls.

Listing 13.9 `LogRoutingDetailsAspect`

```
package ajia.swing;

import ...

public aspect LogRoutingDetailsAspect {
    pointcut duringSyncRouting()
        : cflow(execution(* RunnableWithReturn.run()));

    before() : Swing.uiCall() && duringSyncRouting() {
```

```
        System.out.println("Executing operation synchronously");
    }

    pointcut duringAsyncRouting()
        : cflow(execution(* Runnable.run()))
          && !duringSyncRouting();

    before() : Swing.uiCall() && duringAsyncRouting() {
        System.out.println("Executing operation asynchronously");
    }
}
```

This addition to the aspect logs any calls selected by the `Swing.uiCall()` pointcut that are carried out in the control flow of the `Runnable.run()` method but that aren't in the `RunnableWithReturn.run()` method's control flow.

Let's see how the solution fares. When you compile all the classes and aspects and run the driver program, you get output similar to this:

```
Executing operation asynchronously
Executing:
    void javax.swing.JFrame.setDefaultCloseOperation(int)
    Thread[AWT-EventQueue-0,6,main]

Executing operation synchronously
Executing:
    Container javax.swing.JFrame.getContentPane()
    Thread[AWT-EventQueue-0,6,main]

Executing operation asynchronously
Executing:
    void javax.swing.JFrame.pack()
    Thread[AWT-EventQueue-0,6,main]

Executing operation asynchronously
Executing:
    void javax.swing.JFrame.setVisible(boolean)
    Thread[AWT-EventQueue-0,6,main]

Executing operation asynchronously
Executing:
    void javax.swing.table.DefaultTableModel.setValueAt(Object, int, int)
    Thread[AWT-EventQueue-0,6,main]

Executing operation asynchronously
Executing:
    void javax.swing.JOptionPane.showMessageDialog(Component, Object)
    Thread[AWT-EventQueue-0,6,main]

Executing operation synchronously
Executing:
    int javax.swing.table.DefaultTableModel.getRowCount()
    Thread[AWT-EventQueue-0,6,main]

Row count = 4
Executing operation synchronously
Executing:
    Color javax.swing.JTable.getGridColor()
    Thread[AWT-EventQueue-0,6,main]

Grid color = javax.swing.plaf.ColorUIResource[r=122,g=138,b=153]
```

The output shows that the call to setValueAt(), which was invoked synchronously using the earlier version of the solution, is now being invoked asynchronously. This is what you expect, because it doesn't return any value. But note how JOptionPane.showMessageDialog() is also invoked asynchronously. This isn't the correct behavior; it needs to wait until the user has responded to the message dialog box before continuing. JOptionPane.showMessageDialog() returns void, and therefore your aspect routed it asynchronously. If you had invoked other JOptionPane methods—such as showConfirmDialog(), which returns a non-void return type—you'd get synchronous execution without needing further modifications. If you ran the program yourself, you'd see that getRowCount() and getGridColor() are executed before you close the message dialog box.

As you can see, the modified solution, taking its cue from the return value type, addresses most needs but behaves incorrectly in certain cases. Let's fix that.

THE THIRD VERSION

The idea behind the third version is to let subaspects have explicit control over methods that require synchronous routing. You'll select such methods in a pointcut regardless of their return value type. This way, methods such as JOptionPane.showMessageDialog() that return void can still be routed synchronously. Listing 13.10 shows an aspect that explicitly specifies the methods that must be routed synchronously.

Listing 13.10 Base Swing thread-safety aspect: third version

```
package ajia.swing;

import ...

public abstract aspect SwingThreadSafetyAspect {          ❶ Selects methods that must
                                                            be routed synchronously
    ... uiCall(),nonRoutedCall(), routedCall(),
    ... same as listing 13.4
                                                          Selects synchronous
    public abstract pointcut uiSyncCall();                routing methods ❷

    pointcut syncRoutedCall()
        : routedCall() && (!voidReturnValueCall() || uiSyncCall());

    pointcut asyncRoutedCall()
        : routedCall() && voidReturnValueCall() && !uiSyncCall();

    ... voidReturnValueCall() pointcut,                   Selects asynchronous ❸
    ... around advice to syncRoutedCall() and asyncRoutedCall()   routing
    ... unchanged from listing 13.8                               methods
}
```

❶ You add a new abstract pointcut, uiSyncCall(), to let subaspects define methods that they wish to route synchronously.

❷ You select join points that need synchronous routing by combining the negated voidReturnValueCall() pointcut and the uiSyncCall() pointcut.

❸ You must ensure that all methods selected by the uiSyncCall() pointcut—even those with the void return type—aren't executed asynchronously. You do this by combining the negated `uiSyncCall()` pointcut with the `routedCall()` and `voidReturnValueCall()` pointcuts.

You need to modify the subaspect to add a definition for `uiSyncCall()`. Listing 13.11 shows a modified version of `DefaultSwingThreadSafetyAspect` that explicitly specifies the methods needing synchronous routing.

Listing 13.11 Subaspect that lists synchronous execution join points explicitly

```
package ajia.swing;

public aspect DefaultSwingThreadSafetyAspect
      extends SwingThreadSafetyAspect {
    public pointcut uiCall() : Swing.uiCall();
    public pointcut uiSyncCall() : Swing.uiSyncCall();
}
```

The aspect in listing 13.11 defines `uiSyncCall()` as selected by the same-named pointcut in the `Swing` aspect to select all the calls to any method in `JOptionPane` or its subclasses. Listing 13.12 shows the modifications to the `Swing` aspect to include the `uiSyncCall()` pointcut.

Listing 13.12 Swing aspect

```
package ajia.swing;

import ...

public aspect Swing {
    ...

    public pointcut uiSyncCall()
        : call(* javax..JOptionPane+.*(..))
        /* || ... */;
}
```

You need to select the call join points because you'll want to weave the call sites (your code) instead of the execution site (Swing code).

You can modify the pointcut definition to add other join points that you wish to run synchronously with the caller. Notice the advantage of using a separate aspect to define pointcuts: most likely, such an aspect will become a part of your aspect library, so that any project can use these pointcuts effortlessly.

When you run the driver program, the message dialog box appears before `getRowCount()` and `getGridColor()` are invoked:

```
Executing operation asynchronously
Executing:
    void javax.swing.JFrame.setDefaultCloseOperation(int)
    Thread[AWT-EventQueue-0,6,main]

Executing operation synchronously
Executing:
    Container javax.swing.JFrame.getContentPane()
    Thread[AWT-EventQueue-0,6,main]

Executing operation asynchronously
```

```
Executing:
    void javax.swing.JFrame.pack()
    Thread[AWT-EventQueue-0,6,main]
Executing operation asynchronously
Executing:
    void javax.swing.JFrame.setVisible(boolean)
    Thread[AWT-EventQueue-0,6,main]
Executing operation asynchronously
Executing:
    void javax.swing.table.DefaultTableModel.setValueAt(Object, int, int)
    Thread[AWT-EventQueue-0,6,main]
Executing operation synchronously
Executing:
    void javax.swing.JOptionPane.showMessageDialog(Component, Object)
    Thread[AWT-EventQueue-0,6,main]
Executing operation synchronously
Executing:
    int javax.swing.table.DefaultTableModel.getRowCount()
    Thread[AWT-EventQueue-0,6,main]
Row count = 4
Executing operation synchronously
Executing:
    Color javax.swing.JTable.getGridColor()
    Thread[AWT-EventQueue-0,6,main]
Grid color = javax.swing.plaf.ColorUIResource[r=122,g=138,b=153]
```

The output is nearly identical to that for the conventional solution. The only difference is the additional log statement for monitoring synchronous versus asynchronous execution.

Annotations for routing

An alternative way to write pointcuts for Swing thread safety uses annotations such as `@Sync`, `@Async`, and `@ThreadSafe`. Here, methods carry an appropriate annotation and pointcuts select methods based on the annotations they carry. But for Swing, this won't work well, because the Swing code (as well as your custom components) must be modified to attach such annotations. Any missed annotations in either case will lead to incorrect routing. Therefore, it's best to study the API to define the needed pointcuts. For the more general case, the annotation-based approach often works better. You'll see an example in section 13.2 and 13.3.

You now have a complete solution that implements Swing's single-thread rule without requiring any modification to the core classes. Applying this solution will guarantee compliance with the threading rule without the need to make system-wide modifications. When you apply this aspect to real-world problems, you're likely to need a few enhancements that we consider next.

13.1.4 Improving the solution

In this section, we'll discuss a few enhancements to the previous solution, such as handling exceptions and optimizing the solution using system-specific knowledge.

DEALING WITH EXCEPTIONS

Exception handling poses an interesting challenge when the exceptions are thrown by asynchronously routed calls. For such calls, because the caller isn't going to wait for the execution to be complete, it doesn't have access to the exceptions thrown. Further, exceptions are thrown in the control flow of the event-dispatching thread and not the caller thread. A reasonable strategy to deal with these exceptions is to set a listener that will be notified if the operation fails.

Let's modify the first around advice of the final version of the `SwingThreadSafetyAspect` aspect. All you need to do is surround the `proceed()` statement with a `try/catch` block, as shown in the following snippet. In the `catch` block, you can perform any operations necessary to match your exception-handling policy (such as logging it or passing it to an exception listener). You can also rethrow the exception after wrapping the caught exception in a runtime exception:

```
void around() : asyncRoutedCall(){
    Runnable worker = new Runnable() {
        public void run() {
            try {
                proceed();
            } catch (Exception ex) {
                ... deal with exception
                ... call exception listener, log it, etc.
                ... and then optionally rethrow it after wrapping
            }
        }};
    EventQueue.invokeLater(worker);
}
```

Notice how easy it was to modify the exception-handling strategy. If you weren't using AOP, and you employed anonymous classes, you'd have to modify every method that routed the call asynchronously. If you used named classes to carry out the operations, you'd have to modify each of those classes. With such widespread modifications, ensuring consistent implementation becomes a daunting task. Using a conventional solution, it's possible to implement the expected behavior the first time—with a lot of labor and diligence. But ensuring continual adherence to the policy becomes challenging. With AspectJ, making changes in the exception-handling strategy is easy. For example, if you decide to log an exception in addition to passing it to an exception listener, all you need to change is the aspect and nothing else. This is the power of AOP.

For synchronous invocation, you throw a functionality-specific runtime exception and then write another aspect to unwrap it and throw the exception originally thrown by the operation. This way, the clients need not be aware of the routing and issues related to it.

AVOIDING THE OVERHEAD

In the solution so far, you've selected *all* the calls to the UI methods. This is inefficient because before every call, the aspect invokes `EventQueue.isDispatchThread()` in the `if()` pointcut. Usually the overhead isn't high enough to warrant modifications. But if the overhead is a problem for your system, you can use the typical technique of limiting join points selected by a pointcut to certain packages. For example, when the code updated by a non-event-dispatching thread is limited to certain classes and/or packages, you can limit automatic routing to only those modules. You can do this easily with pointcuts that include `within()` and `withincode()`, as described in chapter 3.

Instead of using `DefaultSwingThreadSafetyAspect`, you can use your own aspect to limit the applicability of the routing advice, as shown here:

```
public aspect LimitedSwingThreadSafetyAspect
    extends SwingThreadSafetyAspect {

    public pointcut uiCall()
        : Swing.uiCall()
          && within(ajia.network..*);

    public pointcut uiSyncCall()
        : Swing.uiSyncCall()
          && within(ajia.network..*);
}
```

In this aspect, you restrict the application of `SwingThreadSafetyAspect` to calls made from `ajia.network` and all its direct and indirect subpackages.

You can also use your own aspect to route a group of calls as a batch. For example, you may want to update multiple components in response to a network event. Although `DefaultSwingThreadSafetyAspect` will get the job done, by routing calls in a batch, you can improve efficiency. To implement such behavior, you need to create a method (perhaps following the Extract Method refactoring) that makes the calls to be routed as a batch. Then, you select that method with either the `uiCall()` or the `uiSyncCall()` pointcut.

If you use these kinds of optimizations, I strongly recommend that you also use the policy-enforcement aspect developed in chapter 11, which detects the violations of Swing's single-thread rule during the development and testing phases. This way, wrong assumptions, if any, will be caught early on.

Let's discuss another usage of the worker object pattern to improve the responsiveness of UI applications.

13.2 Improving the responsiveness of UI applications

Although we've focused on the use of the worker object pattern to ensure thread safety, you can use a small variation on the same theme to improve the responsiveness of UI applications. For example, a common need in UI applications is to avoid locking the GUI when performing a time-consuming task. Let's say you want to implement a time-consuming task, such as sending an email. You don't want to lock up the UI while the email is being sent. Let's consider the example class in listing 13.13.

Listing 13.13 Main.java

```
package ajia.main;

import ...

public class Main {
    public static void main(String[] args) {
        JFrame appFrame = new JFrame();
        appFrame.setDefaultCloseOperation(JFrame.EXIT_ON_CLOSE);
        JButton sendEmailButton = new JButton("Send Emails");
        sendEmailButton.addActionListener(new ActionListener() {
            public void actionPerformed(ActionEvent e) {
                sendEmails();
            }
        });
        appFrame.getContentPane().add(sendEmailButton);

        appFrame.pack();
        appFrame.setVisible(true);
    }

    private static void sendEmails() {
        try {
            // simulate long execution...
            System.out.println("Executing in thread:\n\t"
                               + Thread.currentThread());
            Thread.sleep(20000);
            System.out.println("Completed execution in thread:\n\t"
                               + Thread.currentThread());
        } catch (InterruptedException ex) {
        }
    }
}
```

Compile and run this program, and click the Send Emails button. The whole GUI is locked for about 20 seconds. The reason is that `sendEmails()` is executed in the event-dispatching thread, preventing it from refreshing the GUI. Locking up the GUI in this way is undesirable, and yet you'll see it happen frequently. The reason, I suspect, is the invasiveness associated with implementing a solution that performs operations in the background. The result is that asynchronous executions are often implemented only for *really* time-consuming operations, and other not-so-time-consuming operations are allowed to execute directly in the caller thread.

Implementing the asynchronous execution of a thread is simple when you use AspectJ. All you need to do is use the reusable aspect shown in listing 13.10 and provide concrete subaspects of it. We first introduced this aspect in chapter 12, listing 12.4, to demonstrate the worker object pattern. Let's enhance it to show how you can avoid locking the GUI by asynchronously routing invocations of time-consuming operations. The reusable implementation in listing 13.14 enables the subaspect to improve responsiveness by providing the definition for a pointcut.

Listing 13.14 Abstract aspect to route asynchronously

```
package ajia.concurrent;

import ...

public abstract aspect AsynchronousExecutionAspect {
    private Executor executor = Executors.newCachedThreadPool();

    public abstract pointcut asyncOperation();

    void around() : asyncOperation() {
        Runnable worker = new Runnable() {
            public void run() {
                proceed();
            }
        };
        executor.execute(worker);
    }

    public void setExecutor(Executor executor) {
        this.executor = executor;
    }
}
```

The aspect in listing 13.14 dispatches the operation selected by the `asyncOperation()` pointcut. The `setExecutor()` method lets you plug in an appropriate executor following the classic strategy design pattern. If you're using this aspect in a container that supports dependency injection, you can easily externalize the configuration of this aspect.

Let's apply the annotation-driven participant pattern (ADPP) discussed in chapter 12 to implement a subaspect. Listing 13.15 shows an aspect that selects all operations marked with the `@Slow` annotation.

Listing 13.15 SlowAnnotationDrivenAsynchronousExecutionAspect.java

```
package ajia.concurrent;

import ajia.characteristics.Slow;

public aspect SlowAnnotationDrivenAsynchronousExecutionAspect
        extends AsynchronousExecutionAspect {
    public pointcut asyncOperation()
        : execution(@Slow void *(..));
}
```

As we discussed in chapter 12, using an annotation that describes a subjective characteristic such as `@Slow` may be less desirable than an objective annotation such as `@Timing`. The tradeoff is the simplicity of `@Slow` versus the versatility of `@Timing`. In a given project and with a given team composition, making an appropriate choice is often easy.

The only thing left to do is to mark the `sendEmails()` method with the `@Slow` annotation. Listing 13.16 shows the modified version of listing 13.13.

Listing 13.16 `Main` with slow methods annotated

```
package ajia.main;

import ...

public class Main {
    ...

    @Slow
    private static void sendEmails() {
        ...
    }
}
```

Compile and run the program. When you click the Send Emails button, the GUI won't lock. You'll also see that each call is routed through a separate thread asynchronously (the following output produced after clicking the button three times and then waiting about 20 seconds):

```
Executing in thread:
    Thread[pool-1-thread-1,5,main]
Executing in thread:
    Thread[pool-1-thread-2,5,main]
Executing in thread:
    Thread[pool-1-thread-3,5,main]
Completed execution in thread:
    Thread[pool-1-thread-1,5,main]
Completed execution in thread:
    Thread[pool-1-thread-2,5,main]
Completed execution in thread:
    Thread[pool-1-thread-3,5,main]
```

Let's move our attention away from Swing applications. In the next section, as a sample of modularizing classic thread-safety patterns using AspectJ, we'll examine the read-write lock pattern.

13.3 Modularizing the read-write lock pattern

The read-write lock pattern offers maximal liveliness while ensuring the integrity of objects. It's an appropriate pattern in situations where you expect the reader threads to access the object more frequently than the writer threads, and the operations are expensive (to justify the use of acquiring and releasing locks). The fundamental idea is that any number of readers can simultaneously read the state of the object as long as no thread is modifying the state at the same time.

Implementing this pattern in a conventional way requires adding certain code to each method that reads or modifies the state of an object. In this section, you'll modularize the pattern using AspectJ. We'll introduce a reusable aspect that enables you to implement this pattern with your classes just by adding a simple subaspect.

13.3.1 Implementation: the conventional way

Consider an implementation of the `InventoryService` interface from appendix A that uses a grid-based cache (implemented as the `Map` interface) to avoid round trips to the database. Because inventory is queried more frequently than it's modified, and because access to the grid-based map is expensive, using the read-write lock pattern for such an implementation is appropriate.

The read-write lock pattern uses a pair of locks: the read lock and the write lock. Multiple threads can simultaneously acquire the read lock as long as the write lock hasn't been acquired. Only one thread, on the other hand, can acquire the write lock at any moment as long as no read locks have been acquired. Each operation in the class that needs this pattern must acquire and release the read lock for read-only operations and the write lock for state-altering operations. When the operation is over, it must release the lock that it acquired. Listing 13.17 shows the `InventoryServiceCachedImpl` class with the necessary modifications.

Listing 13.17 `InventoryServiceCachedImpl` with the read-write lock pattern

```
package ajia.service.impl;

import ...

public class InventoryServiceCachedImpl implements InventoryService {
    private Map<Long, InventoryItem> inventory;

    private ReadWriteLock lock = new ReentrantReadWriteLock();     <- Creates read write lock

    public void addProduct(Product product, int quantity) {
        lock.writeLock().lock();                                   <- Acquires write lock
        try {
            InventoryItem inventoryItem
                = inventory.get(product.getId());
            inventoryItem.replenish(quantity);
        } finally {
            lock.writeLock().unlock();                             <- Releases write lock
        }
    }

    public void removeProduct(Product product, int quantity) {
        lock.writeLock().lock();                                   <- Acquires write lock
        try {
            InventoryItem inventoryItem
                = inventory.get(product.getId());
            inventoryItem.deplete(quantity);
        } finally {
            lock.writeLock().unlock();                             <- Releases write lock
        }
    }

    public boolean isProductAvailable(Product product, int quantity) {
        lock.readLock().lock();                <- Acquires read lock
        try {
            InventoryItem inventoryItem
                = inventory.get(product.getId());
            return inventoryItem.getQuantityOnHand() >= quantity;
        } finally {
            lock.readLock().unlock();          <- Releases read lock
        }
```

```
    }

    public void setInventory(Map<Long, InventoryItem> inventory) {
        lock.writeLock().lock();           <-- Acquires write lock
        try {
            this.inventory = inventory;
        } finally {
            lock.writeLock().unlock();     <-- Releases write lock
        }
    }
}
```

You add a lock object of the `ReentrantReadWriteLock` type that allows the same thread to take a lock in a reentrant manner; that way, a thread can take a lock even if it's already in possession of it (you don't need reentrancy for the implementation as shown, but it's a good idea anyway). The `isProductAvailable()` method is a read-only method: you take and release the read lock. In contrast, because the other methods modify the state of the object, you take and release the write lock. The use of `try/finally` ensures that the locks are released even when the operation aborts due to an exception.

Clearly, the implementation is invasive even for a class as simple as `InventoryServiceCachedImpl`. You must similarly modify each class that needs this pattern. Any missed methods will result in potentially fatal program behavior. Further, you must make sure that a method that takes a read lock releases only the read lock and not a write lock, and vice versa.

13.3.2 Implementation: the AspectJ way

The core concept behind the AspectJ-based solution is to create an aspect that encapsulates this pattern. You can then avoid the need to modify each class. Further, because the pattern is reusable, you want the aspect to be reusable as well.

IMPLEMENTING THE BASE ASPECT

To achieve this goal, let's write a base aspect that implements the read-write lock pattern. Listing 13.18 shows the implementation of the pattern in an abstract aspect.

Listing 13.18 Base read-write lock aspect

```
package ajia.concurrent;

import ...

public abstract aspect ReadWriteLockAspect
    perthis(readOperation() || writeOperation()) {          <-- 1 Aspect association

    public abstract pointcut readOperation();               <-- 2 Read operations
    public abstract pointcut writeOperation();              <-- 3 Write operations

    private ReadWriteLock lock
        = new ReentrantReadWriteLock();                     4 Locks object

    Object around() : readOperation() {                     5 Read operation management
        lock.readLock().lock();
        try {
            return proceed();
```

```
        } finally {
            lock.readLock().unlock();
        }
    }

    Object around() : writeOperation() {
        lock.writeLock().lock();
        try {
            return proceed();
        } finally {
            lock.writeLock().unlock();
        }
    }
}
```

(5) Read operation management

(6) Write operation management

(1) Each read-write managed object needs its own lock object. Using the `perthis()` association, you associate a new aspect instance with each `this` object that matches the `readOperation()` or `writeOperation()` pointcut. (See section 6.2.2 to learn more about aspect association.) This arrangement lets you effectively introduce the lock object in each read-write lock managed class without knowing about the specific type of the object.

(2) The concrete subaspects should implement the abstract `readOperation()` pointcut to select methods that don't modify the state of the object.

(3) Similarly, the abstract `writeOperation()` pointcut should select methods that modify the state of the object.

(4) Because a separate aspect instance is created for each `this` object at the matched join point, effectively a separate `lock` object gets associated with each advised object.

(5) The around advice to the `readOperation()` pointcut locks and releases the read lock.

(6) Similarly, the around advice to the `writeOperation()` pointcut locks and releases the write lock.

Now you have a base aspect ready to be extended by subaspects.

IMPLEMENTING SUBASPECTS

To enable the read-write lock pattern, you need to create one or more subaspects, which will make the appropriate classes participate in the base aspect's functionality. Because the subaspects need to select read and write operations, using annotations to simplify the selection is a good idea. Let's pursue this by creating the annotation shown in listing 13.19 that can mark a method as a read operation.

Listing 13.19 Annotation to mark a read-only method

```
package ajia.characteristics;

import ...

@Target(ElementType.METHOD)
public @interface ReadOnly {
}
```

Although you could create an annotation to mark a write operation, you can also infer the same from the lack of `@ReadOnly`. You can also use annotations such `@Static` and `@Stateless` to avoid taking any locks at all for methods that don't need any locks, such as instance methods that don't access the object's state.

`@ReadOnly` is an annotation that describes an objective characteristic and as such says nothing about the locking mechanism. Therefore, to indicate the use of read-write lock pattern, you create the `@ReadWriteLockManaged` annotation, as shown in listing 13.20. Note the use of `@Inherited` to apply the annotation to subclasses.

Listing 13.20 Annotation to mark a class suitable for the read-write lock pattern

```
package ajia.concurrent;

import ...

@Target(ElementType.TYPE)
@Inherited
public @interface ReadWriteLockManaged {
}
```

Finally, you're ready to write the subaspect based on these annotations. Listing 13.21 shows an annotation-driven subaspect to apply the read-write lock pattern.

Listing 13.21 Annotation-driven subaspect for the read-write lock pattern

```
package ajia.concurrent;

import ajia.characteristics.ReadOnly;

public aspect AnnotationDrivenReadWriteAspect
    extends ReadWriteLockAspect {

    public pointcut readWriteLockManaged()
        : execution(* (@ReadWriteLockManaged *).*(..));      ❶ Read-write managed operations

    public pointcut readOperation()
        : execution(@ReadOnly * *(..))
          && readWriteLockManaged();                         ❷ Read operations

    public pointcut writeOperation()
        : !readOperation() && readWriteLockManaged();        ❸ Write operations
}
```

The aspect extends the `ReadWriteLockAspect` base aspect and defines abstract pointcuts to select methods based on the annotations they carry. Let's examine its implementation in detail:

❶ The `readWriteLockManaged()` pointcut selects the execution of any method in a type marked with the `@ReadWriteLockManaged` annotation. Although you could explicitly use the `!static` qualifier to exclude static methods (because they shouldn't be applied with a locking scheme), because the base aspect uses the `perthis()` association, it excludes any static methods making the use of `!static` redundant. If you use an annotation such as `@Static` or `@Stateless` to mark methods that don't need any locks, you augment this pointcut with `&& !execution(@Static * *(..))` or `&& !execution(@Stateless * *(..))`.

2. The `readOperation()` pointcut selects the execution of methods marked with `@ReadOnly` in a read-write lock managed type.
3. The `writeOperation()` pointcut selects methods not selected by the `readOperation()` pointcut. Selecting the write operations using the negation of `readOperation()` is a defensive approach; it's better to err on the side of safety by declaring that all the methods that aren't read-only operations are state-altering operations.

Now comes the fun part of enabling this aspect for the `InventoryServiceCachedImpl` class. As shown in listing 13.22, you need to mark the read-only methods in this class with `@ReadOnly`. You also need to mark the class with the `@ReadWriteLockManaged` annotation (you have a choice in this regard, as you'll see later in this section).

Listing 13.22 Annotated `InventoryServiceCachedImpl` class

```
package ajia.banking;

import ...

@ReadWriteLockManaged
public class InventoryServiceCachedImpl implements InventoryService {
    private Map<Long, InventoryItem> inventory;

    public void addProduct(Product product, int quantity) {
        InventoryItem inventoryItem = inventory.get(product.getId());
        inventoryItem.replenish(quantity);
    }

    public void removeProduct(Product product, int quantity) {
        InventoryItem inventoryItem = inventory.get(product.getId());
        inventoryItem.deplete(quantity);
    }

    @ReadOnly
    public boolean isProductAvailable(Product product, int quantity) {
        InventoryItem inventoryItem = inventory.get(product.getId());
        return inventoryItem.getQuantityOnHand() >= quantity;
    }

    public void setInventory(Map<Long, InventoryItem> inventory) {
        this.inventory = inventory;
    }
}
```

Compared to listing 13.17, you removed the embedded read-write lock-management code and added annotations to denote the read-write lock managed class and read-only operations.

Although this scheme works fine, a potentially undesirable coupling exists between the class and the `@ReadWriteLockManaged` annotation. Unlike marking methods with `@ReadOnly` (which represents an intrinsic characteristic of those methods), classes suggesting a participation in the read-write lock pattern may not be desirable if the same class is to be used in multiple systems with varying concurrency characteristics and needs (as well as the injected grid-based map's implementation). You can solve this problem by using the bridged participation variation of ADPP that we examined in chapter 12. Instead of marking the class with the annotation, you use the aspect in listing 13.23 to supply a set of classes with the needed annotation.

Listing 13.23 Participating aspect to supply annotations

```
package ajia.service.impl;

import ...

public aspect InventoryReadWriteLockParticipation {
    declare @type: InventoryServiceCachedImpl: @ReadWriteLockManaged;
}
```

If you want to provide thread-safe access to other classes, you can modify the declaration or add additional aspects to supply the annotations for those classes. You may, for example, use a type pattern to declare a set of classes as participants in the read-write lock concurrency control.

You now have a reusable implementation for a reusable pattern. You can make these aspects a part of your library and avoid reinventing the wheel each time. By doing so, you'll be assured that the pattern is being implemented correctly and consistently.

13.4 Summary

Concurrency control is inherently complex. The conventional solutions make it even more so by requiring system-wide invasive changes. The conceptual reusability of the few thread-safety patterns is lost in the conventional implementations. AOP fills this gap between concepts and implementation by modularizing the pattern into reusable aspects.

Swing's single-thread rule is simple for component developers but often requires system-wide changes if you're using those components in multithreaded UI applications. The solution we've presented eliminates the need for invasive changes while ensuring consistent behavior. By employing reusable aspects, you make adhering to Swing's thread-safety rule as easy as extending that aspect and providing a few pointcut definitions. With AspectJ, you have a simple model for thread safety that doesn't burden you with complex usage.

Similarly, by introducing a reusable aspect encapsulating the read-write lock pattern, implementing this feature of thread safety is as easy as adding a few simple aspects and marking program elements with annotations. You no longer have to hit the books every time you need to understand exactly how the pattern is supposed to work. Instead, you need to know which methods access the state in a read-only manner and which ones alter the state.

You can extend the ideas presented in this chapter to offer interesting solutions to otherwise laborious work. For example, you can extend aspects from the Swing UI solution to provide thread-safe access to your own classes. You can then ensure that only a preassigned thread is able to access objects of those classes and that other threads route the calls through the preassigned thread using an aspect.

The power of AOP and the patterns should be clear to you by now. In the following chapters, you'll use these patterns to solve other complex crosscutting concerns using AOP.

14 Managing transactions

This chapter covers

- Transaction management overview
- Implementing transaction management aspect
- Implementing Spring's transaction management
- Automatically retrying transactions

Consider the e-commerce example in appendix A. When you add an item to a cart, you remove it from the inventory. What would happen if the operation failed after you added an item to the cart but before it was removed from the inventory? The system would be in an inconsistent state, with the same item counted as being in the shopping cart and in the inventory. To prevent this undesirable situation, you need to execute both operations in a transaction. A *transaction* defines a unit of work that ensures that the system remains in a consistent state before and after its execution. If any operations within a transaction fail, then all of them fail, leaving the system as it was before the transaction started.

Transaction management has four properties: atomicity, consistency, isolation, and durability (ACID). I recommend *Java Transaction Design Strategies* by Mark Richards (Lulu.com, 2006; http://www.infoq.com/minibooks/JTDS) for more information. I also recommend "Distributed transactions in Spring, with and without XA," by David Syer (http://www.javaworld.com/javaworld/jw-01-2009/jw-01-spring-transactions.html).

Transaction management is perhaps the most widely known crosscutting concern in enterprise applications. Most enterprise applications use persistent storage or a messaging system that leads to the need for the transaction management. Traditional implementations of this crosscutting functionality require embedding the transaction management code in many methods. Owing to its crosscutting nature, AOP offers a compelling and elegant solution to implement this functionality.

In this chapter, we'll examine how AOP helps to modularize transaction management. You'll implement an aspect usable with either Spring's proxy-based or AspectJ's byte-code-based AOP. This will provide you a template to implement transaction-like functionality. Although you'll use Spring's transaction-management API for implementation, you should be able to map it to other APIs. We'll also examine Spring's prebuilt aspects for transaction management. Furthermore, you'll implement an AOP solution to retry failed transactions automatically.

Let's begin by examining how transaction management is implemented with conventional and AOP techniques.

14.1 Transaction management implementations

The core idea behind transaction management is simple: start a transaction at the beginning of a unit of work, perform the work, and commit or roll back the transaction. Typically, you commit if no exceptions are thrown during the work. If an exception is thrown, you typically roll back the transaction. Let's see how this scheme translates into implementations.

14.1.1 Conventional implementation

With a conventional implementation, every method that has a transactional requirement must include transaction-management code. The following snippet illustrates this scheme, which uses Spring's transaction-management API (any pseudocode won't be very different):

```
public void businessMethod() {
    TransactionAttribute ta = ...                                        <-- 1 Creates transaction attribute
    TransactionStatus ts = transactionManager.getTransaction(ta);        <-- 2 Starts transaction
    try {
        ... business operation ... uses transactional resources
        transactionManager.commit(ts);                                   <-- 3 Deals with normal outcome
    } catch (Throwable ex) {
        if(ta.rollbackOn(ex)) {
            transactionManager.rollback(ts);
        } else {                                                             4 Deals with exceptions
            transactionManager.commit(ts);
        }
        throw ex;
    }
}
```

Here is roughly what's going on in this snippet:

❶ Transaction attributes specify properties of the transaction about to be started. The common properties include propagation, isolation, read-onlyness, timeout, and rollback behavior for exceptions.

❷ The method gets a transaction from the transaction manager. The propagation attribute governs whether the transaction manager should start a new transaction or continue to use the ongoing one, if any.

❸ Upon successful completion of the operation, the method asks the transaction manager to commit the transaction. Depending on the transaction status, the transaction manager may or may not commit the transaction to the underlying resource. For example, if the status indicates that it isn't a new transaction, no commit takes place at the current level, leaving the decision to the outer transactional method.

❹ Upon throwing an exception, depending on the exception type, the transaction manager is asked to commit or roll back. Similar to ❸, the transaction manager may or may not commit or roll back the transaction yet. The method then throws the caught exception.

The transactional method must use the resources associated with the current transaction throughout its control-flow. For example, if a business operation uses a JDBC connection, it must use the same connection during the entire transaction. Specifically, it must not create a new connection for individual nested operations. In a typical implementation, the transaction manager binds the resources associated with a transaction to a thread-local. The business operations access the thread-local when they need a resource. Of course, a good API hides the use of a thread-local, removing some burden from you.

As you can see, a conventional implementation of transaction management causes code tangling and code scattering. You can correct this situation using AOP.

14.1.2 AOP implementation

With the AOP implementation, aspects take care of transaction management. This allows business modules to focus on their core functionality:

```
public void businessMethod() {
    ... business operation ... uses transactional resources
}
```

The aspect advises such methods with the transaction-management logic.

```
aspect TransactionManagementAspect {
    private TransactionManager transactionManager;

    pointcut transactionalOp() : ...

    Object around() : transactionalOp() {
        TransactionAttribute ta = ...
        TransactionStatus ts = transactionManager.getTransaction(ta);
        try {
            Object ret = proceed();
```

```
                transactionManager.commit(ts);
                return ret;
            } catch (Throwable ex) {
                if(ta.rollbackOn(ex)) {
                    transactionManager.rollback(ts);
                } else {
                    transactionManager.commit(ts);
                }
                throw ex;
            }
        }
        ...
    }
```

The aspect includes a pointcut, and it advises join points selected by the pointcut to surround the selected join points with the transaction-management logic. Notice how closely the around advice resembles a transactional method in a conventional implementation, with the `proceed()` call replacing the business logic.

As usual, the devil is in the details, which we'll explore by writing a complete implementation of a transaction-management aspect in section 14.4. Let's proceed toward that.

14.2 Transaction-management players

Transaction management involves many players that must do a delicate dance to get the desired effect. In this section, you'll gain familiarity with these players to help you implement transaction-management aspects.

14.2.1 Transaction management in architecture

Figure 14.1 shows a typical layering of enterprise applications. The UI layer builds on top of the service layer, which in turn uses the repository layer. The repository uses transactional resources such as a JDBC data source, JPA entity manager, Hibernate session, or JMS session. The service layer demarcates transactions.

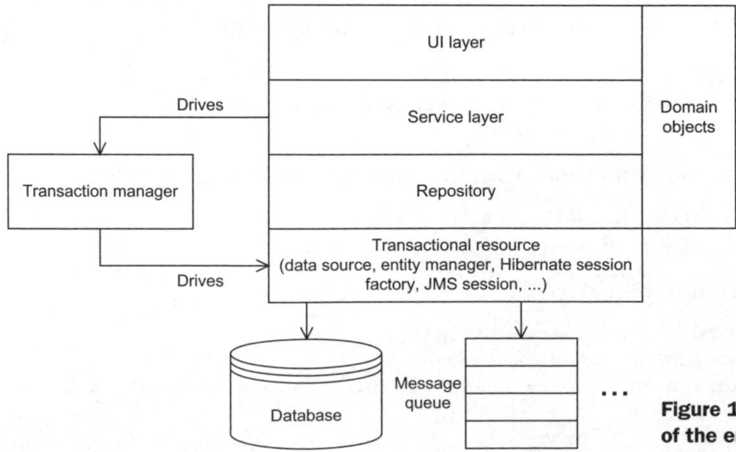

Figure 14.1 Layered architecture of the enterprise system

Typically, the service operations represent use cases that should be atomic. Therefore, those operations drive transactions. Upon starting a transaction, the manager binds the transactional resources to the current thread. The repository layer must use the bound resources throughout the transaction.

Although demarcating transactions at the service layer is common today, it isn't the only possibility. In an alternative design, domain objects may demarcate the transaction boundaries. We'll discuss the reasoning behind such a choice in chapter 16.

14.2.2 Transaction management: one concept, too many implementations

A transaction manager provides a way to start a new transaction and commit or roll back the current transaction. But each transactional resource provides a different way to perform these basic operations. For example, a JDBC connection doesn't have an explicit way to begin a transaction and provides the `commit()` and `rollback()` methods on the `Connection` type. On the other hand, Hibernate requires calling `beginTransaction()` on the `Session` object and provides `commit()` or `rollback()` on the returned `Transaction` object. Similarly, other persistence technologies such as JPA and messaging technologies such as JMS have their own API for transaction management. JTA attempts to provide a unified API. But it targets distributed transaction management and requires you to use a transaction manager typically available in an application server. All of these implementations are different, with no unifying API. Therefore, if you switch from one technology to another, you need to rewrite a good portion of code.

Although transaction management modularized through an aspect hides many issues with incompatible implementations, it's still beneficial to use a layer of abstraction to simplify development of aspects and to let you test aspects separately from the underlying transaction-management implementation. Spring provides one such abstraction with a simple interface and implementations for most commonly used technologies.

14.2.3 Transaction-management abstraction

Let's see an example of a transaction-management abstraction: Spring's `PlatformTransactionManager` interface (listing 14.1) and implementation. You'll later use this abstraction in a transaction-management aspect.

Listing 14.1 Spring's transaction-management abstraction

```
package org.springframework.transaction;

import ...

public interface PlatformTransactionManager {
    TransactionStatus getTransaction(TransactionDefinition definition);
    void commit(TransactionStatus status);
    void rollback(TransactionStatus status);
}
```

The implementation of the `getTransaction()` method obtains a transaction based on the transaction definition (propagation, read-onlyness, isolation, and timeout) provided. By default, the implementation associates the current transaction with the current thread. The returned object contains information about the transaction that must be passed to the `commit()` or `rollback()` method. The return object can also be used to mark the transaction as rollback only.

The Spring Framework provides the implementation of this interface for various transactional technologies such as JDBC, JPA, Hibernate, TopLink, JMS, and JTA. Therefore, it makes a good choice to form a basis for a transaction-management solution.

In the next section, you'll use this abstraction through aspects.

14.3 Aspect implementation choices

To implement transaction management, you can use Spring's proxy-based or AspectJ's byte-code based AOP. In this section, we'll examine the characteristics of both and use this information to implement a transaction-management aspect.

14.3.1 Proxy-based AOP

Consider the typical enterprise application architecture in figure 14.1. Because the service layer encapsulates business functionality, service objects provide a good place to mark transaction boundaries. Furthermore, because service objects are often Spring beans, the proxy-based choice fits the bill well.

Figure 14.2 shows the overall structure of cooperating objects to implement the transaction-management functionality.

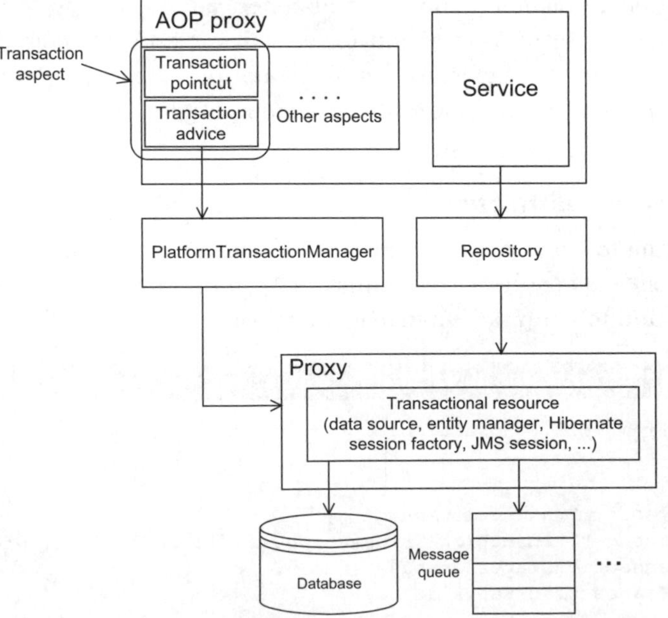

Figure 14.2 Structure of transaction management implemented in a proxy-based AOP framework

Let's examine the roles played by the various objects in the figure:

- An AOP proxy wraps the service bean following the general AOP proxy arrangement discussed in chapter 9. The proxy includes a transactional aspect, whose pointcut selects the transactional methods. The advice uses the transaction manager to start and stop a transaction.
- The transaction manager, in turn, drives the transactional resources. For example, the transaction manager for a JDBC data source may call the `commit()` or `rollback()` method on a `Connection` object.
- The service accesses the repository. The repository uses the same transactional resources as those driven by the transaction manager.
- To satisfy the requirement that the same transactional resources must be used throughout a transaction, a transactional resource is often wrapped in a proxy. The proxy, upon requesting a new resource, looks up a thread-local to check if there is already a resource bound to the current transaction, and returns it. Otherwise, it creates a new resource and binds it to the thread-local.

Although convenient, proxy-based AOP does have some limitations, as discussed in chapter 9:

- Only spring managed beans can be advised.
- Only public methods can be advised.
- Any self-invocations (even to public methods) won't be advised.

Note that the same limitations apply to any proxy-based transaction-management solution, such as an EJB implementation. If these limitations don't suit your applications, you need to resort to byte-code weaving.

14.3.2 Byte-code weaving

Consider a situation where you need to apply transactional boundaries to domain entities (we'll examine cases where applying transaction boundaries at the domain-object level makes sense in chapter 16). In such a case, because domain entities usually aren't Spring beans, you need an approach that avoids the use of proxies. Fortunately, the overall scheme doesn't change much. You still have the same collaboration between the aspect and a transaction manager. If you use the @AspectJ syntax, which is supported in both Spring's proxy-based AOP and AspectJ's byte code based AOP, you can even reuse the same aspects for both kinds of weaving without any changes.

Summarizing, although proxy-based AOP can be sufficient in a majority of cases, you need AspectJ-based AOP in other cases. Therefore, a complete solution should offer both the possibilities. Let's write aspects in both styles to understand the nuances of the solution.

14.4 Transaction-management aspect (almost) from scratch

Although Spring offers a complete solution, one of the goals of this book is to enable you to write your own aspects and not merely learn how to use existing ones. Therefore, you'll create a brand-new transaction-management aspect. This will help you in two ways. First, it will provide an example to follow if you have a crosscutting concern that matches closely to transaction management. Second, if you aren't using Spring, you may have an easier time creating your own aspect by following this example.

> **Interested only in using Spring's transaction management?**
> If you're only interested in how to use Spring's transaction management and not in how to implement a similar support yourself, you may skip this section.

The "from scratch" part will be restricted to aspects only, because that is the focus of the book. For other parts, you'll use ready-made ingredients available in Spring.

14.4.1 Implementing the aspect

Writing a transaction-management aspect entails defining three constructs:

- A pointcut to select transactional operations
- A way to obtain the transactional attribute for a given transactional operation
- Advice that starts and stops the transaction around the advised join points

The first two may vary depending on factors such as the possibility of changing the existing code (to add, say, annotations) and personal preference (such as XML versus annotations). Whichever style you use, the advice needs to perform the same task of starting and stopping transactions. Therefore, you write an abstract aspect, deferring the choice of defining the pointcut and obtaining transactional attributes to its subaspects.

You choose the @AspectJ style to allow the possibility of using Spring's proxy-based AOP (see listing 14.2). Of course, you can weave the aspect using the AspectJ weaver, if desired.

Listing 14.2 Abstract transaction-management aspect

```
package ajia.transaction;

import ...

@Aspect
public abstract class AbstractTransactionManagementAspect {
    private PlatformTransactionManager transactionManager;

    @Pointcut
    protected abstract void transactionalOp();                    ❶ Selects transactional methods

    public abstract TransactionAttributeWithRollbackRules
        getTransactionAttribute(JoinPoint jp);                   ❷ Obtains transactional attributes

    @Around("transactionalOp()")
    public Object transact(ProceedingJoinPoint pjp) throws Throwable {
        TransactionAttributeWithRollbackRules txAttribute
            = getTransactionAttribute(pjp);                       ❸ Advises transactional methods

        TransactionStatus status
```

```
            = transactionManager.getTransaction(txAttribute);

        try {
            Object ret = pjp.proceed();
            transactionManager.commit(status);
            return ret;
        } catch (Throwable ex) {
            if (txAttribute.rollbackOn(ex)) {
                transactionManager.rollback(status);
            } else {
                transactionManager.commit(status);
            }
            throw ex;
        }
    }

    public void setTransactionManager(
        PlatformTransactionManager transactionManager) {
        this.transactionManager = transactionManager;
    }
}
```

3 Advises transactional methods

4 Declares dependency on transaction manager

1. The abstract `transactionalOp()` pointcut defers the selection of transactional operations to subaspects, which may use any criteria such as a naming pattern or annotations.
2. The abstract `getTransactionAttribute()` method defers mapping join points to transactional attributes (propagation, read-onlyness, and so on) to subaspects. Such a method is commonly implemented using an external map (typically defined in XML) or the annotation attributes.
3. The around advice mimics the code from the conventional implementation. You start a transaction and then proceed with the business logic by invoking `pjp.proceed()` in a `try/catch` block. If no exception is thrown, the advice commits the transaction. If the business logic throws an exception, it commits or rolls back the transaction based on the thrown exception and the transaction attribute. In case of an exception, the advice also rethrows the caught exception so that the caller receives the original exception.
4. The aspect declares that it has a dependency on a transaction manager. The aspect must be injected with a suitable implementation of `PlatformTransactionManager`.

Let's define a concrete subaspect, as shown in listing 14.3, that selects transactional operations based on the annotations.

Listing 14.3 Annotation-based transaction-management aspect

```
package ajia.transaction;

import ...

@Aspect
public class AnnotationDrivenTransactionManagementAspect
    extends AbstractTransactionManagementAspect {

    // org..Transactional abbreviation only for better formatting
```

```
    @Pointcut("execution(@org..Transactional * *(..)) " +
              "|| execution(* (@org..Transactional *).*(..))")
    public void transactionalOp() {}

    public TransactionAttributeWithRollbackRules
        getTransactionAttribute(JoinPoint jp) {
        MethodSignature jpSignature = (MethodSignature)jp.getSignature();
        Transactional typeAnnotation
            = AnnotationUtils.
                . findAnnotation(jpSignature.getDeclaringType(),
                                     Transactional.class);
        Transactional methodAnnotation
            = AnnotationUtils.findAnnotation(jpSignature.getMethod(),
                                                 Transactional.class);
        return TransactionManagementUtil
           .createTransactionAttribute(typeAnnotation, methodAnnotation);
    }
}
```

Selects transactional methods (1)

Creates transactional attributes (2)

(1) The `transactionalOp()` pointcut selects methods annotated with the `@Transactional` annotation as well as methods whose declaring type is annotated with `@Transactional`.

(2) The `getTransactionAttribute()` method finds the annotations associated with the method and the defining type of the advised method. It then creates a transactional attribute based on those annotations. The `TransactionManagementUtil.createTransactionAttribute()` method (not shown, but available in the downloadable sources) first creates the attributes based on type-level annotations (if any) and then overrides or augments them with method-level annotations. This allows type-level annotation to declare attributes common to all the methods, but still allows individual methods to override certain attributes.

But does this aspect work? Like all good developers, you'll check it using a test. Later, you'll also see it in action using the JPA-based example in appendix A.

14.4.2 Testing the aspect

To write good tests, let's examine what can go wrong with the implementation. After all, your tests should focus on those scenarios:

- Test that the aspect starts and commits or rolls back the transactions correctly at the methods marked with the `@Transactional` annotation. You should ensure that the aspect doesn't apply its logic to non-transactional methods. This will indirectly check the correctness of the pointcut.
- Test that the aspect handles nested transactional operations correctly.
- Test that the aspect doesn't alter the exception thrown by the business method. For example, if the business method throws `IOException`, then the application of the aspect shouldn't alter that exception in any way.

You need not test the `PlatformTransactionManager` behavior, because that is a concern of its implementers. Although it's crucial that the annotation attribute be passed to the transaction manager correctly, you have that code in a separate class and should unit-test that code separately.

Listing 14.4 shows a JUnit 4–based test that uses mock objects using the Mockito library.

Listing 14.4 Test for transaction-management aspect

```
package ajia.transaction;

import ...

public class TransactionManagementAspectTest {
    @Mock private PlatformTransactionManager transactionManager;
    @Mock private TransactionStatus status1;
    @Mock private TransactionStatus status2;

    private TestService testService;

    @Before
    public void setUp() {
        MockitoAnnotations.initMocks(this);

        when(transactionManager.
            getTransaction(new DefaultTransactionDefinition()))
                .thenReturn(status1)
                .thenReturn(status2);

        testService = new TestService();

        Aspects.aspectOf(
            AnnotationDrivenTransactionManagementAspect.class)
                .setTransactionManager(transactionManager);
    }

    @Test
    public void nonTransactionalMethod() {
        testService.nonTransactional();
        verifyZeroInteractions(transactionManager);
    }

    @Test
    public void transactionNoException() {
        testService.noExceptionMethod();
        verify(transactionManager)
            .getTransaction(new DefaultTransactionDefinition());
        verify(transactionManager).commit(status1);
        verifyNoMoreInteractions(transactionManager);
    }

    @Test
    public void nestedTransactionNoException() {
        testService.nestedTransactionMethod();
        verify(transactionManager, times(2))
            .getTransaction(new DefaultTransactionDefinition());
        InOrder inOrder = inOrder(transactionManager);
        inOrder.verify(transactionManager).commit(status2);
        inOrder.verify(transactionManager).commit(status1);
        verifyNoMoreInteractions(transactionManager);
    }

    @Test(expected=RuntimeException.class)
```

Annotations:
- Annotates mocks to initialize
- Initializes mocks
- Specifies mock transaction-manager behavior
- Injects aspect with mock transaction manager
- Verifies transaction isn't started
- Verifies transaction is started and committed
- Verifies transaction started for each operation
- Verifies commit for outer operation follows commit for nested operation

```
    public void transactionRuntimeException() {
        try {
            testService.runtimeExceptionMethod();
        } finally {
            verify(transactionManager)
                .getTransaction(new DefaultTransactionDefinition());
            verify(transactionManager).rollback(status1);
            verifyNoMoreInteractions(transactionManager);
        }
    }

    ... more tests omitted for brevity ...

    private static class TestService {
        public void nonTransactional() {
        }

        @Transactional
        public void noExceptionMethod() {
        }

        @Transactional
        public void nestedTransactionMethod() {
            noExceptionMethod();
        }

        @Transactional
        public void runtimeExceptionMethod() {
            throw new PersistenceException();
        }

        @Transactional(rollbackFor=IOException.class)
        public void ioExceptionMethodWithRollback()
            throws IOException {
            throw new IOException();
        }

        @Transactional
        public void ioExceptionMethodWithNoRollback()
            throws IOException {
            throw new IOException();
        }
    }
}
```

Verifies transaction started and rolled back

Test class

Note the use of `Aspects.aspectOf()` to obtain the aspect instance of an @AspectJ aspect. Compile this test along with the aspect and related code using the AspectJ compiler (you can use the Java compiler followed by the binary or load-time weaver, as discussed in chapter 8). Running this test shows you a green bar! You can modify the test to verify its correctness when using Spring AOP as well.

14.4.3 Road test for the aspect

Although the test in the previous section illustrated that the basic aspect works fine, you'll take it for a road test with a real application in appendix A. We'll also take this opportunity to show Spring's proxy-based AOP as well as AspectJ's byte code–based weaving with the same aspect.

First, you'll write code common to both AspectJ and Spring AOP. Let's start with a driver, as shown in listing 14.5, so that you can see this aspect in action.

Listing 14.5 Main driver to exercise transaction management

```
package ajia.main;

import ...

public class Main {
    public static void main(String[] args) {
        ApplicationContext context
            = new ClassPathXmlApplicationContext("META-INF/spring/*.xml");

        OrderService orderService
            = (OrderService)context.getBean("orderService");
        ProductService productService
            = (ProductService)context.getBean("productService");
        Order order = new Order();
        Product product = productService.findProduct(1001L);
        orderService.addProduct(order, product, 1);
    }
}
```

Let's write an aspect (listing 14.6) to trace interactions with the transaction manager. You'll also use a variation of `TraceAspect` you developed in chapter 10 to trace domain, service, and repository method executions (The downloadable sources contain this aspect). You'll trace interaction with the transaction manager and the transactional resources (in this case, JPA `EntityManager`) used during a transaction. You also want to log the transaction attributes, where you'll focus on only one property—read-onlyness—because that is the most commonly specified property.

Listing 14.6 Aspect to trace transaction-manager interaction

```
package ajia.tracing;

import ...

@Aspect
public class TransactionTraceAspect {
    private Logger logger = Logger.getLogger(TransactionTraceAspect.class);

    @AfterReturning(value="ajia.transaction.TransactionPointcuts.
➥                   transactionBegin(txDefinition)",
                    returning="txStatus")
    public void traceBegin(TransactionDefinition txDefinition,
                           TransactionStatus txStatus) {
        logger.log(Level.INFO,
                "Starting transaction ["
                + "Read only: "
                + txDefinition.isReadOnly()
                + ", New transaction: "
```

```
                + txStatus.isNewTransaction() + "]");
        NDC.push("  ");
    }

    @AfterReturning(value="ajia.transaction.TransactionPointcuts.
➥                   transactionEnd(txStatus)")
    public void traceEnd(JoinPoint.StaticPart tjpsp,
                         TransactionStatus txStatus) {
        NDC.pop();
        logger.log(Level.INFO,
                   "Ending transaction " + tjpsp.getSignature().getName());
    }

    @Before("ajia.jpa.JPAPointcuts.entityManagerExecution() " +
            "&& !ajia.core.JavaPointcuts.objectExecution() " +
            "&& this(entityManager)")
    public void traceEntityManager(JoinPoint.StaticPart tjpsp,
                                   EntityManager entityManager) {
        logger.log(Level.INFO,
                   "EntityManager ["
                   + tjpsp.getSignature().toShortString()
                   + " on " + System.identityHashCode(entityManager) + "]");
    }
}
```

The trace aspect uses library aspects that define pointcuts for the transaction manager (see listing 14.7), JPA, and the `Object` class. At the start of a transaction, the advice logs the read-only property of the transaction definition as well as the status of the started transaction that indicates if this is a new transaction. For the `EntityManager`, the advice logs the operation carried out and the identity of the entity manager so that you can check whether the same entity manager is used during a transaction.

The aspect uses a library aspect to define the transaction-related pointcuts, as shown in listing 14.7.

Listing 14.7 Reusable aspect with transaction-related pointcuts

```
package ajia.transaction;

import ...

public aspect TransactionPointcuts {
    public pointcut transactionBegin(TransactionDefinition txDefinition)
        : execution(* PlatformTransactionManager.*(TransactionDefinition))
          && args(txDefinition);

    public pointcut transactionEnd(TransactionStatus txStatus)
        : execution(* PlatformTransactionManager.*(TransactionStatus))
          && args(txStatus);

    public pointcut transactionalExecution() :
        : execution(@Transactional * *(..))
          || execution(* (@Transactional *).*(..));
}
```

Next, you need to annotate the classes and methods. Listing 14.8 shows a representative class.

Listing 14.8 Representative service class with @Transactional annotations

```
package ajia.service.impl;

...

@Transactional                                    <-- (1) Specifies type-level transactional attributes
@Service("orderService")
public class OrderServiceImpl implements OrderService {

    ... unchanged since listing A.10

    @Transactional(readOnly=true)
    public Order findOrder(Long orderId) {
        return orderRepository.find(orderId);
    }                                             <-- (2) Overrides to specify method-level transactional attributes

    public void updateOrder(Order order) {
        orderRepository.update(order);
    }                                             <-- (3) Specifies method matching type-level transactional attributes

    ... other methods without annotations unchanged

}
```

(1) You can specify a type-level annotation to execute public methods in that type in a transaction. The annotation attributes (such as `readOnly`, `propagation`, and `isolation`) specified at the type level automatically apply to each public method.

(2) If you need to override an attribute for a specific method, you can specify an annotation at the method level as well. Such attributes override those specified at the type level.

(3) Any public method without the `@Transactional` annotation automatically uses the annotations specified at the type level.

You now have code common to AspectJ byte-code weaving and Spring's proxy-based AOP. They differ only in how you configure the aspect.

ASPECTJ BYTE-CODE WEAVING

You need to configure the aspect to inject a `PlatformTransactionManager` implementation. You do that through the snippet in listing 14.9 (which you can add to any XML file in the META-INF/spring directory on the classpath).

Listing 14.9 Configuring transaction-management aspect for AspectJ weaving

```
<bean id="transactionManagement"
      class="ajia.transaction.AnnotationDrivenTransactionManagementAspect"
      factory-method="aspectOf">
    <property name="transactionManager" ref="transactionManager"/>
</bean>

<bean id="transactionManager"
         class="org.springframework.orm.jpa.JpaTransactionManager">
   <property name="entityManagerFactory" ref="entityManagerFactory"/>
</bean>
```

When you run this code, you get the following log output:

```
EntityManager [AbstractEntityManagerImpl.getTransaction() on 8488470]
Starting transaction [Read only: true, New transaction : true]
  Entering [ProductServiceImpl.findProduct(..)]
    Entering [JpaGenericRepository.find(..)]
      EntityManager: [.Proxy15.find(..) on 6814623]
      EntityManager: [AbstractEntityManagerImpl.find(..) on 8488470]
  EntityManager:
    [AbstractEntityManagerImpl.getTransaction() on 8488470]
  EntityManager:
    [AbstractEntityManagerImpl.getTransaction() on 8488470]
  EntityManager:
    [EntityManagerImpl.close() on 8488470]
Ending transaction commit
EntityManager:
  [AbstractEntityManagerImpl.getTransaction() on 26914410]
Starting transaction [Read only: false, New transaction: true]
  Entering [OrderServiceImpl.addProduct(..)]
    Starting transaction [Read only: false, New transaction: false]
      Entering [InventoryServiceImpl.removeProduct(..)]
        Starting transaction [Read only: true, New transaction: false]
          Entering [InventoryServiceImpl.isProductAvailable(..)]
            Entering [JpaInventoryItemRepository.findByProduct(..)]
              EntityManager:
                [.Proxy15.createQuery(..) on 16093701]
              EntityManager:
                [AbstractEntityManagerImpl.createQuery(..) on 26914410]
            Entering [InventoryItem.getQuantityOnHand()]
        Ending transaction commit
        Entering [JpaInventoryItemRepository.findByProduct(..)]
          EntityManager:
            [.Proxy15.createQuery(..) on 16093701]
          EntityManager:
            [AbstractEntityManagerImpl.createQuery(..) on 26914410]
        Entering [InventoryItem.deplete(..)]
    Ending transaction commit
    Entering [Order.addItem(..)]
      Entering [Order.isPlaced()]
      Entering [Order.getItemFor(..)]
      Entering [Product.getPrice()]
      Entering [LineItem.setQuantity(..)]
  EntityManager:
    [AbstractEntityManagerImpl.getTransaction() on 26914410]
  EntityManager:
    [AbstractEntityManagerImpl.getTransaction() on 26914410]
  EntityManager:
    [EntityManagerImpl.close() on 26914410]
Ending transaction commit
```

First transaction

Second transaction

Second nested transaction

First nested transaction

Second transaction

Notice how the transactions start with the correct read-only properties. For example, when the transaction for the finder operations begins, the transaction is read-only, whereas for `addProduct()`, the transaction isn't read-only. Also notice how nested transactions aren't defined as new. Finally, notice that the same entity manager is used during a transaction. The entity manager with `Proxy` in its type name is a proxy around the real entity manager; it ensures that the business operation uses the same entity manager throughout the transaction, following the scheme shown in figure 14.2.

SPRING'S PROXY-BASED AOP

You can use Spring's proxy-based AOP to get the same effect. Listing 14.10 shows the configuration for the transaction-management aspect.

Listing 14.10 Configuring transaction-management aspect for Spring' proxy weaving

```
<aop:aspectj-autoproxy/>

<bean id="transactionManagement"
      class="ajia.transaction.AnnotationDrivenTransactionManagementAspect">
    <property name="transactionManager" ref="transactionManager"/>
</bean>

<bean id="transactionManager"
      class="org.springframework.orm.jpa.JpaTransactionManager">
   <property name="entityManagerFactory" ref="entityManagerFactory"/>
</bean>
```

Compared to listing 14.9, you no longer use the `factory-method` attribute, because the aspect is a Spring bean. The `<aop:aspectj-autoproxy/>`, as discussed in chapter 9, is an instruction to the Spring container to use beans with the `@Aspect` annotation to apply AOP proxies.

When you run the same driver, you get the following output:

```
Entering [.Proxy25.findProduct(..)]
 EntityManager:
   [AbstractEntityManagerImpl.getTransaction() on 3590613]
 Starting transaction [Read only: false, New transaction: true]      <-- First transaction
   Entering [ProductServiceImpl.findProduct(..)]
     Entering [JpaGenericRepository.find(..)]
       EntityManager:
         [.Proxy21.find(..) on 28989497]
       EntityManager:
         [AbstractEntityManagerImpl.find(..) on 3590613]
   EntityManager:
     [AbstractEntityManagerImpl.getTransaction() on 3590613]
   EntityManager:
     [AbstractEntityManagerImpl.getTransaction() on 3590613]
   EntityManager:
     [EntityManagerImpl.close() on 3590613]
 Ending transaction commit
Entering [.Proxy24.addProduct(..)]
 EntityManager:
   [AbstractEntityManagerImpl.getTransaction() on 28155981]
 Starting transaction [Read only: false, New transaction: true]      <-- Second transaction
   Entering [OrderServiceImpl.addProduct(..)]
     Entering [.Proxy23.removeProduct(..)]
       Starting transaction [Read only: false, New transaction: false]      <-- Nested transaction
         Entering [InventoryServiceImpl.removeProduct(..)]
           Entering [InventoryServiceImpl.isProductAvailable(..)]
             Entering [JpaInventoryItemRepository.findByProduct(..)]
               EntityManager:
                 [.Proxy21.createQuery(..) on 32986216]
               EntityManager:
                 [AbstractEntityManagerImpl.createQuery(..) on 28155981]
             Entering [InventoryItem.getQuantityOnHand()]
```

```
            Entering [JpaInventoryItemRepository.findByProduct(..)]
              EntityManager:
                [.Proxy21.createQuery(..) on 32986216]
              EntityManager:
                [AbstractEntityManagerImpl.createQuery(..) on 28155981]
            Entering [InventoryItem.deplete(..)]
        Ending transaction commit                     <-- Nested
      Entering [Order.addItem(..)]                        transaction
        Entering [Order.isPlaced()]
        Entering [Order.getItemFor(..)]
        Entering [Product.getPrice()]
        Entering [LineItem.setQuantity(..)]
    EntityManager:
      [AbstractEntityManagerImpl.getTransaction() on 28155981]
    EntityManager:
      [AbstractEntityManagerImpl.getTransaction() on 28155981]
    EntityManager:
      [EntityManagerImpl.close() on 28155981]         Second
  Ending transaction commit                        <-- transaction
```

Let's play the "find the differences" game. First, notice the glaring difference of `Proxy` (such as in the first line) in the type name where you would expect a service implementation. Because Spring's proxy-based AOP is in play, and the service objects contain transactional methods, AOP proxies wrap the original service beans. Next, notice that you no longer have a nested transaction started for methods invoked on the self object for `InventoryServiceImpl.isProductAvailable()`. This is due to the self-call limitation of the proxy-based approach, discussed in section 9.2.5.

> **Using your own annotations**
>
> In your service classes, you use the `@Transactional` annotation to mark the transactional types and methods. But you should be able to utilize any other means to select the required join points. For example, you can use the `@Service` annotation to select, say, all public methods of the service layer as transactional. You can combine it with the `@ReadOnly` annotation that you used in chapter 13 to select transactional methods with the read-only attribute. Furthermore, if you use the Model-Driven Architecture (MDA), you can use UML stereotypes that map to Java annotations. Pointcuts can leverage such annotations, as well.

Now that you have a good idea of the AOP implementation of transaction management, we'll examine how prebuilt aspects provided as a part of Spring can simplify this functionality.

14.5 Spring's transaction management

Because most business applications based on the Spring Framework need the transaction-management functionality, Spring provides prebuilt aspects and a simplified way to configure them. Although the solution uses AOP, it hides most of the AOP-related details using the namespace-based configuration.

Spring offers both types of weaving discussed in section 14.3: proxy-based and AspectJ-based. The proxy-based choice restricts demarcating transaction boundaries to Spring-managed beans, whereas the AspectJ-based choice allows the same demarcation at any object, including Spring beans. The focus of this section is on a general understanding of Spring's support for transaction management and how a good aspect library takes the burden off you.

Spring offers two distinct styles to use the transaction-management functionality through proxy-based AOP: XML-driven and annotation-driven. Let's examine both.

14.5.1 XML-driven transaction management

With the XML-driven approach, AspectJ pointcuts specified in XML select the transactional methods. Additional XML elements provide attributes such as propagation and read-onlyness. Listing 14.11 shows the XML configuration needed to add transaction management to the service layer.

Listing 14.11 Configuration for XML-driven transaction management

```
<aop:config>
    <aop:pointcut id="serviceOperation"
        expression="execution(* ajia.service..*Service*.*(..))"/>
    <aop:advisor pointcut-ref="serviceOperation"
                 advice-ref="txAdvice"/>                  Configures ❶
</aop:config>                                   transactional advice

<tx:advice id="txAdvice">
    <tx:attributes>
        <tx:method name="find*" read-only="true"/>
        <tx:method name="is*" read-only="true" />       ❷ Supplies
        <tx:method name="*"/>                             metadata
    </tx:attributes>
</tx:advice>

<bean id="transactionManager"
      class="org.springframework.orm.jpa.JpaTransactionManager">
    <property name="entityManagerFactory"
              ref="entityManagerFactory" />                 Defines ❸
</bean>                                          transaction manager
```

❶ The `<aop:config>` element defines a transaction-management aspect. The embedded `<aop:pointcut>` element specifies an AspectJ pointcut. The other embedded `<aop:advisor>` element specifies a pointcut reference (it could also specify a pointcut expression using the `pointcut` attribute) and a reference to an advisor defined in ❷.

❷ The `<tx:advice>` element specifies the attributes for the transactional methods. The element may specify the `transaction-manager` attribute whose value should be the name of the transaction-manager bean to be used by the aspect. The default name of such a bean is `transactionManager`.

The embedded `<tx:attributes>` elements specify a regular expression for the `name` attribute. For example, the listing specifies `find*` and `is*` as an expression to select methods whose name starts with `find` or `is`, such as `findProduct()` and `isProductAvailable()`. The other attributes specify transactional properties such as propagation, isolation, and read-onlyness for the selected methods. To control rollback behavior when an advised method throws an exception, you can use the `rollback-for` and `no-rollback-for` properties, specifying a list of exceptions.

3 `transactionManager` is the bean used by the transaction-management aspect. The type specified for the bean must implement the `PlatformTransactionManager` interface that we discussed in section 14.2.3 and match the transactional resources used. For example, in the listing, you specify the transaction manager to be `JpaTransactionManager`, because your data access layer uses JPA. If you were to use plain JDBC, you would specify `DataSourceTransactionManager` as the type of transaction manager.

When you run the system with the classes in appendix A, you get the following output. Note that when using the XML-based style, you need not add any `Transactional` annotation to your Java code:

```
Entering [.Proxy20.findProduct(..)]
 EntityManager:
   [AbstractEntityManagerImpl.getTransaction() on 20654997]
 Starting transaction [Read only: true, New transaction: true]      <-- First transaction
   Entering [ProductServiceImpl.findProduct(..)]
     Entering [JpaGenericRepository.find(..)]
       EntityManager:
         [.Proxy15.find(..) on 30710870]
       EntityManager:
         [AbstractEntityManagerImpl.find(..) on 20654997]
   EntityManager:
     [AbstractEntityManagerImpl.getTransaction() on 20654997]
   EntityManager:
     [AbstractEntityManagerImpl.getTransaction() on 20654997]
   EntityManager:
     [EntityManagerImpl.close() on 20654997]
 Ending transaction commit
Entering [.Proxy19.addProduct(..)]                                  Second transaction
 EntityManager:
   [AbstractEntityManagerImpl.getTransaction() on 32412895]
 Starting transaction [Read only: false, New transaction: true]     <--
   Entering [OrderServiceImpl.addProduct(..)]
     Entering [.Proxy18.removeProduct(..)]                          Nested transaction
       Starting transaction [Read only: false, New transaction: false]   <--
         Entering [InventoryServiceImpl.removeProduct(..)]
           Entering [InventoryServiceImpl.isProductAvailable(..)]
             Entering [JpaInventoryItemRepository.findByProduct(..)]
               EntityManager:
                 [.Proxy15.createQuery(..) on 2050852]
               EntityManager:
                 [AbstractEntityManagerImpl.createQuery(..) on 32412895]
             Entering [InventoryItem.getQuantityOnHand()]
           Entering [JpaInventoryItemRepository.findByProduct(..)]
             EntityManager:
               [.Proxy15.createQuery(..) on 2050852]
             EntityManager:
               [AbstractEntityManagerImpl.createQuery(..) on 32412895]
```

```
        Entering [InventoryItem.deplete(..)]
      Ending transaction commit                    <-- Nested
    Entering [Order.addItem(..)]                       transaction
      Entering [Order.isPlaced()]
      Entering [Order.getItemFor(..)]
      Entering [Product.getPrice()]
      Entering [LineItem.setQuantity(..)]
  EntityManager:
    [AbstractEntityManagerImpl.getTransaction() on 32412895]
  EntityManager:
    [AbstractEntityManagerImpl.getTransaction() on 32412895]
  EntityManager:
    [EntityManagerImpl.close() on 32412895]          Second
Ending transaction commit                        <-- transaction
```

The log output shows matching `getTransaction()` and `commit()` invocations. You also see that transaction management with nested operations works as expected.

XML-based transaction management lets you implement the transaction functionality without modifying Java code. But it requires you to keep the two parts of the implementation—Java and XML—in sync. For example, if you rename a method, you must check `<tx:attributes>` to ensure that the specified regular expression continues to select the correct methods.

The fundamental role played by the XML configuration is to select transactional methods and supply transactional properties for those methods. An alternative to the XML-based configuration moves these roles from XML to Java annotations.

14.5.2 Annotation-driven transaction management

With the annotation-driven style, you annotate the types and methods with Spring's `@Transactional` attribute, as shown in listing 14.8 when you developed your own aspect. Alternatively, you can use EJB's `@javax.ejb.TransactionAttribute` annotation.

With the Java code specifying all the details, you no longer need to specify the pointcut and transactional attributes. Listing 14.12 shows the necessary XML configuration.

Listing 14.12 XML configuration for annotation-driven transaction management

```
<tx:annotation-driven/>

<bean id="transactionManager"
      class="org.springframework.orm.jpa.JpaTransactionManager">
    <property name="entityManagerFactory"
              ref="entityManagerFactory" />
</bean>
```

The `<tx:annotation-driven/>` is all that is needed to specify that the types and methods annotated with the `@Transactional` should be considered transactional boundaries and thus subject to transaction-management functionality. Furthermore, the attributes in the annotations specify the transactional properties. The element can use the optional `transactionManager` attribute to specify the name of the transaction manager bean. The default value of this property is `transactionManager`.

If you execute the driver, you'll see identical output compared to the XML-driven version in the previous section.

To cover the cases where a proxy-based solution isn't enough, Spring extends the annotation-driven transaction-management support to use the AspectJ-based weaving.

14.5.3 AspectJ weaver-based transaction management

Enabling AspectJ weaver-based transaction management requires specifying the `mode` attribute for the `<tx:annotation-driven>` element, as shown in the following snippet:

```
<tx:annotation-driven mode="aspectj"/>
```

As in the case of proxy-based transaction management, if you have a bean named `transactionManager`, the aspect uses it to drive transactions. You can always specify the `transactionManager` attribute. For this scheme to work, you must use the AspectJ weaver in one of the forms described in chapter 8 (build-time or load-time weaver, including the Spring-driven load-time weaver).

If you execute the main driver with the AspectJ weaver, you get the following output:

```
EntityManager:
  [AbstractEntityManagerImpl.getTransaction() on 4213679]
Starting transaction [Read only: true, New transaction: true]
 Entering [ProductServiceImpl.findProduct(..)]
   Entering [JpaGenericRepository.find(..)]
     EntityManager:
       [.Proxy15.find(..) on 26551240]
     EntityManager:
       [AbstractEntityManagerImpl.find(..) on 4213679]
 EntityManager:
   [AbstractEntityManagerImpl.getTransaction() on 4213679]
 EntityManager:
   [AbstractEntityManagerImpl.getTransaction() on 4213679]
 EntityManager:
   [EntityManagerImpl.close() on 4213679]
Ending transaction commit
EntityManager:
  [AbstractEntityManagerImpl.getTransaction() on 15900710]
Starting transaction [Read only: false, New transaction: true]
 Entering [OrderServiceImpl.addProduct(..)]
   Starting transaction [Read only: false, New transaction: false]
     Entering [InventoryServiceImpl.removeProduct(..)]
       Starting transaction [Read only: true, New transaction: false]
         Entering [InventoryServiceImpl.isProductAvailable(..)]
           Entering [JpaInventoryItemRepository.findByProduct(..)]
             EntityManager:
               [.Proxy15.createQuery(..) on 15742686]
             EntityManager:
               [AbstractEntityManagerImpl.createQuery(..) on 15900710]
           Entering [InventoryItem.getQuantityOnHand()]
       Ending transaction commit
```

```
        Entering [JpaInventoryItemRepository.findByProduct(..)]
          EntityManager:
            [.Proxy15.createQuery(..) on 15742686]
          EntityManager:
            [AbstractEntityManagerImpl.createQuery(..) on 15900710]
        Entering [InventoryItem.deplete(..)]
    Ending transaction commit                        <-- First nested
    Entering [Order.addItem(..)]                         transaction
      Entering [Order.isPlaced()]
      Entering [Order.getItemFor(..)]
      Entering [Product.getPrice()]
      Entering [LineItem.setQuantity(..)]
  EntityManager:
    [AbstractEntityManagerImpl.getTransaction() on 15900710]
  EntityManager:
    [AbstractEntityManagerImpl.getTransaction() on 15900710]
  EntityManager:
    [EntityManagerImpl.close() on 15900710]          Second
Ending transaction commit                        <-- transaction
```

The most interesting change in the output compared to proxy-based transaction management is the lack of trace output with type names such as `Proxy20` for service beans. With AspectJ-based weaving, Spring doesn't need to create AOP proxies. Instead, byte code is woven with the transaction logic. Another change in the output is the application of the transaction-management logic even for the self-invoked calls (the second nested transaction). Although the example doesn't show it, with byte-code weaving, the transaction-management aspect can apply to package-accessed, protected, and even private methods.

Let's move from the core transaction management to the interesting topic of introducing fault tolerance that works well with the transaction-management concept.

14.6 Implementing fault tolerance for transactional operations

You implemented a fault-tolerance aspect in chapter 4 that retried idempotent operations. Transactional operations are inherently idempotent—if a transactional operation fails, it leaves no change in the system state. Consequently, you can retry transactional operations to implement fault tolerance.

In this section, you'll implement an aspect to retry transactional operations. Later, you'll improve the solution to consider practical realities that require adjustments to the assumption of transactional operations being idempotent. In this section, you'll also see some interesting use of aspects for integration testing.

14.6.1 Base aspect

To simplify code, provide flexibility, and allow better testing, you create a base aspect to encapsulate the essence of the retry crosscutting logic. The base aspect shown in listing 14.13 avoids most of the tough decisions through the use of an abstract pointcut and the strategy design pattern. The subaspects can provide a definition for the pointcut, offering flexibility in terms of the criterion for choosing operations to be retried. The base aspect also makes the aspect reusable beyond transactional operations, such as network operations. The strategy design pattern lets you use a DI container to configure the retry policy. Note that the aspect uses `RetryTemplate` and related types from the Spring Batch project (see http://static.springframework.org/spring-batch for more details).

Listing 14.13 Base aspect to introduce fault tolerance through retries

```
package ajia.faulttolerance;

import ...

@Aspect
public abstract class RetryFaultToleranceAspect {
    @Pointcut
    public abstract void retryOperation();                    ❶ Retry operation pointcut

    private RetryTemplate retryTemplate;

    @Around("retryOperation()")
    public Object retry(final ProceedingJoinPoint pjp)
        throws Throwable {
        RetryCallback<Object> worker
            = new RetryCallback<Object>() {
            public Object doWithRetry(RetryContext retryContext)
                throws Exception {
                try {
                    return pjp.proceed();
                } catch (Exception ex) {
                    throw ex;                                   ❷ Retry advice
                } catch (Error error) {
                    throw error;
                } catch (Throwable t) {
                    throw new IllegalStateException(
                        "Caught throwable that is neither "
                      + "Exception nor Error");
                }
        }};

        return retryTemplate.execute(worker);
    }

    public void setRetryTemplate(RetryTemplate retryTemplate) {
        this.retryTemplate = retryTemplate;
    }
                                               Configurable dependency ❸
}
```

❶ The aspect specifies an abstract pointcut to let subaspects select operations to retry.

❷ The aspect uses the worker object design pattern that we examined in chapter 12. It creates a worker object of the `RetryCallback` type. The work method—`doWithRetry()`—proceeds with the current join point execution. The advice passes the worker object to the retry template. Based on how the retry template is configured, the retry template calls the `doWithRetry()` method multiple times, each time executing the join point.

3 You can configure the aspect with any retry template. The retry template itself may be configured to decide several factors such as which exceptions should be retried, how many times, and how much delay there should be between the successive retries.

The most important question is, which operations should be retried? Let's write a subaspect that answers it.

14.6.2 Using the annotation-driven participant pattern

You can extend the base aspect to provide a definition for the pointcut in a variety of ways. For example, you can use the participant pattern (discussed in chapter 12) to add an aspect per class whose method needs to be retried. But keeping the focus on transaction management, let's use the annotation-driven participant pattern (ADPP) to enable retry logic for the transactional operations.

When working with JPA resources, you need to consider certain characteristics as you design the retry logic. These considerations stem from the fact that JPA exceptions aren't recoverable. When a JPA operation throws an exception, all bets are off, and the entity manager must be discarded. Therefore:

- *You must ensure that the retry logic surrounds the transaction-management logic.* You can achieve this through the aspect-precedence rule, as discussed in chapter 6. In addition, each new transaction must be associated with a fresh entity manager. This is a common practice in many enterprise applications already, so you just need to ensure its adherence. Specifically, you need to watch out for the use of an Open Session in View (or its JPA equivalent—Open Entity Manager in View) filter or other ways to keep the entity manager open longer than the transactions. You can check for this through an enforcement aspect (as discussed in chapter 11) to be extra sure.
- *You should not retry failures in inner transactional operations* (that is, the ones that are in the control flow of an ongoing transaction). Even if an inner operation succeeds after a few retries, the outer operation is still destined for an unrecoverable failure (the transaction is marked for rollback-only in case of an exception), wasting any effort spent in retrying the inner operation. You can satisfy this requirement by using the common idiom of selecting top-level join points, as discussed in section 3.6.2.

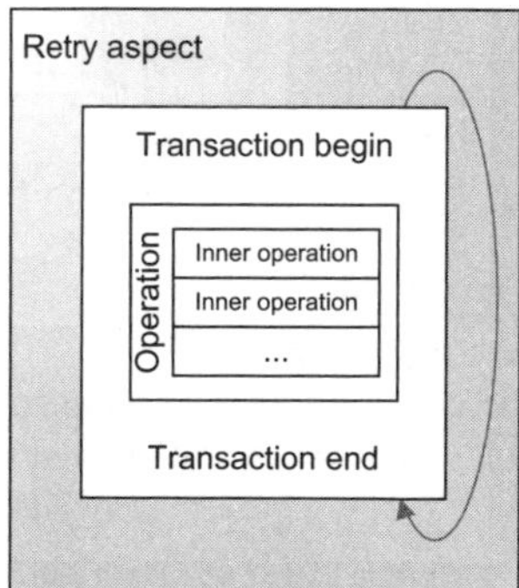

Figure 14.3 Relationship between transactional operations, the transaction-management aspect, and the retry aspect. The retry logic must surround the outermost transactions.

Figure 14.3 shows how the transaction-management aspect relates to the retry aspect.

Let's use this information to write a subaspect, as shown in listing 14.14.

Listing 14.14 Fault-tolerance aspect for transactional operations

```
package ajia.transaction;

import ...

@Aspect
public class TransactionalRetryFaultToleranceAspect extends
        RetryFaultToleranceAspect {
    @Pointcut("TransactionPointcuts.transactionalExecution() "
        + "&& !cflowbelow(TransactionPointcuts.transactionalExecution())")
    private void topLevelTransactionalOp() {}

    @Pointcut("topLevelTransactionalOp()")
    public void retryOperation() { }
}
```

The aspect is simple. You define a private pointcut to select top-level transactional operations through the use of the `cflowbelow()` pointcut. Then, you define the `retryOperation()` pointcut (which is the abstract pointcut in the base aspect) with this pointcut.

14.6.3 Configuring the aspect

The main configuration option is to select the exceptions to be retried, because you should retry only failures that have some chance of succeeding on a reattempt. For example, if the failure is due to insufficient inventory, there is no point in retrying operations within a few milliseconds. On the other hand, concurrency failure exceptions have a better chance of success upon retry.[1] Similarly, failures due to network errors are worth retrying if you're dealing with distributed objects.

Listing 14.15 shows a Spring configuration that sets the retry policy.

Listing 14.15 fault-tolerance-context.xml

```
<beans ...>
    <bean id="faultToleranceAspect"
          class="ajia.transaction.TransactionalRetryFaultToleranceAspect"
          factory-method="aspectOf">
        <property name="retryTemplate" ref="retryTemplate"/>
    </bean>

    <bean id="retryTemplate"
          class="org.springframework.batch.retry.support.RetryTemplate">
        <property name="retryPolicy" ref="retryPolicy"/>
    </bean>

    <bean id="retryPolicy"
       class="org.springframework.
➥          batch.retry.policy.ExceptionClassifierRetryPolicy">
        <property name="policyMap">
            <map>
                <entry key="org.springframework.
```

[1] See *POJOs in Action* by Chris Richardson (Manning, 2006) for an example that handles the specific case of concurrent modification failures.

```
➥                               dao.ConcurrencyFailureException"
                         value-ref="maxAttemptRetryPolicy"/>
                <entry key="org.springframework.
➥                               dao.DataAccessResourceFailureException"
                         value-ref="maxAttemptRetryPolicy"/>
            </map>
        </property>
    </bean>

    <bean id="maxAttemptRetryPolicy"
          class="org.springframework.batch.retry.policy.SimpleRetryPolicy">
        <property name="maxAttempts" value="3"/>
    </bean>
</beans>
```

Let's examine this configuration at a high level (the details are beyond the scope of this book). You define a bean corresponding to `TransactionalRetryFaultToleranceAspect` and inject it with the `retryTemplate` bean. Now, you see DI in full force! The `retryTemplate` bean is injected with a retry policy that uses a map to decide which exception should be retried and how many times. Here you define that `ConcurrencyFailureException` and `DataAccessResourceFailureException` should be retried at most three times. Although you don't use it in this configuration, you can specify a back-off strategy to introduce delays between the successive retries. Such a strategy would come in handy when retrying network failures.

You need to control precedence between transaction management and the retry aspect. You can use a separate aspect with a statement such as the following to specify precedence (this is the traditional syntax; you can use the @AspectJ syntax as well, as discussed in chapter 7):

```
declare precedence: ajia..*, org.springframework..*, *
```

Here, you specify that all the aspects in a direct or indirect subpackage of `ajia` have higher precedence than those in `org.springframework`, which in turn have higher precedence than any other aspects in the system.

Alternatively, if you're using LTW, you can use aop.xml to have the same effect with the following element:

```
<concrete-aspect name="ajia.SystemLevelPrecedence"
                 precedence="ajia..*, org.springframework..*, *"/>
```

Either way, the fault-tolerance aspect will have a higher precedence than the transaction-management aspect, thus ensuring that fault-tolerance logic surrounds the transaction-management logic.

14.6.4 Testing the fault-tolerance aspect

Testing for fault tolerance entails exercising normal test cases, but you need to check that they succeed even when the underlying implementation throws certain exceptions a limited number of times. To do so, you can use a nifty aspect that avoids all the duplication that would otherwise be required for such testing. Listing 14.16 shows the test for the `InventoryService` interface, which uses an aspect that throws faults during testing.

Listing 14.16 Testing fault tolerance through retries

```
package ajia.service.impl;

import ...

public class FaultToleranceInventoryServiceTest
    extends InventoryServiceTest {
    private static aspect FaultInjector percflow(faultTest()) {
        private int faultCount = 0;
        private static int MAX_FAULT_COUNT = 2;

        pointcut faultTest()
            : execution(@Test * InventoryServiceTest.*(..))
              && this(FaultToleranceInventoryServiceTest);

        pointcut faultSite() : call(* EntityManager.*(..));

        before() : faultSite() {
            if (faultCount++ < MAX_FAULT_COUNT) {
                throw new ConcurrencyFailureException(
                    "Simulated failure for testing");
            }
        }
    }
}
```

❶ Declares aspect association

❷ Selects fault tests

❸ Selects fault sites

❹ Injects fault

You create a subclass of your test but include no additional tests because you need to run the same tests with injected faults.

❶ The aspect is declared with the `percflow()` association to attach a fresh aspect instance for each test execution. This way, you can keep track of the number of faults you threw in a test. Note that as discussed in section 6.2.3, the use of `percflow()` causes an implicit restriction on advice matching, selecting only join points in the control flow of `faultTest()`. This is exactly what you want: to inject faults only if the initiator of the flow is your test.

NOTE If you were to apply the retry logic to many classes, you might want to refactor the aspect to extract a base aspect.

❷ The `faultTest()` pointcut selects tests in the base class as long as the `this` object is of `FaultToleranceInventoryServiceTest` type. With this arrangement, if you execute the base test class, you'll see no fault injection. But when you execute the `FaultToleranceInventoryServiceTest` class, the aspect injects faults. Effectively, you have two set of tests: one for the base tests by themselves and another for the fault-injected tests.

❸ The `faultSite()` pointcut selects calls to `EntityManager`. This is where you want to inject simulated faults.

❹ The advice to the `faultSite()` pointcut throws an exception if the fault count hasn't exceeded the max count. Because the aspect uses the `percflow` association, its state—specifically the `faultCount` instance variable—is associated with the control flow for each test. When a new test starts, the `faultCount` is set to zero.

> **Using Jexin to inject faults**
>
> You can use the Jexin open source project (http://jexin.sourceforge.net), which uses AspectJ to inject exceptions to simulate faults.

With AOP helping along the way, you can write surprisingly little code to introduce fault tolerance and even less code to test it.

14.6.5 Improving the solution

Let's complete this chapter by briefly discussing a few improvements to the fault-tolerance aspect. First, we'll examine the use of nontransactional resources such as email notifications, which can challenge the idempotent characteristic of a transactional operation. Next, we'll discuss how you can use Spring AOP to apply the retry aspects.

DEALING WITH NONTRANSACTIONAL RESOURCES

Consider an order-placement operation that sends emails to customers, acknowledging orders. If you retry this operation without special care, you'll end up sending extra emails—one per retry. Note that this problem exists even when you don't intend to retry the transaction. Even in the first attempt, you need to ensure that you perform the nontransactional work only if the ongoing transaction succeeds. If the operations are such that executing them out of order or delaying them is allowed (such as in case of email), aspects can help to improve the situation.

You can take care of such operations by accumulating the work and executing it at the time of transaction commit. If a rollback comes along instead, you empty the accumulated work without executing it. Here is a skeleton aspect to get you started:

```
public aspect NonTransactionalWorkCoordinatorAspect
    percflow(TransactionPointcuts.transactionalExecution()) {
    private List<Runnable> accumulatedWork = ...

    pointcut nonTransactionalWork()
        : execution(@OneWay @NonTransactional void *(..));

    void around() : nonTransactionalWork() {
        Runnable worker = new Runnable() {
            public void run() {
                proceed();
            }
        };
        accumulatedWork.add(worker);
    }

    after() returning : TransactionPointcuts.transactionalCommit(*) {
        for (Runnable work : accumulatedWork) {
            work.run();
        }
    }
}
```

The aspect uses `percflow()` to associate a separate instance of the aspect per transactional operation's control flow. It advises operations marked with the `@OneWay` and `@NonTransactional` annotations (you may, of course, choose any other annotations). Then, the advice creates a worker object and puts it in a queue. When the transaction commits, it executes the accumulated work. Because the aspect uses the `percflow` association, it's a candidate for garbage collection after the transaction is complete. Therefore, you don't need to worry about explicitly clearing the accumulated work.

Note that you aren't implementing a two-phase commit approach here. For example, if the main transaction succeeds, there is a chance that the nontransactional work you accumulated may fail. You need to be ready for such a possibility—for example, you may retry those failures as well. In general, it's best to limit nontransactional work to noncritical activities such as sending email notifications. Enforcement aspects, anyone?

PORTING TO SPRING AOP

You used AspectJ weaving that allowed you to focus more on the high-level problem. But you can use all the ideas and most of the code with Spring's proxy-based AOP. Let's see how you can adjust the code to make it work.

1. Use the `Ordered` interface or the `@Order` annotation to control precedence between transaction management and the retry aspect. Note that you can specify the `<tx:annotation-driven>` element with the `order` attribute so that you can specify its order relative to that of retry aspect. See chapter 9 for details.
2. Replace the use of `call()` with `execution()`, and ensure that the join points selected correspond to Spring beans. Note that you can use `execution()` even with AspectJ byte-code weaving. But if the corresponding method belongs to a third-party jar, it forces the use of LTW or binary weaving of those jars.
3. For the fault-injection aspect, you can't use the `percflow` aspect association. You must replace it with the good old thread-local.

Now, you can choose to use Spring AOP without losing much functionality.

14.7 Summary

Transaction management is one of the most common crosscutting concerns found in enterprise applications. Conventional implementations scatter the transaction-management functionality across many classes and create an undue burden on developers whose primary focus should be business logic. With the aspect modularizing the transaction-management functionality, you can achieve your goal of separation of concerns: aspect developers can focus on implementing transaction functionality, and business logic developers can focus on business functionality.

The widespread use of transaction-management functionality calls for library aspects to avoid duplicated work in multiple projects and organizations. You can configure these aspects in your applications and check off one task in your project with little effort. To illustrate this point, we examined Spring's support for transaction management, which comes in two parts: a transaction-management abstraction and transaction aspects. You can use either the proxy-based or byte code-based AOP with Spring's aspects. Furthermore, you can use XML to specify transaction boundaries and associated attributes or use annotations. If you're using the Spring Framework, that is probably all you need—it's unlikely you'll ever have to implement your own transaction-management aspect.

You also implemented a simple transaction-management aspect from scratch to gain a deeper understanding of its internal workings as well as to use patterns to unit-test the aspects. These patterns should come in handy when you begin implementing your own aspects.

Fault tolerance works particularly well with transaction management. We showed how advanced language features and design patterns help in simplifying implementations of this complex concern. We also used this functionality to show interesting ways you can use aspects to inject faults and avoid rewriting tests.

In the next chapter, we'll examine another common crosscutting concern: security. Much like transaction management, it lends itself to creating aspect libraries.

15 Securing applications

This chapter covers

- Spring Security overview
- Using Spring AOP to secure applications
- Using AspectJ to secure applications

Security is an important consideration in modern, highly connected software systems. Most applications need to expose functionality through multiple interfaces to allow access to the business data and make complex integration possible. But they need to do so in a secured manner. It isn't a surprise that most enterprises spend substantial time, energy, and money to secure applications. Security consists of many components such as authentication, authorization, auditing, protection against web site attacks, and cryptography. In chapter 10, we discussed auditing that you can target for various purposes including security. In this chapter, we'll focus on authentication and authorization.

Implementing security using conventional programming techniques requires you to modify multiple modules to add authentication and authorization code. For instance, to implement access control in an e-commerce system, you must invoke security code from methods of inventory control and procurement modules.

In this chapter, we'll show how Spring Security (formerly known as Acegi) along with AOP can simplify the implementation of the classic crosscutting concern of securing your application. Although we'll use a specific security implementation (Spring Security), given the abstract nature of the API, you should be able to use the solution with other APIs just as well. As in the previous chapter, we'll start with an overview of the problem and follow it with a quick introduction to the underlying implementation (Spring Security). Then, you'll write a few security aspects.

15.1 Securing applications with conventional techniques

The need to secure applications is common, and there are many ways to do so. Modern APIs such as Java Authentication and Authorization Service (JAAS) and Spring Security provide a layer of abstraction over the underlying mechanism and let you separate the configuration from the code. The overall goal of these APIs is to reduce complexity and provide agile implementations. Yet such APIs offer only a part of the solution, leaving you with the task of calling these APIs from many places in the code.

We can classify the conventional solutions in two categories: the do-it-yourself approach, where you explicitly invoke security APIs in appropriate places; and the framework-based approach, where the application framework provides support for common security use cases.

15.1.1 The do-it-yourself approach

In the simplest implementation, the classes implementing the business functionality directly call the authentication and authorization methods. For example, business methods that require an access check directly invoke the security system APIs, as shown in the following snippet:

```
public void businessMethod() {
    SecurityAttribute sa = ...                  // Creates security attribute
    accessManager.checkPermission(sa);          // Checks for permission
    ... business operation ...
}
```

Security attributes specify the privileges needed to execute the business operations. For example, they may specify that the user must be in the admin role. The access manager decides whether the user accessing the method has sufficient privileges. If the user doesn't have sufficient privileges, the `checkPermission()` method throws an exception.

The do-it-yourself approach has many problems:

- It quickly gets cumbersome and repetitious.
- It obscures the intention of business logic and prevents reuse with different security constraints.
- It clutters unit-testing code.
- It's easy to overlook places where the policy is implemented incorrectly.

Frameworks step in to provide some relief.

15.1.2 The framework-based approach

Frameworks often target a specific class of applications and can take advantage of the nature of the applications to offer simplified security solutions. Let's see how two common frameworks do this: servlets and EJBs. Of course, a framework may use AOP as the underlying mechanism as is done in Spring Security. We will discuss such an approach in the sections that follow.

The Servlet specification defines authentication functionality so that applications don't have to deal with it. It also offers a simple role-based authorization to protect URLs. As we discussed in chapter 1, servlet filters implement the *chain of responsibility* design pattern. Authorization is one of the responsibilities that a filter can implement. Such a filter can enforce the access rules based on the URL. For example, it may require that the user possesses the admin role to access URLs starting with */admin*. As we'll discuss in section 15.2, Spring Security uses servlet filters to implement URL-level security. Although it's simple to protect resources based on URLs, a filter-based implementation can't go much beyond that. For example, it can't implement method-level or object-level security.

The EJB framework handles authorization by separating the security attributes into the deployment descriptor or annotations, where you specify the required roles for methods in the EJBs. But you may face situations that require a custom solution for authentication and authorization. Consider, for example, data-driven authorization, where an authorization check considers not only the identity of the user and the functionality accessed but also the data involved. Current EJB frameworks don't offer a good solution to problems that demand this type of flexibility, leaving you to implement the do-it-yourself approach.

How can you improve the security implementation with AOP?

15.2 Modularizing security using AOP

Given the crosscutting nature of security, it shouldn't come as a surprise that AOP offers a simplified and flexible solution. In the same way as aspects in the previous chapter separated the transaction-management logic from the core business logic, you can expect security aspects to offer the same level of separation. Then, business methods can focus on their core logic:

```
public void businessMethod() {
    ... business operation
}
```

The security aspect needs to do the following:

- Select join points that need authentication or authorization.
- Advise the selected join points to perform authentication and authorization.

Here's an example:

```
aspect SecurityAspect {
    private AccessDecisionManager accessManager;

    pointcut secured() : ...
```

```
    before() : secured() {
        SecurityAttribute sa = ...
        accessManager.checkPermission(sa);
    }
}
```

The interesting piece of code is the computation of the security attributes. In the do-it-yourself approach, each method creates a separate security attribute object. In an AOP solution, the same advice applies to all advised join points, yet each join point may require a different attribute. Therefore, the advice may need some cooperation from the advised code or some external configuration to compute a correct attribute at each join point. One way to achieve this collaboration is to use annotations, as you'll see when you implement a complete aspect in section 15.4.2.

You can apply security aspects using either the proxy-based or byte-code based AOP. The considerations behind choosing the appropriate AOP system are identical to those discussed in section 14.3.

As you've seen in previous chapters, the AOP solution relies on an appropriate implementation of the underlying infrastructure. The security aspect acts as a controller that mediates between the core system and the security subsystem. Let's do a quick overview of Spring Security, which you'll use in the subsequent sections to implement your aspects.

15.3 A quick overview of Spring Security

Security requirements vary widely, and many implementations exist to meet these needs. For example, an authentication requirement may vary from simple web-based authentication to a single sign-on solution. Storage for credentials (such as passwords) and authorities (typically roles such as ADMIN or USER) varies widely as well—from a simple text file to a database or Lightweight Directory Access Protocol (LDAP).

These variations make the already complex topic of security even more so. The increased complexity warrants raising the level of abstraction. But creating such an abstraction isn't always an easy task, especially if security isn't your core expertise. This is where Spring Security comes into play. By providing an abstraction layer and an implementation for most commonly used security systems, you can create powerful, portable solutions. If a supplied implementation doesn't meet your needs, you can easily extend it by implementing a few interfaces. Furthermore, Spring Security provides ready-made solutions for a few common scenarios that allow you to implement certain security requirements by including just a few lines of configuration.

We'll now examine Spring Security up close, focusing on the parts you'll use later in this chapter: authentication and authorization.

15.3.1 Authentication

Authentication is a process that verifies that the user (human or machine) is indeed whom they claim to be. For example, the system may challenge the user with a username and password. When the user enters that information, the system verifies it against the stored credentials.

Spring Security supports authentication using a wide range of authentication schemes such as basic, forms, database, LDAP, JAAS, and single sign-on. You can also roll your own authentication to support the specific scheme that your organization is using (and still utilize the rest of the framework, including authorization). After the user credentials have been authenticated, the authenticated user (more generally known as the *principal*) is stored in the *security context*. Figure 15.1 shows the overall structure used in Spring Security for authentication.

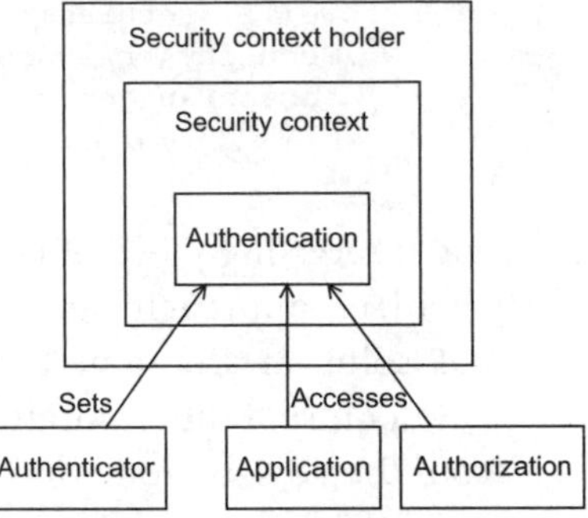

Figure 15.1 Overview of the authentication in Spring Security. The authenticator stores the authentication object in the security context. Other parts of the system, including the authorization subsystem, may access the authentication object from the security context.

As shown in the figure, the authentication system stores an `Authentication` object inside a `SecurityContext`. The `SecurityContextHolder` holds on to one `SecurityContext` object per scope, which may be a thread-local, an inheritable thread-local, or global. The thread-local scope is the default and most useful in web applications. The authenticated user may then be accessed by other parts of the system. For example, a service layer may access the principal authenticated by the web layer so that it can determine whether the user has appropriate privileges for the invoked services. You'll use this fact to access the principal from security-related aspects.

15.3.2 Authorization

Authorization is a process that establishes whether an authenticated user has sufficient privileges to access certain resources. For example, only users with the admin privilege may access certain web pages or invoke certain business methods.

Spring Security provides role-based and object-level authorization. To accommodate potentially complex custom requirements, it provides several components that you can customize. Figure 15.2 depicts the authorization sequence.

As shown in the figure, `AccessDecisionManager` has the overall responsibility to determine access to a given object. It makes the determination based on the current `Authentication` object, the accessed resource (which may be a domain object, an object representing a method, or even a join point), and the security attributes associated with the accessed object. The security attributes specify properties such as the roles required for an authorized access.

`AccessDecisionManager`, in turn, delegates the responsibility to `AccessDecisionVoters` by calling their `vote()` method. Each `AccessDecisionVoter` uses the same information that is passed to the `AccessDecisionManager`'s `decide()` method. Voters may vote to allow, deny, or abstain. Implementations of `AccessDecisionManager` tally all the votes and issue the final verdict.

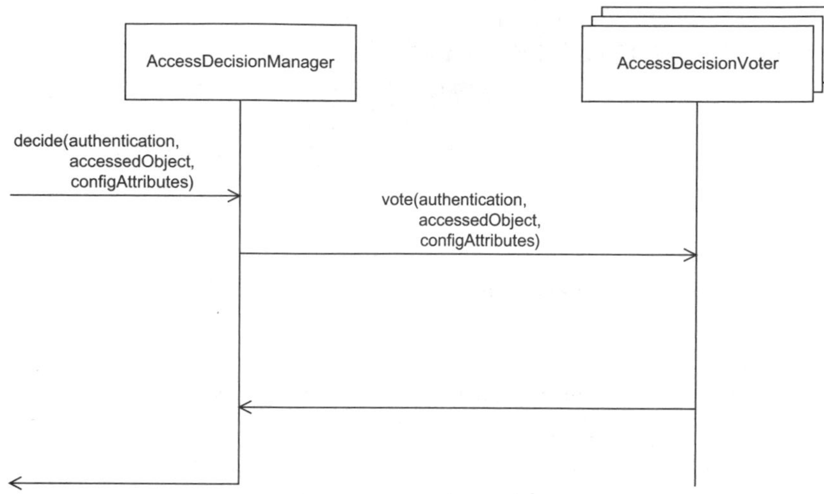

Figure 15.2 Spring Security authorization sequence. The code that needs to check for authorization consults an `AccessDecisionManager`, which in turn conducts a poll among `AccessDecisionVoters` and tallies the result.

Spring Security comes with three `AccessDecisionManager` implementations based on how they tally votes: `AffirmativeBased` (at least one voter returns an affirmative response), `ConsensusBased` (a majority of voters return an affirmative response), and `UnanimousBased` (all voters return an affirmative response). Check the Spring Security documentation for more details on these classes.

In addition to providing support to perform authentication and authorization, Spring Security provides prewritten servlet filters and aspects to enable security in your application with little custom coding. We'll discuss the prebuilt support in Spring Security in section 15.6.

You're now ready to use Spring Security to write a few aspects.

15.4 Implementing a security solution from scratch

Following the template set in the previous chapter, you'll develop a few aspects from scratch. Doing so will serve three purposes:

- It will provide a deeper understanding of how AOP modularizes a security implementation.
- It will help you create custom solutions based on the aspects.
- It will show ideas for implementing security-like solutions.

You'll use Spring Security as the underlying mechanism but drive it through your own aspects. If you need to use a different mechanism, you should be able to modify the aspect easily (although you may configure Spring Security to use that mechanism as well).

You have two separate functionalities to deal with: authentication and authorization. You'll begin with authentication.

Interested only in using Spring security?

As in the previous chapter, if you're only interested in *using* Spring Security, you can skip to section 15.6.

15.4.1 Implementing authentication aspects

When do you authenticate a user? You can do an up-front login when a user visits the web site or starts a UI or console application. You can delay it a bit, for example, when a user visits a secure web page. You can delay it even further, say, when a user accesses a specific functionality leading to a secured method invocation. Yet another style is to perform authentication when the authorization logic throws an exception indicating that the accessing user hasn't been authenticated yet.

Depending on your choice, AOP may or may not be the right implementation technique. For example, if you need to perform authentication only at one specific point, you may not need AOP. In this section, we'll focus on the cases where authentication is performed in response to a method being invoked.

BASE AUTHENTICATION ASPECT

Because join points where you need to perform authentication vary, let's write the base aspect shown in listing 15.1. This lets you defer the selection decision to subaspects. You use the @AspectJ syntax to allow the choice of proxy-based versus byte-code weaving.

Listing 15.1 Base authentication aspect

```
package ajia.security;

import ...

@Aspect
public abstract class AbstractAuthenticationAspect {
    private AuthenticationSupport authenticationSupport;     <-- 1 Support class dependency

    @Pointcut                                                   2 Authentication
    public abstract void authenticationRequired();              pointcut

    @Before("authenticationRequired()")
    public void authenticate() {                                3 Authentication
        authenticationSupport.authenticate();                   advice
    }

    public void setAuthenticationSupport(
            AuthenticationSupport authenticationSupport) {
        this.authenticationSupport = authenticationSupport;
    }
}
```

1 To better facilitate testing, you move most of the authentication-related implementation to a support class, which is declared as a dependency. If you use Spring to configure the application, you can inject this dependency through configuration. Otherwise, you can call the setter directly from the code. See chapter 6 for a discussion of how to access the aspect instance so that you can call a setter on it.

2 The abstract `authenticationRequired()` pointcut lets subaspects specify its definition.

3 The before advice to the `authenticationRequired()` pointcut performs authentication by delegating it to the injected dependency. If authentication fails, the support class throws `AuthenticationException`, which is an unchecked exception.

Thanks to the support class in listing 15.2, there is no Spring Security–related code in the aspect itself.

Listing 15.2 Support class for authentication

```
package ajia.security;

import ...

public class AuthenticationSupport {
    private AuthenticationManager authenticationManager;     <- 1 Authentication manager dependency
    private LoginService loginUI;     <- 2 Login UI dependency

    public void authenticate() {
        Authentication authentication
            = SecurityContextHolder.getContext().getAuthentication();
        if(authentication != null) {
            return;
        }
        Authentication authenticationToken
            = loginUI.getAuthenticationToken();
        authentication
            = authenticationManager.authenticate(authenticationToken);
        SecurityContextHolder.getContext().
            setAuthentication(authentication);
    }     3 Authentication logic

    public void setAuthenticationManager(AuthenticationManager am) {
        this.authenticationManager = am;
    }

    public void setLoginUI(LoginService loginUI) {
        this.loginUI = loginUI;
    }
}
```

Note that a better implementation would declare `AuthenticationSupport` as an interface and create a Spring Security–specific implementation. But for brevity's sake, I skip this step.

1 The class declares a dependency on Spring Security's `AuthenticationManager`. The injected object needs to be configured with the required objects, such as a credential source. This way, you can plug in any authentication mechanism such as a database, LDAP, or single sign-on.

2 The class also declares a dependency on a `LoginService` object. The `LoginService` provides the `getAuthenticationToken()` method that returns an `Authentication` object. It also has a dependency on a strategy that obtains the username and password as the default implementation. For a fat-client UI application, the implementation could put up a dialog box to ask for the username and password.

3 The authentication logic first checks if there is already an authenticated user in the security context. If not, it obtains an authentication token using the login service. It then passes that token to the authentication manager to validate it. The authentication manager throws `AuthenticationException` if the credentials don't match. Otherwise, the method stores the validated authentication object in the `SecurityContext` so that other parts of the system may obtain it.

Let's write a subaspect to see authentication in action.

EXAMPLE SUBASPECT

A good place to authenticate is when the user first invokes a service method. You'll accordingly write a subaspect (listing 15.3) with a pointcut that selects any service method.

Listing 15.3 Aspect for upfront login in a console application

```
package ajia.security;

import ...

@Aspect
public class ConsoleApplicationAuthenticationAspect extends
        AbstractAuthenticationAspect {
    @Pointcut("execution(* ajia.service.*.*(..))")
    public void authenticationRequired() { }
}
```

Before you can use this aspect, you need to configure it. If you're using Spring to configure your application, you'll need to add a snippet similar to listing 15.4 in one of the files that forms the application context. I prefer to add it to a separate file—say, security-context.xml—to keep security-related configuration elements separate from the rest.

Listing 15.4 Configuration for authentication

```
<security:authentication-manager alias="authenticationManager">
    <security:authentication-provider>
        <security:user-service>
            <security:user name="ramnivas" password="aop"
                           authorities="ROLE_USER,ROLE_SUPERVISOR"/>
            <security:user name="rod" password="spring"
                           authorities="ROLE_USER"/>
        </security:user-service>
    </security:authentication-provider>
</security:authentication-manager>

<bean id="authenticationSupport"
      class="ajia.security.AuthenticationSupport">
    <property name="authenticationManager"
              ref="authenticationManager"/>
    <property name="loginUI" ref="loginService"/>
</bean>

<bean id="loginService"
```

```
      class="ajia.security.SysoutLoginService"/>

<bean id="authenticationAspect"
      class="ajia.security.ConsoleApplicationAuthenticationAspect"
      factory-method="aspectOf">
    <property name="authenticationSupport"
              ref="authenticationSupport"/>
</bean>
```

The configuration uses namespace support to reduce the code required (see the Spring Security namespace documentation for more information). The `<security:authentication-manager>` element exposes an authentication manager. The embedded `<security:authentication-provider>` element creates a simple in-memory user service with two users:

- *ramnivas* with *aop* as the password, with the USER and SUPERVISOR roles
- *rod* with *spring* as the password, with the USER role

In real projects, you'll replace this authentication provider with an appropriate one such as that based on a real database, LDAP, or single-sign on. You inject this authentication manager into an authentication support bean, and that bean into the aspect. Remember that you use `factory-method="aspectOf"` only if you use the AspectJ weaver and not when using Spring AOP. If you use Spring AOP, you also need an `<aop:aspectj-autoproxy>` declaration.

When you compile and run these classes and aspects (listings 15.1 through 15.4) along with the driver and `TraceAspect` from chapter 10, you get the following output (user input in italics):

```
Entering [Main.main]
  Entering [AuthenticationSupport.setAuthenticationManager]
  Entering [AuthenticationSupport.setLoginUI]
  Entering [AbstractAuthenticationAspect.setAuthenticationSupport]
  Entering [ProductServiceImpl.findProduct]
     Entering [AuthenticationSupport.authenticate]
        Entering [SysoutLoginService.getAuthenticationToken]
Username: ramnivas
Password: aop
   Entering [JpaGenericRepository.find]
...
```

If you need to authenticate at a different point (say, after the main window is visible in a fat-client application), you have to modify only the pointcut in the subaspect.

Now, let's move to a more interesting and complex topic of authorization.

15.4.2 Implementing authorization aspects

An authorization aspect ensures that the user has sufficient privileges to access the advised join point. As usual, you have two choices for weaving in the authorization logic: proxy-based or byte code–based weaving. To accommodate both choices, you'll use the @AspectJ syntax, exactly as you did for authentication.

Implementing security using proxy-based Spring AOP involves the arrangement shown in figure 15.3.

Compare this to figure 14.2, which implemented transaction management. You'll see similarities due to the common use of AOP as the underlying mechanism. Spring AOP creates a proxy around the service beans, and the security advice ensures authorized access. As discussed in earlier chapters, Spring AOP works only with Spring beans. If you need a more encompassing solution, you'll need to use byte-code weaving.

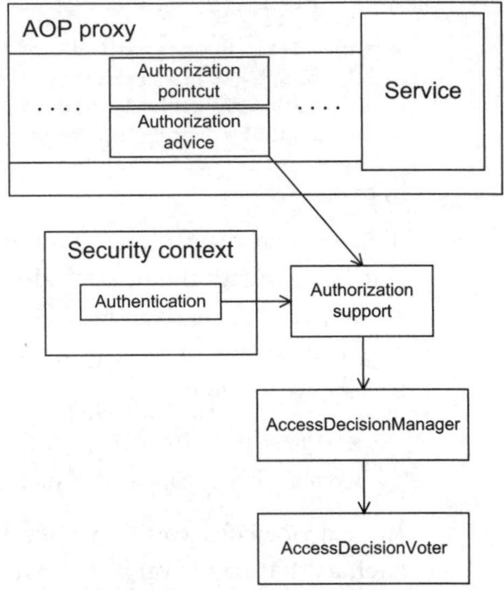

Figure 15.3 Securing the service layer using proxy-based AOP and Spring Security. An aspect consists of a pointcut and an advice. The advice delegates to a support class, which then performs the same task as in figure 15.2.

In the same way as the authentication aspect, the mechanism to choose authorized join points and to obtain security attributes varies. Let's write a base aspect that defers those decisions to subaspects.

BASE ASPECT

To allow flexibility in selecting authorized join points, you implement the abstract aspect shown in listing 15.5.

Listing 15.5 Base authorization aspect

```
package ajia.security;

import ...

@Aspect
public abstract class AbstractAuthorizationAspect {
    private AuthorizationSupport authorizationSupport;      ❶ Injected dependency

    @Pointcut
    public abstract void authorizationRequired();           ❷ Authorization pointcut

    @Before("authorizationRequired()")
    public void authorize(JoinPoint jp) {
        authorizationSupport.authorize(jp);                 ❸ Authorization advice
    }

    public void setAuthorizationSupport(
            AuthorizationSupport authorizationSupport) {
        this.authorizationSupport = authorizationSupport;
    }
}
```

❶ Like the authentication aspect, the authorization aspect delegates to a support class.

❷ The abstract `authorizationRequired()` pointcut allows subaspects to select the join points that need to be authorized.

❸ The advice delegates the authorization logic to the injected support object. Because authorization depends on the join points to compute the security attributes, it passes the current join point to the delegated method.

This aspect uses the support class shown in listing 15.6 to perform authorization. This class essentially implements the collaboration shown in figure 15.2.

Listing 15.6 Support class simplifying implementation and testing

```
package ajia.security;

import ...

public class AuthorizationSupport {
    private AccessDecisionManager accessDecisionManager;          ❶ Injected
    private SecurityMetadataSource securityMetadataSource;          dependencies

    public void authorize(Object securedObject) {
        List<ConfigAttribute> attrs
            = securityMetadataSource.getAttributes(securedObject);
        Authentication authentication
            = SecurityContextHolder.getContext().getAuthentication();
        accessDecisionManager.decide(authentication,
                                     securedObject, attrs);
    }                                               Authorization logic ❷

    public void setAccessDecisionManager(AccessDecisionManager adm) {
        this.accessDecisionManager = adm;
    }

    public void setSecurityMetadataSource(SecurityMetadataSource smds) {
        this.securityMetadataSource = smds;
    }
}
```

❶ The support class declares a dependency on an `AccessDecisionManager` that performs authorization and a `SecurityMetadataSource` that computes the security attributes.

❷ The `authorize()` method obtains a list of `ConfigAttributes`, which are the security attributes for the secured resource. It then obtains the current `Authentication` object from the `SecurityContextHolder`. Finally it passes all this information to the `decide()` method. If the accessing user doesn't have privileges matching the security attributes, the `decide()` method throws an `AccessDeniedException`. If the current user hasn't been authenticated yet, it throws an `InsufficientAuthenticationException`. Both of these are runtime exceptions.

Just in time authentication

You can advise the `AuthorizationSupport.authorize()` method or the advice in the `AbstractAuthorizationAspect` aspect to perform authentication when either throws an `InsufficientAuthenticationException`. Securing web applications through Spring Security uses a similar approach, performing authentication through a servlet filter in response to a thrown exception.

You have a few possible ways to write subaspects based on how you select join points to authorize. The two main selection choices are with or without annotations.

SUBASPECT WITHOUT ANNOTATIONS

A simple choice in writing a subaspect is to define a pointcut and provide a way to compute security attributes for a given join point. Here, you can use the participant pattern discussed in chapter 12, where you implement many simple aspects, each securing a specific class or a set of related classes.

> **Noninvasive crosscutting**
>
> Subaspects that don't use annotations require no changes to the core code. Instead, they rely on existing program structure such as the package structure, inheritance hierarchy, class and method name patterns, and even annotations not related to security. The result is noninvasive security functionality. But these subaspects are a little complex to implement in the absence of security-related information available from the secured program elements. Furthermore, they can be more fragile, because they often rely on fragile naming conventions.

The subaspect as shown in listing 15.7 selects all service methods for authorization.

Listing 15.7 Simple scheme implementing authorized access

```
package ajia.security;

import ...

@Aspect
public class SimpleAuthorizationAspect
    extends AbstractAuthorizationAspect {

    @Pointcut("execution(* ajia.service..*.*(..))")
    public void authorizationRequired() { }
}
```

Although the pointcut itself is simple, you need to implement another puzzle piece to obtain the security attributes for the advised join point. Note that you're applying authorization to the service layer. But nothing stops you from applying it to any other set of objects. Particularly, if you use the AspectJ weaver, you can write a subaspect that applies authorization to the domain entities.

Listing 15.8 shows an implementation of `SecurityMetadataSource` that relies on the method name and an external configuration to compute the security attributes.

Listing 15.8 Mapping-based security attribute definition source

```
package ajia.security;

import ...

public class MappingBasedSecurityMetadataSource
        implements SecurityMetadataSource {
```

```
    private Map<String, String> mapping;

    public List<ConfigAttribute> getAttributes(Object jp) {
        String methodName = ((JoinPoint)jp).getSignature().getName();
        for (String pattern : mapping.keySet()) {
            if(PatternMatchUtils.simpleMatch(pattern, methodName)) {
                String role = mapping.get(pattern);
                return SecurityConfig.createList(role);
            }
        }
        throw new IllegalArgumentException(
            "Unknown mapping for " + methodName);
    }

    public Collection<ConfigAttribute> getAllConfigAttributes() {
        return null;
    }

    public boolean supports(Class clazz) {
        return clazz.isAssignableFrom(JoinPoint.class);
    }

    public void setRoleMapping(Map<String, String> mapping) {
        this.mapping = mapping;
    }
}
```

You use a simple technique to compute security attributes. The role mapping is configured externally (typically, through Spring's application context). The key in the map is a name pattern such as `expire*`, and the value is the required role to access a method matching the name.

You need to configure the aspect (listing 15.9) and its associated objects through Spring's application context.

Listing 15.9 Authorization configuration for simple aspect

```
<bean id="accessDecisionManager"
      class="org.springframework.security.access.vote.UnanimousBased">
    <property name="decisionVoters">
        <list>
            <bean class="org.springframework.security.access.
                         vote.RoleVoter"/>
        </list>
    </property>
</bean>

<bean id="securityMetadataSource"
      class="ajia.security.MappingBasedSecurityMetadataSource">
    <property name="roleMapping">
        <map>
            <entry key="expire*" value="ROLE_SUPERVISOR"/>
            <entry key="reducePrice" value="ROLE_SUPERVISOR"/>
            <entry key="*" value="ROLE_USER"/>
        </map>
    </property>
</bean>
```

1. Defines access decision manager
2. Maps method to role

```
<bean id="authorizationSupport"
      class="ajia.security.AuthorizationSupport">
    <property name="accessDecisionManager"
              ref="accessDecisionManager"/>
    <property name="securityMetadataSource"
              ref="securityMetadataSource"/>
</bean>

<bean id="authorizationAspect"
      class="ajia.security.SimpleAuthorizationAspect"
      factory-method="aspectOf">
    <property name="authorizationSupport" ref="authorizationSupport"/>
</bean>
```

3 Defines authorization support

4 Configures aspect

1 You use the `UnanimousBased` class as the implementation for the access decision manager. You configure it with one voter to decide access based on roles.

2 You use your implementation of `MappingBasedSecurityMetadataSource` and configure it with a map. The mapping specifies that the user accessing the methods with name starting in `expire` or exactly matching `reducePrice` to be in the ROLE_SUPERVISOR role. For all other methods, you set the required role to ROLE_USER.

3 You inject both beans into the `authorizationSupport` bean.

4 You inject the aspect bean with the `authorizationSupport` bean. Note that you'll need to use the `factory-method="aspectOf"` attribute for aspects woven using the AspectJ weaver. If you're using Spring AOP, you shouldn't specify this attribute.

Because your driver program is a console application, you perform authentication through `ConsoleApplicationAuthenticationAspect` (from listing 15.3). You need to ensure that authentication kicks in before authorization if both take place at the same join point. You do that through `SecurityCoordinationAspect`, which declares higher precedence for subaspects of `AbstractAuthenticationAspect` over subaspects of `AbstractAuthorizationAspect`, as shown in listing 15.10. Note that you don't use a subaspect of `AbstractAuthenticationAspect` or the `SecurityCoordinationAspect` if you use a non-aspect solution (such as one based on a servlet filter) for authentication.

Listing 15.10 Aspect to control ordering of authentication and authorization

```
package ajia.security;

import ...

@Aspect
@DeclarePrecedence("AbstractAuthenticationAspect+,"
                 + "AbstractAuthorizationAspect+")
public class SecurityCoordinationAspect {
}
```

If you were to use Spring AOP, you would make each aspect implement the `Ordered` interface or attach the `@Order` annotation to each aspect and configure the order for `ConsoleApplicationAuthenticationAspect` to be a lower number than that for `SimpleAuthorizationAspect`, as discussed in chapter 9.

Let's execute the driver program and log in as the user with the USER role. You expect access to be denied to the `expireProduct()` method:

```
Entering [Main.main]
...
   Entering [ProductServiceImpl.findProduct]
     Entering [AuthenticationSupport.authenticate]
        Entering [SysoutLoginService.getAuthenticationToken]
Username: rod
Password: spring
        Entering [AuthorizationSupport.authorize]
        Entering [MappingBasedSecurityMetadataSource.getAttributes]
     Entering [JpaGenericRepository.find]
  Entering [OrderServiceImpl.addProduct]
...
 Entering [InventoryServiceImpl.expireProduct]
     Entering [AuthenticationSupport.authenticate]
     Entering [AuthorizationSupport.authorize]
        Entering [MappingBasedSecurityMetadataSource.getAttributes]
Exception in thread "main"
➥     org.springframework.security.AccessDeniedException: Access is denied
    at org.springframework.security.access.vote.UnanimousBased.decide(
➥    UnanimousBased.java:74)
    at ajia.security.AuthorizationSupport.authorize(
➥    AuthorizationSupport.java:20)
    at ajia.security.AbstractAuthorizationAspect.authorize(
➥    AbstractAuthorizationAspect.java:19)
    at ajia.service.impl.InventoryServiceImpl.expireProduct(
➥    InventoryServiceImpl.java:53)
...
    at ajia.main.Main.main(Main.java:25)
```

The output for the access by a user with the SUPERVISOR role (username: *ramnivas*, password: *aop*) is similar, except no exception is thrown.

One of the important advantages of the simple aspect is noninvasiveness. The core code is unaware of the security requirements and doesn't need any specific accommodation. This works fine for simple cases where the criterion to select the authorization join points and the logic to deduce the security attributes are simple. But in other cases, it may pose a difficulty in writing a robust pointcut and externalizing the security attributes. In those cases, you may need some collaboration from the core code in the form of annotations.

ANNOTATION-DRIVEN SUBASPECT

The core idea behind the annotation-driven approach is to attach authorized types and/or methods with annotations that specify security-related information such as the expected roles. The aspect can then select all methods that carry such annotations and compute the security attributes based on the annotation values. This idea is similar to how you implemented transaction management in the previous chapter.

Let's write a subaspect that uses annotations, as shown in listing 15.11.

Listing 15.11 Annotation-driven authorization aspect

```
package ajia.security;

import ...

@Aspect
public class SecuredAnnotationAuthorizationAspect
    extends AbstractAuthorizationAspect {

    // The use of the wildcard in org.springframework..Secured,
    // although correct, is used only for better formatting
    @Pointcut(
         "execution(@org.springframework..Secured * *(..))"
    + "|| execution(* (@org.springframework..Secured *).*(..))")
    public void authorizationRequired() {}
}
```

The only change compared to SimpleAuthorizationAspect is the pointcut expression. Instead of selecting every service method, this pointcut selects every method marked with the @Secured annotation as well as every method in a type marked with the @Secured annotation. Spring Security already provides an implementation of SecurityMetadataSource in the form of SecuredMethodSecurityMetadataSource to extract the security attribute from the @Secured annotation.

For this aspect to work, you must mark the type or methods with the @Secured annotation and specify the required role as the attribute. For example, you modify InventoryServiceImpl as follows:

```
@Secured("ROLE_USER")
public class InventoryServiceImpl implements InventoryService {

... unchanged

    @Secured("ROLE_SUPERVISOR")
    public void expireProduct(Product product) {
```

The annotations specify that the expireProduct() method may be accessed only by users with the SUPERVISOR role. Users possessing the USER role may access any other method. You also modify other service classes to add @Secured("ROLE_USER") to ensure that those are accessed only by users with the USER role.

You need to configure this aspect as shown in listing 15.12.

Listing 15.12 Authorization configuration for a simple aspect

```
... accessDecisionManager and authorizationSupport
... unchanged since listing 15.9

<bean id="securityMetadataSource"
      class="org.springframework.security.access.annotation.
➥             SecuredAnnotationSecurityMetadataSource"/>

<bean id="authorizationAspect"
      class="ajia.security.SecuredAnnotationAuthorizationAspect"
      factory-method="aspectOf">
    <property name="authorizationSupport"
              ref="authorizationSupport"/>
</bean>
```

That's it. You're now ready to run the application:

```
Entering [Main.main]
...
   Entering [ProductServiceImpl.findProduct]
     Entering [AuthenticationSupport.authenticate]
        Entering [SysoutLoginService.getAuthenticationToken]
Username: rod
Password: spring
   Entering [JpaGenericRepository.find]
...
   Entering [InventoryServiceImpl.expireProduct]
     Entering [AuthenticationSupport.authenticate]
     Entering [AuthorizationSupport.authorize]
Exception in thread "main"
➥  org.springframework.security.AccessDeniedException:
➥  Access is denied
    at org.springframework.security.access.vote.UnanimousBased.decide(
➥  UnanimousBased.java:74)
    at ajia.security.AuthorizationSupport.authorize(
➥  AuthorizationSupport.java:20)
    at ajia.security.AbstractAuthorizationAspect.authorize(
➥  AbstractAuthorizationAspect.java:19)
    at ajia.service.impl.InventoryServiceImpl.expireProduct(
➥  InventoryServiceImpl.java:56)
...
    at ajia.main.Main.main(Main.java:25)
```

The output is identical to that of the subaspect that didn't use annotations.

Now that you've implemented simple authentication and authorization, let's get a bit more adventurous and see how you can stretch aspects to complex security requirements.

15.5 Implementing field-level authorization

Consider a health-care application that manages entities such as doctors, patients, prescriptions, lab results, diagnoses, and insurance claims. Although many users may access diagnoses, not all may see every field. For example, an insurance agent may see when a lab test was performed but not the test results. Similarly, a patient may see the result only after the doctor approves it. In such situations, security is at the individual field level and not at the object level.

Because the security-access logic applies to the fields of domain objects, proxy-based AOP doesn't cut it. You must use AspectJ-based weaving. (Note that Spring Security currently doesn't provide this functionality out of the box, but a future version may.)

The decision to determine access may be based on roles, object state, or a combination thereof. For example, a user with ROLE_DOCTOR may be able to see any test results (role-based decision), or you may have a more stringent requirement that only the doctor who ordered the test may see its results (object-state and role-based decision). Furthermore, it's likely that you'll want to have doctors with ROLE_EMERGENCY_DOCTOR to be able to see results regardless of their relationship to the patients.

The core idea behind implementing field-access checks is similar to method access. The only real difference is that instead of using method-level annotations, you use field-level annotations. By using a field-access pointcut (discussed in chapter 3), you can enforce the access check.

Annotation isn't the only choice

As you've seen for authorization, the use of annotations isn't the only choice for field-level security. It's valid to enforce access checks based on packages, inheritance hierarchy, and so on. For example, if you need to control access to all fields whose type extends the `Document` type, you can use `get(Document+ *)` to select the access-controlled fields. You can also repurpose existing non-security annotations. For example, if you need to control access to the fields whose type is marked with the `@HIPAAData` annotation,[1] you can use the `get((@HIPAAData *) *)` pointcut.

It boils down to understanding the join point model and the pointcut expression language. This is why I made you read the long, detailed chapter 3.

Let's see how this is implemented in your e-commerce application. First, you'll define an annotation (listing 15.13) that can be attached to fields.

Listing 15.13 Custom annotation to mark secured fields

```
package ajia.security;

import ...

@Target(ElementType.FIELD)
@Retention(RetentionPolicy.RUNTIME)
public @interface Access {
    String[] value();
}
```

This annotation is similar to the `@Secured` annotation. The only difference is that you allow the annotation target to be a field. Listing 15.14 shows a test that you'll follow with an implementation to make it pass.

Listing 15.14 Test to verify field-level security

```
package ajia.security;

import ...

@RunWith(SpringJUnit4ClassRunner.class)
@ContextConfiguration
public class AccessFieldSecurityAspectTest {
    private Product product;
```

[1] The Health Insurance Portability and Accountability Act—HIPAA—in the USA, among other things, mandates certain privacy policies. See http://en.wikipedia.org/wiki/HIPAA for details.

```
    @Before
    public void setup() {
        setupAuthentication("ROLE_SUPERVISOR");
        product = new Product("TestProduct",
                              "Test Description", 20);
    }

    @Test
    public void regularAccess() {
        setupAuthentication("ROLE_ANONYMOUS");
        product.getName();
        product.setName("new name");
    }

    @Test
    public void securedAccessSufficientAuthority() {
        setupAuthentication("ROLE_SUPERVISOR");
        product.getPrice();
        product.setPrice(0);
    }

    @Test(expected=AccessDeniedException.class)
    public void securedReadAccessInsufficientAuthority() {
        setupAuthentication("ROLE_USER");
        product.getPrice();
        product.setPrice(0);
    }

    @Test(expected=AccessDeniedException.class)
    public void securedWriteAccessInsufficientAuthority() {
        setupAuthentication("ROLE_USER");
        product.setPrice(0);
    }

    private void setupAuthentication(String role) {
        Authentication authentication
            = new TestingAuthenticationToken(
                    "ramnivas", "", role);
        SecurityContextHolder.getContext().
            setAuthentication(authentication);
    }
}
```

In this test, you exercise three scenarios: uninhibited access to an unsecured field, successful access for users with a correct role, and preventing access to users with an incorrect role. The test assumes that the `price` field in the `Product` class is a secured field that requires ROLE_SUPERVISOR as the expected role. You fulfill this assumption by marking that field with the `@Access` annotation, as shown in listing 15.15.

Listing 15.15 Domain entity with secured fields

```
package ajia.domain;

...

public class Product extends DomainEntity {
```

```
    private String name;
    private String description;
    @Access("ROLE_SUPERVISOR") private double price;

    ... unchanged from listing A.2

}
```

Let's write a simple aspect that advises fields marked with the `@Access` annotation to authorize access to those fields (see listing 15.16).

Listing 15.16 Aspect advising access to secured fields

```
package ajia.security;

import ...

@Aspect
public class AccessFieldSecurityAspect {
    private AuthorizationSupport securitySupport;

    @Pointcut("(get(@Access * *) || set(@Access * *)) "
            + "&& @annotation(access)")
    public void secureFieldAccess(Access access) {}                  ❶ Selects field access

    @Before("secureFieldAccess(access)")
    public void secure(Access access) {                              ❷ Secures field access
        securitySupport.authorize(access);
    }

    public void setSecuritySupport(
            AuthorizationSupport securitySupport) {
        this.securitySupport = securitySupport;
    }
}
```

❶ The pointcut selects read and write access to any field annotated with the `@Access` annotation. It also collects the annotation associated with the field.

❷ The advice consults the injected `securitySupport` object to make an access decision.

Next, you configure the aspect with a context that is loaded by the test (AccessFieldSecurityAspectTest-context.xml), as shown in listing 15.17.

Listing 15.17 Configuration of the aspect for the test

```
<beans ...>
    <bean id="securityMetadataSource"
         class="ajia.security.AccessAnnotationMetadataSource"/>

    <bean id="accessDecisionManager"
         class="org.springframework.security.access.vote.UnanimousBased">
        <property name="decisionVoters">
        <list>
            <bean class="org.springframework.security.
➥                         access.vote.RoleVoter" />
          </list>
        </property>
    </bean>
```

```
    <bean id="fieldSecurityAspect"
          class="ajia.security.AccessFieldSecurityAspect"
          factory-method="aspectOf">
        <property name="securitySupport" ref="securitySupport"/>
    </bean>

    <bean id="securitySupport"
          class="ajia.security.AuthorizationSupport">
        <property name="accessDecisionManager"
            ref="accessDecisionManager" />
        <property name="securityMetadataSource"
            ref="securityMetadataSource"/>
    </bean>
</beans>
```

When you run this test, you see a green bar!

Now, let's examine how Spring Security uses AOP to provide out-of-box solutions.

15.6 Spring Security prebuilt solutions

Spring Security provides ready-made solutions that enable developers to secure applications with a few lines of configuration. These solutions target different parts of application: web, service layer, and domain objects. Let's take a look at these solutions. Note that full details of Spring Security are beyond the scope of this book. I strongly recommend that you read the documentation provided as a part of its download.

15.6.1 Web security

Securing web applications is a common task, therefore, Spring Security provides special support for this scenario. With namespace-based configuration, a few lines can configure URL level security that ensures that the user has the right authority to access the URLs. For example, the following Spring configuration provides authentication using a default login page and ensures that any URLs that end with "delete.htm" are accessible only by users with the ADMIN role. Other URLs are accessed only by users with the USER role.

```
<security:http auto-config="true">
    <security:intercept-url pattern="/*delete.htm" access="ROLE_ADMIN"/>
    <security:intercept-url pattern="/**" access="ROLE_USER"/>
</security:http>

... declaration of user service to provide username/password
```

Typically, you'll start with a simple snippet as shown, modify various attributes, and add additional elements to tailor to your specific needs. For many applications, it's sufficient to secure just the UI layer. But you may want to secure the service layer as well, to prevent any errors in the UI security configuration from compromising the system. It also allows secured access through non-web interfaces.

15.6.2 Service level security

Because most enterprise applications utilize a service layer as the exclusive way of accessing business functionality, it makes sense to secure this layer. Spring Security provides prebuilt aspects along with namespace-based configuration support to secure the service layer with minimal code (more precisely, you can secure any Spring bean, not just those in the service layer). It offers two options to specify the access-control information: through the XML-based configuration and through annotations.

EXTERNAL CONFIGURATION OPTION

With the external configuration option, XML code specifies the secured methods as well as the mapping between methods and roles. This approach is similar to what we presented in section 15.4.2. The following snippet shows how you can limit method access to users with specific roles:

```
<security:global-method-security>
    <security:protect-pointcut
        expression="execution(* ajia.service.*.delete*(..))"
        access="ROLE_ADMIN"/>
</security:global-method-security>
```

Notice something that should look familiar to you by now: a pointcut expression. The `protect-pointcut` element specifies a pointcut and the required privileges to access the join points selected by that pointcut. For example, this snippet specifies that only users with the ADMIN role may access any method whose name starts with `delete` in a class in the `ajia.service` package. Behind the scenes, this snippet leads to the creation of a proxy for the service beans along with a security aspect, as shown earlier in figure 15.3.

ANNOTATION-BASED OPTION

Annotations provide another way to enable method-level security. Instead of writing a pointcut, you attach types and methods with annotations that specify the security attributes, as shown in listing 15.18.

Listing 15.18 Example class with security annotations

```
package ajia.service.impl;

import...

@Secured("ROLE_SUPERVISOR")                                    <-- 1 Type-level annotation
public class InventoryServiceImpl implements InventoryService {
    ...

    public void addProduct(Product product, int quantity) {
        ...
    }

    public void removeProduct(Product product, int quantity) {
        ...
    }
                                                  Method-level annotation 2
    @Secured("ROLE_USER")                                      <--
    public boolean isProductAvailable(Product product, int quantity) {
        ...
    }
}
```

❶ The type-level annotation specifies the security attribute required for all methods in the type. For `InventoryServiceImpl`, the `@Secured` annotation at the type level specifies that user must have the SUPERVISOR role to access any method, unless the method also specifies its own annotation.

❷ The method-level annotation specifies the security attribute for the annotated method. For `InventoryServiceImpl`, the `@Secured` annotation for the `isProductAvailable()` method overrides the role specified at the type level to be the USER role.

The XML configuration reduces to this:

```
<global-method-security secured-annotations="enabled">
```

Instead of the `@Secured` annotation, you can use Java Specification Requests (JSR) 250 annotations from the `javax.annotation.security` package, such as `@RolesAllowed`, `@PermitAll`, and `@DenyAll`. The XML configuration enables the use of JSR 250 annotation as follows:

```
<global-method-security jsr250-annotations="enabled">
```

Whichever way you choose, the underlying mechanism involves Spring AOP along with Spring Security players, as shown earlier in figure 15.3.

What about prescreening?

A common way to handle access control is to apply *anticipatory* restrictions. For example, in a web application, you may hide certain links after you determine that the user doesn't possess sufficient authority to successfully access the associated functionality. Disabling that functionality has the additional advantage of not letting a user attempt access only to be presented with an unfriendly message indicating that they shouldn't have clicked that link.

But this scheme has a few limitations and flaws:

- It doesn't work for non-UI applications.
- For bookmarkable URLs, it doesn't prevent the possibility of someone sharing a link.
- It's cumbersome to implement prescreening where a free-form UI interaction is expected based on, say, the outcome of a search result.
- It relies on due diligence of the UI programmers to put security checks in the right places. Any lapse on their part may lead to security holes.

Even if prescreening is used, it's still critical that the backend expect the unexpected, always suspect all requests, and apply security on its own. Of course, you should add prescreening whenever possible; but its purpose should be to provide a better user experience, not to secure applications.

GOING BEYOND ROLES

In some situations, the role alone isn't sufficient to determine access. Moreover, the role required to access some functionality may depend on the data at the time of access. Therefore, Spring Security offers a way to protect domain entities through an access control list (ACL). With it, you can limit access to certain objects only to users with specific authorization to those objects.

Spring Security, starting with version 3.0, also offers a way to specify scripts that describe access rules. For example, as shown in the following snippet, you can specify that expiring an item in the inventory requires that the user be the manager for the department of the product being expired:

```
@PreAuthorize("#product.department.manager.name.equals(
➥              #authentication.name)")
public void expireProduct(Product product) {
    ...
}
```

The implementation behind the script-based support is similar to that for caching in chapter 4, where you used a script to compute the cache key. Scripts can use method arguments and the authentication object to define access rules. The script-based authorization also supports post authorization (which can also access the object returned by the advised method) as well as filtering of arguments and returned objects.

For some applications, securing the service layer isn't sufficient; you need to secure domain objects as well.

15.6.3 Domain-object security

You need to apply security to domain objects such as an account, customer, and line item. In many applications, every operation is funneled through the service layer, so service-layer security suffices. But such use of the service layer can be a burden on the architecture (especially if that is the only purpose of the service layer). Therefore, it can be valuable to apply security directly to domain objects.

As you saw in section 15.3, Spring Security offers an infrastructure that is flexible enough to be applied to domain objects with little effort. Currently, Spring Security doesn't include prebuilt aspects targeted toward domain objects; but this may change in a future version. Meanwhile, you can use the aspects developed in listings 15.5–15.17 to secure your domain objects. Of course, because typically domain objects aren't managed by Spring, you can't use Spring's proxy-based AOP; that job is best left to the AspectJ weaver.

Let's end this chapter with a discussion of what else aspects can do to implement a wide range of security requirements.

15.7 Additional ideas in implementing security

As I mentioned earlier, security requirements vary a lot—and when you cross the comfort zone of basic authentication and authorization, it's wild out there! Enterprises tend to have specific requirements to enforce various facets of security, such as auditing access to sensitive data and filtering collections returned as part of a query.

This section will discuss a few ideas and ways to approach these requirements. When you implement your specific requirements, I recommend that you start with the presented approach and modify it as needed.

15.7.1 Auditing access

For privacy monitoring and regulatory compliance, you may need to monitor access to important data and operations. For example, although a user may have access to a piece of data, it may be important to audit when and in which context they access that data. If things go wrong or suspicious activities take place, such auditing may save people and organizations; that's the world we've come to live in.

Implementing auditing with AOP is a piece of cake. We've already discussed all you need to know in chapter 10. Essentially, you extend the monitoring aspects presented in that chapter to audit security-related fields and operations. The audit record may need to include the accessing context, such as the top-level method that led to an access to a sensitive field. You may also need the join point context associated with the top-level method. The `cflow()` pointcut combined with the wormhole pattern discussed in chapter 12 comes in handy here.

15.7.2 Filtering field content

Consider an inventory-management service in which you want to expose only inventory items that the user is entitled to see. For example, the users can see only products associated with their department. In this case, you don't want to completely reject access to the field. Instead, you need to filter the content. Spring Security provides a mechanism known as `AfterInvocationManager` as well as the `@PostFilter` annotation for scripting-based filtering. But you can also implement your own filter using an `around()` advice.

The scheme of filtering returned data may exhibit a performance problem if the returned value is a large collection. Filtering essentially pulls all the information from the underlying source and removes elements that don't match a security criterion. A better scheme may apply some prefiltering. If you use an ORM technology such as Hibernate, you can enable filters that augment SQL queries with a `where` clause. For example, you can enable a filter upon entering a service method so that when eventually a query is executed at the data layer, the clause limits the returned data. The ORM technologies also offer the concept of *criteria* that play a role similar to filters but apply to individual queries. By advising the queries' creation to augment the additional criteria, you can easily limit access to data.

15.8 Summary

Security is a classic example of a crosscutting concern—the same concern needs to be implemented and applied across many chunks of the same code base. Although security frameworks such as Spring Security and JAAS isolate you from the details of the underlying security mechanism, the *application* of the security check can still lead to code tangling and scattering.

An AOP solution modularizes this crosscutting concern. By driving the security APIs through aspects, it keeps the security code away from the main-line business code. This offers a good separation of responsibility: security experts can focus on writing security aspects, and developers with business knowledge can focus solely on business logic.

Security solutions using aspects come in various forms. The simplest form uses a servlet filter to secure the UI layer or proxy-based AOP to secure the service layer. But many applications need to go beyond securing the UI or the service layer. This is where the general nature of an AOP solution outshines all the alternatives. By targeting the aspect to domain objects, you can easily implement domain-object security. You can even target fields of an object so that information doesn't leak to unauthorized users. This provides enormous flexibility in designing your application and avoids having to make architectural decisions just to provide a convenient funnel in which security is applied.

Annotations can simplify implementing security functionality. A solution that uses annotations isn't as transparent, because business code carries security-related annotations. But many developers see this arrangement as a good compromise between a completely noninvasive solution and directly embedded security code. With a completely noninvasive solution, business developers wonder how security is implemented and how to influence security requirements. Aspect developers also need to work hard on writing a good pointcut and potentially require business classes to include an aspect following the participant pattern. Annotations provide a good collaboration point, where classes contain annotations and aspects consume those through pointcuts.

For any kind of situation, AOP offers a broad range of possibilities for making authorization decisions. You can use AOP's modularization and simplicity to address any security requirements during application evolution—all you need is good knowledge of the underlying security APIs and AspectJ.

So far in this book, we've focused mostly on infrastructural aspects. But aspects are also useful in domain logic. In the next chapter, we'll examine a few ways aspects can help with that.

16 Improving domain logic

This chapter covers

- Empowering objects using DI
- Implementing crosscutting business logic
- Avoiding unnecessary DTOs

So far in this book, we've established that AOP is useful for implementing crosscutting infrastructure functionality such as monitoring, concurrency control, transaction management, and security. Those crosscutting concerns are often the first you'll implement with AOP. But AOP is also useful in improving the implementation of domain logic in several ways. First, aspects help in implementing dependency injection (DI) for objects not explicitly managed by a DI container. This enables the implementation of complex behavior that would otherwise be tedious. Second, by modularizing crosscutting business logic, AOP provides the same benefits it offers to crosscutting infrastructure concerns. Furthermore, AOP helps enforce design rules targeted toward the domain objects, improving the overall quality of the software system.

Unlike infrastructure aspects, these aspects are specific to the target domain. Consequently, most of the aspects aren't reusable. In this chapter, we'll focus on general concepts so that you can map them to your own domain. The examples in this chapter rely on a certain notion of the business domain and may not match yours. But the precise nature of the business domain isn't the main point. This chapter is about identifying solutions that remove limitations from the current architecture styles. It strives to trigger a thought process so that you can apply and expand on the ideas presented.

In this chapter, we'll focus on empowering objects with a combination of DI enabled through AOP and modularizing crosscutting business logic. We will also examine a way to avoid the use of Data Transfer Objects (DTOs) in many cases without sacrificing benefits they offer.

16.1 Empowering objects

One of the main premises of object-oriented programming is that objects should have both data *and* behavior. But the reality is often different. Many objects, especially domain objects, act as simple data carriers lacking rich behavior—thus creating an anemic domain model (see http://www.martinfowler.com/bliki/AnemicDomainModel.html for a detailed discussion). As a result, implementations often shift the behavior to the service layer. The core problem is that implementing rich behavior requires collaboration with other objects, and accessing those objects isn't as easy as it may appear at first.

Let's revisit the `Order` class you've been using in this book. For the most part, this class is a data carrier: it includes a list of `LineItem`s and the status of the order indicating if it has been placed. Essentially, it contains all the information that is persistent in nature. It includes some trivial behavior to obtain the total of the entire order, but there is a catch. You're getting away with using a simple implementation for this behavior: the order total is the sum of the individual line-item costs. In the real world, this implementation is unlikely to fly. The order total must consider various factors such as a bulk discount, a special discount due to a coupon, or special pricing based on the status of the customer.

The same level of complexity applies to other pricing-related functionality: obtaining discount details, obtaining possible discounts if the customer adds more items or acquires a special status, and so on. Similar complexity may crop up in other classes such as `LineItem`. You certainly don't want to burden the domain objects with pricing-related logic. Doing so would tangle the pricing logic with the domain objects and make it difficult to share pricing computations between related classes such as `Order` and `LineItem`.

In the last few years, the Domain Driven Design (DDD) approach has gained popularity. The main premise of the DDD approach is that the design, especially for complex systems, should be based on a domain model, and the primary focus should be on domain logic and not technological factors. Because the domain models for complex systems have rich behavior, the corresponding design and implementation should have the matching rich behavior. See *Domain-Driven Design: Tackling Complexity in the Heart of Software* (Addison-Wesley, 2003) by Eric Evans for more information. But implementing the DDD approach has some practical difficulties. As you'll see in this chapter, AOP substantially helps you implement the DDD approach by overcoming these difficulties.

> **Spring Roo and domain-driven design**
> The Spring Roo (http://www.springsource.org/roo) project uses AspectJ to promote domain-driven design. Through a judicious use of annotations along with aspects, it offers improved productivity, elegant design, and simpler implementation without locking user applications to Roo.

16.1.1 Enabling rich behavior

Implementing rich behavior in a reasonable manner requires the `Order` class to delegate the pricing computation to a separate class. Essentially, you need an arrangement such as the following:

```
public class Order extends DomainEntity {
    private transient PricingStrategy pricingStrategy;

    ...

    public double getTotalPrice() {
        return pricingStrategy.getPrice(this);
    }
}
```

You include a field of the `PricingStrategy` type. To avoid serializing this field, you mark it as `transient`. With an object-relational mapping (ORM) framework such as JPA, marking the field as `transient` avoids persisting it into database. The `getTotalPrice()` method uses this field to call the `getPrice()` method, passing the `this` object as the parameter. You can similarly implement methods such as `getAdjustments()` to obtain details of the currently applied discounts, `getPossibleAdjustments()` to obtain possible discounts the customer may receive, and so on.

The question is how to initialize the `pricingStrategy` field. You have a few options.

- *Hard-coded dependency*—Set the `pricingStrategy` field to an instance of a specific class:

  ```
  private transient PricingStrategy pricingStrategy
      = new SimplePricingStrategy();
  ```

  The hard-coded dependency makes it difficult to swap a pricing strategy or perform unit testing.

- *Locator*—Introduce a locator class (commonly known as a *service locator*) with a method to obtain a reference to a shared object. At the application or container level, you register various objects with the locator. Doing so removes the hard-coded dependency between the `Order` class and a pricing strategy implementation.

  ```
  private transient PricingStrategy pricingStrategy
      = (PricingStrategy) Context.get("pricingStrategy");
  ```

Such an arrangement makes it easier to swap the implementation by registering a different object with the locator. But the domain objects now depend on the locator class—`Context`, in turn, adds a dependency on the environment that supplies a locator. Compared with the hard-coded dependencies approach, such an arrangement doesn't fare much better with unit testing. Unit tests need to somehow coerce the `Context` object into returning the expected mock or stub object, because you may need to set the `pricingStrategy` to a different mock or stub object in each test.

- *Dependency injection*—Add the necessary structure to domain objects to enable DI. For example, you can add a setter for each injected dependency. Then, you let a container inject dependencies upon instantiating the object. With this setup, the object has no knowledge of the mechanics of the DI. You can swap one service for another by modifying the configuration. For unit testing, you can set the dependencies directly by calling setters from the test code, without needing any special mechanism.

Static field dependency injection?

You can add a static field to the domain classes and initialize this field through an external mechanism. But this approach suffers from a few drawbacks:

- It forces all objects of the same type to share the same dependency.
- It makes it awkward to share common logic in an inheritance hierarchy that needs to delegate work to a different dependent object.
- It makes all objects of a class depend on a single object. Swapping that object at runtime in a synchronized manner is difficult.
- Unit testing—especially parallel execution of tests—becomes difficult, if not impossible.

With beans such as controllers, services, and repositories, a DI container such as Spring instantiates the objects and injects dependencies. But a DI container doesn't instantiate domain objects (such as entities and value objects). Instead, you or other frameworks such as ORM can directly instantiate objects (using `new` or the reflection API). Consequently, the container doesn't have an opportunity to inject dependencies. AspectJ comes to the rescue by extending the container services to the domain objects. Let's examine an implementation of this technique available in Spring.

16.1.2 Injecting dependencies with Spring and AspectJ

Spring uses the AspectJ weaver to provide a prebuilt solution to inject dependency into any objects—even those that are instantiated outside of Spring. An aspect injects dependencies whenever an instance of a specified class is instantiated or deserialized. Figure 16.1 shows how an aspect injects dependencies into domain objects.

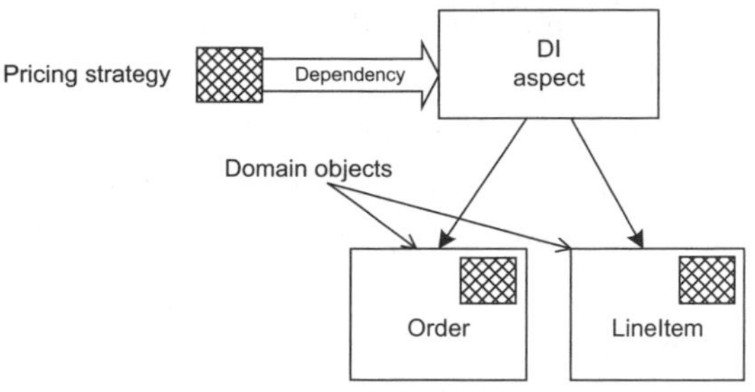

Figure 16.1 Domain object DI through an aspect. Upon creating domain objects, the aspect performs DI on them. The aspect itself has dependencies injected into it, which it injects into the domain objects.

Spring offers two ways for you to specify classes to participate in such a DI mechanism: by annotating the class and through domain-specific interfaces along with custom sub-aspects. Let's examine each in detail.

ANNOTATION-BASED DI

With this style, you mark each class that needs DI with the `@Configurable` annotation. You also specify through configuration how Spring should inject dependencies. As you'll see later in this section, you can avoid most of the configuration through Spring's autowiring feature.

Let's apply this style to the `Order` class. You'll inject each instance of `Order` with a `PricingStrategy` bean. Listing 16.1 shows the modifications to the `Order` class.

Listing 16.1 Preparing `Order` for DI

```
package ajia.domain;

import ...
import org.springframework.beans.factory.annotation.Configurable;

@Entity
@Table(name="orders")
@Configurable                                        <-- 1 Annotates class for DI
public class Order extends DomainEntity {

    ...

    private transient PricingStrategy pricingStrategy;

    ...

    public double getTotalPrice() {
        return pricingStrategy.getPrice(this);       <-- 2 Uses injected dependency
    }

    public void setPricingStrategy(PricingStrategy pricingStrategy) {
        this.pricingStrategy = pricingStrategy;
    }                                                Declares dependency 3
}
```

1. You mark the class with the `@Configurable` annotation to signal that this class should be configured by the Spring container, even though it's not instantiated as a Spring bean.

2. You use the injected pricing strategy to implement the getTotalPrice() method to delegate the computation.
3. You add a setter to allow Spring to inject the dependency.

Although you'll be creating Orders outside of Spring, you need to instruct Spring how to configure an Order instance. You do that through a prototype bean definition; see listing 16.2.

Listing 16.2 Configuration to inject dependencies

```
<beans ...>
    <bean id="pricingStrategy"
          class="ajia.domain.SimplePricingStrategy"/>      <- 1 Bean to inject

    <bean class="ajia.domain.Order" scope="prototype">      2 Specification of domain object DI
        <property name="pricingStrategy" ref="pricingStrategy"/>
    </bean>

    <context:spring-configured/>      <- 3 Instruction to inject dependencies
</beans>
```

1. The pricingStrategy bean is a regular Spring bean that you'll inject into the Order objects.
2. You declare a bean of the Order type. The prototype scope instructs Spring to not create a bean for this definition upon creating the application context. In your setup, you'll never request a bean for this definition; hence, no bean will ever be created for the definition. Alternatively, you can use the abstract="true" attribute to the same effect. In either case, the bean definition serves only as the specification for the injected dependencies. You use a <property> element to declare that the dependency should be wired to the pricingStrategy bean. If there were more dependencies to be injected, you would have one <property> element for each of them, just like any other Spring bean.
3. The <context:spring-configured/> element instructs Spring to inject dependencies for the classes annotated with the @Configurable annotation. Behind the scenes, it instantiates an aspect and configures it. Now, whenever an Order instance is created or deserialized, this aspect will call the setPricingStrategy() method and pass it the pricingStrategy bean as the argument.

Let's check this through a simple integration test, as shown in listing 16.3.

Listing 16.3 Integration test to check the DI mechanism

```
package ajia.domain;

import ...

@RunWith(SpringJUnit4ClassRunner.class)
@ContextConfiguration
public class PricingStrategyInjectionTest {
    @Test
    public void lineItemInjection() {
```

```
        Order testOrder = new Order();
        Assert.assertNotNull(
            ReflectionTestUtils.getField(testOrder,
                                         "pricingStrategy"));
    }
}
```

The test creates an Order and checks whether the dependency has been injected into it.

Unit-testing with @Configurable objects

When you're using unit testing, unlike integration testing, you don't want to involve any infrastructure, including Spring. Therefore, you should manually inject dependencies (typically, mock or stub objects) by calling the appropriate setters.

Spring's autowiring mechanism offers an additional technique based on the @Autowired annotation that eliminates the associated configuration. Let's modify the Order class as shown in listing 16.4 to use the @Autowired annotation.

Listing 16.4 Using @Autowired mechanism to avoid explicit configuration

```
package ajia.domain;

import ...

@Configurable
public class Order extends DomainEntity {

    ...

    private transient PricingStrategy pricingStrategy;

    ...

    @Autowired
    public void setPricingStrategy(PricingStrategy pricingStrategy) {
        this.pricingStrategy = pricingStrategy;
    }
}
```

With the @Autowired annotation, you no longer need a prototype bean in the configuration. In listing 16.5, you don't see any beans corresponding to the Order class.

Listing 16.5 Configuration with the @Autowired annotation

```
<beans ...>
    <bean id="pricingStrategy"
          class="ajia.domain.SimplePricingStrategy"/>

    <context:spring-configured/>
</beans>
```

Spring detects any property marked with the @Autowired annotation and injects that dependency using the configuration specified in the XML file. You don't even need the setter method; you can mark the field itself as autowired, as shown in the listing 16.6.

Listing 16.6 Simplifying code through the use of @Autowired fields

```
package ajia.domain;

import ...

@Configurable
public class Order extends DomainEntity {
    ...

    @Autowired private transient PricingStrategy pricingStrategy;

    ... no setPricingStrategy() method
}
```

With the field itself marked with the `@Autowired` annotation, you no longer need a setter. This will, however, require you to use reflection to set such fields for unit-testing purpose as you have done in listing 16.3.

All Spring container services now showing in objects near you

The `@Configurable` annotation extends the Spring container functionality to any object—not just Spring beans. This is why the `@Autowired` mechanism, which is a general Spring feature, worked for the `Order` class. Similarly, other DI-related annotations such as `@PostConstruct` and `@Required` also work with `@Configurable` objects (but not `@PreDestroy`, because the Spring container can't know when an object is being destroyed, similar to the way Spring deals with prototype beans).

But be careful. The more services you use from the Spring container, the more dependency you have on it. You need to be careful when extending the container services to the domain objects such as `Order` and `LineItem`. A pragmatic approach requires that you consider the convenience offered by annotations and the purity of the code without them. As always, start with what makes sense at a given moment, and refactor when necessary.

`@Configurable`-based DI uses reflection to inject all dependencies. For objects that are created often, this may cause a performance problem. Furthermore, the `@Configurable` annotation is Spring specific, creating a dependency between the domain objects and the framework. An alternative style promotes the use of domain-specific interfaces.

DOMAIN INTERFACES-BASED DI

You can avoid the performance problem and the object's dependency on Spring using domain interface-based DI. This requires writing aspects, but if you've come this far in reading this book, it should be of no big concern to you!

A way to look at the `Order` and `LineItem` classes is that they're clients of the injected dependencies. The classes may indicate this relationship by implementing specific interfaces. A typical interface would include setter methods that set dependencies. This style allows using domain-specific interfaces instead of the Spring-specific `@Configurable` annotation. Listing 16.7 shows the interface that a client of `PricingStrategy` would implement.

Listing 16.7 Interface to be implemented by PricingStrategy clients

```
package ajia.domain;

import ...

public interface PricingStrategyClient {
    void setPricingStrategy(PricingStrategy pricingStrategy);
}
```

Spring includes `GenericInterfaceDrivenDependencyInjectionAspect` that implements the core logic to inject dependencies. You can extend this aspect to apply DI on classes that implement your domain specific interface(s). For example, listing 16.8 shows the `Order` class that implements the `PricingStrategyClient` interface.

Listing 16.8 Order class implementing domain-specific interface

```
package ajia.domain;

import ...

public class Order extends DomainEntity implements PricingStrategyClient {

    ...

    private transient PricingStrategy pricingStrategy;

    ...

    public void setPricingStrategy(PricingStrategy pricingStrategy) {
        this.pricingStrategy = pricingStrategy;
    }
}
```

Notice that you no longer need a Spring-specific annotation in this class. Listing 16.9 shows an aspect that injects dependencies into the object of the classes that implement `PricingStrategyClient`.

Listing 16.9 Aspect to inject dependencies into object of PricingStrategyClient type

```
package ajia.domain;

import ...

public aspect PricingStrategyDependencyInjectionAspect
    extends GenericInterfaceDrivenDependencyInjectionAspect
                <PricingStrategyClient> {                          ❶ Declaring subaspect

    private PricingStrategy pricingStrategy;

    public void configure(PricingStrategyClient bean) {
        bean.setPricingStrategy(this.pricingStrategy);
    }                                                              ❷ Injecting dependencies

    public void setPricingStrategy(PricingStrategy pricingStrategy) {
        this.pricingStrategy = pricingStrategy;
    }                                                              ❸ Declaring dependencies
}
```

This code implements what we may call the *dependency distribution pattern*. You inject the aspect with dependencies and the aspect will distribute those dependencies into other objects. Let's see the parts of the aspect in more details.

❶ The `PricingStrategyDependencyInjectionAspect` subaspect extends `GenericInterfaceDrivenDependencyInjectionAspect` and binds its generic parameter to `PricingStrategyClient`. This indicates that objects of the `PricingStrategyClient` type and its subclasses will be configured by the subaspect. Notice how simple it is to write the subaspect.

❷ The `configure()` method provides a definition for the abstract method in the base aspect. The base aspect will call this method whenever a configurable object matching the generic parameter type is either created or deserialized. The method calls the appropriate setter to inject the dependency. In your case, there is only one dependency to set. But you may configure the object in whatever way appropriate. Note that, dependency injection is done by direct method calls instead of reflection, thus offering better performance.

❸ The aspect includes a setter to declare a dependency that it will distribute to the advised objects. Alternatively, you can mark the `pricingStrategy` field with `@Autowired` and avoid the setter.

Of course, you'll need to configure each aspect to inject the dependency into it. Listing 16.10 shows the bean definition corresponding to the aspect.

Listing 16.10 Dependency injection into the aspect

```
<beans ...>

    <bean id="pricingStrategy" class="ajia.domain.SimplePricingStrategy"/>

    <bean class="ajia.domain.PricingStrategyDependencyInjectionAspect"
          factory-method="aspectOf">
        <property name="pricingStrategy" ref="pricingStrategy"/>
    </bean>
</beans>
```

You don't need a prototype bean defined in the application context, because each DI aspect knows how to inject dependencies.

If you run the same test, you should see a green bar. Although this works, you can do better. First, you can move the aspect inside `PricingStrategyClient` interface, explicitly promoting the relationship between the two. Second, you can use the interface implementation idiom discussed in chapter 5 to relieve each class of the burden of implementing the client interface. When you make these changes, you get the implementation in listing 16.11.

Listing 16.11 Improved DI through use of a nested aspect

```
package ajia.domain;

import ...

public interface PricingStrategyClient {
```

```
    static aspect Impl {
        private transient PricingStrategy
            PricingStrategyClient.pricingStrategy;

        public void PricingStrategyClient.setPricingStrategy(
            PricingStrategy pricingStrategy) {
            this.pricingStrategy = pricingStrategy;
        }

        public PricingStrategy
            PricingStrategyClient.getPricingStrategy() {
            return this.pricingStrategy;
        }
    }

    public static aspect DependencyInjectionAspect
        extends GenericInterfaceDrivenDependencyInjectionAspect
            <PricingStrategyClient> {
        ... unchanged since listing 16.9
    }
}
```

Interface implementation idiom

Nested DI aspect

With this change, the `Order` and `LineItem` classes don't need to implement the `setPricingStrategy()` method. You need to adjust the configuration for the nested aspect's fully qualified name. Listing 16.12 shows the modified configuration.

Listing 16.12 DI into the aspect

```
<beans ...>

    <bean id="pricingStrategy" class="ajia.domain.SimplePricingStrategy"/>

    <bean
       class="ajia.domain.PricingStrategyClient$DependencyInjectionAspect"
       factory-method="aspectOf">
        <property name="pricingStrategy" ref="pricingStrategy"/>
    </bean>
</beans>
```

It may seem that routing requests, such as for the `getTotalPrice()` method in the `Order` class, through the domain objects offers only superficial advantages. But on closer examination, you start to see several advantages. By making domain objects offer rich functionality (even when achieved by delegating to other objects), you can achieve real encapsulation and autonomy within the domain classes. You also reduce the amount of collaboration that needs to be carried outside those classes. For example, the clients don't have to know the existence of a pricing strategy to compute prices. They get pricing from the order objects—just as it would appear natural to do. This kind of arrangement also conforms to the Law of Demeter, also referred to as the Principle of Least Knowledge (http://www.ccs.neu.edu/home/lieber/LoD.html), which promotes the motto "Only talk to your friends."

So far, we've only focused on computing pricing using a (dependency-injected) strategy. Where else can you take advantage of DI in the domain objects?

> **A right-sized approach to design**
>
> I use varied approaches when it comes to designing a system. If the domain logic is complex, I lean heavily toward a rich domain-object model. But if the application is simple, essentially performing create, read, update, and delete (CRUD) operations with simple business logic, I may go for a more rote approach with an anemic domain model. Of course, the trick is knowing which category your application belongs in. But judging application complexity is difficult. As you will see throughout this chapter, AOP makes moving from anemic to rich domain model in an incremental manner a much simpler process.

16.1.3 Possibilities enabled by domain-object DI

You now have a good idea of how to inject dependencies. Let's see how else the e-commerce domain can benefit. In all these cases, you'll use one of the DI mechanisms discussed earlier.

ENRICHING DOMAIN OBJECT BEHAVIOR

Take a look at the `OrderServiceImpl` class in appendix A, listing A.10. The `addProduct()` and `removeProduct()` methods delegate their work of adding a line item to or removing it from the `Order` class. It also updates the inventory by invoking a method on the inventory service. You could make the `Order` take on the responsibility of notifying the inventory service, if you could inject an inventory service into the `Order` instance.[1] Using the DI mechanism discussed earlier in the chapter, you can modify the `Order` class as shown in listing 16.13. Although the code shown uses `@Configurable` and `@Autowired` annotations, the overall scheme would work just fine with either of the domain-object DI approaches discussed in section 16.1.2. Note that downlodable sources include automated tests for the code in this section.

Listing 16.13 Order implementation with inventory management

```
package ajia.domain;

import ...

@Configurable
...
public class Order extends DomainEntity {
    ...
    @Autowired private transient InventoryService inventoryService;

    public void addProduct(Product product, int quantity) {
        ... unchanged since listing A.4
        inventoryService.removeProduct(product, quantity);
    }
```

1 There is of course the danger of including *too* many concerns. For example, is it an order's responsibility to notify inventory? This is where your domain model comes into the picture. If the domain concept of order describes notifying inventory, it's a good idea to mirror that in the implementation, but not otherwise.

```
    public void removeProduct(Product product, int quantity) {
        ... unchanged since listing A.4
        inventoryService.addProduct(product, quantity);
    }
}
```

The `addProduct()` and `removeProduct()` methods take on the responsibility of notifying the inventory service of the changes. The `Order` object itself is now capable of implementing any behavior that makes sense for the domain.

> **Package arrangement with domain object DI**
>
> When you start to inject services into domain objects, if you continue to use the existing package structure, you get a circular dependency: services refer to domain objects, and domain objects refer to the services. You can resolve this by making the service interfaces belong to the same package as the domain classes they're injected into. Service implementations should stay in a separate package, because those implementations refer to domain objects, but not vice versa. The same issue and resolution apply to any other injected objects, such as repositories.

With this modification, the service layer no longer needs to deal with the inventory management, as shown in listing 16.14.

Listing 16.14 `OrderService` implementation without inventory management

```
package ajia.service.impl;

...

public class OrderServiceImpl implements OrderService {
    ...

    public void addProduct(Order order, Product product, int quantity) {
        order.addProduct(product, quantity);
        updateOrder(order);
    }

    public void removeProduct(Order order, Product product, int quantity) {
        order.removeProduct(product, quantity);
        updateOrder(order);
    }
    ...
}
```

Any client must still funnel all requests to add or remove products through `OrderServiceImpl`, because it still updates the `Order` (makes the persistence framework reattach the entity) as well as manages the transactions. You can make the `Order` take care of notifying the repository of the changes, if you inject the `OrderRepository` into the `Order` class as shown in listing 16.15.

Listing 16.15 `Order` class updating the repository

```
package ajia.domain;

import ...

@Configurable
...
public class Order extends DomainEntity {
    ...
    @Autowired private transient InventoryService inventoryService;
    @Autowired private transient OrderRepository orderRepository;

    public void addProduct(Product product, int quantity) {
        ... unchanged since listing A.4
        inventoryService.removeProduct(product, quantity);
        orderRepository.update(this);
    }

    public void removeProduct(Product product, int quantity) {
        ... unchanged since listing A.4
        inventoryService.addProduct(product, quantity);
        orderRepository.update(this);
    }
}
```

With this change, `OrderServiceImpl` reduces to nothing more than a plain delegation, as shown in listing 16.16.

Listing 16.16 `OrderService` implementation without inventory or repository update

```
package ajia.service.impl;

import ...

public class OrderServiceImpl implements OrderService {
    ...

    public void addProduct(Order order, Product product, int quantity) {
        order.addProduct(product, quantity);
    }

    public void removeProduct(Order order, Product product, int quantity) {
        order.removeProduct(product, quantity);
    }
    ...
}
```

The application configuration still sets up the transactions around this service class. It also contains other methods such as finding an order or all orders, or deleting an order. In those cases, each operation is delegated to the repository. You could easily apply transactions to `Order` and `OrderRepository`'s methods. If the unit of work encompasses multiple repository operations, you can always set transaction boundaries at the methods that represent the unit of work. In such an arrangement, transactions at the repository level participate in the outer transactions. See chapter 14 for more information about how transaction management works with nested operations.

Inject repositories?

Injecting repositories into the domain objects may make you uncomfortable. This may be due to the kind of architecture you've been implementing for many years. In general, understand the possibilities and make your own decisions.

So, with `OrderServiceImpl` reduced to pure delegation and not even taking care of transaction management, does it still need to exist?

DISCUSSION: RETHINKING THE SERVICE LAYER

After the business logic and transaction management is removed from the service object, the service layer serves no technical function. From this perspective alone, you may remove the service layer. In a web application, this means that the web UI controllers access the domain objects and the repository layer directly.

The service layer *should* exist if you need it as a façade to encapsulate implementation-specific knowledge of the underlying business logic. Furthermore, you may need a service object to expose the business functionality to remote clients. But in that case, the purpose and design constraints of such a service object are different from those used by a web controller. Many times, in current architectures, the service layer exists because it lets you apply infrastructure functionality such as transaction management and security through a proxy-based interception framework (including Spring AOP). With AspectJ paving the way to invoke these kinds of functionality where they naturally should occur, the service layer's reason for the existence is no longer so strong.

Another way to look at services is to categorize them into two kinds: technical and integration. Technical services exist only due to the technical architecture of the system. Integration services, in contrast, allow exposing functionality to logically or physically external components. The system needs integration services regardless of the underlying architecture. However, we have leeway on dealing with technical services.

If you're new to the full power of AspectJ-based AOP, I suggest that you keep a thin service layer. You may even want to keep transaction boundaries at the service layer.

Implication on service-oriented architecture

In a service-oriented architecture (SOA), an application is composed of well-defined services. How does focusing away from services and toward domain objects affect this? It doesn't in any significant way.

Services designed in SOA have a different focus than services defined only to serve a technical purpose. You wouldn't take a service designed to serve a co-located web layer and make it available as it is to other clients in a SOA-based application. Instead, you'd carefully craft a service, paying attention to factors such as forward compatibility and suitability by access through remote clients. With the domain-focused approach enabled by AOP, the services exposed in this manner can delegate to rich domain objects.

Over time, as you feel more confident with this approach, you can move toward using domain objects directly or through other services. The goal of enriching domain objects isn't the removal of the service layer; it's making objects map more closely to the domain model.

SIMPLIFYING THE DOMAIN OBJECT API

A look at the `Order` class reveals that the client must obtain product objects (through the product repository) to add or remove items. If you inject a product repository into the order object, you can implement methods that take the product id, obtain the product using the repository, and pass it to the method that takes the `Product` object as an argument. Listing 16.17 shows such implementation.

Listing 16.17 Simplified API to order through the use of an injected repository

```
package ajia.domain;

import ...

public class Order extends DomainEntity {
    @Autowired private transient ProductRepository productRepository;

    public void addProduct(Long productId, int quantity) {
        Product product = productRepository.find(productId);
        addProduct(product, quantity);
    }

    public void removeProduct(Long productId, int quantity) {
        Product product = productRepository.find(productId);
        removeProduct(product, quantity);
    }

    ...
}
```

Now the classes that use `Order` don't need to access `ProductRepository`. By reducing the number of objects the clients have to deal with, you offer a simpler API and you gain implementation flexibility.

There is an alternative to adding the new APIs directly in the target class. Using static crosscutting, you can separate the simplification API from the main API. Listing 16.18

> **Humane interfaces**
>
> This kind of client-centric API is also referred to as a *humane interface*. In contrast, a *minimal interface* provides only the basic methods that enable but don't provide clients to write convenience methods. A humane interface considers typical uses of the interface and provides convenience methods as a part of the interface itself. See http://martinfowler.com/bliki/HumaneInterface.html for details. Also see http://ramnivas.com/blog/index.php?p=20 for an aspect-oriented way of implementing humane interfaces.

shows an aspect that introduces the id-based API that internally uses a repository to obtain the product and call the product-based API.

Listing 16.18 Aspect to introduce the id-based API

```
package ajia.domain;

import ...

public aspect OrderSimplificationAspect {
    private ProductRepository productRepository;

    public void Order.addProduct(Long productId, int quantity) {
        Product product =
          OrderSimplificationAspect.aspectOf().getProduct(productId);
        addProduct(product, quantity);
    }

    public void Order.removeProduct(Long productId, int quantity) {
        Product product =
          OrderSimplificationAspect.aspectOf().getProduct(productId);
        removeProduct(product, quantity);
    }

    public void setProductRepository(ProductRepository productRepository) {
        this.productRepository = productRepository;
    }

    private Product getProduct(Long productId) {
        return OrderSimplificationAspect.aspectOf()
                .productRepository.find(productId);
    }
}
```

Note that you inject the `ProductRepository` into the aspect itself. As a result, you need not inject the repository into the `Order` class. A further refinement of this scheme would put the aspect directly inside the `Order` class. This way, the main and the simplification API reside in their own compartments (the class and the aspect).

16.2 Implementing business logic

Some business logic exhibits *micro-crosscutting concerns*—they spread over a few small chunks of code, often just a few methods in one class. In these cases, AOP can avoid code scattering and tangling at a smaller level. Let's see two examples of such concerns in the e-commerce domain: implementing inventory monitoring and checking order-level constraints.

16.2.1 Improving inventory management

Consider the inventory-management subsystem in an e-commerce application. Real-time monitoring of inventory enables businesses to respond to changing demands in an agile manner. For example, an inventory-monitoring system could detect the inventory level of the products and the rate of depletion to start the process of procuring additional items.

Listing 16.19 shows the `InventoryMonitoringAspect` aspect that monitors the `InventoryService` to track inventory updates.

Listing 16.19 Monitoring inventory changes through an aspect

```
package ajia.service.impl;

import ...

public aspect InventoryMonitoringAspect {
    @Autowired private InventoryMonitor inventoryMonitor;

    public pointcut inventoryUpdate(Product product)
        : (execution(* InventoryService.addProduct(Product, ..))
           || execution(* InventoryService.removeProduct(Product, ..)))
          && args(product, ..);

    after(Product product) returning : inventoryUpdate(product) {
        inventoryMonitor.notify(product, thisJoinPoint);
    }
}
```

Because this aspect advises the service-layer objects, which are defined as Spring beans, you can use Spring AOP along with the @AspectJ aspects.

Alternatively, if your architecture so dictates, you can apply the aspect to the domain objects and advise the methods in the `InventoryItem` class. Listing 16.20 shows an aspect that monitors changes in the inventory and updates an inventory monitor.

Listing 16.20 Inventory-monitoring aspect

```
package ajia.service.impl;

import ...

public aspect InventoryMonitoringAspect {
    @Autowired private InventoryMonitor inventoryMonitor;

    public pointcut inventoryUpdate(InventoryItem item)
        : (execution(* InventoryItem.replenish(..))
        || execution(* InventoryItem.deplete(..)))
        && this(item);

    after(InventoryItem item) returning : inventoryUpdate(item) {
        inventoryMonitor.notify(item.getProduct(), thisJoinPoint);
    }
}
```

This scheme works fine for the `InventoryService` or `InventoryItem` class, because you can select the two methods that modify the object state. But if a class has a large number of methods, such selection will lead to the fragile pointcut problem. In those situations, it's best to lean on annotations as discussed in chapter 12.

This implementation has a caveat: notifications are sent even when the ongoing transaction fails (adding a product to or removing it from inventory). You can fix this problem in a variety of ways. First, you can use Java Transaction API (JTA) and ensure that the notification implementation participates in the transaction; but for most use cases, using JTA for such a scenario is overkill. Alternatively, you can accumulate the notifications until the transaction commit time, as we discussed for the retry logic in chapter 14. Finally, you can make the response to the notifications immune to false notifications. For example, the notification processor can check the database for changes before proceeding.

16.2.2 Checking for the order-level constraint

Depending on your domain, what constitutes a valid order may be complex. For example, perhaps only certain kinds of line items may be mixed, an order amount or weight may not exceed a certain threshold, the type or count of items that may be bought is limited, certain customers may not purchase hazardous materials, and so on. In short, there are business constraints on domain objects. It's best to detect violations as they take place so you can provide feedback. The aspect in listing 16.21 shows how AOP can help implement such business rules.

Listing 16.21 Order-validation aspect

```
package ajia.domain;

import ...

public aspect OrderValidationAspect {
    private OrderValidator orderValidator;

    public pointcut orderUpdate(Order order)
        : execution(* Order.*(..))
          && this(order)
          && !cflow(execution(* OrderValidator+.*(..)));

    after(Order order) returning : orderUpdate(order) {
        orderValidator.validate(order);
    }

    public void setOrderValidator(OrderValidator orderValidator) {
        this.orderValidator = orderValidator;
    }
}
```

The `cflow()` pointcut ensures that calls initiated from the `OrderValidator` aren't validated. Without the `cflow()` pointcut, you'll get an infinite recursion.

You may consider the order-validation logic to be part of the `Order` class. In that case, you may want to embed the aspect inside the `Order` class to signify the stronger relationship between the two. With such a structure, the nested validation aspect helps to untangle the validation logic from the main-line logic. You'll see an example of such arrangement in the next section.

You can apply the aspect to the service layer, as long as you ensure that all the modifications to the order are funneled through the service. In that case, you can use Spring AOP instead of AspectJ weaving.

> **ORM and validation**
>
> ORM frameworks such as Java Persistence API (JPA) allow applications to install event listeners and notify them when updating an entity to the database. You can use these notifications to validate the entities. But these notifications are limited to persistent entities and occur only when entities are committed. The AspectJ-based approach lets you detect violations to any objects as soon as they occur, which is a much more natural fail-fast implementation.

For the purpose of illustration, you'll use a simple rule where the order total can't exceed a prespecified amount, as shown in listing 16.22 (see downloadble source for automated tests).

Listing 16.22 Simple order validator

```
package ajia.domain;

import ...

public class OrderValidatorTotalPrice implements OrderValidator {
    private float MAX_ORDER_VALUE = 100f;

    public void validate(Order order) {
        if(order.getTotalPrice() > MAX_ORDER_VALUE) {
            throw new OrderValidationException();
        }
    }
}
```

Note that you may choose to send a notification instead of throwing an exception to alert users, but still allow temporary violations. The separation of concerns implemented by the code simplifies any such changes—all you need to do is modify the `OrderValidator` class.

16.2.3 Refactoring using aspects

Refactoring is a way to modify an internal implementation without affecting the externally observable behavior. With recent interest in Extreme Programming (XP), refactoring techniques are gaining well-deserved attention. With AOP, you get added opportunities for refactoring.

Consider the `Order` class, which implements the *freezing* of a placed order. Currently, the `addProduct()` and `removeProduct()` methods check whether the order is frozen before changing the order. The same code is spread over two places. In a more realistic implementation, it's likely to be scattered in even more locations. You can write a simple aspect that implements the freezing functionality. Typically, you'll place the aspect inside the class, similar to a private method. But you may not recognize the need to create an aspect for such functionality right away; instead, you may start with a conventional implementation and then refactor through aspects.

Aspects used to refactor crosscutting code differ from mainstream aspects in the following ways:

- Aspects used for refactoring are narrowly scoped to crosscut a class or two as opposed to potentially crosscutting the whole system. Essentially, these aspects deal with micro-crosscutting concerns.
- Because refactoring aspects are tightly bound to classes they're refactoring, it's okay for these aspects to depend on implementation details of the classes being refactored. In fact, such an aspect is an implementation detail of a class.

Let's refactor the `Order` class to extract the freezing of an order into a nested aspect (listing 16.23) through the application of a technique known as *Extract Method Calls.*[2]

Listing 16.23 Refactored `Order` class

```
package ajia.domain;

import ...

public class Order extends DomainEntity {

    ...

    public void addProduct(Product product, int quantity) {
        ... no checking for placed order
        ...
    }

    public void removeProduct(Product product, int quantity) {
        ... no checking for placed order
        ...
    }

    private static aspect Freezing {
        before(Order order)
            : (execution(* Order.addProduct(..))
               || execution(* Order.removeProduct(..)))
              && this(order) {
            if(order.isPlaced()) {
                throw new IllegalStateException(
                    "Order once placed may not be modified");
            }
        }
    }
}
```

The order-validation and order-freezing functionality use the same overall template. They both implicitly implement the observer design pattern through aspects to monitor the changes in the underlying objects and respond to those changes in a functionality-

[2] See http://www.theserverside.com/tt/articles/article.tss?l=AspectOrientedRefactoringPart1 and http://www.theserverside.com/tt/articles/article.tss?l=AspectOrientedRefactoringPart2 for more aspect-oriented refactoring techniques.

specific way (such as validating or checking for a frozen order). When you apply aspect-oriented refactoring to your domain objects, you'll find this pattern useful.

We'll now move to the last idea for improving the domain logic implementation that ensures that objects are accessed only in the intended way.

16.3 Managing access to objects

Consider how the web layer may access an `Order` object for display purposes. Perhaps the service layer provides the web with the `Order` object. Consequently, the web layer also gets access to the contained `LineItem` objects. But you don't want the web layer to modify the `LineItem` objects directly. Doing so may potentially violate the constraints at the `Order` level as discussed in section 16.2.2. You want these kinds of checks to be performed at the `Order` level—in Domain Driven Design (DDD) parlance, at the aggregate root level.

You have two choices: use a Data Transfer Object (DTO) for the order and line item, where the line item DTO is immutable and the order DTO provides an API to modify those (in turn checking constraints for each modifications); or use the exposed domain model[3] and somehow ensure that the web layer uses the objects correctly. Although DTO is a good pattern, it may be cumbersome to write a DTO for each class. You may even need a set of DTOs for each use case to expose the right amount of information. For example, should `OrderDTO` always include `LineItemDTOs`? The extra code needed by the DTO pattern may not be justifiable if your web layer is co-located with the domain layer (where you don't typically have constraints imposed when transferring objects over the network). AspectJ provides an easier solution, where you continue to expose domain objects to the web layer without the fear of invalid usages. Essentially, the same object can exhibit multiple personalities based on the accessing layer.

16.3.1 Applying specific policies

First, you'll implement an aspect that targets the `Order`→`LineItem` relationship. This implementation will apply some specific rules. Later, you'll develop a more general aspect to enforce aggregate boundaries.

Listing 16.24 shows an aspect that ensures that a `LineItem` isn't modified except in the control-flow of an `Order` method. The implementation follows the aspects developed in chapter 11, where you applied a similar policy for runtime enforcement of EJBs.

Listing 16.24 Controlling exposure to the aggregate root

```
package ajia.enforcement;

import ...

public aspect LineItemExposureControlAspect {
    pointcut lineOrderModification() : execution(* LineItem.set*(..));

    pointcut duringOrder() : cflow(execution(* Order.*(..)));
```

[3] See *POJOs in Action* by Chris Richardson (Manning, 2006) for more information about various way for the web layer to access the domain model.

```
    before() : lineOrderModification() && !duringOrder() {
        throw new AggregateBoundaryViolationException(
            "A LineItem may not be modified except through an Order");
    }
}
```

By checking whether the line item is modified in the control flow of an operation of the `Order` class, you enforce the access-control rule. Note that an alternative definition for the `lineOrderModification()` pointcut is `set(* LineItem.*)` that selects field modifications instead of setter methods. You can generalize this rule to avoid a specific implementation for each set of domain classes.

16.3.2 Applying general policies

The general rule for aggregate boundaries is that for each set of classes, there is a designated aggregate root class. All modifications to any aggregate member must be through its aggregate root. From the implementation point of view, you need to enforce two rules:

- *No modifications to a non-root entity from another architectural layer*—For example, the web layer must not directly modify a `LineItem` object.
- *No foreign aggregate root access*—Any access through an aggregate root must match the aggregate root for the modified entity. For example, a `LineItem` may be modified only during an operation in its aggregate root: `Order`. It would be a violation if a `LineItem` is modified from another aggregate root such as `Customer`.

Figure 16.2 shows the overall access scheme.

If these rules are broken, you can get subtle bugs in the system. Given the crosscutting nature, aspects should help here. The aspect you're about to implement is fairly complex; but because this is the last chapter with code, you should be ready for such an aspect by now!

A challenge in implementing an enforcement aspect is identifying aggregate roots, aggregate members, and modifying operations. You can meet this challenge through annotations. First, let's create the `@AggregateRoot` annotation as shown in listing 16.25.

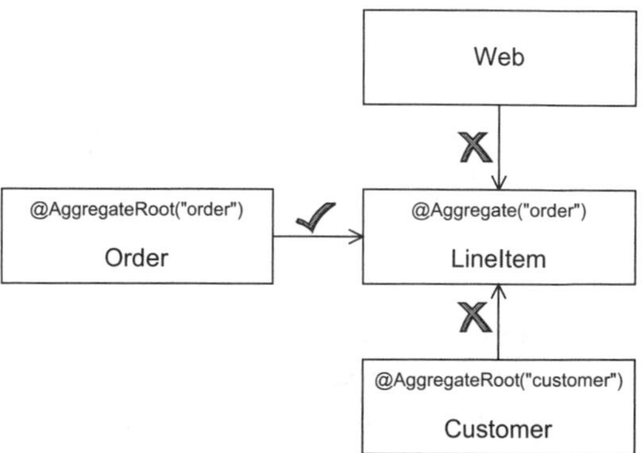

Figure 16.2 Managing access to an aggregate. All access to an aggregate member must originate from the aggregate root designated for the same group.

Listing 16.25 `AggregateRoot` annotation interface

```
package ajia.enforcement;

import ...
```

```
@Retention(RetentionPolicy.RUNTIME)
public @interface AggregateRoot {
    String value();
}
```

You can mark aggregate root types with this annotation, whose `value` property specifies an identifier for the aggregate. For example, you can mark the `Order` type with the `@AggregateRoot("order")` annotation, as shown in listing 16.26.

Listing 16.26 Order class with the `@AggregateRoot` annotation

```
package ajia.domain;

import ...

@AggregateRoot("order")
...
public class Order extends DomainEntity {
    ...
}
```

The attribute for the annotation must uniquely identify each type of aggregate in the system. A good choice is the name of the root class. You can choose to automatically determine this by relying on a convention (for example, the package structure, if all members belong to the same package) and omit specifying an explicit value.

Next, you create the `@Aggregate` annotation, as shown in listing 16.27. Then, you mark the non-root members of an aggregate with this annotation, whose `value` attribute specifies an identifier matching the root they belong to.

Listing 16.27 Aggregate annotation to declare membership to an aggregate

```
package ajia.enforcement;

import ...

@Retention(RetentionPolicy.RUNTIME)
public @interface Aggregate {
    String value();
}
```

For example, you mark the `LineItem` class to belong to the `order` aggregate, as shown in listing 16.28. You also reuse the `@ReadOnly` annotation developed in chapter 13 to mark the read-only operations in non-aggregate types (you could mark any other types as well, but you don't need to do so for the aspect developed in this section).

Listing 16.28 Marking a non-root class

```
package ajia.domain;

import ...

@Aggregate("order")
...
public class LineItem extends DomainEntity {
    ...
```

```
    @ReadOnly
    public int getQuantity() {
        return quantity;
    }

    public int setQuantity(int quantity) {
        return this.quantity = quantity;
    }

    ...
}
```

Note that as an alternative, you can use naming conventions to select read-only methods. You can also apply the bridged participation pattern discussed in chapter 12 to use the `declare @method` construct to supply the `@ReadOnly` annotation. With such arrangement, although the class avoids a repeated use of the `@ReadOnly` annotation, the aspect itself doesn't have to rely on a naming convention. If you take this route, you may want to supply the annotation through a nested aspect inside a class, following the annotation-driven participant pattern discussed in chapter 12 and shown in listing 16.29.

Listing 16.29 Marking a non-root class

```
package ajia.domain;

import ...

@Aggregate("order")
...
public class LineItem extends DomainEntity {

    ...

    public int getQuantity() {
        return quantity;
    }

    public int setQuantity(int quantity) {
        return this.quantity = quantity;
    }

    ...

    private static aspect ReadOnlyDesignator {
        declare @method
            : * LineItem.get*(..) : @ReadOnly;
    }
}
```

Finally, you use these annotations to implement the aspect to enforce aggregate boundaries, as shown in listing 16.30.

Listing 16.30 Generalized aspect to enforce aggregate boundary policies

```
package ajia.enforcement;

import ...

public aspect AggregateBoundaryEnforcementAspect  {
```

```
    private Logger logger
        = Logger.getLogger(AggregateBoundaryEnforcementAspect.class);

    pointcut nonAggregateRootModification(Aggregate aggregate)      ❶ Selects non-
        : execution(!@ReadOnly * *(..)) && @within(aggregate);        aggregate
                                                                      modifications
    pointcut aggregateRootOperation(AggregateRoot aggregateRoot)
        : execution(* *(..)) && @within(aggregateRoot);
                                                        Selects ❷   ❸ Selects
    pointcut directModification()          aggregate root operations   direct
        : nonAggregateRootModification(*)                               modifi-
          && !cflowbelow(aggregateRootOperation(*));                    cations

    pointcut throughRootModification(AggregateRoot aggregateRoot,      Selects
                                     Aggregate aggregateNonRoot)    ❹ modifi-
        : nonAggregateRootModification(aggregateNonRoot)               cations
        && cflowbelow(aggregateRootOperation(aggregateRoot));          through
                                                                       root
    before() : directModification() {
        throw new AggregateBoundaryViolationException(
            "Non-root entity modified without going through"    ❺ Monitors direct
            + "its aggregate root");                               modifications
    }

    before(AggregateRoot aggregateRoot, Aggregate aggregateNonRoot)
        : throughRootModification(aggregateRoot, aggregateNonRoot) {
        if(!aggregateRoot.value().equals(aggregateNonRoot.value())) {
            throw new AggregateBoundaryViolationException(
              "Non-aggregate root object not accessed though its root");
        }
    }                                        Monitors mismatched ❻
}                                                aggregate roots
```

❶ The `nonAggregateRootModification()` pointcut selects method execution in non-aggregate root entities (marked with `@Aggregate`) that don't carry the `@ReadOnly` annotation. It also collects the `@Aggregate` annotation so that you can use it in the advice that enforces that the modifications happen through its root entity.

❷ The `aggregateRootOperation()` pointcut selects method executions within an aggregate root. It also collects the annotation to use in the advice.

❸ The `directModification()` pointcut selects modifications to non-root objects that don't occur in the control flow of a root object's operation. The use of the `cflowbelow()` pointcut accommodates intermediate classes (such as utility classes) between root and non-root objects. This pointcut doesn't collect any context because a direct modification is a violation regardless of the annotation values.

❹ The `throughRootModification()` pointcut, in contrast to `directModification()`, selects modifications to non-root objects that occur in the control flow of a root object's operation. Because the advice must check for the matching attribute values, you collect the annotation associated with both root and non-root objects. Note the use of the wormhole pattern (discussed in chapter 12) to collect the annotation for the root object.

❺ The advice to the `directModification()` pointcut throws an exception to enforce the policy.

❻ The advice to the `throughRootModification()` pointcut compares the annotation values to ensure that the aggregate roots match. For example, if a `LineItem` is modified during an operation in the `Customer` class, it's a violation, because the aggregate roots for the two classes (`customer` and `order`) don't match. If they don't match, the advice throws an exception.

Let's complete this implementation by writing the test in listing 16.31.

Listing 16.31 Testing enforcement of the aggregate boundary policy

```
package ajia.domain;

import ...

public class AggregateBoundaryEnforcementTest {
    @Test(expected=AggregateBoundaryViolationException.class)
    public void directModification() {
        LineItem nonRoot
            = new LineItem(Mockito.mock(Order.class),
                           Mockito.mock(Product.class), 1);
        nonRoot.setQuantity(2);
    }

    @Test(expected=AggregateBoundaryViolationException.class)
    public void throughInvalidRootModification() {
        TestRoot root = new TestRoot();
        root.operation();
    }

    @Test
    public void throughValidRootModification() {
        Order order = new Order();
        order.addProduct(Mockito.mock(Product.class), 2);
    }

    @AggregateRoot("test")
    private static class TestRoot {
        public void operation() {
            LineItem nonRoot
                = new LineItem(Mockito.mock(Order.class),
                               Mockito.mock(Product.class), 1);
            nonRoot.setQuantity(2);
        }
    }
}
```

In this test, you run through a few scenarios: direct access, access through an invalid root (`order` versus `test`), and access through a valid root.

With the enforcement aspect watching your back, you can be sure that the objects are used only as intended. You can also avoid writing extra classes just to ensure the correct access. Overall, you get higher-quality implementation with a lot less code.

16.4 Summary

AOP is useful not only for infrastructural aspects but also for improving domain logic. Crosscutting concerns exist even for the domain logic, and AOP can help modularize those.

One of the common problems faced in designing enterprise applications is the inability to create behavior-rich objects, which leads to anemic domain models. The main reason behind the existence of an anemic domain model is the difficulty in making the collaborating objects available to the domain objects. Extending DI to domain objects allows them to collaborate with the injected dependencies to implement rich behavior. These domain objects offer simpler APIs to the client, improve testability, and simplify the overall architecture.

AOP also helps to modularize crosscutting business logic. The focus of such an implementation is separating the main-line business logic from the crosscutting business rules. Typical implementations use the observer design pattern. By observing changes in the domain or service objects, you can provide additional business services. This gives you flexibility in choosing monitored objects and responding to notifications.

Extending enforcement aspects to implement the ideas in DDD helps you avoid creating unnecessary classes while ensuring the correct use of the existing classes. This speeds up the development process by letting you focus on what is important: your domain logic.

By now, you should be convinced of the power and versatility of the aspect-oriented programming. In the next chapter, we'll deal with adoption issues so that you can put all this information to good use.

17 Taking the next step

This chapter covers

- Approaching AOP adoption
- Applying AOP in various development phases

As we come to the end of this book, let's consider some issues and practical solutions that will help your organization embrace AOP. In the last few years, having gone through its hype cycle, most developers and managers understand AOP's value proposition. This is especially true for organizations that have embraced lightweight technologies such as Spring. Others still need convincing, especially when applying AOP that involves byte-code weaving. The industry could also use more guidance toward using an aspect-oriented approach in analyzing new problems and designing solutions.

In this chapter, we'll address the adoption issue head on. I'll make a few specific recommendations to help you be successful with AOP while managing risks with it. I'll also discuss analysis and design based on AOP concepts.

17.1 The adoption path: technologies

Successfully adopting any technology requires that you take a pay-as-you-go approach. Such a path avoids undue risk, requires minimum upfront cost, and provides benefits at each stage. Let's discuss a typical adoption path applied to enterprise application development. This path typically starts with Spring AOP.

17.1.1 Spring AOP

If you're using the Spring Framework as the basis for your application, using Spring AOP is a risk-free way to introduce AOP. You need no special compiler, no modifications to launch scripts, and, perhaps more important, no management approval—it's just Java as far as development and deployment are concerned! Furthermore, Spring provides pre-built aspects for common enterprise crosscutting concerns such as transaction management and security, to get you started quickly.

Spring AOP is limited in the kind of crosscutting it supports—it can advise only public methods of Spring beans. This makes it difficult to make mistakes (especially in over-applying aspects). I recommend that you use the @AspectJ syntax if you're developing applications using Java 5 or later. This will help you to move to the AspectJ weaving, because you would have already learned a majority of the syntax.

Spring AOP will enable you to implement a few useful applications of AOP as you have seen throughout the book. You may stay with Spring AOP, until you come across a need for more complex crosscutting that needs the full power offered by AspectJ.

17.1.2 AspectJ

A typical tipping point for the use of AspectJ in Spring applications is a crosscutting functionality that applies to objects beyond just Spring beans. You may also be attracted to AOP due to the architectural possibilities it offers as discussed in chapter 16. If you aren't using Spring as the basis for your application, AspectJ will be the starting point.

When you decide to use AspectJ, you face choices of syntax and the weaving mechanism. The right choices depend on multiple factors such as your team's experience level, the IDE you use for development, and the kind of crosscutting functionality you need to implement. Please see the guidelines in chapter 7 and 8 for a more detailed discussion. Of course, you may use AspectJ weaving along with Spring AOP in the same application.

Whether you use Spring AOP or AspectJ, you still don't need to dive in head first. You can dip your toes using development aspects and then move to production aspects. Let's see how.

17.2 The adoption path: applications

You'll typically start with simpler applications of AOP, gain experience, and then apply it to problems that are more complex. You may want to start with aspects meant to be used only during development and then later develop aspects for production use. In either case, you can use Spring AOP or AspectJ.

17.2.1 Development aspects

Development aspects help to simplify the development process without having to be included in the production system. Because aspects won't be a part of production, the perceived risk of using a new technology is substantially lower. You'll also likely have a better chance of getting approval from management (most of the time, you may not need any approval).

Development aspects also offer a way to gain experience with AOP if you're new to it. While you're learning it, your main purpose should be to improve your individual productivity and gain confidence in AOP. Let's see a few categories of development aspects.

HELPING WITH DEBUGGING

Consider your options when you face a concurrency-related issue such as deadlocks or corrupted data. Due to the unpredictability of the issue and modifications of the concurrency dynamics due to breakpoints, using a debugger isn't a good choice. In such cases, you can write a few tracing aspects and execute the system (run your test suite or perform manual testing). You can periodically examine the log output to see if you've hit the concurrency problem. Based on that information, you can fix the problem. When the problem is fixed, you no longer need the aspect. Of course, you can add it back periodically to see if there are other problems lurking as the application evolves.

MONITORING PERFORMANCE

Similarly, you can use aspects to spot performance bottlenecks. Although a profiler may help with this problem, many performance issues are uncovered only during close-to-real deployment. Such an environment usually isn't available during development phases. By enabling performance-monitoring aspects during pre-production testing, you can perform dynamic profiling in a near-real environment. You then have the option to either continue using those aspects in the deployed system or take them out.

ENFORCING POLICIES

When you're developing complex applications, you definitely need to ensure that the program elements adhere to certain policies. In chapter 11, we discussed several examples of enforcement that you can implement using AOP. The real value of those examples is in the techniques they present. Whenever you come across a new policy, implement it using aspects. Over time, you'll collect a repertoire of aspects that you can use in existing and new projects without much effort.

HELPING WITH TESTING

You can use aspects to introduce simulated faults (such as exceptions and delays) and use those when you test the system's fault tolerance, as we showed in chapter 14. You can also use a tracing aspect to get the most out of the testing effort. During the testing phase, when you expect to uncover problems, you can use aspects to collect context information and not just exception call stacks. When it's time to ship the product, you can take out the context-collecting aspects. With an AOP-based approach, you have a flexible way to collect context and maintain better control over the inclusion or exclusion of the collection logic.

When you have enough experience with development aspects, you'll be ready to move to production aspects.

17.2.2 Production aspects

Production aspects require a bigger commitment, because unlike development aspects, you must use them in production. You can't, for example, have an option to exclude transaction management or security aspects.

INFRASTRUCTURE ASPECTS

These aspects represent a major portion of production aspects, as you saw in chapters 13 through 15. Common aspects include those used for transaction management, security, and concurrency control. You may find pre-built solutions for many of these functionalities in frameworks such as Spring. If not, you should strive to create reusable aspects, because many other projects will need the same functionality.

When you're comfortable implementing infrastructure aspects, you can look for subtler crosscutting concerns such as those in the domain logic.

CROSSCUTTING DOMAIN LOGIC

Recognizing crosscutting concerns in domain logic is complex. You can start with domain-object dependency injection implemented using AspectJ. Although the injection is a crosscutting concern, using the dependency isn't; but it provides significant leeway in how you architect your system.

As we discussed in chapter 16, you may find business logic that applies to a few classes or a set of methods in a class. You can use aspects to modularize such logic, leading toward a cleaner implementation. Often, you may not recognize the crosscutting nature of domain logic until you've already implemented it. In those cases, you can use refactoring aspects.

REFACTORING ASPECTS

Refactoring aspects are produced through the application of the refactoring process to extract crosscutting logic. Because the code is already implemented along with tests, the refactoring process provides a way to modify the implementation with an assurance that the code works the same way as it did before the refactoring, even with the new aspects.

When you implement a new crosscutting concern using aspects, you'll face challenges in approaching it. Let's discuss a typical way.

17.3 Applying AOP to new problems

After you've committed to using AOP in your organization, you need to decide whether it's appropriate for each target problem. You must consider an approach that will incorporate AOP while causing minimal destabilization of the overall system. Typically, you want to apply aspects to a restricted subsystem and then, when the solutions are proven, expand the use of AOP to the whole system. In this section, we'll examine the two phases of applying AspectJ to a problem: deciding to use it and then using it.

17.3.1 Talking the talk

How do you decide whether a concern is better addressed by AOP compared to a conventional solution? In other words, how do you know if a concern is crosscutting? You can use the following as a guide:

- *Will a non-AOP alternative cause code scattering?* Code scattering is usually a sure sign of a crosscutting concern. If you have to copy and paste nearly identical code in multiple places or insert complementary blocks of code for a concern in several modules, AOP is a good choice. It will immediately yield a cleaner design and substantial code savings.
- *Will a non-AOP alternative cause code tangling?* Code tangling generally accompanies code scattering, but you may see code tangling by itself. For example, you may have just one service that uses the read-write lock based concurrency control. A conventional implementation tangles the two functionalities: concurrency code and the service's business logic. Using aspects separates these two functionalities, makes them simpler to understand, and allows them to evolve separately. It's much like refactoring code into private methods even when you know there is only one caller. Over time, you'll find more modules that call for the same separation of crosscutting concerns.
- *Exercise caution when an AOP solution is meant to patch the underlying implementation.* It's better to address the underlying problem than to use aspects to get around it.

17.3.2 Walking the walk

When you determine that a certain functionality is a possible crosscutting concern, and you decide to use AOP to implement it, you can follow this approach:

1. *Study the conventional solution.* In this step, you sketch out, design, and even prototype the conventional solution. Although illustrating the conventional solution makes you (or your manager!) appreciate the AOP solution, it mainly helps you understand the design required to implement aspects. The idea is to first sketch the code tangling and code scattering, and then modularize it. After you become reasonably experienced at this, you can reduce the emphasis on this step or even eliminate it.
2. *Limit the implementation.* By limiting the solution to only modules that currently need the functionality, you eliminate the impact—both positive and negative—on other modules. The goal is to leave as much of the system unaffected as possible and reduce the testing effort required. To do this, you can either use pointcuts such as `within()` to specify only join points in the modules you want to weave, or you can configure your build system to include only those modules.

   Alternatively, you can use annotations to target specific program elements. The pointcuts can select the join points that carry the annotations. This also offers the benefit of making the class developers comfortable with AOP; they get to control the application of aspects by choosing to annotate program elements explicitly, as we discussed in chapter 12.
3. *Let it loose.* When you're comfortable with the solution and its impact, you should modify the pointcuts or build configurations that have been limiting applicability. For example, instead of restricting monitoring to certain modules, you lift those restrictions to let monitoring span the whole system. This way, if a new module joins the system, it starts benefiting from the aspects right away.

This systematic approach helps you tackle almost any problem with little risk. Experience will be your best guide in determining how much weight you should assign to each step in your system.

17.4 Employing AOP in development phases

Each phase of a software project—design, implementation, testing, and maintenance—emphasizes certain activities. AOP plays a different role in each of the phases. Let's look at some typical ways AOP helps in each situation.

17.4.1 AOP in the design phase

If you start using AOP in the design phase, you'll reap the maximum benefits. From an architectural perspective, the separation of concerns offered by AOP simplifies designing both the business logic and crosscutting concerns. Furthermore, as discussed in chapter 16, AOP offers alternative architectural choices promoting a more domain-driven approach.

Here is a typical way to use AOP during a design phase:

1. *Recognize crosscutting concerns.* This step is part of mapping requirements to modules. As a rule of thumb, consider concerns described with an adjective or adverb starting with *every*, such as *every time* or *everywhere*, as possible crosscutting concerns. Recognizing these concerns ahead of time lets you avoid the effort needed to modularize crosscutting concerns in the conventional fashion.
2. *Design the mainline business functionality first.* Apply standard conventional design techniques to the business functionality. The better you design the business functionality, the easier it will be to apply crosscutting concerns, because it will simplify the specification of the weaving rules.
3. *Design crosscutting concerns.* Address the prominent and immediate crosscutting concerns. It's also a good idea to sketch out the crosscutting concerns that you're aware of but don't need to address immediately. This approach helps you avoid overdesign; and because you'll use AOP to implement the crosscutting concerns, deferring the decision won't lead to huge code changes.

Design is only as good as its implementation. Let's see how AOP helps during the implementation phase.

17.4.2 AOP in the implementation phase

When you use AOP in the implementation phase, you should place additional emphasis on certain common practices, as well as follow a few new guidelines to make the process of implementing the core and crosscutting concerns as easy as possible.

IMPLEMENTING CORE CONCERNS

The decision to use AOP affects how you'll implement the core concerns. Fortunately, if you're using AOP, much of the process and methodology is largely unchanged from OOP. But paying attention to a few practices will make your job easier. You should follow these common principles regardless of whether you use AOP:

- *Write well-factored code.* Ideally, each operation implements a specific core functionality. Because in AOP most pointcut definitions specify join points for method invocations, methods can be considered units of crosscutting granularity. Therefore, if each method maps to a specific functionality, you can select join points at the right level of granularity; this allows you to apply AOP consistently throughout your project.
- *Use consistent naming conventions.* Sticking to a consistent naming convention throughout your project will help you write pointcuts that use wildcards to select join points. Using wildcards instead of fully specifying each join point not only makes writing aspects easier but also ensures that the aspects automatically apply to any new modules that you may add to the system later.
- *Favor annotations over alternatives.* Most technologies such as JPA, EJB3, and Spring MVC offer a choice between annotating program elements and specifying external XML configuration. From AOP's perspective, using annotations is a better choice, because you can use those annotations in pointcut expressions.

In addition to these common good practices, here are some guidelines that are specific to AOP:

- *Separate the crosscutting concerns from the core modules in the initial phase.* When you come across a concern that affects multiple modules, apply the questions in section 17.3.1 to determine whether you should use aspects to implement the functionality. You may decide to implement the functionality using aspects immediately or wait until the functionality is really needed.
- *Watch out for any visible tangling and scattering.* Be on the lookout for code tangling and code scattering while implementing the core concerns; consider them a symptom of possible crosscutting concerns being implemented using OOP techniques that may be candidates for AOP. Initially, you'll be looking for well-known crosscutting concerns, such as tracing or security. Later on, with experience, you'll be able to spot more subtle crosscutting concerns and modularize them.

These steps will help you to better implement crosscutting concerns.

IMPLEMENTING CROSSCUTTING CONCERNS

When you implement crosscutting concerns, you need to perform the following tasks. It's typical to iterate over them during the implementation phase:

- *Identify the join points.* In this step, you identify the places in the code that need the crosscutting behavior. Then, you need to decide the best way to express the pointcuts that select the required join points: signature-based pointcuts, annotation-based pointcuts, control flow–based pointcuts, and so on. If required, to help in selecting pointcuts, you may have to implement custom annotations and attach them to program elements.
- *Choose the underlying technology.* To implement a crosscutting concern, you often have to decide what the underlying implementation will be. Your choice

will be largely influenced by the overall system architecture and specific project requirements.

- *Design the aspects.* In this step, you design the aspects. You may want to consider using one or more of the patterns presented in chapter 12 (as well as any new patterns you've discovered) as a template. Pay particular attention to using consistent naming conventions for aspects; that will simplify the process of selecting join points inside the aspects. It will also help you when you want to specify aspect precedence. Finally, you also need to decide whether you can create reusable aspects so that you can leverage them the next time you deal with the same crosscutting concern.

Another issue to consider is how to organize the aspects so that your build configurations are flexible and easy to work with. To use aspects in a plug-and-play manner, you must separate them according to the functionality they implement (typically by adding them to separate packages). A proper separation of aspects will help you to more easily configure the build system to include or exclude certain aspects in your builds. To do this, pay attention to these two factors:

- *Deployment*—Certain aspects are most useful during the development phase, such as those that perform tracing for debug/profiling purposes and policy enforcement. You'll probably want to group these developmental aspects under a separate package so that you can easily add them to and remove them from your builds as you choose. That way, you can take advantage of those aspects during the development phase while ensuring they don't affect the deployed system.
- *Correctness*—The most fundamental characteristic of any software system is its correctness—the other characteristics, such as efficiency, are secondary. For example, transaction-management support is fundamental to the correctness of the system, whereas efficiency gained by caching isn't. Although you may choose to remove some aspects that you used in development from your deployment build system, you must ensure that the aspects that are necessary for correctness are always included in any build target.

After the system has been implemented and deployed, the maintenance phase commences.

17.4.3 AOP in the maintenance phase

The maintenance phase consists primarily of two activities: adding implementations to satisfy new requirements and fixing bugs found in the deployed systems. AOP can handle the following tasks during the maintenance phase:

- *Creating protection walls*—A big challenge during the maintenance phase is making sure that new changes don't break other parts of the system. Policy-enforcement aspects ensure that the new features don't violate the policies, thus helping in preventing the introduction of new bugs.

- *Implementing new features*—Just like during the implementation phase, AOP can implement new crosscutting concerns in a noninvasive manner. Using AOP helps minimize code changes to the core of the system for these concerns, thus minimizing the possibility of adding new bugs.
- *Creating emergency patches*—You may encounter situations where you need to augment or find an alternative behavior to a few methods in an existing system. The urgency of such a need may prevent you from implementing a proper solution. In these cases, AspectJ can provide a simpler way to *patch* these methods. But you should exercise caution. Emergency patches have a tendency to remain as "solutions" forever. If too many patches are added to a system, eventually they often lead to maintenance nightmare.

If you're like most developers, as much as you wish otherwise, you have to deal with legacy projects. Let's see how AOP can make your life better during that phase.

17.4.4 AOP in legacy projects

Legacy projects can be a challenge primarily for two reasons. First, the core code may lack the clean separation of functionality that allows you to use AOP. Second, certain crosscutting concerns may already be implemented using conventional techniques. This may mean that you must first remove the concern from the core code and put it into aspects before improving its implementation. Through all these steps, you need to exercise care to avoid altering the core system behavior in an undesirable way. Here are some ways to ease the process:

1. *Start out with no-commitment aspects.* Begin with simple aspects, such as policy enforcements and tracing. These aspects enable you to introduce new behavior without requiring any modifications to the core modules. This way, you minimize the risk of inadvertently affecting the core system behavior. The application of these aspects is limited to development, and you don't need a commitment to use AOP in deployment. This no-commitment, no-risk approach helps you use AOP immediately in almost any system. For such usages, AspectJ's LTW is often the best choice to get started.
2. *Refactor the code.* Any serious use of AOP requires that the core code within each module implement relatively clear responsibilities. Ensuring that this is the case and refactoring the code if necessary may require considerable effort. Fortunately, it will help your system regardless of whether you use AOP. For messy code bases, you may want to apply techniques described in *Working Effectively with Legacy Code* by Michael Feathers (Prentice Hall, 2004) to clean code before adding aspects to it. Policy-enforcement aspects also help during application of these techniques to protect you against inadvertent violations.
3. *Refactor the crosscutting concern.* While refactoring the core concern, you'll see code-tangling and code-scattering symptoms. Work your way through the modularization of a few prominent crosscutting concerns. A test suite will help during this step to ensure continual conformity to core system functionality.

Now that you've seen how to approach AOP, let me share a few final thoughts.

17.5 Parting thoughts

Here are some additional recommendations as you move forward on your path toward becoming an AOP and AspectJ expert:

- *Start simple.* If you're new to AOP, start simple. In particular, don't worry about reusable aspects in the beginning; adding these features later, even as an afterthought, is usually better than paying an upfront cost. Most aspects in this book are reusable, but I didn't design them that way in my first attempts. The typical process is to come up with the overall design, implement simple aspects that solve the problem, and then see how to generalize them into reusable aspects. Remember your first encounter with OOP? You most likely didn't create interfaces, function objects, and delegate objects right away. The same applies to AOP adoption. You can refactor aspects just like you can refactor classes!
- *Join the community.* Learning from other people's experience can be useful. There are a couple of good mailing lists and forums that you should consider joining. Visit http://eclipse.org/aspectj, http://aosd.net, and http://forum.springframework.org for more details. On these mailing lists, you'll find that committers and users for the projects are ready to help anyone facing problems. I'll be available on Author Online at http://www.manning.com/laddad2 to help you with your questions.
- *View AOP as augmenting technology.* Use the underlying conventional classes as much as possible. Throughout the book, solutions are based on available technologies: logging toolkits for logging, Spring's transaction-management and security infrastructure, and so on. These technologies have been used by thousands of developers worldwide for several years, and such heavy usage results in mature solutions. You can use AOP to fill in the missing pieces of these technologies.
- *Experiment.* I learned most techniques through experimentation. Start with the examples in this book. Try them outside of real projects. You'll get valuable insight into the AOP philosophy and its logistical issues. You'll gradually become more comfortable with it and be ready to solve more complex problems.
- *Develop a repertoire of reusable aspects.* When it comes to productivity, nothing beats reusing modules that have already been developed. Many crosscutting concerns apply not only to multiple modules but also to multiple systems. As you gain more experience, start paying attention to reusable parts and create reusable libraries to benefit various projects. But keep in mind that you should always start simple.

Aspect-oriented programming helps to bring order to the chaos introduced by crosscutting concerns. When you use it, the design is more clearly mapped to the implementation. AOP isn't a silver bullet that will solve all your programming problems. Nevertheless, you have to make progress—one step at a time. Over the last decade, AOP has influenced enterprise technologies (EJB3 interceptors, monitoring solutions, transaction and security implementation), and I expect it to influence many more changes over the next decade. AOP has come a long way, has ironed out its kinks, and is destined to gain a strong foothold in most enterprise applications.

appendix A: Setting up the example

To let you work with an application that represents a real-world application, this appendix sets up a base example that you'll use throughout the book. You'll create an e-commerce site whose UI allows users to view product details and buy products. On the back end, the application provides a rudimentary inventory-management service. It uses the following technologies to implement this system: Spring Framework version 3.0, including Spring MVC, and the Java Persistence API (JPA) version 1.0 with Hibernate version 3.3 as the implementation. The example also uses many other packages (directly and indirectly).

The downloadable sources contain a Maven build script that automates downloading dependencies and building the required artifacts. The script shows the specific version of each of the packages used. It also includes an Eclipse project that will let you easily experiment within the IDE environment.

The example in this appendix doesn't use any aspects except the transaction-management aspect supplied by Spring. I'll only show interesting parts of the system, leaving out some details to avoid distracting from the main goal of the system: introducing various crosscutting functionalities. You can download the complete code from the book's web site.

Domain classes

Because the domain objects form the core of an application, you'll start with those classes. You'll set up a simple class structure with `Product`, `Order`, `LineItem`, and `InventoryItem` classes and their superclass, `DomainEntity`. In chapter 3, this inheritance helps you understand the join points that occur in the method and constructor invocation between the base and derived classes.

Domain classes use JPA annotations to express persistence-related information. Whenever appropriate, they rely on default mapping to avoid an annotation overload.

Let's start with the abstract base class `DomainEntity` in listing A.1. It represents a potentially persistent entity that has an `id` property. The purpose of this class is to avoid duplicating the id-related code in each entity class.

Listing A.1 `DomainEntity`: shared support for persistent entities

```
package ajia.util;

import javax.persistence.GeneratedValue;
import javax.persistence.GenerationType;
import javax.persistence.Id;
import javax.persistence.MappedSuperclass;

@MappedSuperclass
public abstract class DomainEntity {
    @Id
    @GeneratedValue(strategy=GenerationType.AUTO)
    private Long id;

    public Long getId() {
        return id;
    }
}
```

The use of the `@MappedSuperClass` annotation lets mapping information come from the derived classes. Next comes the `Product` subclass in listing A.2, which represents a product such as a book. It includes the `name`, `description`, and `price` properties.

Listing A.2 `Product`: something you can buy

```
package ajia.domain;

import javax.persistence.Entity;
import javax.persistence.Table;

import ajia.util.DomainEntity;

@Entity
@Table(name="products")
public class Product extends DomainEntity {
    private String name;
    private String description;
    private double price;

    public Product() {
    }

    public Product(String name, String description, double price) {
        this.name = name;
        this.description = description;
        this.price = price;
    }

    public String getName() {
        return name;
    }
```

```
    public void setName(String name) {
        this.name = name;
    }

    public String getDescription() {
        return description;
    }

    public void setDescription(String description) {
        this.description = description;
    }

    public double getPrice() {
        return price;
    }

    public void setPrice(double price) {
        this.price = price;
    }

    @Override
    public String toString() {
        return "Product: " + name;
    }

    ... hashCode() and equals() methods
}
```

There isn't much JPA-related code because I chose to use default column names for each field.

Anemic domain model?

This application uses an *anemic domain model*, where the domain model classes don't contain interesting behaviors. Chapter 16 deals with this question by looking into alternative architecture styles enabled by AspectJ.

A `LineItem` represents an entry for a given product in an order. Listing A.3 shows the implementation.

Listing A.3 `LineItem`: order entry describing the product and its quantity

```
package ajia.domain;

import javax.persistence.CascadeType;
import javax.persistence.Entity;
import javax.persistence.ManyToOne;
import javax.persistence.Table;

import ajia.util.DomainEntity;

@Entity
@Table(name="lineItems")
public class LineItem extends DomainEntity {
    @ManyToOne(cascade=CascadeType.ALL)
    private Product product;

    @ManyToOne
```

```
    private Order order;

    private int quantity;
    private double unitPrice;

    private LineItem() {
    }

    public LineItem(Order order, Product product, int quantity) {
        this.order = order;
        this.product = product;
        this.quantity = quantity;
        this.unitPrice = product.getPrice();
    }

    public int getQuantity() {
        return quantity;
    }

    public int setQuantity(int quantity) {
        return this.quantity = quantity;
    }

    public Product getProduct() {
        return product;
    }

    public double getUnitPrice() {
        return unitPrice;
    }

    public double getLineTotal() {
        return getQuantity() * getUnitPrice();
    }
}
```

The annotations are a bit more interesting here due to management of the relationship between `LineItem`, `Product`, and `Order`. You also include a no-arg, private constructor to work with object-relational mapping (ORM) solutions.

Because the product price may change after you create a line item, the product price is stored when the line item is created. Next, the `Order` class in listing A.4 includes a collection of `LineItems`.

Listing A.4 `Order`: collection of line items

```
package ajia.domain;

import java.util.ArrayList;
import java.util.Collection;

import javax.persistence.CascadeType;
import javax.persistence.Entity;
import javax.persistence.FetchType;
import javax.persistence.OneToMany;
import javax.persistence.Table;

import ajia.util.DomainEntity;

@Entity
@Table(name="orders")
```

```
public class Order extends DomainEntity {
    @OneToMany(cascade=CascadeType.ALL, fetch=FetchType.EAGER,
            mappedBy="order")
    private Collection<LineItem> lineItems = new ArrayList<LineItem>();
    private boolean placed;

    public void addProduct(Product product, int quantity) {
        if (isPlaced()) {
            throw new IllegalStateException(
                "Once placed, the order may not be modified");
        }
        LineItem lineItem = getItemFor(product);

        if (lineItem != null) {
            lineItem.setQuantity(lineItem.getQuantity() + quantity);
        } else {
            lineItem = new LineItem(this, product, 1);
            lineItem.setQuantity(quantity);
            lineItems.add(lineItem);
        }
    }

    public void removeProduct(Product product, int quantity) {
        if (isPlaced()) {
            throw new IllegalStateException(
                "Once placed, the order may not be modified");
        }

        LineItem lineItem = getItemFor(product);

        if (lineItem == null) {
            throw new IllegalArgumentException(
                    "Failed to get line item");
        }
        int currentQuantity = lineItem.getQuantity();
        if (currentQuantity < quantity) {
            throw new IllegalArgumentException(
                    "Removing more quantity than present");
        }
        if (currentQuantity == quantity) {
            lineItems.remove(lineItem);
        }
        lineItem.setQuantity(currentQuantity - quantity);
    }

    public boolean isPlaced() {
        return placed;
    }

    public void place() {
        placed = true;
    }

    public void cancel() {
        placed = false;
    }

    public Collection<LineItem> getLineItems() {
        return new ArrayList<LineItem>(lineItems);
    }

    public double getTotalPrice() {
        double totalPrice = 0;
```

```
        for (LineItem lineItem : getLineItems()) {
            totalPrice += lineItem.getLineTotal();
        }
        return totalPrice;
    }

    private LineItem getItemFor(Product product) {
        for (LineItem lineItem : lineItems) {
            if (lineItem.getProduct().equals(product)) {
                return lineItem;
            }
        }
        return null;
    }
}
```

The main functionality this class offers is adding and removing products. It ensures that adding a product for which a line item already exists leads to updating the line item's quantity instead of creating a new line item. Similarly, it removes the line item when its product quantity is reduced to zero. It also prohibits modifying an already-placed order.

For inventory-management functionality, you implement `InventoryItem` as shown in listing A.5. Like `LineItem`, it models the inventory associated with a product.

Listing A.5 Inventory item modeling product availability

```
package ajia.domain;

import javax.persistence.Entity;
import javax.persistence.OneToOne;
import javax.persistence.Table;

import ajia.util.DomainEntity;

@Entity
@Table(name="inventoryItems")
public class InventoryItem extends DomainEntity {
    private @OneToOne Product product;
    private int quantityOnHand;

    private InventoryItem() {
    }

    public InventoryItem(Product product) {
        this.product = product;
    }

    public int getQuantityOnHand() {
        return quantityOnHand;
    }

    public void deplete(int quantity) {
        quantityOnHand -= quantity;
    }

    public void replenish(int quantity) {
        quantityOnHand += quantity;
    }
}
```

InventoryItem lets you deplete and replenish inventory to account for bought items, cancelled orders, and arrival of new products. In a more complete implementation, you would have the ability to reserve items and consider items being procured. We won't implement those features here, to keep things simple.

That completes the mapping of domain entities for persistence. Next, you'll implement the repository and service layers.

Repository layer

The repository, also known as the Data Access Object (DAO) layer, is responsible for allowing access to persistent objects. Because many repositories share common methods to find, delete, and update entities, you can create a reusable interface and its implementation. For simplicity, this implementation assumes that an entity's id is always of the Long type. Listing A.6 shows the GenericRepository interface.

Listing A.6 Reusable generic-based repository interface

```
package ajia.util;

import java.util.List;

public interface GenericRepository<T> {
    public List<T> findAll();
    public T find(Long id);
    public void update(T entity);
    public void delete(T entity);
}
```

Nothing terribly interesting here; it lets you find all entities or a single entity with the given id, update an entity, and delete it. Subinterfaces, if required, may add methods specific to the associated entity type as shown in listing A.7.

Listing A.7 Repository for InventoryItem

```
package ajia.repository;

import ajia.domain.InventoryItem;
import ajia.domain.Product;
import ajia.util.GenericRepository;

public interface InventoryItemRepository extends
                 GenericRepository<InventoryItem> {
    public InventoryItem findByProduct(Product product);
}
```

This interface adds the ability to find the inventory item associated with a product.

All repositories can use the common implementation shown in listing A.8 as the base class. A specific implementation may choose to override the base implementation.

Listing A.8 Reusable generic-based repository implementation

```
package ajia.util;

import java.lang.reflect.ParameterizedType;
import java.util.List;
```

```
import javax.persistence.EntityManager;
import javax.persistence.PersistenceContext;

import ajia.util.DomainEntity;
import ajia.util.GenericRepository;

public class JpaGenericRepository<T extends DomainEntity>
    implements GenericRepository<T> {

    private Class<T> entityType;
    @PersistenceContext protected EntityManager em;

    @SuppressWarnings("unchecked")
    protected JpaGenericRepository() {
        this.entityType
            = (Class<T>)
              ((ParameterizedType)getClass().getGenericSuperclass())
                 .getActualTypeArguments()[0];
    }

    public T find(Long id) {
        return em.find(entityType, id);
    }

    @SuppressWarnings("unchecked")
    public List<T> findAll() {
        return em.createQuery("select o from " + entityType.getName() +
                              " o ").getResultList();
    }

    public void update(T entity) {
        em.merge(entity);
    }

    public void delete(T entity) {
        em.remove(entity);
    }
}
```

Next, you implement the repository for `InventoryItem`, as shown in listing A.9.

Listing A.9 Inventory repository based on a common JPA repository

```
package ajia.repository.impl;

import javax.persistence.NoResultException;
import javax.persistence.Query;

import org.springframework.stereotype.Repository;

import ajia.domain.InventoryItem;
import ajia.domain.Product;
import ajia.repository.InventoryItemRepository;
import ajia.util.JpaGenericRepository;

@Repository(value="inventoryItemRepository")
public class JpaInventoryItemRepository
        extends JpaGenericRepository<InventoryItem>
        implements InventoryItemRepository {
    public InventoryItem findByProduct(Product product) {
        Query query
            = em.createQuery("select o from InventoryItem o "
                           + "where o.product = :product");
```

```
        query.setParameter("product", product);
        try {
            return (InventoryItem) query.getSingleResult();
        } catch (NoResultException ex) {
            return null;
        }
    }
}
```

Most of the implementation inherits from `JpaGenericRepository`. Therefore, you implement only the `findByProduct()` method. You similarly have `JpaOrderRepository` and `JpaProductRepository` implementations (not shown here). In those cases, you don't need any additional code.

> **Spring annotations**
>
> Notice the use of the `@Repository` annotation. This annotation, along with annotations such as `@Service` and `@Controller`, simplifies configuration using component scanning. All you need to do is add a `<context:component-scan>` element. In listing A.9, for example, Spring automatically creates a bean with the `inventoryItemRepository` id of `JpaInventoryItemRepository` type. These annotations, along with `@Autowired`, can significantly reduce the amount of XML you need to write. In this book, it also allows us to focus on the core topic: the use of aspects.

You'll now move one level up and implement the service layer.

Service layer

The service layer encapsulates business logic. This is also where you typically demarcate the transaction boundary (we'll discuss that in chapter 14). The first implementation is `OrderService` in listing A.10, which is responsible for managing orders: adding products to an order, placing or cancelling an order, as well as creating, querying, and deleting orders. This example takes a simple approach to inventory management, where adding an item to an order removes it from the inventory. This simplification allows us to focus on the core goals of the book. A comprehensive approach would include the notion of reserving items until finalizing the order, and so on.

Listing A.10 `OrderService` implementation

```
package ajia.service.impl;

import java.util.List;

import org.springframework.beans.factory.annotation.Autowired;
import org.springframework.stereotype.Service;

import ajia.domain.Order;
import ajia.domain.Product;
import ajia.domain.LineItem;
import ajia.repository.OrderRepository;
import ajia.service.InventoryService;
```

```
import ajia.service.OrderService;

@Service(value="orderService")
public class OrderServiceImpl implements OrderService {
    @Autowired private OrderRepository orderRepository;
    @Autowired private InventoryService inventoryService;

    public Order findOrder(Long orderId) {
        return orderRepository.find(orderId);
    }

    public void updateOrder(Order order) {
        orderRepository.update(order);
    }

    public void deleteOrder(Long orderId) {
        orderRepository.delete(orderRepository.find(orderId));
    }

    public List<Order> findOrders() {
        return orderRepository.findAll();
    }

    public void addProduct(Order order, Product product, int quantity) {
        inventoryService.removeProduct(product, quantity);
        order.addProduct(product, quantity);
        updateOrder(order);
    }

    public void removeProduct(Order order, Product product, int quantity) {
        inventoryService.addProduct(product, quantity);
        order.removeProduct(product, quantity);
        updateOrder(order);
    }

    public void cancelOrder(Order order) {
        for (LineItem lineItem : order.getLineItems()) {
            removeProduct(order, lineItem.getProduct(),
                          lineItem.getQuantity());
        }
        order.cancel();
        updateOrder(order);
    }

    public void place(Order order) {
        order.place();
        updateOrder(order);
    }
}
```

The `OrderServiceImpl` class delegates most operations to the repository. To add and remove products, it adjusts inventory appropriately. Before cancelling an order, it puts the products in the order back in inventory. `OrderServiceImpl` uses `InventoyService`, which you implement next as shown in listing A.11.

Listing A.11 Inventory management service implementation

```
package ajia.service.impl;

import org.springframework.beans.factory.annotation.Autowired;
import org.springframework.stereotype.Service;
```

```
import ajia.domain.Product;
import ajia.service.InventoryService;
import ajia.domain.InventoryItem;
import ajia.repository.InventoryItemRepository;
import ajia.service.InventoryException;

@Service("inventoryService")
public class InventoryServiceImpl implements InventoryService {
    @Autowired InventoryItemRepository inventoryRepository;

    public void addProduct(Product product, int quantity) {
        InventoryItem inventoryItem
            = inventoryRepository.findByProduct(product);
        if (inventoryItem == null) {
            inventoryItem = new InventoryItem(product);
        }
        inventoryItem.replenish(quantity);
        inventoryRepository.update(inventoryItem);
    }

    public void removeProduct(Product product, int quantity) {
        if (isProductAvailable(product, quantity)) {
            InventoryItem inventoryItem
                = inventoryRepository.findByProduct(product);
            inventoryItem.deplete(quantity);
            inventoryRepository.update(inventoryItem);
        } else {
            throw new InventoryException(
                "Insufficient inventory to fulfill"
              + "request for " + product.getName()
              + " quantity " + quantity);
        }
    }

    public boolean isProductAvailable(Product product, int quantity) {
        InventoryItem inventoryItem
            = inventoryRepository.findByProduct(product);
        if ((inventoryItem == null)
                || (inventoryItem.getQuantityOnHand() < quantity)) {
            return false;
        }
        return true;
    }
}
```

You now have all the classes required to implement a basic application. Let's create a Spring configuration to use these classes.

Application configuration

Following Spring best practices, you'll split this configuration across multiple files and put them in a META-INF/spring directory. Following another best practice, you'll use two application contexts related by a parent-child relationship: the web application context is a child of the business application context. The former includes web-related artifacts such as controllers and views; the latter includes backend objects such as services, repositories, data sources and transaction management, configuration of the ORM framework, as well as applying transaction management to the service layer.

Due to the use of @Repository, @Service, and @Autowired annotations, the application configuration is simple. The first context file in listing A.12 uses Spring's component-scanning feature to scan the classpath, create components, and wire them up.

Listing A.12 application-context.xml: using component scanning

```
<beans xmlns="http://www.springframework.org/schema/beans"
    xmlns:xsi="http://www.w3.org/2001/XMLSchema-instance"
    xmlns:context="http://www.springframework.org/schema/context"
    xmlns:aop="http://www.springframework.org/schema/aop"
    xsi:schemaLocation=
       "http://www.springframework.org/schema/beans
        http://www.springframework.org/schema/beans/spring-beans-2.5.xsd
        http://www.springframework.org/schema/context
        http://www.springframework.org/schema/context/spring-context-2.5.xsd
        http://www.springframework.org/schema/aop
        http://www.springframework.org/schema/aop/spring-aop-2.5.xsd">
    <context:component-scan base-package="ajia">
        <context:exclude-filter expression="ajia.web..*" type="aspectj"/>
    </context:component-scan>
</beans>
```

You exclude the ajia.web package to let web components be created in the web context, which is a child of the application context. Next, you set up the datasource as shown in listing A.13.

Listing A.13 datasource-context.xml: setting up the datasource

```
<beans ...>
    <bean id="dataSource" class="org.apache.commons.dbcp.BasicDataSource">
        <property name="driverClassName" value="${jdbc.driverClassName}" />
        <property name="url" value="${jdbc.url}" />
        <property name="username" value="${jdbc.username}" />
        <property name="password" value="${jdbc.password}" />
    </bean>
</beans>
```

Following another best practice in Spring, you externalize data-source-related information in a property file, as shown in listing A.14.

Listing A.14 jdbc.properties: externalizing datasource information

```
jdbc.driverClassName=org.hsqldb.jdbcDriver
jdbc.url=jdbc:hsqldb:file:eCommerce
jdbc.username=sa
jdbc.password=
```

You use the datasource through JPA, as shown in listing A.15.

Listing A.15 jpa-context.xml: configuring JPA provider

```
<beans ...>
    <bean id="entityManagerFactory"
          class="org.springframework.orm.jpa.
➥                LocalContainerEntityManagerFactoryBean">
```

```
        <property name="dataSource" ref="dataSource" />
        <property name="jpaVendorAdapter">
            <bean
             class="org.springframework.orm.jpa.vendor.
➥                    HibernateJpaVendorAdapter" />
        </property>
    </bean>

    <bean id="transactionManager"
          class="org.springframework.orm.jpa.JpaTransactionManager">
        <property name="entityManagerFactory"
                  ref="entityManagerFactory" />
    </bean>
</beans>
```

Here, you set up a JPA entity manager with Hibernate as the underlying implementation. You also create a transaction manager based on the entity manager. Configuring JPA requires specifying a persistence.xml file that describes the domain entities being managed by JPA and the properties for the underlying implementation, as shown in listing A.16.

Listing A.16 persistence.xml: configuring a JPA provider

```
<persistence version="1.0"
    xmlns="http://java.sun.com/xml/ns/persistence"
    xmlns:xsi="http://www.w3.org/2001/XMLSchema-instance"
    xsi:schemaLocation="http://java.sun.com/xml/ns/persistence
➥          http://java.sun.com/xml/ns/persistence/persistence_1_0.xsd">

    <persistence-unit name="eCommerce">
        <provider>org.hibernate.ejb.HibernatePersistence</provider>
        <class>ajia.domain.Product</class>
        <class>ajia.domain.LineItem</class>
        <class>ajia.domain.Order</class>
        <class>ajia.domain.InventoryItem</class>
        <properties>
            <property name="hibernate.dialect"
                      value="org.hibernate.dialect.HSQLDialect"/>
            <property name="hibernate.hbm2ddl.auto" value="create-drop"/>
            <property name="hibernate.show_sql" value="false"/>
            <property name="hibernate.format_sql" value="true"/>
            <property name="hibernate.show_sql_parameters" value="true"/>
            <property name="hibernate.cache.provider_class"
                      value="org.hibernate.cache.HashtableCacheProvider"/>
            <property name="hibernate.ejb.event.merge"
                      value="org.springframework.orm.hibernate3.
➥                             support.IdTransferringMergeEventListener"/>
        </properties>
    </persistence-unit>
</persistence>
```

Finally, you set up infrastructure services—in this case, transaction management—and apply it to the service layer, as shown in listing A.17.

Listing A.17 infrastructure-context.xml: setting up transaction management

```
<beans xmlns="http://www.springframework.org/schema/beans"
       xmlns:xsi="http://www.w3.org/2001/XMLSchema-instance"
       xmlns:context="http://www.springframework.org/schema/context"
```

```
       xmlns:tx="http://www.springframework.org/schema/tx"
       xmlns:aop="http://www.springframework.org/schema/aop"
       xsi:schemaLocation="http://www.springframework.org/schema/beans
         http://www.springframework.org/schema/beans/spring-beans-2.5.xsd
         http://www.springframework.org/schema/tx
         http://www.springframework.org/schema/tx/spring-tx-2.5.xsd
         http://www.springframework.org/schema/context
         http://www.springframework.org/schema/context/
➥              spring-context-2.5.xsd
         http://www.springframework.org/schema/aop
         http://www.springframework.org/schema/aop/spring-aop-2.5.xsd">
    <context:property-placeholder
        location="classpath:META-INF/spring/**/*.properties"/>

    <tx:advice id="txAdvice" >
        <tx:attributes>
            <tx:method name="find*" read-only="true" />
            <tx:method name="is*" read-only="true" />
            <tx:method name="*"/>
        </tx:attributes>
    </tx:advice>

    <aop:config>
        <aop:pointcut id="serviceOperation"
                      expression="execution(* ajia.service.*.*(..))"/>
        <aop:advisor advice-ref="txAdvice"
                     pointcut-ref="serviceOperation"/>
    </aop:config>
</beans>
```

The infrastructure-context.xml file also loads property files using a wildcard pattern. In this case, it loads jdbc.properties. For transaction management, you use an XML-based configuration. When we discuss transaction management in chapter 14, you'll modify this configuration to use annotation-based alternatives.

That does it for the backend application context. Let's move our attention to the web layer.

The web layer

The web layer specifies view-related beans such as controllers and views. The web application context, which is a child context of the backend application context, configures these beans. Because it's a child context, it can use beans such as services from the parent context.

You'll use a recommended approach from the annotation-based Spring MVC. Listing A.18 shows a controller that lets you view an order, add products to it, and place the order.

Listing A.18 Controller to view and update an order

```
package ajia.web;

import javax.servlet.http.HttpSession;

import org.springframework.beans.factory.annotation.Autowired;
```

```
import org.springframework.stereotype.Controller;
import org.springframework.web.bind.annotation.RequestMapping;
import org.springframework.web.bind.annotation.RequestMethod;
import org.springframework.web.bind.annotation.RequestParam;

import ajia.domain.Order;
import ajia.service.OrderService;
import ajia.service.ProductService;

@Controller
public class OrderController {
    @Autowired private OrderService orderService;
    @Autowired private ProductService productService;

    @RequestMapping("/viewCart.htm")
    public Order viewCart(HttpSession session) {
        return getCurrentOrder(session);
    }

    @RequestMapping(value="/addToCart.htm", method=RequestMethod.POST)
    public String addToCart(@RequestParam("id") Long productId,
                            HttpSession session) {
        Order currentOrder = getCurrentOrder(session);
        orderService.addProduct(currentOrder,
                                productService.findProduct(productId), 1);
        return "redirect:productSummary.htm";
    }

    @RequestMapping(value="/place.htm", method=RequestMethod.POST)
    public String place(HttpSession session) {
        orderService.place(getCurrentOrder(session));
        session.removeAttribute("currentOrder");
        return "redirect:/";
    }

    private Order getCurrentOrder(HttpSession session) {
        Order currentOrder = (Order) session.getAttribute("currentOrder");
        if (currentOrder == null) {
            currentOrder = new Order();
            orderService.updateOrder(currentOrder);
            session.setAttribute("currentOrder", currentOrder);
        }
        return currentOrder;
    }
}
```

You similarly have controllers for viewing products, editing orders, and administrative functionality.

You create a web application context based on the controller classes, as shown in listing A.19. You also provide a view resolver to map view names into a JSP view.

Listing A.19 web-context.xml: configuring the web layer

```
<beans ...>
    <context:component-scan base-package="ajia.web"/>

    <bean class="org.springframework.web.servlet.mvc.
➥               annotation.DefaultAnnotationHandlerMapping"/>
    <bean id="viewResolver"
          class="org.springframework.web.servlet.view.
```

```
➥                 InternalResourceViewResolver">
        <property name="prefix" value="/WEB-INF/views/"/>
        <property name="suffix" value=".jsp"/>
    </bean>
</beans>
```

You also have additional artifacts: JSP files and web.xml. See the downloadable sources for complete details.

Logging configuration

You write a basic logging configuration, as shown in listing A.20. When you add AOP functionality, you'll modify this base configuration appropriately.

Listing A.20 log4j.xml: basic logging configuration

```
<log4j:configuration xmlns:log4j="http://jakarta.apache.org/log4j/">
    <appender name="console" class="org.apache.log4j.ConsoleAppender">
        <param name="Target" value="System.out" />
        <layout class="org.apache.log4j.PatternLayout">
            <param name="ConversionPattern" value="%m%n" />
        </layout>
    </appender>

    <logger name="ajia">
        <level value="info" />
    </logger>

    <logger name="org.springframework">
        <level value="warn" />
    </logger>

    <logger name="org.hibernate">
        <level value="warn" />
    </logger>

    <root>
        <priority value="warn" />
        <appender-ref ref="console" />
    </root>
</log4j:configuration>
```

The system includes many other classes and configuration files especially related to unit and integration testing. But we don't need them for our purpose of explaining the use of AOP.

Building and running the application

Thanks to Maven, building and running application is easy. You don't need to download anything other than the Java Development Kit (JDK) and Maven.

To build the war file, issue the following command, which also runs the tests before packaging:

```
> mvn clean package
```

To deploy the application, assuming Tomcat is your web server, you can copy the war file (in the target directory) as Commerce.war to Tomcat's webapps directory and start Tomcat (a similar process will work for other web or application servers). Alternatively, you can run the application using embedded Tomcat by issuing the following command:

```
> mvn tomcat:run
```

Then, launch your browser, and visit http://localhost:8080/Commerce. You should be able to view products, add a few to the shopping cart, and view the shopping cart.

appendix B: Using Ant with AspectJ

Most developers use either Ant or Maven to build their projects. This appendix shows various weaving scenarios implemented using Ant. Appendix C does the same for Maven. Note that the focus of this appendix is the use of AspectJ weaver; therefore, we use the simplest Ant structure to get things done.

You'll use the classes from chapter 2's listing 2.1 and 2.2 and the profiling aspect in listing 2.4 to exercise various weaving scenarios. Let's start with the simplest scenarios of building using source code build-time weaving.

Weaving sources

As discussed in chapter 8, in source code build-time weaving, you supply the ajc compiler with classes and aspects in source-code form. The aspects may be expressed using either traditional syntax or @AspectJ syntax. Listing B.1 shows an Ant build file that compiles classes and aspects together.

Listing B.1 Source-coded build-time weaving through Ant

```
<project name="Source code build-time weaving" default="run">
    <property file="../../../build.properties"/>

    <taskdef classpath="${aspectj.home}/lib/aspectjtools.jar"         ❶ Defines iajc task
        resource="org/aspectj/tools/ant/taskdefs/
                 aspectjTaskdefs.properties"/>

    <path id="project.class.path">
        <pathelement location="${aspectj.home}/lib/aspectjrt.jar"/>
    </path>

    <target name="compile">
        <mkdir dir="classes"/>
        <iajc destdir="classes" source="1.5"                           ❷ Compiles sources
              classpathref="project.class.path">
            <sourceroots>
                <pathelement location="src/main/java"/>
```

```
            </sourceroots>
        </iajc>
    </target>

    <target name="run" depends="compile">
        <java classname="ajia.main.Main" classpath="classes"
              classpathref="project.class.path"/>
    </target>
</project>
```

❷ Compiles sources

❸ Runs program

❶ You make the AspectJ Ant tasks available by setting the value of the `resource` attribute to the org/aspectj/tools/ant/taskdefs/aspectjTaskdefs.properties file. This properties file, which is part of aspectjtools.jar, specifies the mapping of the Ant compile tasks to their corresponding classes. Specifically, it defines the `iajc` task.

❷ You define the `compile` target by using the `iajc` task and specify `sourceroots` as a nested element. You use the `destdir` attribute to specify the destination directory for the class files produced. Alternatively, you could use the `outjar` attribute to specify a jar file as the destination. The jar file produced using the `outjar` attribute is identical to the classes produced using the `destdir` attribute followed by a `<jar>` Ant task.

❸ You define the `run` target using the java task element and specify `ajia.main.Main` as the class to execute.

When you execute the build file, you get output similar to the following:

```
> ant
Buildfile: ...\build.xml
compile:
run:
     [java] Wanna learn AspectJ?
     [java] void ajia.messaging.MessageCommunicator.deliver(String)
➥              took 454806 nanoseconds
     [java] Harry, having fun?
     [java] void ajia.messaging.MessageCommunicator.deliver(String, String)
➥              took 139962 nanoseconds
     [java] void ajia.main.Main.main(String[]) took 7164039 nanoseconds
BUILD SUCCESSFUL
Total time: 1 second
```

Note that the `iajc` task allows additional options that match those of the ajc compiler. See chapter 8 for more information about each compiler option.

Because profiling is a reusable functionality, you want to create an aspect library out of it so that you can weave it into any application that needs that functionality.

Creating an aspect library

The mechanics of creating an aspect library differ from source code build-time weaving only in that you don't pass the classes to be woven to the `iajc` task. Note that if you use the @AspectJ syntax to develop a library, you can use `javac` to compile the aspects (optionally, you can package using the `jar` task). The Ant file in listing B.2 assumes that the profiling aspect is in a separate project (along with any support classes).

Listing B.2 Creating an aspect library using Ant

```
<project name="Aspect Library" default="compile">
    ... unchanged since B.1

    <target name="compile">
        <mkdir dir="dist"/>
        <iajc source="1.5" classpathref="project.class.path"
              outjar="dist/profiling.jar">
            <sourceroots>
                <pathelement location="src/main/java"/>
            </sourceroots>
        </iajc>
    </target>
</project>
```

The iajc task definition hasn't changed much since listing B.1. The main change is the use of the outjar attribute instead of the destdir attribute. Note that you could use the same definition as in listing B.1. But because it's best to package a library as a jar, you use the outjar option. As described in section earlier, the outjar option is merely a shortcut for compiling the classes followed by a jar task.

When you execute the build file, you see output as following:

```
> ant
Buildfile: ...\build.xml
compile:
     [iajc] warning at ...\src\main\java\ajia\profile\ProfilingAspect.aj:6::0
➥    advice defined in ajia.profile.ProfilingAspect has not been applied
➥    [Xlint:adviceDidNotMatch]
BUILD SUCCESSFUL
Total time: 1 second
```

If you check the dist directory, you see profiling.jar. Note the warning issued by the AspectJ weaver: it tells you that the profiling advice didn't apply to any join points. The warning is correct but not useful for a library aspect, because the advice will be applied only when the library is woven into other parts of the system. To stop this warning, you need to create a file as shown in listing B.3.

Listing B.3 Property file to specify the levels for various warnings (xlint.properties)

```
adviceDidNotMatch=ignore
```

The file in listing B.3 uses the property file syntax, where the key is the name of the lint[1] warning and the value is the level at the compiler should report. The levels you specify must be error, warning, or ignore. See the AspectJ documentation for possible lint errors and warnings.

You need to specify the xlintfile properties of the iajc task to modify its error and warning reporting, as follows:

```
<iajc source="1.5" classpathref="project.class.path"
      outjar="dist/profiling.jar" xlintfile="xlint.properties">
```

[1] Lint is a program that flags potential problems in code written in the C programming language. Similar programs have been implemented for many other languages. See http://en.wikipedia.org/wiki/Lint_(software) for more details.

The `iajc` task allows the `outxml` attribute to specify whether the aop-ajc.xml file should be created. Such a file enlists all the aspects supplied as the input to the compiler. This option is useful with load-time weaving (LTW) because it obviates the need to use a separate aop.xml file (see chapter 8 for more about LTW):

```
<iajc source="1.5" classpathref="project.class.path"
      outjar="dist/profiling.jar" xlintfile="xlint.properties"
      outxml="true">
```

Next, you weave this library into a jar file.

Weaving into jar files

To use an aspect library, you must weave it into an application. To illustrate such weaving, you first create a jar file for your application classes without weaving any aspects in them. Listing B.4 assumes a project with the classes by themselves. Note that there is nothing special in this Ant file from the AspectJ perspective; you're only interested in the final product—a jar file. In a real application, you'll probably start with a jar file handed to you.

Listing B.4 Producing a jar file for Java sources

```
<project name="Java Library" default="compile">
    <target name="compile">
        <mkdir dir="dist"/>
        <javac source="1.5" destdir="classes" srcdir="src/main/java"/>
        <jar destfile="dist/application.jar" basedir="classes"/>
    </target>
</project>
```

When you execute this Ant file, you get an application.jar file in the dest directory. Note that AspectJ doesn't require that the input be a jar file; it works fine with classes.

Let's weave application.jar with profiling.jar, which was produced in the previous section. Listing B.5 shows an Ant file that uses the `iajc` task to accomplish this goal.

Listing B.5 Weaving an aspect library into jar files

```
<project name="Weaving into Java Library" default="run-woven">
    ...

    <target name="weave">
        <mkdir dir="dist"/>
        <iajc injars="dist/application.jar"
              aspectpath="dist/profiling.jar"
              outjar="dist/profiled-application.jar"
              classpathref="project.class.path">
        </iajc>
    </target>

    <target name="run-normal" depends="weave">
        <java classname="ajia.main.Main" classpathref="project.class.path">
            <classpath>
                <pathelement location="dist/application.jar"/>
            </classpath>
        </java>
```

```
    </target>

    <target name="run-woven" depends="weave">
        <java classname="ajia.main.Main" classpathref="project.class.path">
            <classpath>
                <pathelement location="dist/profiled-application.jar"/>
                <pathelement location="dist/profiling.jar"/>
            </classpath>
        </java>
    </target>
</project>
```

The `iajc` task in the `weave` target specifies application.jar as the jar file to be woven in using the `inpath` attribute and profiling.jar as the aspect library using the `aspectpath` attribute. Each of these attributes can be specified as nested elements, which comes in handy if you need to specify multiple jar files. Each option also comes with a reference variation—`inpathref` and `aspectpathref`—which lets you refer to Ant variables defined elsewhere.

The `iajc` task specifies profiled-application.jar as the output jar file. As with any `iajc` task, you could specify the `destdir` attribute to produce class files instead of a jar file.

The `<run-normal>` and `<run-woven>` targets show how to execute the application with or without the woven jar file. Note that we show these tasks for illustration purpose only. In a typical enterprise application, you'll deploy the woven jar file to the application or web server.

When you execute the Ant file for both these targets, you get the following output:

```
> ant run-normal run-woven
Buildfile: build.xml

run-normal:
     [java] Wanna learn AspectJ?
     [java] Harry, having fun?

weave:

run-woven:
     [java] Wanna learn AspectJ?
     [java] void ajia.messaging.MessageCommunicator.deliver(String)
➥              took 327136 nanoseconds
     [java] Harry, having fun?
     [java] void ajia.messaging.MessageCommunicator.deliver(String, String)
➥              took 166781 nanoseconds
     [java] void ajia.main.Main.main(String[]) took 2951213 nanoseconds

BUILD SUCCESSFUL
Total time: 1 second
```

The `run-normal` target shows the output without any profiling information. The `run-woven` target, on the other hand, shows the effect of the woven aspect.

appendix C: Using Maven with AspectJ

The previous appendix examines various weaving options enabled through Ant. In this appendix, you perform the same tasks using Maven.[1] As in appendix B, you'll use the classes from listings 2.1 and 2.2 and the profiling aspect from listing 2.4 to exercise various weaving possibilities.

Weaving sources

Maven, through the open source codehaus.org project, provides a plugin to work with AspectJ (visit http://mojo.codehaus.org/aspectj-maven-plugin for details). Let's see this plugin in action through the Maven pom.xml file in listing C.1.

Listing C.1 Maven pom.xml to perform source code build-time weaving

```
<project xmlns="http://maven.apache.org/POM/4.0.0"
         xmlns:xsi="http://www.w3.org/2001/XMLSchema-instance"
         xsi:schemaLocation="http://maven.apache.org/POM/4.0.0
                             http://maven.apache.org/maven-v4_0_0.xsd">
    <modelVersion>4.0.0</modelVersion>
    <groupId>ajia.helloworld</groupId>
    <artifactId>helloworld</artifactId>
    <packaging>jar</packaging>
    <version>1.0-SNAPSHOT</version>
    <name>helloworld</name>
    <dependencies>
        <dependency>
            <groupId>org.aspectj</groupId>
            <artifactId>aspectjrt</artifactId>
            <version>1.6.5</version>
        </dependency>
    </dependencies>

    <build>
        <plugins>
```

❶ Declares dependency on AspectJ runtime (aspectjrt.jar)

[1] Please use Maven 2.2.0 or later. I've encountered a few problems with older versions.

```
            <plugin>
                <groupId>org.codehaus.mojo</groupId>
                <artifactId>aspectj-maven-plugin</artifactId>
                <executions>
                    <execution>
                        <goals>
                            <goal>compile</goal>
                        </goals>
                        <configuration>
                            <source>1.5</source>
                            <target>1.5</target>
                        </configuration>
                    </execution>
                </executions>
            </plugin>
```

❷ Sets up Maven AspectJ plugin

```
            <plugin>
                <groupId>org.codehaus.mojo</groupId>
                <artifactId>exec-maven-plugin</artifactId>
                <executions>
                    <execution>
                        <goals>
                            <goal>java</goal>
                        </goals>
                    </execution>
                </executions>
                <configuration>
                    <mainClass>ajia.main.Main</mainClass>
                </configuration>
            </plugin>
        </plugins>
    </build>
</project>
```

❸ Runs program

❶ The pom.xml file declares a dependency on aspectrt.jar. ❷ It adds the Maven AspectJ plugin to participate in the compile phase. ❸ It also includes a plugin to let you run the `ajia.main.Main` class.

When you execute the build file to install the compiled sources and execute the main class, you get output similar to the following:

```
> mvn install exec:java
...
[INFO] [aspectj:compile {execution: default}]
...
Wanna learn AspectJ?
void ajia.messaging.MessageCommunicator.deliver(String) took 145549
     nanoseconds
Harry, having fun?
void ajia.messaging.MessageCommunicator.deliver(String, String)
➥    took 79619 nanoseconds
void ajia.main.Main.main(String[]) took 2176533 nanoseconds
```

Next, you'll create an AspectJ library.

Creating an aspect library

As with the Ant version, building an aspect library is nothing special, except for a few additional options. If you use the @AspectJ syntax, you don't need to use the Maven

AspectJ plugin; simply declare dependency on aspectjrt.jar and compile the sources. Listing C.2 shows how to build an aspect library. (The project includes only the profiling aspects.)

Listing C.2 Maven pom.xml to create an aspect library

```
<project xmlns="http://maven.apache.org/POM/4.0.0"
         xmlns:xsi="http://www.w3.org/2001/XMLSchema-instance"
         xsi:schemaLocation="http://maven.apache.org/POM/4.0.0
                             http://maven.apache.org/maven-v4_0_0.xsd">
    <modelVersion>4.0.0</modelVersion>
    <groupId>ajia.helloworld</groupId>
    <artifactId>profiling</artifactId>
    <packaging>jar</packaging>
    <version>1.0-SNAPSHOT</version>
    <name>profiling</name>
    <dependencies>
        <dependency>
            <groupId>org.aspectj</groupId>
            <artifactId>aspectjrt</artifactId>
            <version>1.6.5</version>
        </dependency>
    </dependencies>

    <build>
        <plugins>
            <plugin>
                <groupId>org.codehaus.mojo</groupId>
                <artifactId>aspectj-maven-plugin</artifactId>
                <executions>
                    <execution>
                        <goals>
                            <goal>compile</goal>
                        </goals>
                        <configuration>
                            <source>1.5</source>
                            <target>1.5</target>
                        </configuration>
                    </execution>
                </executions>
                <configuration>
                    <outxml>true</outxml>
                </configuration>
            </plugin>
        </plugins>
    </build>
</project>
```

Compared to listing C.1, the only difference is the use of the `<outxml>` element. You set that element to `true` to automatically generate aop-ajc.xml and include it in the output jar. When you execute the build file, the profiling jar is installed in your Maven repository.

Next, you'll weave this aspect library jar into another application jar file.

Weaving into jar files

Let's build a plain Java application based on listing 2.1 and 2.2, which creates the application-unwoven artifact (a jar file); see listing C.3.

Listing C.3 Maven pom.xml to create unwoven HelloWorld application jar

```
<project xmlns="http://maven.apache.org/POM/4.0.0"
         xmlns:xsi="http://www.w3.org/2001/XMLSchema-instance"
         xsi:schemaLocation="http://maven.apache.org/POM/4.0.0
                             http://maven.apache.org/maven-v4_0_0.xsd">
    <modelVersion>4.0.0</modelVersion>
    <groupId>ajia.helloworld</groupId>
    <artifactId>application-unwoven</artifactId>
    <packaging>jar</packaging>
    <version>1.0-SNAPSHOT</version>
    <name>application-unwoven</name>
</project>
```

Let's weave an application-unwoven artifact with the profiling artifact produced in the previous section. Listing C.4 shows the Maven pom.xml file that weaves these to produce a woven jar.

Listing C.4 Weaving application-unwoven artifacts with profiling artifact

```
<project xmlns="http://maven.apache.org/POM/4.0.0"
         xmlns:xsi="http://www.w3.org/2001/XMLSchema-instance"
         xsi:schemaLocation="http://maven.apache.org/POM/4.0.0
                             http://maven.apache.org/maven-v4_0_0.xsd">
    <modelVersion>4.0.0</modelVersion>
    <groupId>ajia.helloworld</groupId>
    <artifactId>application-woven</artifactId>
    <packaging>jar</packaging>
    <version>1.0-SNAPSHOT</version>
    <name>application-woven</name>
    <dependencies>
        <dependency>
            <groupId>org.aspectj</groupId>
            <artifactId>aspectjrt</artifactId>
            <version>1.6.5</version>
        </dependency>

        <dependency>
            <groupId>ajia.helloworld</groupId>
            <artifactId>profiling</artifactId>
            <version>1.0-SNAPSHOT</version>
        </dependency>

        <dependency>
               <groupId>ajia.helloworld</groupId>
               <artifactId>application-unwoven</artifactId>
            <version>1.0-SNAPSHOT</version>
        </dependency>
    </dependencies>

    <build>
        <plugins>
            <plugin>
                <groupId>org.codehaus.mojo</groupId>
                <artifactId>aspectj-maven-plugin</artifactId>
                <executions>
                    <execution>
                        <goals>
                            <goal>compile</goal>
                        </goals>
```

```
                    </execution>
                </executions>
                <configuration>
                    <weaveDependencies>
                        <weaveDependency>
                            <groupId>ajia.helloworld</groupId>
                            <artifactId>application-unwoven</artifactId>
                        </weaveDependency>
                    </weaveDependencies>

                    <aspectLibraries>
                        <aspectLibrary>
                            <groupId>ajia.helloworld</groupId>
                            <artifactId>profiling</artifactId>
                        </aspectLibrary>
                    </aspectLibraries>
                </configuration>
            </plugin>
        </plugins>
    </build>
</project>
```

The Maven AspectJ plugin requires that the project declare a dependency on the artifacts to be woven in and the aspect libraries.[2] In the configuration, you specify the artifacts to be woven in (equivalent to the `-inpath` ajc option) under the `<weaveDependencies>` section and the aspect libraries to weave in (equivalent to the `-aspectpath` ajc option) under the `<aspectLibraries>` section. When you execute this build file, the application-woven artifact is installed in your Maven repository.

---

[2] Version 1.1 of the aspectj-maven-plugin has a bug that requires the project to include sources. Therefore, in the downloadable sources, you'll find a blank interface included in the src/main/java directory.

index

Symbols

B

C

K

L

M

T

U

V

W

X

Y

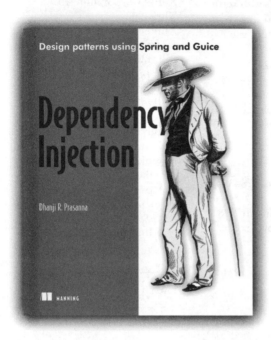

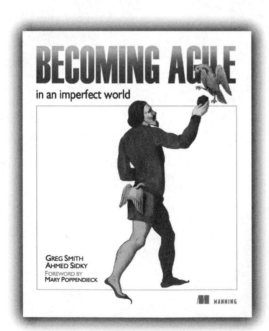

MORE TITLES FROM MANNING

Spring in Action
Second Edition
by Craig Walls
with Ryan Breidenbach

ISBN: 1-933988-13-4
768 pages
$49.99
August 2007

Spring in Practice
by Willie Wheeler and John Wheeler

ISBN: 1-935182-05-6
600 pages
$44.99
January 2010

For ordering information go to www.manning.com

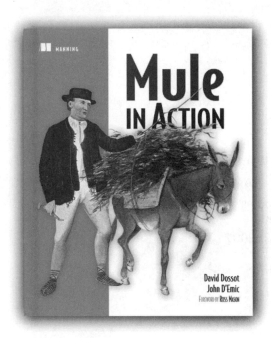

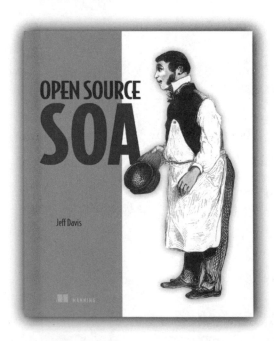